DOSTOEVSKY

Dostoevsky in 1872, by V. G. Perov

DOSTOEVSKY

The Miraculous Years

1865-1871

JOSEPH FRANK

PRINCETON UNIVERSITY

PRESS

Copyright © 1995 by Princeton University Press
Published by Princeton University Press,
41 William Street, Princeton, New Jersey 08540
In the United Kingdom:
Princeton University Press, Chichester, West Sussex

Library of Congress Cataloging-in-Publication Data

Frank, Joseph (1918–)
Dostoevsky : the miraculous years, 1865–1871 / Joseph Frank.
p.   cm.
Includes bibliographical references and index.
ISBN 0-691-04364-7
1. Dostoyevsky, Fyodor, 1821–1881—Biography.
2. Novelists, Russian—19th century—Biography.
3. Russia—Intellectual life—1801–1917.
I. Title.
PG3328.F68   1995   891.93′3—dc20   [B]   94-43403

This book has been composed in Adobe Utopia
Designed by Jan Lilly

Princeton University Press books are printed on
acid-free paper, and meet the guidelines for permanence and
durability of the Committee on Production
Guidelines for Book Longevity of the
Council on Library Resources

Printed in the United States of America

3   5   7   9   10   8   6   4   2

This book is dedicated to "Richard"

R. P. Blackmur (1904–1965)

A great critic, an irreplaceable friend,
who encouraged me to believe I
could someday write books
he would wish to read

CONTENTS

CONTENTS

LIST OF ILLUSTRATIONS

Unless otherwise noted, all illustrations are from *Feodor Mikhailovich Dostoevsky v Portretakh, illyustratsiyakh, dokumentakh*, ed V. S. Nechaeva (Moscow, 1972).

The present work is the fourth volume in the series that I am writing on the life and works of Dostoevsky. The next volume, the last, will deal with the final ten years of his life. During the years covered here, Dostoevsky wrote three major novels and two novellas; these not only rank among his best works, but are among the greatest in Russian and in world literature as a whole. It is the production of such masterpieces that makes Dostoevsky's life worth recounting at all, and my purpose, as in the previous volumes, is to keep them constantly in the foreground rather than treating them as accessory to the life per se. The aim of literary biography, as I conceive it, is to furnish readers with a context, drawn from the writer's personal life, as well as from the social, cultural, literary, and philosophical background of his or her time, that will help toward a better understanding of the work. Without such application of its researches to the works themselves, literary biography, at least for me, loses much (if not all) of its presumed point. Hence I have included lengthy analyses of these celebrated novels and stories in the course of my narrative; and this has led to the present volume being rather bulkier than its predecessors, in which there were fewer works to discuss and ones that required less elucidation. But I found that I could not avoid placing this extra demand on the reader without infirming the very purpose of my endeavor.

Indeed, precisely because of the stature of the creations that it deals with, this fourth volume is a crucial one for my whole undertaking. I began with the idea, many years ago, that a close and exhaustive study of the Russian social-cultural context would yield more fruitful results for a better understanding of Dostoevsky than the usual approaches that had been taken, especially in Western criticism. These approaches had been mainly biographical in a narrowly personal sense, or psychological and psychoanalytical, or, influenced by Russian émigré and Symbolist criticism, primarily religious and theological. Indigenous Russian criticism had paid more attention to Dostoevsky's social-cultural environment, but reactions to his writings in his own time were naturally colored by the fierce political enmities of the period, which made any relatively objective appraisal of them impossible from this point of view. Later Russian criticism of this type, up to and through the Soviet period, only continued to reiterate the positions on the right and the left staked out in Dostoevsky's own day. Or, as in the case of the Symbolists and the Formalists, who were determined to give Dostoevsky's art its just due, the social-cultural context (except for its literary component) was swept aside as entirely irrelevant and, for the Symbolists, even demeaning to the universality of Dostoevsky's thematic range and his inspired exploration of the eternal dilemmas of the human condition. Far be it from me to wish to diminish such an appreciation of Dostoevsky's genius by one iota! But even more remarkable, I continue to think, is that he rose to such greatness from precisely those by-now musty arguments taking place among a handful of the intelligentsia in the long-ago Russia of the 1840s, 1860s, and 1870s. Without some knowledge of these bitter quarrels, destined to reverberate throughout the world up to our own time in Dostoevsky's pages and those of others, and whose ultimate consequences are now being played out with the collapse of communism, we do not truly understand the sources of his inspiration or the passions—and apprehensions—which, combined with his own life experiences and literary gifts, gave birth to his greatest work.

This was the point at which I started, and I well remember the words of my late and deeply lamented friend Irving Howe, whose own writings I admired and whose praise I greatly cherished, shortly after I had published my third volume and was chatting with him about the fourth. What he told me, in sum, was that my fourth, in which I should have to tackle three literary landmarks, would be the acid test of my belief that new and valuable light could be shed on them by an intensive study of their social-cultural genesis. These words rang in my ears as an inspiring challenge in all the years I have been writing this volume; and I looked forward to the pleasure—now, alas, foreclosed—of presenting him with a copy to see if he thought the challenge had been met. Other readers will come to their own conclusions, and I can only hope that these will continue to be as favorable as they have been in the past.

DURING the period in which I have worked on this book, I have been fortunate in being surrounded by friends and colleagues whose knowledge and interests have provided support for my own efforts. Lazar Fleishman and Gregory Freidin of the Stanford Slavic Department have been an invaluable source of encouragement and insight, and I could rely on their native knowledge of Russian culture to buttress my own. Theodore and Renée Weiss of Princeton and Ian and Ruth Watt of Stanford were also friends to whom I could turn for literary stimulus and insight. Gary Saul Morson of Northwestern University and Caryl Emerson of Princeton University have been generous Slavic interlocutors as well, and offered welcome reassurance that I had not gone astray. Donald Fanger of Harvard, a major Dostoevskian himself, whose classic *Dostoevsky and Romantic Realism* has lost none of its value in thirty years, turned out to be a reader of the present book for Princeton University Press. His appreciative comments were a source of considerable pleasure and, as always, of great value. Another eminent fellow Dostoev-skian, Jacques Catteau of the Sorbonne and the Institut d'Études Slaves, helped to make my Paris sojourns, with the aid of his wife, Jacqueline, personally pleasurable as well as scholarly profitable; and I have benefited a great deal from his own work and enlightening conversation in addition to the resources of the Institut d'Études Slaves, over which he presides.

As I was writing this preface, word reached me of the death of another cherished friend, Ralph Ellison, and I should like to record here how grateful I have always been to him over the years for our conversations about Dostoevsky just as I was on the point of launching out on a book (!) about him. The enthusiastic support he offered to such an idea was greatly heartening, and I still have the volume of Dostoevsky's essays that he plucked off his bookshelf (we shared neighboring offices in Rutgers University) and gave me as a gift. I never pick it up without re-membering the warmth of his friendship and the brilliance of his own assimilation of Dostoevsky, both in his magnificent *Invisible Man* and in his critical essays.

Other friends also come to mind whose responses, as it were, made my day from time to time, especially in moments of difficulty. Intensely involved letters from E. M. Cioran and the late Jean Hélion about my third volume helped to spur on my sometimes flagging spirits as I strug-gled with the fourth. A Paris friend René Chenon, now also passed away, was a faithful and discerning reader, whose vast culture gave his com-ments particular weight in my eyes, and I felt his anticipation of future volumes as a great compliment. Nor should I forget to express my grati-tude to the ordinary readers who wrote to inquire when the next volume would be available and sometimes just to wish me good luck. Nothing gave me more pleasure than to receive such letters, which confirmed my long-held conviction that there are nonspecialist readers all over Amer-ica who are willing (and even eager) to tackle scholarly works written to be understood rather than to display a mastery of the latest academic jargon.

Calvin Radl undertook the final typing of the bulky manuscript with a smiling patience at my continual revisions. Gretchen Oberfranc, my edi-tor at Princeton, pored over the text with appreciation and a sharp eye for awkwardnesses and omissions. I am also indebted to the former liter-ary editor of the Press, Robert Brown, for his gentle prodding, which never let me forget that both he and a public were waiting for my next installment.

I am grateful to the National Endowment for the Humanities, which awarded me a fellowship in 1990–1991 to work on this volume, and also to the Center for International Studies at Stanford University for a travel grant allowing me to visit St. Petersburg (Leningrad) and make a Dostoevsky pilgrimage. I am happy to acknowledge the financial help afforded by the Division of Arts and Sciences of Stanford University, the Stanford Humanities Center, the Center for Russian and East European Studies at Stanford, and the Marguerite Eyer Wilbur Foundation (especially Russell Kirk) to defray the expenses of preparing this massive manuscript for publication. I should also like to express my thanks to the Bibliothèque des Langue Orientales and the Bibliothèque of the Institut d'Études Slaves in Paris, whose facilities considerably lightened the task of my researches for this volume and the previous ones.

To my wife, Marguerite, who has always taken time from her own professional work (in mathematics) to give me the benefits of her advice, counsel, and criticism, I can only once again express my deepest gratefulness. Her suggestions led to a greatly improved reorganization of Chapters 19 and 20, and, as my first reader and editor, the rigor and discrimination of her mind and her stylistic sensitivity have always helped immeasurably to improve my pages.

Joseph Frank

Stanford, California—Paris, France, 1994

The problem of transliteration is always a difficult one, and I have opted for the simplest solution. For all Russian words, names, or otherwise, I use System I in the transliteration chart contained in J. Thomas Shaw, *The Transliteration of Modern Russian for English Language Publications* (Madison, Milwaukee, and London, 1967), 8–9. I have, however, occasionally inserted a "y" to indicate a soft sound where this would not be the natural pronunciation of the transliterated word in English, even though System I does not pay any attention to this feature of Russian. And I have always used English forms, rather than transliteration, where such exist and have become customary (Alexander rather than Aleksandr, for example).

Citations to Dostoevsky's texts and correspondence are made to the volumes of the great Academy of Sciences edition: F. M. Dostoevsky, *Polnoe Sobranie Sochinenii*, 30 vols. (Leningrad, 1972–1980). For the novels, I have consulted various translations: those of Constance Garnett, Jessie Coulson, Richard Pevear and Larissa Volokhonsky for *Crime and Punishment*; for *The Idiot*, Constance Garnett; for *The Gambler*, Victor Terras and Constance Garnett; for *The Eternal Husband*, Constance Garnett; for *The Devils*, David Magarshack and Constance Garnett. I have also used the *Selected Letters* translated by Andrew McAndrew and the relevant volumes of the *Complete Letters* translated by David Lowe.

All citations have been checked with the Russian texts, and alterations made whenever necessary.

PART I

Some "Strange, 'Unfinished' Ideas"

Can our civilization actually survive without the belief that the distinction between good and evil, between the prohibited and the mandatory, does not depend on our respective decisions and thus that it does not coincide with the distinction between the advantageous and the disadvantageous? Since something that may be beneficial to one human being or group may obviously be unfavorable to others (and by the same token, something that is disadvantageous to a person or group at some point in time may turn out to be advantageous to that person or group in the long run); in short, since there is after all no concept of what is advantageous or disadvantageous *tout court*, the notion that moral precepts coincide with utilitarian criteria eivdently amounts to nothing but the tenet that moral precepts do not exist. Kant knew that, of course; thus by turning against the popular utilitarianism of the Enlightenment, he also knew exactly that what was at stake was not any particular moral code, but rather a question of the existence or nonexistence of the distinction between good and evil and, consequently, a question of the fate of mankind.

Leszek Kolakowski, *Modernity on Endless Trial*

Умом Россию не понять,
Аршином общим не измерить:
У ней особенная стать —
В Россию можно только верить.

Russia cannot be understood by reason,
Nor measured by a common rule:
It has its own configuration—
Russia, you can only take it on faith.

F. I. Tyutchev, November 28, 1866

CHAPTER 1

Introduction

During an earlier period of Dostoevsky's life, in the years of his arrest for political conspiracy, imprisonment, and exile to Siberia—the period covered in the second volume of the present series, *The Years of Ordeal*—he had been buffeted about by a succession of unexpected and quite sensational events. Compared to those years, the seven to which the present volume is devoted are rather quiet and unexciting. He remarried, fled Russia to escape from importuning creditors and grasping dependents, and lived obscurely in Germany and Switzerland until his return in 1871. His seclusive life of unremitting literary labor was shared only by his young bride, who twice made him a father; and his toilsome existence was unrelieved except by occasional—and invariably unsuccessful—jaunts to various gambling casinos. There he experienced the cathartic thrill of excitement that made roulette so irresistible a passion for him, and futilely pursued his hope of obtaining enough funds to allow him to return home.

Despite their relatively pedestrian external character, however, these six years are among the most remarkable in Dostoevsky's career, and mark a high point in the annals of nineteenth-century literature. For it was in this short span of time that he produced three of his greatest novels—*Crime and Punishment, The Idiot,* and *The Devils*—and two of his best novellas, *The Gambler* and *The Eternal Husband.* From a literary point of view, these were the miraculous years of Dostoevsky the writer; and the more one learns about the conditions under which he lived, the more incredible it seems that he was capable of producing so many masterpieces so rapidly. For he had to cope not only with grinding poverty and continual changes of residence, but also with recurring fits of epilepsy that incapacitated him for days at a stretch.

At just about the time we begin this volume, Dostoevsky said in a letter to a friend that, for all the hardships he was then facing, he still was not discouraged and felt himself to possess "the vitality of a cat."[1] One of the most frequently reiterated motifs in his work is precisely that of an instinctive and unquenchable love of life, a blind and passionate commitment to a belief in its supreme value, which no unhappy experiences could ever shake or undermine. "Life is a gift, life is happiness, every minute can be an eternity of happiness," he had written to his brother

3

Mikhail, in a soul-searching letter composed just after having undergone a ceremony of mock execution.[2] For an agonizing interval that he would never afterwards forget (and which he enshrined in *The Idiot*), he believed that he would be shot within the next twenty minutes. Dostoevsky's astonishing resilience in adversity, his ability to spring back and recover from the worst blows and disappointments, certainly were linked with this revelation of the unsurpassable beauty of life itself—a revelation that overwhelmed him as he stood in the shadow of death. But even before this epochal event, we can observe a toughness and tenacity in Dostoevsky's character that boded well for a creative career requiring him to triumph over daunting obstacles.

Dostoevsky's determination to become a writer had been evident from the years of his early adolescence, and was stimulated by the literary upbringing provided by his parents. He had also received an excellent education in private schools, and then, through the culture proffered to a future Russian Army officer and gentleman, in the Academy of Military Engineers. As a boy he had absorbed Karamzin, Zhukovsky, Derzhavin, Anne Radcliffe, Walter Scott, and Schiller, and had stoutly defended Pushkin against his parents' preference for the more sentimental Zhukovsky. When Pushkin died in the same year as Dostoevsky's mother, he said that if he were not already in mourning he would don it for the poet—so intimately did he feel the loss of his literary idol! Although accepting his father's decision that he prepare for an Army career, he made up his mind, along with his older brother Mikhail, to become a writer; and he retired from the Army the moment he felt it financially possible to do so. He counted on his pen to make a living in the future, and was to rely on it as his major source of income for the remainder of his life.

Dostoevsky's faith in his talent was strikingly confirmed by the resounding success of his first novel, *Poor Folk*, which was the sensation of the 1845 literary season. Hailed later by Alexander Herzen as the first Socialist novel in Russian literature, it was immediately praised by Vissarion Belinsky, the leading progressive critic of the time, as a brilliant response to his call for a literature inspired by social-philanthropic themes. But Belinsky found Dostoevsky's next work, *The Double*, too exclusively psychological for his tastes; and as Dostoevsky continued to experiment with various forms and styles throughout the 1840s, rather than overtly stressing a social thematic, his reputation suffered a precipitous decline. Moreover, his combination of personal timidity and literary vanity made him a laughingstock in literary coteries, and he became the butt of many comic anecdotes as well as of a mocking poem. But he resolutely went his own way, refusing to kowtow even to the powerful Belinsky, with whom he quarreled on both literary and ideological (that is, religious) grounds.

Dostoevsky's refusal to follow Belinsky's literary prescriptions did not mean that he had lost interest in the social issues so apparent in his first novel, and still present, in a subtle and implicit manner that Belinsky overlooked, in the psychological dilemmas of characters in later works as well. In 1847 he began to frequent the Petrashevsky Circle, a discussion group dominated by Fourierists in which all sorts of "advanced" ideas were bruited about. What distinguished Dostoevsky's participation in these public debates was his intense abhorrence of serfdom. A year or so later, under the influence of Nikolay Speshnev—who may be considered a real-life prototype of Stavrogin in *The Devils*—he joined a small, secret group dedicated to stirring up a peasant revolution to abolish serfdom, no matter what the cost in blood. The existence of this group, and Dostoevsky's enlistment in its ranks, was kept secret throughout his lifetime; it became known only when revealed by documents published in 1922. He would put this experience as a secret revolutionary conspirator to good use when he came to write *The Devils* twenty-one years later. But the otherwise harmless activities of the Petrashevsky Circle, in the menace-filled atmosphere created by the revolutions of 1848 in Europe, led to the roundup of the members and their confinement and questioning for almost a year. Taken out to be sentenced and presumably shot, Dostoevsky, after the mock-execution ceremony already mentioned, was condemned to four years in a labor camp, to be followed by service in the Russian Army.

Nothing better illustrates the native staunchness of Dostoevsky's character than his exemplary behavior under the pressure of interrogation, during which he refused to betray either himself or others. Nor, as happened in some instances, did the terrible physical and emotional strains of prison-camp life cause him to go to pieces. These strains are brilliantly depicted in his prison-camp memoirs, *House of the Dead*, which provide an indispensable clue to that "regeneration of [his] convictions" which he later said began to occur during these years. Such a "regeneration" ended, once and for all, any revolutionary illusions he may still have clung to; these simply evaporated when he ran headlong into the indiscriminate hatred of the peasant convicts for *all* the educated (and hence upper-class) prisoners like himself! But he also gained a new appreciation of, and insight into, the deeply rooted moral world of the peasantry, who lived inside their native Christianity as they did in their skins, and whose moral instincts were never obliterated even in the midst of their worst criminal excesses. He also obtained a revelatory insight into the irrational, ineradicable needs of the human personality—the need, strongest of all, for a sense of internal freedom, of the autonomy of one's own being, which comes to individuals through the exercise of what is felt as free will. And mankind, he became convinced, also harbored an irresistible need to live in a cosmos from which hope (and there-fore some sort of ultimately religious meaning) had not been entirely eradicated.

On returning to St. Petersburg and the literary life after a ten-year hia-tus, Dostoevsky found an entirely changed political and social-cultural climate. The abolition of serfdom by Alexander II in 1861 blotted out the social evil that Dostoevsky had hated the most, and against which he had been willing to rebel at the risk of his life. The other reforms launched in the early years of that regime also seemed to promise the birth of a new and more just society. Throwing himself fervently into the literary fray from which he had been removed for so long, Dostoevsky, along with his older brother Mikhail, founded a new journal *Time* (*Vremya*). It quickly became one of the leading periodicals, despite the intense jour-nalistic competition on both the right and the left, certainly to a great extent because of Dostoevsky's own contributions (*The Insulted and Injured, House of the Dead, Winter Notes on Summer Impressions*), not to mention numerous polemic interventions on issues then being hotly debated.

Dostoevsky's journal advanced an ideology known as *pochvenni-chestvo*, a return to the soil (*pochva*), a return to one's native roots. His main purpose was to stimulate an effort to bridge the immense gap, from which he had personally suffered so much in Siberia, between the peas-antry and the Westernized upper class. His four years of life on a level of equality with the peasant convicts, he believed, had given him a unique insight into the mentality of the Russian peasant, and shown him how chimerical were all the revolutionary expectations of the radical intelli-gentsia. And though Dostoevsky was always willing to acknowledge the moral passion by which the radicals were inspired, their new ideology, which had come to the fore in his absence (most notably in the writings of N. G. Chernyshevsky), could not have been more inimical to his own convictions.

Composed of a mixture of English Utilitarianism, French Utopian So-cialism, Feuerbachian atheism, and crude mechanical materialism and determinism, this odd amalgam ran smack against the worldview that Dostoevsky had so painfully acquired in his prison-camp years. But his opposition to this ideology, which may roughly be called Russian Nihil-ism in a broad sense, only gradually became apparent in the first five years of the 1860s. It was at the end of this period, in 1864, that he first attacked it head-on in *Notes from Underground*, and worked out the ar-tistic strategy he would use for a similar purpose in his two great novels of the 1860s (*Crime and Punishment* and *The Devils*). This strategy con-sisted of creating characters who *accepted* one or another tenet of Russian Nihilism, and then exhibited in their lives how disastrous were its consequences as they attempted to put such precepts into practice. Dostoevsky, however, did not portray these precepts merely as guides to ordinary social behavior; for him they raised profound moral-philosophical questions far transcending their sources in the material on which he drew, and he traced them back to their ultimate roots in the clash between the fundamental principles of Judeo-Christian morality and the secular alternatives offered by Nihilism. It is this imaginative capacity to raise the social to the tragic, combined with his psychological genius, that gives his greatest works such universal scope and still-undiminished power.

Time was on the point of gaining financial security for its editors when, on the erroneous assumption that one article had supported the Polish uprising of 1863, the journal was mistakenly suppressed by the government. This was an unexpected and undeserved blow from which Dostoevsky's fortunes never fully recovered; but the Dostoevsky brothers did not lose heart. They obtained permission to publish a new journal *Epoch* (*Epokha*), which was launched under the worst possible economic circumstances; and just as this new venture was getting under way, Dostoevsky's personal world also collapsed completely. His first wife, Marya Dimitrievna, died in April 1864 after a long and harrowing illness. The pair had long been emotionally estranged, but Dostoevsky had never ceased being devoted to a person he had once passionately loved and who provided him with a modicum of familial stability. Three months later, his beloved brother Mikhail, who looked after the financial affairs of their journals, was struck down suddenly and unexpectedly. The two people to whom Dostoevsky had been closest in the world thus disappeared within this very short space of time; and he was left alone to provide for himself and his stepson Pasha, as well as for Mikhail's widow and children.

It was at this disastrous moment of his life, and under the stress of his cherished brother's death, that he made the decision that would adversely affect him for the remainder of his days. Dostoevsky could have closed down the journal, assigned its assets to its creditors for whatever they might yield, and then depended on his talents as a writer for an income without worrying about the huge burden of debt that Mikhail had accumulated to finance *Epoch*. Instead, encouraged by his success with *Time*, and certainly overestimating his capacities to act as literary editor, chief contributor, and financial manager all in one, he decided to continue publication. Investing his own inheritance from his wealthy aunt A. F. Kumanina in the journal, he rashly also assumed personal responsibility for his brother's contracts; and these debts, as well as his obligations to Mikhail's family, were primarily the cause of the distressing poverty in which he lived throughout the remainder of the 1860s (though his gambling sprees did not help either). This is the point at which we now pick up the thread of his career, as he forlornly struggles to keep *Epoch* afloat and despondently seeks to begin a new life for himself to replace the one that had vanished.

CHAPTER 2

"The Unhappiest of Mortals"

The deaths of his wife and elder brother in the spring of 1864 deprived Dostoevsky of the two people who had shared his life most closely. Never an expansive or gregarious personality, lacking any intimate friends who might have helped to alleviate his grief, Dostoevsky now survived in desperate loneliness, devoting all his energies to the single-handed struggle to keep the faltering *Epoch* alive. The financial future of Mikhail's large family depended on his labors, and he expended himself unstintingly in the vain attempt to rescue the sinking publication from extinction.

During the remainder of *Epoch*'s existence (the last issue was published in March 1865), Dostoevsky's life became one unending round of unrelieved drudgery. According to the commiserating account furnished by his younger brother Nikolay to one of their sisters in Moscow, "he works all night, never goes to bed before five in the morning . . . all day he does nothing but sit and look after the editorial business of the journal." As Nikolay saw it, although his brother never complained, "in my opinion, he is the unhappiest of mortals."[1] It is hardly surprising, under these conditions, that Dostoevsky should have cast around for some female companionship to relieve the bleakness of his solitude, or that the two attempts he initiated in this direction should both have been made possible by contacts established in the course of carrying out his editorial labors.

2

Dostoevsky first heard of Martha Panina, also known by the name of Martha Brown, from the man with whom she was then living, a minor contributor to *Epoch* named Peter Gorsky. He was one of the numerous denizens of St. Petersburg's literary Grub Street who clustered around the various publications, eking out a beggarly existence on the edge of destitution and often supplementing their literary labors with manual work. All that we know of the relations between Dostoevsky and Martha Panina is contained in a handful of letters written by her between November 1864 and January 1865. Although it cannot be stated with certainty that the two became lovers, the letters reveal a growing degree of intimacy that distinctly raises such a possibility. And they also give us a rare glimpse of Dostoevsky's willingness to become charitably involved in the personal lives of at least some of his contributors—without even the slightest suggestion, in the beginning, that he harbored any amatory interest whatever in the much-buffeted and considerably shopworn Martha Panina.

Her real name, which Dostoevsky may well never have learned, was Elizaveta Andreyevna Chlebnikova, and she was the wayward daughter of a landowning family who had received some education and could write a literary Russian. An adventurous existence had taken her over most of Western Europe in the company of various men—a Hungarian, an Englishman, and a Frenchman among others. On first setting foot in England, without a penny and completely ignorant of the language, she had tried to take her life in despair and was saved by the police. For some weeks she lived under the bridges of the Thames among other vagabonds, and, if we believe her account, became an innocent accomplice of a gang manufacturing and distributing counterfeit money. Thanks to the zeal of various missionaries concerned to save her soul, she acquired English very rapidly; and a charitable Methodist pastor, impressed by her knowledge of the Bible and ability to recite the Lord's Prayer in English, took her to live with his family on the Isle of Guernsey. With the blessing of her patron, she married a sailor named Brown who worked on a boat whose home port was Baltimore, and she then lived (one assumes as Mrs. Brown) in Weymouth, Brighton, and London. When or why the marriage ended is unknown; equally obscure is what brought Martha Brown back to Russia, where, as she remarks, many people no longer thought she was Russian at all.

On returning to her homeland, she became the mistress of a much older man named Flemming, who served in some subordinate capacity on one of the literary journals, and then transferred her affections to Gorsky. A retired army officer, he enjoyed a minor literary reputation as a specialist in physiological sketches depicting the pitiable lives of the poorest inhabitants of St. Petersburg, and the title of one of his contributions to *Time* conveys their flavor: *Poor Lodgers. In the hospital and out in the cold. From the notes of a martyr.* Dostoevsky had a certain sympathy for Gorsky's literary endeavors, which probably reminded him of some of his own writings in the 1840s, and he commented favorably on one of them published in the first issue of *Epoch*. "Gorsky's [piece] pleased me very much" he wrote Mikhail. "As a defense against all attacks on him, one can say that this is not at all literature and it is stupid to look at it from this point of view. These are simply *facts*, and as such are useful." Ever alert to reader opinion, Dostoevsky adds that "the piece of Gorsky produced some effect here [in Moscow]. It was liked."[2]

Gorsky, a confirmed alcoholic, lived on much the same miserable level as the figures who peopled his sketches, and Panina told Dostoevsky that her life with him, which sometimes reached "the furthest limits of vagabondage," rivaled her English experiences in the utter extremity of their destitution.[3] Hoping to capitalize on her linguistic abilities, Gorsky brought her to the editorial offices of *Epoch* one day, introduced her to Dostoevsky, and suggested that he might use her as a translator. Her first letter to him is a purely formal reply to an offer of such work conveyed through Gorsky; the second, a month later, is of a more personal nature, but still without any hint of a greater intimacy.

Nonetheless, Panina appeals to Dostoevsky, as someone with position and moral authority, to intervene with Gorsky and attempt to bring him to his senses. By this time she was occupying a bed in the Peter and Paul Hospital, where Gorsky had shown up to exhibit his displeasure and make a drunken scene. One source of contention between them was her refusal, despite Gorsky's pressure, to write an autobiographical account of her European travels for publication. Perhaps, as she insists, she lacked the literary capacity to undertake such a task; but she was also inwardly reluctant to expose her disreputable past to public scrutiny. "I never intended to wander," she assures Dostoevsky, "and wandered only because things turned out that way."[4] Gorsky's scandalous public behavior had now thrown her into despair, and seriously affected her health. "Ever since Mr. Gorsky turned up in a drunken condition, I have suffered from insomnia and some sort of terribly feverish condition, and I feel a total loss of strength and courage. All the same, Mr. Gorsky is not at all to blame, only destiny and in part myself, since all is a punishment for the past."[5] Dostoevsky could hardly have remained unresponsive to such sincere accents of contrition and Panina's refusal to blame others, even the obstreperous Gorsky, for her numerous woes.

Dostoevsky had already entrusted Panina with reading some of the proofs of *Epoch*, though she complains that Gorsky's confusion and disorder had so far prevented her from correcting those portions for which she was responsible. Another letter sent the same day asks Dostoevsky to connive at deceiving Gorsky, but only for the purpose of leading him to abate his demands that Panina exploit her shameful memories for the sake of earning a few rubles. Accompanying this letter was a manuscript, which Dostoevsky was requested to flourish before Gorsky as a sample of Panina's compliance with his wishes, but without allowing him to consult its contents. It is from this manuscript that we glean all our information concerning Panina's past; and Dostoevsky was to inform Gorsky that, in his editorial judgment, it was unsuitable for publication. Whether Dostoevsky fell in with this plan remains unknown, but he must certainly have read the text; a few days later he visited the hospital and left some money for the proofreading. Her next letter refers gratefully to this visit, and also mentions some additional money and a further letter sent without the knowledge of Gorsky. To guard Dostoevsky's reputation, she assures him she will send all messages from the hospital as if they came from a male patient.

Two letters written a week later indicate that Panina had no intention of, or at least was hoping to avoid, returning to live with Gorsky. Indeed, although now fully recovered, she preferred to remain in the disease-ridden hospital rather than lapse back into a life of misery and abuse. Again, though, she pleads with Dostoevsky to forgive Gorsky's behavior; it would seem, as she explains, that "he imagines, entirely without foundation, that if I leave the hospital and he has no funds, I will choose to live in debauchery." During Dostoevsky's call, he had advised her to remain with Gorsky at least for the time being; and she reluctantly agrees with such counsel because "the last thing in the world I like, and what I fear most in life, are scandals, and especially the scandals of Mr. Gorsky."[6]

Two weeks later, another letter discloses that Gorsky had shown up in the hospital once again, behaved like a madman, shamefully insulted her in public, and shouted that he would track her down even if it meant going to the bottom of the sea. Such words could only mean that he knew their relationship was at an end; and she accordingly asks Dostoevsky whether she can come directly to him on leaving the hospital, or get in touch with him from where she will be staying, "in the confident hope that you will not refuse to give me, for the last time, at least your friendly advice." With this letter was enclosed another to Gorsky (probably unsealed), which she asked Dostoevsky to dispatch, and also a letter of Gorsky's about which she desired to have Dostoevsky's opinion. He had clearly assumed the role of trusted confidant of the troubled Martha (as she now signs herself), and she writes apologetically: "Forgive me for so boldly entrusting you with all the secrets of our commonplace liaison."[7]

The last letter, dated sometime in the second half of January 1865, reveals an entirely new state of affairs. Panina, living in the city, is no longer with Gorsky; and she feels obliged to clarify the motives inspiring her willingness to acquaint Dostoevsky with the most intimate details of her decidedly unsavory situation. "You have already shown me so much consideration and sympathy," she writes, "and your trust is so extremely valuable to me, that I, for my part, would consider it ungrateful and base if I were not fully frank with you. Since my relation to Mr. Gorsky is more conventional than intimate, my aim was to allow you, on the basis of my letters to him, to obtain some knowledge concerning me and my circumstances." At this point, the letter continues in a fashion suggesting some previous conversation between the pair about the possibility of Martha Panina coming to stay with Dostoevsky as his mistress. "In any case," she goes on, "whether I can succeed or not in satisfying you in a physical sense, and whether there will exist between us that spiritual harmony on which will depend the continuance of our acquaintance, believe me when I say that I shall always remain grateful that you favored me with your friendship even for a moment or a certain period of time. I swear to you that I have never, until now, resolved to be as frank with anyone as I have ventured to be with you."

"Forgive me for this egoistic admission, but so much grief, despair, and hopelessness has accumulated in my soul during these past two years, which I have spent in Russia as in a prison, that, as God is my witness, I am happy, I am fortunate, to have met a man possessing such calmness of soul, such patience, such good sense and righteousness as could be found neither in Flemming nor in Gorsky. I am absolutely indifferent at present as to whether our relation will be long or short. But I swear to you that what I value, incomparably more than any material gain, is that you were not squeamish about the fallen side of my personality, that you placed me higher than I stand in my own estimation."[8] Martha Panina concludes by urging Dostoevsky to show *this* letter to Gorsky; and whether it led to the love affair she so obviously desired, or whether such an affair had already begun, cannot be determined. One may perhaps see a transposition of this relationship, and of the behavior that inspired Martha with such gratitude, in Dostoevsky's portrayal of Prince Myshkin's attitude toward the abused Nastasya Philippovna—who, like Martha, could not forgive herself, but was unable to follow Martha's example in extending forgiveness to others.

3

———

Just about the same time as this final letter from Martha Panina, Dostoevsky also received another from a young woman with whom he was soon to fall in love. Her name was Anna Korvin-Krukovskaya, and two of her short stories—one entitled *A Dream*, the other *Mikhail*—had been printed in *Epoch* during the previous months; but both had appeared under the pseudonym of Yury Orbelov. For Miss Korvin-Krukovskaya, who had sent the stories in secret to the magazine, was the elder daughter of a retired lieutenant-general with strict principles about the behavior of his female folk. A gentleman of the old school, strongly imbued with the sense of his own importance and the dignity of his family, he lived with his much younger wife and two daughters in the depths of the countryside near Vitebsk on the Polish-Russian border. Young Anna, then all of twenty-two, had hidden her literary exploits from her father, if not from her sister Sofya—later to become famous under the name of Kovalevskaya as the first woman to hold a chair of mathematics in Europe—and dispatched them with the conspiratorial aid of the estate steward, who was devoted to his young mistress and had agreed to receive any reply in his name. Sofya's memoirs allow us to peer into the recesses of this isolated nest of gentlefolk in the Russian provinces, out of which would emerge two extraordinary women with whom Dostoevsky maintained cordial relations throughout the remainder of his life.

General Korvin-Krukovsky, who raised pure-blooded cattle and ran a liquor distillery on the family estate, had very little taste for the social frivolities of Petersburg. But, in deference to the desires of his more convivial spouse for some diversion, and also to introduce his daughters to a wider range of suitors, he allowed them to plunge into the fashionable Petersburg whirl each year for a period of a month or, at most, six weeks, while he remained behind impatiently awaiting their return. The letter Dostoevsky received from Anna on February 28 signified that one of these annual descents on Petersburg relatives was impending, and informed him that the Korvin-Krukovskys would be glad to receive a visit if notified in advance of his intention to call. Since Dostoevsky was a noted author who had accepted, and encouraged, the fledgling literary efforts of their daughter, such an invitation would seem the least that might be expected. In fact, however, permission to extend it had been granted to Anna only after a long struggle against the deeply rooted prejudices of her suspicious and disgruntled father.

The General had met one Russian literary lady as a young man, the then reigning society belle Countess Rostopchina, and he had chanced on her again years later at the gambling tables of Baden-Baden behaving in a distinctly unladylike manner. Such was the inevitable fate of all Russian authoresses; and when he discovered by accident that his own Anyuta was glorifying in this dubious appellation, he flew into such a rage that his frightened family feared he would be felled by a stroke. To make matters worse, the encouraging letter from Dostoevsky that he inadvertently read also contained payment for Anna's contributions to *Epoch*. "Anything can be expected from young ladies who are capable, unbeknownst to their father and mother, of entering into correspondence with an unknown man and receiving money from him!" he thundered. "Now you are selling your stories, but the time may come, perhaps, when you will sell yourself!"[9]

After this first paroxysm of wrath, the General relapsed into sullen silence; but he gradually gave way to the mollifying influence of his wife, who had been inclined to side with him at first, but then began to feel rather proud that her daughter had become a successful Russian authoress. He finally consented to his wife's plea that he at least listen to a reading of *A Dream*, which contained a pathetic account of the heroine's struggle to escape from the stifling constraints of family tyranny. This subject hit so close to home, according to Sofya's recollections, that at the conclusion, when the young Lilenka dies regretting the waste of her life, tears sprang to the General's eyes and he hastily left the salon without a word. Nothing further was said about Anna's literary career, but from that moment the entire situation changed. The guilty steward was restored to the post from which he had been ignominiously evicted, and permission was given to Anna to meet Dostoevsky on the next trip to Petersburg. But the General, though kindhearted enough under his forbidding exterior, still felt uneasy, and prudently admonished his wife to be on her guard. "Remember, Lisa, that you have a great responsibility," he told her before departure. "Dostoevsky is not a person of our society. What do we know about him? Only that he is a journalist and former convict. Quite a recommendation! To be sure! We must be very careful with him."[10]

4
———

Such were the origins of the letter that Dostoevsky received inviting him to call on the Korvin-Krukovsky family in Petersburg. Of course he knew nothing about the preceding drama, or only what he might have guessed from Anna's missives; but the secrecy surrounding her contributions, and the correspondence carried on under an assumed name, probably allowed him to surmise something about her background. He knew that she was proud and ambitious, since she had asked him, on sending her first story, whether he could judge if she would develop into an *important* Russian authoress. He also guessed, from the nature of the story itself, that she was young and inexperienced, and he refers to reading it "under the fascination of that youthful directness, that sincerity and warmth of feeling, which fills your story." Without responding to the question about her future literary promise, he adroitly used it to obtain more information about his mysterious contributor. "I would be genuinely happy" he writes, "if you found it possible to tell me more about yourself; how old you are and in what circumstances you live. It is important for me to know all this in order accurately to evaluate your talent."[11]

The original of this letter, which has been lost, does not appear in Dostoevsky's correspondence; but Anna displayed it, in the strictest secrecy, to the bedazzled eyes of her sister Sofya, who read it over so many times that she felt able to transcribe it word for word in her memoirs many years later. The pages of these memoirs also contain a vivid and delightfully perfidious portrait, painted by an admiring but envious younger sister, of the strong-willed, talented, and beautiful Anna, who fought fiercely with the French and English governesses employed to turn her into a "brilliant, worldly society belle,"[12] and who constantly sought to assert her independence. Not that she had any objection at first to the nature of her education; but she refused to submit to discipline from strangers, and was even bold enough to protest openly against her father's decision to rusticate in the boring isolation of the provinces. Eagerly seeking some distraction, at fifteen Anna threw herself on the pile of English novels yellowing in the family library—mostly Gothic or historical romances retailing the derring-do of knights in the Middle Ages—and promptly began to head her letters with the place-name "Château" Palibino. Her favorite room was located in a turret under the eaves, from whose vantage point she could scan the road for the knight coming to rescue her from the tedium of provincial captivity.

A new phase began with the reading of a more recent novel, Edward George Bulwer-Lytton's *Harold*, set in the time of the Norman Conquest of England. King Harold perishes during the Battle of Hastings, unshriven of mortal sin and thus condemned to eternal suffering. His fiancée, the ravishing Edith Swan-Neck, secretly enters a convent, takes a vow of perpetual silence, and devotes her life to prayer and the tireless care of the afflicted and unfortunate. But when, on her deathbed, she asks for a sign from Heaven that Harold will be forgiven as recompense for *her* life of saintly devotion, no such sign is forthcoming; and she dies with a curse against God on her lips. This novel brought Anna face-to-face with the "accursed questions of human life" at the age of sixteen, and suddenly revealed to her the vanity of earthly endeavors and the unsolved mystery of human destiny.* The result was an access of religious questioning in which Anna wept uncontrollably over the unhappy fate of humanity as a whole—a problem, as she assured Sofya, the younger girl was not yet mature enough to understand—and spent her time reading Thomas à Kempis's *Imitation of Christ*. Now she treated the

---

* This account of *Harold* is based on Sofya's recollection and hardly jibes with the novel itself. After leafing through its pages (to *read* its floridly fustian text is quite impossible now), I could find nothing to bear out this version of the theme. Edith is the betrothed of Harold, but they are unable to marry because too closely related; in the final chapter she discovers his body on the battlefield. " 'Wed, wed,' murmured the betrothed; 'wed at last? O Harold, Harold! the words of the Vala were true,—and Heaven is kind!' and laying her head gently on the breast of the dead, she smiled and died." Edward Bulwer-Lytton, *Harold, Last of the Saxon Kings*, 2 vols. (Boston, 1896), 2: 326.

Harold's romance with Edith is in fact a minor subtheme in a work largely devoted to the political and cultural struggle over England between Saxons and Normans. But no doubt this romance is what struck Anna, who may have transposed the impossibility of marriage between Harold and Edith into a self-sacrifice on her part. It was God (or his Church) that stood in the way of her happiness, and hence, the issue of God's injustice.

household servants with particular attention and delicacy, and assumed a refined politeness toward the English governess that drove the poor lady out of her mind. Shortly afterward, though, the preparations for the French play to be given on her mother's name day swept everything else aside. Anna turned out to have considerable dramatic talent, enjoyed her triumph at the festivities to the hilt, and entreated her father to allow her to enter a theatrical school and become an actress.

Living as she did in faraway Palibino, and carefully shielded from the subversive new ideas then stirring all of young Russia, the highly impressionable Anna was unaware that her girlish infatuation with the Middle Ages and her metaphysical despair had long since fallen out of fashion. But the modern world finally loomed on her horizon in a form made classic by Russian literature: incarnated in the son of the local priest. The young man, a model student, had graduated at the top of his class in the seminary; but then, despite the pleas of his father and the weighty intervention of the local bishop, he had refused to become a clergyman. Instead, he had enrolled in the faculty of natural sciences at Petersburg; and on returning home for the summer holidays, he not only exhibited a scandalous desire to be treated as an equal by the all-powerful General, but proclaimed to all and sundry that man was descended from the apes! Had not the revered Professor Sechenov, the famous physiologist at the University, denied that any such entity as the soul really existed?—it was all, he had proven, just a matter of nervous reflexes! Russian Nihilism of the 1860s thus made its appearance on the local scene; and Anna was soon observed taking long walks and plunged deep in eager and prolonged conversation with the ungainly young man, whose lowly social origins precluded any suspicion of romantic interest.

It was through him that she first obtained copies of the radical journals *The Contemporary* (*Sovremennik*) and *The Russian Word* (*Russkoe Slovo*), and he eventually turned up with a precious copy of Herzen's illegal weekly *The Bell* (*Kolokol*), published in London and smuggled into the country. Anna began to wear simple dark dresses with smooth collars, pulled her wavy and luxuriant blond hair straight back, and engaged the local peasant women in conversation; even more, she organized morning classes to teach their children how to read. Cases of books arrived dealing with the most serious subjects—no longer novels, but works like *The Physiology of Everyday Life* by G. H. Lewes (mentioned in *Crime and Punishment* and a great favorite with the radicals) and the *History of Civilization*, perhaps by Guizot but more likely by the less conservative T. H. Buckle, whose name crops up in *Notes from Underground*. Finally catching up with her century and generation, Anna now demanded, not that her father allow her to become an actress, but that he consent to her pursuing studies while living by herself in Petersburg.

To the General, such an idea was sheer madness; no well brought up and unmarried young lady could live by herself outside the protection of the family domicile!

Anna's two contributions to *Epoch* were clearly projections of her own restive rebelliousness. *A Dream* deals with the sad life of a young girl of modest family, oppressed by the gloomy and tedious monotony of her toilsome existence, who one day goes to a nearby church and observes the funeral of a poor student with no family or real friends. Suddenly she finds herself sobbing, and is overcome with desolation when she feels her own life to be equally hopeless and futile. In a dream, she sees herself living together with the dead student, poor but happy in their loving union and a life that has some purpose; but then, waking to find that nothing has changed or can possibly change, she wastes away and dies.

Mikhail, which betrays the influence of her religious phase, centers on a wealthy young boy, left an orphan, who feels some religious stirrings and is sent to live in a monastery with an uncle, an ex-dandy once a riotous young Guards officer but now an ascetic monk. Mikhail accidentally meets a charming young princess on a visit to the monastery who turns out to be a friend of his family; and he is suddenly stirred by a craving for life. But when he returns to the world, he finds that the princess is about to marry his cousin, also a fashionable Guards officer, and that his monastic years have destroyed any capacity to enjoy mundane pleasures. He dies of tuberculosis in his cell, gazing at his impassive uncle who represents death-in-life, and leaves his fortune to the princess. Both stories indicate the author's own need to break out of her confines, and her fear of being stifled by the restrictive routine of her isolated circumstances.

Dostoevsky apologized in his letter for some cuts made in *Mikhail* at the request of the ecclesiastical censorship, but he consoles Anna with the assurance that the elided passages were superfluous. Brevity is always a virtue, and "all the great writers," he declares sententiously, "write in the most concise way." Otherwise, he is lavish in his praise, and also cites supporting confirmation for his favorable judgment. "Your story *Mikhail* was very much liked by all of our editors and our regular contributors. One of them, Strakhov (he writes 'The Notes of a Chronicler'), and whose opinion I value most of all, finds that you have a great innate mastery and diversity. Diversity as, for example, in *A Dream* and *The Life of a Monk* [the original title of *Mikhail*]. All in all, *Mikhail* was liked by many people, *A Dream*, not by all. You know my opinion. Not only may you, but *you must*, take your talents seriously. You are a poet." Dostoevsky advises Anna to read and study, and also, as he adds, "it is necessary to believe. Otherwise, one arrives at nothing. Your ideal appears quite well, although *in a negative way*. Mikhail was not able, *by* *reason of his very nature* (that is, unconsciously) to accept something *lower than his ideal*; this is a strong and profound idea."[13] Dostoevsky here is presumably referring to Mikhail's rejection of a world with no higher purpose or exalted aim, and, though the context is unclear, advocating a more positive and distinct belief in "the ideal."* But he will soon find that Anna, despite the deference expressed in her letters, would be anything but a docile pupil, and that she was much more infected by the virus of Nihilism than her writings might have led him to surmise.

5

Shortly after their arrival in Petersburg in the early spring of 1865, the Korvin-Krukovskys received Dostoevsky for the first time; and the long-awaited visit, anticipated by Anna with such eagerness and trepidation, turned out to be a catastrophe. Strictly conforming to her husband's parting injunctions, Anna's mother insisted on being present; Sofya too, consumed with curiosity, had received permission to remain in the living room; two elderly Russian-German aunts (Mme Korvin-Krukovskaya came from German stock), finding one pretext or another to enter and catch a glimpse of the famous author, finally installed themselves there for good. Furious at this solemn assemblage, Anna exhibited her displeasure by silence. Dostoevsky too, taken aback at being forced to confront such a forbidding gathering, totally failed to respond to Mme Korvin-Krukovskaya's polite conversation, uttered in her most ingratiating and worldly style. "He seemed old and sickly that day," Sofya recalled, "as was always the case, incidentally, when he was in low spirits."[14] After half an hour of this slow torture, Dostoevsky seized his hat and hastily departed. Anna ran to her room, uncontrollably burst into tears, and her reproaches soon reduced her mother to the same lachrymose condition.

Five days later, Dostoevsky called again unexpectedly and found only the two girls at home. He and Anna immediately engaged in eager conversation, as if they had been old friends, and matters could not have

---

* There has been some speculation in the Dostoevsky literature that this story of Anna Korvin-Krukovskaya, *Mikhail*, may have had some influence on the creation of Alyosha Karamazov. The possibility was raised by Sofya in a conversation with Dostoevsky: " 'Well yes, this could be true!' Feodor Mikhailovich said, striking his forehead, 'but, take my word for it, I forgot about Mikhail when I invented Alyosha. Perhaps, maybe, unconsciously he appeared to me,' he added musingly."

It is difficult to take this statement as more than a gesture of conversational politeness toward an old friend. The resemblance in situation is so external and superficial that it is hardly worth mentioning. A much more likely source for Alyosha, if one is necessary, may be found in George Sand's *Spiridion*. See S. V. Kovalevskaya, *Vospominaniya*, 67–68; T. I. Ornatskaya, "Dostoevsky i Rasskazi A. V. Korvin-Krukovskoi (Zhaklar)," in *Dostoevsky, Materiali i Issledovaniya*, ed. G. M. Fridlender (Leningrad, 1985), 6: 238–241; for George Sand, see my first volume, *Dostoevsky: The Seeds of Revolt, 1821–1849* (Princeton, N.J., 1976), 130.

gone more swimmingly. He seemed to Sofya to be quite another person, much younger than before and marvelously kind and clever; she could hardly believe that he was all of forty-four years old! When their mother returned home, she was startled and a little frightened to find Dostoevsky ensconced there alone with her daughters; but the two were so radiantly happy that she promptly invited him to stay for dinner. The ice was thus finally broken, and Dostoevsky now began to call on the Korvin-Krukovskys two or three times a week.

According to Sofya, Dostoevsky often spoke about his past when others were not present, and what she reports poses some problems for the historian. For her memoirs contain disturbing factual anomalies that may come either from Dostoevsky's own embellishments or lapses of memory (such lapses were quite frequent with him, partly as a result of his epilepsy), or perhaps from misremembrance on her part. It should also be kept in mind that many stories about Dostoevsky's earlier years were freely bandied about among his admirers and acquaintances, and accepted as true. In reporting Dostoevsky's words about the moment when he was awaiting death before the firing squad, for example, Sofya has him actually blindfolded, tied to a stake, and awaiting the command to be executed. In fact, Dostoevsky was not among the three Petrashevtsy placed in this position, though he would have been among those next in line if the execution had really taken place.*

Similarly, Sofya cites Dostoevsky as asserting that his epilepsy had begun only *after* his release from prison camp, which contradicts all the other evidence at our disposal dating his initial attack to the first year of his arrival there. Sofya also depicts Dostoevsky describing his first seizure as the culmination of an argument with an old friend, an atheist visiting Siberia from Petersburg, against whom Dostoevsky had been defending the existence of God. The conversation, begun on Easter Eve, had continued the whole night through; and as the church bells rang for Easter matins, Dostoevsky for the first time felt the ecstatic surge of the pre-epileptic "aura." "And I felt," he said, "that heaven had come down to earth and swallowed me. I really grasped god and was penetrated by him."[15] No such visit is known from other sources, and one can well believe that Dostoevsky improvised such a story, with its suspiciously symbolic details and its reminiscences of *Faust*, for the benefit of the enraptured Anna and her younger sister. But the words he is supposed to have added about the "happiness" experienced in the moment of "aura" also remarkably resemble a passage in *The Idiot*, as well as Strakhov's account of witnessing one of Dostoevsky's epileptic seizures published in 1883 (Kovalevskaya's memoirs appeared four years later). Either Dos-

* For an account of the circumstances of Dostoevsky's mock execution, see my second volume, *Dostoevsky: The Years of Ordeal, 1850–1859* (Princeton, N.J., 1983), chap. 5.

toevsky had already formulated almost the exact words of this passage in his mind, or Sofya was filling in from already published descriptions.*

It would seem, as well, that Dostoevsky once told his spellbound female audience about a novel he had intended to write in the days of his youth. He had wished, he said, to depict an educated and cultivated gentleman, obviously a member of the gentry, who had caroused as a young man but then settled down and was now an honorable and respected paterfamilias. Traveling abroad, and sampling with delectation all the art treasures of Europe, he wakes one morning in his sunny hotel room filled with a sense of physical contentment and self-satisfaction. "He saw again the wonderful band of light falling on the bare shoulders of St. Cecilia in the Munich gallery. He also recalled an especially intelligent passage in a book he had recently read, *On the Beauty and Harmony of the World*." But he suddenly begins to feel uneasy, as if troubled by some long-dormant twinge of pain (though he can detect no such source of discomfort), and as he concentrates his thoughts, he suddenly recalls an incident from the distant past. Once after a riotous night, and spurred on by drunken companions, he had violated a ten-year-old girl . . . But at this moment Mme Korvin-Krukovskaya broke in with a horrified shriek: "Feodor Mikhailovich! For pity's sake! There are children present!"[16]

This story, if true, obviously foreshadows a number of scenes in still-unwritten novels: Svidrigailov's recollections in *Crime and Punishment* of a young girl who had drowned herself, evidently one of the victims of his lust; Stavrogin's confession, written for *The Devils* but not published in Dostoevsky's lifetime, of the seduction of the twelve-year-old Matryosha, who also kills herself, and whose memory returns to haunt him under almost the same circumstances of sybaritic aesthetic complacency; and of course the rape of the simpleton Lizaveta by the elder Karamazov after a drinking bout. That Dostoevsky had intended to write such a novel, as Sofya says, "in his youth" certainly raises some question; this phrase presumably refers to the 1840s, and nothing in the work of that time remotely resembles the *tonality* of the episode narrated. It seems closest of all to Stavrogin's confession, which Sofya could not have known; and while this resemblance supports the authenticity of her words, it hardly accords with her placement of the time. It is true, of course, that Dostoevsky hints at such a theme of child violation in

---

* Jacques Catteau has printed the passages from Strakhov and Kovalevskaya side by side and noted not only the linguistic resemblances between them but also that the incident Strakhov records took place on Easter Eve as well. Catteau plausibly suggests that Kovalevskaya's "recollection" may well be a collage of Strakhov's account and some words in *The Idiot* on Muhammad and the Koran. He remarks in a footnote: "this is not the first time that we have had doubts about the *Memoirs* of the great mathematician." My own attempt to check the *Harold* references would seem to justify such skepticism. Jacques Catteau, *La Création littéraire chez Dostoevski* (Paris, 1978), 156–157.

A Christmas Tree and a Wedding (1848), which lashes out at the forced marriage of an adolescent girl to a much older husband. But the juxtaposition of refined aestheticism and lustful depravity emerges in Dostoevsky's works sharply only after his return from Siberia in the 1860s.

Yet his lifelong preoccupation, and what some have considered his pathological obsession, with this scabrous theme can hardly be doubted. Some recent and little-known information helps to throw new light on what has frequently been interpreted as Dostoevsky's suspiciously unhealthy fixation on this loathsome perversion. Sometime in the late 1870s, Dostoevsky was sitting in another drawing room when the question arose of what should be considered the greatest crime on earth.

> Dostoevsky spoke quickly, agitatedly and stumblingly. . . . The most frightful, the most terrible sin—was to violate a child. To take a life— that is horrible, Dostoevsky said, but to take away faith in the beauty of love—that is the most terrible crime. And Dostoevsky recounted an episode from his childhood. When I lived in Moscow as a child in a hospital for the poor, Dostoevsky said, where my father was a doctor, I played with a little girl (the daughter of a coachman or a cook). She was a delicate, graceful child of nine. . . . And some disgraceful wretch violated the girl when drunk and she died, pouring out blood. I recall, Dostoevsky said, being sent for my father in the other wing of the hospital, but it was too late. All my life this memory has haunted me as the most frightful crime, the most terrible sin, for which there is not, and cannot be, any forgiveness, and I punished Stavrogin in *The Devils* with this very same terrible crime.[17]

6

As can be seen from Sofya's recollections, Dostoevsky's verbal comportment may well have led Anna's mother to regret having admitted him into the intimacy of the family circle. Another occasion when she undoubtedly had second thoughts about her tolerance occurred during a farewell party, at which, after much urging, Dostoevsky had agreed to be present. The society was mostly Russian-German, very staid, official, and stuffy—exactly the sort of group in which Dostoevsky felt most uncomfortable. He resented that Anna, in her role as elder daughter, shared the obligations of receiving with her mother and was not allowed to confine her attentions exclusively to himself. Even worse, he conceived a furious jealousy for a handsome young officer present among the guests, who was obviously attracted to Anna, and to whom, he convinced himself, Anna would be forced to become engaged against her will. He expressed his displeasure and created a scandal by unpleasant remarks uttered in a loud voice (for example, that the Bible had not been written for society women to read) and by a generally boorish behavior. It was after this evening, according to Sofya, that Anna's previous reverence for Dostoevsky sharply altered. The private conversations between the two changed in tone; now they seemed to be disputing, sometimes acrimoniously, rather than engaging in a friendly exchange of ideas.

As the moment approached for Anna's return to Palibino, Dostoevsky became more censorious and despotic, and Anna less docile and more assertive. "The continual and very burning subject of their argument," writes Sofya, "was Nihilism. The debate over this question continued sometimes long after midnight; the longer they spoke, the more they became excited, and in the heat of the argument they expressed views far more extreme than they actually held."[18] As a sample, Sofya cites the following exchange: "'All of contemporary youth is stupid and backward!' Dostoevsky once shouted. 'Shiny boots are more valuable for them than Pushkin!' To which Anna retorted coolly that 'Pushkin has in fact become out of date in our time,' knowing that nothing could drive Dostoevsky into more of a fury than a lack of respect for Pushkin."[19]

All the same, one evening when Sofya was bravely struggling with Beethoven's *Sonate Pathétique*, which she knew to be among Dostoevsky's favorites, he and Anna treacherously slipped away to another room unobserved. And when the disconsolate pianist, heartbroken at such desertion, went to find her lost audience, she burst in on a proposal of marriage. There is some uncertainty whether Anna accepted, in the emotion of the moment, and then was freed from her pledge by Dostoevsky (that is the story he told his second wife), or whether she ever gave any reply at all. Sofya does not mention an engagement, and one assumes that, if it had existed, Anna's family would have been informed.

Whatever the truth, Anna soon told Sofya: "I do not love Dostoevsky in such a way as to marry him." Besides the difference in age and ideas, Anna realized, with salutary insight, that Dostoevsky needed a wife entirely submissive to his will. "Look," she told her younger sister, "I am sometimes surprised at myself that I cannot love him! He is such a good man! . . . But he does not at all need someone like me as a wife. His wife must devote herself to him entirely, give all her life to him, think only of him. And I cannot do that, I want to live myself! Besides, he is so nervous, so demanding!"[20] Dostoevsky would find exactly the sort of wife he needed a year later, but he always continued to maintain extremely cordial relations with Anna and her sister.

Indeed, he saw a good deal of Anna in the mid-1870s, even though, in the interim, she had married a well-known French radical named Charles Victor Jaclard and committed herself wholeheartedly to a life of revolutionary activity. Not only was she the first translator of parts of Karl Marx's *Capital* into French, but she also established warm personal relations with Marx and played a leading role among the women (they included a surprising number of Russians) who participated courageously in the defense of the Paris Commune of 1870. It is quite likely that Dostoevsky drew on his courtship of her for the portrait of Aglaya Epanchina in *The Idiot*, whose engagement to Prince Myshkin upset her respectable family as much as Anna's friendship with Dostoevsky had initially done with hers. And some of the scenes depicting Prince Myshkin's awkwardness in "good" society may well have originated in Dostoevsky's own misadventures at the receptions and soirées of the Korvin-Krukovskys. Once more, however, after his attempt to win Anna's hand had come to an amicable but irreversible end, Dostoevsky was thrown back on the isolation from which he so achingly longed to escape.

CHAPTER 3

Khlestakov in Wiesbaden

All through the gloomy winter and spring of 1864–1865, as he was vainly struggling to keep *Epoch* alive, Dostoevsky dreamed of finding some relief from his exhausting labors in a voyage to Europe. Writing to Turgenev in Baden-Baden just before the new year, in the hope of obtaining a contribution to the journal, he also speaks of his plans for the near future. "I work day and night," he writes, "I scurry around, I write, I edit, I struggle with typesetters and censors, etc. I can hardly say that my health is good, but I have decided that, at the end of April, I will spend three months abroad to look after myself. I will come to visit you. And by Autumn, I will have gotten back into form. While abroad I wish to write a long story."[1] No further information is given about this intended work; but the reference may well be to what later became *Crime and Punishment*, which began as an idea for a long story rather than a novel.

Several months later, while sadly describing the final collapse of *Epoch* to his old friend Baron Wrangel—now secretary to the Russian embassy in Denmark—Dostoevsky again speaks longingly of the prospect of a European respite. Each time he had been to Europe in the past, he explains, "my health improved with remarkable rapidity." For this reason, he had planned, before his life fell to pieces, to pass three months of every year abroad, "particularly since, given the cost of living here, it is very advantageous to do so from the financial point of view."[2] But his brother's death had interfered with this intention, and now the failure of *Epoch* had left him without a penny. All the same, he assures Wrangel that he still hoped to get away; but when he finally succeeded in doing so, the anticipated relief from his worries turned into a nightmare of humiliation because of his gambling losses. It was in the midst of the emotional turmoil caused by such events that he set to work on the first draft of *Crime and Punishment*.

2

What Dostoevsky says about his life in the various letters just cited certainly explains part of his eagerness to travel abroad; but there was still another and very powerful reason that he could hardly confess to Turgenev, or even now to someone like Wrangel, for whom his private life had once been an open book. Dostoevsky's thoughts turned irresistibly toward Europe because it was there that he could hope to meet his ex-mistress Apollinaria Suslova, the young feminist writer who had never been entirely out of his mind during the past two years. He had carried on a secret correspondence with her even while his wife was dying; and if he was so attracted to Anna Korvin-Krukovskaya, it was at least partially because she seemed another (and more upper-class) incarnation of Suslova.

Dostoevsky and Suslova had become intimate during the winter of 1862–1863; but after a few months, her passion for the considerably older Dostoevsky, who may well have been an unsatisfactory lover, rapidly began to wane. While awaiting his arrival in Paris during the late spring of 1863, she had allowed herself to be seduced by a Spanish medical student; and though she traveled together with Dostoevsky for several months during the summer of 1863, she proved unwilling to restore him to his previous status as lover. But she did not break with him entirely, and, during their trip, constantly held out the hope that he might regain her favors. Suslova had remained in Europe when Dostoevsky returned to Russia, and letters between the pair constantly went back and forth: nine were sent in 1864; in 1865 Dostoevsky wrote six more and Suslova eleven. Unfortunately, all of this correspondence has been lost (except for the draft of one letter preserved in Suslova's *Diary*); and although some of this epistolary exchange may have involved editorial matters, since Suslova published a story in the sixth issue of *Epoch*, there can be little doubt that it also touched on more personal affairs as well.

That Dostoevsky still dreamed of renewing his relations with Suslova is amply evident from a letter he sent her younger sister Nadezhda, soon to become famous as the first Russian woman to obtain a medical degree (and who later became a very close friend of Anna Korvin-Krukovskaya). Nadezhda Suslova was then pursuing her medical studies in Zurich, and since Apollinaria, living in Montpellier, was scheduled to join her there, Dostoevsky wrote letters to both addresses. His covering letter to Nadezhda is the only document to have survived; but this is enough to offer a glimpse into his tortuous relations with his former mistress.[3]

Nadezhda herself, whom Dostoevsky greatly admired and whom he had often visited while she was still in Petersburg, had evidently criticized him quite harshly for his supposed ill treatment of her sister. He thus asks her to read his letter to Apollinaria, in which "you will find a clear reply to all the questions that you ask me in your letter, namely, whether 'I enjoy savoring the sufferings and tears of others,' etc. Also, responses with regard to cynicism and dirtiness." These words evidently

1. Apollinaria Suslova

refer to accusations made by Apollinaria, who may well have mingled personal reproaches with her reaction to *Notes from Underground*; and Dostoevsky appeals to Nadezhda's firsthand knowledge of his character to counter their damaging effect. For the past several years, he reminds her, "I have come to seek in your company some peace for my soul during all the times of trial, and recently it was only to you that I came when my heart was too full of grief. You have seen me in my sincerest moments and you can judge: do I feed on the sufferings of others, am I brutal, (inwardly), am I cruel?" Dostoevsky apparently was convinced that an impartial answer could only be in the negative.

Apollinaria, he tells her sister, is herself "a great egoist. Her egoism and her vanity are colossal. She demands *everything* of other people, all the perfections, and does not pardon the slightest imperfection in the light of other qualities that one may possess; as for herself, she recognizes no obligations, even the very slightest, toward people." Recalling what had happened in Paris, Dostoevsky turns Apollinaria's accusation of cruelty back against herself. Not because she fell in love with someone else, he hastens to explain, but "because of the four lines that she wrote to my hotel and the brutal phrase: 'You have arrived a bit too late.'" And yet, just fifteen days before, "she was writing that she loved me passionately." Dostoevsky predicts that she will always be unhappy, because "the person who demands everything of others but recognizes no obligation can never be happy." What little we know of Apollinaria Suslova's later life would seem to bear out this prophecy.*

Despite such bitter words, Dostoevsky confesses that "I still love her, I love her very much, but already I wish not to love her. She *does not deserve* such a love." The letter about which she had complained to Nadezhda was not insulting, Dostoevsky insists, but simply contained Dostoevsky's protests against ill treatment at her hands. "What she finds insulting in it is that I have dared to oppose her, dared to tell her I was suffering. . . . She has no humanity at all in her relations with me. She knows that I still love her. Why then does she torture me? Don't love me, but also don't torture me." If, as psychoanalytic commentators often

---

* Not much information exists concerning Suslova in later years (born in 1839, she died in 1918), and what little there is comes from a very biased source—her husband V. V. Rozanov, now recognized as one of the most original philosophical essayists of turn-of-the-century Russian culture. His book, *The Legend of the Grand Inquisitor*, still stands as a pioneering work of Dostoevsky criticism of considerable insight and influence. But Rozanov was also a very morally dubious figure, who sometimes advocated a vicious anti-Semitism and wrote simultaneously for both progressive and reactionary newspapers under different pseudonyms.

Rozanov and Suslova were married when he was twenty and she forty. After six years she ran away, apparently with a Jewish lover of good family and education working in the book trade. Terribly broken up by this desertion, according to his account, Rozanov refused to give her a legal separation in the hope that she would return; she then refused to grant him a divorce even when he later fathered several children by a woman he wished to marry. When Suslova continued to refuse a divorce, and Rozanov appealed to her father with whom she was then living, the old man replied that "the enemy of the human race has moved in with me now, and it [has become] impossible for me to live here." One of Rozanov's friends, who went to plead with Suslova when she was past sixty, mentioned the fierce implacability of her hatred.

In a letter written in 1902, Rozanov describes their first meeting when he was seventeen and she thirty-seven, obviously giving an impression of her character affected by their disastrous entanglement. Dressed severely in black on this occasion (she was in mourning for a dead brother), and still retaining traces of her former remarkable beauty, she spoke coldly and calmly. As a seasoned coquette, she could see that the inexperienced youth was "troubled" and had fallen under her spell; but he adds that she possessed the power of fascinating and subduing others, not only a pubescent adolescent. Her opinions by this time were those of a patriotic Russian legitimist, who expected the Bourbons to triumph in France, and in Russia loved only "aristocratism, tradition." He compares her with Catherine de Medici, claiming that she would be perfectly capable of committing a murder with complete indifference, and would have enjoyed shooting at the Hugenots from a window on St. Bartholomew's Eve.

She was, he writes, "sublime . . . I have never yet seen such a Russian woman, and if Russian, then a *raskolnitsa* of the *pomorskaya soglasiya*, or even better—a Mother of God of the flagellants." The *raskolnitsi* of the type mentioned by Rozanov had abolished the rites of marriage, and, as Leroy-Beaulieu remarks, "put into practice in their humble *izbas* the troubling Utopia of George Sand's *Jacques*." A Mother of God of the flagellant sect exercised absolute autocratic power over those belonging to her group. See Leonid Grossman, *Put Dostoevskogo* (Moscow, 1928), 134–137; and Anatole Leroy-Beaulieu, *L'Empire des Tsars et les Russes* (Paris, 1990), 1197. I cite the most recent edition of Leroy-Beaulieu's great work, first published in 1881–1883, which I shall draw on several times again. It does for Russia what Tocqueville did for the United States, and like that classic study has lost none of its value.

maintain, Dostoevsky's behavior patterns exhibit a strong masochistic component, such words illustrate that there was clearly a limit to his presumed enjoyment of suffering; but neither could he forget that Suslova had once loved him, nor relinquish the tantalizing hope that she might surrender herself again. For all his misgivings, he could not let slip what seemed his last chance for personal happiness; and the pursuit of Apollinaria was certainly among the reasons why he determined, at whatever cost, to return to Europe during the summer of 1865.

3

The major obstacle to such a plan was simply a lack of funds, and just how hard-pressed Dostoevsky was at this time can be seen from a little incident involving one of the minor contributors to *Epoch*. In June 1865 he received a letter from Arthur Benni, then sitting in debtor's prison, asking if Dostoevsky could pay the forty-five rubles owed him by the magazine, which the unfortunate Benni could now use to very good advantage. A mysterious but attractive personage, Arthur Benni figured briefly in the annals of Russian social-cultural history during the 1860s and unhappily acquired a rather dubious reputation.

The son of a Polish pastor and a Scottish mother of good family, Benni had been brought up in Poland and sent to school later in England; there he had studied engineering and obtained a post in the civil service. After meeting Alexander Herzen in London, however, Benni decided to devote himself to the cause of social-political progress, and he returned to Russia carrying a petition (composed with the aid of Turgenev) asking Alexander II to grant a constitution and establish a parliamentary democracy. Benni traveled through the Russian countryside attempting to obtain signatures for this document; and it was probably his endeavor to import the habits of political democracy into Russia—as Turgenev, perhaps with a twinge of guilt, suggested after Benni's death[4]—which led to the rumor that he was an agent in the pay of the Russian secret police. His petition gathered few signatures, and he earned a meager living as a translator and contributor to periodicals of a progressive complexion, including *Time* and *Epoch*. Benni was of a candid and generous nature, as one gathers from the naive initiative of his petition, and his friend, the major novelist Nikolay Leskov, joined Turgenev in Benni's posthumous defense by depicting him, in a sketch called *The Mysterious Man*, as a type of secular saint.[5]

Perhaps Benni's personality was one reason why, rather than replying to the letter, Dostoevsky went in person to the prison and paid Benni as much as he could afford to spare. As another letter of Benni's makes clear, Dostoevsky also took the occasion to pour out his heart to a sympathetic listener about *his own* financial woes. The well-bred Benni, writing to thank Dostoevsky both for the pleasure of his company and the partial payment, adds that, after listening to Dostoevsky's tale of disaster, "I even feel sorry that I wrote you about this matter" (his own need for funds), and tells Dostoevsky not to worry about him any further.[6] Apparently, even Benni's imprisonment, under oppressive and insalubrious conditions, did not outweigh what he learned about the collapse of *Epoch* and the disastrous consequences it had brought down on Dostoevsky's hapless head.

Indeed, just a few days after his visit to Arthur Benni, Dostoevsky received a notice from the local police official in charge of his district warning him to pay his creditors without delay a sum amounting to six hundred rubles. In case of default, he could expect a visit from the police to make an inventory of his personal belongings preparatory to their sale at auction. One of the creditors filing the complaint was of the peasant class, the other an attorney, who also lent money at interest, by the name of P. Lizhin; and Dostoevsky certainly remembered the name, and perhaps the personage, when creating the unctuous, oily, and totally unscrupulous lawyer Peter Petrovich Luzhin in *Crime and Punishment.*

To meet this immediate threat, Dostoevsky turned for help to the Literary Fund, which had been established to aid needy writers and scholars. Just a month earlier he had resigned as a member of the committee administering the fund (actually, he had been its secretary for two years) because another member had publicly questioned the propriety of two earlier loans accorded him, most of which he had repaid. Despite this embarrassing contretemps, he saw no other alternative but to appeal to the fund once more. The loan of six hundred rubles was happily granted and rescued him from the loss of all his household effects.

Continuously subjected to such harassment, Dostoevsky was all the more eager to leave the country for a time. On June 8 he wrote to A. A. Kraevsky, his old editor of the 1840s and still at the head of *Notes of the Fatherland,* to offer him the plan for a new work and to request an advance of three thousand rubles. "My novel is called *The Drunkards,*" Dostoevsky explains, "and will deal with the present problem of alcoholism. It will not only expose the question but present it in all its branches, particularly depictions of families, the education of children under such conditions, etc. etc."[7] Dostoevsky promised to have the first chapters ready by October 1865; in case of death, or if he failed to meet the deadline, he offered as guarantee the right in perpetuity to *all* his previous works, and he specified other conditions protecting the rights of the publisher. But Kraevsky replied that the sum demanded was not available in his editorial coffers (although Dostoevsky had asked for only half the amount as an immediate payment), and in any case the journal had a large backlog of belles lettres awaiting publication. Kraevsky, incidentally, had no reason to manifest any goodwill toward Dostoevsky, who just a few months earlier had published a mocking attack on him in *Epoch* for having known how to turn Russian literature into a profitable business.

It is quite likely that Dostoevsky's plan for *The Drunkards* came to little more than the idea he mentions in his letters. Totally hemmed in by the affairs of *Epoch*, he would hardly have had time to work out ideas for a new novel, and he probably suggested the subject both because it was topical (as he remarks) and also because it might capitalize on his reputation as a writer who had specialized in portraying the world of the Petersburg "poor folk" among whom such a story would presumably be set. Alcoholism was then at the center of public attention because a recent change in the manner of licensing drinking establishments, intended to combat the ravages of drunkenness, had only served to make it more widespread; in April 1865 a special commission had been appointed to examine the law and recommend measures to restrain "the excessive [use of alcohol] among the people."[8] Dostoevsky was referring to this background in his proposal, and was counting on Kraevsky's knowledge of his earlier work as well. After all, one of the most appealing characters in *Poor Folk*, old Pokrovsky, had been a confirmed drunkard; and in the story *An Honest Thief*, Dostoevsky had compassionately depicted a hopeless alcoholic who, after stealing a pair of breeches from an equally poverty-stricken benefactor to obtain some vodka, dies of a broken heart over the theft.

Aside from the letter to Kraevsky, only one other bit of information exists concerning this plan, a few lines in a notebook under the title, *The Drunkards*:

—We drink because there is nothing to do.
—You lie!—It's because there is no morality.
—Yes, and there is no morality—because for a long time (150 years) there has been nothing to do. (7: 5)

This snatch of dialogue reads as if intended as an epigraph for the novel as a whole; and the theme recalls a point of view Dostoevsky had expressed long ago in his Petersburg feuilletons of 1847. There he had written that "when a man is dissatisfied, when he is unable to express himself and reveal what is best in him (not out of vanity, but because of the most natural necessity to become aware of, to embody and fulfill his Ego in real life), he at once [may] ... take to the bottle in a big way" (18: 31). Drunkenness here is also seen as a consequence of the lack of anything to do (*delo*); but at that time Dostoevsky considered this lack a result of the totally despotic political regime of Nicholas I, which had kept the country frozen in a terrified immobility. Now, however, he interprets such inactivity more consistently with his ideology of *pochvennichestvo*, which, like Slavophilism, traced all the problems of Russia to the split between the educated class and the people caused by the reforms of Peter the Great. *The Drunkards* as such, however, was never written, but provided the subplot involving the Marmeladov family in *Crime and Punishment.*

Meeting with no success at Kraevsky's journal, Dostoevsky turned, as a last resort, to a tightfisted publisher named Stellovsky, well known and ill famed for driving very hard bargains. Stellovsky had already approached Dostoevsky with an offer of two thousand rubles in return for the right to publish a single edition of his works with no royalties accruing. Dostoevsky had initially turned down this miserly proposition; but, driven back to Stellovsky by necessity, he now agreed to accept even more severe conditions. The publisher would advance three thousand rubles in exchange for the right to print an edition of Dostoevsky's complete works. In addition, Dostoevsky agreed to furnish a new novel of specified format by November 1, 1866; and in case of failure, Stellovsky would have the right to publish *all* of Dostoevsky's future works without compensation to the author for a period of nine years. Despite the risks of entering into such a contract, which might greatly reduce his only source of income for a substantial period, Dostoevsky was forced to accept. After revising his works for Stellovsky's new edition, and obtaining a provisional promise from the journal *Library of Reading* (*Biblioteka dlya Chtenia*) to forward him an advance in return for a story or some travel articles, he left for Europe at the end of July.

4
———

Each time Dostoevsky had gone abroad in the past, he had hurried to the roulette tables shortly after crossing the frontier; and the same pattern was repeated on this occasion as well. By the time he arrived in Wiesbaden on the twenty-ninth of July to try his luck, the three thousand rubles obtained from Stellovsky had been distributed among his most pressing creditors and also parceled out to meet the needs of Mikhail's family and Dostoevsky's stepson Pasha; only one hundred and seventy-five silver rubles had been retained for the voyage. Dostoevsky, with the typical superstition of the gambler, had probably chosen Wiesbaden as his destination because he hoped to repeat the success of three years earlier, when he had racked up winnings there of twelve thousand francs in one glorious hour of play. Five days later, however, he lost everything down to his last penny, and was even forced to pawn his watch. For help he turned first to Turgenev in Baden-Baden, whom he had seen just the month previous in Petersburg and with whom he was on the friendliest footing.

Two years earlier, after receiving an admiring letter from Dostoevsky about *Fathers and Children*, Turgenev had expressed his gratitude and replied that Dostoevsky was one of the two people (the other was the important but little-known V. P. Botkin) who had really understood the book.* The excellent article on the novel in *Time*, which viewed Turgenev's hero Bazarov primarily as a tragic figure torn by the conflict between his Nihilist reason and "his great heart," certainly expressed Dostoevsky's own point of view, even though it was written by N. N. Strakhov. More recently (February 1865), Dostoevsky had scrupulously dispatched three hundred rubles to the wealthy landowner Turgenev in payment for *Phantoms*, published in the first number of *Epoch*, at a moment when his own financial position and that of the journal could not have been more precarious. Writing from Wiesbaden, Dostoevsky first explained his unfortunate circumstances and then apologetically added that, while feeling "aversion and shame" at disturbing his fellow novelist, he had nowhere else to appeal for help. And "since you are more intelligent than the others, it is morally easier to turn to you. Here is what is involved: I appeal to you as one human being to another, and I ask for one hundred thalers." Dostoevsky promised to repay within a month out of funds he expected to receive from the *Library of Reading* and also from "someone who *must* help me."[9] This someone is perhaps Apollinaria Suslova, with whom he had kept in constant touch and who, very shortly afterward, arrived in Wiesbaden for a brief visit.

Turgenev very rapidly sent fifty thalers, which was all he could afford at the moment. Dostoevsky gratefully acknowledged the loan: "although [it] has not entirely cleared me, all the same it is of great help. I hope to pay you back very soon."[10] But Dostoevsky neglected to do so within the specified time, assailed as he was by other obligations, and this embar-

---

* Vassily Petrovich Botkin (1810–1869) was the son of a wealthy tea merchant. Although lacking a formal higher education, he acquired a knowledge of French, German, and English, and developed into one of the finest Russian connoisseurs of the new literature, art, music, and philosophy of the first half of the nineteenth century. As a member of Belinsky's *pléiade* in the mid-1840s, to which he was admitted despite his lowly commercial origins, he became one of the critic's chief informants about German Left Hegelian philosophy and French Utopian Socialism, translating a number of relevant texts on these subjects for Belinsky's benefit.

Botkin's own writings, which include a volume called *Letters from Spain* and articles of literary, art, and music criticism, were highly appreciated by his contemporaries. In later life he became a great admirer of Thomas Carlyle, whom he translated and whose ideas he espoused; and this did not endear him to the radical intelligentsia of the 1860s, whose Utilitarianism he abhorred. Although almost forgotten through most of the late nineteenth and twentieth centuries, a collection of his criticism, including his correspondence with other notables, has recently been published. See V. P. Botkin, *Literaturnaya Kritika, Publitsistika, Pisma* (Moscow, 1984).

rassment only aggravated his hostility when, two years later, they met face-to-face and quarreled over Turgenev's harsh indictment of Russia in his next novel, *Smoke*. This dispute ended all personal relations between them, and the unpaid loan remained a hidden irritant that festered for the next ten years.

In addition to Turgenev, Dostoevsky also appealed to Herzen in Geneva, with whom his relations in the recent past had been very cordial; but he received no immediate reply. Meanwhile, Suslova appeared on the scene to spend a few days with her still amorous ex-lover, whose circumstances were hardly propitious for renewing his efforts to regain her affections. During the intervening two years, Suslova had become friendly with the novelist and woman of letters Evgeniya Tur (the pseudonym of Countess Salias de Tournemire), as well as with Natalie Tuchkova-Ogareva, Herzen's mistress and the legal wife of his intimate friend Nikolay Ogarev. Although frequenting their circle of friends and acquaintances, which included many luminaries active among the Russian radical opposition in Europe, Suslova's desultory and wandering life in France and Switzerland had been unhappy and frustrating.

It was shadowed by bitterness over her abrupt abandonment in Paris by her Spanish lover, and by the dispiriting emotions attendant on the various flirtations and abortive love affairs recorded in her *Diary*. Her first and deepest amorous relation had been with Dostoevsky, and she tended to blame him for her inability to establish more satisfactory ones with other men. After a tentative effort to attract a French physician who was treating her for some unspecified female complaint, she writes: "If I hadn't loved before, if my physician were not my doctor, our relationship would be quite different. Where has my courage gone? As I remember what happened two years ago, I begin to hate D[ostoevsky]. He was the first to kill my faith. But I want to shake off this sadness."[11] In what sense Dostoevsky had killed her "faith" is not clear; but she probably means her radical "faith" that life could be simple, uncomplicated, and happy once the trammels of conventional morality had been discarded.

These words were written eight months before Suslova came to meet Dostoevsky again, and her depression had not lightened substantially. Her feelings about Dostoevsky had always been ambivalent, as the unbroken correspondence between them amply proves, and her reluctance to break with him entirely is confirmed by her stopover in Wiesbaden in early August for a reunion with her still-persistent suitor. What passed between them unfortunately remains unknown; but since he continued to harbor the hope of joining her in Paris after escaping from Wiesbaden, the encounter could not have gone too badly. Also, their meeting may well be connected with a decision that Suslova came to shortly afterward. On September 17, after three disillusioning weeks in Paris mulling over the ill-fated past, she confided to her diary that she had firmly resolved to return to Russia. "I should live in a prov[incial] to[wn], have my circle, organize a private school on the model of antiquity, but not in Petersburg, for it is better to be important in the country, etc., not [just to exist] in the country and die of boredom."[12] Such an intention sounds very much like a personal application of what Dostoevsky had been advocating in his journals, namely, that the "superfluous men" of the Russian intelligentsia should put aside their titanic ambitions to change the universe entirely and teach just one small child to read.

Dostoevsky could hardly have anticipated that his eagerly awaited rendezvous with Suslova would occur under such inglorious circumstances, reduced as he was to utter destitution and living in fear of being expelled from his hotel at any moment and taken to the police. One quite naturally thinks of *Notes from Underground*, where the underground man finds himself in a similarly humiliating situation when the repentant prostitute Liza, before whom he had posed as a person of some importance, comes to visit him unexpectedly and catches him in all the unedifying reality of his actual existence. The result in the story is an outburst of hatred and resentment on his part, but nothing of the kind occurred in real life. Dostoevsky's letters to Suslova after her departure are filled with concern over her welfare, and it is likely that, leaving herself with barely enough to continue her journey, she aided Dostoevsky with whatever funds she had available. "Dear Polya," he writes, "in the first place I do not understand how you managed to arrive [in Paris]. To my disgusting anguish about myself has been added the anguish about you.... At Cologne the hotel, the carriages, the voyage—even if you had enough for the train, you were probably hungry. All this hammers in my head and gives me no rest."[13]

Dostoevsky had no secrets from Suslova, and it is from his letters to her that we obtain the most graphic image of the debasing conditions under which he was temporarily forced to live and which cut his pride to the quick. "Meanwhile," his letter continues, "my situation has gotten so bad that it is unbelievable. Scarcely had you left when on the next day, early in the morning, the hotel declared to me that they would no longer give me any meals, neither tea nor coffee. I went for an explanation and the stout German owner explained to me that I did not 'deserve' the meals and that he would send me tea. So that since yesterday I no longer eat and only drink tea. Yes, and they give awful tea, made without any samovar; my clothes and shoes are no longer cleaned, nobody responds to my summons, and all the staff treat me with an inexpressible, totally German contempt. There is no greater crime for a German than to be without money and not pay on time. All this would be comic, but all the same it is very unpleasant."

35

Two days later, Dostoevsky adds some new details in another letter sent without postage. "My affairs are terrible *nec plus ultra*; it is impossible to go any further. Beyond, there must be another zone of misfortunes and filthiness of which I still have no knowledge. . . . I am still living without meals, and this is already the third day that I live on morning and evening tea—and it's curious: I do not at all really wish to eat. The worst is that they hem me in and sometimes refuse me a candle in the evening [especially] when some bit of the previous one is left over, even the smallest fragment. But I leave the hotel every day at three o'clock and only return at six, so as not to give the impression that I do not dine at all. How much like a Khlestakov!"* Dostoevsky concludes with a plea to Suslova to raise some money for him from her friends in Paris if possible, and adds, as a despairing postscript: "now I no longer see at all what will become of me."[14]

To the distress induced by his circumstances was added the humiliation of failing to receive any answer from Herzen; what disturbed him was not so much the lack of financial succor as the disrespect for his person implied by such silence. At first, Dostoevsky assumed—what in fact turned out to be the case—that Herzen had left Geneva for the summer and that the letter had not yet reached its destination. As time went on, though, and even while struggling against his suspicions, the possibility that Herzen was treating him negligently continued to pursue him. "And yet Herzen torments me," he admits to Suslova. "If he received my letter and *does not wish* to respond—what a humiliation and what behavior! really, did I deserve this, and for what reason? My disorder? Agreed, I was disorderly, but what sort of bourgeois morality is this?" A postscript to this letter announces with relief that Herzen has finally replied; and though he could not spare the full amount requested, he had offered to send a lesser sum if this would help. Dostoevsky wonders why Herzen has not simply dispatched the smaller sum and decides forgivingly that he was probably short of funds; but now, he tells Suslova, it is impossible to bring himself to answer with another pleading entreaty.

5
―――――

Despite the bleak picture of solitary misery that emerges from Dostoevsky's letters, he was not as isolated as might be assumed. There were other Russians in Wiesbaden with whom he struck up an acquaintance,

---

* Khlestakov is of course the main character of Gogol's play, *The Inspector-General* (*Revisor*). When the spendthrift young civil servant arrives penniless in a provincial town and is mistaken for an inspector-general from the capital, he plays the role to the hilt and is treated royally until exposed as a fraud. Like Khlestakov, Dostoevsky pretends to have enough money to dine outside the hotel.

and they played a crucial part in helping him to escape from the debasement of his penury. Of particular importance was the priest in charge of the Russian Orthodox Church of the locality, Father I. L. Yanishev. A man of unusual culture, he had studied physics and mathematics as well as theology at the Petersburg Ecclesiastical Academy, and just a year later he would be appointed rector of that key clerical institution. After teaching theology and philosophy at the University of Petersburg between 1855 and 1858, Yanishev was assigned to various Russian churches abroad; but he was by no means an ordinary officiating priest, and while serving in Copenhagen was entrusted with an extremely important task. He tutored the Danish princess Dagmar, who was engaged to the Russian crown prince Alexander, in the precepts of the Orthodox faith; and this diplomatic assignment gives some indication of his worldly polish and cultivation.

Father Yanishev became well known in Orthodox theological circles because of his endeavors to ground moral theology on the psychological analysis of human character, and in one book, he paid special attention to a problem of vital concern to Dostoevsky: the freedom of the will. His writings and teachings met with some opposition because he broke with the usual scholastic expositions of dogma and tried to bring Orthodox doctrine closer to ordinary human life. Father George Florovsky, in his great work on the history of Russian theology, writes about him with a shade of disapproval because his teachings were "above all, a justification of the world. 'Earthly blessings' are accepted as the *necessary* milieu *outside of which moral awakening is impossible*—'without which virtue is impossible.' . . . Monasticism and asceticism cannot be approved of from this point of view. In the contemplative mysticism of the ascetics, Yanishev found only quietism" (italics in original).[15]

Instead of such "quietism" (of which Prince Myshkin will be mistakenly accused), Yanishev favored a Christianity understood primarily as charitable love for others—a love that he called "the center and crown of the Christian faith."[16] Just how much Yanishev may have influenced Dostoevsky's ideas about Christianity, it is impossible to say. The novelist certainly did not need Yanishev to teach *him*, the erstwhile Christian Socialist, that Christianity was primarily "charitable love"; but if the two talked of such matters, Dostoevsky would certainly have been pleased to find such a conception defended by so eminent a clergyman. And when the young novice Alyosha Karamazov is told by his mentor Father Zosima to quit the monastery and test his Christianity in the hurly-burly of everyday life, he is being instructed to follow one of the chief tenets of Father Yanishev's teachings. The sharp contrast between the relatively latitudinarian Father Zosima and the fanatical, crazed ascetic Father Ferapont in the same novel certainly conforms with Father Yanishev's aversion to the excesses of monastic rigor. Dostoevsky remained in contact with Father Yanishev even after Wiesbaden, and two years later wrote of him to Apollon Maikov: "He is a rare person, worthy, meek, with a sense of his own dignity, of an angelic purity of soul and a *passionate* believer."[17] It was Father Yanishev who presided at the religious services accompanying Dostoevsky's burial in 1881.

More immediately pressing issues than theological ones were naturally on Dostoevsky's mind when the two men first met, and Father Yanishev aided the distraught man of letters not only with spiritual counsel but also with a down-to-earth loan. Even better, they discovered a mutual friend in Baron Wrangel, whom the priest had met while residing in Copenhagen; and Father Yanishev was able to inform Dostoevsky that his old friend, who had helped him so unstintingly in the past, was to return from his summer holidays in September. Dostoevsky had written to Wrangel a month or two earlier, probably planning to visit Copenhagen in the course of his travels; but no reply had been forthcoming. Now he turned to Wrangel with a plea to rescue him by the loan of one hundred thalers. Two weeks later, he wrote again: "I have nothing" he declares. "I owe money to the hotel, I have no credit, and I am in a frightful situation. It is always the same thing as before, the only difference being that it is now twice as bad." Promising to repay the loan within a month, Dostoevsky explains that "I count on my story, which I am writing day and night. But instead of three folio sheets it is spreading out to six, and the work is not yet finished."[18]

This is the first reference to such a work in the letters sent out by Dostoevsky pleading for financial succor; another was made in a letter, now lost, to Alexander Milyukov, part of which Milyukov cites in his memoirs. Dostoevsky had asked Milyukov to attempt to obtain the promised advance from the *Library of Reading*, and also to make the rounds of the journals with the offer of a new composition, which is "widening out and becoming richer" under his hands but about which he regrettably says nothing further. He is certain, though, that "people will pay attention to it, talk about it . . . nothing of this kind has yet been written among us; I guarantee its originality, yes, and also its power to grip the reader."[19]

None of the Petersburg journals to which Milyukov turned was interested in Dostoevsky's offer. Indeed, the editors of the radical *Contemporary*, at Milyukov's first word, abruptly cut him short: they would have nothing to do with the man who had thrown stones at Nikolay Chernyshevsky, the leading radical publicist who had been arrested three years earlier and sent into exile and forced labor in the late spring of 1864. As Dostoevsky learned some years afterward, this reaction was inspired by the erroneous view, which he later took the trouble to deny in print, that his satirical short story *The Crocodile* had ridiculed Chernyshevsky in a manner considered personally insulting.

6
———

It was during this period of protracted mortification that Dostoevsky, while strolling one day among the linden trees at Wiesbaden, poured some of his troubles into the sympathetic ears of Princess Shalikova, a distinguished lady who also frequented the company of Father Yanishev and was herself an authoress under various pseudonyms. As it turned out, she was also a distant relative of M. N. Katkov, the powerful antiradical editor of the *Russian Messenger* (*Russkii Vestnik*), and she encouraged Dostoevsky to apply to him as a possible publisher. If the idea had crossed his own mind earlier, he had been unable to overcome an understandably strong resistance against making overtures to this old ideological opponent—one who had never concealed his scorn for what he considered the cloudy and confused precepts of *pochvennichestvo*—in his present plight. Eight years before, Katkov had given him an advance for a story (*The Village of Stepanchikovo*), but had then rejected the work and recovered the money from Dostoevsky (or rather from his older brother Mikhail). During the period of *Time* and *Epoch* (1861–1865), Dostoevsky and Katkov had frequently engaged in sharp polemics, and Dostoevsky had published an article (*A Ticklish Question*) containing an unmistakable lampoon at which Katkov could well have taken offense. Moreover, it was Katkov's campaign against *Time* for pro-Polonism that had contributed to the banning of the journal (although he later retracted the dire accusation).

All these powerful reasons had so far inhibited Dostoevsky from addressing himself to this highly successful editor; but the words of Princess Shalikova may well have conveyed some indication of Katkov's more recent appreciation of Dostoevsky *as a writer*. Whatever was said, the result is well known: Dostoevsky wrote to Katkov sometime during the first two weeks in September. Although the original of this letter has been lost, the copy of a draft containing the first outline of the conception of what became *Crime and Punishment* was found among Dostoevsky's papers. At this stage, Dostoevsky was not thinking of a novel but of a story or novella, which he has been working on "for two months" and is on the point of completing. He promises Katkov that it will be finished in one or two weeks, at most a month, and then outlines its central theme.

The idea of the work, he assures Katkov,

> so far as I can judge, in no way contradicts [the policy] of your journal; rather the contrary. It is the psychological report of a crime. The action is contemporary, set in the present year. A young man, expelled from the university, a petty bourgeois in origin and living in

the direst poverty, through light-mindedness and lack of steadiness in his convictions, falling under the influence of the strange, "unfinished" ideas afloat in the atmosphere, decides to break out of his disgusting position at one stroke. He has made up his mind to kill an old woman, the wife of a titular counselor who lends money at interest. The old woman is stupid, stupid and ailing, greedy, takes as high a rate of interest as a Yid, is evil and eats up other lives, torturing a younger sister who has become her servant. "She is good for nothing," "Why should she live?" "Is she at all useful for anything?" etc.—These questions befuddle the young man. He decides to kill her in order to bring happiness to his mother living in the provinces, rescue his sister, a paid companion in the household of a landowner from the lascivious advances of the head of this gentry family— advances that threaten her ruin—finish his studies, go abroad, and then all his life be upright, staunch, unbendable in fulfilling his "humane obligation to mankind," which would ultimately "smooth out" his crime, if one can really call a crime this action against a deaf, stupid, evil, sickly old woman who does not herself know why she is on earth and who perhaps would die herself within a month.

Although crimes like this are terribly hard to carry out—i.e., almost always loose ends and pieces of evidence stare one in the face, and an awful lot, being left to chance, almost always betrays the guilty, he succeeds in completing his undertaking quickly and successfully in a totally accidental fashion.

Almost a month passes after this until the final catastrophe. No one suspects or can suspect him. Here is where the entire psychological process of the crime is unfolded. Insoluble problems confront the murderer, unsuspected and unexpected feelings torment his heart. Heavenly truth, earthly law take their toll and he finishes by *being forced* to denounce himself. Forced because, even though he perishes in *katorga*, at least he will be reunited with people; the feeling of isolation and separation from mankind, which he felt right after completing the crime, has tortured him. The law of truth and human nature took its [text illegible]. . . . The criminal himself decides to accept suffering in order to atone for his deed. . . .

In my story there is also a hint of the idea that the prescribed judicial punishment for the crime frightens the criminal much less than lawgivers think, partly because he himself morally demands it.

I have seen this even among very uneducated people, in the crudest circumstances. I wanted to show this especially in an educated member of the new generation, so that the thought would be clearer and more palpable. Several recent instances have convinced me that my *subject* is not at all eccentric. Especially that the murderer is an educated and even well-inclined young man. Last year in Moscow I heard a story (a true one) of a student excluded from the university after the student incidents —he decided to attack the post and kill the postman. There are still many traces in the newspapers of the unheard-of lack of steadiness in convictions, which leads to terrible deeds. (That seminary student, who killed a girl by agreement with her in a shed and was captured an hour later having breakfast, etc.) In a word, I am convinced that my subject is in part justified by our own time.

It is understood that I have left out, in this present account of the idea of my story—the whole subject [which may mean the plot details—J.F.]. I guarantee that it will grip the reader, but about the artistic execution I will not take it on myself to judge. It has too often happened that, because of haste, I wrote very, very wretched things. However, I have not written this thing hastily but with passion. I will try, *if only for myself,* to finish it in the best possible way.[20]

In conclusion, Dostoevsky asks to be paid the quite modest sum of one hundred and twenty-five rubles per folio sheet, although it was well known that writers like Turgenev and Tolstoy received a good deal more, and he pleadingly requests an immediate advance of three hundred rubles to rescue him from his present difficulties, whose details he leaves unspecified. No reply arrived immediately, and with the help of Wrangel and Father Yanishev Dostoevsky managed to pay his bills and return to Russia. When Katkov finally sent the advance to Wiesbaden, Dostoevsky was already back in his native land, having broken the trip with a visit to Copenhagen before proceeding home. Father Yanishev forwarded the money, and this was the beginning of Dostoevsky's long relationship with *The Russian Messenger,* which published all his major novels except *A Raw Youth.* It was also the beginning of a much more prolonged period of literary labor than Dostoevsky had imagined when he promised to complete his "story" in a few more weeks.

CHAPTER 4

"Our Poor Little Defenseless Boys and Girls"

Dostoevsky may well have believed, when he wrote to Katkov, that he would be able to complete the project on which he was working in about a month. It had been conceived as a short story or novella, and his notebooks contain a substantial draft of this initial plan in almost finished form. But the work continued to grow and widen under his hands, and metamorphosed into a large novel shortly after he returned to Petersburg. As a result, the book took another year to write, and the course of its creation was embedded in a series of circumstances affecting both Dostoevsky's private life and that of Russia itself. The first attempt on the life of the Tsar by a member of the radical intelligentsia occurred when Dostoevsky had completed about half the novel, and it was the deed of an ex-student who could easily be identified with Dostoevsky's main character. This shattering event increased the impact made by Dostoevsky's portrayal of the crime committed by *his* ex-student, and certainly affected the mood in which the final sections of the book were composed.

2

Dostoevsky's return to St. Petersburg in mid-October immediately plunged him back into the swarm of menacing creditors from whose persecution he had fled to Europe. "Until now," he writes Wrangel, "I have not been able to come to any agreement with them, and I am not sure I can succeed; while the majority are reasonable and accept my offer to spread the payments over five years, with others I have not been able to work things out."[1] To make matters worse, Dostoevsky's epileptic attacks increased in frequency shortly after his return (as if, he remarked bitterly, to make up for the three months' respite afforded him in Europe). He was also incapacitated by a severe attack of hemorrhoids, an affliction that had made its appearance three years before and prevented him from writing because he could not sit comfortably upright when it recurred. All this misery was further aggravated by "family disagreements, the countless troubles connected with the affairs of my late brother, of his family, and of our deceased journal."

The "disagreements" to which Dostoevsky refers arose from the resentment of Mikhail's widow and her children at their straitened economic situation, for which they held Dostoevsky primarily responsible. The failure of *Epoch* had deprived them, as well as Dostoevsky, of their only secure source of income, and they bitterly regretted his decision to continue the journal after Mikhail's death. Dostoevsky, on the other hand, felt that he had done his utmost to look after their interests by continuing publication, and he was deeply aggrieved at their hostility. From his point of view, the assumption of Mikhail's debts, and the investment of his own inheritance in the journal, had mortgaged his future and represented a sacrifice for which he was now having to pay very dearly indeed. The rights and wrongs of this family quarrel need not be decided here; but Dostoevsky firmly believed that the resentment of Mikhail's family was thoroughly unjust. Nonetheless, he conscientiously assigned them a portion of whatever income he received from his writings (to be sure, never enough in their eyes) all through the remainder of the 1860s.

Dostoevsky complains sadly about the difficulties of literary composition under such nerve-racking conditions, and it might be thought that he would have avoided complicating them further in any way. But instead, even though most of the story he had proposed to Katkov already existed in a next-to-final draft, he decided to recast his entire plan. "At the end of November," he explained to Wrangel two months later, "a good part (of the initial plan) had been written and was ready; but I burned it all; I can confess this to you now. I didn't like it myself. A new form, a new plan carried me away, and I started afresh."[2] This new plan involved writing a much longer work, a novel in six parts (five are also mentioned) whose title would be *Crime and Punishment*. A more extensive discussion of this change will be provided in the next two chapters.

It would be an exaggeration to speak of Dostoevsky as maintaining any normal sort of social life during the second half of 1865, and he remarks himself that "I have not visited anyone all winter. I have not seen anybody or anything, and have gone to the theater only once for the première of *Rogneda*" (an opera by the composer Alexander Serov, a friend of Dostoevsky's and a contributor to *Epoch*).[3] In fact, however, his days were not as bare of conviviality as such words might lead one to assume. Apollinaria Suslova was now living in Petersburg, and he continued to pursue her, though with results that hardly alleviated his loneliness. On November 2, 1865, Suslova confided to her diary: "Today F[eodor] M[ikhailovich] was here and we argued and contradicted each other all the time. For a long time now he has been offering me his hand and his heart, and he only makes me angry doing so. Speaking of my character, he once said: 'If you were to get married, you'd begin to hate your husband three days later, and leave him.' Remembering Gaut [a French physician with whom she had flirted], I said that he was the only man I knew who did not try to get somewhere with me. He said, in his usual manner: 'This Gaut may have been trying it too.' Then he added: 'Someday I am going to tell you something.' I began pestering him to tell me what. 'You can't forgive me that you gave yourself to me, and so you are avenging yourself; that's a feminine trait.' This upset me very much." Dostoevsky then invited Suslova to the theater, and she hit back by saying: "I'm not going to the theater with you, since I've never been there with you before; you can ascribe this whim to the reason you have pointed out to me earlier."[4]

Dostoevsky had attributed Suslova's exasperating behavior to a need for revenge, and her words contain an obvious reference to the humiliations that *she* had endured in the early days of their relationship. Dostoevsky's first wife had then still been living, and he had gone to great pains to conceal his illicit affair; of course he and Suslova had never appeared together in public. Another diary entry a few days later tells of a visit by Dostoevsky. In the only conversation recorded, Suslova taunts Dostoevsky about his religious convictions. "I said that I was going to become a holy woman," she writes, "that I would walk through the Kremlin gardens in Moscow in my bare feet, telling people that I was having conversations with the angels, etc. I talked a lot." Another person present remarked that one prophet of this kind had confessed to having been "talking through his hat," and Suslova comments that "the idea occurred to me how quickly and how easily one can become a source of annoyance to these people" (among whom Dostoevsky of course took first place).[5] Obviously, she did everything in her power to annoy and provoke him, and their relationship ended when his offers of marriage were persistently refused. But Dostoevsky would soon re-create the strained intensity of their love-hate bickering in *The Gambler*—where, however, he acquires imaginatively what he had failed to achieve in reality. For there the beautiful and contemptuous Polina is genuinely in love with the feckless and self-destructive gambler.

3

The first and second parts of *Crime and Punishment* were serialized in the January and February issues of *The Russian Messenger*, and Dostoevsky had every reason to be pleased with the public response. "I have already heard many enthusiastic utterances [about it]. It contains daring and original things" he proudly told Wrangel.[6] To be sure, "these daring and original things" were by no means to everyone's taste, and the radicals on *The Contemporary*, just as they had done with Turgenev's *Fathers and Children* four years earlier, responded immediately to Dostoevsky's challenge. "Has there ever been an instance in which a student killed someone in order to commit a robbery?" asked its critic G. Z. Eliseev. "If such an instance ever occurred, what can it prove regarding the state of mind of the students as a group? What would Belinsky have to say about this new 'fantasy' of Mr. Dostoevsky, a fantasy according to which the entire student body is accused without exception of attempting murder and robbery?" A month later the same critic wrote that, from the artistic point of view, Dostoevsky's depiction of a sordid murder, "in the sharpest exactitude and with all the most minute particulars," was "the purest absurdity," and no justification for it could be found in the annals of either ancient or modern art.[7]

Such predictable reactions did not prevent the book's installments from being a sensational success with the reading public; many years later Strakhov still recalled the furor they had created. "Only *Crime and Punishment* was read during 1866," he testifies, "only it was spoken about by lovers of literature, who often complained about the stifling power of the novel and the painful impression it left, which caused people with strong nerves almost to become ill and forced those with weak ones to give up reading it altogether."[8] Strakhov also remembers what he considers "most striking of all": the coincidence "with reality." On January 12, 1866, a student named A. M. Danilov killed a moneylender and his manservant in order to loot their apartment, and many of the details surrounding the crime instantly brought Raskolnikov's deed to everyone's mind.

In fact, however, Danilov made no claim to be a compassionate soul oppressed by the suffering of humanity; his motive seems to have been pure and simple robbery, and his aim solely to acquire enough wealth to indulge an inordinate taste for luxurious living. Unlike Raskolnikov, moreover, Danilov committed his crime in cold blood rather than feverish hysteria, and his conduct at the trial exhibited no signs of remorse. Nonetheless, because the crime was the work of a student, the widespread impression prevailed, as reported by Strakhov, that "it was carried out under the general nihilistic conviction that all means were permitted to improve an unreasonable state of affairs." A survey of the press of the time supports this assertion, and Dostoevsky himself, interpreting the remarkable conjuncture in this light, "often spoke about it and took pride in the triumph of his artistic perspicacity."[9] Several years later, with obvious reference to the Danilov case, he wrote to Apollon Maikov that what was deprecatingly called "my idealism has even predicted facts. It has happened."[10]

Despite the furor aroused by these early chapters, which, as Dostoevsky later learned from Katkov, had brought *The Russian Messenger* at least five hundred new subscribers, his financial arrangements with the journal were a constant source of anxiety. Pressed by urgent need, he had offered the original idea for *Crime and Punishment* at a very low rate per folio sheet, and the magazine, in any case, had agreed only to purchase a novella of limited size. As the manuscript increased in length, there were disturbing indications that the journal editors hoped to lower the price so as to decrease their overall outlay. In view of the public acclaim, Dostoevsky understandably wished to retain the higher rate to which, more than ever, he now felt fully entitled. And all the more so, since he had learned that his novel had been of great help to *The Russian Messenger* at a difficult moment. His manuscript had come along just when regular contributors like Turgenev and Tolstoy had failed to supply the belle-lettristic reading matter obligatory for every number of a "thick" Russian journal. "Turgenev is not writing anything," Dostoevsky explained to Wrangel in a letter of February 1866, "and they have quarreled with Tolstoy." As a result, "we [Katkov and Dostoevsky] are engaged in a silent conflict" over page rates.[11]

To settle the matter, Dostoevsky believed it would be necessary to travel to Moscow and talk to Katkov personally; but he did not wish to make a move before at least half the work had been published. "With the help of God," he remarked fervently, "this novel can be the most splendid thing." Nor did he wish to request any more advances, since these would only obligate him morally and tie his hands when the time came to negotiate. Dostoevsky thus continued to live on the very edge of poverty, haunted by the fear that his creditors would press him to the wall and ruin everything. In response to some friendly advice from Wrangel counseling him to enter government service, and thus assure himself a guaranteed income, Dostoevsky sketched for Wrangel's benefit his hopes for a substantial economic return. "But here's the trouble," he adds sadly: "I may spoil the novel, and I have a presentiment that this may happen. If I am locked up in prison for debt, then I will certainly spoil it and maybe not even complete it at all; everything will then go to pieces."[12]

By mid-March, deciding that the time was now ripe, Dostoevsky made the voyage to Moscow; and after a satisfactory interview with Katkov, he was promised a further advance of a thousand rubles. He also took the occasion to visit the family of his second sister Vera, whose husband, Doctor A. P. Ivanov, served as a physician in the Konstantinovsky Land

Surveying Institute and with whom he was on the very best of terms. The friendly and hospitable Ivanovs always had a houseful of guests, and one of them was an attractive twenty-year-old woman by the name of Marya Sergeevna Ivanchina-Pisareva, a friend of one of the Ivanov daughters. Just a month before, Dostoevsky had written gloomily to Wrangel that "at least you, my good friend, are happy with your family, while fate has so far denied me this great and *sole* human happiness."[13] We know that Dostoevsky had, all this time, been eagerly seeking some remedy for his emotional solitude, and he was very much taken with the "lively and pert" Marya Sergeevna. One morning, when the family had gone to Easter matins, he remained at home with her and formally proposed marriage; but in view of the difference in their ages (Dostoevsky was then forty-five), the sprightly young lady turned him off by an unmistakably discouraging quotation from Pushkin's *Poltava.*[14]* This incident reveals how intent Dostoevsky was on remarrying as rapidly as possible and, as he had indicated to Wrangel, fulfilling his desire to found a family.

4

It was just a day or two after Dostoevsky's return from Moscow that the shattering event occurred which left all of Russia aghast. The Tsar's habit, well known to his adoring subjects, was to walk his dog every day in the Summer Gardens adjacent to the Winter Palace; and a small crowd was watching on April 4, 1866, as he was about to enter his carriage after completing his constitutional. At that moment a pale and desperately poor ex-student, with long flowing hair falling over his shoulders, pushed his way through the multitude of spectators, took aim with a pistol, and fired a shot. Whether Dimitry Karakozov was a faulty marksman or whether someone—a tradesman named Osip Kommissarov, who became a national hero overnight—had jostled his arm, the shot went wild, and Karakozov was overpowered by the crowd. Saved by the police from a lynching at the hands of the outraged mob, he was dragged to Alexander II, who personally took his pistol from him and asked if he were a Pole. It seemed inconceivable to the Tsar that an attempt on his life would be made by anyone but a foreigner; yet Karakozov, who came from a family of small, impoverished landowners and who had been expelled from the university, like Raskolnikov, for failing to pay his fees, replied: "Pure Russian."

News of Karakozov's unsuccessful attempt stunned all of Russia and produced a spontaneous outpouring of devotion and fidelity to the monarch rivaling the manifestations of patriotism exhibited during major

* The quotation, "Okameneloe godami / Pylaet serdtse starika," can be literally translated as: "Petrified by the years / The heart of the old man flames up."

historical catastrophes such as the Napoleonic invasion. Like many others, Dostoevsky was shocked into a state of near hysteria by the unbelievable report, and he rushed to the home of his oldest and closest friend, Apollon Maikov, to share his agitated feelings. P. I. Weinberg, who was visiting Maikov, has left this image of how Dostoevsky burst in on them with the terrible tidings:

> Feodor Mikhailovich Dostoevsky ran headlong into the room. He was terribly pale, looked in an awful fright, and he was shaking all over as if in a fever.
> "The Tsar has been shot at," he shrieked, not greeting us, in a voice breaking with emotion.
> "Killed?" Maikov cried out in some sort of strange inhuman voice.
> "No ... He was saved ... Fortunately ... But shot at ... shot at ... shot at ... "
> We gave him a little something to quiet himself—though Maikov too was close to fainting—and we all three ran into the street.[15]

What dominated in Dostoevsky's reaction was simply the horror of the news itself; but he must certainly have been filled with foreboding at the severe consequences that he knew would now automatically ensue. Herzen, who strongly repudiated Karakozov's action, wrote forebodingly in *The Bell* that "we expect only calamity from it, and are dumbfounded at the thought of the responsibility that this fanatic has taken upon himself."[16] Turgenev hastened to write P. V. Annenkov that "one cannot but shudder at the thought of what would have happened in Russia if the dastardly deed had succeeded."[17]

What *did* happen was bad enough: Count N. M. Muraviev, who had suppressed the Polish rebellion of 1863 with bloody ferocity—thus acquiring the infamous cognomen of "the Hangman of Vilna"—was appointed head of a commission to investigate the background of the assassination attempt and given virtually the powers of a dictator. Simultaneously, Katkov launched a ferocious press campaign against all those liberal and particularly radical organs of opinion whose nefarious influence had led to the horrendous crime. As Herzen accurately foresaw, the government, aided by the demagogic jeremiads of Katkov, now would "mow down everything right and left, mow down its enemies first of all, mow down the freedom of speech that has not yet fully emerged, mow down independent thought, mow down all proudly forward-looking heads, mow down 'the people' who at present are being so flattered, and all this under the name of saving the Tsar and avenging him."[18] The reigning atmosphere of terror is well conveyed in the memoirs of one of the editors of *The Contemporary*, G. Z. Eliseev, the same who had criticized the early chapters of *Crime and Punishment*. "Every day, almost always in the morning," he recalled, "news arrived that during the night this or that literary man had been taken, and the next morning they took so-and-so and so-and-so. Little by little half of the literary men I knew had been taken.... All of these rumors, the constantly growing apprehension and the sleepless nights had so enervated me and brought me so near the point of complete prostration that I considered going and asking them to lock me up in the fortress."[19]

Another editor of *The Contemporary*, Dostoevsky's erstwhile friend Nikolay Nekrasov, behaved under these nerve-shattering circumstances in a manner that has always been considered especially reprehensible. As a man of letters and a poet, Nekrasov had been personally associated with all the eminent representatives of Russian radical opinion beginning with Belinsky; and it was Nekrasov, indeed, who had entrusted the editorial fate of his journal to Nikolay Chernyshevsky and Nikolay Dobrolyubov. Moreover, his own poems had been filled with what the Russians call "civic themes," those social-humanitarian motifs expressing the convictions of the radical intelligentsia; and several of them—one of which Dostoevsky parodistically used as an epigraph to the second part of *Notes from Underground*—had taken on symbolic stature as fervidly lyrical declarations of radical ideals. Despite all this, in a desperate effort to preserve *The Contemporary* from extinction, he read a poem in honor of Muraviev at a banquet given in the count's honor at the exclusive English Club (his left-wing sympathies did not prevent Nekrasov from frequenting the very highest Russian society). His eulogy concluded with the threatening words: "Spare not the guilty ones!" And to heighten the disgrace, Nekrasov also composed a poem in honor of the pitiable and drink-sodden Kommissarov, who was everywhere being celebrated as "the instrument of God" chosen to avert a great calamity from the Russian people. All these demeaning efforts, which severely tarnished Nekrasov's reputation and poisoned the remainder of his days, proved to be distressingly futile. The implacable Muraviev, after the public obeisance of the poem, is reported to have told Nekrasov, with condescending contempt: "I would like to protect you from collective responsibility for the evil we are combating, but that is hardly within my power."[20] And he promptly closed down *The Contemporary* for good and all.

5

Dostoevsky too may well have felt a shudder of fear during these frightening days of grim repression. As an ex-convict, he was still under police surveillance; he was also the ex-editor of a journal that had incurred official displeasure and been banned only two years earlier, at the time of the Polish uprising, for political unreliability. Nor did Dostoevsky have any illusions about the authorities' powers of discernment; he knew very well that they were too obtuse to distinguish between various shades of social-political opinion, and that he would be lumped in the same suspicious category as the radicals he had been polemically combating in *Epoch*. Nothing untoward occurred to him personally, however, though he blamed his difficulty in obtaining a passport to go abroad "on the present circumstances."

This remark is made in an extremely important letter (April 1866) to Katkov, which contains a lengthy appraisal of the situation in the country brought on by the measures taken in the wake of Karakozov's fateful shot. One should remember that Dostoevsky was writing to the leader of the violent assault against all shades of liberal and radical opinion, and that he was now financially dependent on the raging editor for his very sustenance. It is thus all the more praiseworthy that he felt impelled to speak out, even if very diplomatically, against the wave of repression sweeping the country. Although Dostoevsky is usually considered to have become a hardened reactionary by this time, such a judgment is hardly borne out by the evidence of this document.

The letter begins with an expression of gratitude for receipt of the thousand rubles agreed upon, and some words of praise for the policy of the *Moscow Gazette* (*Moskovskii Vedomosti*), the newspaper also owned and edited by Katkov. Dostoevsky congratulates Katkov on the "independent" line taken by the newspaper, which has now proven that it is not, as was formerly widely believed, merely a government mouthpiece supported by subsidies from the authorities.[21] Such words probably refer to Katkov's conviction that the assassination attempt could only have originated in a Polish plot (even though Karakozov was thoroughly Russian), and his insinuation that a complicity with the Poles existed in the very highest court circles—an Aesopian reference to the Grand Duke Konstantin Nikolaevich, the Tsar's brother, who had been Governor-General of Poland before the uprising and was known to have advocated a liberal policy.

Although warmly approving such "independence," and certainly harboring no sympathy for the Poles, Dostoevsky nonetheless expresses some reservation about Katkov's insistence on assigning guilt exclusively to foreign sources. As a preface, he remarks that there are fundamental issues on which he and Katkov, the erstwhile Anglophile and pro-Westerner, would never be in accord. "I will tell you frankly," he confides, "that I am, and probably always will be, an authentic Slavophil by conviction, except for some slight disagreements; and there are certain points on which I can never agree with the *Moscow Gazette*." Such a confession of allegiance may seem, at first sight, to be rather superfluous; but it is firmly linked to what Dostoevsky will tell Katkov in a moment. For the Slavophils had always insisted that the Russian people were God-fearing, loyal, and obedient subjects of the Tsar, and that there was thus no necessity for the authorities to regard them with suspicion and mistrust. Before suggesting such an idea, however, Dostoevsky assures Katkov of his "heartfelt gratitude" for the editor's "marvelous activity ... especially at this moment."[22]

All the same, as Dostoevsky continues, he begins discreetly to voice certain objections to the emphasis of Katkov's press campaign. "I have heard the opinion expressed," he remarks with affected candor, "that the *Moscow Gazette* underestimates the importance of nihilism; that, of course, the center and foundation of the evil lies not within but without; but that the nihilists are quite capable of anything even by themselves. The doctrine of 'shaking everything up by *les quatre coins de la nappe*, so that, at least, there will be a *tabula rasa* for action,'—does not require any roots. Socialism (and particularly in its Russian reworking)—demands precisely the cutting of all ties. You know they are completely convinced that on a *tabula rasa* they will immediately construct a paradise. Fourier you know believed that if only one phalanstery were built, the whole world would immediately be covered with phalansteries; those were his words. And our Chernyshevsky often used to say that, if he could only talk to the people for a quarter of an hour, he would immediately convince them to become socialists."[23]

One would imagine, on reading such words, that Dostoevsky was wholeheartedly approving of Katkov's merciless excoriation of the native radicals. And so he was, up to a point; but it then appears that if the Nihilists have been successful in influencing Russian youth, it is for reasons that can hardly be considered evil. "And among us Russians," he goes on, "our poor little defenseless boys and girls, we still have our own, eternally present *basic* point on which Socialism will long continue to be founded, that is, their enthusiasm for the good and their purity of heart. There are countless rogues and scoundrels among them. But all those high school pupils, those students, of whom I have seen so many, have become nihilists so purely, so unselfishly, in the name of honor, truth, and genuine usefulness! You know they are helpless against these stupidities, and take them for perfection."[24]

Dostoevsky's focus has thus shifted from agreement with Katkov's outrage against the Nihilists (whose influence he implicitly, and quite rightly, connects with Karakozov's deed) to sorrow and pity for all the innocents who are being misled by such doctrines. The captive Karakozov was being interrogated and tried in secret, and very little information was available about what those doctrines may have been; but if

Dostoevsky had had more information, he would have been surprised (and perhaps pleased as an artist, if not as a public-spirited Russian) to discover how accurately he had intuited the consequences of that "unsteadiness" of moral convictions he was then portraying in Raskolnikov. Karakazov was a member of a small underground group of radicals headed by Nikolay Ishutin, all students or ex-students, and all inspired by the extremism of the revolutionary ideas of the 1860s as Dostoevsky had just described them. "Plans were made [by this group]," writes Franco Venturi, "to rob a merchant and attack the post, thus raising in theory the problem of individual expropriation. One member of the group . . . thought of poisoning [his father] so as to be able to give his legacy to the cause." Venturi comments on "the Machiavellian note" struck by such plans, combined with "the desire for self-sacrifice" on behalf of the people also evident in the same circle; and it was out of such a milieu that Karakozov had emerged.[25]*

Unlike Katkov, though, Dostoevsky did not believe that such ideas, and the desperate actions to which they gave rise, could be suppressed by force or would make way in time for other, less noxious convictions as a result of education. "But when *at last* will that be? How many sacrifices will Socialism consume until that time? And after all: a healthy science, even if it takes root, will not destroy the weeds so quickly—because a healthy science is still only a science, *not a direct form of civic and social activity* [italics added]. And the innocents are convinced that nihilism—gives them the most complete chance to exhibit their civic and social activity and freedom."[26] The only possible answer, implied though not stated, is to provide more scope for "civic and social activity" within the Russian state, to allow more freedom for the idealism of youth to express itself in some socially permitted fashion.

---

* There can be little doubt that Ishutin's group prepared the way for Sergey Nechaev a few years later, and many of the people Nechaev recruited had been initiated into revolutionary activity by Ishutin. This earlier group was organized in two sections: one, called the "Organization," was devoted to agitation and propaganda; the second, called "Hell," was dedicated to terrorism against the landowning classes and government, and the final aim was the assassination of the Tsar. "A member of 'Hell,'" according to Ishutin, "must live under a false name and break all family ties; he must not marry; he must give up his friends; and in general he must live with one single exclusive aim: an infinite love and devotion for his country and its good." Ishutin also used a purely fictitious identification with a supposed European Revolutionary Committee, whose aim was to wipe out all monarchs, in order to strengthen the prestige of his group. It should be mentioned, though, that the group opposed Karakozov's decision and tried to dissuade him from carrying it out.

Ishutin and those like him were implacably opposed to the liberation of the serfs and to any attempt to promote or implement democratic reforms because they would prevent a more thoroughgoing revolution. As Venturi remarks, "this violent opposition to reforms inevitably coincided with the opinion of the most reactionary nobles who always opposed the emancipation of the serfs and who now continued to criticize it." We shall soon see Dostoevsky making exactly the same equation between left and right extremes both in his letters and in *The Devils*. Franco Venturi, *Roots of Revolution* (New York, 1966), 334–338.

Dostoevsky is thus really disagreeing with Katkov beneath the surface of seeming accord; and he continues to do so in the same covert fashion as the letter proceeds. Katkov had remarked scoffingly that certain quarters were interpreting the repressive measures just instituted as a sign that the government, once bent on liberal reforms, was now turning toward reaction, and Dostoevsky agrees that such a view has become very widespread. But then he indicates, in the course of pretending only to supply more information about opinions prevalent in Petersburg, that he too fears exactly the reaction dismissed by Katkov as a liberal bugaboo.

"Do you know what some people are saying?" he asks, again adopting the pose of naïveté. "They say that April 4th has proven mathematically the powerful, extraordinary, sacred union of the Tsar with the people. And such union should allow certain governmental personalities to show more faith in the people and in society. Meanwhile, everybody now awaits with fear more constraints on speech and thought. They expect administrative controls. But how can nihilism be fought without freedom of speech? Even if they, the nihilists, were given freedom of speech, even then it would be more advantageous: they would make all Russia laugh by the *positive* explanation of their teachings. While now they are given the appearance of sphinxes, an enigma, wisdom, secrecy, and this fascinates the unexperienced.

"Why not, some say, even make the investigation [of Karakozov] public? In the ministries, you know, there is perhaps not one man among them who knows how to speak to the nihilists. And here, with publicity, the whole society could help, and the people's enthusiasm would not be swallowed up, as now, in administrative secrecy. They see clumsiness in this, a timidity on the part of the government, a devotion to outmoded forms. So they lose trust and begin to fear reaction."[27]

This remarkable letter, written at a moment when the clamor for more severity against the radicals was resounding on all sides, throws a good deal of light on the complexity of Dostoevsky's relation to them and on the state of mind in which he was composing his novel. Unquestionably, he had now come to believe that the ideas and influence of the radical intelligentsia were disastrous for the country; but he never questioned for a moment that the vast majority of its members were inspired by a profound moral impulse. And while totally condemning the Russian brand of Socialism, which he equates with a call for total destruction (we shall see that he had some justification for this suspiciously tendentious interpretation), he also cherished a great sympathy for the genuine "enthusiasm for the good . . . and purity of heart" that he knew inspired so many of the radical young. However destructive the consequences of their actions might be both for society and for themselves, he well understood that these sprang from an irrepressible need of youth to express itself in some socially constructive manner. Since no such possibility existed, they threw themselves into the arms of revolution. One senses here the anguish of the ex-revolutionary Dostoevsky over the vain self-sacrifice (as he could only judge it to be) of the idealistic and pure-hearted young men and women who were treading the same dangerous path that had led him to Siberia. It was impossible for him to look on indifferently while so many were being led to disaster by the pied pipers of Nihilism, to whose tunes the youth danced with so much self-sacrificing dedication and moral fervor.

6

During the next few months, straining himself to the limits of his endurance, Dostoevsky continued to work without respite, even though continually harassed by his creditors. To Father Yanishev, whose loan he finally repaid out of the additional thousand rubles obtained from Katkov, he wrote at the end of April: "My epilepsy has worsened so much that if I work for a week without interruption I have an attack, and the next week I cannot work because the result of two or three attacks will be—apoplexy. And yet I must finish. That's my situation." Dostoevsky also adds that "my novel has been a great success and raised my reputation as a writer."[28] But this triumph only plunged him into deeper despair over the conditions under which he was forced to create. He had hoped, as he told Wrangel in another letter, to spend the summer in Dresden and finish his novel there without disturbance. "Otherwise, here in Petersburg it is impossible to finish ... as for the creditors, the more one pays, the more insolent they become."[29] But the threat of war between Austria and Prussia, delays in obtaining a passport, and, most important of all, a fall in the value of the ruble ruled out such a trip.

In a letter to Anna Korvin-Krukovskaya—who had, with the approval of her father, invited him to vacation in Palibino—Dostoevsky explains that his novel will probably keep him pinned to Petersburg throughout the summer. Trying to draw some consolation from this unappealing prospect, he suggests that "in truth, the melancholy, sleazy and foul-smelling Petersburg of summer time fits with my mood and may even provide me with some pseudo-inspiration for my novel; but it's too oppressive."[30] As the spring wore on, Dostoevsky finally decided that Petersburg would indeed prove intolerable, though he hesitated to go to Palibino because, as he remarks to Anna in mid-June, "it would be impolite for me to visit and work all day long."[31] He finally decided to give Moscow a try, but then, finding the heat and the loneliness unbearable after a few days, moved to the nearby village of Lublino, where the Ivanovs had rented a dacha and were able to find accommodations for Dostoevsky.

Lublino, a well-known summer resort about three or four miles from Moscow, was surrounded by a picturesque park and bordered by a large lake on one side and an extensive forest on the other. The Ivanovs' ten children had all brought along friends, and there were other young people whom the benevolent Dr. Ivanov had taken under his wing. Since Dostoevsky needed peace and quiet in order to work, a spacious room was found nearby to which he could retire in tranquillity. Several letters from Moscow in late June reveal Dostoevsky's concern for, and exasperation with, his stepson Pasha Isaev, whom he invited to join him but then castigated for his irresponsibility in failing to reply promptly. Pasha, however, finally accepted his stepfather's invitation, and they installed themselves in Lublino at the beginning of July.

Two memoirs have been left of this relatively blithe summer of 1866: one by Dostoevsky's niece Marya Alexandrovna Ivanova, then eighteen years old and already displaying outstanding musical talent (she later became a brilliant pianist); the other by the then fifteen-year-old N. Von-Voght (or Fon-Fokht, to use the Russian spelling), a student at the Konstantinovsky Institute whom the Ivanovs had befriended and invited for the summer. Both depict the lighthearted, untroubled atmosphere of those carefree days, when much time was spent in long walks to neighboring villages during the soft, summery, moonlit evenings, on word games and amateur theatricals to while away the hours after dinner, and on the inevitable good-humored chaffing and jesting of high-spirited youth. The usually gloomy and care-worn Dostoevsky evidently blossomed in this rejuvenating atmosphere, and, despite his age and forbidding reputation (everyone there had some knowledge of his early works and knew of his legendary aura as a Siberian survivor), he is depicted as playing the part of master of the revels with great relish. Just two months before, in writing to Father Yanishev, he had detailed the familiar litany of his woes, but then interjected that "life and hope have not yet dried up for me."[32] The image we obtain of him during these summer months amply confirms such words.

"Although he was forty-five years old," writes his niece, "he behaved with surprising unaffectedness toward the young company, and was the initial organizer of all the distractions and pranks. Even externally he appeared much younger than his years. Always elegantly dressed, with starched collars, gray trousers and a dark-blue, loose-fitting jacket, Dostoevsky carefully looked after his appearance and was very unhappy, for instance, that his small beard was so scanty."[33] The young people did not hesitate to tease him about his modest dandyism, nor to reply boldly to his often provocative sallies; and sometimes there were more serious discussions, which did not, however, spoil the reigning atmosphere of camaraderie. "With the youth present among the Ivanovs Dostoevsky often quarreled about the modish 'nihilism,' and over the question of which was superior: 'boots or Pushkin,'" his niece reports. "He eloquently defended the importance of Pushkin's poetry."[34]

Much diversion was afforded the assembled company by Dostoevsky's ability to turn out reams of mocking light verse, most of it directed against a young nephew of the Ivanovs, Dr. Alexander Karepin, who was also the butt of impromptu skits and pantomimes equally flowing from Dostoevsky's tireless pen. Despite his perfectly respectable medical career, Dr. Karepin was in all other aspects an amiable simpleton; as Dostoevsky's niece remarked, "all the adventures of Dickens's Pickwick happened to him."[35] Still unmarried, Dr. Karepin was an opponent of the new ideas about women's emancipation advocated by Chernyshevsky in *What Is To Be Done?*, and Dostoevsky once worked him into a fury by asserting that the government had set up an organization to encourage women to desert their husbands and come to Petersburg for the purpose of learning how to operate sewing machines (an allusion to the dressmaking establishment successfully organized by the heroine of the novel, Vera Pavlovna). Dr. Karepin took all this with solemn literalness, and flew into a rage against such interference with family stability until reassured that it was only a joke.

Dostoevsky here was ridiculing Chernyshevsky (as well as Dr. Karepin) with some of the same zest he displays in portraying the character of the simpleminded but essentially well-meaning Utopian Socialist Lebezyatnikov in *Crime and Punishment*. And some of the mockery directed against the doctor, which occasionally led to rather cruel embarrassment, would later be aimed against the character of Trusotsky in *The Eternal Husband*—a novella in which Dostoevsky introduces the country-house surroundings and the youthful high spirits of his Lublino summer.

Among the other guests present in the Ivanov household was Dr. Ivanov's ailing brother, generally considered to be on the point of death, and his wife Elena Pavlovna, whose married life had been a far from happy one. Dostoevsky's desire to remarry was well known, and everyone in the Ivanov entourage had of course learned of his sudden and unexpected proposal to Marya Ivanchina-Pisareva just a few months earlier. Probably he had complained to his sister Vera more than once, just as he had done in his letter to Wrangel, about being deprived of the joys of family happiness; and it occurred to her that the long-suffering and sweet-tempered Elena Pavlovna, soon to become a widow, would make a very suitable match. Dostoevsky fell in with this idea, and one day asked Elena whether, if she were free, she would consider him a satisfactory bridegroom. The embarrassed lady gave no clear-cut answer to this rather macabre inquiry, and Dostoevsky, since he had not met with a flat refusal, now considered himself to be morally engaged; but the situation hardly bound him to anything specific.

7

Despite all the amusements in which he took so active a part, Dostoevsky nonetheless could hardly forget either about his novel or, as time went on, about the new work that he had promised to Stellovsky by the beginning of the year. His plan had been, as he rather swaggeringly confided to Anna Korvin-Krukovskaya in late June, "to do an unheard of and eccentric thing: write 30 signatures [a signature consisted of sixteen pages] in 4 months of two different novels, one in the morning and the other in the evening, and to finish on schedule." Dostoevsky pretends that such "eccentric and extraordinary things" rather pleased him, though admitting that since he had no choice he might as well take pride in the conditions under which he had to work. "I am convinced that not a single one of our writers, whether past or present, ever wrote under the conditions in which I am *continuously* forced to write. Turgenev would die at the very thought."[36] These words indicate what Dostoevsky had hoped to accomplish, but not at all what actually occurred. In mid-July he confides to A. P. Milyukov: "I have worked very little, and in general—I am still only preparing to work—although in the past two weeks I have been *very* busy. But it's possible to be even busier (twice as much), and I am saving my strength for the last period, that is, the month of August."[37]

Dostoevsky's announced intention of working both morning and evening probably explains why Fon-Fokht describes him as sitting down to his desk shortly after breakfast and continuing to lunch time, while his niece speaks of him as working only in the stillness of the night. It was more usual for him to compose at night, and his morning labors were presumably spent in sketching ideas for *The Gambler*, which, however, he completed only several months later. According to one anecdote, the late evening hours were indisputedly reserved for pressing ahead with *Crime and Punishment*. A lackey of the Ivanovs, assigned to sleep in Dostoevsky's dacha so as to aid him in case of an epileptic attack, announced after a few days that he would refuse to reside with the author any longer. The reason, he explained, was that Dostoevsky was planning to kill somebody—"all through the night he paced up and down in his room and spoke about this aloud."[38]

Dostoevsky made weekly visits to Moscow for consultation with the editors of *The Russian Messenger*, and "always returned dissatisfied and upset. He explained this as the result of being almost always forced to correct his text, or even simply to throw out certain parts because of censorship pressure."[39] Such words refer to a situation that Dostoevsky mentions in the mid-July letter to Milyukov, where he further specifies that the worst "censorship pressure" came not from the legal authorities but from Katkov and his assistant editor N. A. Lyubimov, who were insisting that he rewrite the chapter containing the scene in which Sonya reads to Raskolnikov the passage from the Gospel concerning the raising of Lazarus. This time-consuming task was one reason why Dostoevsky's hope of being able to write his novel for Stellovsky during the summer, while still continuing to forge ahead with *Crime and Punishment*, proved to be overly optimistic. Dostoevsky admitted to Milyukov that "I have *not yet tackled* the novel for Stellovsky, but I will. I have worked out a plan— a quite satisfactory little novel, so that there will even be traces of characters. Stellovsky upsets me to the point of torture, and I even see him in my dreams."[40] In fact, however, Dostoevsky made no further progress that would enable him to fulfill the terms of the threatening contract.

On October 1, shortly after Dostoevsky's return to Petersburg, Milyukov called and found his friend walking up and down his study in terrible agitation. It was then, for the first time, that Dostoevsky frankly revealed to him the prejudicial terms of the Stellovsky agreement and confessed that he was hopelessly entrapped. Just a month was left to satisfy his part of the bargain and nothing had yet been written; even if he managed to write a first draft, it would be almost physically impossible to transcribe and correct it in time to meet the deadline. Milyukov, horrified at what might occur, suggested that a group of Dostoevsky's friends take the plan already prepared and each write a section; this collective effort could then be submitted and published under Dostoevsky's signature. "No!" Dostoevsky answered firmly. "I will never sign my name to other people's work."[41] Milyukov then advised him to find a stenographer and dictate the novel; this would speed up the process of composition considerably and, in particular, shorten the amount of time necessary for the physical preparation of the manuscript. Never having dictated any of his work before, Dostoevsky was quite reluctant and doubted whether he could create in this fashion; but he finally agreed to make the attempt as perhaps the one possible solution to his dilemma.

Luckily, Milyukov had contact through a friend with a professor of stenography who had recently established the first such course for women in Russia. A day or two later, one of his star pupils, Anna Grigoryevna Snitkina, turned up in Dostoevsky's flat with newly sharpened pencils and a portfolio especially purchased for this epochal occasion, ready to assume her duties. This businesslike visit of the outwardly cool young lady proved to have a decisive effect on Dostoevsky's entire life. Anna

Snitkina became his second wife in a very short space of time, henceforth devoting herself heart and soul to his welfare and exercising a salutary influence on the remainder of his career. Their courtship will be narrated in a later chapter; for the moment it is only necessary to know that *The Gambler* was completed on schedule and that, after this feat, the final chapters of *Crime and Punishment* were easily taken in stride. Dostoevsky now found dictating so much to his taste that he employed it, with Anna Grigoryevna as amanuensis, in all his future work. The completion of *Crime and Punishment* thus marked a crucial moment in Dostoevsky's life both as man and as artist. With this novel he stepped forward, once and for all, into the front rank of Russian writers; and in the next chapter we shall begin to examine the history of its creation.

CHAPTER 5

The Sources of
Crime and Punishment

Crime and Punishment began as the idea for a long short story, the first-person confession of a murderer, presumably planned to be somewhat the same length as *Notes from Underground*. It would also have resembled this earlier work in that the psychology of the protagonist would be inextricably interwoven with his "ideology," his acceptance of certain ideas that "befuddle" his moral conscience and justify his crime. This basic conception remained unchanged even as the work blossomed under Dostoevsky's hands and turned into the first great artistic synthesis of his post-Siberian career.

Such a synthesis took place when the protagonist of Dostoevsky's novella, an ideological murderer, became involved with the Marmeladov family, who had been originally destined for the novel *The Drunkards*. The deeply affecting social realism of Dostoevsky's depictions of Petersburg slum life, and the psychological mastery he had always displayed in the portrayal of acute moral conflict, thus were combined with an attack on the moral-philosophical foundations of the reigning radical ideology. Moreover, as we shall see, his grasp of this ideology evolved from the simplistic Utilitarianism sketched in the letter to Katkov into a much more complex and brilliantly imaginative projection of the destructive and self-destructive possibilities embodied in the very latest version of the radical faith. Far from attempting to vilify the radicals, as Eliseev had charged, Dostoevsky was rather striving to warn them against the calamitous results he could foresee flowing from the ideas by which they were now being inspired.*

Crime and Punishment is thus an extremely rich work composed of many strands, and any adequate account of its history must try to weave them all together. The present chapter will sketch the experiential, the literary-thematic, and, most of all, the ideological context within which the novel was conceived. Only a knowledge of these contexts can help to

---

* See the comment of N. N. Strakhov, who wrote of the book in 1867, certainly after conversations about it with Dostoevsky: "This is not laughter at the young generation, reproaches and accusations but—a tearful lament over it." Quite surprisingly, the editors of the Academy edition remark that these words of Strakhov "to a large extent truly characterize the relation of the writer to his hero" (*PSS* 7: 353).

throw some light on the many vexing questions concerning the book's interpretation. The next chapter will analyze, with the help of Dostoevsky's notebooks, the gestation of the work itself, from its modest inception through the various drafts and recastings that led to the discovery of its definitive structure and appropriate narrative technique.

2

Tradition has always associated the origins of *Crime and Punishment* with the period of Dostoevsky's internment in a Siberian prison camp; and Dostoevsky himself appears to support such a linkage by ending the book with Raskolnikov's precipitate conversion to Christian values in precisely such a locale. In addition, Dostoevsky had lived side-by-side with common criminals during these years, many of them murderers, and it has been presumed that the impressions he gathered of his fellow inmates stimulated his interest in the psychology of crime and ultimately gave birth to his novel. There is no doubt that the experiences of these years provided a very important substratum of the book; but this must not be confused with the notion that *Crime and Punishment* is the *direct* realization of a creative idea conceived at that time.

In a letter dating from October 1859, Dostoevsky referred to a plan for a novel that would be a "confession," and also wrote that "I conceived it in *katorga*, lying on the plank bed, in painful moments of sorrow and self-criticism."[1] L. P. Grossman, one of the best early Dostoevsky scholars, suggested that *Crime and Punishment*, also a "confession," was the fulfillment of this plan; but more recent scholarship, in my opinion quite justifiably, has rejected this identification.[2] Dostoevsky also mentions, in the same letter, another idea for a novel about "a young man who murdered and landed in Siberia," but this is quite separate from the confession project. The "confession" has nothing to do with a murder, and probably refers to what became the second part of *Notes from Underground.* As for the young man who murdered and landed in Siberia, nothing at all is said about his motivation; at best he provides only the barest schema for the later work. There is thus no convincing evidence that *Crime and Punishment* began, in any artistically relevant fashion, as the realization of an idea that first came to birth while Dostoevsky was serving his prison-camp sentence.

But if it will not do to imagine *Crime and Punishment* as having begun to take shape in Siberia in some unmediated fashion, neither will it serve simply to deny that the observations and experiences gathered there provided a powerful stimulus for essential aspects of Dostoevsky's creation. Even though his prison-camp term was now fifteen years in the past, he had, just three years before, brought its relevatory impact back to life with stunning force in *House of the Dead*; and he obviously drew on certain of his encounters there to nourish his novel.

As a first example, we may adduce his acquaintance with the bandit chief Orlov, "who had murdered old people and children in cold blood," and who provided Dostoevsky with a chillingly vivid image of what it meant to be a Napoleonic personality. Orlov was, as Dostoevsky wrote, "a man of terrible strength of will and proud consciousness of his strength." Becoming aware, on one occasion, that Dostoevsky "was trying to get at his conscience and discover some sign of penitence in him," he looked at his educated fellow prisoner "with great contempt and haughtiness, as though I had suddenly in his eyes become a foolish little boy with whom it was impossible to discuss things as you would with a grown-up person. There was even a sort of pity for me to be seen in his face. A minute later he burst out laughing at me, a perfectly open-hearted laugh free from any irony." As Dostoevsky saw it, Orlov "could not really help despising me, and must have looked upon me as a weak, pitiful, submissive creature, inferior to him in every respect" (4: 47–48). These are precisely the feelings of Raskolnikov when he measures himself against the image of the "extraordinary" personality that he has tried to emulate so unsuccessfully; no matter how airtight the conclusions of his logic, he finds it impossible to transform himself into an Orlov.

Orlov's connection with the book, no matter how plausible, still remains only a hypothesis; but there is no doubt about the role assigned to another denizen of the camp. No one there was more repellent to Dostoevsky than a convict of the noble class named Aristov, who served as a spy and informer and was "the most revolting example of the depths to which a man can sink and degenerate, and the extent to which he can destroy all moral feeling in himself without difficulty or repentance." Aristov had been sent to prison for having falsely denounced other people as political malcontents, and then using the funds obtained from the secret police on this pretext to lead a life of wild debauchery. Dostoevsky described him as "cunning and clever, good-looking, even rather well-educated and [someone] who had abilities"; but his thorough viciousness made this deceptively pleasing outward appearance, marked by an "everlasting mocking smile," only more sinister (4: 62–63). When the character of Svidrigailov first makes an appearance among the notes for *Crime and Punishment*, he is called Aristov.[3] But while some of the scoffing cynicism and yet attractive outward features of the original are retained, as well as his total unscrupulousness, the world-weary *ennui* that Dostoevsky imparts to the character proves, if proof were necessary, that he invariably reshaped his external models freely to accord with his thematic and artistic aims.

Less obvious, but in my view equally certain, is the relation of an important subplot in the novel with the history of a prisoner named Ilinsky, who had been convicted, presumably on unimpeachable evidence, of the murder of his father. But something about his character and light-hearted behavior suggested to Dostoevsky, despite his knowledge of all the accusatory circumstances, that the carefree young officer might truly be innocent; and this psychological intuition turned out to be accurate when the real murderer confessed some years later. The house painter Nikolay in *Crime and Punishment* is also suspected of murder on quite damaging material evidence, but Razumikhin, who often speaks directly for the author, refuses to believe in his guilt on the basis of psychological impressions very similar to those which prompted Dostoevsky to question Ilinsky's sentence. Later, the history of Ilinsky will furnish additional inspiration for *The Brothers Karamazov*.

3

Such linkages between the novel and Dostoevsky's Siberian years are not difficult to establish; but there are also more surreptitious connections that have escaped the vigilance even of the horde of zealous source-hunters who have pored over this relationship. No one has noted, so far as my knowledge goes, the analogy that exists between Raskolnikov's psychology before and after the crime with Dostoevsky's description of what frequently occurred in the case of real-life peasant murderers. Such a peasant, house serf, soldier, or workman often has lived in peace for most of his life; but suddenly, at a certain point, "something in him seems to snap; his patience gave way and he sticks a knife into his enemy and oppressor." Such an event is "criminal but [still] comprehensible"; what follows, however, is much less so. Now the same quiet and previously peaceable person begins to kill indiscriminately, "for amusement, for an insulting word, to make a round number, or simply 'out of my way, don't cross my path, I am coming!' The man is, as it were, drunk, in delirium. It is as though once having overstepped the sacred limit, he begins to revel in the fact that nothing is sacred to him" (4: 87–88). But once the fit is over, such criminals calm down and very quickly reassume their original docile nature.

Here is the pattern of much that happens to Raskolnikov, although transposed into terms more suitable to his status as an educated member of the intelligentsia. It is not so much the murder itself that releases his "delirium" as the *idea* of "overstepping the sacred limit," and it is this idea that allows him "to revel in the fact that nothing is sacred to him." Once the murder has been committed—and he kills two people, instead of one, as originally planned—the formerly reticent and retiring Raskol-nikov unexpectedly exhibits a defiant rage and hatred for all those he believes might suspect him, and even for those who come to his aid (like his friend Razumikhin) or whom he had previously loved (like his mother and sister). He becomes, as it were, a new personality, parading a dis-dainful arrogance that surprises even himself, but which, ultimately, he finds it impossible to sustain. What occurs to Raskolnikov is an exact moral-psychic counterpart of the transformation of the convicts who had run amok; and the resemblance, whether conscious or not, is too striking to be ignored.

Another passage in the prison memoirs, equally overlooked in the commentaries, seems to me to cast the most light on the initial inception of *Crime and Punishment*. At this point, Dostoevsky is lamenting the in-herent injustice of assigning the same legal penalty for crimes whose motives may have been entirely dissimilar, and of sentencing criminals to identical punishment even though they differ profoundly in moral character. One, for example, may feel no guilt or remorse whatever over a savage murder, and "never once, during the entire duration of his im-prisonment, reflects upon the crime he has committed. He even consid-ers himself to be in the right." But others respond quite differently—for example, "an educated man with a sensitive conscience, with awareness, heart. The pain in his heart will be enough to do away with him, long before any punishment is inflicted upon him. Far more mercilessly, far more pitilessly than the sternest law, he condemns himself for his crime" (4: 43).

Here, in all likelihood, is the germ of his novella about "a young man who murdered," and who would represent the type of personality he de-fines: "an educated man with a sensitive conscience" that punishes him far more severely than the rigors of the sternest law. If this speculation is correct, then the origins of *Crime and Punishment* may well be traced back and seen as a creative aftermath of Dostoevsky's Siberian years— but only in the sense that these years provided a truly unique experien-tial gauge, as it were, allowing him to measure the dangerous illusions of the radicals about the human personality in general and themselves in particular. And if the murderer of the novella would also, in the long run (Dostoevsky mentions the period of a month), find himself unable to en-dure "the pain in his heart," the motivation for his voluntary self-surren-der would be that terrible sense of freezing isolation, that withering awareness of separation from the remainder of mankind, which the au-thor himself had felt in prison camp because of the "obstinate, irrecon-cilable hatred" displayed toward him and all the members of his class by the implacable peasant convicts.

Additional aspects of Dostoevsky's life in Siberia will also be utilized in his novel. The prototype of the character Marmeladov has often been identified as the husband of Dostoevsky's first wife, Alexander Ivanovich Isaev, who was still alive when Dostoevsky fell hopelessly in love with his blonde, pretty, highly intelligent, and long-suffering consort. Isaev had been a schoolteacher and a customs official, but lost both posts because of inveterate drunkenness; and he spent his time carousing with the riffraff in the taverns of Semipalatinsk while his neglected wife and seven-year-old son lived on the edge of beggary. Dostoevsky, however, valued Isaev's human qualities, and wrote to his brother Mikhail that "he suffered from much undeserved persecution at the hands of local society." Unable to discipline himself, he had "sunk very low. And yet he was highly cultivated and the kindliest of persons. . . . He was, despite all the dirt, exceptionally noble."[4] It is remarkable to what extent Dostoevsky manages to capture this incongruous set of attributes in his fictional personage.

Isaev's wife, Marya Dimitrievna, was not only attractive, but, as Dostoevsky's friend Baron Wrangel wrote, she also possessed "a passionate nature given to quite exalted feelings."[5] Already stricken by tuberculosis when Dostoevsky met her, she died after a long and racking agony in April 1864. There can be little doubt that she served as the prototype for Katerina Ivanovna Marmeladova, whose torments, sufferings, and despairing courage in misfortune Dostoevsky paints with such powerfully moving strokes. Marya Dimitrievna was given to tempestuous outbursts of rage, and Dostoevsky excused them by reassuring her that "for a person with your force of character it is impossible not to rebel against injustice; that is an honest and noble trait. It is the foundation of your character."[6] He characterized her to Baron Wrangel as "a knight in female clothing,"[7] and the fiery, combative Katerina Ivanovna, eternally protesting so futilely against the world's injustice, can well be seen as a poignantly magnified realization of such an image. Marmeladov's description of the desperate situation that forced her to accept him as a husband ("and she was left [a widow] . . . with three children in a wild and remote district where I happened to be . . . and in such hopeless poverty that . . . I don't feel equal to describing it") also corresponds roughly, but by no means literally, to the general circumstances in which Dostoevsky's own marriage took place (6: 15–16).*

These are some of the threads that can be discerned stretching from the Siberian years to the novel on whose draft Dostoevsky had been feverishly working as he sat, penniless and hungry, in his room at Wies-

---

* For the circumstances of Dostoevsky's first marriage, see my *Dostoevsky: The Years of Ordeal, 1850–1859* (Princeton, N.J., 1983), chap. 15.

baden, surely boiling inwardly with some of the same rage as his future Raskolnikov against the heartlessness of a world in which poverty led only to endless humiliation.

4
———

Dostoevsky himself never linked the theme of his proposed novella with his Siberian years except perhaps by implication, when he told Katkov that he had seen the inner need for punishment manifest itself "even among very uneducated people, in the crudest circumstances." In fact, however, he offered no example of such a need among the peasant convicts, and had spoken of it only as an attribute of an "educated conscience." It was such a conscience that Dostoevsky now wished to portray in "an educated member of the new generation," someone who, having fallen under the influence of the "strange, 'unfinished' ideas afloat in the atmosphere," has been betrayed into committing a murder "through light-mindedness and lack of steadiness in his convictions." Dostoevsky thus clearly connects his novella with the ideological ambience of the time, and in his original proposal to Katkov he cites several newspaper accounts of recent crimes committed by students, which, in his opinion, indicated that the age-old injunction against murder had begun to lose its prohibitive force in their milieu. The crimes he singles out were all committed in cold blood and after careful thought; they were not crimes of passion, or revenge, or crude rapacity; they were diligently carried out by persons with, presumably, consciences refined by education. It may well have been such accounts that gave the original jolt to Dostoevsky's imagination: he always paid the closest attention to the annals of crime, and considered them telltale symptoms of the prevailing moral climate.

If these news stories made such an impact on Dostoevsky, however, it was because he had long been fascinated with the figure of the intellectual criminal who justifies—or pretends to justify—his criminality in terms of a theory. Five years earlier, in one of the early issues of *Time*, Dostoevsky had run a series of articles about famous French criminal trials, which, as he wrote in a prefatory note, are "more exciting than all possible novels because they light up the dark sides of the human soul that art does not like to approach, or which it approaches only glancingly and in passing" (19: 89). The first of the series dealt with the famous murderer Pierre-François Lacenaire, whose story gripped Dostoevsky because of the alliance between his obvious culture and refinement and the monstrosity of his deeds. Lacenaire, he wrote, "is a remarkable personality, enigmatic, frightening and gripping. Base instincts and cowardice in the face of poverty made him a criminal, and he dared to set himself up as a victim of his century. All this joined to a boundless vanity; it is the type of a vanity developed to the utmost degree" (19: 90). Such remarks indicate Dostoevsky's fascination with the type of the intellectual-murderer, which was probably also stimulated by his traumatic encounter with Aristov in the prison camp.

This recollection of Lacenaire may well have provided Dostoevsky with some sort of character-schema; but if so, it was one that he filled out in purely Russian terms. For the ideology that he places at the root of that "lack of steadiness . . . in convictions" among the youth unmistakably refers to the attempt of the radical intelligentsia of the 1860s to base morality on a Utilitarian foundation. The protagonist of Dostoevsky's as yet unnamed work decides to kill the old pawnbroker because she is evil, cruel, and merciless; but he does not use his moral revulsion at her conduct as a justification for his deed. Rather, he persuades himself that her existence is "useless," thus substituting a Utilitarian standard for his instinctive moral reaction. Such a Utilitarian criterion "befuddles" the young man, and he resolves to rescue his family by murdering the wretched woman and pilfering her coffers, after which he plans to devote the remainder of his days to good deeds (fulfilling his "humane obligations to mankind") as a means of compensating for his crime. But Dostoevsky also represents him—using in his outline the same technique of "narrated monologue"[8] that he will employ so masterfully in the novel— as inwardly questioning whether such a murder should be considered a "crime" at all ("if one can really call a crime this action against a deaf, stupid, evil, sickly old woman" etc.). If not, then the character should have no compunctions whatever about disposing of her life; no moral considerations of *any* kind need disturb him, since Utilitarian reason, not old-fashioned biblical notions of good and evil, have now become the basis of morality. This conflict between the old morality of conscience and the new morality based on Utilitarian reason is what "befuddles" Dostoevsky's character and shapes the manner in which his personality is portrayed.

Dostoevsky's idea for a story thus neatly takes its place in the main line of development that his work had assumed since his return from Siberia in 1860. This line may be defined as an exploration both of the moral deficiencies of the progressive ideology he had himself accepted during the 1840s, and of the public and personal dangers lurking in the more recent radical ideas that had become dominant in the 1860s. His first post-Siberian novel, *The Insulted and Injured*, had exposed the sentimentalism of his own early work to critical scrutiny, and already contained a concealed attack on the doctrine of "rational egoism" propagated by N. G. Chernyshevsky. As the leading radical publicist, Chernyshevsky had popularized the view, derived from Jeremy Bentham and

J. S. Mill, that the ultimate criterion of morality was "utility." Mankind, Chernyshevsky had declared, seeks primarily what gives it pleasure and satisfies its egoistic self-interest; but since men are also rational creatures, they eventually learn through enlightenment that the most lasting and durable "utility" consists in identifying their personal desires with the welfare of the majority of their fellows. In the character of the villainous Prince Valkovsky, who mouths ideas taken from Chernyshevsky, Dostoevsky had revealed how easily a morality based on the acceptance of Utilitarian egoism could be perverted into an apologia of the blackest iniquity. But since such evil is depicted only in the guise of a corrupt aristocrat, it is obvious that Dostoevsky did not yet wish to lay it squarely at the door of the radicals themselves.

During the next several years, Dostoevsky continued to polemicize with radical doctrines—sometimes overtly, as in his journalistic sallies, and sometimes indirectly, simply taking for granted that his readers would catch his drift and make the necessary connections. In *House of the Dead*, for example, there is an obvious thrust against "rational egoism" in the description of a widow living near the prison camp who had devoted herself heart and soul to easing the lot of the convicts. "Some people maintain," Dostoevsky writes, "that the purest love for one's neighbor is at the same time the greatest egoism. What egoism there could be in this instance I can't understand" (4: 68). Less explicitly, a polemic with Chernyshevsky runs through the entire book, since Dostoevsky demonstrates in its pages, with overwhelming clarity and indelible force, the *opposition* between egoism and reason rather than their harmonious interaction. Rational considerations, on which Chernyshevsky so ingenuously relied, are shown to be impotent when confronted by the entire gamut of emotional responses—some of which, at first sight, seem entirely *irrational*—through which the human personality expresses its irrepressible needs, especially its need to possess a sense of its own autonomy.

Notes from Underground launched a much more vehement onslaught against radical ideology—though still in a highly allusive and indirect fashion—by once again dramatizing its possible human consequences if taken literally as a guide to conduct. Reason, in radical ideology, had come to be identified with the belief in a thoroughgoing determinism, which denied the existence of free will and hence the very possibility of moral choice; but Dostoevsky had become convinced that the human personality would never accept such a limitation on its freedom. He thus attacks this dogma by creating an imaginary character (the underground man) who *accepts* as an axiom Chernyshevsky's unqualified denial of the existence of any such human capacity as free will. The result is an explosion of irrational egoism on the part of the underground man simply because it is humanly impossible to live by such a doctrine; the personality will *always* refuse to surrender its moral autonomy, its right to *choose* between good and evil, even though reason may have decided that any such right has been eliminated by the irrefutable discoveries of science about the laws of nature. In the second part of *Notes from Underground*, the eruption of egoism is provoked by the underground man's absorption of the Russian variety of European Romantic Byronism.

The tone of *Notes from Underground*, however, is so satirical and parodistic, its theme so wrapped in an inverted irony, that Dostoevsky can hardly be said here to have confronted the doctrines of the radicals straightforwardly and head-on. His new idea for a story, though, represented a much more serious and much blunter assault on Utilitarian morality than any he had mounted so far. Now he wished to pillory it as the cause of so much confusion and chaos, as so blurring the line between good and evil, that it could mislead an idealistic and highly compassionate young man, revolted by suffering and injustice, into the commission of a brutal murder. Initially, as we have seen, Raskolnikov's aim was only to extricate himself and his family from their tormenting difficulties; but in the final text, this intention becomes subordinate to a more complex ideological motivation that is no longer identified with the ideas that Dostoevsky had attacked in *Notes from Underground*. If we are to understand *Crime and Punishment*, we must thus place it back into the context of this pivotal mutation of radical ideology, which led to the growth of what may properly be labeled as Russian Nihilism.

As Dostoevsky well knew, the Utopian Socialist Chernyshevsky was not a Nihilist at all in the sense in which this term came to be understood in the mid-1860s. And to comprehend what Nihilism means, we must turn to the furious polemics carried on by *The Contemporary*, which spoke for the Chernyshevsky tradition in Russian culture, with another left-wing, and initially friendly periodical, *The Russian Word* (*Russkoe Slovo*). Only the contributors to this second journal can be considered the genuine spokesmen for the Nihilist position; and Dostoevsky's plan for a story, whatever its initial scope may have been, eventually developed into a response to the significant change in radical ideology marked by the ascension of *The Russian Word* as a stridently independent voice. This ascension signaled a move from Chernyshevsky's Utopian Socialism and "rational egoism" (relatively anodine, at least in theory and as depicted in his enormously influential novel *What Is To Be Done?*) to a much harsher doctrine that encouraged an élite of superior individuals to step over all existing moral norms for the sake of advancing the interests of mankind as a whole.

The first notable manifestation of this new variety of radical thought—which led to what Dostoevsky, in a very important article, eventually labeled as "The Schism [*Raskol*] among the Nihilists"—is ordinarily dated as beginning with the publication of Turgenev's *Fathers and Children* in the spring of 1862. In fact, however, it began a year earlier with the first major appearance in print of a young critic and publicist, the high-strung, emotionally unstable, but extremely talented Dimitry I. Pisarev. His significance was immediately spotted by the alert N. N. Strakhov, the chief commentator on the current cultural scene for Dostoevsky's journal *Time*. Strakhov gleefully pointed out that Pisarev had gone farther than other radicals along the path of total negation, and he cited as evidence the words that Pisarev had declared, with youthful bravado, to be "the ultimatum of our [the radical] camp." These words boldly exhorted the young generation: "strike right and left, no harm can come of it and no harm will come," because "what resists the blow is worth keeping; what flies to pieces is rubbish."[9] Strakhov also noted, quite perceptively, the new accent of individualism underlying Pisarev's text, a longing for some form of *personal* fulfillment quite absent from the writings of either Chernyshevsky or Dobrolyubov. Pisarev had vigorously proclaimed "the emancipation of the individual" to be the ultimate aim of all of modern thought; and Strakhov interprets this to mean, quite in accord with more recent historians of Russian culture, that Pisarev "rejects everything in the name of one general authority, in the name of *life*, and life he obviously understands as *the alluring variety of lively and unlimited pleasures.*"[10]

Pisarev's extremism and individualism, which initially had provided only a divergent nuance in the radicalism of the 1860s, led to a much more dramatic disagreement in the aftermath of the publication of Turgenev's *Fathers and Children*. This quarrel marked a watershed in the evolution of radical thought, and ultimately exercised a decisive influence on the creation of *Crime and Punishment*. Chernyshevsky was persuaded that Turgenev had conceived the work as a means of revenge against Dobrolyubov, ignobly caricaturing the young publicist personally in the central character Bazarov; and he continued to cling to this conviction to the very end of his life.[11] Even though erroneous, such a view received some justification from Turgenev's openly expressed displeasure at Dobrolyubov's critical disparagement of his novels and stories, and his resentment at a personal dislike that the abrasive Dobrolyubov made no effort to conceal. As a result, *The Contemporary* printed a slashing attack from the vitriolic pen of M. A. Antonovich, who castigated Turgenev's masterpiece as a disastrous artistic failure and, even worse, a slander on the radical movement. Pisarev then leaped into the fray with a sensational article strongly defending Turgenev's novel and declaring that, in the main character Bazarov, the novelist had faultlessly delineated an accurate image of the new radical hero of the time.

Dostoevsky, as we know, was a great admirer of *Fathers and Children*, and both he and Strakhov considered Turgenev to have written a poignantly lyrical indictment of the very same human limitations of radical ideology against which Dostoevsky had already begun to protest. Naturally, he would have carefully read and weighed every word of Pisarev's endorsement of Bazarov as a flawless portrayal of the evolving self-image of the young radicals—a self-image whose widespread acceptance entailed momentous consequences for the immediate social-cultural future. It was the possible moral effects of this metamorphosis of radical ideology that Dostoevsky came to depict in *Crime and Punishment*; and if we are to comprehend the ideas and behavior of Raskolnikov, whom Dostoevsky began to conceive only three years later, it is to Pisarev's article that we must turn first of all.

Antonovich had indignantly dismissed Bazarov as an ignoble caricature of the ideals of the Russian radicals; but Pisarev greeted him as their sterling, exemplary realization. Pisarev thus established that identification of radicalism with Nihilism, and hence with the ambition of creating a *tabula rasa* by total destruction, on which we have seen Dostoevsky drawing in his letter to Katkov. For it was Bazarov who had first declared himself to be a "Nihilist" and who announced that, "since at the present time, negation is the most useful of all," the Nihilists "deny—everything."[12] Also, Pisarev stresses an aspect of Bazarov's personality that Dostoevsky will later exploit with masterly effect. "Bazarov is extraordinarily conceited," Pisarev wrote, "but his conceit is inconspicuous precisely because of its immensity . . . he is so full of himself, he stands so securely on such a height, that he is almost completely indifferent to the opinions of other people." One character in Turgenev's novel refers to Bazarov as possessing a "Satanic pride," and Pisarev hastens to agree that "this expression is very felicitously chosen and is a perfect characterization of our hero."[13] Dostoevsky—and most emphatically not by chance—will employ exactly the same phrase in his notes to describe the aspect of Raskolnikov's personality that comes to the fore after the murder.

Most important of all, Bazarov's immense personal superiority to the world surrounding him is then generalized by Pisarev and given the status of a universal law marking out two sharply opposed types of human beings. The first group, a very small one, consists of people like Bazarov, who not only exhibit extraordinary personal qualities but refuse to be bound by anything external to themselves and their desires.

Bazarov, as Pisarev interprets him, "everywhere and in everything does only what he wishes, or what seems to him useful and attractive. He is governed only by personal caprice and personal calculation. Neither over him, nor outside him, nor inside him does he recognize any regulator, any moral law, any principle." Even more, "nothing except personal taste prevents him from *murdering and robbing*, and nothing except personal taste stirs people of this stripe to make discoveries in the field of science and social existence" (italics added).[14] After thus placing Bazarov on such a solitary proto-Nietzschean height above and beyond the moral law, Pisarev then contrasts his lonely grandeur with "the masses," who "in every period have lived contentedly, and with their inherent placidity have been satisfied with what was at hand." Consequently, "the mass *does not make discoveries or commit crimes*; other people think and suffer, search and find, struggle and err on its behalf—other people eternally alien to it, *eternally regarding it with contempt*, and at the same time eternally working to increase the amenities of its life" (italics added).[15]

These passages from Pisarev call for commentary on two points. One is the use of the word "contempt" to characterize Bazarov's attitude toward the people, whose future welfare is presumably to be the primary concern of his own life. Nothing similar to such disdain, mingled with such dedication, can be found in the radicalism of *The Contemporary*; but it will be amply evident both in the ideas and in the behavior of Raskolnikov. Moreover, in accepting Bazarov as the ideal image of the new "hero of his time," and thus giving a *positive* value to those aspects of his character that had most outraged the Chernyshevsky faction, Pisarev indicated his approval of the famous scene in which Bazarov expresses the tragic contradiction between his own need for self-fulfillment and the indistinct hope of some future social bliss. When his liberal friend Arkady looks forward to the far-distant attainment of such bliss for the peasantry, Bazarov admits to a surge of intense "hatred for this poorest peasant, this Philip or Sidor, for whom I'm to be ready to jump out of my skin, and who won't even thank me for it.... Why, suppose he does live in a clean hut, while nettles are growing out of me—well, what then?"[16] Raskolnikov too will reject the similarly self-sacrificial long view of the Utopian Socialists and think feverishly: "No, life is only given to me once and I shall never have it again; I don't want to wait for 'the happiness of all'" (6: 211). Such resemblances can hardly be fortuitous: Pisarev's essay, as well as the controversy to which it gave rise, unquestionably served as a major source of Dostoevsky's inspiration.

Indeed, one of the mysteries of Dostoevsky scholarship is why this perfectly obvious relationship has attracted so little attention. Scholars have ransacked the culture of past and present in pursuit of "sources" for

Raskolnikov's division of mankind into "ordinary" and "extraordinary" people, and searched high and low for precedents anticipating his theory that the second category possessed the *right* to disregard the injunctions of the moral law prohibiting murder. Dostoevsky was of course thoroughly familiar with the Romantic Titanism of such writers as Schiller and Byron, whose proud and solitary heroes, often inspired by the noblest ideals of humanity, gloomily bear the onus of having committed the most atrocious crimes. In *Die Räuber* (*The Robbers*), a drama that Dostoevsky had known since childhood, Schiller's Robin Hood protagonist Karl Moor revolts against the injustice of creation but finally surrenders, of his own free will, to the higher majesty of God's law.

And in one of Dostoevsky's favorite novels, Balzac's *Le Père Goriot*, he had long ago come across the ringing tirades of the master criminal Vautrin, who proclaims that wealth and power belong by right to those strong enough to grasp them unhindered by moral compunctions. The same novel comes even closer to *Crime and Punishment* in the famous scene during which Rastignac, taking a leaf from Rousseau, asks his friend, the impoverished medical student Bianchon, whether he would agree to be responsible for the death of a decrepit mandarin in China if, at the mandarin's demise, a million francs would suddenly appear and allow him to fulfill all his desires. Rastignac needs money to lavish on an elegant mistress (hardly a concern of Raskolnikov's), but also to provide a dowry for his two lovely but impoverished sisters (this is much closer to Raskolnikov's worry over the fate of his sister Dunya). The Utilitarian nature of this question, which postulates the trading of a "useless" human life for a fortune, is quite similar to Dostoevsky's theme; and the resemblance is reinforced when Bianchon responds in the negative on the ground that he has no aspirations to become a great man.*

Turning to Russian literature, an obvious forerunner of Dostoevsky's novel may be found in Pushkin's *The Queen of Spades*, whose young and insignificant hero, also consumed by a burning desire for wealth and power, is said to be endowed with "the profile of Napoleon and the soul

---

* Bianchon's answer is worth quoting in full, since it also brings in Napoleon as a comparison: "'But you ask a question,' he tells his friend, 'that everyone confronts at the entrance to life, and you want to cut the Gordian knot with a sword. To act in this way, my dear fellow, you have to be Alexander [the Great]; otherwise you land in jail. As for myself, I am happy with the modest existence that I will create for myself in the country, where I shall quite stupidly take over from my father. Human affections are satisfied as fully in the smallest circle as in an immense circumference. Napoleon did not eat his dinner twice, and could not have any more mistresses than a medical student intern at the Capucins. Our happiness, my dear fellow, is always located between the soles of our feet and our cranium; and whether it costs a million a year or a hundred louis, the intrinsic perception within us is the same. I decide to let the Chinaman live.'" Balzac, *La Comédie Humaine*, ed. Pierre Citron, preface Pierre-Georges Castex, 10 vols. (Paris, 1965), 2: 260.

The relation between *Crime and Punishment* and Balzac's novel was first pointed out in a famous essay by Leonid Grossman, *Balzac and Dostoevsky*, trans. Lena Karpov (n.p., 1973).

of Mephistopheles."[17] He too kills a defenseless old woman in order to obtain a secret formula for success in gambling, and is driven mad by his conscience. More recently, Russian scholarship has drawn attention to a life of Julius Caesar written by Napoleon III. This book, much discussed in the European and Russian press in 1865, takes the same line as Hegel's characterization of "the world-historical individual," defending the right of great historical figures to accomplish their world-transforming role unhampered by the narrow standards of conventional social morality.[18] Dostoevsky certainly read the articles about this book appearing in the Russian press, which was unanimously hostile to its thesis; but they would only have refurbished for him a symbolic image of Napoleon already well established in Russian literature.

A verse in *Evgeny Onegin* reads: "We all now pose as Napoleons / Millions of two-legged creatures / For us are the instrument of one."[19] The investigating magistrate Porfiry Petrovich is alluding to these lines when he admonishes Raskolnikov: "Oh, come, don't we all think ourselves Napoleons now in Russia?" (6: 204). Napoleon had thus long been familiar to Dostoevsky as the embodiment of a ruthlessly despotic unconcern for other "two-legged creatures"; and what this meant in practice is illustrated by an anecdote recorded by Apollinaria Suslova during her travels with Dostoevsky in the fall of 1863: "As we were taking dinner [in Turin], he said, looking at a little girl who was doing her lessons: 'Well, imagine, there you have a little girl like her with an old man, and suddenly some Napoleon says: "I want this city destroyed." It has always been that way in the world.'"[20] Dostoevsky's image of Napoleon as the incarnation of a merciless disregard for human life and the ordinary laws of morality was hardly a novelty by the time he came across the book by Napoleon III.

It would be foolish to contend that all such sources, especially the works of literary predecessors whom Dostoevsky knew and admired, may not have exercised any influence on the conception of his latest novel. But if such models recurred to his imagination, and entered into his text through one or another allusion or turn of phrase, it was because they had been mobilized by his attempt to come to grips with the dangers he perceived in the new Nihilist ideology. For the Bazarov-image eulogized in Pisarev's essay draws together all the components of the future Raskolnikov: the belief that he can rise superior to the dictates of conscience; the conviction that he would not allow himself to be affected by any "moral regulator"; the contempt felt for that portion of mankind who placidly accept the fate from which the élite of "other people" are struggling to set them free; the unwillingness to sacrifice the present for the future. One or another of these traits may be found elsewhere, but scarcely all of them taken together. No other source provides so perfect a fit as Pisarev's exalted celebration of Bazarov, and, most important, none envisages the superior individual who is glorified as a typical Russian radical intellectual, a *raznochinets* of the 1860s.

6
———

Published in the spring of 1862, Pisarev's article marked the beginning of an increasingly harsh polemic between *The Contemporary* and *The Russian Word* that Dostoevsky followed with the closest interest. And as the conflict raged, the position of the "immoderate Nihilists" of *The Russian Word* (as Dostoevsky labeled them) revealed even more glaringly some of the attitudes he was soon to embody in Raskolnikov. If Pisarev had felt no qualms about Bazarov's "contempt" for the tranquil, unthinking masses, his even less inhibited colleague V. A. Zaitsev minced no words in bluntly expressing such contempt in the most insulting fashion. The people, he wrote (and though he was nominally talking about Italy, no Russian reader would mistake the reference to home), are "coarse, stupid, and, as a result, passive; this is of course not their fault, but so it is, and it would be strange to expect any sort of initiative from them."[21] To make matters worse, Zaitsev even inclined for a time to accept Social Darwinism, and he defended Negro slavery on the ground that the mental inferiority of the colored races would lead to their disappearance if they were not protected by their white masters. "Only tender-hearted gentlewomen like Harriet Beecher Stowe," he remarked sarcastically, "can insist on brotherhood between the races."[22]

Quite consistently with such an unflattering view of the masses, Pisarev and *The Russian Word*, although radical in their opposition to the political status quo, also favored the capitalist industrialization of Russia. To be sure, they desired such development to take place under the guidance of "enlightened" members of the intelligentsia, who would use the benefits of economic progress to bring about a more just and equable social-political order. By contrast, Chernyshevsky and his followers had looked forward rather to a Socialist transformation of the Russian commune (the *obshchina*), by which they meant modernizing the agricultural economy while retaining the Socialist values of equality and mutuality. For they believed that these values, the very heart of the Socialist ideal, had been miraculously preserved at the core of Russian folk-life. Dostoevsky too cherished the notion that such values had continued to exist in the *obshchina*; but since for him they were grounded in the inherited Christianity of the Russian peasantry, they would, he feared, inevitably vanish once the religious faith of the peasant population had been undermined.

75

Still, Dostoevsky and the "moderate Nihilists" shared common ground in their conviction that the Russian people, far from being tranquil, passive, and worthless, embodied essentially Socialist principles in their way of life; and regardless of whether this morality of communality was defended on the basis of "rational egoism" or Christian self-sacrifice, the values upheld and cherished in each case were much the same.* But now, in the writings of the "immoderate Nihilists," Dostoevsky saw the very foundations of any such morality being destroyed in the name of an egoism asserting the right of superior individuals to override the moral law at their own sweet will—in the interests of humanity as a whole, of course! If some of Raskolnikov's lucubrations have so often been compared with Nietzschean ideas of a Superman, it is because they both develop the same logic of an egoism imbued with the notion of its inherent superiority and guided by a will-to-power convinced of its supreme historical importance.

Dostoevsky's acute and almost instantaneous responsiveness to this disturbing transformation of radical ideology, and his fear of what it might portend for the future, was manifest even before *Crime and Punishment* in a slight, unfinished work called *The Crocodile*. This amusing sketch is usually considered only an insignificant episode in Dostoevsky's skirmish with the radical satirist M. E. Saltykov-Shchedrin, which began in 1863 and, flaring up again in 1865, provoked the article already mentioned on "The Schism among the Nihilists." In fact, though, this unpretentious grotesque is Dostoevsky's first reaction to the implications of the new radical line beginning to make its appearance among the publicists of *The Russian Word*.

The Crocodile concerns the fantastic adventure of a conceited bureaucrat of "advanced" opinions, who is accidentally swallowed by a crocodile on exhibition in St. Petersburg and quite contentedly takes up residence in his belly. From this secure vantage point, whose isolation allows him the leisure to concentrate his mind, he decides to proclaim a whole new set of ideas about the future improvement of mankind. As he explains with enthusiasm, "you have only to creep . . . into a crocodile . . . shut your eyes, and you immediately devise a perfect millennium for mankind" (5: 197). This mockery of a visionary Utopianism, however, is not Dostoevsky's main target; rather, he focuses on the futile attempt made by a naive friend of the crocodile-dweller, concerned about his

---

* This concordance of views between the "moderate Nihilists" and Dostoevsky's *pochven-nichestvo* was recognized by the opponents of both. "Dobrolyubov," wrote Zaitsev, "reminds us of the *pochvenniki* when he talks about the people. In him too peeps out that mystical opinion of the people, that idea of some sort of extraordinary gifts that distinguish the mass. Ultimately, it is true that an ideal notion of the people sometimes led Dobrolyubov into error, and induced him to expect too much from the people." V. I. Zaitsev, *Izbrannye Sochineniya v Dvukh Tomakh*, ed. B. P. Kozmin (Moscow, 1934), 1: 30.

health and welfare, to initiate a rescue effort before he dissolves entirely in the reptile's gastric juices. This well-meant humanitarian aim is opposed by a highly placed bureaucrat, who has recently been convinced by an important capitalist that Russia is greatly in need of new foreign investments. The crocodile is the property of a visiting German entrepreneur, and any injury to it would only discourage the flow of capital into the country and hinder Russian economic expansion.

The crocodile-dweller himself, though "progressive" to the tips of his toes, nonetheless agrees with the capitalist's reasoning; before all else, "the principles of economics" must be respected. All considerations of simple "humanity" are thus swept aside, and the logic of utility, the logic of economics, triumphs over the plight of a human being. The advocate of capitalist enterprise and the inventor of a new millennium are in complete accord; both right and left in Russia, as Dostoevsky saw it, had now accepted exactly the same chilling and inhumane prescriptions for human conduct. Much the same point will soon be made, but no longer in a jesting or satirical context, in the encounter between the unscrupulous lawyer Luzhin and the rebellious humanitarian murderer Raskolnikov in the work that Dostoevsky began to block out just a half-year later.

7

Historians of Russian culture agree that the views championed by Pisarev and *The Russian Word* gained more and more followers during the mid-1860s, and that *Pisarevshchina* became the prevailing intellectual mode.* One reason, quite simply, was the superior literary quality of Pisarev's prose, the brilliance of his lashing wit compared to anything that his opponents on the right or left could muster (though Saltykov-Shchedrin was no mean adversary). In addition, the mistrust of the people evinced so bitingly by Pisarev and Zaitsev corresponded to an increasingly widespread mood among the intelligentsia, who had confidently expected a revolution in the spring of 1863. This was the moment at which the newly liberated peasants were required to sign their final agreements with the landowners; and it had been widely believed that,

* The dominance of Pisarev was noted, four years after his death in 1868, by the censorship authorities, who were sometimes shrewd observers of the cultural scene. One official wrote that "of all the Russian socialist writers, Pisarev seems to be the most popular among the younger generation; their immaturity is such that they not only read his works but study them, and every line serves as an occasion for heated and passionate debates." Cited in E. Lampert, *Sons Against Fathers* (Oxford, 1965), 295.

Lampert's lively, vigorous, and highly informative book is the best in English on Russian radical thought of the 1860s. For some critical considerations, however, see my *Through the Russian Prism* (Princeton, N.J., 1990), 201–208.

desiring more land than they had been allotted or could afford to purchase, the defiant peasants would finally rise up and smash the hated Tsarist regime once and for all. When nothing of the sort occurred, a profound sense of disillusionment swept over the young radicals, who lost that faith in the revolutionary potentialities of the peasantry which, under the influence of *The Contemporary*, they had once accepted as the cornerstone of their convictions. Now they realized they could count only on themselves to obtain some social justice for the unhappily quiescent people, and the Bazarovian "contempt" that Pisarev had singled out so presciently became a much more widespread social attitude. It was out of this despairing frame of mind that Karakozov had fired his lonely shot against Alexander II.

Once set within this context, Raskolnikov's ideas and actions, as finally depicted in Dostoevsky's novel, can be seen as quite accurate extrapolations of the mentality of the moment among the radical youth. Moreover, Dostoevsky's choice of a main protagonist also dovetailed very neatly with the dominant literary trend of the time. In one of the last issues of *Epoch*, N. N. Strakhov had noted that Russian literature was now preoccupied with the question of the "new people," that is, the radical *raznochinets* intellectuals who had recently emerged at the forefront of the Russian social-cultural scene. "The first who began," he wrote, "was the keenly alert Turgenev, who with his Bazarov intended to portray the new man. Then Mr. Pisemsky wrote his *The Unruly Sea*, in which, by the natural course of events, figures of the new people made their appearance. . . . In *The Russian Messenger*, *Marevo* [*The Mirage*, by V. P. Klyuzhnikov] appeared, in *The Contemporary*—*What Is To Be Done?* . . . All of these revolved around one fundamental fulcrum—the image of the new man; and if matters proceed along the same lines, then we obviously have to anticipate more than a few novels of the same type."[23] This perceptive prediction, which Dostoevsky had read and approved for publication, was to be fully realized in his own creation.

Strakhov mentions only the most notable novels that had been inspired by, and written in the wake of, *Fathers and Children*. A whole group of minor writers, themselves of the same *raznochintsy* origin as the characters in their sketches and stories, also depicted the lives of the growing intellectual proletariat of the 1860s in ways that anticipate some of Raskolnikov's ideas and attitudes. In N. G. Pomyalovsky's unfinished novel *Brother and Sister*, for example, a note of protest can be heard that illustrates how much of Raskolnikov emerged from the actual social situation of the group to which he belonged. The main character of this novel, Peter Potesin, bitterly regrets that "an aversion to vileness has held me down," and he dreams of summoning up enough courage some day to steal a considerable fortune. "And then honorable people will be

my friends, I will help writers, artists, establish schools, go on a binge."
To rob the rich, he argues, is really no crime: "Lord, what they have has
also been stolen, it belongs to others, not to them. . . . The capital lying
in their coffers is not really property that belongs to them. It belongs to
no one. Whoever acquires it, he is in command." But all this is just talk,
and Potesin dies regretting his own failure to turn word into deed: "Useless rectitude—what an anomaly in life on earth!"[24]

Some of Pomyalovsky's early work had been published by Dostoevsky
in *Time*, and other writers of the same school were printed in *Epoch*;
both as editor and as someone passionately concerned with the drift of
Russian opinion, Dostoevsky always kept a sharp eye on the production
of such new young writers. But in *Crime and Punishment* he would take
the sporadic questionings of such impoverished representatives of the
educated youth, struggling despairingly to keep their heads above water
amid the imperial splendors of Petersburg, and raise them to the level of
a tragic confrontation between man's ambition to change the world for
the better and the age-old moral imperatives of the Christian faith.

CHAPTER 6

From Novella to Novel

The main outlines of Dostoevsky's conception of *Crime and Punishment* were set very early, but the full dimensions of his final text were very far from being apparent to him all at once. It was only as the work developed and expanded under his hands that it took on the multifaceted richness whose sources we explored in Chapter 5. A decisive moment in the creation of the book occurred in November 1865, when Dostoevsky decided to shift from a first-person narrator telling his own story to a carefully defined third-person narrator external to the events themselves.

Let us follow this process of gestation, so far as possible, by returning to the embryonic version sketched in the letter of September 1865 to Katkov and, with the aid of Dostoevsky's notebooks, tracing its growth into the finished masterpiece.

2

In the splendid complete edition of Dostoevsky's writings published by the Academy of Sciences of the former Soviet Union, the editors have reassembled the disorderly confusion of the notebooks that Dostoevsky kept while working on *Crime and Punishment* and printed them in a sequence roughly corresponding to the various stages of composition. Dostoevsky, as we know, was in the habit of casually flipping open his notebooks and writing on the first blank space that presented itself to his pen; and since he also used the same pages to record all sorts of memorabilia, the extraction of this material was by no means a simple task. Thanks to these meritorious labors, however, we now possess a working draft (unfortunately, only a fragmentary one) of the story or novella as originally conceived, as well as two other versions of the text. These have been distinguished as the Wiesbaden version, the Petersburg version, and the final plan embodying the change from a first-person narrator to the indigenous variety of third-person form invented by Dostoevsky for his purposes.

The Wiesbaden version coincides roughly with the story that Dostoevsky described in his letter to Katkov, and a draft of six short chapters has been reconstructed from his notes. Written in the form of a diary or journal, the events it records correspond more or less accurately to what eventually became the conclusion of Part I and Chapters 1–6 of Part II in the definitive redaction. The action of this part of the novel begins with Raskolnikov's return to his room after the murder. He first restores the axe to the house porter's lodge; then he conceals his plunder in a hole in the wallpaper and frenziedly tries to erase bloodstains from his clothes. Utterly worn out by nervous tension and illness, he falls into a feverish sleep until awakened by a summons from the local police station. He drags himself to the station in terror, learns that the summons is merely about a debt to his landlady, but faints from physical weakness combined with fright when he hears talk about the murder between two police officials. This collapse arouses suspicion, and, fearing a search of his room, he hurries home to remove the spoils of his crime, which he hides under a large stone near a urinal for workmen. Losing consciousness for four days, he awakens to find himself in the care of his friend Razumikhin and the recipient of money from his mother. But finding the presence of others, and particularly the spontaneous effort to aid him, irksome and burdensome, he slips out of his room unobserved and goes to a café, where he turns to newspaper accounts of the crime and encounters the police clerk Zametov. At this point the manuscript breaks off.

What strikes one about the six Wiesbaden chapters is how much of the later text they already contain. Here are almost all the secondary characters in their final form: the sympathetic and simple peasant girl Nastasya, an amused and astonished observer of the goings-on of the city folk among whom she has been cast; the rowdy, boisterous, but pure-hearted ex-student Razumikhin, who comes of a noble family and is also penniless; the two police officials, one peaceable and kindhearted, the other vain, irritable, and explosive; the elaborately gowned German brothel-keeper Luisa Ivanovna, preposterously striving to assert the impeccable decorum maintained in her establishment; the dandified and corrupt police clerk Zametov; the self-important young doctor, an acquaintance of Razumikhin, who has a special interest in nervous diseases and has come to advise about the narrator's condition. Details suggesting a bloody criminal deed are given, and the fright and terror of the narrator vividly conveyed; but it is not indisputable, as one commentator assumes, that the missing first chapter contained a depiction of the murder itself.* It is possible that the story began *after* the crime, whose events

---

* "The [first] chapter which included the preparations for the murder and the murder itself is lost." See Gary Rosenshield, *Crime and Punishment* (Lisse, 1978), 15. On p. 17, though, Rosenshield suggests another possibilty: "the narrator's preoccupation with his present memory of the past perhaps indicates that *Crime and Punishment* was originally a psychological study of a criminal only after the murder." The question remains open, though the

would be gradually disclosed retrospectively through the narrator's account of its unbearable effects on his emotions.

This first draft concentrates entirely on the moral-psychic reactions of the narrator after the murder—his panic, his terror, his desperate attempts to control his nerves and pretend to behave rationally while consumed by a raging fever and constantly at the mercy of his wildly agitated emotions. What continually haunts him, in moments of lucidity, is his total estrangement from his former self, from his own past, and from the entire universe of his accustomed thoughts and feelings. And it gradually dawns on him that he has been severed from all this by one stroke—the stroke that killed the repulsive pawnbroker and, by a horrible mischance, her long-suffering and entirely blameless sister Lizaveta, who, to make matters worse, is said to have been pregnant. This emphasis, of course, corresponds to the original motivation that Dostoevsky gave Katkov for the criminal's surrender: "The feelings of isolation and separation from humanity which he felt immediately after committing the crime wear him down."

This theme dominates in the early draft, and is expressed in three scenes of a growing order of magnitude. The first takes place at the police station, when the narrator, offended at being treated discourteously, snaps back at the police official for his rudeness. In a marginal note, Dostoevsky adds the narrator's reflections: "Yes, I was trembling with indignation and nothing could distract me; I even forgot everything. To be sure I was still saying it all from old habit (but all the same how could I) not yet understand anything. My God, did I think that I could (really), that I had the right to breathe freely, and that everything had already been taken off my chest, only because all the traces had been hidden?" (7: 18).* The narrator, an educated person and ex-student, had responded to official insolence with the same anger as he would have done in the past, still oblivious of the total change in his relations to others. No longer could he morally assert a right to be treated with respect, weighed down as he was by the terrible burden of the crime he had committed.

This realization comes to the narrator only by hindsight; but a much more instant recognition occurs when, after concealing the spoils of the crime, he decides to pay a visit, on the impulse of the moment, to his friend Razumikhin. Something very odd occurs as the narrator climbs

---

second hypothesis seems to me more plausible; it is difficult to imagine Dostoevsky beginning with an unmotivated murder. Rosenshield's careful and perceptive analysis of the techniques of narration is one of the best studies devoted to the novel, and should be better known.

The lost first chapter was probably contained in a notebook that Dostoevsky mislaid. There is a reference to this missing notebook in *PSS*, 28/Bk. 2: 157; May 9, 1866.

* The words and phrases printed in parentheses are corrections and additions that Dostoevsky made in the various drafts of his text.

the stairs—something which, as he writes, "I don't quite know how to put into words." For he felt a sensation that "if there is (now) for me on earth something (especially) hard (and impossible) then it is to talk and have relations ... with other (people, as before, I don't know how, in short, to express exactly what I felt then, but I know it). . . . And (the consciousness of all that) was my instant of the most oppressive anguish for perhaps all that month, in which I went through so much endless torture" (7: 35–36). These words indicate the moment at which the narrator realizes that even the simplest and most ordinary human relations have now become impossible for him; and Dostoevsky drew a circle around the paragraph to indicate its importance.

The final epiphany of this experience occurs in a sequence that begins when the narrator, quitting Razumikhin and walking through the busy streets on the way home, is lashed by the whip of a passing coachman whose path he is blocking: "The whip's blow made me so furious that, having jumped to the railings, I angrily ground and (gnashed) my teeth." He also is aware of the laughter of the onlookers who had witnessed this insulting chastisement. "But as soon as I realized what the point [of the laughter—J.F.] was (then the rage in me immediately disappeared. It seemed to me that it was no longer worthwhile concerning myself with that)." Just as in the police station, his first reaction was one of outraged pride; but he realizes almost at once how inappropriate such a response was in his present predicament. "The thought came to me immediately that it would have been a lot better (perhaps even good) if the carriage had crushed me (completely)" (7: 38). These words may well be the origin of what later occurred to Marmeladov, who in fact dies after being crushed by the wheels of a carriage.

Among the onlookers was a merchant's wife and her little daughter, who slip a twenty-kopek piece into the narrator's hand because "the blow had awakened their pity for me." Clutching the coin, the narrator walks toward the Neva in the direction of the Winter Palace while gazing at the cupola of St. Isaac's Cathedral and "all that splendid panorama." In the past, as a student, he had walked by the same vista many times, and had always felt that "despite this unexampled splendor and this astonishing river, this whole view was worth nothing" because there was "a (complete) coldness (and deadness) about it ... a quality that destroys everything ... an inexplicable cold blows from it." But now, as he stands in the same place that he knew so well, "suddenly the same (painful) sensation which oppressed my chest at Razumikhin's half an hour ago, the same sensation oppressed my heart here." He realizes that "there was no reason for me (any longer) to stop here or anywhere). . . . Now I had something else to concern me, something else, but all those, all those former sensations and interests and people were far away from me as if from another planet" (7: 39–40). As he leans over the railing of a canal, the narrator lets the twenty-kopek piece slip into the water, thus symbolizing his break with all these emotions and values of the past.

Although the effects of estrangement are clearly intended to dominate in the resolution of the action, they are reinforced by other episodes. One such is the narrator's half-dream, half-hallucination, kept almost unchanged in the novel, which reveals both his self-revulsion at the crime and his fear of pursuit. Lying in bed, he suddenly hears "a terrible cry" and opens his eyes; slowly he realizes that it is one of the police officials he has just met who is beating the landlady on the staircase. "I had never heard such unnatural sounds, such yelling, grinding of teeth, curses, and blows. . . . What is it all about, I thought, why (is he beating her), why? Fear like ice penetrated me to the core . . . (soon they will come for me (also) I thought). . . ." Imagining all this to be real, the narrator asks Nastasya about the frightening occurrence; but he is told that nothing of the sort had happened—it had all been a delusion, despite the narrator's conviction that he had been fully awake. "A yet greater tremor seized me," he writes, presumably at this evidence of his derangement. When Nastasya tells him "(that) is the blood in you crying out" (7: 41–43), she takes this bit of folk wisdom literally, while to the narrator the word "blood" immediately evokes the crime. Such an experience, added to his estrangement, was surely meant to provide further incentive for the narrator's eventual confession.

3
———

Why Dostoevsky abandoned his story can only remain a matter for speculation, but one possibility is that his protagonist began to develop beyond the boundaries in which he had first been conceived. All through the extant text, the narrator is crushed and overcome by the moral-psychic consequences of his murderous deed; but just as the manuscript breaks off, he begins to display other traits of character. Instead of fear and anguish, he now exhibits rage and hatred against all those who have been looking after him in his illness and decides to slip away from their oppressive care. The conversation about the murder at his bedside, he explains, "made me feel unbearable malice . . . and what is more remarkable still is that during these agonies, this terror, I never thought a single time with the slightest compassion about the murder I had committed" (7: 73). Here is a character entirely different from the one previously portrayed, and Dostoevsky may have stopped writing at this point because his figure had begun to evolve beyond his initial conception. In some notes for the immediate continuation of this version, he jots down: "Recovered. Cold fury, calculation. Why so much nerves?" (7: 76). This last phrase is obviously a scornful question of the narrator addressed to himself.

Once Dostoevsky had begun to see his character in this light, alternating between despair and "cold fury," it became increasingly difficult to imagine a purely internal motivation for his self-surrender; and this may have led Dostoevsky to fuse the story with his previous idea for the novel called *The Drunkards*. An early plan already includes "the episode with the drunkard on Krestovsky," and references to "Marmeladov's daughter" now appear in all the outlines of the action. "He (the narrator) went to the daughter. Like a prostitute. Then the daughter herself came. The daughter helps the mother. Takes the money. Pity for the children" (7: 80). It is this note of pity that the Marmeladovs introduce into the narrative, or rather, since the narrator also pities the plight of his own mother and sister, a totally different manner of expressing pity than the one he has chosen.

After the narrator has committed the crime, it is he who feels a need for pity, which he cannot imagine being offered except by a Sonya capable of loving and forgiving even her ignominious father. One note shows how important "pity" has now become for Dostoevsky's character: "Who then will take pity?" he asks himself. "No one? No one? I am a base and vile murderer, laughable and greedy. Yes, precisely, is such a one to be pitied? Is there someone to take pity? No one, no one! And yet this is impossible" (7: 85). Of course it is Sonya who will "take pity." What is explicitly articulated here will remain implicit, though perfectly discernible, in the final text and underlies Raskolnikov's irresistible impulse to turn to her with his confession.

"The civil servant's daughter," as Sonya Marmeladova is initially labeled, now becomes linked with the narrator's decision to give himself up, though Dostoevsky has great difficulty imagining how this action will be motivated. One alternative envisages the narrator invoking a "picture of the golden age" and then asking: "But what right have I, a vile killer, to desire happiness for people and to dream of a golden age. I want to have that right. *And following this* (this chapter) he goes and gives himself up. He stops by only to say good-bye to her, then he bows down to the people and—confession" (7: 91). Another note sketches a different scenario of the same resolution: "Mother, sister, the story of the love. Why can't I become a Gaas [a saintly Moscow doctor who aided convicts—J.F.]? Why is everything lost? The baby. Who will forbid me to love this baby? Can't I be good? Prayed. Then *the dream* [which contained a vision of Christ—J.F.]. The next day he went [to confess—J.F.]. . . . In the evening the civil servant's daughter brought to him . . . " (7: 80).

Such edifying resolutions, however, clashed much too obviously with the manner in which the narrator had begun to evolve. "About the mother and sister. No, for you, for you, my dear creatures! But people are base. Consoles himself completely" (7: 78). This denigration of mankind as a whole, not only its more "useless" specimens, now begins to appear quite frequently. For example: "(The misfortunes of his father, mother). How nasty people are! Are they worth having me repent before them? No, no, I'm going to remain silent." Or again: "How disgusting people are! And just now the letter from his mother. (That keeps him from becoming embittered)" (7: 82). Most important of all, Dostoevsky now links such misanthropy with the motif of power: "How low and vile people are.... No: gather them up into one's hands, and then do good for them. But instead [he is thinking of his confession—J. F.] to perish before their eyes and inspire only sneers" (7: 83).

All these notes portray the character's own thoughts and feelings. In others, Dostoevsky sets down instructions for himself, and these suggest that he has begun to see how these two divergent aspects of his protagonist might be portrayed as more than a simple alteration. "N.B. *Important.* After the sickness, a kind of cruelty and complete justification of himself, and when that was shaken, the letter from his mother" (7: 78). This observation is indeed "important" because it implies a significant character shift after the murder and the resulting illness. Now a "kind of cruelty" comes to the surface that was not evident before; a new aspect of personality, previously hidden, unexpectedly emerges. Another note reveals all the weight that Dostoevsky attributed to this discovery. "So that there is then a *coup de maître*," he writes with pardonable pride. "At first there was danger, then fear and illness, and his whole character did not show itself, and then suddenly his (whole) character showed itself in its full demonic strength and all the reasons and motives for the crime become clear" (7: 90). The handling of the character is thus conceived not so much in terms of any deep-seated modification but rather as the bringing to light of potentialities always present but hitherto only lying dormant in the background.

4

There has been a perpetual quarrel in Dostoevsky criticism over whether the motives finally attributed to Raskolnikov are or are not contradictory. At first, his crime appears to be the result of his Utilitarian logic, set in motion by his own economic straits, the desperate plight of his family, and a desire to aid others with the spoils of the murder. A good bit later, we learn about the article in which he has justified the right of "extraordinary people" to step over the moral law in order to bring benefits to humanity as a whole. In the confession scene with Sonya, however, Raskolnikov gives as his motive simply the desire to obtain power for himself alone, solely to test whether he is entitled to take his place among those superior individuals who possess the innate right to overstep the moral law.

The notion that these varying rationalizations are contradictory derives from the days when Dostoevsky was considered a writer who frantically turned out sensational novels from deadline to deadline, and was not too concerned, or lacked the time to be concerned, with such artistic matters as the internal consistency of his characters' motivation. Now that the notebooks have revealed how carefully he worked over every detail of his text, and how he always refused to sacrifice artistic integrity to editorial pressure, such an assumption is quite clearly erroneous. But the information contained in the notebooks has not even yet, in my opinion, been adequately utilized for the purposes of critical interpretation. For the notes we have been citing, as we shall try to show in the next chapter, suggest that the differing explanations offered by Raskolnikov represent different phases of the inner metamorphosis he undergoes after committing the murders—a metamorphosis that results from his gradually dawning *grasp* of the full implications of what he has done. Not only does his horrified conscience continue to operate on the moral-psychological level, but he also comes to understand the inner contradictions contained in the ideas in which he has believed. As Dostoevsky writes in another note: "N.B. His moral development begins from the crime itself; the possibility of such questions arise which would not then have existed previously" (7: 140).

Whether the novel actually answers the questions that arise for Raskolnikov has often been doubted. Another note, entitled "the chief anatomy of the novel," is frequently cited to prove Dostoevsky's indecisiveness on this crucial question; but in my view it proves just the opposite. "After the illness, etc. It is absolutely necessary to establish the course of things firmly and clearly and to eliminate what is vague, that is, explain the whole murder one way or another, and make its character and relations clear." The phrase "one way or another" would seem to confirm the worst suspicions about Dostoevsky's lack of clarity; but a marginal jotting, keyed to the word "murder," reads: "pride, personality, and insolence" (7: 141–142). This could not be more specific: here we have the forces unleashed in Raskolnikov by the unholy amalgam then typical of Russian radical ideology—an altruistic desire to alleviate social injustice and suffering thrown together with a supremely Bazarovian contempt for the masses. It is the danger of self-delusion and moral-psychic tragedy lurking in this perversely contradictory mixture that Dostoevsky was trying to reveal through Raskolnikov's fate.

Dostoevsky, as we have seen, speaks of Raskolnikov's character as suddenly exhibiting "its full demonic strength"; other references change this significantly to "Satanical pride" (7: 149). Pisarev used exactly the same expression for Bazarov; and though the notes are regrettably sparse with information about the ideological context within which Dostoevsky was working, his use of this phrase, as should be clear by now, is far from accidental. It reveals that Dostoevsky's character was being created in relation to Pisarev's deification of the new *raznochinets* "hero of our time," and that the ideas attributed to Raskolnikov can be traced primarily to the famous article on Bazarov in *The Russian Word*. Moreover, the course of radical ideology itself, evolving from the relative humanitarianism of *The Contemporary* (represented in Dostoevsky's novel by the ridiculous, obtuse, but good-hearted Lebezyatnikov) to the contemptuous élitism and worship of the superior individual exhibited by Pisarev and Zaitsev, duplicates precisely the mutation in Raskolnikov on which Dostoevsky was now basing the portrayal of his character. Psychology and ideology thus fuse together once again into the seamless unity that Dostoevsky called "idea-feelings"; and his ability to intuit these syntheses of emotion and ideology constitutes much of his particular genius as a novelist.

Luckily, we need not base the contention that such a fusion took place in *Crime and Punishment* solely on one phrase. There is a specific allusion to Pisarev's ideas in the early version of a speech by Luzhin, the unscrupulous businessman who wishes to marry Raskolnikov's sister Dunya. In this note he is still called Chebalov, but the content of his words is identical with those of the preening suitor in Part II, Chapter 5; and this homily, it should be noted, is recognized by Raskolnikov as expressing the identical pattern of ideas that had led him to the murder. "Chebalov says to Raskolnikov. *Tant que* I've put my affairs in good order, I am useful to others, and therefore, the more I am an egoist, the better it is for others. As for the old beliefs: you loved, you thought of others, and you let your own affairs go down the drain, and you ended up being a weight around the neck of your neighbors. It's simply a matter of arithmetic. No, you know, I like the realists of the new generation, the shoemaker and Pushkin; and although I do not agree with them in part, still the general tendency" (7: 151). This last, unfinished sentence unmistakably refers to Pisarev, who had launched the slogan of "Realism" as a social doctrine in 1864 and, following Bazarov, had resoundingly declared a shoemaker to be more useful than Pushkin. It was manifestly within this specific ideological framework that Dostoevsky was now conceiving the tormented course of Raskolnikov's career and interweaving these ideas with his psychology.

Crime and Punishment came to birth only when, in November 1865, Dostoevsky shifted from a first-person to a third-person narrator. This was the culmination of a long struggle whose vestiges can be traced all through the early stages of composition. Some of the problems of using the first person are already apparent from the earliest version, whose first chapter is supposedly written five days after the murder (committed on June 9). The narrator dates the beginning of his diary as June 14 because, as he explains, to have written anything earlier would have been impossible in view of his mental and emotional confusion. Indeed, even when he begins to write, this same state of confusion continues to plague him, and Dostoevsky reminds himself that "in all these six chapters (the narrator) must write, speak and appear to the reader in part as if not in possession of his senses" (7: 83).

Dostoevsky thus wished to convey the narrator's partial derangement while, at the same time, using him as a focus on the external world and portraying the reactions induced by his crime as the action proceeds. All this posed serious difficulties, and the manuscript version shows Dostoevsky's constant uncertainty about how to hold the balance between the narrator's psychic disarray and the needs of his story. He writes, for example, in the first chapter: "I had already started up the stairs, but (suddenly) I remembered the axe. I don't understand how I could even for a single moment have forgotten about it; (it was after all necessary). It tortures me now. It was the last pressing difficulty I had to take care of" (7: 5–6). Dostoevsky crosses out the last three sentences because they obviously show a narrator reflecting on actions that had taken place in the past; and such reflections indicate a composure that the writer was not yet supposed to have attained.

This problem of time perspective bothered Dostoevsky from the very start, and he moves the second chapter back several more days, to June 16, in order to give his narrator more time to come to his senses; but such a change could only be a temporary stop-gap. The distance between past and present was still not great enough, and this led to an inevitable clash between the situation in which the narrator was immersed and his function as narrator. As Edward Wasiolek has rightly pointed out: "Raskolnikov is supposed to be ... fixed wholly on his determination to elude his imaginary pursuers. But the 'I' point of view forces him to provide his own interpretations, and, even worse, his own stylistic refinements. Every stylistic refinement wars against the realism of the dramatic action."[1] Moreover, there would be serious doubts about the verisimilitude of a narrator who presumably is in a state of semi-hysteria, and yet is able to remember and analyze, to report long scenes as well as lengthy dialogues, and in general to function as a reliable observer. This problem was only made more acute when the Marmeladovs entered the picture and fragments of the drunkard's extensive monologues began to appear among the notes.

Dostoevsky was acutely aware of this issue, and the first expedient he thought of is indicated by a brief note: "The *story* ends and the *diary* begins" (7: 81). Since no trace of such a dual form can be found, this idea was probably abandoned very quickly; but one understands how Dostoevsky's mind was working. He wished to separate a recital of events, set down by the narrator after they had been completed, from another account of the same events written by someone still caught in their flux. This would have eliminated the disturbing clash between one and the other so noticeable in the Wiesbaden version. The same purpose inspires the next alternative, the Petersburg version, which is entitled "On Trial" and whose author is now in the custody of the legal authorities.

In this text, the narrator begins: "(I was on trial and) I will tell everything. I will write everything down. I am writing this for myself, but let others and all my judges read it, (if they want to). This is a confession (a full confession). I am writing for myself, for my own needs and therefore I will not keep anything secret" (7: 96). This draft continues with Marmeladov's monologic recital of his woes (preserved almost *verbatim* in the novel); and by this time the schema of events has been recast so that this scene clearly precedes the murder. Most important, though, the position of the narrator, sitting in jail and sadly contemplating his errors, allows him both to respond and to reflect without unduly straining credibility. But even in this plan, the time gap between the termination of all the events and the composition of the narrative is very small (roughly a week), and Dostoevsky continued to remain uneasy. After all, the narrator can hardly be completely tranquil, for the trial has not yet taken place.

The notebooks thus contain a third possibility, which is attached to a near-definitive outline of the action concerning Raskolnikov during the first two-thirds of the novel. "A New Plan," Dostoevsky announces, "The Story of a Criminal. Eight years before (in order to keep it completely at a distance)!" (7: 144). The phrase in parenthesis indicates just how preoccupied Dostoevsky was with this issue of narrative distance, and how clearly he saw all of the problems involved. In this new plan, the narrator would be writing after the conclusion of his prison term (eight years), and what was probably the subtitle would indicate the profound moral alteration induced by the passage of time: the narrator now calls *himself* a criminal, no longer maintaining that the murder could not be considered a "crime" at all. The narrator is now so far removed from his previous self that it would require only a short step to shift from an I-narrator to the third person.

6
—————

This narrative shift, however, did not occur all at once, and Dostoevsky debates the reasons for it in pages that, lying in close proximity to those just cited, were probably written at about the same time. "Rummage through all the questions in this novel," he admonishes himself, and then he proceeds to do so. "If it is to be a confession," he muses, "then everything must be made overly clear to the *utter extreme*. So that at every instant of the story everything must be entirely clear." The recognition of this necessity leads Dostoevsky to some second thoughts: "*For consideration*. If a confession, then in parts it will not be chaste (*tselomudrenno*) and it will be difficult to imagine why it was written." The use of the term "chaste" (which can also be translated broadly as "proper") in this context is rather odd; but it refers to the question of why the narrative has been written at all. Why should the narrator have wished to engage in so painful an act of self-exposure? At this point, Dostoevsky comes to the conclusion that his narrative technique must be altered.*

"But the subject is like this. The story from oneself [the author], and not from *him* [the character]" (7: 148–149). What Dostoevsky means by "subject" is left ambiguous; but he may be thinking about his conception of a main character who, after the crime, reveals unexpected aspects of himself—aspects of which, previously, he had not been fully aware. If, in a first-person narration, "everything must be made clear *to the utter extreme*" at every instant, then it would be difficult to obtain such an effect of self-surprise; at best, the revelations could be referred to and explained, but hardly presented with full dramatic force. Taken in conjunction with the problem of justifying his narrative, such considerations would explain why Dostoevsky, despite his desperate economic straits, could not resist making a fresh start and transferring to a third-person narrator.

But there still remained the question of exactly what kind of narrator this should be. Contemporary narratologists have hailed, as a recent

---

* The use of this word *tselomudrenno* has also attracted the attention of L. M. Rosenblyum, whose unpretentious but close and careful study of Dostoevsky's notebooks is one of the best works of recent Russian Dostoevsky scholarship. She believes that Dostoevsky employs the term to stress the impropriety of a first-person narrator depicting the murder in all its repulsive naturalistic crudity. It may also, in her view apply to the *rapidity* with which Raskolnikov, as originally sketched, resolves the moral problem caused by the murder through his repentance. See Rosenblyum, *Tvorcheskie Dnevniki* (Moscow, 1981), 272–273.

triumph of their discipline, the discovery that authorial narrators are not just loose, amorphous presences who know how to spin a yarn; they are, rather, "implied authors," with distinct profiles and attitudes that decisively shape the novelistic perspective. Dostoevsky, as it turns out, was fully conscious of this important truth and tried to define exactly the stance that his authorial narrator would adopt. No such problem had arisen earlier because the narrator was the central character. Everything had been presented from his own point of view, which meant that, though guilty of a terrible crime, he would inevitably arouse a certain sympathy because of his altruistic impulses, his inner sufferings, and his final repentance. What sort of third-person narrator could play the same role in relation to the reader? As Dostoevsky pondered the choice between the first and third person, he wrote: "But from *the author*. Too much naiveté and frankness are needed." Why this should be so is hardly self-evident; but the context suggests that Dostoevsky may still have been thinking of some sort of confessional novel, which, even if cast in the third person, would involve the total identification of the narrator with the main protagonist. Such an assumption would help explain the emphasis of the next sentence, which insists on the *separation* of the author from the character: "It is necessary to assume *as author someone omniscient and faultless*, who holds up to the view of all one of the members of the new generation" (7: 149).

The narrator will thus be undertaking a specific historical task: to exhibit for scrutiny an example of the very latest Russian type, the successor to Bazarov and the other "new men" of Russian literature. But Dostoevsky may have felt that such a narrator would be *too* coolly detached, too "omniscient and faultless" to serve his purposes ("faultless" translates the Russian *ne pogreshayuschim*, which literally means "sinless" and can be taken to imply an accusatory or condemnatory posture). He therefore alters his narrator, in another notation, merely to a "sort of invisible and omniscient being, *who doesn't leave his hero for a moment*, even with the words: 'all that was done completely by chance'" (7: 146; italics added). By attaching the narrator as closely as possible to the protagonist's point of view, Dostoevsky retains the advantages of I-narration, which automatically generates the effect of sympathy created by all inside views of a character; and he reminds himself to maintain such inside views, as far as possible, even when moving from the direct portrayal of consciousness into summary and report. At the same time, he retains the freedom of omniscience necessary to dramatize the process of Raskolnikov's self-discovery, to reveal the character gradually, to comment on him from the outside when this becomes necessary, and to leave him entirely when the plot-action widens out.

This narrative technique fuses the narrator very closely with the consciousness and point of view of the central character as well as other important figures (though without, as Mikhail Bakhtin was inclined to maintain, eliminating him entirely as a controlling perspective).[2] Dostoevsky had used a similar narrative approach earlier in *The Double*, and such a fusion was by no means unprecedented in the history of the novel (in Jane Austen, among others). But in *Crime and Punishment* this identification begins to approximate, through Dostoevsky's use of time-shifts of memory and his remarkable manipulation of temporal sequence, the experiments of Henry James, Joseph Conrad, and later stream-of-consciousness writers such as Virginia Woolf and James Joyce. Brilliantly original for its period, this technique gives us the gripping masterpiece we know, whose intricate construction and artistic sophistication can only cause us to wonder at the persistence of the legend that Dostoevsky was an untidy and negligent craftsman. Some light on this legend may be cast by the remark of E. M. de Vogüé, a novelist himself, who wrote of *Crime and Punishment* with some surprise in 1886 that "a word . . . one does not even notice, a small fact that takes up only a line, have their reverberations fifty pages later . . . [so that] the continuity becomes unintelligible if one skips a couple of pages."[3] This acute observation, which expresses all the disarray of a late nineteenth-century reader accustomed to the more orderly and linear types of expository narration, helps to account for the tenacity of such a critical misjudgment; but we have now begun to attain a more accurate appreciation of Dostoevsky's pathbreaking originality. Even so, *Crime and Punishment* still has not yet been read with sufficiently close attention to the interweaving of those "reverberations" on whose connection its meaning depends.

7

Once having decided to recast his novel in this new form, Dostoevsky began to rewrite from scratch; but he did not, as he told Wrangel in February 1866, burn everything he had written earlier. On the contrary, he was easily able to integrate sections of the earlier manuscript into his final text—especially those scenes in which his narrator had acted as an observer and reporter—simply by shifting them from the first to the third person. The remainder of Dostoevsky's notes concern the finished novel and need not be discussed here. There is, however, one additional question on which they help to throw some light.

The writing of the novel went smoothly and steadily except for a clash with the editors of *The Russian Messenger* already referred to, about which, regrettably, very little is known. Dostoevsky mentions it in a letter of July 1866 to A. P. Milyukov, in which he explains that Katkov and his assistant N. A. Lyubimov had refused to accept the initial version of the chapter of *Crime and Punishment* containing the famous scene in which Sonya reads to Raskolnikov the Gospel story of the raising of Lazarus. "I wrote [this chapter]," Dostoevsky confides, "with genuine inspiration, but perhaps it's no good; but for them the question is not its literary worth, they are worried about its *morality*. Here I was in the right— nothing was against morality, and *even quite the contrary*, but they saw otherwise and, what's more, saw traces of *nihilism*. Lyubimov declared firmly that it had to be revised. I took it back, and this revision of a large chapter cost me at least three new chapters of work, judging by the effort and the weariness; but I corrected it and gave it back."[4] By the time this letter was written, the revision had already been completed.

Since the original manuscript has unfortunately been lost, it is very difficult to determine just what the editors had objected to in the text. The only other information available is a remark made at the end of the century (1889) by the editors of *The Russian Messenger*, who, in publishing Dostoevsky's letter, commented that "it was not easy for him [Dostoevsky] to give up his intentionally exaggerated idealization of Sonya as a woman who carried self-sacrifice to the point of sacrificing her body. Feodor Mikhailovich substantially shortened the conversation during the reading of the Gospels, which in the original version was much longer than what remains in the printed text."[5] It seems clear, then, that Dostoevsky had initially given Sonya a much more affirmative role in this scene; and this led to what Katkov considered her unacceptably "exaggerated idealization."

What Katkov found inadmissible may perhaps be clarified by a passage in Dostoevsky's notebooks, where Sonya *is* presented occasionally as the spokeswoman for the morality that Dostoevsky wished to advocate. In one scene, she explains to Raskolnikov that "in comfort, in wealth, you would perhaps have seen nothing of human unhappiness. The person God loves, the person on whom he really counts, is the one to whom He sends much suffering, so that he sees better and recognizes through himself why in unhappiness the suffering of people is more visible than in happiness." Immediately following this speech, Raskolnikov retorts bitterly: "And perhaps God does not exist" (7: 150). This reply is included in the Gospel-reading chapter, and we may assume that Sonya's words were meant for the same context. It is quite possible that other speeches of the same kind in the notes were also included in the rejected version.

If so, it is not difficult to understand why the worthy editors of *The Russian Messenger* might have been upset. For Dostoevsky is depicting a fallen woman as the inspired interpreter of the Gospels, the expositor of the inscrutable purposes of Divine Will. Moreover, if the logic of Sonya's words is taken literally, it would mean that God had ultimately brought about, for His own ends, her degradation and Raskolnikov's crime. Such a bold reversal of the ordinary tenets of social morality could well have been seen by the editors as being tainted with "nihilism," since it could provide an opening for an implicit accusation against God Himself. Indeed, exactly such an accusation will soon be made by the death-stricken Ippolit Terentyev in *The Idiot* and later by Ivan Karamazov.

If these speculations have any validity, they may help to clarify why Dostoevsky was accused by the editors of blurring the boundaries between good and evil. "*Evil* and *good* are sharply separated," he assures Lyubimov, "and it will be impossible to confuse or misinterpret them. . . . Everything you spoke about has been done, everything is separated, demarcated and clear. *The reading of the Gospels* is given a different coloring."[6] Katkov probably improved Dostoevsky's text by insisting that he shorten Sonya's preachings; and the novelist may well in the end have recognized this himself. As he returned the proofs in mid-July, he remarked: "For 20 years I have painfully felt, and seen more clearly than anyone, that my literary vice is: *prolixity*, but I can't seem to shake it off."[7] There is, however, nothing prolix about *Crime and Punishment*, whose every word stems from the acute artistic self-awareness illustrated in the preceding pages.

CHAPTER 7

A Reading of
Crime and Punishment

This was the time, when, all things tending fast
To depravation, speculative schemes—
That promised to abstract the hopes of Man
Out of his feelings, to be fixed thenceforth
For ever in a purer element—
Found ready welcome. Tempting region that
For Zeal to enter and refresh herself,
Where passions had the privilege to work,
And never hear the sound of their own names.

William Wordsworth, *The Prelude*

Crime and Punishment is the second of Dostoevsky's full-length novels after Siberia, and the first of the truly great novels of his mature period. *Notes from Underground*, though unquestionably a masterpiece, is more of a "dialectical lyric" (to borrow a term from Kierkegaard) than a short story or a proper novella. But in *Crime and Punishment* we witness the full flowering of the narrative form that Dostoevsky had begun to use in the two works he wrote just after leaving prison camp, *Uncle's Dream* and *The Village of Stepanchikovo*, and then in his first large novel, *The Insulted and Injured*. *Uncle's Dream* had begun as a play, and Dostoevsky's two novellas both use the tightly plotted form, full of unexpected surprises and sharp reversals of situation, typical of the mid-nineteenth-century stage and still favored by Ibsen. The action unrolls in a relatively short space of time, and dialogue and scenic confrontation dominate over narrative exposition and description.

In *The Insulted and Injured*, Dostoevsky's tendency to adapt dramatic techniques for his narrative purposes had led him to the *feuilleton-novel*—so called because it appeared as a regular serial in French newspapers—which itself emerged from the tradition of melodrama and ultimately from the Gothic novel of the eighteenth century. The technique of this genre, also used by Balzac and Dickens, invariably involves a central intrigue with some mystery to unravel or some criminal to be brought to justice, and employs an urban setting as a symbolic environment much as the Gothic novel had used the mysterious, ghost-haunted ruins of medieval castles. Just as with Dickens's London or Balzac's Paris, Dostoevsky too is able to distill a haunting Baudelairian poetry out of the sordid Petersburg slums, and to convey a unique sense of "la fourmillante cité, cité pleine de rêves / Où le spectre en plein jour raccroche le passant!"* Indeed, it is only after he has come to the "cité pleine de rêves" that Raskolnikov begins to dream *his* grandiose and frightening dreams; and he will find himself inescapably haunted by the specter of his crime as he wanders the streets of the "most abstract and premeditated city in the world" (5: 101).**

From his earliest work, to be sure, Dostoevsky had known how to use cityscapes very effectively, and he had always shown a preference for dramatic over expository narrative. Even when employing a seemingly objective narrator, as in *The Double*, he had blended this narrator with the consciousness of the main character to such an extent that his exposition tended to take on the form of a semi-monologue. The *feuilleton*-novel thus offered Dostoevsky a larger structure that corresponded to the natural tendencies of his talent; but it took him some time to learn how to use it for his own purposes. In *The Insulted and Injured*, there is a disturbing clash between a plot machinery motivated by a love intrigue and a pattern of relationships with ideological implications; these exist side by side without being integrated and in fact work at cross purposes. It is only in *Notes from Underground*, where the psychology of the underground man is seamlessly shaped by certain ideas and cultural values, that Dostoevsky first succeeds in fusing the personality of his character with his new, antiradical ideological thematics.

Crime and Punishment clearly draws on this achievement, and the main plot line, involving the commission of a murder as the result of ideological intoxication, depicts all of the disastrous moral-psychic consequences that result for the murderer. The psychology of Raskolnikov is placed squarely at the center, and carefully interwoven with the ideas ultimately responsible for his fatal transgression. Every other feature of the work as well, in one way or another, illuminates the agonizing dilemma in which Raskolnikov is caught, with its inextricable mixture of

---

* "Swarming city, city full of dreams / Where the specter in full daylight intercepts the passer-by." Charles Baudelaire, *Oeuvres Complètes*, ed. Y.-G. Le Dantec (Paris, 1954), 159.

** Hovering in the background of *Crime and Punishment*, as Gary Rosenshield has perceptively noted, is the outline of a much more conventional novelistic schema. "Raskolnikov's story, in a way, fits the sentimental pattern of the innocent young provincial who comes to seek his fortune in the capital, where, waylaid by the forces of evil, he succumbs to corruption and loses all traces of his former freshness and purity. Only Raskolnikov succumbs not to the temptations of high society like Balzac's Rastignac or Stendhal's Julien Sorel, but to those of rationalistic Petersburg." In this context, Dostoevsky is writing another variation on the great nineteenth-century theme that Lionel Trilling called the Young Man from the Provinces. See Gary Rosenshield, *Crime and Punishment* (Lisse, 1978), 76.

tormenting passions and lofty rationalizations. The main character is surrounded by others who serve as oblique reflectors of his inner conflicts, and even the subplots serve as implicit thematic commentary. Figures such as Razumikhin, Dr. Zosimov, and the investigating magistrate Porfiry Petrovich sometimes sound like the *raisonneurs* of the French classical stage; and the development of the plot action, as we shall try to show, is organized so as to guide the reader toward a proper grasp of the significance of Raskolnikov's crime.

Every element of the book thus contributes to an enrichment of its theme and to a resolution of the deepest issues that are posed. At the center of the plot action, of course, is the suspense created by Raskolnikov's inner oscillations and the duel between him and Porfiry Petrovich; but this must be placed in the context of all those "reverberations" generated by the novel's extraordinarily tight-knit ideological-thematic texture. No detail or event seems casual or irrelevant—included only to obtain what Roland Barthes has scornfully called "l'effet du réel," the illusion that the novelist is conveying what the reader will recognize as "real life" in all its diffuse abundance.[1] Dostoevsky managed to convey such a sense of the verisimilar nonetheless, and was very much concerned to remain within its boundaries; but the more closely we read, the more clearly we see how superbly he has succeeded in reshaping such conventions of realism for his own purposes.

Even though *Crime and Punishment*, as we have already sufficiently argued, is a work conceived in direct relation to the perfervid ideological climate of Russia in the mid-1860s, Dostoevsky did not create his new novel out of wholly new materials. Raskolnikov himself (the name evokes the Russian word for a schismatic religious dissenter, a *raskolnik*), though he has no exact precursor in the gallery of Dostoevsky's earlier characters, can well be seen as a fusion of two previous figures. One is Mr. Golyadkin in *The Double*, who also attempts to revolt against the established moral-social order and discovers that his personality is not robust enough to support his timidly rebellious insurgence. Golyadkin goes mad as a result of the psychic strain of his inner conflict; and Raskolnikov suffers a temporary mental derangement for the very same reason. But Golyadkin was only an overambitious government bureaucrat, not a member of the intelligentsia, and so Dostoevsky turned to other figures from the 1840s—the "dreamer"-narrator of *White Nights* and the young philosopher-dreamer Ordynov in *The Landlady*—to provide the additional traits he needed. The "dreamer" of the 1840s, lost in solitary revery, had become alienated from ordinary human life and lived in a world of Romantic fantasy; but he also wished to make contact with "reality," and even to transform the world and bring it more into conformity with his visionary longings. In *The Landlady*, the dismal failure of the main character to accomplish such a feat anticipates Raskolnikov's final acceptance of Sonya's faith: "He [Ordynov] would lie for hours together as though unconscious on the church pavement" (1: 318). This edifying conclusion is an admission of defeat in the 1840s, rather than, as in *Crime and Punishment*, a resurrection and the beginning of a new life of hope and regeneration in the 1860s.

Dostoevsky also drew on previous works for other characters as well as for Raskolnikov. The hopelessly alcoholic Marmeladov, whose very name indicates his lack of willpower, is the superb culmination of a line that begins with old Pokrovsky in *Poor Folk*—the excruciatingly self-conscious derelicts and outcasts who manage, despite all the moral-psychic ravages of their debased condition, to retain an agonizingly acute moral sensibility. Sonya too is a much-elaborated version of the young prostitute Liza in *Notes from Underground* (not to mention a long array of pure-hearted prostitutes in the French social novel), who futilely appeals for help to the underground man and reveals, by her spontaneous gesture of love, her moral superiority to his sadistic vanity. Raskolnikov's loyal friend, the open-hearted, generous, and boisterous Razumikhin, whose name contains the Russian word for "reason," *razum*, indicates Dostoevsky's desire to link the employment of this faculty not only with the cold calculations of Utilitarianism but also with spontaneous human warmth and generosity. His character bears some resemblance to the sturdy and sympathetic Arkady Ivanovich of *A Weak Heart*, who similarly protects and shelters his much more sensitive and vulnerable comrade Vasya.* Svidrigailov continues the line of cynical, wealthy, intellectually sophisticated, and self-aware villains begun with Prince Valkovsky in *The Insulted and Injured*; here he becomes deepened by more than a modicum of Byronic self-disgust and metaphysical despair. All these types, familiar to anyone acquainted with Dostoevsky's earlier writings, are taken up once again, raised to the moral-religious level, and firmly integrated into the intricate unity of his first great novel-tragedy.

---

* In Dostoevsky's notes (7: 71), through what is evidently a slip of the pen, he once writes Rakhmetov instead of Razumikhin. Rakhmetov is the underground revolutionary hero of Chernyshevsky's *What Is To Be Done?*, who possesses great physical strength, trains himself to endure extreme physical hardship, and maintains an iron self-control. Razumikhin is endowed with the first two of these qualities, and Dostoevsky's mistake reveals his obvious desire to create a nonrevolutionary counterpart to Chernyshevsky's *bogatyr* (the Herculean hero of the Russian folk-epic).

At one point, Razumikhin says that his name is only a shortened form of his real one, Vrazumikhin (6: 93). The verb *vrazumit* means to teach or to make understand, and while Razumikhin does not understand a good deal of what is happening to his friend, his own behavior in coping with adversity provides a lesson that Raskolnikov will ultimately have to learn.

2
—————

Crime and Punishment is a novel of riveting power, one of the greatest of
the nineteenth century, and it has been at the center of critical controversy ever since the day of its publication. This is not the place to examine the history of its reception, though some references will of course be
made to various critics and their views as we proceed. Without imagining
for a moment that it is possible to give even a remotely adequate account
of so rich a work from one point of view alone, my own will nonetheless
be circumscribed by the perspective already outlined in Chapter 5. Dostoevsky's letter to Katkov leaves no doubt that his immediate inspiration
was a desire to counteract the nefarious consequences he could foresee
arising from the moral-social doctrines of Russian Nihilism; and he remained faithful to this inspiration even after his original plan had blossomed into a much more ambitious creation.

The doctrines of the Russian Nihilists from which Dostoevsky began
can only be considered jejune when judged in terms of any larger philosophical horizon; but his genius enabled him to elevate them to artistic
heights equaling the greatest creations of Greek and Elizabethan tragedy.
His novels are, as Vyacheslav Ivanov called them long ago, "novel-trage-
dies" both in their scenic technique and in the uncompromising power
with which they pose the clash of conflicting moral-religious alternatives.[2] But such alternatives arise out of the social-cultural conflicts of
Dostoevsky's own time and place; and if we are concerned with understanding Dostoevsky himself, rather than the innumerable ways in which
he has entered into the consciousness of the modern world, it is indispensable to return to these origins as our point of interpretive departure.
Otherwise, we are apt to go sadly astray in assessing the meanings he
wished to convey, and even miss the artistic structures through which
this meaning is conveyed.

Dostoevsky approached Russian Nihilism with a troublingly keen perception of the dangers lurking within its seemingly meritorious aspirations—a perception sharpened by his observations of aberrant human
behavior during his prison-camp years in Siberia. It is not surprising,
however, that the radicals refused to recognize themselves in his pages,
or that Eliseev's early charges of bias, distortion, and slander (sometimes
softened to misunderstanding and incomprehension) should continue
to be repeated up to the present day. Pisarev himself, in a famous article,
ridiculed the notion that Raskolnikov's ideas could be identified with
those of the radicals of his time, though we know from his sister that he
wept while reading *Crime and Punishment*.[3]* Whether these were tears

* "Pisarev's sister," writes E. Lampert, "reports that he read Dostoevsky's novel in a state

of recognition, however, cannot be affirmed. Perhaps not, since Dostoevsky portrayed Nihilist ideas, not on the level at which they were ordinarily advocated, but rather as they were refashioned by his eschatological imagination and taken to their most extreme (though quite consistent) consequences. The aim of these ideas, as he very well knew, was altruistic and humanitarian, inspired by pity and compassion for human suffering; at their root was what Dostoevsky believed to be the innately Christian moral nature of the Russian people. But these aims were to be achieved by suppressing entirely the spontaneous outflow of such feelings, relying on reason (understood in Chernyshevskian terms as Utilitarian calculation) to master all the contradictory and irrational potentialities of the human personality, and, in its latest variety of Bazarovism, encouraging the growth of a proto-Nietzschean egoism among an élite of superior individuals to whom the hopes for the future were to be entrusted.

Raskolnikov was created to exemplify all the potentially disastrous hazards contained in such an ideal; and the moral-psychological traits of his character incorporate this antinomy between instinctive kindness, sympathy, and pity on the one hand and, on the other, a proud and idealistic egoism that has become perverted into a contemptuous disdain for the submissive herd. All the other major figures in the book are equally integrated with Raskolnikov's fluctuations between these two poles; each is a "quasi-double" who embodies, in a more sharply accentuated incarnation, one or another of the clashing oppositions within Raskolnikov's character and ideas. Bakhtin aptly remarks that each character Raskolnikov encounters becomes "for him instantly an embodied solution to his own personal question, a solution different from the one at which he himself had arrived; therefore every person touches a sore spot in him and assumes a firm role in his inner speech."[4] It is not only in "inner speech," however, that such characters function; they structure the novel through the unrolling sequence of encounters generated by the plot action. And these encounters, which present Raskolnikov with one or another aspect of himself, work to motivate that process of self-understanding so crucial for Dostoevsky's artistic purposes.

Crime and Punishment has often been likened to a modern detective story or criminal adventure thriller, and the *feuilleton*-novel that influenced Dostoevsky is historically the ancestor of both these subgenres. At first sight, since there is no ambiguity about the identity of the murderer, comparison with a detective story may seem less appropriate than with a thriller, in which someone overtly commits a crime at the start and the

---

of anguish ... that he wept when he was reading it, and that the reading nearly finished him." E. Lampert, *Sons Against Fathers* (London, 1965), 337.

interest lies in the working out of the adventures that flow from this initial misdeed.[5] In fact, however, *Crime and Punishment* is focused on the solution of an enigma: the mystery of Raskolnikov's motivation. For Raskolnikov himself, as it turns out, discovers that he does not understand *why* he killed; or rather, more accurately, he becomes aware that the moral purpose supposedly inspiring him cannot really explain his behavior. Dostoevsky thus internalizes and psychologizes the usual quest for the murderer in the detective story plot and transfers this quest to the character himself; it is now Raskolnikov who searches for *his own* motivation. This search provides a suspense that is similar to, though of course much deeper and more morally complex than, the conventional search for the criminal. To be sure, there is an investigating magistrate, Porfiry Petrovich, whose task it is to bring Raskolnikov to justice; but this purely legal function is subordinate to his role of spurring on the course of Raskolnikov's own self-questionings and self-comprehension.

Dostoevsky also brilliantly adapts another feature of the detective story, though this particular technical feat has gone largely unremarked. Such a narrative always contains clues, some pointing to the real criminal, others to perfectly innocent characters who are falsely suspected and are meant to mislead the reader temporarily. Innocent characters are also arrested here for the murders; but the reader knows better, and Dostoevsky, as we shall see, uses these erroneous charges both for technical purposes and to obtain a thematically important contrast. Moreover, since the central mystery is that of Raskolnikov's motivation, he also uses such blunders to plant clues to *this* enigma that both guide and misguide the reader. The guiding ones, carefully woven into the background of the action from the very start (but so unobtrusively that they are easy to overlook, especially on first reading), point to what Raskolnikov will finally discover about himself—that he killed, not for the altruistic-humanitarian motives he believed he was acting upon, but solely because of a purely selfish need to test his own strength. The false clues, particularly prominent in Part I, are suggestions that Raskolnikov was acting in response to material, social, or purely psychopathic causes; but such a deterministic point of view is openly combated in the book itself.

These clues are false in the sense that they lead away from the true answer to the question of Raskolnikov's motivation; but the motivations they suggest are not false in any absolute sense (as is the more usual confusion of an innocent person with a guilty one). On the contrary, such imputed possibilities exert a very strong pressure on Raskolnikov and add greatly to the sympathy he evokes in the reader. Clues of this kind should thus perhaps not be called false, but accessory or ancillary rather than primary; and their validity is constantly challenged both dramatically and, through such characters as Razumikhin, Dr. Zosimov, and

Porfiry Petrovich, directly and discursively. Built into the narrative of *Crime and Punishment* is thus a view of how it should be read, a hermeneutic of its interpretation, which is an integral part of its antiradical theme and expresses Dostoevsky's oft-expressed belief in the importance of ideas and their power to influence human behavior. No one, so far as my knowledge goes, has ever paid the slightest attention to this aspect of the book, and it is high time to remedy such a glaring oversight.

3

Crime and Punishment begins *in medias res*, two and one-half days before Raskolnikov commits his crime, and continues through a duration estimated to be approximately two weeks. Time in the novel, so far as it is felt through Raskolnikov's consciousness, contracts and expands freely according to the importance for him of the events being depicted. It thus seems to lack any objective dimension; and it is also manipulated very freely to obtain certain thematic effects by what Ian Watt, writing about Conrad, has called "thematic apposition," that is, the juxtaposition of events occurring at different times in order to establish connections between them without explanatory authorial intrusion.[6] This Bergsonian fluidity of time has often, and quite rightly, been noted as Dostoevsky's anticipation of a narrative technique that will become widespread later in the century (partly as a result of Dostoevsky's influence). But the structure of the novel as a whole is not that of Raskolnikov's consciousness, and it is a mistake to confuse the two. For one thing, there are important episodes in which Raskolnikov is not present and the narrator's point of view dominates. For another, the objective chronology of events (what Russian Formalists call the *fabula*, the time sequence of events *before* they are reshaped for the artistic purposes of the novel) plays a crucial part in illuminating the mystery of Raskolnikov's motivation. It is this *fabula* that is gradually uncovered, with all its psychic-ideological implications, as the double time structure of the mystery plot (the time of the action in the present disclosing what occurred in the past) proceeds on its way.

The famous opening section of *Crime and Punishment*, filled with some of the most powerfully affecting pages that Dostoevsky ever wrote, is also a subtle construction whose various thematic strands it is very important to disentangle. At the center is the inner conflict of Raskolnikov, torn between his intention to commit a crime in the interests of humanity and the resistance of his moral conscience against the taking of human life. He is a sensitive young intellectual, whose fineness of sensibility is conveyed both through his instinctive impulses of compassion for the suffering he sees all around him and also through the intensity of his self-revulsion at his own intentions. He has, when we first encounter him, been brooding over the crime for six weeks; and though he lives in appalling poverty, it is perfectly clear that he would not have thought of committing it simply for purely selfish reasons. It is the fate of suffering humanity that concerns him, as revealed in the tavern scene (we shall return to this scene several times), where the Utilitarian-altruistic justification for the proposed crime is clearly expressed.

Why not kill a wretched, rapacious, and "useless" old moneylender and employ the funds to alleviate the human misery so omnipresent in Raskolnikov's world? This is the thought that was dawning in his mind when he hears it uttered by a student and a young officer in a casual conversation after a game of billiards. Dostoevsky sets this scene in such a public place of recreation, and depicts Raskolnikov as overhearing it simultaneously with the birth of his own exactly similar "strange idea," in order to show just how widespread and commonplace this Utilitarian type of reasoning and its conclusions had become. They were by no means the solitary invention of Raskolnikov's tormented and disordered brain, though there are certain elements in his character that designated *him* as someone who would put them to the test.

The depiction of the Petersburg background in *Crime and Punishment* is justly famous, and Dostoevsky does everything in his considerable artistic powers to accentuate the squalor and human wretchedness that pass before Raskolnikov's eyes, or filter through his sensibility, as he walks through the streets filled with pothouses, brothels, and reeling drunks. His encounter with the hopeless drunkard Marmeladov, abject and guilt-stricken at his own degradation, embodies for Raskolnikov everything in the world that he finds intolerable, especially when Marmeladov explains to all and sundry that he, as well as his starving family, are being kept alive by the self-sacrifice of his prostitute daughter Sonya. On the level of plot, Marmeladov thus seems only to strengthen Raskolnikov's desire to act against the horrifying misery that surrounds him; but on the level of ideological theme, Dostoevsky uses the encounter to uncover in advance both the heartlessness of Raskolnikov's own convictions (not yet specifically introduced) and the alternative set of values to be posed against them.

When Marmeladov describes going to a moneylender for a loan he would obviously never repay, he well understands that his inevitable failure to obtain one is quite in accord with "modern" views. Should the moneylender give him the loan out of "compassion"? "But Mr. Lebezyatnikov, who keeps up with the modern ideas, explained the other day that compassion is forbidden nowadays by science itself, and this is what is done in England, where there is political economy" (6: 14). Raskolnikov's own reasoning is based on exactly the same Utilitarian notions of "political economy," which exclude any feeling of compassion for the "useless" individual marked out as the sacrificial victim. By contrast, the ecstatic vision of the drunkard before he collapses provides the very starkest antithesis to the inhuman tenor of the ideas that Raskolnikov is dreaming of putting into practice. For here Marmeladov, in a mixture of freely altered citations from the Gospels, envisions Christ returning at the Last Judgment and pardoning even the "children of shame" like himself because "not one of them believed himself worthy of this." It is certainly not accidental that Christ's all-forgiving love is opposed "by the wise ones and those of understanding" (this last word translates *razumnie*), whereby Dostoevsky ingeniously turns the Pharisees of the New Testament into precursors of the Russian radicals of the 1860s (6: 21).

The symbolic weight of this Petersburg setting, largely confined to the swarming and tawdry lower-class district in which Raskolnikov lives, reinforces the social-humanitarian motivation that is the nominal justification for Raskolnikov's crime; and up to Chapter 3 (Part I), this is the sole reason indicated for his intention. But Dostoevsky then increases the weight of this more or less impersonal incitation ("One death, and a hundred lives in exchange—it's simple arithmetic") with a much more intimate motive: the letter from Raskolnikov's mother (6: 54). Here he learns about the desperate circumstances of his own family, the misadventures of his sister Dunya with the philandering landowner Svidrigailov, and her decision, clearly against her inclinations, to marry the tight-fisted and domineering lawyer Luzhin solely to help her adored brother. Her resolve thus places Raskolnikov, as he realizes only too piercingly, in exactly the same debasing (though outwardly more respectable) position as the drunken Marmeladov living off Sonya's earnings.

Dostoevsky's portrayal of the agonies of a conscience wrestling with itself, as Raskolnikov struggles to suppress his moral scruples and steel himself for murder, has no equal this side of *Macbeth*. His horrified recoil after the trial visit to the pawnbroker's flat, so as to spy out the ground in advance, is only the first of several reactions that increase in severity: "Oh God! how loathsome it all is. . . . And how could such an atrocious thing come into my head?" (6: 10). The unforgettable dream sequence in Chapter 5, which evokes a childhood recollection of the savagely sadistic beating and killing of a "useless" old mare by the drunken peasant Mikolka, epitomizes Raskolnikov's lacerating conflict with remarkable vividness. On the one side, there is the little boy who "loved that church, the old-fashioned icons for the most part without frames, and the old priest with his trembling head" (the incident takes place on the outskirts of a cemetery, with a nearby church) (6: 46). This little boy, who still exists in the depths of Raskolnikov's psyche, furiously breaks away from his father's grasp, puts his arms around the head of the dead horse to kiss her lips and wounded eyes, and finally flies "in a frenzy with his little fists out at Mikolka" (6: 49).* On the other, there is the grown Raskolnikov dreaming this dream, who now plans to behave exactly like Mikolka—and not in a drunken rage, but according to a carefully thought out, "rational" theory. The combat within Raskolnikov between these two aspects of himself is so rending that he wakes in a state of terror and self-loathing, believing (mistakenly) that he has at last conquered the obsessive temptation to kill.

The reader, for the most part, remains immersed in Raskolnikov's consciousness all through Part I and tends to identify with his point of view. What dominates the foreground is Raskolnikov's primarily Utilitarian-altruistic intentionality, which the reader inclines to take (and is meant to take, in large measure) as perfectly genuine. But Dostoevsky is far from wishing such motivation to be viewed as exclusive. Interwoven with the major episodes of Raskolnikov's inner struggle are background incidents whose purpose can only be to indicate that, in reality, Raskolnikov is quite purblind to the subconscious psychic-emotive forces that have been stirred up in his personality. In all such incidents, Raskolnikov behaves in a fashion that shows his emotions being mobilized *against* the feelings that inspire his Utilitarian-altruistic aims. Here we see a Raskolnikov quite different from the one whose heart is torn by human suffering—a Raskolnikov who, just after springing to the aid of someone in distress (as when he helps Marmeladov to stagger home and leaves some kopeks on the windowsill, or calls a policeman to protect a tipsy young girl in the street being followed by a lecherous fat "dandy"), undergoes an abrupt reversal of attitude. The compassionate Raskolnikov of one moment becomes a coldly unconcerned and contemptuous egoist in the next, totally indifferent to the misfortunes that had stirred his pity.

Egoism as an ingredient of Raskolnikov's character is indicated very early in the "expression of profoundest disgust" that passes over his face as he walks through "the revolting misery" of the stinking streets. He is also said to have maintained "a sort of haughty pride and reserve about him" in relations with his fellow students, behaving "as though he were

---

* This dream is linked to an incident that occurred when Dostoevsky, at the age of sixteen, was traveling from Moscow to Petersburg with his older brother to enter school in the capital. On the way, they saw a government courier beating a peasant driver, and the peasant then lashing his horse into a frenzy. Dostoevsky recalls this traumatic scene in his notes for *Crime and Punishment*: "My first personal insult," he writes, "the horse, the courier" (7: 138). For more information, see *Dostoevsky: The Seeds of Revolt* (Princeton, N.J., 1976), 69–73.

Scholars have also traced some details of this dream to a poem of Nekrasov's, *At Twilight* (*Do Sumerek*), which contains a very similar depiction of a peasant beating a disabled horse; here too the horse is struck on its "weeping, gentle eyes." This line of the poem will later be referred to by Ivan Karamazov (14: 219). See S. V. Belov, *Roman F. M. Dostoevskogo 'Prestuplenie i Nakazanie,' Kommentarii* (Leningrad, 1979), 97.

superior [to them] in development, knowledge, and convictions, as though their beliefs and interests were beneath him" (6: 6, 43). Raskolnikov's precipitous shifts of behavior have usually been taken merely as a manifestation of the psychological antinomies of his personality; but for Dostoevsky, psychology and ideology were now inseparable, and each such reversal is correlated with some reference to radical doctrine. Just after his trial visit, reeling both with fever and self-disgust, Raskolnikov stops at the pothouse where he meets Marmeladov and drinks a glass of beer. Instantly feeling better, he attributes his previous moral discomposure to lack of nourishment and shrugs it off: Chernyshevsky had taught that morality was just a product of physiology.

Raskolnikov also has second thoughts about the kopeks he left the Marmeladovs. " 'What a stupid thing I have done,' he reflects. ' . . . They have Sonya, and I need the money myself' " (6: 25). This Utilitarian consideration checks the spontaneous outflow of pity, and with "a malignant laugh" he ponders on the infinite capacity of mankind to adapt itself to the most degrading circumstances. Much the same happens when, after calling the policeman to help the girl (whom he identifies with his sister Dunya being pursued by Svidrigailov), he unexpectedly turns away in disgust. Suddenly "something seemed to sting Raskolnikov; in an instant a complete revulsion of feeling came over him," and he swings to the other extreme: "Let them devour each other alive—what is it to me?," he mutters to himself (6: 42). What "stings" Raskolnikov is the bite of these Darwinian reflections, which view the triumph of the stronger as right and just and any help to the weaker as a violation of the laws of nature. This scene is then duplicated internally as Raskolnikov first imagines the girl's probable future of prostitution, venereal disease, and ruin at eighteen or nineteen, but then caustically dismisses this resurgence of pity because "a certain percentage, they tell us, must every year . . . go that way . . . somewhere . . . to the devil, it must be, so as to freshen up the rest and leave them in peace" (6: 43).

4

Radical ideas, identical in their Utilitarian logic to those expressed in the tavern scene, thus continually act to reinforce the innate egoism of Raskolnikov's character and to turn him into a hater rather than a lover of his fellow humans. It is not only that his *ideas* run counter to the instinctive promptings of his moral-emotive sensibility; these ideas momentarily transform him into someone for whom moral conscience ceases to operate as part of his personality. Not that his moral aim is insincere; but in steeling himself to accomplish his purpose, we become aware, Raskolnikov must suppress in himself the very moral-emotive feelings from which this aim had originally sprung. What occurs in these scenes thus illustrates the manner in which Raskolnikov's ideas have been affecting his personality; and they cast an important light on what has been taking place within him emotively ever since he fell under their influence.

If we examine the *fabula* of the novel, disregarding for the moment its *siuzhet* (the Russian Formalist term for the *artistic* manipulation of narrative structure, that is, the order in which this structure unfolds for the reader), we realize that radical notions began to influence Raskolnikov approximately six months before the events of the novel begin. It was then that he wrote his fateful article "On Crime," which recasts and extends Pisarev's reflections on Bazarov, and divides people into two categories: the "ordinary" and the "extraordinary." The first group, the masses, are content with their lot and docilely accept whatever established order exists; the second, a small élite, is composed of individuals who "seek in various ways the destruction of the present for the sake of the better" (examples given are Newton and Kepler, Lycurgus, Solon, Muhammad, and Napoleon). Such "extraordinary" people invariably commit crimes, if judged by the old moral codes they are striving to replace; but because they work "for the sake of the better," their aim is ultimately the improvement of mankind's lot, and they are thus in the long run benefactors rather than destroyers. So that, Raskolnikov argued, "if such a one is forced for the sake of his idea to step over a corpse or wade through blood, he can find in himself, *in his conscience*, a sanction for wading through blood" (6: 199–200; italics added). Since writing that article, Raskolnikov had become fascinated with the alluringly majestic image of such a Napoleonic personality who, in the interests of a higher social good, believes that he possesses a moral right to kill.

Five months later, Raskolnikov makes his first visit to the abhorrent pawnbroker and then drops in at the tavern where he overhears the conversation between the student and the young officer. This marks the moment of the appearance of his "strange idea," which is based on exactly the same Utilitarian logic expounded in his article: murder can be sanctioned by conscience in the name of a higher social good. And looming behind the sudden birth of Raskolnikov's intention ("pecking at his brain like a chicken in the egg") are thus the long months of gestation during which he had dreamed of becoming such a Napoleonic personality and acquiring homicidal privileges (6: 53). His encounter with Alyona Ivanovna simply concretized the possibility of applying this ambition, which had been germinating in his subconscious, to the local Petersburg conditions of his own life.

Commentators still continue to maintain that there is a fundamental opposition between the ideas uttered in the tavern scene and those presented in the article; and it is true that there is a different *stress* in the two versions of the same basic doctrine. At first, Dostoevsky emphasizes Raskolnikov's humanitarian-altruistic aims; later, it is the Napoleonic personality that comes to the fore. But this is in accordance with Dostoevsky's handling of his *siuzhet*, his mystery story technique of gradual disclosure, which orchestrates the process of Raskolnikov's piecemeal self-discovery. Both aspects of the doctrine are present in each instance, and it is only the accent that shifts as Raskolnikov comes to understand how the temptation of incarnating a Napoleonic personality has run athwart of his supposedly unselfish purposes.

The first overt mention of Raskolnikov's article occurs during his interview with Porfiry Petrovich in Part III; and it is a common error to assume that no allusions to its contents have been made earlier.* But in fact, during the very tavern conversation usually taken as the antithesis of the article, the narrator indicates the need for a Napoleonic personality to put into practice the ideas being discussed. For when the young officer objects that the injustice of the pawnbroker's existence is simply "nature," the student retorts vehemently: "we have to correct and direct nature, and but for that we should drown in a sea of prejudice. *But for that there would never have been a single great man.* They talk of duty and conscience;—but the point is, what do we mean by them?" (6: 54; italics added).

The notion of a "great man," who possesses the moral right to give a new meaning to "duty" and "conscience," is thus involved from the very first in Raskolnikov's "strange idea"; and there is even a generally unnoticed allusion to this grandiose ambition on the opening page. As Raskolnikov stealthily slips past his landlady's door, afraid of being confronted with his failure to pay the rent, he caustically jeers at his own timidity: "I want to attempt such a thing, and at the same time am frightened by such trifles. It would be interesting to know what it is men are most afraid of. Taking a new step, uttering *their own word* is what they fear most" (6: 6; italics added). Raskolnikov will later define his "extraordinary" people precisely by their ability to utter a "new word"; he is thus placing the drably scruffy crime he intends to commit in such an exalted perspective.

Another and more extended reference to the article is inserted as Raskolnikov frantically makes his final preparations for the killing. Long ago, we are told, he had been concerned about the "psychology of the criminal" (which is how the subject of his article is later described) and why

---

* In a guide to the novel, Gary Cox writes of this article, which he rightly says "contains some of the chief rationalizations for the murder," that "there is no mention of it in Part 1, where Raskolnikov is planning the crime and talking about the inception of the idea." He thinks it "hard to escape the conclusion" that "Dostoevsky simply did not think of the article until after Parts 1 and 2 were published" (?). See Gary Cox, *Crime and Punishment* (Boston, 1990), 73.

run-of-the-mill lawbreakers were invariably overcome by "a failure of reason and willpower" just before committing their offense. This failure was like a disease that attacked them, and then passed off like any illness; but as a result, they left clues scattered about the scene of the crime that made them easy to identify and arrest. Raskolnikov was convinced that nothing of the sort would happen in his case: "his reason and will would remain unimpaired at the time of carrying out his design, for the simple reason that his design was 'not a crime.'" "We will omit," adds the narrator tantalizingly, "all the process by means of which he arrived at this conclusion; we have run too far ahead already" (6: 58–59). But this process of reasoning is manifestly contained in Raskolnikov's article, whose "extraordinary" people did not commit "crimes" precisely because they had a *moral right* to disregard existing laws; "ordinary" criminals were perturbed by conscience and thus gave themselves away. Raskolnikov's belief that he would be immune to such agitations indicates his long-held self-classification as one of the "extraordinary" élite.

Nonetheless, as Dostoevsky so powerfully shows, Raskolnikov is very far from being able to conquer the "irrational" responses of his conscience. During the past six weeks, weeks filled with "monologues in which he jeered at his own incompetence and indecision" (6: 7), he had instead worked himself into a psychopathic state labeled as *monomania* by the narrator—a state that Dostoevsky portrays with his usual skill at depicting characters afflicted with mental disorder. Monomania is clinically defined as an irrational obsession with one particular object, event, idea, or person—which in this case results from Raskolnikov's uncertainty over whether he can bring himself to act in accordance with his self-image as an "extraordinary" person. So far, crippled by the stubborn opposition of his moral conscience, he has on the contrary been assailed by a frustrating paralysis of will and a gradual replacement of conscious volition by the subconscious compulsions of his monomania. These provide another motivation for Raskolnikov that has attracted the attention of scores of psychiatrists and psychoanalysts; but while Raskolnikov undoubtedly suffers from a form of mental illness, the *cause* of this malady cannot be understood solely in terms of psychopathology. It is a product of the *moral*-psychological warfare taking place between his conscience and the effect of his ideas on his personality.

There is abundant evidence in these early pages of Raskolnikov's mental imbalance, which has caused his grip on external reality to weaken. This loss is illustrated by a number of telling details (such as the battered top hat of German make that he wears, which makes him easily identifiable) and the direct reference to his walking in the street muttering to himself, "sunk in thought, or more accurately, as if into a kind of unconsciousness" (6: 6). Raskolnikov's self-imposed isolation is compared to that "of a tortoise in its shell." "Even the sight of the servant girl who had to wait upon him and looked sometimes into his room stirred him to bilious convulsions." The narrator explains that "in the present state of his spirits" (that is, during the past six weeks) he had even begun to take a masochistic pleasure in the squalid disorder of his miserable little room, finding such slovenliness to be "positively agreeable" (6: 25–26). As so often in Dostoevsky, Raskolnikov's self-hatred at his own impotence thus turns outward into a sadistic hatred of others (even of the cheerful peasant servant Nastasya, who obviously feels sorry for the starving ex-student and tries to aid him in her way). He has now become too embittered to respond to kindness except with resentment; moreover, his monomania has focused all his emotions on the desire to kill, further stirring up all the latently aggressive inhumanity of his egoism.

Raskolnikov is thus shown, throughout these chapters, falling more and more into the grip of his monomania, and this means into the grip of his desire to prove to *himself* that he truly belongs to the "extraordinary" category. At the same time, he has no awareness of the deadly dialectic taking place in his personality, which requires him to muster a pitiless egoism in order to bring about a humanitarian and morally beneficent end. This lack of awareness is of course essential for Dostoevsky's artistic strategy, and it is emphasized by the manner in which Raskolnikov's inner struggle is finally resolved. Just at the moment when, after the mare-killing dream, Raskolnikov believes that his conscience has won and that he has at last shaken off "that spell, that sorcery, that fascination, that obsession" (the careful choice of words indicates to what extent he felt in the power of a subliminal psychic compulsion), he accidentally overhears a conversation revealing that his intended victim, Alyona Ivanovna, who lives with her younger sister Lizaveta, will be alone at a certain hour the next day (6: 50).

This chance encounter, acting on an already deranged psyche strained to the breaking point, releases the mechanism of his monomania in a manner that will later be described by Dr. Zosimov (whose diagnosis is reliable as far as it goes and deserves more attention than it usually receives). Those suffering from monomania, the doctor explains, sometimes "perform actions . . . in a masterly and very cunning way, while the direction of the actions, the origin of the actions, are deranged and dependent on various morbid impressions. As in a dream" (6: 174). On hearing of this miraculous opportunity, which certainly can be considered a "morbid impression," Raskolnikov accordingly "felt suddenly in his whole being that he had no more freedom of thought, no will. . . . It was as if a part of his clothing had been caught in the cogs of a machine and he was being dragged into it" (6: 52, 58). Fate thus takes a hand, but it is fate acting on a pathological psychic predisposition to kill conditioned by ideological self-intoxication.

This surrender of Raskolnikov to the grip of fatality, one of the pivots of the novel, has elicited a good deal of speculative interpretation. Its specific *thematic* function, however, is to obviate any possibility that Raskolnikov will be understood to have acted on the basis of a conscious, willed, rational decision. Rather, he is controlled by the psychic forces released through the struggle to overcome the moral resistance of his conscience. Raskolnikov is thus portrayed as being governed by compulsions he does not understand (though the reader has been afforded a glimpse of what they amount to *in practice*), and whose true meaning it will take him the remainder of the book to unravel. Moreover, the gap between Raskolnikov's self-deception and the perspective of the reader is further widened by Dostoevsky's little-noted but masterly manipulation of time sequence in the chapter just preceding the murder.

The all-important tavern scene, so often referred to already, is placed at Chapter 6, Part I, of the *siuzhet* even though this event occurred six weeks earlier in the *fabula*. Why this time shift? Evidently, so that the reader can receive the strongest impression of the enormous gap between Raskolnikov's nominally humanitarian-altruistic aim, which has just been clearly enunciated for the first time, and the blood-soaked horror that will be depicted a few pages later in Chapter 7. The discrepancy between abstract idea and concrete human reality, between intention and actualization, could not have been driven home more dramatically. And this effect is then reinforced by another time shift that soon follows, which refers to matters antedating the murder even farther back in the *fabula*—six months instead of six weeks. For an intercalation contains the references already mentioned to Raskolnikov's article, on the basis of which he believes in his own invulnerability to "irrational" agitations because, as the narrator rather mockingly notes, "as regards the moral question . . . his analysis was now complete; his casuistry had become as sharp as a razor, and he could not find any conscious objections in himself" (6: 58). Both his original theory and its Petersburg embodiment are thus brought into very close "thematic apposition" to the crime itself.

These time shifts create a profound effect of dramatic irony that works both backward and forward in the text. All through the past six weeks, it becomes clear, Raskolnikov himself had been prey to the symptoms of the "ordinary" criminal, assailed by the same "eclipse of reason and failure of willpower . . . that reached [its] highest point just before the perpetration of the crime" (6: 58). Indeed, Raskolnikov is ailing not only psychologically but also physically, suffering from a state of high fever that only augments the "eclipse of reason and failure of willpower" to which he had believed himself immune. The extent to which he had been self-deluded in the past thus becomes manifest; and since he has by no means succeeded in vanquishing his "ordinary" moral conscience, he will obviously not succeed either in attaining the nerveless self-mastery that theoretically flows from his doctrine.

The dramatic irony employed in this chapter receives sensational confirmation in the murder scene, which shocked Dostoevsky's contemporaries by the crudity and unsparing realism of its depiction. Nothing goes according to what few plans Raskolnikov had made in advance, and the unexpected necessity of also killing the meek and good-hearted Lizaveta glaringly illustrates the contingency of human reality that Raskolnikov had imagined he could so easily dominate. He acts in a state of terrorized panic, though behaving with the cunning and seeming consequentiality of a monomaniac. The narrator leaves no doubt that Raskolnikov's reasoning faculties were in complete abeyance. Only at the last moment, after killing Lizaveta, does he realize that he had failed to latch the door!

In most of this brutal murder scene, the narrator remains close to Raskolnikov's point of view and superbly conveys the almost hypnotic nature of his behavior. But he notes at one point that "fear gained more and more mastery over him," and adds that Raskolnikov would have given himself up if he could have realized all the "hopelessness" and "hideousness" of his position. Not from fear, however, "but from the simple horror and loathing of what he had done. This feeling of loathing especially surged up in him and grew stronger every minute" (6: 65). Once more Raskolnikov's moral conscience rises up in revolt, but he is no longer able to suppress it by the casuistry of his Utilitarian logic; the crime itself is what this logic has brought him to in reality. What emerges instead is the rampant egoism justified by such logic, and now fully released in his monomania. As the two men who had come to visit Alyona Ivanovna rattle at the locked door behind which Raskolnikov stands, axe in hand, "he was in a sort of delirium. He was even making ready to fight when they should come in. . . . Now and then he was tempted to swear at them, to jeer at them, while they could not open the door!" (6: 68).

This moment behind the door, when Raskolnikov's egoism reaches a self-destructive pitch of hatred for and defiance of everyone, will be used again as a flashback, and becomes a leitmotif. It represents all those emotive forces that, stirred up by his theory and then unleashed in the crime, have now become detached from their previous moral mooring. The two antithetical parts of Raskolnikov's personality, held together earlier by the razor-sharp dialectic of his casuistry, had persuaded him that it was possible to reconcile murder and morality. No longer is such a belief tenable; and he will continue to fluctuate between these two poles for the remainder of the book, with only the faint glimpse of a possible resolution at the end.

5
———

Part I of *Crime and Punishment*, customarily passed over merely as a "prologue" to the main action, is in fact far more important to the structure of the work than generally realized. It is simply not true, as K. Mochulsky believes, that at the end of this section "neither the hero nor the readers know the real reason for the crime."[7] Raskolnikov certainly acted in a state of psychopathic oblivion, but Dostoevsky has surely conveyed a sense to the reader of what this "real reason" will turn out to be. Raskolnikov's point of view and that of the reader, despite the widespread opinion to the contrary, do *not* coincide—or at least were not *meant to* coincide, if we have read Dostoevsky aright so far. And while readers may not, especially on first perusal, be able to detach themselves sufficiently from Raskolnikov to pick up all the foreshadowings, they nonetheless cannot avoid receiving the stunning impact of the discrepancy between events and his declared aims and expectations. In Part II of the novel, which runs from the immediate aftermath of the crime to the arrival of Raskolnikov's family in Petersburg, Dostoevsky will begin to close the gap between Raskolnikov's awareness and that already imparted to the reader by the narrator.

In Chapters 1 and 2 of Part II, Raskolnikov is still in the same blurred state of consciousness as during the crime itself; but when, on awakening from his feverish doze, he discovers bloodstains on his clothes and realizes he had not removed the arm-loop for the axe from his sleeve, some of the confusion in which he has acted begins to dawn on his distraught sensibility. The brilliant plot twist of the summons to the police station to pay his IOU brings him into contact with the legal authorities, and the sense of being pursued and hounded will never leave him in the future. Most important of all is what occurs when he appeals for mercy to the police clerk and suddenly realizes that his entire relation to the normal moral-social world has irremediably changed. "A gloomy sensation of agonizing everlasting solitude and estrangement took conscious form in his soul . . . he felt clearly that . . . he could never appeal to these people . . . even if they had been his own brothers and sisters" (6: 81–82). The reference to "brothers and sisters" foreshadows Raskolnikov's meeting with his family, when he will experience this sense of solitude with agonizing acuity.

The immediate consequence of this encounter with moral-social isolation, of his exile from the human community, is an overwhelming impulse to confess to the humane police officer Nikodim Fomich; and this involuntary need to overcome his glacial sense of alienation, which will continue to war with his vanity and egoistic pride, is what will soon cause him to seek the solace of human companionship through Sonya. But when Nikodim Fomich plunges into a conversation with his subordinate, the explosive but easily pacified Lieutenant Gunpowder, about the murder of Alyona Ivanovna, Raskolnikov collapses into a dead faint. This brings him under suspicion, though his feverish physical state provides a plausible alibi; but the incident also begins the process of objectifying past events for Raskolnikov by means of Dostoevsky's ingenious variation on the convention of eavesdropping. The conversation concerns the two men who had come to visit the pawnbroker just after Raskolnikov had locked the door and who then, each in turn, had left to call the house porter. They had been arrested as suspects, and the two policemen, in discussing whether they could be guilty, reconstruct Raskolnikov's actions as he furtively left the flat and slunk down the staircase.

It is in this way that Raskolnikov will gradually learn about his own behavior; but such conversations also serve as indirect authorial commentary and constitute one of the hermeneutic subtexts already mentioned. For all these discussions turn on the issue of whether criminal guilt should be gauged on the basis of what seem to be obviously incriminatory facts (why did the two men *both* leave the door?), or whether one should also take into account other evidence that is purely "psychological"—how the suspects behaved in public just before entering the building, and so on. These arguments examine the question of guilt in terms of an opposition between immediately evident and easily ascertainable causes, based on obvious material facts, and conclusions derived from intuiting the inner states of consciousness of the suspect. Such a question is analogically linked to Raskolnikov's own motivation, and implicitly points to the importance of paying the closest attention to *his* "state of consciousness" as revealed through, and affected by, his ideas.

The events at the police station lead Raskolnikov to begin the process of exploring his own motivation, which the crime has shown him could hardly be the one he had previously imagined. After hurrying to remove the booty from his room and burying it under a large stone, "a new, utterly unexpected and exceedingly simple question perplexed him"; and this query is the first step toward undermining the humanitarian-altruistic rationale given so much prominence in the tavern scene: "If really all this was done *consciously* [*sozhnatelno*]," he thinks, "and not like a fool, if you really had a definite and unwavering goal, how is it that you never even looked in the purse, and have no idea of what you gained, or why you shouldered all this torment and consciously embarked on such a base, vile, and ignoble business?" (6: 86). What sweeps over Raskolnikov in response to this uncertainty is "a new and irresistible sensation of boundless, almost physical repulsion for everything around him, an obstinate, hateful, and malevolent sensation ... growing stronger and stronger every minute. He loathed everyone he met" (6: 87). This "irresistible sensation" in fact contains much of the answer he was seeking, though he was not yet conscious of what it signified.

The entirely new moral-psychic situation in which Raskolnikov finds himself is then underlined by the visit to his only friend, the warm-hearted, generous, ebullient Razumikhin, who was introduced earlier and obviously serves as a contrast to the introspective, gloomy, embittered Raskolnikov. Their social-economic circumstances were exactly the same; but Razumikhin "was straining every nerve to improve his circumstances in order to continue his studies" (6: 44). Despite Razumikhin's lively banter and offer of aid to a friend who, as he quickly realizes, is "delirious," the visit only increases Raskolnikov's tormenting sense of irremediable solitude. Two other incidents are then used to broaden this motif. One is the famous panorama of the "magnificent spectacle" (6: 90) of Petersburg, which in the past had always filled Raskolnikov with "a gloomy and mysterious impression" (6: 90) he could never fathom. Now, along with "all his past, all his *old ideas*, and problems and thoughts and sensations," he felt even more alienated from it than before (ibid.; italics added). The symbolic meaning of this break with "all his past" is then expressed when, with a sweep of his arm, he unthinkingly throws into a canal the twenty-kopek piece given him as charity by a little girl "in Christ's name."* This gesture indicates how little he can identify himself any longer with the charitable aims expressed in the tavern scene. What remains is the raw terror of the dream that follows, when he imagines hearing the volatile Lieutenant Gunpowder mercilessly beating the landlady on the staircase.

At this juncture, there is a hiatus of three days, during which Raskolnikov lies in a semiconscious delirium, only confusedly aware of his surroundings and awakening once the peak of his illness has passed. Razumikhin, taking charge of his ailing friend during this time, had brought in for consultation the young and highly competent Dr. Zosimov, who as a hobby took a special interest in psychiatric disorders. Through Razumikhin's clumsy efforts to cheer up his ailing and morose friend, Raskol-

---

* A little girl giving some kopeks to a person in need had a poignant resonance for Dostoevsky, since he recorded in *House of the Dead*, it had happened to himself. Once, while walking in the street with a guard, a little girl "came running after me. 'Here, "unfortunate," take a kopek in the name of Christ!' she cried, running out ahead of me and pressing the coin in my hand. ... I kept that kopek for a long time" (4: 19).

Dostoevsky's wife later commented on this scene in *Crime and Punishment*: "This is a personal recollection of Feodor Mikhailovich. He spoke any number of times of this kopek and regretted that he had not succeeded in keeping it" (*PSS*, 4: 289).

nikov learns that the bribe-taking Zametov had visited his room and that, in his feverish ravings, he had given away some fragmentary details of his effort to conceal the traces of the crime.

He also learns, through the conversation between Razumikhin and Zosimov (as well as from the interjection of Nastasya), not only that the slaughtered Lizaveta had mended his shirt but also just how oblivious he had been during the murders. For the house painter Nikolay has been arrested as a suspect, and an argument breaks out over this new solution to the crime. Nikolay had been seized after pawning some jewels he had found in the empty flat where Raskolnikov had taken refuge before slipping down the stairs. Raskolnikov himself (as well as the reader) had been totally ignorant of this loss; and nothing could have brought home to him so forcibly his utter lack of self-possession, his total failure to live up to his anticipatory image of rational self-mastery. The information comes as a terrible shock, and Raskolnikov reacts with a frightened start while "staring with troubled, terrified eyes at Razumikhin" (6: 108).

Once again Raskolnikov's reactions are accompanied by a thematic-hermeneutic counterpoint. Razumikhin defends the innocence of Niko-lay, despite all the incriminating evidence (Nikolay had also tried to hang himself out of fear of the police), with the argument that such evidence must be weighed against other, less palpable factors relating to the "psychology" of the suspect. Nikolay had been wrestling playfully in the entrance of the apartment house with his work partner at the approximate time the murders had been committed; and Razumikhin argues passionately that it would have been *humanly* impossible for him to have killed two women just a few moments before engaging in such lighthearted horseplay. But the Russian legal authorities, he raps out, are incapable of "accepting such a fact—based solely on psychological impossibility alone, and on a state of mind alone—as an irrefutable fact, demolishing all incriminating material facts whatsoever" (6: 110). Dostoevsky thus explicitly states the issue already broached in the police station, and emphasizes the importance of a "state of mind" rather than "all incriminating and material facts whatsoever" in ascertaining guilt. The reference to the problem of Raskolnikov's own motivation can hardly be doubted.

The climax of this sequence is the visit of Peter Petrovich Luzhin—the fiancé whom Dunya Raskolnikova had accepted only after a sleepless night spent praying on her knees fervently before an icon—to Raskolnikov's dingy and squalid "cabin." Luzhin himself is a self-made man, a lawyer with a high rank in the civil service, pompous, self-satisfied, and filled with an overwhelming sense of his own importance. He is also a petty tyrant who looks forward gloatingly to bending the proud but penniless Dunya to his will. As Raskolnikov had learned from his mother's letter, Luzhin likes to consider himself as "sharing the convictions of the younger generation" (6: 31), though he does so out of fear of their influence rather than from any genuine sympathy. Raskolnikov thus finds himself confronted with someone who is not only personally hateful, but who also glaringly reveals the moral dubiousness of exactly the same Utilitarian logic to which he had become so ruinously committed.

The elegantly attired Luzhin tries to impress the ragged but insouciant Razumikhin, distressingly unawed by the visitor's imposing hauteur, by declaring his sympathy with "the younger generation" and his approval of "the new, valuable ideas, [the] new valuable works . . . circulating instead of the old dreamy and bookish ones." Progress, he declares sententiously, is being made "in the name of science and economic truth." For example, in the past the ideal of "love thy neighbor" had been accepted, and the chief result was that "it came to tearing my coat in half to share with my neighbor and we both were left half-naked." Now, on the contrary, science had shown that "everything in the world rests on self-interest," and "therefore in acquiring wealth solely and exclusively for myself, I am acquiring, so to speak, for all, and helping to bring to pass my neighbor's getting a little more than a coat; and that not from private, isolated liberality, but as a consequence of the general advance" (6: 115–116). One understands why the radicals resented seeing their ideas placed in the mouth of so unsavory a character as Luzhin; but Dostoevsky accurately captures their reliance on Utilitarian egoism, their aversion to private charity (as demeaning to the receiver), and their rejection of the Christian morality of love and self-sacrifice (in theory if not in practice). Luzhin is so evidently hypocritical in pretending to be concerned about "my neighbor" that Raskolnikov is forced to confront the awful possibility that his own cherished beliefs could also well have concealed such purely self-serving ends.

Luzhin's unctuousness is carefully interwoven with a renewed discussion of the crime, during which Raskolnikov learns even more humiliating details about his blunders and his blindness. Under the pressure of the emotions produced by such additional glimpses of his failure, he finally intervenes in the conversation about the increase of crime in general and among the educated class in particular. Luzhin had asked what explanation there might be for "the demoralization of the civilized part of our society," and when he begins to speak of "morality . . . and so to speak principles," Raskolnikov cuts him short: "But why do you worry about it. . . . It's in accordance with your theory—carry out logically the theory you were advocating just now and it follows that people may be slaughtered" (6: 118). Raskolnikov himself, of course, had carried out the theory logically; he too had rejected the old-fashioned "dreamy and bookish" morality of "love thy neighbor" for the Utilitarian version advocated by the radicals and parroted by Luzhin. And when he implicitly recognizes himself in Luzhin's words, he indicates his awareness that the ideas he had adopted so pure-heartedly could equally well (and even better) justify arrant selfishness, a greedy desire for personal gain and a bent for sadistic domination. This encounter with Luzhin finally breaks the thread linking Raskolnikov's Utilitarian reasoning with its supposedly altruistic-humanitarian goals.

Openly expressing outrage at Luzhin's treatment of his sister and mother, Raskolnikov brutally drives him away along with his other visitors, who are equally included in his self-hating rage. Furtively leaving his room, he plunges into the streets with a frenzied, inchoate feeling "that all *this* must be ended today . . . he *would not go on living like that*" (6: 120–121). A series of street encounters duplicate those of Part I, but reveal the change in Raskolnikov that has now begun to take place, his need to seek relief from the solitude of his guilt and reestablish links with humanity. He pauses to listen to an adolescent street singer, whose costume prefigures the first appearance of Sonya ("a crinoline, a mantle, and a straw hat with a flame-colored feather"), and he gives her a five-kopek piece with no Utilitarian afterthoughts (6: 121). Instead of avoiding people, he engages a stranger in conversation and startles him with a strange evocation of a Petersburg winter scene in the midst of the sweltering summer heat (using the imagery of the Natural School of the 1840s, hence of Dostoevsky's earlier work, with its sentimental-humanitarian overtones). His inquiry after the vanished huckster, from whom he had learned by chance that Alyona Ivanovna would be alone, indicates his urge to retrace the recent past, about which, as he now realizes, he possesses only a very confused notion.

The climax of this sequence is the meeting with the still-attractive prostitute Duclida, who asks for six kopeks without offering him her favors in return. Another prostitute rebukes her for descending to outright beggary; and this grotesque assertion of a surviving modicum of self-respect, even in the midst of ultimate degradation, recalls to Raskolnikov a book (Hugo's *Notre Dame de Paris*) in which a condemned man imagines he would prefer to live on a small ledge for a thousand years rather than die within a few hours. "No matter how—only to live! . . . What scoundrels men are!" (6: 123), he thinks, in words similar to his reaction on leaving the Marmeladovs and regretting his instinctive charity. But he is no longer quite the same person, and such a reaction is transformed into an all-embracing pity for humankind and a twinge of guilt: " 'And he is a scoundrel who for this reason calls them scoundrels'—he added a moment later" (6: 123).

Raskolnikov's sensibility has thus now thrown off the grip of the Utilitarian dialectic, which had instantly converted all his previous impulses of compassion into an attitude of contempt. At the same time, the egoistic component of Raskolnikov's character, which had been inflated into megalomania by the "great man" aspect of his doctrine, is no longer held in check by the mirage of serving any moral cause; it operates solely to aid his self-defense and becomes a naked defiance of the law. This is the moment in the book when Dostoevsky brings into play his *coup de maître*—the master stroke of which he had spoken in his notes—and begins to develop Raskolnikov's "Satanical pride" (7: 149), kept subordinate up to this point to his poverty, the initial accentuation of his predominantly altruistic purposes, and the desperate situation of his family: "And then suddenly his [whole] character showed itself in its full demonic strength, and all the reasons and motives for the crime become clear" (7: 90).

This newly prominent feature of his character first emerges in the scene that takes place in the café, ironically called the "Palais de Cristal," where Raskolnikov goes to consult the newspapers in his quest for self-knowledge.* There he stumbles upon the mistrustful police clerk Zametov, who suspects him, and this menace drives him into a towering rage. He cannot resist taunting and baiting Zametov in words calculated to fuel his suspicions even further; and he boasts of being able to commit a crime (the passing of counterfeit bills in a bank) with exactly that state of nerveless self-possession his theory had persuaded him he could preserve. But both he (and the reader) know how dismally he had fallen short of such braggadocio, and his false posturing accentuates the sense of his failure.

For Raskolnikov, his dangerous game with Zametov allows him to relive the crime in miniature; the claim to flawless self-mastery precedes an upsurge of explosive hatred in which he loses control and blurts out a confession—though, recovering an instant later, he pretends only to have been provoking Zametov to admit his suspicions. It is the narrator who compares the challenge to Zametov and the murder by describing Raskolnikov as breaking "into nervous laughter. . . . And in a flash he remembered, with an extraordinary intensity of feeling, another instant not long ago, when he had stood behind a door with an axe, while the bolt rattled, and outside the door people were swearing and trying to force a way in, and he was suddenly filled with a desire to shriek at them, and laugh, laugh, laugh" (6: 126). This momentary flashback, which en-

---

* This name is an ironic allusion to the Crystal Palace of the London World's Fair, built in 1851, which Dostoevsky had visited in the summer of 1862. Extremely innovative from a technological point of view, the huge cast-iron and glass building became a symbol of the luxurious housing to be provided in the Utopian community of the future in Chernyshevsky's novel *What Is To Be Done?* Dostoevsky, in *Winter Notes*, had seen it as an image of the triumph of the flesh-god Baal, "some sort of Biblical illustration, some prophecy of the Apocalypse" (5: 67–70). For more information, see my *Dostoevsky: The Stir of Liberation* (Princeton, N.J., 1986), 238–242.

larges on the briefer notation in the murder scene, starkly illuminates the fierce and totally self-absorbed egoism that had driven Raskolnikov and lights up the true nature of his motivation.

Raskolnikov, however, can sustain such a bellicose attitude only when confronted by a concrete threat to his freedom. Left to himself, and painfully aware of his self-deception, he plunges back into total despair. Overcome by the same sense of icy desolation that had assailed him in the police station, he decides to settle for "the square yard of space," the life of ignominy he had refused to condemn a little while before. Turning his steps toward the police station to confess, he realizes he is passing the tenement in which the crime took place; and his eerily somnambulistic return to the scene of the murder climaxes his compelling need to play detective toward the confused tangle of his own deed. He is "terribly annoyed" that the old wallpaper is being replaced and that "everything was so altered." It is as if he wished to reverse time, or at least arrest its flow, and return to the beginning of what had gone so badly awry (6: 133). His odd behavior arouses suspicion, and he challenges those who question him, in a repetition of his behavior with Zametov, to come with him to the police station. Finally, he sets off alone for the last step; but while still hesitating, in the midst of a world in which "all was dead and silent like the stones on which he walked, dead to him, *to him alone*" (6: 135; italics added), another masterly plot twist occurs, which again reverses the course of the action. His attention is suddenly caught by the commotion of an accident, and he rushes toward it to find the dying Marmeladov crushed by the wheels of a passing carriage.

Raskolnikov leaps to Marmeladov's aid, as he had done earlier with all other victims of misfortune before being inwardly checked, and suddenly finds himself thrust into a world in which his aching need to establish bonds of emotive solidarity can be amply gratified. His crime, intended to benefit humanity, had cut him off from others by an invisible wall; but now he pours all his altruism, unhindered by Utilitarian reconsiderations, into easing (if only momentarily) the terrible lot of the Marmeladovs, whose misery Dostoevsky depicts with a laconic, almost unbearable power. A sharp contrast is also drawn between Raskolnikov's impulse to give them his last penny and the pious platitudes of the priest summoned to perform the rites for the dying, whose ritually consoling words drive the half-crazed and tubercular Katerina Ivanovna into a despairing rage. The gratitude and affection lavished upon Raskolnikov open the floodgates of all his previously suppressed Christian sentiments, and he asks little Polechka, Sonya's half-sister, to "pray for me sometimes: 'and Thy servant, Rodion'—just that" (6: 147). The need for absolution, which he will soon seek through Sonya, is already evident here.

This direct release of Raskolnikov's pent-up Christian emotions leads to a remarkable recovery from hopelessness; and a symbolic contrast, focusing on the image of blood, is deftly introduced to highlight his resurgence. Raskolnikov had been spattered with Marmeladov's blood while helping to carry the body, and the police official Nikodim Fomich remarks, " 'But what is this? You are soaked with blood . . . ' 'Yes I am . . . I've got blood all over me!' said Raskolnikov with a peculiar look; then he smiled, nodded his head, and turned down the stairs" (6: 145). Raskolnikov is indeed "soaked with blood" in another sense, which had left him in a state of abject despair; but the bloodstains of Marmeladov fill him with "a strange, new feeling of boundlessly full and powerful life—a feeling which might be compared with that of a man condemned to death and unexpectedly reprieved" (6: 146).

This new sense of "full and powerful life," it has hardly been noticed, is expressed by Raskolnikov no longer in terms of his previous desire to attain some larger, impersonal, Utilitarian-altruistic goal but solely as a refusal to accept personal defeat. "My life did not die with the old woman. . . . Now comes the reign of reason and light . . . and . . . freedom and power . . . now we shall see" (6: 141). This is the first mention of the concealed relation between "reason" and "power" that had been working on Raskolnikov's psyche all along; but once again Raskolnikov's conscious ideas clash with the emotive forces stirring in his personality. Earlier, he had refused to allow his moral conscience to govern his feelings because Utilitarian reason had demanded its repression; now the renewal of hope that springs from having given free rein to his conscience is used to support a brazenly egoistic self-concern. The contradiction is flagrant, and when Raskolnikov reassures himself "that it was possible to live . . . that his life had not died with the old woman," the narrator is quick to demur: "Perhaps," he remarks, "he had been in too much haste to reach this conclusion, *but of this he did not think*" (6: 147; italics added). The narrator's ominous note is then confirmed by the arrival in Petersburg of Raskolnikov's mother and sister, who bring him back to the agonizing awareness that his horrible secret has cut him off from those he loves the most, and whose plight had contributed to drive him to the fearsome slaughter.

6

The appearance of Raskolnikov's family checks the upsurge of hope he had felt on leaving the Marmeladovs and plunges him back into his desperate solitude. The impossibility of communicating with his mother and sister, the anticipation of their shock and horror if they learned what he had done, the unthinkability of any explanation that might lessen their dismay —all this makes their frightened solicitude unbearable for him, and leads to flashes of hatred for those he loves the most. The meeting between Avdotya Raskolnikova and Razumikhin marks the beginning of a touchingly normal romance (the only one in Dostoevsky's novelistic corpus), which is depicted with a quiet humor. Raskolnikov's vehement objections to his sister's proposed marriage to Luzhin develops the plot parallelism between his situation and that of the Marmeladov family in their dependence on Sonya, and he violently refuses to countenance obtaining any aid for himself through his sister's marriage.

He exhibits no such repugnance, however, in the case of Sonya's aid to her family. Quite the contrary, he introduces her to his mother and sister, and is immensely pleased when Dunya makes a deep and courteous bow to the social outcast. What infuriates him with Dunya, though, is that she pretends not to be making a sacrifice at all but claims to be acting only for self-advantage. "Proud creature! She won't admit that she wants to do it out of charity! Too haughty! . . . They [his mother and sister] even love as if they hate" (6: 170). By this time, Raskolnikov has begun to understand how easily a prideful egoism can begin with love and turn into hate. He thus senses in Dunya, who is constantly compared with him both physically and morally, a more intimately personal incarnation of the dialectic that had led him to catastrophe.

At this point in the text, clearly as a preparation for the full disclosure of the article "On Crime," Dostoevsky begins to fill in those aspects of Raskolnikov's past that help to illuminate his self-identification with the "extraordinary" people. Razumikhin here provides a description of his friend's split personality, which combines "a noble nature and kind heart" with moments when he is "cold and inhumanly callous to the point of inhumanity; it's as though he were alternating between two characters" (6: 165). Such words are often taken as a conveniently handy psychological explanation of the vagaries of Raskolnikov's behavior and of the crime itself. But Razumikhin's description, it should be noted, is carefully limited only to "the last year and a half," that is, exactly the period when Raskolnikov had fallen under the influence of radical ideas. Moreover, even though he had certainly been "egoistic" earlier, we learn in the same conversation that this character trait had not previously determined him to be "inhumanly callous to the point of inhumanity."

Just how his egoism had manifested itself becomes clear when his mother, going farther back into the preradical past, recalls his plan to marry the landlady's daughter—a subplot sometimes considered only a superfluous digression, but in fact of considerable thematic significance. Since Raskolnikov had planned to marry despite "my [his mother's] tears, my entreaties, my illness, my possible death from grief, from poverty," the urge to rescue his family could hardly have been a primary motive (6: 166). His concern for his family had always been subordinate to an immutable egoism of personal self-affirmation; but this egoism, as his abortive romance well shows, had previously been combined with a whole-souled acceptance of Christian values quite the opposite of callous inhumanity. Still, the innate extremism of Raskolnikov's temperament had been evident even in this commitment. The girl, Razumikhin remarks with some perplexity, was "positively ugly . . . and such an invalid . . . and strange" (6: 166). But Raskolnikov explains that " 'she was fond of giving alms to the poor, and was always dreaming of a nunnery. . . . I believe I would have liked her better still if she had been lame or a hunchback' (he smiled dreamily)" (6: 177). These disturbing words indicate a desire to embrace and comfort what others would find repellent, and suggest a desire for self-sacrifice bordering on martyrdom; it is as if Raskolnikov looked on his proposed marriage as some sort of self-exalting as well as morally heroic deed. His conversion to radicalism involved no change in the moral aims of these ambitions and supplied a similar outlet for his egoism; but it inspired a different sort of heroism in terms of Utilitarian principles. Six months after burying his fiancée, with whom, as he tells Dunya, he had argued about his new convictions, he wrote the article expressing this new self-image.

It is now Dr. Zosimov who, in these scenes, takes up the role of hermeneutic commentator. Zosimov tells Raskolnikov's family that "the patient's illness, aside from *his difficult material circumstances* during the last few months," had some moral causes, "was, so to speak, the product of many complex moral and material influences, anxieties, apprehensions, troubles, *certain ideas* . . . and so on" (italics added). Zosimov thus stresses the psychological, nonmaterial causes of Raskolnikov's condition, and he insists that "certainly the patient had some fixed idea, something indicating monomania" (6: 159). To Raskolnikov himself, Zosimov remarks that "it is necessary to eliminate the original, so to speak, radical causes that influenced the onset of your ill condition." He is sure that Raskolnikov knows what these causes are, "because you are an intelligent man and, of course, have observed yourself." Such causes can thus hardly be Raskolnikov's "difficult material circumstances," which are plain for all to see; and Zosimov correctly infers that "the beginning of your disorder to some extent coincides with your leaving the university" (6: 171). This is precisely the moment at which Raskolnikov had written his article "On Crime."

It is against this background that Raskolnikov comes for his first meeting with Porfiry Petrovich, who, as he knows from remarks let drop by Razumikhin, has been "very anxious to make his acquaintance" (6: 189). Porfiry Petrovich takes a distinguished place in the gallery of law enforcers in the nineteenth-century novel and is extremely original as an example of the type. Unlike Poe's Dupin, he is far from being a monster of rationality; nor is he, like Hugo's Javert, a relentless incarnation of the Law. Razumikhin describes him as of a "rather peculiar turn of mind. . . . He is incredulous, skeptical, cynical. He likes to mislead people, or rather to baffle them" (6: 189), and he is very fond of role playing. Once, having purchased a new suit of clothes, he persuaded his friends that he was on the point of getting married; in an argument with the Socialists, he takes their side "simply to make fools of them" (6: 198). One recognizes here an analogue to Dostoevsky's own artistic assumption of radical ideas (through his characters) for the purpose of exposing their catastrophic consequences; and Porfiry's role-playing is very much like that of a novelist, who embodies his own personality in a whole range of characters.

Porfiry is highly cultivated (the very first words he utters include a quotation from Gogol), and, since he has come across Raskolnikov's article and made inquiries about the author, he has obviously been closely following the movement of contemporary ideas. He thus has an understanding of Raskolnikov's cast of mind, which, taken along with everything he has learned from Zametov and others, convinces him that Raskolnikov is the murderer. Even though Razumikhin considers Porfiry to be employing the "old, material method" of criminal investigation, in fact the very opposite is true: he understands that the cause of Raskolnikov's crime is ultimately "psychological" (that is, ideological) and cannot be understood in "material" terms at all.

Indeed, this understanding is conveyed, if somewhat elliptically, in the conversation that precedes the introduction of Raskolnikov's article. Razumikhin has been storming against the Socialists, in his usual tempestuous fashion, because they believe that "crime is a protest against the abnormality of the social organization and nothing more . . . no other causes are admitted! . . . Human nature is not taken into account, it is excluded, it is not supposed to exist! . . . They don't want a living soul!" In his usual provoking manner, Porfiry contradicts Razumikhin by asserting that "'environment' counts for a great deal in crime." When the irate Razumikhin furiously asks if environment can explain "a man of fifty [who] violates a child of ten," Porfiry replies "with noteworthy gravity" that "strictly speaking . . . a crime of that nature can very well be ascribed to the influence of 'environment'" (6: 197). One may take this as just another instance of Porfiry's playacting; but it can also be read as a preparation for the redefinition of "environment" that then follows. For at this juncture, Porfiry turns to Raskolnikov and says: "All these questions about crime, environment, children, recall to my mind an article of yours"—and plunges into his interrogation (6: 198). By this shift of subject, Porfiry turns from the "material" environment—the only one given importance by the Socialists—to, as it were, the social-cultural and "psychological" environment created by such articles as Raskolnikov's and *their* possible effects on a "living soul."*

The dialogue about Raskolnikov's article finally discloses the original Pisarevian complex of ideas to which Raskolnikov had become committed and which, in leading him to believe that he could behave like a "great man," had led to the murders. It is very likely that, on a first reading, the novelty of the information given here overshadows everything else; but rereading enables one to appreciate the many subtle ways in which the moral-psychic *effects* of this doctrine have already been shown at work in Raskolnikov. Porfiry goes to the heart of the matter when he suggests to Raskolnikov, as "a playful, psychological idea," that "when you were writing your article, surely you couldn't have helped, he-he! fancying yourself . . . just a little, an 'extraordinary' man, uttering a *new word* in your sense. . . . That's so, isn't it?" Nor does Raskolnikov deny such a likelihood: " 'Very possibly,' [he] answered contemptuously" (6: 204; italics in text). Porfiry's question thus highlights all the foreshadowing of Part I; but by this time Raskolnikov has become *aware* of his abysmal failure, and his responses to Porfiry reflect this new stage of his development.

When Porfiry sarcastically asks by what signs "extraordinary" people are to be recognized, and whether or not a mistake is possible, Raskolnikov replies with a disconsolate admission: "Quite a number of them [ordinary people] by some freak of nature such as is not impossible even among cows . . . like to fancy that they are progressives, 'destroyers,' and propagators of the 'new word,' and all this quite sincerely" (6: 207). Raskolnikov can by now only be referring to himself with these words, and the effect of such self-recognition is made clear by his response when Porfiry inquires about the "conscience" of those who mistake their category. "Any man who has one [a conscience]," Raskolnikov replies, "must suffer if he is conscious of error. This is his punishment—in addition to hard labor" (6: 203). Razumikhin then wonders why the "real geniuses," those who have the moral right to kill, ought not to suffer some pangs as well over their victims. Although Raskolnikov had once believed them to be entirely immune from such antiquated travails, he now revises his image of "greatness" to take his own torments into account: "Why the word *ought*? . . . He will suffer if he is sorry for his victims. Suffering and pain are always obligatory on those of wide intellect and profound feeling," he says pensively to himself. "Truly great men must, I think, experience a great sorrow on earth" (6: 203).

This is a decidedly new version of "greatness," which is now linked

* It is worth noting that, in this exchange, Porfiry's use of the word "environment" (*sreda*) is twice put into quotation marks, to indicate that for him it has a different sense than the one used by the Socialists and attacked by Razumikhin (6: 197).

with Raskolnikov's primordial Christian sensibility; no longer does greatness consist in the power entirely to wipe out the sufferings of conscience through the wonder-working omnipotence of Utilitarian reason.
But the impossibility of amalgamating the qualms of Christian conscience with Raskolnikov's previous image of "greatness" is revealed in
the very next scene, when he follows a workman in the street who had
been making inquiries about him. "Wearing a long waistcoat and looking
at a distance remarkably like a woman," the workman at first refuses to
answer Raskolnikov's questions and then suddenly blurts out: "murderer" (6: 209). Porfiry's attempt to trick Raskolnikov, by a sudden question, into admitting that he had been in the house on the day of the murders (which would have trapped him in an outright lie) had already
shown him that his guilt was an open secret; and this blunt accusation
strikes the final blow to his tottering self-control.

The thoughts that now flow through his mind in a seemingly disconnected stream, after he sinks down on his couch "with a weak moan of
pain" (6: 210), climax the process of self-confrontation that has been occurring all along; and Raskolnikov's eyes are finally opened to the tragic
antinomy on which he has become impaled. The mystery of the tradesman's knowledge of the murder (which later turns out to be only suspicion) recalls to him the jewelry dropped unawares and how far he had
fallen short of his expectations; but even more, how foolish it had been
for him to believe he could succeed when he continued to cling to the
moral purpose of his intended deed. True great men like Napoleon cared
not a whit about any such purpose, and acted solely out of a supreme
conviction in their right to do whatever they pleased. "No, these men are
not made so. The real *Master* to whom all is permitted storms Toulon,
carries out a massacre in Paris, *forgets* an army in Egypt, *wastes* half a
million men in the Moscow expedition and gets off with a jest at Vilna.
And altars are set up to him after his death, and so *all* is permitted. No,
such people it seems are not of flesh but of bronze!" (6: 211).

Fragmentary ideas now race through Raskolnikov's consciousness as
he lies in a state of "feverish exaltation," at times feeling "that he was
raving" in his delirium. At first calling himself a "louse" because of the
"aesthetic" incongruity between the pettiness of his own deed ("a vile,
withered old woman, a moneylender, with a red box under the bed") and
the grandeur of the figure whose name and destiny had hung before him
like a lodestar ("Napoleon, the pyramids, Waterloo"), Raskolnikov then
repeats the self-accusation for other than "aesthetic" reasons: "I am a
louse, nothing more," he says, "because ... I have been importuning
Providence for a whole month, calling on it to witness that it was not for
my own, so to speak, flesh and lust that I proposed to act but for a noble
and worthy end ... from all the lice on earth I picked absolutely the most
useless, and when I killed her, I intended to take from her exactly as

much as I needed for the first step, neither more nor less." It is the real-ization of *this* incongruity that makes him exclaim: "I killed a principle, but as for surmounting the barriers, I did not do that, I remained on this side" (6: 211). Raskolnikov had killed the "principle" of the old moral law against taking human life; but his very purpose and choice of victim showed that he had not been able "to surmount the barriers." He had attached a moral aim to his desire to achieve "greatness"; he had re-mained a man of flesh, who had failed to become one of bronze.

It is in the midst of these self-lacerations, when Raskolnikov sees clearly for the first time the self-opposing tangle of his Pisarevian pre-cepts, that Dostoevsky chooses to contrast him with the Utopian Social-ist followers of Chernyshevsky. These will soon appear in the caricatural figure of Lebezyatnikov, who shares Raskolnikov's faith in Utilitarian reason and his universally altruistic aims but whose ideology does not contain the *new* egoistic note, so conspicuous in Pisarev, of a Bazarovian need for *personal* self-fulfillment and self-aggrandizement. Raskolnikov thinks to himself:

> Why was that foolish fellow Razumikhin railing at the Socialists just now? They are industrious and business-like people; they work for the "common weal." . . . No, I have only one life given to me, and it will never come again; I do not want to wait for the "common weal." I want to have my own life, or else it's better not to live at all! (6: 211)

Far from any longer being concerned about the "common weal," Ras-kolnikov fiercely envies those strong enough to disregard it entirely. "Oh, how well I understand the 'Prophet' with his sabre on his steed. The 'Prophet' is right . . . when he sets a marv-el-ous battery across a street somewhere, and mows down the innocent and the guilty, without deign-ing to explain! It's for you to obey, trembling creatures and—*do not will*, because—that is not your affair" (6: 211). But Raskolnikov—even though he exclaims to himself, "Ah, how I hate the old woman [the murdered Alyona Ivanovna] now! I feel I should kill her again if she came to life!"—cannot sustain this hostility for very long; and his thoughts modulate into recollections of Lizaveta and Sonya ("poor, gentle things, with gen-tle eyes"). His inner struggle then terminates in the dream (drawing on details from Hugo's *Le dernier jour d'un condamné*) that ends Part III, in which he unsuccessfully tries to rid himself of the ghost of his victim. Fearfully reliving the moment of the murder, he tries to kill Alyona Iva-novna again but finds her impervious to his blows. Huddled in a chair, with her head drooping and face concealed, she was "overcome with noiseless laughter" and simply "shook with mirth" (6: 213) as he redou-bled his blows. He had murdered her in the flesh but not in his spirit, and she continues to haunt his conscience. He had failed to become one of the "great men" who had gone beyond good and evil altogether.

7
_____

Dostoevsky is a master in the art of arousing interest and suspense by the early, fleeting evocation of characters who then enter the main action only at a later moment in the narrative. This time-tested device, like many others from popular fiction, is not used in his work solely for external effect, however, but is most often given a solid thematic significance. Svidrigailov thus emerges from the shadows at the beginning of Part IV, when Raskolnikov has finally glimpsed the incongruity of attempting to place an all-powerful egoism into the service of moral ends. Materializing in Raskolnikov's room almost as if part of the dream repetition of the murder, Svidrigailov seems to be an apparition; and Raskolnikov asks Razumikhin whether the latter had actually *seen* Svidrigailov in the flesh. Nothing similar had occurred in the case of Luzhin; and Svidrigailov's emergence from, as it were, Raskolnikov's subconscious suggests that he stems from a more deeply rooted level of Raskolnikov's personality than Luzhin, who embodies his ideas. Svidrigailov mirrors the elemental thrust of that egoism which, concentrated in Raskolnikov's monomania, had ultimately led to the murders; and he now confronts Raskolnikov as someone who has *accepted* the thoroughgoing egoistic amorality which, as Raskolnikov now has begun to realize, he had unwittingly been striving to incarnate himself.

One of Dostoevsky's most strangely appealing characters, a sort of monster à la Quasimodo longing for redemption to normalcy, Svidrigailov is much less a melodramatic villain than his predecessor, Prince Valkovsky. His Byronic world-weariness signifies a certain spiritual depth, and the contradictions of his personality, which swing between the blackest evil and the most benevolent good, perhaps can best be understood in Byronic terms. Is he not similar to such a figure as Byron's Lara, in the poem of the same name, "who at last confounded good and ill," and whose supreme indifference to their distinction made him equally capable of both? One can well say of Svidrigailov:

> Too high for common selfishness, he could
> At times resign his own for other's good,
> But not in pity, not because he ought,
> But in some strange perversity of thought,
> That sway'd him onward with a secret pride
> To do what few or more would do beside;
> And thus some impulse would, in tempting time,
> Mislead his spirit equally to crime.[8]

Svidrigailov thus embodies the same mixture of moral-psychic opposites as Raskolnikov, but arranged in a different order of dominance. What rules within him is the conscious acceptance of an unrestrained egoism acting solely in the pursuit of personal and sensual pleasure; but his enjoyments are tarnished by self-disgust. What dominates in Raskolnikov are the pangs and power of conscience even in the midst of a fiercely egoistic struggle to maintain his freedom. Svidrigailov also resembles Raskolnikov in the sophistication and sharpness of his intellect; he is a brilliant and witty talker who does a great deal to enliven the final sections of the book.

Nominally, Svidrigailov arrives in Petersburg in hot pursuit of Dunya; but though he pretends to be driven only by the pleasure of sensual passion ("something present in the blood, like an ever-burning ember, forever setting one on fire"), his desire for Dunya, whatever it may have been initially, has now become a quest for personal salvation (6: 359). The plot parallelism with Raskolnikov-Sonya is obvious, and could hardly have been carried through if Svidrigailov had been a less complex character. The disabling workings of *his* self-disgust may be gathered from his picture of eternity as a little room, "something like a bathhouse in the country, black with soot, with spiders in every corner.... I sometimes imagine it like that, you know," he confesses to Raskolnikov. When the latter, "with a feeling of anguish," protests that he might imagine something "juster and more comforting than that," Svidrigailov only responds that perhaps this would be just, "and, do you know, it's what I would certainly have made it deliberately!" (6: 221). For all his assumed moral insensibility, Svidrigailov is unable to escape a sense of self-revulsion, which he wishes to extend to humanity as a whole.

Dostoevsky, however, reserves the full deployment of the Raskolnikov-Svidrigailov relation for a later thematic stage. The torments of his unbearable moral-social isolation have already been eased for Raskolnikov by his second encounter with the Marmeladov family, and he hopes to continue to find relief and support through Sonya. As yet, however, he does not seek only pity and forgiveness from her, but adopts the attitude already suggested in his dialogue with Porfiry. He sees himself as someone who, like Sonya, has taken on the burden of suffering to aid a humanity trapped in helpless misery; and he thus tries to bring her round to regarding *his* crime as identical with *her* pathetic infringement of conventional morality. Dostoevsky manages to capture Sonya's innocence in the midst of degradation, her gaucherie and burning purity of religious faith, with a remarkable surety of touch. What she offers to Raskolnikov is an unsullied image of the self-sacrificing Christian love that had once also stirred him to his depths. She is the *existential reality* of that love for suffering mankind which, when amalgamated with the Utilitarian reason of radical ideology, had become perverted into the monstrosities of his crime.

In the marvelous scenes between the two, Raskolnikov clearly reveals his desire to embellish his own deed with the halo of Christian self-sacrifice. This is what makes him so susceptible to "the sort of *insatiable* compassion . . . reflected in every feature of her [Sonya's] face"; it is what throws him on his knees to kiss her feet "because of your great suffering" (6: 243, 246). But even as he yields in this way to her example, the unalloyed faith of Sonya does not fail to arouse his educated scorn. When he learns that she and his victim Lizaveta had met to read the New Testament together (as was frequently done by groups of the *raskolniki*, the Old Believers), he calls them *yurodivie* (holy fools, usually considered simpleminded, if not demented) but finds himself irresistibly drawn to their unshakable faith in God's ultimate goodness—the faith that, against all reason, miraculously supports Sonya in the midst of vice as she struggles to help the deranged Katerina Ivanovna and the starving children.

Under the effect of this emotion, Raskolnikov thinks sarcastically: "I shall become one [a *yurodivi*] myself here. It's catching"; and it is then that he commands Sonya to read from the copy of the New Testament given her by Lizaveta (6: 249). What he wishes to hear is the passage from the Gospel of Saint John narrating the resurrection of Lazarus, which symbolically holds out the possibility of his own moral resurrection. In pages that have evoked a mountain of commentary, Dostoevsky depicts, with the bleakly reverential simplicity of a Rembrandt etching, "the candle end [that] had long since burnt low in the twisted candlestick, dimly lighting the poverty-stricken room and the murderer and the harlot [*bludnitsa*], who had come together so strangely to read the eternal book" (6: 251–252). Dostoevsky is careful to use the Church Slavonic word *bludnitsa*, rather than a more colloquial one, and thus associates Sonya with Mary Magdalene as Raskolnikov blends with Lazarus. Nowhere perhaps do we come closer to Dostoevsky's own tortuously anguished relation to religious faith than in the mixture of involuntary awe and self-conscious skepticism with which Raskolnikov reacts to Sonya. But the moment he shakes off the emotions stirred by the Gospel reading, the clash of values between the two recommences.

Raskolnikov appeals to Sonya because it is only she to whom he can reveal the truth—because she too is a flagrant sinner and has become an outcast in the eyes of society. It is she, and not his uprightly virtuous family clinging to their self-respect, who might be able to accept him without shock and horror, and even sympathize with his purpose, if not its results. "You too have stepped over the barriers . . . you were able to overstep!" he says to Sonya (6: 252). But exactly the opposite is true: Raskolnikov had not been able to "step over" because he had still clung to moral conscience; Sonya had violated the moral law totally against her will and desire. For all her debasement, Sonya is not inwardly torn because her sin has been redeemed by the purity of her *self*-sacrifice. It is this difference that Raskolnikov desperately tries to wipe away when he says, with wonderful sophistry, "you have laid hands on yourself, you destroyed a life . . . *your own* (it's all the same)!" (ibid.). With a grandeur equaling that of *Antigone*, in which the law of the family and the gods clashes with that of the state and *Realpolitik*, Dostoevsky here depicts the conflict between the intransigent imperatives of Christian love and the demand for a more equitable social justice. On the one side, there is the ethic of Christian *agape*, the total, immediate, and unconditional sacrifice of self that is the law of Sonya's being (and Dostoevsky's own highest value); on the other, Raskolnikov's rational Utilitarian ethic, which justifies the sacrifice of *others* for the sake of a greater social good.*

Raskolnikov's attitude in this scene, in which he asks Sonya to link her fate with his ("so we must go together, by the same path!") is an inconsistent admixture reflecting a new phase of his moral-psychic struggle. After undermining Sonya's hope that God will protect little Polechka from Sonya's fate ("'but, perhaps, there is no God at all,'" Raskolnikov had said "with a sort of malignance"), he illustrates the awfulness of this prospect by referring to children as "the image of Christ" and citing the Gospel: "Theirs is the Kingdom of Heaven." When the hysterically weeping Sonya, wringing her hands, asks, "What then must we do?" he replies: "Demolish what must be demolished, once and for all, *and take the suffering on ourselves*" (6: 252–253; italics added). This assumption of suffering, however, is immediately countered by a more despotic assertion of egoism than any he has yet consciously uttered so far: "What? Don't you understand? . . . Freedom and power, but above all, power! Power over all the trembling creatures, over the ant-heap . . . that's the goal!" he tells the bewildered Sonya (6: 253). With this phrase—"above all, power"—he involuntarily reveals the truth about himself that has begun to pierce through to his consciousness.

---

* Just how conscious Dostoevsky was of this theme of *agape*—the theological term for a limitless, spontaneous, unquestioning, self-sacrificing Christian love—is revealed in a minor episode. Sonya, who provides the moral standard of the novel, never blames herself for being a prostitute, which is her only possible way of practicing *agape* in relation to her family; but she bitterly regrets having failed to give Katerina Ivanovna some cuffs that she had bought ("pretty, new, embroidered") to adorn herself. Katerina had asked to be given them ("'Please do,' she said, she wanted them so much"). But Sonya refused with the chilling Utilitarian question, "What use are they to you, Katerina Ivanovna?" and had never forgiven herself for this betrayal of *agape*, this chance to give the dying woman a moment of happiness (6: 245).

The importance of this little-noted incident is stressed in Dostoevsky's notes, in which, when Sonya says "I am a great sinner," Raskolnikov thinks she is talking about her prostitution. But she replies: "'*I am not speaking of that* . . . but I have sinned against love many times' and she narrates here a story—write it well (touchingly) how once Mrs. Marmeladova, humiliated and downtrodden, had taken a liking to an embroidered collar of hers, and had asked for it; but Sonya had not given it to her. . . . Now if she only had the collar and if she were to ask for it, she would give it to her; she would give everything to her. . . . N.B. Create all this" (7: 135).

The scenes with Sonya alternate with equally brilliant ones involving Porfiry, who, on Raskolnikov's second visit, again provokes and torments him with slyly mocking insinuations. His words indicate that he knows all about Raskolnikov's suspicious movements and behavior and considers him the murderer. But he continues to treat his suspect as a personal acquaintance, almost a friend, and professes great concern about the state of his nerves and the frenetic agitation he exhibits in response to double-edged intimations. Porfiry's own tactics are revealed when he professionally explains to Raskolnikov, as a student of the law interested in such matters, that the best method of investigation is to play on the suspect's nerves: "but let him know or at least suspect every moment that I know all about it and am watching him day and night, and if he is consciously in continual suspicion and terror, he'll be bound to lose his head" (6: 261). Porfiry's strategy is nothing if not "psychological," and he sums up Raskolnikov's situation when he remarks, "you, my dear Rodion Romanovich, are still a young man ... and therefore you esteem the human intellect above all things, like all young people." To which he adds: "reality and human nature, sir, are very important things, and oh how they sometimes bring down the most perspicacious calculations!" (6: 263).

With a fine irony, Dostoevsky shows Porfiry's words applying not only to Raskolnikov but also to his own intended "surprise." His "perspicacious calculation" had been to work Raskolnikov up to a pitch of nervous frenzy and then confront him with the workman who had called him "murderer." Under this shock, Raskolnikov's already jangled nerves might have collapsed entirely. Instead, the house painter Nikolay erupts into Porfiry's chambers and, also for "psychological" reasons, confesses to the murders. Nikolay is carefully characterized as a religious *raskolnik* who has been tormenting himself because of his accidental connection with the crime. His misadventures with the jewels and his arrest had only deepened a sense of sinfulness brought on by exposure to the unfamiliar temptations of urban life, and, deciding to take "suffering" on himself in an *imitatio Christi*, he falsely confesses.

Nikolay's confession, which seems to exonerate Raskolnikov once and for all, allows Dostoevsky to shift his attention to various subplots for several chapters; and he relieves the tension somewhat by furnishing comic and tragi-comic variations on his major theme. The ridiculous mediocrity Lebezyatnikov mouths the Utopian Socialist platitudes of the early 1860s, which had been largely absorbed into, and replaced by, the ideas expressed through Raskolnikov. But even though sharply caricatured, Lebezyatnikov is still depicted with a certain sympathy. Like Raskolnikov, his immediately humane responses to concrete situations contradict his rational Utilitarian principles, and he plays a crucial part in unmasking Luzhin's despicable attempt to turn Sonya into a thief. The scandal scene at the wake following Marmeladov's funeral turns into a ludicrous but sadly grotesque contest of wills between the haughty Katerina Ivanovna, desperately clinging to her last shred of prideful status, and the outraged German landlady. Egoism is not confined to the likes of Raskolnikov, Luzhin, and Svidrigailov, and it brings on a tragicomic squabble over a social prestige equally nonexistent on both sides: the furious Russian insists that her father was a governor while the irate German promotes *her* father to the exalted rank of *Burgomeister*.

The culmination of the scandal scene also prepares the way for an intensification of the moral confrontation between Sonya and Raskolnikov at their next meeting, which follows hard on the rowdy commemoration. Luzhin, attempting to frame Sonya by secretly slipping money into her pocket, had accused her of theft; and Raskolnikov seizes on this incident as an additional self-justification. If Sonya had the choice, would she, he asks, decide that "Luzhin should live and commit abomination," even if this meant "the ruin of Katerina Ivanovna and the children"? To which the distraught Sonya can only reply, with the instinctive penetration of uncorrupted moral feeling: "But I can't know God's intentions. . . . how could it depend on my decision. . . . Who made me a judge of who shall live and who shall not?" (6: 313). With an artistry that cannot be too highly praised, Dostoevsky manages, without a false note, to portray the uneducated Sonya countering Raskolnikov with the argument that no puny human could arrogate to herself the power over human life traditionally exercised solely by God.

This reply is the prelude to Raskolnikov's final confession, which he makes to Sonya while alternating between feelings of hatred and love—hatred because he is exposing himself to her judgment, love because what he encounters in her eyes is only "a look of anxiety and anguished care." And when she finally comprehends the truth, which he is unable to bring out in words, her first reaction, after a childlike fear reminiscent of Lizaveta as he approached with his axe, is to throw herself into his arms and exclaim, with a total identification: "'What have you done, what have you done to yourself? . . . There is no one, no one, unhappier than you in the whole world' . . . and suddenly she broke into hysterical sobbing" (6: 376). But when Sonya promises to follow him to prison, he recoils, "and the same hostile, almost mocking smile played on his lips. 'Perhaps, Sonya, I don't mean to go to prison yet,' he said." The narrator, now fused with Sonya (here and throughout this scene), remarks: "In his changed tone she suddenly heard the voice of the murderer." This is the voice of Raskolnikov's egoism, the "Satanic pride" released in his personality first by his ideas and then through the crime and its aftermath (6: 316–317).

The admission of the murder itself is only the beginning of this great scene. Raskolnikov's struggle to explain the cause of his crime not only to Sonya but, more importantly, to himself equals in poetic force some of the final soliloquies of Shakespeare. Those who maintain, like Philip Rahv, that even after this scene "we are still left with a crime of indeterminate origin and meaning" simply refuse to read it in the context of the book as a whole.[9] Raskolnikov knows by this time that all the reasons for the crime he had previously given himself are false; and we have seen his dawning awareness of the clash between his assumed moral purpose and the purely egoistic qualities of personality that the idea of his crime had encouraged uninhibitedly to come to the fore. But, in the midst of his torments and his struggles, he had never paused to answer the question he had raised when concealing the loot from the murders. Now, faced with giving an account of himself to Sonya, he gropingly tries to break through to some sort of self-understanding.

When Sonya, drawing on her own life, speaks of "poverty," his recollection of burying the money recurs, and he says emphatically, "if I'd simply killed her because I was hungry, ... I should be *happy* now" (6: 318). But the reasons he then offers (the needs of his family and his desire to "start a new career and enter on a life of independence") all remain on this same rational, common-sense level of material need. Even when he says, "I wanted to become a Napoleon," he imagines Napoleon asking himself whether he should murder "some ridiculous old hag, a pawnbroker . . . to get money from her trunk (for his career, you understand)" (6: 319). In fact, though Raskolnikov had indeed dreamed this Napoleonic dream, it was not at all to obtain money "for his career" in any personally self-serving sense, or to come to the aid of his mother and sister. Sonya instinctively refuses to accept any of these proffered explanations, and Raskolnikov finally admits himself that "I am lying, Sonya. . . . I've been lying for a long time. . . . There are quite different reasons here, quite, quite different!" (6: 320).

Up to this point Raskolnikov has been speaking with a certain sadness and a touch of self-mockery, "as though it were a lesson" (6: 319). But now "his eyes shone with a feverish brilliance," and "he was almost delirious; an uneasy smile strayed on his lips. His terrible exhaustion could be seen through his excitement" (6: 320). Raskolnikov is sinking back into his illness and the pathological state of mind it had created; he is reliving the monomania to which he had become a prey, and this leads him to sketch a portrait of himself at last conforming to the image given in Part I. Now he diagnoses the moral-psychological effects of his "great man" obsession, the *willful* manner in which he had worsened his material circumstances ("I didn't go out for days together, and I wouldn't work, I wouldn't even eat, I just lay there doing nothing"), and the resulting transformation of his personality so that sympathy and compassion changed to contempt and hate: "And I know now, Sonya, that whoever is great in mind and spirit will have power over them [the "ordinary" people]. Anyone who is greatly daring is right in their eyes." Identifying with Sonya again to reinforce Raskolnikov's words, the narrator comments: "Sonya felt that this gloomy catechism had become his faith and his credo" (6: 320–321).

Raskolnikov, however, had not accepted previously that might alone could make right, and he is formulating here what he had come to understand through his own sense of failure. He knows very well that this "credo" had not been his point of departure; and so he shifts, with self-tormenting sarcasm, to a description of the inner struggle with his conscience, whose values he still believed he was obeying even as he contemplated murder: "And don't suppose that I went into it headlong like a fool! I went into it like a wise man, and that was just my destruction." It was just because he was assailed by the question of whether "I had the right to gain power—I certainly hadn't the right," or "whether a human being is a louse," that his failure became inevitable. "If I worried myself all those days, wondering whether Napoleon would have done it or not, it means I must have felt clearly that I wasn't Napoleon" (6: 311).

It was "the agony of that battle of ideas" that impelled Raskolnikov finally to throw it off entirely. With the wisdom of hindsight, he breaks through to a comprehension of the compulsion that had been at work in and through his monomania: "I wanted to murder *without casuistry*, to murder for my own sake, for myself alone!" (italics added). And Raskolnikov then sweeps away any and every motivation except the testing of his own strength: "I didn't murder either to gain wealth or to become a benefactor of mankind. Nonsense! I just murdered . . . and whether I became a benefactor to others, or spent my life like a spider catching everyone in my web and sucking the life out of others, *must have been of no concern to me at that moment . . . I know it all now*" (italics added). Raskolnikov's real aim was solely to test "whether I was a louse like everyone else or a man. . . . Whether I am a trembling creature or whether I have the *right*" (6: 321–322). With these climactic words, Raskolnikov's understanding finally coincides with what has long since been dramatically conveyed by Dostoevsky.

This act of self-recognition, however, does not persuade Raskolnikov to accept Sonya's injunction to "go at once, this very minute, stand at the crossroads, bow down, first kiss the earth which you have defiled and then bow down to all the world and say to all men aloud, 'I have killed!'" (6: 322). Quite the contrary, even though acknowledging the pure egoism that had motivated him "at that moment," he refuses to imagine surrendering to the legal authorities, who themselves represent for him the same amoral egoism operating on a vastly larger scale. The very self-contradictory nature of the forces motivating Raskolnikov, of which he has only just become fully aware, would humiliate him further in the eyes of the law. "'And what should I say to them—that I murdered her, but did not dare to take the money and hid it under a stone?' he added with a bitter smile. 'Why, they would laugh at me, and would call me a fool for not getting it. A coward and a fool!'" (6: 323). Raskolnikov thus decides to continue to fight for his freedom.

Part V ends with the painfully sublime scene of the death of Katerina Ivanovna, one of the most genuinely heartrending in the entire nineteenth-century novel. Sonya had described her as someone "whose mind is quite unhinged," but who "is seeking righteousness, she is pure. She has such faith that there must be righteousness everywhere and she expects it" (6: 243). Driven to desperation after being evicted from her room by the irate German landlady, she rushes into the street with her children, forcing them to sing and dance as street performers in her determination to shame the world into "righteousness." "And that general [who had discharged the drunken Marmeladov] will lose his post, you'll see! We shall perform under his windows every day, and if the Tsar drives by, I'll fall on my knees, put the children before me, show them to him, and say, 'Defend us, father.' He is the father of the fatherless, he is merciful, he'll protect us, you'll see" (6: 329). Katerina Ivanovna, in her defiant and demented way, is an analogue of Raskolnikov, and her crazed hopes have the effect of softening the atrocity of his guilt. Even if misguided, there is no doubt that he had initially wished to provide the world with some of the "righteousness" that Katerina Ivanovna was so vainly and frenziedly seeking.

8

Raskolnikov's confession to Sonya climaxes his quest for knowledge about himself. From this point on, the action of the novel is oriented toward the future rather than toward uncovering the meaning of the past, and its thematic structure is well defined in Dostoevsky's notebooks: "Svidrigailov—the most desperate cynicism. Sonya—the most unrealizable hope. (It is Raskolnikov himself who must express this.) He has passionately attached himself to both" (7: 204). These are the two alternatives between which he oscillates, knowing that Svidrigailov, who eavesdropped on his confession to Sonya, is privy to his secret. Both are aware that he is a murderer, and each, in effect, indicates an opposing path along which he can choose to decide his fate. At last aware that he had unknowingly killed only as an egoistic test of strength, Raskolnikov is linked to Svidrigailov by this self-discovery; his own ideas have led him to the same result as Svidrigailov's unalloyed cynicism. But, at the same time, it is impossible for him to accept such cynicism with Svidrigailov's casual complacency and seeming indifference.

Sonya, while waiting to share his fate, can only imagine the future as being his voluntary acceptance of punishment. Her pleas are reinforced by Porfiry Petrovich, who, in his final interview with Raskolnikov, speaks frankly and openly instead of with the mocking hostility intended to provoke his suspect into self-betrayal. After the two interviews in which he tried to break down the arrogance so evident in Raskolnikov's article, Porfiry had come to understand his character better and to take pity on the gifted young man, whose terrible crime, as he had come to understand through all the manifestations of his psychic disarray, had hardly been the deed of a callous or unredeemable malefactor. "I regard you," he assures Raskolnikov, "as a man of noble character and not without rudiments of magnanimity, though I don't agree with all your convictions" (6: 344). Raskolnikov notes, at the beginning of their talk, that "a serious and careworn look came into his [Porfiry's] face; to his surprise Raskolnikov saw it covered by sadness. He had never as yet seen and never suspected such an expression in his face" (6: 343). Porfiry's "sadness" may well be taken as that of the author himself, contemplating with melancholy a new, youthful incarnation of the revolutionary illusions that had once sent *him* to Siberia. Such a supposition can find support in the striking sense of identification with Raskolnikov that Porfiry expresses, as if he too had experienced the very same temptations ("I, too, have felt these feelings so that your article seemed familiar to me"); and he identifies Raskolnikov's mood at the time of writing his article with a garbled citation from Gogol's *Diary of a Madman*, a work that had profoundly influenced the young Dostoevsky (6: 345).

However that may be, Porfiry's speech, with its penetrating analysis of the "psychology" of Nikolay, also serves to bring out both the social-cultural contrast, as well as the similarity in extremism, between the radical intellectual Raskolnikov and the peasant sectarian Nikolay, who comes from a family of *beguny* (Wanderers or Runners, convinced that the world was in the grip of Antichrist). Not long before, Nikolay had been under the spiritual guidance of an elder (*staretz*) for two years, "was full of fervor, prayed at night, read the old books, the 'true ones,' and read himself crazy" (6: 347). Raskolnikov, too, it might be said, had "read himself crazy"; but Nikolay is ready to accept suffering to atone for his own sinfulness and that of the world, while Raskolnikov, though enduring agonies of conscience, still cannot bring himself to follow its injunctions. This is why, as Porfiry declares, his crime "is a fantastic, gloomy business, a modern case, an incident of today when the heart of man is troubled. . . . Here we have bookish dreams, a heart unhinged by theories." Here we have "a murderer [who] looks upon himself as an honest man, despises others, poses as a pale angel" (6: 348). Raskolnikov himself is the murderer, Porfiry affirms softly, and urges him to confess voluntarily under the best possible conditions—that is, so as to free an innocent man and thus obtain the goodwill and leniency of the court. Besides, Porfiry informs Raskolnikov, he has found a piece of material evidence (though whether this is true never becomes known) and plans to arrest him in a few days.

In this final section, Raskolnikov's attention turns toward Svidrigailov. Dostoevsky provides ample reason in the plot intrigue to justify Raskolnikov's involvement with the libertine (whose knowledge of Raskolnikov's guilt may allow him to blackmail Dunya, and so on), but the relation between the two has a subtler ideological-thematic connection. Svidrigailov's past is wrapped in a cloud of atrocious rumors, and he was, as Raskolnikov concludes, "a very unpleasant man, evidently depraved, undoubtedly cunning and deceitful, possibly malignant" (6: 354). Raskolnikov refuses to see any connection between Svidrigailov's sinister past and his own crimes, and believes—what is of course true—that "their very evil-doing is not of the same kind" (ibid.). All the same, we see him "hastening to Svidrigailov" and somehow "expecting something *new* from him, directions, a way out" (ibid.). Svidrigailov, after all, is the only person who knows that Raskolnikov is guilty and has not urged him to confess; indeed, he seems completely unconcerned, amused rather than shocked, and it is through this total cynicism that Raskolnikov feels he might perhaps offer "a way out."

The encounter between the two provides the first great example of Dostoevsky's dialogues in a tavern, which, begun rather limply in *The Insulted and Injured*, will reappear in *A Raw Youth* and *The Brothers Karamazov*. The use of such a sordid setting, whose shabby and disreputable aspect is always accentuated, allows him to obtain a titillating effect of dissonance between the squalidness of the environment and the seriousness and importance of the ideas being debated. Under the influence of champagne, Svidrigailov reminisces about his criminally libertine past, and the morally fastidious Raskolnikov cannot help being shocked. But when he asks, "Have you lost the strength to stop yourself?" Svidrigailov justly retorts that Raskolnikov is hardly in a position to set up as a moral arbiter: "You preach to me about vice and aesthetics. You—a Schiller, you—an idealist! Of course that's all as it should be and it would be surprising if it were not so, yet it is strange in reality" (6: 362).

For all his assumed indifference to morality, however, Svidrigailov has reached a state of boredom relieved only by sensuality; but now vice too has begun to pall, and the withering tedium of metaphysical *ennui* thus threatens Svidrigailov with self-destruction. He cherishes the secret hope of finding redemption through Dunya, who had not been unresponsive to his advances;* but the final scene between them, after he entraps her into coming to his quarters, plays out the somewhat melodramatic dénouement of their subplot and brings him to the realization that her conquest is impossible. Moved by her refusal to shoot him in cold blood after missing twice, he gains control over himself sufficiently to allow her to leave unmolested. His rebuff at the hands of Dunya snaps the last thread attaching Svidrigailov to existence, and this scene is shortly followed by his suicide.

Before taking his life, however, he continues, as he has already done, to make financial arrangements ensuring the future of the Marmeladov children and of Sonya. Svidrigailov's generosity has appeared inconsistent to some commentators; but as the passage from Byron has already suggested, Svidrigailov's total amoralism makes him *equally* capable of good and evil, and he certainly took a "secret pride" in confounding the image held of him by others. When he had earlier offered Raskolnikov a gift of ten thousand rubles for Dunya, to rescue her from Luzhin, he remarked, in an ironic paraphrase of Goethe's Mephistopheles, that he was acting only "on the basis that I do not really claim the privilege of doing nothing but harm" (6: 223). But while rejecting such a criticism of Svidrigailov, we must level another and more important one. The munificence of Svidrigailov disposes much too facilely of all the social misery that Dostoevsky has so unflinchingly depicted, and to sweep it away only through Svidrigailov's caprices causes a serious thematic imbalance that cannot be overlooked.

Svidrigailov's last hours are described in some of the most evocatively dreary pages that Dostoevsky ever wrote. First attempting to amuse himself in a shabby "pleasure garden," he takes refuge in a sordid hotel as a thunderstorm breaks, while in the city, threatened by flooding, he foresees that "the cellar rats will come to the surface" (6: 392). The "cellar rats" of his own past swim out of his subconscious in various dreams, one of which evokes the funeral bier of a young girl who had drowned herself, "crushed by an insult that had appalled and amazed that childish soul . . . and torn from her a last scream of despair" (6: 391). In another dream, he comes across a young girl "not more than five years old," shivering and soaked to the skin. Taking her back to his room, he puts her to bed wrapped in his blanket and, before leaving, turns to see if she is asleep. She smiles at him, but "there was something shameless, provoca-

---

* Svidrigailov's description of how he countered her protests against seducing the peasant girls on the estate recalls the tactics used by Valmont in *Les Liaisons dangereuses* to overcome the virtuous Mme de Tourvel. "I, of course, threw it all on my destiny, posed as hungering and thirsting for light, and finally resorted to the most powerful weapon in the subjection of the female heart, a weapon which never fails one. It's the well-known resource—flattery" (6: 366).

tive in that quite childish face; it was depravity, it was not the face of a child but that of a shameless French harlot. . . . 'What, at five years old?' Svidrigailov muttered in genuine horror"—and then awakes (6: 393). For him there is no natural innocence left in the world; everything he touches turns into the corruption of unashamed vice. With this awareness of his living damnation, Svidrigailov shoots himself before the astonished eyes of a Jewish fireman, incongruously wearing the standard "Achilles helmet" of his uniform.

Svidrigailov's mockingly provocative account of his sexual philanderings had revolted Raskolnikov to the very roots of his being; and his well-aimed sneers at Raskolnikov's reproaches had brought home to the murderer that he had lost any right to distinguish himself morally from his shameless interlocutor. How could he convincingly oppose the ravages of Svidrigailov's unrestrained libido when his own ego had equally refused to recognize any moral limits? Raskolnikov thus realizes that he cannot follow *this* degrading path, which leads to the depths plumbed by Svidrigailov, and decides instead to yield to Sonya's entreaties and take Porfiry's advice. Before doing so, he goes to his mother for a last farewell. She blesses him with the sign of the cross, and "for the first time after all these awful months his heart was softened. He fell down before her, he kissed her feet, and both wept, embracing" (6: 397). There is bitter irony as she tells him that she has read his article three times, is now convinced that he will have a brilliant intellectual career, and, speaking of his strange behavior, says of the article: "that's the solution of the mystery!" (6: 395). Indeed it is, though in a fashion that she is quite incapable of comprehending.

With Dunya, however, there is a last flare-up of Raskolnikov's pride, and he rebels against acknowledging that he has committed any "crime" at all. What he has learned from his failure is only his own weakness, his own inability to subdue his conscience *completely* and place it in the service of his "idea." But his own failure was not a refutation of this "idea," in which he still could not see any logical flaw; there was no reason why a true "great man," untroubled and secure in his absolute right to overstep existing moral bounds, could not *also* be a "benefactor of mankind." "I too wished to do good and would have done hundreds, thousands of good deeds to make up for this one piece of stupidity." His failure was a purely personal one: "but I . . . I couldn't carry out even the first step, because I am contemptible, that's what's the matter. He had placed himself in the wrong category, and this has nothing to do with the validity or justice of his unshaken beliefs (6: 400). Dostoevsky will return to cope with this contention in the Epilogue.

In the final chapter, Raskolnikov goes to Sonya to accept Lizaveta's cross from her, and the tangle of his feelings is indicated in the implicit

2. The Haymarket, St. Petersburg

reproach of his words and his wonder at her grief. "You wanted me to go yourself," he says. "Well, now I am going to prison you'll have your wish." But then, seeing her tears, "his feeling was stirred; his heart ached, as he looked at her. . . . 'What am I to her? Why does she weep?'" (6: 403). Raskolnikov bows down and kisses the earth at the Haymarket, as Sonya had admonished, in a gesture of repentance typical of the *raskolniki*, only to be met with the laughter and jeers of people who think he is either drunk or about to embark as a pilgrim for the Holy Land. Then he goes to confess to Lieutenant Gunpowder, unwilling to accept the humiliation of surrendering to Porfiry, and hears, in the midst of a friendly flow of chatter about various radical fads, that Svidrigailov had killed himself the night before. Raskolnikov is so overcome that he stumbles out into the courtyard without saying a word; but there stood Sonya, on her face "a look of poignant agony, of despair" (6: 409), and he returns to make the confession. His fate and that of Svidrigailov, whose pitiful demise has been so superbly depicted outside of Raskolnikov's purview, thus form a continuous parallel up to the very end.

9

In accordance with the tradition of the nineteenth-century novel, Dostoevsky provides an Epilogue in which the lives of his main characters are followed beyond the limits of the plot action, which here culminates in Raskolnikov's confession. Many features of *Crime and Punishment* have been disputed over the years, but none has been more vigorously condemned than this Epilogue, which a majority of influential commentators have rejected as seriously flawed. Much of this censure, however, seems to me wide of the mark because it focuses too exclusively on the question of Raskolnikov's "conversion." As a result, no attention has been paid to the quite essential thematic function that the Epilogue actually performs.

It has been too easily assumed that the main aim of the Epilogue is to provide a reassuring outlook on Raskolnikov's future; in fact its purpose is to offer an authorial perspective on the major thematic issues that, Dostoevsky felt, required either reinforcement or completion. One such issue is the decisive role that must be ascribed to the effect of Raskolnikov's ideas on his psyche. These ideas, in bringing on his monomania, had ultimately provided the motivating force for the crime; and the Epilogue points once again to their centrality. Another issue is the gap that still exists between the moral-psychic emotions that led Raskolnikov to confess and his continued belief that his ideas, whatever his own personal defeat, have not been invalidated.

The Epilogue leaps ahead to a year and a half after the crime, when Raskolnikov already had been in a Siberian prison camp for nine months. But the narrator immediately returns to the time of the trial, which followed hard on the heels of Raskolnikov's admission of guilt. "There had been," we are told, "little difficulty about his trial," at which Raskolnikov explained all the circumstances and events very clearly. The court, however, found it incredible that he had not looked into the purse he had taken, and wondered why he should lie on this minor point; but "finally some of the lawyers more versed in psychology" admitted that this declaration could be true. From which recognition "they immediately drew the deduction that the crime could only have been committed as a result of temporary mental derangement, through homicidal mania, without object of purpose or gain. This fell in with the most recent fashionable theory of temporary insanity, so often applied in our day to criminal cases." Even more, the defendant's psychopathic condition was amply confirmed and "led strongly to the conclusion that Raskolnikov was not quite like an ordinary murderer and robber, but that *there was another element in the case*" (6: 410–411; italics added). The irony of this last phrase should by now be obvious. The other "element in the case," which had brought on Raskolnikov's "temporary insanity," was his self-intoxication with radical ideology; but of course nobody (except Porfiry) had paid any attention to this element whatsoever.

Raskolnikov himself, moreover, "to the intense annoyance" of advocates of "the most recent fashionable theory," refused to offer any plea of "temporary insanity." Quite the contrary, "he answered very clearly with the coarsest frankness that the cause was his miserable position, his poverty and helplessness, and his desire to provide for his first steps in life." The court was quite satisfied with this self-evident explanation, but it was manifestly Raskolnikov's way of avoiding any further probing of his true motives. Nor are we hardly supposed to take at face value his admission that "he had been led to the murder through his shallow and cowardly nature," and that his confession had been caused by "his heartfelt repentance." All this, the narrator remarks, so as to signify its unreliability, "was almost coarse" (6: 411). The "coarseness" comes from the very banality of Raskolnikov's self-condemnation, his obvious desire to tailor the complexities of his situation to the limited comprehension of his judges and to confound those jurists "more versed in psychology." Dostoevsky's tongue-in-cheek resumé of the court proceedings is thus intended to undermine, for the last time, any acceptance of Raskolnikov's pathology or of his poverty, *taken by themselves*, as satisfactory explanations of what had led him to disaster.

The reader, if not the court, knows full well that Raskolnikov's so-called "heartfelt repentance" is really a crushing sense of defeat; and the depression that marks his behavior in the prison camp, where he even rebuffs Sonya's effort to comfort and console him, is the result not of the hardship of his lot but of the collapse of belief in himself. He falls ill for a long time, and "it was wounded pride that made him ill." What tortures him is that he cannot see any flaw in his theory but finds it only in himself: "he did not repent of the crime at all," and "his exasperated conscience found no particularly terrible fault in his past, except a single *blunder* which might happen to anyone. Not being able to find any flaw in his ideas, he could thus see no value in the 'continual sacrifice leading to nothing' that he had accepted. Of course he had committed a crime, but 'what is meant by crime? My conscience is at rest. . . . Well, punish me for the letter of the law . . . and that's enough. Of course in that case many benefactors of mankind who snatched power for themselves instead of inheriting it ought to have been punished at their first steps. But those men succeeded and *so they were right*, and I didn't, and so I had no right to have taken that first step' " (6: 416–417; italics added). Raskolnikov thus still believes that there is nothing *inherently* incompatible between the ruthless acquisition of power by an "extraordinary person," who never questions for a moment that his ego is superior to all moral laws, and the possibility of that person then becoming (and being regarded as) a "benefactor of mankind."

To resolve this particular thematic crux Dostoevsky has recourse to the famous final dream of Raskolnikov, the dream in which he sees "the whole world . . . condemned to a terrible new strange plague that had come to Europe from the depths of Asia." This dream, like all the others in the book, emerges from the depths of his moral-emotive psyche, and like them is the response of his conscience to his ideas. His logic is answered not by any sort of rational refutation but by the vision of his horrified subconscious (which in Dostoevsky is usually moral, as it also is in Shakespeare). What the dream represents is nothing less than the *universalization* of Raskolnikov's doctrine of the "extraordinary people," the imaginary materialization of a world whose inhabitants all believe they are "extraordinary" and in which *all* attempt to put this belief into practice. The plague is caused by "some sort of new microbes . . . attacking the body, but these microbes were endowed with intelligence and will"; and those attacked became "mad and furious" while believing they had reached new heights of wisdom and self-understanding. "Never had men considered themselves so intellectual, and so completely in possession of the truth as these sufferers. Never had they considered their decisions, their scientific conclusions, their moral convictions so infallible." The disease obviously allows each person to preserve "moral convictions" and inspires a desire to enlighten others with the truth of such convictions so as to become a benefactor of humanity. "Each thought that he alone had the truth and was wretched looking at the others, beat himself on the breast, wept, and wrung his hands" (6: 419–420).

But the certainty of each ego in its own infallibility, and the absolute assurance and authority imparted by such certainty, leads to the breakdown of all common norms and values. "They did not know how to judge and could not agree what to consider evil and what good; they did not know whom to blame, whom to justify. Men killed each other in a sort of senseless spite." No form of social cohesion could resist the contagion of the plague; even when men were not destroying each other, it was impossible for them to collaborate in any common task. "Men met in groups, agreed to do something, swore to keep together, but at once began something different from what they proposed." The plague thus removes the implicit basis of consensus on which human society is based, and the final result is total social chaos. "There were conflagrations and famine. All men and all things were involved in destruction." "Only a few men could be saved in the whole world," and "they were a pure chosen people, destined to found a new race and a new life, to renew and purify the earth, but no one had seen these men, no one had heard their words and their voices" (6: 420). The myth of a new élite race thus emerges again, on the ruins of a world demolished by the spread of the very same belief in "extraordinary people."

Here we see Dostoevsky destroying the last shreds of Raskolnikov's stubborn conviction that a supreme egoism could be combined with socially benevolent consequences. On the contrary, the universal reign of such an egoism would lead to the collapse of society altogether. Let all presume they were "extraordinary people" and the result would be the Hobbesian world of Raskolnikov's feverish nightmare, the war of all against all. This is the world of Western society as Dostoevsky had described it in *Winter Notes*, the world in which "the ego sets itself in opposition, as a separate, self-justifying principle, against all of nature and all other humans; it claims equality and equal value with whatever exists outside of itself" (5: 79). It is, in fact, not only equality that each ego now claims but absolute superiority; and this is the plague that has come to Russia, not from Asia but from Europe itself, to infect the radical intelligentsia: the plague of a moral amorality based on egoism and culminating in a form of self-deification. Dostoevsky thus uses the typical technique of his eschatological imagination to dramatize all the implicit dangers of the new radical ideology.

Raskolnikov's dream provides an impressive climax to the main ideological theme of the book and is, in effect, its proper ending. The further effort to show some inner stirrings in Raskolnikov himself toward the adoption of a new set of values is much less successful. He is depicted as wondering at the "inexplicable" phenomenon of the irrational love of life displayed by the peasant convicts despite all the hardships of their lot. He is tormented because of the hatred he encounters among the peasants, whom he does not, like the other educated prisoners (Poles), regard only as "ignorant slaves" (6: 418). Without knowing anything about his beliefs, they consider him an "infidel," even though he takes the sacraments with them at Lent and prays with all the others; and they shout at him during a quarrel: "You don't believe in God." On the other hand, they all admire Sonya, whom they grow to trust and love; and even the worst criminals call her "our dear, good little mother" (6: 419). One understands that Dostoevsky is trying to indicate how Raskolnikov's pride and egoism have alienated him from an instinctive, unquestioning attachment to life, as well as from the faith of the people, who refuse to accept him as a genuine Christian.

But all this is brushed in too rapidly and perfunctorily to be really persuasive. More effective is the growing need for Sonya that Raskolnikov feels after the desolation of his dream; she offers him not only a means of renewing his life personally but also, perhaps, a way of achieving some sort of assimilation to the people. In the final pages, though, just before Raskolnikov flings himself at Sonya's feet to embrace her and weep, he is sitting on the riverbank, gazing at the steppe, where he sees the tents of nomads in the distance. It seemed as if time had stood still, and he was back in the "age of Abraham and his flocks" (6: 421), the age of untroubled faith. It is only after this comparison occurs to him that he turns to Sonya, but Dostoevsky knew very well that Raskolnikov could not become another Sonya or return to "the age of Abraham," and that it would be a daunting task to find an adequate artistic image of a possible new Raskolnikov. This task could hardly be undertaken in his brief concluding pages; and so the Epilogue, if by no means a failure as a whole, invariably leaves readers with a quite justified sense of dissatisfaction. It was, moreover, a sense evidently shared by Dostoevsky, whose narrator speaks of Raskolnikov's "gradual regeneration" as being "the theme of a new story" (7: 422); and it would be a story that continued to preoccupy Dostoevsky throughout the remainder of his creative life. For time and again we shall see him returning to the challenge of creating a regenerated Raskolnikov—of creating, that is, a highly educated and spiritually developed member of Russian society who conquers his egoism and undergoes a genuine conversion to a Christian morality of love.

PART II

Remarriage

CHAPTER 8

"A Little Diamond"

The publication of *Crime and Punishment*, which created even more of a sensation than had *House of the Dead* five years earlier, marked a new era in Dostoevsky's literary career. Once again he was in the forefront of Russian literature, and it was now clear that he, Turgenev, and Tolstoy were in competition for the palm as the greatest Russian novelist. The final chapters of the novel had been completed with the aid of Anna Grigoryevna Snitkina, the stenographer who had worked with him on *The Gambler*; and by this time a major change had also occurred in his personal life. He had proposed marriage to Anna Grigoryevna and been accepted.

Ever since the death of his first wife, we have seen Dostoevsky eagerly seeking to remarry and to establish the normal family life for which he yearned so fervently and seemingly so vainly. Three women had rejected him in the past two years, and he had even entered into a tentative engagement with the docile and long-suffering Elena Pavlovna while she waited for the demise of her ailing spouse. Dostoevsky's great problem, of course, was that his occasions for meeting eligible and marriageable young women were few and far between. The demanding constraints of his literary life left him with little time for society and hardly any energy. The few women with whom he became seriously involved, and even his passing affair with Martha Brown, had all been connected with his literary and editorial activity; and the same proved to be the case with Anna Snitkina.

The charming story of their meeting and courtship, recounted in the *Reminiscences* edited and published after her death (and now supplemented by the shorthand diary that she kept during the first year of their marriage),* is one of the most luminous episodes in a life otherwise filled

---

* The so-called memoirs of Anna Grigoryevna, *Vospominaniya*, were never completed by her, and a selection of the manuscripts was first published in 1925 by L. P. Grossman. A revised and improved version appeared in 1971, edited by S. V. Belov and V. A. Tunimanov. It is this version that has been translated into English under the title of *Reminiscences*.

In 1973, a volume of the invaluable literary-historical annual *Literaturnoe Nasledstvo* published new material and researches concerning Dostoevsky, among them a hitherto undeciphered portion of Anna Dostoevsky's diary. To occupy herself during her first year in Europe as Dostoevsky's wife, she put down, on the exact date at which they had occurred a year earlier, her recollections of the courtship period. This account fills out, as well as sometimes diverges from, what she included in the memoirs written in the later years of her life.

with gloom and misfortune. Difficulties and hardships aplenty would continue to plague Dostoevsky and his new bride, particularly in the early years of their marriage when they lived abroad. But thanks to the sterling moral qualities and sturdy good sense of Anna Grigoryevna, the erratic and turbulent Dostoevsky would finally attain that relatively tranquil family existence he so much envied in others.

2

The pert, reserved, and quite attractive young lady who turned up at Dostoevsky's flat at half-past eleven on the morning of October 4, 1866, prepared to take dictation, came from a comfortable but by no means wealthy family of mixed Ukrainian and Swedish origin. Her father's ancestors had left Ukraine several generations back, had risen in the world, and had provided him with a good education in the Jesuit school at Petersburg. In a remark that would have pleased her husband, Anna hastens to add that "he did not become a Jesuit, but he remained all his life a good and open-hearted man" who served "in one of the magistracies and departments of the civil services."[1] Her mother was quite proud of her learned Swedish ancestry (one of her forebears had been a Lutheran bishop) and had grown up in Finland in a Swedish-speaking environment before the family moved to Petersburg. Her daughter reports, as family tradition, that "she spoke Russian badly" at the time of her courtship by Anna's father.[2]

Another family tradition helps to throw light on Anna's own decision to marry the much older Dostoevsky. Her mother had been engaged at the age of nineteen to an officer who was soon killed in action in Hungary, and after a period of mourning the family duly arranged for her to meet other eligible young suitors. But there was also an older man at one of these parties whom she preferred to the younger swains because "he kept telling stories and laughing."[3] This was Anna's then forty-two-year-old father, not considered a prospect because of his age and because, as was well known, he had decided not to marry while his mother was still living. The interest of the beautiful young woman, however, overcame his hitherto staunch resolution, and the two plighted their troth. There was thus for Anna nothing unusual or unacceptable about a marriage with a considerably older man; it was, on the contrary, the pattern of her own family. It should also be noted that her mother, though a devout Lutheran, decided to convert to Orthodoxy after experiencing what she took to be a sign from God in answer to her prayers for help about the problem. This incident tells us something about the pious atmosphere in which Anna was nurtured, and also about the prin-

3. Anna Grigoryevna Dostoevsky, ca. 1863

ciple of self-sacrifice for the sake of family concord instilled in her by her mother.

Anna Grigoryevna was raised in a strict but, according to her own account, harmonious family atmosphere, in which the children (she had an older sister and younger brother), though not spoiled and pampered, were well and justly treated. "My parents loved us all very much, and never punished us without cause. Life in our family was quiet, measured and serene, without quarrels, dramas or catastrophes."[4] Between the ages of nine and twelve she was sent to a school in which, except for the lessons in religion, all instruction was given in German; and her fluency in that language stood the Dostoevskys in good stead when they lived in Germany during the years just after their marriage. Anna was also growing up in the period when higher education began to become available for Russian women. The first secondary school had been opened for them in Petersburg in 1858, and Anna entered in the fall of that year, graduating in 1864 with honors. "My studies," she remarks, "came easily to me,"[5] and evidently her family encouraged her to continue in the learned footsteps of her mother's ancestors.

The first Pedagogical Institute for women opened in 1863 for those wishing to continue their education, and Anna eagerly entered in the fall of 1864. "At that time," she writes, "a passionate interest in the natural sciences had arisen in Russian society, and I too succumbed to the trend. Physics, chemistry and sociology seemed a revelation to me, and I registered in the school's department of mathematics and physics."[6] Anna was thus a young woman of her time; but while such enthusiasm for the natural sciences often led to a conversion to political radicalism and its accompanying obligatory atheism, there is no trace of any such tendency in Anna's development. Indeed, she soon found that the sciences were not her forte and that she much preferred reading novels to observing the crystallization of salts. The zoology lectures were interesting enough at first; but alas, when it came to laboratory work and she was required to observe the dissection of a cat, she embarrassedly fainted dead away! What she enjoyed most were the brilliant lectures on Russian literature by a Professor V. V. Nikolsky, which she attended assiduously; one wonders whether he made any reference in them to the work of her future husband.

By this time, Anna's father had fallen ill, and it was clear he would not recover. Dropping out of school to help with his care, she spent many hours reading to him from the novels of Dickens. One suspects that she was not too unhappy to leave her scientific studies; but her behavior also exhibits a sense of duty and capacity for self-subordination that was to mark her conduct as Dostoevsky's spouse. Her father, however, regretting the abandonment of her education, urged her to look for other possibilities; and then she came across the announcement of a course in stenography given relatively late in the evening after her father was asleep. With his encouragement she enrolled, but at first found the work difficult—stenography was just a lot of "gibberish"[7]—and continued only because her father insisted. His death was such a wracking event that she interrupted her attendance; but the kindly Professor Olkhin, though the course was terminated, continued to work with her by correspondence when he discovered how grief-stricken she was and the cause of her disappearance. These private lessons enabled her to catch up rapidly and turned her into an excellent secretary capable of taking dictation at reasonable speed. When Professor Olkhin was asked to find a stenographer to aid the noted writer Dostoevsky, he immediately thought of the young and determined Anna Grigoryevna, who had become his favorite pupil and disciple.

Anna was naturally very excited at the prospect of embarking on her first job, which for a woman in those days was a very important event. "I felt that I was setting out on a new road, that I would be earning money by my own labor, that I would become independent. And the idea of independence for me, a girl of the 1860s, was a very precious idea." Even more, her first assignment, marking "my transformation from a schoolgirl into an independent practitioner of my chosen profession," would be to work with a writer whose books she admired and by whom she had been deeply affected.[8] Her father had been a great reader of *Poor Folk*, and had spoken feelingly about the sad fate of the young writer Dostoevsky when she was still a girl. On learning that the vanished Dostoevsky had reappeared and was to publish a new magazine, her father gleefully pointed out to the family: "You see, Dostoevsky did come back."[9] Anna and her sister disputed the issues of *Time* that were bought every month, and at the age of fifteen she tearfully pored over installments of *The Insulted and Injured*. The narrator of that novel, the tenderhearted but hapless Ivan Petrovich, particularly appealed to her, and she identified his deplorable fate with that of the author. Later she told her husband that she had been in love with him in that guise ever since those early years. More recently, she had been reading *Crime and Punishment*, and as she entered the apartment house in which Dostoevsky resided, "I was immediately reminded of the house . . . where Dostoevsky's hero Raskolnikov had lived."[10] The maidservant who opened the door wore a green checked shawl around her shoulders, and Anna wondered whether this was not the prototype of the famous green shawl of Katerina Ivanovna in the novel.

The flat that Anna entered was decently but very modestly furnished, except for two large and beautiful Chinese vases in Dostoevsky's study (some remains from his Siberian years, when he had lived close to the Chinese border). The study itself she found "dim and hushed; and you felt a kind of depression in that dimness and silence." The first person she saw, beside the maidservant, was a half-dressed young man "with hair disheveled and shirt open at the chest," who emerged from a side room and rapidly vanished when he caught sight of her.[11] This young man was Pavel (Pasha) Isaev, Dostoevsky's stepson by his first wife, and Anna, much to her sorrow, was to get to know him all too well when she replaced his mother as Dostoevsky's spouse. Dostoevsky himself soon appeared, but also quickly quit the room to order tea, leaving Anna to mull over her impressions. He had seemed quite old at first sight, but when he returned and began to speak, he suddenly "grew younger at once." Anna estimated his age to be between thirty-five and thirty-seven (in fact he was forty-five). Her description of his external appearance is worth quoting entire: "He was of medium height and very erect posture. His chestnut-colored hair, faintly tinged with red, was heavily pomaded and carefully smoothed. But it was his eyes that really struck me. They weren't alike—one was dark-brown, while the other had a pupil so dilated that you couldn't see the iris at all. [Dostoevsky had recently fallen during an epileptic attack and temporarily injured his right eye—J.F.] This dissimilarity gave his face an enigmatic expression. His face [was] pale and sick-looking. . . . He was dressed in a blue cotton jacket, rather worn, but with snow-white collar and cuffs."[12]

Dostoevsky, who had agreed to try working with a stenographer only with great reluctance and as a last resort, was nervous and distraught, obviously at a loss on how to treat this newly intrusive presence. To break the ice, he began to question Anna about her study of stenography, then a relatively new method of transcribing speech, and one of his comments anticipates an important thematic motif in *The Gambler*. Anna informed him that her class had begun with more than a hundred students, but only twenty-five were left at the end; many, thinking that stenography could be mastered in a few days, had dropped out when this supposition proved false. "'That's always the way in our country with every new undertaking,' said Dostoevsky, 'They start at fever heat, then cool off fast and drop it altogether. They see that you have to work— and who wants to work nowadays?'"[13] Another remark may possibly be taken as a corollary to this observation about the Russian aversion to sustained labor. Dostoevsky informed Anna that he had been very glad when Professor Olkhin had recommended a female stenographer, and he challenged her to guess why. The answer was "because a man would likely as not start drinking, while you won't fall into any drinking habits, I hope?" The very proper Anna could scarcely contain herself from bursting into laughter, but she managed to preserve her decorum and reassured Dostoevsky on this score "with perfect seriousness."[14]

Dostoevsky's difficulty in adjusting himself to Anna, and finding just the right footing in relation to her, is vividly revealed by another incident. He smoked continuously during this first interview, as he continued to do later, stubbing out one cigarette and lighting another even before the first was finished; at one point he offered Anna a cigarette. Ladies, of course, did not smoke in the mid-nineteenth century—at least not in public—but neither did ladies hire themselves out as stenographers and visit the apartments of perfect strangers unattended. By inviting Anna to take a cigarette, Dostoevsky thus indicated that he thought she might be a completely emancipated Nihilist à la Kukshina, always puffing away at a cigarette in Turgenev's *Fathers and Children*. When Anna refused, he inquired whether she were merely doing so out of politeness. "I was quick to assure him," she writes, "that I not only didn't smoke, but didn't even like to see other women smoke."[15] This firm reply signaled to Dostoevsky that she had no sympathy with such breaches of the accepted social code, despite her own assertion of a relative independence through employment. A bit later, he told Anna that "he had been pleasantly surprised by my knowledge of correct behavior. He was used to meeting Nihilist women socially and observing their behavior, which roused him to indignation."[16]

Once this uncomfortable moment had passed, Dostoevsky continued to converse, but in a dispirited fashion. "He looked exhausted and ill" to the observant Anna, and had difficulty in collecting his thoughts; he kept asking her name and then forgetting it a moment later. Such lapses in memory were quite frequent after his epileptic seizures, and with a frankness that astonished Anna he informed her almost at once that he suffered from epilepsy and had undergone an attack just a few days before. At last remembering why she had come, he read her a passage from *The Russian Messenger*, which she took down and transcribed, and he corrected two minor errors rather sharply. He was also concerned by the amount of time it took to put her shorthand into words, not realizing that she would do this at home rather than during their working hours together. After the first stab at dictation, however, he walked around the room for some time sunk in thought, "as if unaware of [Anna's] presence," and then gave up the attempt to concentrate altogether. Telling Anna he was in no condition to work, he asked her to return in the evening at eight o'clock, when he would begin to dictate his novel. This was extremely inconvenient for Anna, who lived at the other end of the city; but she was so eager to make her first job a success that she agreed, deciding to spend the intervening time with some relatives who lived closer to Dostoevsky's location.[17]

On her return that evening, Dostoevsky began by offering her tea and cakes, as he had done before, asked her name again and proffered a cigarette, apparently totally forgetful of what had occurred just a few hours earlier. The dictating sessions usually began with such social preliminaries, and then turned to the work to be done. Dostoevsky was now evidently in a calmer frame of mind, and this time Anna's rather negative reaction to him was totally reversed. "All at once, it seemed to me that I had known Dostoevsky for a long time, and I began to feel more natural and at ease."[18] As often happened when Dostoevsky wished to establish some intimacy with others, he began to reminisce about his past, vividly evoking his arrest and condemnation in the Petrashevsky case—which culminated in his belief, on being taken from the Peter and Paul Fortress, that he would be executed in a few minutes. While the youthfully impressionable Anna listened with reverential rapture, he described all the details now so well known but then still more or less wrapped in legend; and he dwelt on some of his emotions at the time (soon to be used in *The Idiot*). "How precious my life seemed to me, how much that was fine and good I might have accomplished! My whole past life came back to me then, and the way I had sometimes misused it; and I so longed to experience it all once again and live for a long, long time . . . " Dostoevsky's narrative left Anna with an "eerie feeling," and a sense of great surprise that he should confide such intimate details to someone he scarcely knew. It was only later that she came to understand the reasons for such disconcerting frankness. "At that time Feodor Mikhailovich was utterly alone and surrounded by persons who were hostile to him. He felt too keenly the need to share his thoughts with those whom he sensed as kind and interested in him."[19]

Dostoevsky finally began to dictate the opening paragraphs of *The Gambler* but stopped very soon, and Anna left for home to transcribe the text. The next day she arrived a half-hour late to find Dostoevsky in great agitation. He had thought she might not return at all, and he would have lost not only a stenographer but also the small fragment of manuscript he had managed to compose! Every page was precious to him because, as he explained, he had agreed to provide a novel of a specified length by the first of November, "and I haven't even worked out a plan for it."[20] This was Anna's first knowledge of Dostoevsky's perilous dilemma and the reasons she had been engaged. "Stellovsky's behavior," she writes, "made my blood boil,"[21] and she determined to do everything within her power to rescue the intended victim from his clutches. Learning the menacing details of Dostoevsky's precarious practical situation only reinforced the feeling he had inspired in Anna the night before. "This was the first time I had ever known such a man: wise, good, and yet unhappy, apparently abandoned by everyone. And a feeling of deep pity and commiseration was born in me."[22]

On the second day, Dostoevsky began dictating with more determination; but "it was obviously difficult for him to get into the work. He stopped often, thought things over and asked me to reread what he had already dictated."[23] After an hour he felt tired, decided to rest, and began to chat with Anna again. Once more forgetting her name, and absent-mindedly offering her another cigarette, he brightened up considerably when she began to question him about contemporary Russian writers. He was warm in his praise of Maikov, whom "he loved not only as a talented poet, but also as the finest and most intelligent of men." Maikov was indeed one of Dostoevsky's oldest and most faithful friends, on whose help he could—and did—rely when he could turn to no one else. Nekrasov "he bluntly called a cheat, a terrible gambler, someone who talks about the sufferings of mankind, but who drives around himself in a carriage with trotters."* A remark about Turgenev, toward whom Dostoevsky felt extremely ambivalent, prefigures the bitter quarrel between them the very next year, which would end their relations until shortly before Dostoevsky's death. "He mentioned Turgenev as a first-rate talent, but regretted that as a result of his long residence abroad he had lost some of his understanding of Russia and the Russian people."[24] This opinion would be strongly confirmed for Dostoevsky a year later by the publication of *Smoke*, the most bitterly condemnatory of all Turgenev's novels about his native land.

4
———

Dostoevsky was fidgety and distracted during his first few sessions with his new collaborator, wondering whether her services would really help him to meet his looming deadline; but very quickly, encouraged by her cool determination, he settled down to a regular routine. Anna arrived at his house every day at twelve and stayed until four. "During that time we would have three dictating sessions of a half-hour or more, and between dictations we would drink tea and talk."[25] Dostoevsky, as Anna noticed, now was much calmer when she arrived, and became more and more cheerful as the pages piled up and she estimated that the manuscript would be ready for submission by the appointed date. Dostoevsky's mood certainly improved when this became clear; it also lightened as, in the midst of his total isolation (though Maikov did show up one day for a visit), he began to pour out his heart to an avid, attentive, and devotedly sympathetic listener. "Each day, chatting with me like a friend, he would lay bare some unhappy scene from his past. I could not help being deeply touched at his accounts of the difficulties from which he had never extricated himself, and indeed could not." Each day, as well, his attitude toward Anna, whose name he no longer forgot, became kindlier, warmer, more personal. "He often addressed me as '*golubchik*' (or 'little dove,' his favorite affectionate expression)," and in response to Anna's inquiries recounted many of the details of his past life, not only those involving his arrest and Siberian exile but also ones of a more private character.[26]

Anna had noticed, on her first visit, the portrait of a rather cadaverous-looking woman in a black dress and cap hanging in Dostoevsky's study, and assumed this to be his existing wife; the young man of whom she had caught a glimpse would be their son. Now she learned that Dostoevsky's wife had died two years before and that the young man was his

---

* These words from Anna's diary, expressing Dostoevsky's view of Nekrasov in 1866, were softened in the *Reminiscences*, which merely say: "He considered Nekrasov the friend of his youth and had a high opinion of his poetic gift" (p. 26).

stepson. This information pleased her greatly because, once meeting Pasha Isaev by chance in the courtyard of the apartment house, he had been rude and patronizing, snatching her portfolio from her grasp to investigate the mysterious "stenography" and impressing her very unpleasantly with his appearance as well. "From close up he looked even less attractive than at a distance. He had a sallow, almost yellow face, dark eyes with yellowish whites, and teeth yellowed with tobacco stains."[27] Dostoevsky's conversations with Anna thus began to turn more and more to questions concerning his present trying situation and depressed state of mind, saddled as he was with debts and struggling to make ends meet. Anna noted how bad things were with her own eyes when the Chinese vases suddenly vanished and the silver spoons of the dining set were replaced on the table by wooden ones. Dostoevsky explained that both had been pawned to pay some pressing creditors who no longer could be put off.

For the most part, Anna indicates, "Feodor Mikhailovich always spoke about his financial straits with great good nature"; but the general tenor of all his stories was invariably "so mournful" that she could not help asking why he never recalled moments of joy or happiness. His reply was designed to cater to Anna's evident sympathy for his misfortunes, as well as to indicate the hopes for a happier future that, we may surmise, he had already begun to associate with her appealing person. "Happy?" he replied. "But I haven't had any happiness yet. At least, not the kind of happiness I always dreamed of. I am still waiting for it. A few days ago I wrote to my friend Baron Wrangel, that in spite of all the grief that has come to me I still go on dreaming that I will begin a new, happy life."[28] In fact, Dostoevsky had written Baron Wrangel many months before, and in the letter his dream of a "new, happy life" was specifically linked to remarriage and the founding of a family.

Dostoevsky now also began to acquaint Anna Grigoryevna with some of the details of his more recent sentimental life—such as his attraction to, and presumed engagement with, Anna Korvin-Krukovskaya. He forgivably embellished the story by making their engagement somewhat more explicit than it really had been; no doubt he wished to intimate that a highly desirable young woman *could* agree to link her life with his own. He had, according to this version of events, released the other Anna from her promise only because the sharp divergence of their social-political views excluded the possibility of happiness. Nothing is said in the *Reminiscences* about Suslova, but the diaries reveal that Dostoevsky showed her portrait to Anna Grigoryevna; and when Anna called her a "remarkable beauty," Dostoevsky disparagingly observed that she had changed a good deal in the past six years.[29]

As the talk between the two dwelt more and more on Dostoevsky's present circumstances, he depicted himself, with all his skill in melodrama, as having reached a crucially decisive moment in his life, as being at a point of crisis that would soon decide his future fate for good and all. With more than a touch of Romantic Byronism, he told Anna that "he was standing at a crossroad and three paths lay open before him." He could go to the East—Constantinople and Jerusalem—and remain there, "perhaps forever"; he could "go abroad to play roulette," and "immolate himself in the game he found so utterly engrossing"; or he could "marry again and seek joy and happiness in family life."[30] Since Anna had already shown so much friendliness for him, would she give him the benefit of her advice? Which path should he follow?*

Dostoevsky was evidently testing the temperature of the water into which he very soon planned to plunge, and the reply he received from the sturdily commonsensical Anna was the one he had hoped would come. It may be doubted whether she really believed that he might become a religious pilgrim, or lose himself entirely, like the protagonist of the novella on which they were both working, in the intoxicating world of gambling (though the second scenario, as Anna was very soon to learn to her sorrow, contained far more plausibility than the first). But Anna had no leaning toward such "vague and somewhat fantastic notions," as she calls them, and told her anxious questioner that marriage and family happiness were what he needed. At which Dostoevsky instantly responded with a further question: since Anna had indicated that he might still be able to find a wife, should he seek for an intelligent one or a kind companion? Anna came down on the side of intelligence; but Dostoevsky, knowing himself far better than she did at this point, replied that he would prefer "a kind one, so that she'll take pity on me and love me."[31] Anna Grigoryevna little knew then how much pity and love she would be required to lavish on Dostoevsky in the future.

Once the talk turned to the subject of marriage, Dostoevsky asked Anna why she had not married herself. Neither of the two suitors seriously pursuing her, she replied, inspired more than respect, while she wanted to marry for love. Dostoevsky hastened to agree that love was all-important, that "respect alone" was not sufficient for a happy life together. The *Reminiscences* remain silent about what Anna Grigoryevna thought of such conversations, and why Dostoevsky was dwelling on such matters so insistently; but the diaries disclose that she was very well aware of their drift. "Even then," she writes, "it seemed to me that he would certainly propose, and I really did not know whether I would accept or not. He pleases me very much, but all the same frightens me

---

* Dostoevsky's reference to a trip to the Near East was not *entirely* made up of whole cloth; there is evidence that he had been thinking of such a journey at least since 1863. In that year, he was given a letter of introduction to the head of the Imperial Russian Mission in Constantinople, presumably as a preparation for such a voyage. The letter was written by E. P. Kovalevsky, then head of the Literary Fund, who had also been an important diplomat and traveler in the Balkans and Siberia. See *PSS*, 28/Bk. 2: 573.

because of his irascibility and illness." She noticed how often he shouted at the maidservant Fedosya, though adding that the rebukes were on the whole very well deserved. Despite the growing intimacy between the pair, which led Anna to such speculations about the future, a strict decorum was carefully maintained. "Not once during all that time was there any talk of love or a single improper word."[32]

The daily meetings with Dostoevsky now became the center of Anna's life, and everything she had previously known seemed to her uninteresting and insipid by comparison. "I rarely saw my friends," she writes, "and concentrated wholly on work and on those utterly fascinating conversations we used to have while we were relaxing after our dictation sessions. I couldn't help comparing Dostoevsky with young men I used to meet in my own social circle. How empty and trivial their talk seemed to me in comparison with the ever fresh and original views of my favorite writer." Anna was clearly falling under the spell of her intimacy with Dostoevsky and the exciting stimulation provided by his constant presence. "Leaving his house still under the influence of ideas new to me," she confesses, "I would miss him when I was at home and lived only in the expectation of the next day's meeting with him. I realized with sorrow that the work was nearing its end and that our acquaintance must break off." The deadline of November 1 was fast approaching; and since Dostoevsky too was feeling the same sense of impending loss, he put into words what both had been mulling over in their minds. Confessing how much he enjoyed Anna's companionship and "our lively talks together," he remarked on what a pity it would be if all this were now to end. "I shall miss you very much. And where shall I ever see you again?" Anna fumbled for some reply, and could only come up with "theatres and concerts" as possible meeting places in the future; but Dostoevsky brushed these aside for lack of time, and because they allowed for little more than social chatter to be exchanged. Why did not Anna Grigoryevna invite him to meet her family? Such a request was certainly a harbinger of serious amatory intentions, and Anna agreed on the spot; but she would set the time for such a visit only after work on the manuscript had been terminated.[33]

There now remained no doubt that *The Gambler* would be completed by the due date, but the finished manuscript would only be ready perilously close to the deadline. Stellovsky would stop at nothing to prevent Dostoevsky from meeting the terms of his contract, and Dostoevsky "began to be afraid that Stellovsky would contrive some kind of trick . . . would find a pretext for refusing to accept the manuscript."[34] The resourceful Anna consulted a lawyer about the matter, who advised registering the manuscript with a notary or with the police officer of the district in which Stellovsky lived. The same advice was given by a lawyer Dostoevsky went to see, perhaps at Anna's urging; and the instructions stood him in very good stead. Meanwhile, elated at having been able to complete the novella at all, Dostoevsky planned a victory dinner for his friends in a restaurant and of course invited Anna, without whom, as he justly said, his triumph would not have been possible. But she refused because she had never been to a restaurant in her life, and she was afraid that her shyness and awkwardness would impede the general merriment.

Stellovsky, true to his reputation, attempted by every possible means to prevent Dostoevsky from delivering the manuscript on time. The dictation was finished on October 29, and Anna brought the manuscript to Dostoevsky on the thirtieth, which happened to be his birthday; he was to make the final corrections on the thirty-first and hand in the work on the following day. Arriving on the thirtieth, Anna was confronted with Emilya Feodorovna, the widow of Dostoevsky's brother Mikhail, come with birthday greetings; and the lady snubbed the employee Anna unmercifully, even though Dostoevsky was warm in his praise of Anna's indispensable aid. This was only the first of Anna's many unhappy experiences with this dependent relative, who had also been cordially disliked by Dostoevsky's first wife, Marya Dimitrievna. Upset by his sister-in-law's haughty rudeness, Dostoevsky insisted, as he said good-bye to Anna at the door, that she now set the date for his visit to her home. The diary records that he spoke to her in an impassioned manner during this leave-taking, and even jestingly suggested that they run away together to Europe; from which Anna concluded "that he loves me very much."[35]

Two days later, Dostoevsky tried to deliver the manuscript to Stellovsky's home but was told that he had left for the provinces; nor would the manager of his publishing firm accept it, on the pretext that he had not received specific authority to do so. By this time it was too late for a notary, and the police officer of the district would not be returning to his office until ten o'clock in the evening. The frantic Dostoevsky, watching the precious hours slip away, just managed to meet his deadline two hours before its expiration. At last, however, he held the all-important receipt in his hands, and the ordeal was over.

5

By this time, Anna's whole life had begun to revolve around Dostoevsky, and the few days between the end of her employment and Dostoevsky's promised visit on November 3 were a stretch of dreariness and anxiety. Their earlier talks together had been so natural and spontaneous, so much a product of their work together, and now she would be obliged to play hostess and lead the conversation herself! What could they possibly talk about? Anna well knew that neither she nor her mother was skilled in the social graces, and she was saddened by the thought that Dostoevsky might pass a dull and dispiriting evening in their company. She justifiably calls herself, however, "a person of naturally buoyant spirits,"[36] and she fought against her mood by visiting friends and attending one of Professor Olkhin's lectures. He greeted her with warm congratulations, and said that Dostoevsky had written to express his gratitude for Olkhin's recommendation of a stenographer whose help had proved so invaluable. This new method had proved so successful, moreover, that Dostoevsky intended to continue to use it in the future. If nothing else, this letter indicated to Anna that Dostoevsky had no intention of letting her drop out of sight.

The great day of the visit finally arrived; but, alas, Dostoevsky appeared at Anna's doorstep an hour late. The cab driver, with no idea of how to find the rather remote street, had circled about futilely until a passerby led him personally to the address. Despite Anna's anxieties, the evening passed off very well. Dostoevsky gallantly kissed the hand of Mme Snitkina, who surely needed no explanation of his intentions, and immediately plunged into an account of his adventures with Stellovsky. Once that theme had been exhausted, he proposed that Anna continue to work with him on the completion of *Crime and Punishment* after about a week of rest. She gladly agreed, if Professor Olkhin, who might wish to recommend another pupil, would give his consent. Dostoevsky took this proviso very badly and remarked, "perhaps the truth is you don't want to work with me any longer?"[37] Anna certainly knew that he was talking about much more than stenography as he pressingly urged her to consult Olkhin on the matter the very next day. By this time, Anna's situation was hardly secret from those who knew her best. Her sister Masha, after spending the next day with Anna and listening to her talk of Dostoevsky "with extraordinary animation," easily discerned the truth. "It's all for nothing, Netotchka," she told Anna with solid practicality, "your having such a crush on Dostoevsky. For your dreams can't ever come about, and thank goodness they can't—if he's that ill and overloaded with family and debts!"[38]

Anna vehemently denied having any such "crush" on Dostoevsky, but her sister's words led to some reflections all the same. Might she really have fallen in love? And, if so, should she stop seeing Dostoevsky and "try to forget about him little by little?"[39] But, with an instinctive casuistry that furthered her true desires, she also reasoned that what Masha had said might *not* be true. Would it be pardonable then to deprive herself of employment—not to mention the innocent pleasure of Dostoevsky's company? And why withdraw the stenographic help he so desperately needed—especially since, as she well knew, the only other competent stenographers trained by Olkhin were already fully engaged? So went the ebb and flow of her thoughts, which were interrupted by an unannounced visit from Dostoevsky three days later, while she was idly picking away at the keys of the piano and waiting for a cab to arrive. Dostoevsky had not been able to spend more than one or two days without her company; and though he had firmly decided not to give way to his impulse to call, realizing that it might seem "strange" to Anna and her mother, once having "resolved not to come under any circumstances . . . as you see, here I am!"[40] Dostoevsky's inability to resist the prompting of his emotions could hardly have seemed, in this instance, anything other than charming and eminently excusable to Anna; but she would soon encounter other evidences of the same trait of character that drove her to the brink of despair.

The day following this impromptu visit, November 8, had nominally been set as the time when Anna and Dostoevsky would fix a schedule for the completion of *Crime and Punishment*; but Dostoevsky himself had other plans in mind. On her arrival, Anna noticed that he was "excited about something. The expression on his face was heightened, fervid, almost ecstatic, and made him look much younger."[41] The exuberance of his mood, on which Anna commented with pleasure, he ascribed to a happy dream. Pointing to a rosewood box given him by a Siberian friend—the Kirghiz sultan Chokan Valikhanov, who had served as an officer in the Russian army and later became a widely recognized ethnographer—Dostoevsky explained that he had dreamed he was rearranging his papers there (in other words, attempting to organize and reorder his past), when he suddenly came across, buried in the midst of the heap, "a little diamond, a tiny one, but very sparkling and brilliant." This discovery had cheered him immensely, since he attributed "great meaning" to dreams and believed firmly that "my dreams are always prophetic." Whenever he dreamed of his father or his brother Misha, he knew that some catastrophe was impending; but his dream of "the little diamond" had been "a good dream," one that seemed to foreshadow some happy change in the present grimness of his circumstances. Anna, however, remarked jocularly "that dreams are usually explained as having the opposite meaning," and this brought about an instant alteration in Dostoevsky's buoyancy. "'So you think no happiness will ever come to me? All that—all that is only a vain hope?' he said pitifully."[42]

Just what Dostoevsky hoped that his dream foretold (assuming it had not been invented to prepare Anna for what lay ahead) was revealed as the conversation proceeded. Dostoevsky, it would seem, had had the idea for a new novel, one in which "the psychology of a young girl" played a crucial part, and he found it difficult to work out the ending; he needed some help, and appealed to Anna for her aid. This of course flattered her enormously, and she proudly settled in a chair to give her assistance to the distinguished novelist. The hero of Dostoevsky's novel turned out to be a man about his own age, "no longer young," and also a writer. His life, transposed very slightly, bore a remarkable resemblance to Dostoevsky's own (a "serious malady," for example, had torn him away from his work for ten years, exactly the term of Dostoevsky's imprisonment and exile), and Anna soon realized that "the further he [Dostoevsky] went, the clearer it grew to me that he was telling about his own life." All the travails she had heard about previously only in snatches were now brought together into a consecutive account; and running through the narrative was the passionate longing of the hero to find at last the happiness that had so far eluded his grasp. But was this still possible? "Dostoevsky did not spare the darker shades in delineating his hero," Anna comments. He was described as "a man grown old before his time, sick with an incurable disease (a paralyzed hand), gloomy, suspicious; possessed of a tender heart, it is true, but incapable of expressing his feelings; an artist and a talented one, perhaps, but a failure who had not once in his life succeeded in embodying his ideas in the forms he dreamed of, and who never ceased to torment himself over this fact."[43] This last detail, incidentally, was by no means merely an appeal designed to elicit an extra drop of sympathy from Anna Grigoryevna; it represented a view of his own work that Dostoevsky held up to his dying day.

Just at this critical period of his life, the writer meets a young girl roughly of Anna's age, perhaps a year or two older; the provisional name Dostoevsky had given her was Anya. Whether, as the *Reminiscences* pretend, Anna Grigoryevna took this as a reference to Korvin-Krukovskaya may well be doubted; the diary shows that Dostoevsky had told Anna a few days before that he wished to call *her* Anya or Anechka.[44] In any case, the heroine Anya was painted in the most glowing colors and said to be "gentle, wise, kind, bubbling with life and possessed of great tact in personal relationships." When Dostoevsky remarked of his heroine that, though "not a real beauty ... she is very nice-looking [and] I love her face," Anna Grigoryevna could not (supposedly) suppress a pang of jealousy, and "something pinched in my heart." Dostoevsky's unhappy author naturally fell in love with this irresistible young girl, and began to be tormented by whether she could possibly respond to his own feelings. "What could this elderly, sick, debt-ridden man give a young, alive, exuberant girl?" Would not the very idea of uniting her fate with his be asking her to make a "terrible sacrifice?"[45] Here was the point at which Dostoevsky wanted Anna Grigoryevna to give him the benefit of her feminine counsel. Would she consider it psychologically plausible for such a young girl to fall in love with the artist?

Anna replied to the query with the full emotional force of her own passionate longings. "But why would it be impossible? ... Where is the sacrifice on her part, anyway? If she really loves him she'll be happy, too, and she'll never have to regret anything!" This was the moment Dostoevsky had been waiting for, and these the words he had used all his literary skill to bring to her lips; once having heard them, he threw aside his fiction of a fiction and came to the dénouement. "'Imagine,' he said, 'that the artist is—me; that I have confessed my love for you and asked you to be my wife. Tell me, what would you answer?'" Anna Grigoryevna understood, from the inner torment manifest in Dostoevsky's countenance, that "if I gave him an evasive answer I would deal a deathblow to his self-esteem and pride. I looked at his troubled face, which had become so dear to me, and said 'I would answer that I love you and will love you all my life.'"[46] Anna Grigoryevna's refusal to hesitate even for a moment, to ask for a little time to reflect on what would be, after all, a momentous and risky decision, reveals both the firm resoluteness of her character and her overriding concern to spare Dostoevsky any further anguish. His welfare, under conditions that few other women would have borne so resiliently, would always continue to be her major preoccupation; and she remained unstintingly faithful to her pledge that she would love Dostoevsky for the remainder of her life.

6

The newly engaged pair, once the joyful excitement of the moment had passed, decided to keep their decision secret for a time, except from Anna's mother. Although warning her daughter of the many hardships that could easily be predicted for the couple, Mme Snitkina did not attempt to dissuade Anna from her perilous choice. Dostoevsky called the very next day to obtain her formal consent, and presented his suit in due and proper form. The mother tearfully acquiesced, and Anna Grigoryevna, to end Dostoevsky's obvious discomfiture, cut the touching scene short by calling for some tea. The pair had decided on secrecy ostensibly because Dostoevsky's circumstances could not as yet allow them to fix a date for the wedding ceremony; but Dostoevsky also wished to keep the news from his various Petersburg relatives for as long as possible. If so, his purpose was foiled by his uncontrollable need to communicate his happiness to someone, anyone, in lieu of those who ordinarily should have shared his rejoicing. The cab driver who drove him to and from Anna's house every day became his confidant, to whom he chattered about his future marriage; and this information quickly reached the ears of Fedosya, the servant in Dostoevsky's home, before a week had gone by. The supposed secret was thus disclosed very quickly, and caused a great deal of displeasure among those who had become accustomed to counting on Dostoevsky's earnings for their own support.

Anna Grigoryevna had known that Dostoevsky was in dire financial straits, but it was only after their engagement that she fully realized to what extent his indigence was caused by the demands made on him by others. He wholly supported his stepson Pasha, then twenty-one years of age and quite content to allow this situation to continue indefinitely; he provided in good part for his brother Mikhail's widow, Emilya Feodorovna, who had four grown children; and he also helped his younger brother Nikolay, a trained architect but a confirmed alcoholic who was often on his uppers.* The results of their combined exactions was vividly illustrated for Anna Grigoryevna one cold evening in late November when Dostoevsky arrived at her home chilled to the bone and, after imbibing large quantities of tea, also took several glasses of sherry. He had, it seems, worn his light fall overcoat instead of the fur greatcoat necessary for winter weather; and he confessed to having pawned his greatcoat for a few days when all three dependents converged with pleas for help at the same time. Anna Grigoryevna was so outraged that she broke into tears "and talked like a madwoman, without choosing my words."[47] Dostoevsky calmed her by promising not to leave his house until the greatcoat was redeemed. This was only the beginning of Anna's struggle to wrest Dostoevsky free from those who, she believed, were unduly exploiting his generosity and sense of obligation.

The most immediate obstacle to Dostoevsky's marriage was simply that, in addition to being saddled with his brother Mikhail's debts, he had assumed so much financial responsibility for his family. Anna Grigoryevna realized to her dismay that "the moment Feodor Mikhailovich got hold of any money, all his relatives . . . would instantly put forward their sudden but urgent needs; and out of the three or four hundred rubles received from Moscow for *Crime and Punishment* no more than thirty or forty would remain to Feodor Mikhailovich by the next day. Of this sum, moreover, nothing would be paid off on his promissory notes except the interest."[48] It would clearly be impossible, if this pattern continued, for Dostoevsky ever to discharge his debts, no matter how much he wrote and how successful his works might be. Once she became his wife, Anna Grigoryevna decided, she would take their finances into her own hands and put a brake on this self-defeating beneficence; but for the moment there was little she could do except remonstrate.

For the marriage to take place, a considerable sum would be required over and above the payments accruing from *Crime and Punishment*.

---

* Mikhail Dostoevsky had also kept a mistress named Praskovya Petrovna Anikieva, by whom he had had a son, and Dostoevsky contributed to their support as well. There is a reference to her in A. G. Dostoevskoi, *Dnevnik A. G. Dostoevskoi 1867 g.* (Moscow, 1923), 111.

Since literature was Dostoevsky's only source of income, he decided to travel to Moscow over Christmas and offer his next novel to Katkov in return for an advance sufficient to provide for the ceremony and a new establishment. *Crime and Punishment*, still in the course of publication, continued to hold readers riveted to the pages of *The Russian Messenger*, and there was good reason to believe that Katkov would be forthcoming with funds. In case of failure, Dostoevsky planned to begin another novel immediately, write a good part of it as rapidly as possible, and then offer it to the first taker; but this might mean postponing the wedding for as long as a year. (The trip to Moscow would also allow Dostoevsky to have a final talk with the despondent Elena Pavlovna, whose ailing husband was still dragging out his life but to whom, nonetheless, Dostoevsky still felt a certain commitment.) Happily, Katkov readily acceded to Dostoevsky's request and promised two thousand rubles, which would start arriving in installments in January; the date of the wedding was thus set for mid-February. But the first installment of seven hundred rubles instantly vanished in the usual fashion; and after estimating that the wedding would cost between four and five hundred rubles, Dostoevsky prudently entrusted this part of the second installment to Anna for safekeeping. He knew full well that, if left in his hands, it would immediately be disbursed to his importuning relatives.

Dostoevsky's first marriage had taken place in a miserable little Siberian village, in the most humble and modest circumstances, among people he scarcely knew, and with the acknowledged ex-lover of his bride as one of the witnesses. His second was celebrated amidst the splendors of the Izmailovsky Cathedral, brilliantly illuminated for the occasion and resounding with the voices of a superb chorus, surrounded by his family and closest friends and, at his side, a radiant young bride who adored and revered him as man and artist. He could hardly believe his good fortune, and when introducing Anna to his friends at the wedding reception in her mother's home, he kept repeating: "Look at that charming girl of mine! She's a marvelous person, that girl of mine! She has a heart of gold!"[49] There are few moments in Dostoevsky's life when we catch him enjoying unalloyed happiness, and this is certainly one of those rare occasions. Nor were his hopes disappointed or his expectations betrayed; the marriage was to prove a solid and enduring one, with the bonds of affection between the couple only increasing and strengthening with the passage of time. But Anna, as perhaps Dostoevsky was even then uneasily aware, would indeed need "a heart of gold" to cope with and surmount what lay ahead for her in the immediate future, both in Russia and in her life with Dostoevsky abroad.

CHAPTER 9

The Gambler

With Anna Grigoryevna's devoted assistance, Dostoevsky was able to win one of the most serious gambles he had ever made in his life: he accomplished the spectacular feat of composing a lengthy novella within a month, met Stellovsky's deadline, and retained the publication rights to his literary works. In fact, Dostoevsky had long thought of using gambling as a theme for a novella, and he had probably made some preliminary notes for such a story at Lublino during the summer of 1866. *The Gambler*, originally entitled *Roulettenberg*, was no doubt more clearly defined in his mind than he may have led Anna to believe in the fall. The result, in any case, was one of the liveliest, brightest, and most amusing of his shorter creations.

2

The first mention of this theme goes back to the summer of 1863, when Dostoevsky was traveling in Europe with his erstwhile mistress Apollinaria Suslova. Consumed with bitterness and resentment at having just been humiliatingly abandoned by her Spanish lover, a medical student known only as Salvador, she was withholding her sexual favors from Dostoevsky and engaging in a cat-and-mouse game of advance and withdrawal. Dostoevsky was gambling furiously all during this trip, and he thought of recouping his losses by turning them into literature. While in Rome, he wrote to N. N. Strakhov outlining a work for which he hoped Strakhov could obtain an advance. "I have in mind," he wrote "a man who is straightforward, highly cultured, and yet in every respect unfinished, a man who has lost his faith but *who does not dare not to believe*, and who rebels against the established order and yet fears it." The letter then continues:

> The main thing, though, is that all his vital sap, his energies, rebellion, daring, have been channeled into *roulette*. He is a gambler, and not merely an ordinary gambler, just as Pushkin's Covetous Knight is not an ordinary miser. . . . He is a poet in his own way, but the fact is that he himself is ashamed of the poetic element in him, because deep down he feels it is despicable, although the need to take risks

ennobles him in his own eyes. The whole story is the tale of his playing roulette in various gambling houses for over two years.

Dostoevsky then compares his projected story with *House of the Dead*,
which "was a portrayal of convicts who had never been portrayed *graph-
ically* by anyone before." Similarly, "this story is bound to attract attention as a *graphic* and very detailed representation of gambling at roulette." Aside from the fact that "materials of this type are read with
considerable curiosity in our country, gambling at spas, especially where
Russian expatriates are concerned, has some (perhaps not unimportant)
significance."[1] This last comment hints that a passion for gambling possesses some sort of symbolic national (that is, Russian) meaning.

Most commentators tend to view *The Gambler* in purely biographical
terms, as a transcription of Dostoevsky's tormenting relations with Suslova at this period (as well as an unrivaled portrayal of the onset of Dostoevsky's own gambling mania, which has since become a setpiece in
psychiatric textbooks). Or, focusing on the first sentence of the above
quotation, they have tried to force the events into some sort of religious
framework.[2] But neither of these alternatives is satisfactory: Dostoevsky never wrote a fictional work whose significance was *merely* autobiographical; nor can the religious reading, which construes Aleksey's
pathological gambling as the result of a loss of faith in God, be supported
by a single line in the text. On the contrary, when Aleksey steps into a
gambling casino for the first time, he writes: "As for my innermost moral
convictions, there is no place for them, of course, in my present reasoning [about gambling]. I'll leave it at that. I am saying this to relieve my
conscience" (5: 218).

Aleksey thus confirms that he retains both his "innermost moral convictions" and his "conscience"; there is not a trace of any questioning of
the accepted moral code or of God, from whom that code derives. Moreover, such a religious-metaphysical approach clashes with the *tonality* of
the novella, which is jaunty, bouncy, and full of a certain youthful high
spirits (as befits the narrator, despite his unhappy fate). The focus of its
theme is on the vagaries of the Russian national character rather than on
the results of a loss of faith in God; and the first of these subjects could
be treated with a certain levity.

My own view is that, by the time Dostoevsky came round to using the
idea outlined in his letter, he had altered his thematic aim. The religious
motif had dropped by the wayside, and instead he developed what had
been mentioned only as an afterthought—namely, that the gambling of
Russian expatriates "has some (perhaps not unimportant) significance."
In the novella, this significance becomes linked to the remark about the
gambler being "a poet in his own way," who "is ashamed of the poetic

element in him ... although the need to take *risks* ennobles him in his own eyes." Dostoevsky explains this idiosyncratic notion of "poetry" by a reference to Pushkin's Covetous Knight, who amasses a fortune not for the sake of the money itself but solely for the psychological sense of power it enables him to acquire over others. "Poetry" in this Dostoevskian sense means acting not for immediate self-interest or for the gratification of any fleshly material desire, but solely to satisfy a powerful psychic craving of the human personality, whether for good or evil.

Dostoevsky believed that the Russian character was peculiarly susceptible to this kind of "poetry," and much of the story is taken up with illustrating the contrasts between the Russian national character and others (French, English, German). No one, so far as my knowledge goes, has paid the slightest attention to this important aspect of the text; but it makes *The Gambler* the only work of Dostoevsky's that is "international" in the sense of that word made familiar by, for example, the fiction of Henry James. It is, in other words, a story in which the psychology and conflicts of the characters not only arise from their individual temperaments and personal qualities but also reflect an interiorization of various national values and ways of life. In Russian literature, there is the German-Russian contrast in *Oblomov*, the French-Russian contrast in *War and Peace*, and the Caucasian-Russian contrast in *The Cossacks*. Dostoevsky's *The Gambler*, far from being only a self-exposing dramatization of one of the problems of his personal life, belongs with such books as a spirited but by no means uncritical meditation on the waywardness of the Russian national temperament.

3

Written in the form of a first-person confession or diary, like *Notes from Underground, The Gambler* recounts a decisive series of events in the life of the narrator, Aleksey Ivanovich. This cultivated and highly intelligent young Russian nobleman is serving as a tutor in the entourage of a Russian General Zagoryansky, who is temporarily living abroad. He imagines himself to be in love with the General's stepdaughter Praskovya (or Polina, as she is more familiarly called), and their romance constitutes the central plot line. Commentators have been so bemused by the biographical overlappings that they have simply identified Aleksey with Dostoevsky and taken Polina as the supposedly "demonic" Suslova.

In fact, however, as D. S. Savage pointed out long ago, Aleksey is an unreliable narrator, and the picture he gives of Polina is woefully distorted by his own frustrations and grievances.[3] The two characters who serve as moral yardsticks—the allegedly moribund Auntie, a wealthy Russian matriarch who erupts on the scene as large as life, and the English lord and prosperous manufacturer Mr. Astley—both speak of Polina in the very highest terms. Their view of her character is totally different from that of the presumably love-struck and embittered Aleksey, who vehemently insists that he would throw himself down from the Schlangenberg mountaintop, a local tourist attraction, if she would but give the command. Yet he resents her at the very same time and cannot overcome his conviction that she looks down on him, from the height of her superior social position, with the utmost indifference.

The characters in *The Gambler* break down easily into two groups—the Russians and the Europeans—and they are contrasted along lines that may be described, to use Dostoevsky's own category, as "poetic" and "nonpoetic." Among the Europeans are the fake (or exceedingly dubious) Count or Marquis de Grieux and his supposed cousin, Mlle Blanche de Cominges; her presumably noble origins are quite clearly sham, and she is in fact a high-priced *cocotte*. Both of these French figures are linked with the family of the widowed General, who is residing in grand patriarchal style at a German gambling spa called Roulettenberg and squandering money right and left. The General has given promissory notes to de Grieux on all his Russian estates in return for loans and is completely in the Frenchman's power. The sensual and provocative Mlle Blanche would also dearly love to improve her social position by becoming *madame la générale*; and as long as the smitten General is in funds, she allows him to pay his court. All the hopes of the General depend on Auntie, whose momentarily expected demise will pour a considerable fortune into the General's lap. Even after paying off his debts, he would still remain an extremely wealthy Russian *barin*; and what de Grieux has not taken will be left to Mlle Blanche.

Both de Grieux and Mlle Blanche are thus moved by exclusively mercenary motives (though the latter has a few upsurges of sentimental generosity); and Mlle Blanche's relation to the General is paralleled by that of de Grieux to Polina. He had seduced her earlier in the belief that she was a wealthy heiress; but he becomes increasingly cool as the General's financial prospects grow dimmer. Unlike the aging General, who is deeply and genuinely smitten with Mlle Blanche (this is *his* way of being a "poet"), Polina no longer has any illusions about de Grieux. "The moment he finds out that I, too, have inherited something from her [Auntie]," she tells Aleksey, "he will immediately propose to me. Is that what you wanted to know?" (5: 213). The only other important foreign character is Mr. Astley, an exemplar, it is true, of all the gentlemanly virtues, but also a partner in a sugar refining firm and thus limited by his English world of prosaic practicality and common sense.

The Russian characters, on the other hand, are all moved by feelings whose consequences may be practically disastrous but in every case

4. A gambling room in Wiesbaden

involve some passion transcending practicality. Both the General and Polina have been stirred by love, and Polina has now transferred her affections to Aleksey—though he is too self-absorbed and self-preoccupied to understand that her presumed coldness would dissolve in an instant if he did not continually insist on his slavish subservience to her supposed tyranny. What obsesses Aleksey is the sense of his own social inferiority as a humble tutor in the General's household, where, despite his culture, education, and status as a Russian nobleman, he is treated little better than a servant. He *is* treated outrightly as a servant by the de Grieux–Mlle Blanche tandem, as well as by the hotel staff, and he totally misunderstands Polina because he believes that she disdains him for the same reasons. He cannot possibly imagine that she might favor him over two other much more imposing suitors, de Grieux and Mr. Astley, and he exhibits a rankling acrimony to which she responds in kind. The dialogues between the two crackle with the tension of this love-hate relationship, though the supposed "hate" is really caused by Aleksey's wrongheaded view of Polina's feelings.

Even before arriving, Aleksey had been convinced that "something would happen to me in Roulettenberg, that there would be something, quite without fail, that would affect my destiny radically and definitively" (5: 215). Roulette would thus change his life; and he explains to Polina, when she challengingly inquires what transformation would occur, that "with money I'll be a different man, even for you, not a slave" (5: 229). Aleksey begins to gamble, presumably as a means of winning Polina, but more from a need for egoistic self-affirmation than a genuine desire for love. When Polina rightly accuses him of counting on "buying me with money," he indignantly rejects the charge; but her reply hits the nail on the head. "If you aren't thinking of buying me, you certainly think you can buy my respect with money" (5: 230). Polina already knows that de Grieux's "love" waxes and wanes depending on his estimate of her financial status; and she is wounded to the quick by Aleksey's assumption that *her* feelings toward him could be swayed for the same reason. At the climax of the plot action, Aleksey's behavior toward Polina in fact comes to parallel that of de Grieux.

Aleksey's conduct, however, will not be the result of the same "non-poetic" acquisitive motives displayed by the suavely elegant Frenchman. For when Aleksey begins to gamble, the excitement of the play causes him to lose sight entirely of his presumed goal of winning the funds necessary to change his life and gain Polina. Far from stopping when luck is in his favor, he continues to gamble because "some kind of strange sensation built up in me, a kind of challenge to fate, a kind of desire to give it a flick on the nose, or stick out my tongue at it" (5: 224). The thrill of this "strange sensation," which may be taken as his means of overcoming his perpetual sense of abasement, overpowers every other consideration; and he invariably continues to gamble until he is entirely wiped out.

Those who win, on the other hand, behave like the emblematic Frenchwoman who, in one scene, places "her bets quietly, coolly, and calculatingly, taking notes with a pencil and sheet of paper of the numbers that were coming up and trying to find the patterns according to which the chances fell at a given moment. . . . Every day she would win a thousand, two thousand, or at most three thousand francs . . . and . . . she would immediately walk away" (5: 262). But once Aleksey experiences the excitement of gambling "poetically," that is, the excitement of his "challenge to fate," he finds the sensation so exhilarating that he never wishes it to end; and so he becomes not only an incorrigible gambler but also an inveterate loser.

Aleksey has been shown very early in the text to be an ardent Russian patriot, who vehemently defends his country's very unpopular policies against French and Polish critics (*The Gambler* is set just after the suppression of the Polish rebellion of 1863–1865). But when de Grieux remarks "caustically and spitefully," referring to the tutor's losses, that "Russians were . . . lacking in talent even in gambling," Aleksey at first seems to agree (5: 223). This insulting observation, however, is then turned around into an encomium of the Russians' refusal to dedicate their lives entirely to the accumulation of wealth. "Roulette is simply made for Russians," Aleksey declares, because "the faculty of amassing capital has become, through a historical process, virtually the main point in the catechism of the virtues and qualities of civilized Western man." Russians have never learned to revere such amassing of capital as an end in itself; but they need money too, and so "are very fond of, and susceptible to, methods such as, for example, roulette, allowing one to get rich suddenly in two hours, and without work. And since we gamble to no purpose, and also without real effort, we tend to be losers!" (5: 223).

All the same, Aleksey declares roundly, "I would much rather spend my whole life in a Kirghiz nomad's tent . . . than worship the German idol," that is, "the German method of saving money by honest work." This "German idol" is then amusingly caricatured in imagery taken from the pastoral-idyllic strain of German literature (for example, Goethe's *Hermann und Dorothea*). "They have here, in every house, a *Vater*, who is extraordinarily honest. . . . Every such *Vater* has a family, and in the evening they read instructive books aloud to each other. Elms and chestnut trees rustle over the little house. Sunset, storks on the roof, and all of it is so extraordinarily poetic and touching." But the honest *Vater* keeps his family "in a condition of complete servitude and submission," and "they all work like mules and all save money like Jews." Any personal happiness they might possibly obtain in their lives is relegated to a far-distant future. Such an appalling prospect fills Aleksey with dread because, as he declares, "I am [not] willing to consider my person as a necessary accessory to capital" (5: 225–226).*

One might be inclined to take Aleksey's peroration merely as a clever riposte to de Grieux's withering disdain; but Dostoevsky certainly meant it to have a wider application. This becomes clear from the quite diverting episode involving Auntie (also called Grandmother), who, instead of expiring on schedule in Moscow, explodes unexpectedly on the Roulettenberg scene and sends all the hopes pinned on acquiring her fortune flying out the window. The blunt old matriarch, despotic and high-handed but fundamentally humane and kindhearted, represents the tra-

---

* This passage of *The Gambler* is quoted even more extensively in the fascinating and pathbreaking article of the economic historian Alexander Gerschenkron, "Time Horizon in Russian Literature." By an economic time horizon, Gerschenkron means the amount of rational economic planning and forecasting for the future that goes beyond present needs and immediate wants. In his view, "the greater the degree of economic backwardness of a given area, the lower the time horizon of economic agents within it."
Because information on such a subject is hard to come by, Gerschenkron examines Russian literature for data and singles out Aleksey Ivanovich's tirade as representative of the extremely low economic time horizon of the Russian relation to money. A similar Russian-German contrast is of course found in *Oblomov*, and Gerschenkron cites passages of the same kind from Gogol and Saltykov-Schchedrin. See Alexander Gerschenkron, "Time Horizon in Russian Literature," *Slavic Review*, 4 (1978), 692–715.

ditional down-to-earth virtues of the Russian gentry unspoiled by any truckling to foreign tastes and fashions. Her commanding presence inspires immediate respect and deference even in the imposing Oberkellner of the fashionable hotel, used to receiving the best European society.

Auntie's behavior, so far as gambling is concerned, provides a textbook illustration of Aleksey's view concerning the Russian attraction to roulette. Instantly tempted by such a miraculous and seemingly effortless enrichment, she pays no attention to Aleksey's warnings and promptly begins to play. What possesses Auntie is the imperious pride of someone used to issuing commands and being obeyed, the pride of a Russian landowner all-powerful on her estates. "'There, look at it,' Grandmother said angrily, 'how long will I have to wait until the miserable little zero comes up. For the life of me, I'm not going until the miserable little zero comes up!'" (5: 263). It finally does, and she is hooked. Unwilling to stop until she imposes her will on the velleities of the wheel, she loses heavily, stubbornly cashes all her securities at a ruinous rate to continue to play, and loses every penny. A loan from Mr. Astley enables her to limp home contritely to Russia, where she plans to rebuild the local parish church in penance for her gambling sins (thus additionally dismantling the notion that gambling is somehow connected with a loss of faith in God).

One other aspect of this Auntie episode provides important foreshadowing of the dénouement of the Aleksey-Polina romance. On her first visit to the casino, Auntie embarrasses everyone by insisting on entering its august precincts accompanied by her majordomo Potapych and her peasant maid Marfa. "So she is a servant, so I have to leave her behind!" she retorts to the General's warnings about propriety. "She is a human being too, isn't she? . . . How could she go anywhere, except with me?" (5: 259). Later, when gambling has taken over, she loses all concern for Marfa and snappishly dismisses the maid when she devotedly begins to escort her mistress again. Once the passion for gambling has gained the upper hand, all other human feelings and relations just cease to exist.

4

The arrival and departure of Auntie creates a crisis in the lives of the other characters, since it is clear that she will not give a cent to the General and that her funeral mass will hardly be said tomorrow. De Grieux thus announces his intention to leave for Russia and claim the General's property. Before departing, he sends a letter to Polina explaining ceremoniously that he must renounce all further hopes for *their* future, but that, as a man of honor, he would turn over fifty thousand francs to the General on her behalf. Aleksey finds her sitting in his room that night and realizes that her presence could only mean one thing. "Why that meant that she loved me! . . . she had compromised herself before everybody, and I, I was just standing there, refusing to understand it!" (5: 291). How he might have behaved is indicated the next day by Mr. Astley, who remarks acidly that Polina "was on her way here yesterday, and I should have taken her to a lady relative of mine, but as she was ill, she made a mistake and went to you" (5: 300). Far from thinking of how best to protect the reputation of his alleged beloved, Aleksey rushes off to play roulette and win the fifty thousand francs neeeded to wipe out de Grieux's insult. Nothing had changed in their relations, and he still behaved as though it were necessary to "buy her respect."

At the casino, Aleksey hits a sensational winning streak, playing frantically and frenziedly in the "Russian" style—"haphazard, at random, quite without thought" (5: 293). His luck continues to hold, and "now I felt like a winner *and was afraid of nothing, of nothing in the world*, as I plunked down four thousand on black" (ibid.; italics added). Staking on impossible odds, his usually crushed personality is freed from its crippling limits; he is aware of nothing except the intoxication of this release, and he breaks off play only accidentally when he hears the voices of onlookers marveling at his winnings. "I don't remember," he remarks, "whether I thought of Polina even once during all this time" (5: 294).

Just as he had forgotten Polina while gambling, so he becomes aware, on the way back, that what he now feels has little to do with her plight. What dominates his emotions is "a tremendous feeling of exhilaration—success, triumph, power—I don't know how to express it. Polina's image flitted through my mind also. . . . Yet I could hardly remember what she had told me earlier, and why I had gone to the casino" (5: 295). When his first remark to her is about the best place to conceal the money, she breaks "into the sarcastic laughter I had heard so often . . . every time I made one of my passionate declarations to her" (ibid.). Polina had sensed the falsity of his so-called passion in the past, and now she sees its bogusness confirmed even more glaringly. It is at this moment, when she realizes that Aleksey's attitude is not really different from that of de Grieux—both men gauge her most intimate sentiments only in terms of money—that her ulcerated pride and dignity bring on a hysterical crisis. Turning on Aleksey with detestation, she says bitterly: "I won't take your money. . . . You are giving too much. . . . de Grieux's mistress is not worth fifty thousand francs" (ibid.). But the true pathos of her condition is then revealed when she breaks down completely, caresses Aleksey in delirium, and keeps repeating: "You love me . . . love me . . . will you love me?" (5: 297).

Aleksey spends the night with Polina in his room, and on waking, "with infinite loathing" (5: 298), she flings the fifty thousand francs in his face as she had wished to do with de Grieux. Aleksey is still puzzling over this event while composing his manuscript a month later, and his pretended lack of comprehension (really a guilty self-deception) is reminiscent of the underground man's self-excuses for the mistreatment of the prostitute Liza, who had come to him for aid. "To be sure," he is honest enough to admit, "it all happened in a delirious state, and I knew it too well, and . . . yet I refused to take that fact into consideration." But then he tries to reassure himself that "she wasn't all that delirious and ill. . . . So it must be she knew what she was doing" (5: 298–299). What Polina *did* know was that Aleksey's love had not been genuine enough, nonegoistic enough, to resist taking sexual advantage of her deranged and helpless condition.

5
———

What occurs at this point, when Aleksey goes off with his winnings to Paris in the company of Mlle Blanche, has been found by some commentators to be quite unconvincing. "The act confounds us," the usually insightful Edward Wasiolek has written, "and seems unprepared for in any way."[4] But Aleksey's initial description of Mlle Blanche strongly suggests that he is far from being impervious to her well-displayed attractions. Nor does the prescient Mr. Astley, "in a tone as if he were quoting information from a book," have any doubt about Aleksey's destination: "All Russians, when they have some money, go to Paris!" (5: 300). Aleksey will follow the usual Russian path and kick up his heels in Paris, but Dostoevsky motivates him a little more individually all the same. Mlle Blanche is not lacking in either psychological acumen or a smattering of education, and she propositions the newly affluent Aleksey with a quotation from Corneille's *Le Cid*, asking him if he has the courage to dare. Since his personality is still under the spell of the psychic afflatus provided by his gambling exploit, he goes off with her on the spot. "I can't say I felt very cheerful," he confesses, "but, since the previous day, I had been conditioned to risking everything on one card" (5: 302).

The Paris pages of *The Gambler* are more or less a blur of impressions, similar to the scenes in Turgenev's *A Nest of Gentlefolk* describing the reactions of an idealistic gentry-landowner whose frivolous and unfaithful wife has plunged him into the Parisian maelstrom as a sickened spectator. Mlle Blanche is honest enough in her own way, and, while spending Aleksey's money hand over fist, she introduces him to a friend Hortense, who keeps him occupied in a manner suggested by her nickname, *Thérèse-philosophe*—the title of a well-known eighteenth-century pornographic novel. Still, Aleksey becomes terribly bored at Mlle Blanche's parties, where he is forced to play host to the dullest businessmen with newly minted fortunes, insolent and ignorant military types, and "a bunch of wretched minor authors and journalistic insects" with "a vanity and conceit of such proportions as would be unthinkable even back home in Petersburg—and that is saying a great deal!" (5: 304). (How Aleksey might have known this is not clear; but Dostoevsky was certainly in a position to make such a comparison.) The escapade comes to an end, and Aleksey is sent on his way once all his money—to which he displays a total indifference ("un vrai Russe, un calmouk!" Mlle Blanche says admiringly)—has been dissipated, much to the benefit of Mlle Blanche's social prestige (5: 308).

Although the main story of *The Gambler* ends with this episode, a final chapter, dating from a year and eight months later, provides a pointed commentary. Aleksey has now become an addicted gambler, traveling around Europe and picking up odd jobs as a flunkey until he can scrape together enough money to return to the tables. He is completely dependent on the "strange sensation" afforded by gambling, the thrill that enables him to affirm his identity and triumph momentarily over his gnawing sense of inferiority. "No, it wasn't the money I craved. . . . I only wanted that the next day all these Hinzes [another employer], all these Oberkellners, all these magnificent Baden ladies, should all be talking about me, tell each other my story, wonder at me, admire me and bow before my new winnings" (5: 312). Nonetheless, he also feels that "I have grown numb, somehow, as though I were buried in some sort of mire" (ibid.). This feeling was particularly aroused by a meeting with Mr. Astley, supposedly accidental but in fact carefully arranged at the instigation of Polina.

Auntie had died meanwhile, leaving Polina a comfortable inheritance, and she has been keeping a concealed but protective eye on Aleksey all this while. Mr. Astley, covertly sent to see if Aleksey has changed in any way, discovers that he is much the same—if not worse. He still believes that Polina is in love with de Grieux, and reiterates his opinion that "young Russian ladies" invariably mistake a Frenchman's "elegance of form" for that of "his own soul," whereas in reality it is only "an external garment" (5: 316). At this, exploding with rage, Mr. Astley reveals that he has come to see Aleksey expressly on Polina's behalf; it is really Aleksey she has loved all along. "What's worse, even if I were to tell you that she still loves you, why, you would stay here just the same! Yes, you have destroyed yourself. You had some abilities, a lively disposition, and you are not a bad man. *In fact, you might have been of service to your country, which needs men so badly.* . . . I am not blaming you. It seems to me that all Russians are like that, or are disposed to be like that. If it isn't roulette, it's something else but similar to it. . . . You are not the first who does not understand what work is (I'm not talking about your plain people). Roulette is preeminently a Russian game" (5: 317; italics added).

Aleksey himself had said the same thing earlier in his rejection of the "German idol"; but now Mr. Astley shows the obverse side of this refusal to discipline the personality in some way and harness it to achieve a desired result. The "poetic" character of the Russian personality, if left to operate unchecked, can lead both to personal disaster and the obliteration of all sense of civic or moral obligation. Aleksey apparently wants to take this lesson to heart, and with the ten louis d'or left him at parting by Mr. Astley he thinks of gambling in a new way for the first time: "Yes, all it takes is to be *calculating and patient* just once in a lifetime—that is all! *All it takes is to keep control of yourself just once, and your whole life will be changed in an hour!*" This last phrase, however, betrays the old, incorrigibly Russian Aleksey; and what he remembers in the last paragraph is the exhilaration he had once felt when he bet the small sum he had been saving for dinner and won one hundred and seventy gulden. "And what if I had lost heart that time, if I had not dared to take that chance?" (5: 318; italics added). He will, it appears, continue to gamble in the "Russian" style.

Read in such ethnic-psychological terms, *The Gambler* may be seen as Dostoevsky's brilliantly ambivalent commentary, inspired by his own misadventures in the casino, on the Russian national character. Disorderly and "unseemly" though the Russian character may be, it still has human potentialities closed to the narrow, inhuman, and Philistine penny-pinching of the Germans; the worldly, elegant, and totally perfidious patina of the French; and even the solidly helpful but unattractively stodgy virtues of the English. "For the most part," as Aleksey remarks to Polina, "we Russians are so richly endowed that we need genius to evolve our own code of manners. And genius is most often absent, for, indeed, it's a rarity at all times. It's only among the French and perhaps some other Europeans that the code of manners is so well defined that one may have an air of dignity and yet be a man of no moral dignity whatever" (5: 230).

But if Russians have not yet worked out their own code of manners, and if the dangers of such a lack have become quite obvious, they can only demean themselves by attempting to imitate any of the European models. For all his weaknesses, Aleksey arouses sympathy both because of his honesty about himself (except in the case of his night with Polina, which she has presumably forgiven) and because of his unerring eye and refreshing disrespect for the hypocrisies, pretensions, and falsities by which the Europeans cover up their shortcomings. One of the most amusing episodes, which can be mentioned only in passing, involves Aleksey's "insult" to an insufferably pompous German baron and baroness; he refuses to apologize and ties everybody into knots by pretending to insist on the punctilio of the European gentlemanly code of *politesse* and *point d'honneur*. There is an engaging brashness and sincerity about him that wins the friendship of all the "positive" characters (Polina, Auntie, Mr. Astley), and Dostoevsky certainly hoped the reader would share some of their sentiment. Nor was Aleksey perhaps meant to be seen as *entirely* a lost man, if we judge by his reaction upon learning that Mr. Astley had been sent by Polina: "'Really, Really!,' I exclaimed, as tears came gushing from my eyes. I just could not hold them back. I believe that it was the first time in my life this had happened" (5: 317). Such tears may presage something for the future, and they surely indicate an access of undistorted feeling of which the earlier Aleksey had been incapable; but whether this is to be taken as a hint of possible recovery may be left undecided.

6

The Gambler, as we have said, should not be read in simple biographical terms; but it nonetheless allows us to catch a glimpse of how Dostoevsky may well have rationalized his gambling addiction to himself. From this angle, the work may be considered both a self-condemnation and an apologia at the same time. No doubt it must have been some consolation to believe, as Dostoevsky probably did, that his own losses, which almost always resulted from a failure to stop playing when he was ahead, were the consequence of a national Russian trait carried to excess and not merely a personal defect of character. He was, after all, a "poet" in both the literal and the symbolic senses of that word; and his "poetry" was proof that he found it impossible to subordinate his personality to the flesh-god of money, before whom, as he had written in *Winter Notes*, all of Western civilization was now prostrate. He lost materially, but in some sense he gained a certain reaffirmation of national identity from his very losses. One should also keep in mind that, at the time Dostoevsky wrote *The Gambler*, his yielding to this weakness had so far injured no one but himself, and he referred to it with a certain bravado. It was only after his second marriage that the addiction began to elicit feelings of acute guilt and remorse.

The Gambler, in any case, is a sparkling little work, whose style and technique are in the vein of satirical social comedy familiar from Dostoevsky's Siberian novellas (*Uncle's Dream* and *The Village of Stepanchikovo*). The relation of Aleksey and Polina, and the portrayal of the treacherous allurements of gambling, strike a deeper note than these earlier and relatively lighthearted productions; but while Aleksey's gambling may be a "challenge to fate," this challenge is not developed into the moral-religious questionings of the major novels. The gambling scenes are in a class by themselves, and no one, before or since, has depicted the intoxicating delirium of a gambling obsession with such intimate mastery. The rather risky use of an unreliable first-person narrator has led to much misunderstanding, especially when it later was combined with what became known of Dostoevsky's biography; but the recognition that Aleksey's view of Polina should not be taken at face value is now generally accepted. The real blemish of *The Gambler* is Dostoevsky's unpardonably vicious smear of the Polish exiles supposedly hanging around Roulettenberg, all of whom are shown to be nothing but abjectly servile scroungers and petty crooks. Under the circumstances of the time, this slander displays an embittered chauvinism that is a deplorable regression from the equable and even admiring portraits of Polish fellow prisoners in *House of the Dead*.

Not the least interesting aspect of *The Gambler*, finally, is that it points both backward and forward in Dostoevsky's artistic development. Aleksey's obsession with the hope of winning somewhat resembles Raskolnikov's fascination with his theory of crime; and neither character can maintain the total, rational self-control of the emotions that is the prerequisite of success. The thrill and excitement that Aleksey momentarily feels may also be taken as another, more muted variant of the absolute power that Raskolnikov believes he has the right to arrogate for himself. There is also a reminder of *Crime and Punishment* when Mr. Astley, commenting on the incapacity of the Russian educated class to understand the importance of work, sounds very much like Razumikhin attributing the rise in crime among this group to exactly the same cause.*

Pointing to the future is the figure of Polina, the pure-souled woman degraded and almost driven mad (in this case only a temporary breakdown) by the violation of her deepest feelings when she finds herself in the position of being bought and sold. The outlines of the queenly Nastasya Philippovna in *The Idiot*, consumed with pathological self-hatred for the same reasons, are already visible here; so, more faintly, is Aglaya Epanchina in Aleksey's remarks about "young Russian ladies" and their sentimental illusions about Europeans. In the tenaciously long-lived Auntie, the warm and lovable matriarchal tyrant, we can see a first sketch for the similarly sympathetic and choleric Mme Epanchina. Dostoevsky was thus already feeling his way toward some of the characters of his next great novel; but when he wrote *The Gambler*, he had not yet the faintest idea of what this new major undertaking would turn out to be.

---

* "Well, what did that Reader [an academic title] of yours in Moscow answer when he was asked why he had counterfeited the tickets?" Razumikhin asks. " 'Everybody else gets rich by various means, and we wanted to get rich too as quickly as we could.' ... The idea was to do it at other people's expense, as quickly as possible, *and without work*. They were used to having everything found for them, to being in leading-strings, to being spoon-fed" (6: 118; italics added).

CHAPTER 10

Escape and Exile

Dostoevsky's courtship of Anna Grigoryevna was a whirlwind affair: only four months elapsed between their first meeting and the wedding. During most of this period Anna spent a good part of every day alone with Dostoevsky, on whom his family did not intrude while he was at work, and she was thus removed from the normal course of his day-to-day existence. The two were totally absorbed by their efforts to complete *The Gambler*, and their intimacy was certainly fostered by this relative isolation. Anna's contacts with Dostoevsky's family and friends had been very few and fleeting, but this seclusion naturally ended once their impending wedding was announced. Work still continued, however, on the final chapters of *Crime and Punishment*, and the happy pair were also much taken up with planning their future life together.

Once the wedding festivities were over, though, Anna found herself part of a pattern of life established long before she came on the scene, and one to which, much against her will, she was now forced to adapt. Her presence, moreover, was resented as that of an interloper who threatened to undermine the expectations of those accustomed to live off Dostoevsky's by no means secure or uninterrupted income. Her position as wife thus became increasingly burdensome and frustrating; and it was largely because of her dissatisfaction, as well as her determination to save her marriage at all costs—even at the price of some personal financial sacrifice—that the Dostoevskys decided to go abroad in the spring of 1867. There were other reasons for this decision as well: Dostoevsky's epilepsy had recently taken a turn for the worse, and he was convinced that his attacks lessened when he lived in Europe. Also, he sought some respite from the constant harassment of his creditors. But without the stimulus provided by Anna's unhappiness, as well as the funds that she raised to make the trip possible, the Dostoevskys probably would not have embarked on what turned out to be, quite unexpectedly, four years of European *Wanderjahre*.

2

The days immediately following the wedding were filled with postnuptial celebrations, and Anna Grigoryevna remarks "that I drank more goblets of champagne during those ten days than I did all the rest of my life." So too did her new husband; and those celebratory libations brought on Anna's first face-to-face encounter with the frightening physical manifestations of Dostoevsky's dread disease. Dostoevsky had spoken of his epilepsy at their very first meeting; but his attacks usually occurred at night in his sleep, and Anna as yet had not been confronted with a daytime onset. It overtook him at the home of her sister, just as Dostoevsky, "extremely animated," was telling some story. Suddenly, "there was a horrible, inhuman scream, or more precisely, a howl—and he began to topple forward."[1] A similar incident had occurred just after Dostoevsky's first marriage, as he and his bride were journeying back to Semipalatinsk; and Marya Dimitrievna never quite recovered from the shock of the shattering event, which cast a pall over their life together from the very start.

Nothing so undermining overcame Anna Grigoryevna, though she was younger, had been more sheltered, and might have been expected to be even more frightened. Although her sister became hysterical and fled from the room with a "piercing scream," Anna seized Dostoevsky firmly by the shoulders, tried to place him on the couch, and, when this failed, pushed aside the obstructing furniture and slid his body to the floor. There she sat holding his head in her lap until his convulsions ceased and he began to regain consciousness. The attack was so severe that he could hardly speak, and the words he succeeded in uttering were gibberish. An hour later he suffered another onslaught, "this time with such intensity that for two hours after regaining consciousness he screamed in pain at the top of his voice. It was horrible."[2] Such repeated attacks were mercifully infrequent, and Anna Grigoryevna attributes the one she describes to the nervous strain, as well as the obligatory overindulgence in drink, of the postnuptial visits. Drinking invariably had a bad effect on Dostoevsky, and he rarely allowed himself more than an occasional glass of wine.

Anna Grigoryevna proved quite capable of coping with such severe tests of her own equilibrium and did not allow them to dampen her joy at being Dostoevsky's bride. But she found herself initially helpless before a much more insidious and covert threat to her happiness—one that arose partly from the objective circumstances of Dostoevsky's life, partly from her bruising contacts with other members of Dostoevsky's family, most notably his stepson, Pasha.

Dostoevsky's routine, as Anna Grigoryevna discovered, made it almost impossible to spend any time with him alone. He wrote or read at night, slept through most of the morning, and rose in the early afternoon. An early riser, Anna busied herself with household matters while he slept, but found that it was usual for his young nieces and nephews, all attractive and some quite musically gifted, to drop in during the late morning and stay for lunch. In the afternoon, other friends and relatives arrived, and very often remained for dinner. Anna Grigoryevna, with no experience in managing a household, found this unceasing round of hospitality wearisome and burdensome. The only people she found interesting and enjoyed entertaining were Dostoevsky's literary friends. But the younger people often found their conversation boring, and Anna, closer in age to the young, was asked to take them to another room and look after their amusement.

The hostility of Emilya Feodorovna, which Anna had felt so acutely at their first meeting, slackened because of Anna's kindness toward, and tolerance of, the visits of her children. But her attitude remained patronizing if no longer outrightly inimical, and she spared no occasion to comment within Dostoevsky's hearing on Anna Grigoryevna's all too evident shortcomings as a housekeeper—of course only for the purpose of helping her to improve! Her obtrusive presence became a constant source of irritation despite her seeming goodwill; but the irksomeness of Dostoevsky's sister-in-law was nothing compared to the machinations of Pasha, who bitterly resented the intrusion of this outsider on what he considered his foremost claim to Dostoevsky's concern and financial resources. Pasha, who continued to live with his stepfather after the marriage, had been accustomed to take charge of the household himself; and Dostoevsky had been only too content to leave such domestic matters in his hands. The appearance of Anna Grigoryevna put an end to this (so far as Pasha was concerned) very convenient arrangement. According to Anna Grigoryevna, whose testimony concords with what little is known about Pasha Isaev's unattractive character, he carried on a veritable campaign designed to undermine the marriage and protect his hitherto unchallenged power over the Dostoevsky household management.

In her memoirs, Anna Grigoryevna goes into considerable detail about the various maneuvers used by Pasha to suborn her authority. One tactic was to make daily life as difficult as possible, and then to place the blame for everything that went wrong on her faulty supervision. There is no need to dwell on all the petty details of this family warfare; it is enough that Anna very quickly came to feel that the daily aggravations were part of a larger purpose. "With these continual unpleasantnesses of his [Pasha's], his squabbling and the tales he carried to Feodor Mikhailovich, he was counting on embroiling my husband and myself in quarrels and forcing us to separate."[3] Worst of all, while Dostoevsky was present, Pasha carefully concealed his hostility under a surface of attentiveness and amiability; but he did not restrain himself from coarsely expressing his resentment to Anna's face once they were alone. Dostoevsky, who was infinitely patient with his stepson's shortcomings—a patience probably nourished by a sense of guilt toward Pasha's dead mother—was completely hoodwinked, and even commented happily on the improvement of his manners as a result of Anna's influence.

All these tensions made the first weeks of Anna's new life very far from the blissful period she had anticipated, and even led her to question the viability of her marriage. There were doubts about her own ability properly to master her new tasks; fear that her shortcomings had already made Dostoevsky regret his choice; and also anger that "he, 'the great master of the heart,' failed to see how difficult my life was and kept pressing his boring relatives on me and defending Paul, who was so hostile to me."[4] The growing sense of estrangement from Dostoevsky that Anna began to feel took on major importance because of the very nature of their relationship. On her part, as Anna explains, this was more "cerebral" than physical; her passion for Dostoevsky was "not a passion which might have existed between persons of equal age." It was, rather, "an idea existing in my head . . . it was more like adoration and reverence for a man of such talent and such noble qualities of spirit," and "a searing pity for a man who had suffered so much without ever knowing joy and happiness, and who was so neglected by all his near ones."[5] The very basis of Anna's love for Dostoevsky was threatened by the conditions of their life together, which fell back into the very pattern Anna had hoped to change and whose alteration had been, in her eyes, the justification of their marriage.

Matters came to a head about a month after the wedding, when Anna Grigoryevna felt too tired and upset to accompany Dostoevsky to an evening party at the Maikovs. The moment his stepfather had left, Pasha assailed her with more than his usual vehemence. Roundly declaring that Dostoevsky's marriage had been a "colossal folly," he accused her of spending too much of "the funds intended for all of us," and ended with the terrible charge that Dostoevsky's epilepsy had worsened recently through the fault of Anna Grigoryevna.[6] The beleaguered Anna broke down completely, retreated to her room in tears, and was still sobbing inconsolably in the darkened chamber when Dostoevsky returned. In reply to his anxious inquiry, Anna finally poured out all her griefs, to which he listened in surprise and astonishment. Apparently he had no inkling of how matters really stood, and had been completely taken in by Pasha's maneuvers. He acknowledged that their life together since the wedding had proved onerous to him as well, especially the constant visits of the young people; but he thought they provided distraction for Anna Grigoryevna. When Anna expressed fears that he had ceased to love her, he was quick with reassurances and proposed a trip to Moscow to allow them to escape from the pressures of their Petersburg routine.

Dostoevsky had been thinking of such a trip to see Katkov and to explore the possibility of obtaining a further advance that would allow them to travel abroad in the summer. The reunited pair left the very next day, to the surprise but not the objection of the household retinue, who assumed quite correctly that Dostoevsky was applying to Katkov for additional funds but had no idea how these were intended to be spent. The Moscow trip enabled Dostoevsky to introduce Anna to the Ivanovs, relatives with whom he was on the friendliest terms, and who were pleasantly surprised that he had married a very presentable young woman and not "a Nihilist, with bobbed hair and spectacles" (the information that Anna was a "stenographer" had led to such suspicions).[7] There was some prejudice against Anna Grigoryevna because she had definitely ended all hope of a future marriage between Dostoevsky and Elena Pavlovna; and the younger people missed no opportunity, in the midst of the obligatory cordiality, to make her feel their displeasure under the guise of jokes and quips. Nothing untoward occurred, however, and Dostoevsky later used some of this chafing for *The Eternal Husband*, which depicts the atmosphere of the Ivanov household.

One incident during their visit made a great impression on Anna Grigoryevna, and taught her a lesson she was never to forget. Taking part in a card game one evening, she was seated next to a lively and amusing young man who spoke to her without the calculated snippishness of the others, and to whom she responded with animation and pleasure. Dostoevsky, playing in a different room, looked in frequently to see how Anna was faring; and his mood as the evening wore on became gloomier and gloomier. On returning to their hotel, in response to Anna's attempts to cheer him up, he turned on her furiously with the accusation of being a "heartless coquette" who had flirted with a younger man all evening solely to torment her husband.[8] Apollinaria Suslova had of course discarded Dostoevsky for a younger lover, and he obviously lived in fear of the same misfortune befalling him once again. This little scene ended with Dostoevsky comforting Anna Grigoryevna and begging forgiveness for his unjustified accusations; but it revealed the bottomless depths of his anxieties, and she resolved to be more careful in the future. During this trip Anna also visited her younger brother Ivan, a student in the Petrovsky Agricultural Academy on the outskirts of the city. It was here, a few years later, that Sergey Nechaev and his radical group murdered a classmate of Ivan Snitkin's, an event that Dostoevsky would place at the center of *The Devils*.

Katkov continued to be as obliging as ever and readily accorded Dostoevsky another advance of a thousand rubles. It seemed that the hope of going abroad would finally be realized, and Anna returned to Petersburg glowing with a secret sense of satisfaction and triumph. Nothing was said as yet publicly about their future plan, but matters came to a head very quickly when Emilya Feodorovna suggested renting a large house for the summer in Pavlovsk. To this proposal, Dostoevsky replied that he and Anna would be abroad at that time; and the news created consternation in the ranks of the assembled family. Conversation stopped instantly, Emilya Feodorovna went to speak with Dostoevsky privately in his study, and a furious Pasha flatly told Anna Grigoryevna that *he* would not tolerate such a trip, whose expenses would seriously deplete the funds on which all the family drew. His remonstrances with Dostoevsky proved unavailing, however, and the family finally fell back on *demanding* that advance sums for their expenses be left before the couple's departure.

By the time these sums were totaled up, the amount far exceeded the thousand rubles that Katkov had promised. Matters were made worse when one of Dostoevsky's creditors, who previously had been satisfied with interest, now suddenly insisted on at least partial repayment of a debt under the threat of seizing and selling Dostoevsky's belongings. The financial obstacles to a trip seemed insuperable, and Dostoevsky was willing to abandon it and accept Pavlovsk—with the promise to Anna of writing something over the summer that would, he hoped, pay for a trip abroad in the fall. Anna's heart sank when Dostoevsky explained how impossible their planned journey had turned out to be, and she hurried away more oppressed than ever with the weight of her despairing thoughts. She was convinced that "if we were to save our love, we needed to be alone together if only for two or three months . . . [and] that then the two of us would come together for the rest of our lives, and that no one could separate us again." With the determination that always marked her actions, she decided to raise the travel money herself by pawning her dowry. This involved a considerable risk of losing possessions that she cherished, and the elderly Anna Grigoryevna looks back with some bemusement as she re-creates her feelings of that time. "Possessions—furniture, fancy clothes—have great importance when one is young. I was extremely fond of my piano, my charming little tables and whatnots, all my lovely things so newly acquired."[9] But she was convinced that the future happiness of her marriage was at stake, and this belief crowded out every other sentiment in guiding her course of action.

Anna immediately went to consult her mother, whose disapproval she feared, but who readily agreed that such a radical step was necessary to ensure the future of the union. What Anna says about her mother's attitude goes a long way toward explaining the formation of the daughter's character and values. "She was a Swede," Anna comments, "her view of life was more Western, more cultured; and she feared that the good habits inculcated by my upbringing would vanish thanks to our Russian style of living, with its disorderly hospitality." Dostoevsky had always refused to take a penny of Anna's belongings and was harder to persuade; but she prepared the ground carefully by first going to pray with him in a chapel during a walk and only then broaching her idea. As anticipated, he instantly rejected her proposal to pawn her property; it was only after she broke down and began to sob in the street, imploring him to "save our love, our happiness," that he hastily agreed.[10] Already well acquainted with the waverings of his will, Anna insisted that they go straightaway to apply for a foreign passport (as an ex-convict, Dostoevsky had to get special permission to travel abroad, and this often took time). Luckily, the clerk was an admirer of Dostoevsky and promised that the document would be ready in a few days. Anna's mother gathered up the jewelry, silver, and other valuables the very same evening, and an appraiser came a day later for the furniture.

Dostoevsky then announced that he and Anna were going abroad after all—and no later than two days hence! Pasha's instantaneous objections were cut short, and Dostoevsky told his dependents that they would receive the sums asked for but not a kopek more; the extra money was Anna Grigoryevna's, and he had no right to dispose of it except in accordance with what had already been decided. The pair packed very quickly, entrusting all future financial arrangements to Anna's mother, and took along only a necessary minimum since they expected to be gone for no longer than three months. In fact, they were not to return for four years.

Although Anna Grigoryevna was later able to write that "I shall be eternally grateful to God for giving me strength in my decision to go abroad," this gratitude was often tempered by bitter afterthoughts in the years closer to the event. "There [abroad]," she writes somewhat ingenuously in her memoirs, "a new, happy life began for Feodor Mikhailovich and me which strengthened our mutual friendship and love and continued up to the day of his death."[11] All this is true of the remainder of their life as a whole, but hardly of the period following their departure. A "new" life certainly began for them, but one that could be called unqualifiedly "happy" only in the harmonizing light of a memory evoking a cherished and now-vanished past. What occurred, in truth, was to test Anna Grigoryevna's devotion and moral stamina to the uttermost, and it was her ability to measure up to the challenge that, in the long run, forged an unshakable foundation for her marriage.

4
———

The Dostoevskys left for their European "vacation" on April 12/26, 1867, accompanied to the railroad station by Anna Grigoryevna's relatives as well as by Emilya Feodorovna, her daughter Katya, and Dostoevsky's old friends the Milyukovs (Milyukov had come to say good-bye to him in the Peter and Paul Fortress before he left for Siberia, and had greeted him at the railroad quay on his return). Pasha, in a fit of pique, was not among the party; he refused to join in wishing Godspeed and a pleasant voyage to his stepfather and his new bride.

The Dostoevskys took the train from Petersburg to Berlin, and then moved on to Dresden, where they rented three rooms in a private home and apparently intended to settle. Dostoevsky, heavily in debt to Katkov, planned to set to work there on his next novel, and also to write an article on V. G. Belinsky for which he had received an advance from another editor. But the distractions entailed by their first weeks of living abroad, and particularly by a disastrous ten-day expedition to the roulette tables at Hombourg just a month after arriving, prevented him from progressing at all on the novel. During the spring and summer, however, Dostoevsky was gathering impressions and undergoing experiences that would enter into its creation in one form or another, though he was hardly aware that they would have any direct relation to its composition.

Anna Grigoryevna had promised her mother to keep an account of the trip, and she purchased a notebook at the station just before departure to fulfill that obligation. This shorthand diary, which she kept until the birth of her first child a little over a year later, provides a more extensive and detailed account of the day-to-day events in Dostoevsky's life than we possess for any other period of his existence. Unfortunately, Anna Grigoryevna concentrates largely on the externalities of their circumstances and encounters, or on explaining her own reactions to events rather than on illuminating those of her husband. If we are to judge from her pages, Dostoevsky hardly spoke to her at all about his work; even when she had some knowledge of it—he dictated his lost article on Belinsky to her, for example—she simply records the fact and says not a word about its content. Again, she often refers to the spats and quarrels between them in these early days, when she defended her opinions or took umbrage at some of his behavior, but she never offers details that might help to reveal his ideas and attitudes. What preoccupied her—and not without good reason—was the immediate and quite straitened circumstances in which they lived, the problem of adjusting to Dostoevsky's continually changing moods, and the difficulties of living in a foreign environment where they did not know a soul and were constantly thrown back on themselves for companionship.

Dostoevsky was not an easy person to get along with even under the best conditions, and his continually recurring epilepsy, though most of the attacks were relatively mild, invariably made him irritable, intolerant, and quarrelsome. Nor was his temper improved by his rabid xenophobia, which manifested itself in an intense dislike of the Germans among whom he lived and whose language he spoke very brokenly. He was constantly offended by what he considered negligent or disrespectful treatment in hotels and restaurants (the Dostoevskys took all their meals in restaurants, with the exception of breakfast), and he often complained about the food in a provocative and offensive manner. Of one such incident in a pastry shop, Anna herself remarks: "He seems to take a perfect delight in saying uncivil things to the Germans." Indeed, on these occasions his command of the language improved remarkably, as Anna notes amusedly of an altercation over a seat in a railway carriage. Anna Grigoryevna was much more peaceable and less bigoted; but she joins Dostoevsky in denouncing the congenital "stupidity" of Germans (someone was always giving them wrong directions!) or fretting bitterly about the petty cheating from which they suffered at the hands of waiters, landlords, and tradespeople.[12]

What Anna called Dostoevsky's "irritable, volcanic nature" also led to continual disagreements between the two. Dostoevsky was vexed at having his utterances or judgments challenged, and often upbraided Anna quite harshly when she differed with him. Despite such rebukes, she took a certain youthful pleasure in provoking him nonetheless. On one occasion, he was railing against the Germans, "and as we happened to pass by a German Hussar, got into a frenzy over the King of Saxony and his guard of fifty thousand men. I said I didn't see why he shouldn't have it, if he had the money. (As a matter of fact, I cared not a rap if the King had a guard or not, or whether he lived or died; I only contradicted for the sake of something to say.) But Feodor was all the more seriously annoyed with me and told me if I was as stupid as that I had better hold my tongue." At other times, they quarreled about a "sunset" (!), or because Anna, forgetting Dostoevsky's years in the Russian army, questioned whether he could hit the bullseye at a shooting gallery. Having fully demonstrated his marksmanship, Dostoevsky then snapped out that her remark "only confirmed a thought he had long had, that a wife was the natural enemy of her husband." This led to another dispute, and Anna jots down dispiritedly a day or two later: "What does it all mean, this perpetual quarreling between us?"[13]

To focus exclusively on the bickerings of the couple, however, would be to present a quite distorted image of their actual relations. Anna was infinitely tolerant of her husband's bad-tempered reactions and never forgot—how could she, being a pityingly pained witness to his frequent epileptic convulsions—that much of his irascibility was caused by the deranged state of his nerves. She never really took such abuse seriously, and writes, just after having been called "stupid," "I simply can't be cross with him; sometimes I show a severe face, but I've only to look at him for all my wrath to melt away." Dostoevsky's rages, as she depicts them, were all on the surface; the moment he saw her truly upset or disturbed he would shift instantly from rancor to tenderness. Just after the shooting-gallery incident, for example, Anna stalked off to return home alone,

and Dostoevsky arrived to find her in tears; whereupon he began to in-
veigh against the lonely life they were living and declared he was certain
that Anna "deplored ever having married him and a lot more silly nonsense of this kind." Clearly, he had been brooding over the possible consequences of his splenetic behavior, and his repentant words led to "a
heart-to-heart talk, and I felt so much more easy in my mind." It was
Dostoevsky's habit to wake her and say good-night before going to bed
(she retired earlier), and then "we talk together for ages, and he says
pretty things to me and we joke and laugh, and that is the time we seem
to come nearest together and is most precious to me of all the hours of
the day."[14] All of their disputations, so far as can be judged from Anna's
diary, ended with such renewed pledges of affection, and thus did not
leave any lasting scars.

Whatever the strains and stresses of daily life with Dostoevsky under
such trying conditions, Anna Grigoryevna was doggedly determined to
make her marriage a success. What she feared most, rather than the
hardships arising from their poverty or Dostoevsky's mercurial personality, was that she might lose him to his earlier passion for Suslova. Anna
kept a watchful eye on her husband and knew very well that he was
keeping in touch with his ex-mistress. Just before leaving for Dresden,
Dostoevsky had received a letter from Suslova, to which he replied
shortly after arriving there. Suslova had been living abroad for a year,
and he brings her up to date on what has been occurring in his life—his
contract with Stellovsky and the writing of *The Gambler*, the recent wors-
ening of his epilepsy, the extreme financial pressure caused by having
assumed his brother's debts, his isolation and loneliness, and finally his
marriage and decision to go abroad. Of Anna Grigoryevna, he writes that
she has "a remarkably good and open character. . . . The difference in
age is terrible (20 and 44), but I am more and more convinced that she
will be happy. She has a heart and knows how to love." This laconic observation could well be an implicit reproach to Suslova; and such an in-
ference can be supported by Dostoevsky's concluding words, which respond to Suslova's complaints about her own sadness and melancholy.
"Oh, my dear, I do not invite you to a secondhand *obligatory* happiness,
I respect you (and have always respected you) for your rigorousness, but
I know that your heart *cannot* but demand love, and you consider people
to be either infinitely radiant, or the next moment scoundrels and vul-
garians. I judge by the facts. Draw your own conclusion."[15] Dostoevsky
knew that Anna would not evaluate him in such exacting terms, and that
inexhaustible tolerance, rather than implacable stringency, was what he
required most of all.

Dostoevsky made rather perfunctory efforts to conceal his correspondence with Suslova from Anna, and perhaps he believed that she remained ignorant of his epistolary infidelity. Anna was not deceived for a

moment, and when Dostoevsky was absent—he spent a good deal of time alone in cafés reading French and, whenever possible, Russian newspapers—she did not scruple to look through his letters. "It isn't the thing, I know, to read one's husband's letters behind his back," she remarks guiltily, "but I couldn't help it. The letter was from S[uslova]. After I had read it, I felt cold all over, and shivered and wept with emotion. I was so afraid the old inclination was going to revive and swamp his love for me. Dear God, do not send me this miserable fate! Just to think of it makes my heart stand still."[16] Suslova's letter has regrettably been lost, along with a later one that Anna picked up at the post office just after seeing Dostoevsky off for Hombourg. Carefully opening the flap so that it could be resealed, she decides that "it was a very stupid, clumsy letter and says but little for the understanding of the writer. I am quite sure she is furious about Feodor's marriage, and her annoyance is easy to see from the tone of the letter. . . . I went over to the looking-glass and saw how my face was covered with little red spots from excitement."[17] Such a possible challenge to her marriage certainly fortified Anna's resolve patiently to endure all the onerous burdens that it entailed.

5

The romance of Dostoevsky and Anna Grigoryevna had blossomed in the course of their work together on *The Gambler*, and there is a certain irony in their future union being inaugurated under the auspices of this creation. Nothing placed more of a strain on Anna Grigoryevna than the renewed onset of Dostoevsky's gambling obsession once they began living abroad; and this work, if she could only have known it, foreshadowed what was to become the worst enemy of her marital happiness. Dostoevsky, to be sure, had spoken to her of his infatuation with gambling and identified himself with the feckless protagonist of his story; but he had also exposed its dangers—both through the fate of Aleksey Ivanovich and through the condemnatory diagnosis of Mr. Astley. Anna could well have believed that the novella had exercised a cathartic effect, and that Dostoevsky's gambling days were over. Besides, he had spoken to her of his future life as involving a choice between losing himself in gambling or remarrying; and since he had now chosen the second, it might have seemed that he had renounced the first. In fact, however, it was another of his utterances that presaged the future more accurately. When Anna expressed a "contempt" for Aleksey Ivanovich, "whose irresoluteness I could not forgive," Dostoevsky told her that "it is possible to possess a strong character, to prove that fact by your own life, and nonetheless lack the strength to conquer in yourself the passion for roulette."[18] Dostoevsky here was unquestionably speaking of himself, and

soon nothing was to be more important for him than to cling to his conviction that yielding to such a human weakness as roulette did *not* justify
a total moral condemnation.

Three weeks after settling in Dresden, Dostoevsky began to speak of
making a trip to Hombourg to try his luck, and Anna Grigoryevna,
though dreading the prospect ("when I think of his going away and leaving me here alone, cold shivers run down my spine"), raised no objection. Instead, she assured him that she could look after herself quite satisfactorily, and confided to her diary: "I see how this place begins to
weary him and put him in a bad temper. It's so natural; here he is all
alone, and no men to whom he could talk a little. . . . And, as the thought
of this trip fills his mind to the extinction of everything else, why not let
him indulge in it?"[19] For Dostoevsky, the passion and excitement of the
play, which he conveys so vividly in *The Gambler*, was obviously the lure;
but there were always perfectly solid objective reasons allowing him to
rationalize his desire, and these reasons had just recently acquired a new
urgency.

Not only was there hanging over him, as in the past, the staggering
load of debt he had assumed and his obligations to his dead brother's
family; now his very freedom was at stake. Just before leaving, two of his
creditors filed charges that could have led to his arrest and incarceration
in debtor's prison. As he wrote a bit later to Apollon Maikov, "it was
touch and go that I wasn't seized."[20] Dostoevsky could thus no longer
return to Russia without risking imprisonment, and his only chance of
regaining his homeland was to obtain enough money to pay his debts. In
addition, there was his hope of establishing a family, with all the new
expenses that this would entail (for Anna Grigoryevna had become pregnant sometime shortly after their departure from Russia). Never had
Dostoevsky been under greater psychic pressure to obtain funds quickly,
and he was haunted by the image he had seen (or believed he saw) of
others easily doing so at the roulette tables. His own addiction to gambling, combined with the ever-reviving hope of emerging from his financial quagmire in one miraculous stroke, thus made the attraction of the
casinos irresistible.

Dostoevsky took the train to Hombourg on May 4/16, filled more with
trepidation and remorse than anticipatory excitement as he left Anna
Grigoryevna in tears at the station. He wrote her a day later: "I was terribly sad yesterday. How I would have liked to take you in my arms, to
have you with me, and though the thought came to me, I didn't turn
back. I am acting stupidly, stupidly, even more, badly and out of weakness, but there is just a minuscule chance and . . . to hell with it, that's
enough."[21] Dostoevsky hardly was going off to Hombourg with a light
heart, as if on a joyous escapade, and his mood became considerably

worse as the inevitable began to happen. In his second letter, he accurately foresees the future: "But I imagine my torment if I lose and leave without accomplishing anything . . . even more of a beggar than when I arrived."[22]

Even though planning just a three- or four-day interval, Dostoevsky remained in Hombourg for ten days, winning and losing but never able to break away in time when luck was in his favor, and finally being wiped out entirely. He pawned his watch at one point, managed to redeem it a day or so later, but then lost it again for good; and so, as Anna remarks on his return, she never knew what time of day or night it was. The agitated letters he wrote her daily are painful to read, and continually oscillate between self-castigation for yielding to temptation and frantic reassertions of the possibility of winning if one could manifest the self-control shown in *The Gambler* to be so antithetical to the Russian national character. "Here is my definitive observation, Anya: if one is prudent, that is, if one is as though made of marble, cold, and *inhumanly* cautious, then definitely *without any doubt*, one can win *as much as one wishes*." Someone in the casino was always performing such a feat successfully; this time it was a Jew who played "with horrible, *inhuman* composure" and "rake[d] in the money," leaving every day with a thousand gulden. Dostoevsky reports that he has short stretches of such composure, and always wins while they last; but very soon, confirming his view of Russians, he loses control and is carried away into disastrous recklessness. Like Aleksey Ivanovich, he finds the whole business morally repugnant, and implores his wife: "Anna, promise me never to show these letters to anyone. I do not want tongues to wag about this abominable situation of mine. 'A poet remains a poet.'"[23]

What is so striking about these letters, aside from their pathetic disclosure of Dostoevsky's weakness and capacity for self-delusion, is the depth of the guilt-feelings they express. Dostoevsky had berated himself in the past because of gambling losses he could ill afford, but he had never given way to such extreme self-flagellations. Never before, to be sure, had anyone been so helplessly dependent on him as Anna Grigoryevna, and never before had he felt so morally reprehensible in sacrificing her to his compulsion. As he remarks himself, after confessing to gambling away the money she had sent for his return fare: "Oh, if only the matter concerned just me, I wouldn't even be wondering now; I would have laughed, given it up as a bad job, and left. One thing and *one thing only* horrifies me: what will you say, what will you think about me? And what is love without respect? After all, because of this our marriage has been shaken. Oh, my dear, don't blame me permanently!" Entreating Anna to send him the fare again, he pleads with her not to come herself out of mistrust. "Don't even think of *coming* here *yourself* because of not trusting me. Such a lack of trust—that I will not come back—will kill me."[24]

In one of these letters, as scholars have long noted, Dostoevsky strikes off a passage that he will use verbatim in *The Idiot*. Exclaiming over how well and unaffectedly Anna's letters express her feelings, he complains: "I can't write like that and express my heart, my feelings that way. Both in reality and when we're together I'm sullen, uncommunicative, and do not at all have the gift of expressing all of myself. I don't have form, gesture."[25] This last sentence will eventually be uttered by Prince Myshkin; but Dostoevsky's letters from Hombourg, and the whole torturing experience they convey, can be linked to his next novel in a less external manner as well.

Dostoevsky had always depicted characters whose external behavior or lowly social position was no indication of their true moral worth. Raskolnikov, the murderer torn by remorse, whose crime was at least partly a wrathful revolt against human suffering, is morally superior to the totally selfish, unscrupulous, and impeccably respectable attorney Luzhin. There is always a gap for Dostoevsky between a surface conformity to accepted conventions of conduct and a genuine moral sensibility; the first is never a gauge of the second, and his characters sometimes behave in the most reprehensible fashion while inwardly acknowledging with remorse their guilt and their shame. Nowhere will such characters be more prominent than in *The Idiot*, where a whole host of figures abruptly swings back and forth between arrant rascality and contrite apologia. The often incongruous seesawing of such characters may well be seen as a transposition of Dostoevsky's own attempts, in the midst of his gambling frenzy, to maintain a minimum of self-respect, and to reassure himself that he was not entirely a worthless reprobate.

Indeed, one can go even further in speculating about such connections between his gambling and his next novel. For Dostoevsky now began to feel, not as a longed-for ideal but as a blessed moral-psychic reality, the soothing and consoling effects of Anna's all-forgiving love. "I'm not the one who has a saintly soul, my radiant angel," he writes, "but you, you have the saintly soul. . . . In my situation a letter like [yours] is like manna from heaven. At least I know that there is a being who loves me for my whole life."[26] Is it any wonder that the theme of compassion stands so firmly at the center of the next artistic universe that Dostoevsky was very soon to create?

If one aspect of Dostoevsky's misadventures in Hombourg recalls Aleksey Ivanovich (without, to be sure, that character's bounciness and bravado), another evokes Mr. Astley. As his losses mounted and the hopelessness of his situation became self-evident, what appeared to be the only means of salvation was the panacea of getting back to work. "My darling, we will have very little money left," he writes, "but don't grumble, don't be downcast, and don't reproach me. . . . I'll write Katkov right away and ask him to send me another 500 rubles to Dresden. . . . As for me, I'll get down to work on the article about Belinsky and while waiting for a reply from Katkov will finish it. My angel, perhaps this is even all for the best; I'll be rid of that cursed thought, the monomania, about gambling. Now again, just as the year before last (before *Crime and Punishment*), I'll triumph through work."[27] Such resolutions were invariably the result of Dostoevsky's gambling misfortunes.

Dostoevsky at last returned to a long-suffering and lonely Anna Grigoryevna, who had valiantly tried not to give way to despair in his absence. He wrote his promised letter to Katkov requesting another advance, and life resumed its ordinary round while the pair waited for a reply and lived frugally on some money (much less than they had expected) sent by Anna's mother. Pleas for funds from Pasha and Emilya Feodorovna also arrived, and, much to Anna's concealed resentment, Dostoevsky answered them patiently. She could not help but feel that their demands were at least in part responsible for his gambling mania, which she had now come to fear and abhor.

Toward the end of May, Dostoevsky was greatly upset by the news of an unsuccessful attempt made on the life of Alexander II by a Polish exile, Anton Berezowski, as the Tsar was visiting Paris for the opening of a world's fair. "God be thanked—that is indeed a piece of good fortune for all us Russians," Anna jots down after learning that the Tsar had not, as first reported, been wounded. Then she adds: "Feodor was dreadfully excited at the attempt on the Tsar's life. He loves and honors him a great deal."[28] This news, which provoked an epileptic fit that night, only increased Dostoevsky's already virulent anti-Polish sentiments and hardened his animosity toward the Russian radicals who had supported the Polish cause a few years before.

Dostoevsky's intention had been to move to Switzerland after receiving the funds from Katkov; but in planning the trip, the alluring idea of a stopover at Baden-Baden to recoup his gambling losses tempted him once again—especially since, in his letters to Anna from Hombourg, he had complained that his concern over her welfare was a source of emotional disturbance that prevented him from putting his infallible "method" for winning into practice. The desire to return to her, to get things over with as quickly as possible, constantly led him into overeagerness and loss of control. It had been a mistake not to have brought her along; if they were together in Baden, this obstacle to success would be eliminated. As Anna Grigoryevna writes sadly in her memoirs, "he spoke so persuasively, cited so many examples in proof of his theory, that he convinced me too," and she agreed to spend two weeks in

5. Attempt on the life of Alexander II in Paris, 1867

Baden-Baden, "counting on the fact that my presence during his play would provide a certain restraining influence. Once this decision was made, Feodor Mikhailovich calmed down and began to rewrite and finish the article he was having so much trouble with," the piece on Belinsky.[29] The pair left Dresden for Baden-Baden on June 21/July 3 and arrived a day later; but an account of this eventful interlude must be reserved for the next chapter.

6

Despite the deficiencies of Anna Grigoryevna's *Diary*, which barely gives a glimpse of Dostoevsky the writer and cultural personality, some useful information of this kind can still be gleaned from her pages. When, upon first settling in Dresden, Dostoevsky saw a copy of Herzen's *My Past and Thoughts* (*Byloe i Dumi*) in a window on one of his strolls, he hesitated to buy it because of the price. Later, when Anna persuaded him to spend the two thalers, they returned to find the work no longer in stock; instead they procured two volumes of Herzen's periodical almanac *The Polar Star* (*Polyarnaya Zvezhda*), though Anna soon located a copy of the memoirs elsewhere. *My Past and Thoughts* was indispensable for Dostoevsky at this time because it contained a celebrated portrait of Belinsky in the famous section portraying the generation of the 1840s; and it was Herzen's delineation of the tempestuous Belinsky, always exploding either with moral indignation or with rapture at some new enthusiasm, that Dostoevsky was planning to supplement. In Herzen's memoirs,

Dostoevsky also read about the far less well-known but extremely color-ful and almost legendary figure of Father Vladimir Pecherin, a Russian who had become a Roman Catholic and a priest of the Redemptorist Order.

Vladimir Pecherin had been a fellow student of Herzen's at the University of Moscow in the 1830s, and, though the two never met there, they had many friends in common. Like other members of his generation, Pecherin was attracted to the moral-religious ideals of Utopian Social-ism, and he also wrote poetry that circulated in manuscript among his university companions and their circle. A brilliant student of the classical languages, Pecherin was sent abroad for two years on a government scholarship to complete his education. On his return, he was appointed, even before completing his degree, Professor of Greek language and an-tiquities. He gave an impressive opening lecture and was an inspiring teacher; but after one term he left for Europe, explaining to the authori-ties in a letter that he would never return to a country among whose inhabitants it was impossible to find the imprint of their Creator.

After four years of wandering in the West, sometimes reduced to the utmost poverty, Pecherin converted to Catholicism and joined the rigor-ous Redemptorist Order, whose mission is to to work among the poor (Herzen erroneously calls him a Jesuit). Thirteen years later, when Herzen had taken up residence in London, he learned by chance that Pecherin was living in a monastery in nearby Clapham. Curious to inves-tigate the enigma of this remarkable career, Herzen arranged to call on his fellow Russian, and he recounts the visit with his usual inimitable mastery of evocative detail. The letters exchanged between the two after Pecherin had read some of Herzen's works reveal, as might be expected, a sharp clash of views concerning the future of mankind and the founda-tions of human society.

Noting that Herzen seemed to rely on "philosophy and literature" to create a more desirable world order, Pecherin objects: "the evidence of history is entirely against you . . . only religion has ever served as the foundation of a state." Herzen countered by expressing his usual belief that Russia, with its "communistic people," was destined to create a new world, and that only science provided the hope for future betterment. "The masses have been left by their teachers in the state of cattle. Sci-ence, nothing but science, can correct that now and give them a piece of bread and a roof." But Pecherin then expresses horror at the prospect of such a world, based on "a limited, narrow science, a materialistic science that analyses and dissects matter and knows nothing else. . . . Woe to us if *that* science triumphs." What Pecherin feared most, he declares, was to be forced to participate in a world dominated exclusively by materialistic interests and the "tyranny of matter." To which Herzen ripostes that the triumph of Pecherin's principles would lead to the entire suppression of whatever freedom already exists and the reign of total tyranny. "And what is there to fear?" he queries Pecherin ironically. "The rumble of the wheels bringing its daily bread to the hungry, half-clad crowd?"[30]

That Dostoevsky read this exchange with the utmost care is quite clear from an unmistakable allusion in *The Idiot*, where the drunken buffoon Lebedyev, who is at the same time an interpreter of the Book of Revelation, explicitly refers to the disagreement in the course of a tipsy tirade. There is, he exclaims, "one secluded thinker" (Pecherin) who has complained that "mankind has grown too busy and commercial," and he has been answered by another thinker "who is always moving among his fellows" (Herzen). This second thinker, with a flourish of triumph, retorts that "the rumble of the wagons bringing bread to starving humanity is better, maybe, than spiritual peace"—after which thrust he "walks away . . . conceitedly." Lebedyev, who in my opinion speaks for Dostoevsky here, comments on this dispute with bibulous solemnity: "But vile as I am, I don't believe in the wagons that bring bread to humanity. For the wagons that bring bread to humanity without any moral basis for conduct, may coldly exclude a considerable part of humanity from enjoying what is brought" (8: 311–312). Dostoevsky certainly had no idea, when he came across this Herzen-Pecherin dialogue, that he would soon use it for his next novel; nor is there any mention of it in his notes. But its employment indicates how, even when still very far from having discovered his new theme and central character, his creative subconscious was absorbing a controversy concerning the relation of the Christian moral ideal to a world consumed by the "materialistic interests" from which Pecherin had fled in dismay.

Herzen's pages on Father Pecherin not only provided Dostoevsky with some of the inspiration for *The Idiot* but also flowed into *The Devils* as well. In the course of their conversation, Herzen refers in passing to several poems by Pecherin that he recalled having read in Moscow and asks for permission to print them if copies of the manuscripts can be found. Pecherin, who had no copies himself and denied being able to dictate them from memory, refused to give any definite answer about publication while affecting indifference toward his youthful effusions. Herzen managed to obtain them, however, and they appeared in an anthology published by his Free London Press. Dostoevsky had resolved, as we know from Anna Grigoryevna, "to read through all the censored publications" published abroad, believing that "it [was] essential for his future works that he should do so";[31] and this poetic anthology was not neglected. Evidently, he found in one of Pecherin's poems, "The Triumph of Death," a superbly expressive example of the overheated Romantic lyricism of the 1830s. There is a delightful parody of this work in the opening chapter of *The Devils*, devoted to the glorious career of Stepan Trofimovich Verkhovensky, where the poem is adduced as one of the literary peccadillos of his youth, fearfully circulated in manuscript, in defiance of the authorities, "among two dilettanti and one student" (10: 9).

While in Dresden, Dostoevsky also advised Anna Grigoryevna to read *Les Misérables*, which they found in the local library, and she remarks that "Feodor has a tremendous opinion of it and always likes to read it again. It was he who recommended it to me and explained lots of things to me about the character of the hero."[32] Dostoevsky thus re-read Hugo's book himself, and so gained a refreshed impression of the character of Jean Valjean, whom he soon mentioned as one of the few attempts in the novel to create an embodiment of the Christian moral ideal comparable to Prince Myshkin. Anna also read Dickens on the advice of her husband; and though she mentions only *Nicholas Nickleby* and *The Old Curiosity Shop*, it is quite likely that they also spoke of Mr. Pickwick, whom Dostoevsky a few months later would cite as a comic portrayal of an ideal Christian character. But it was not only from literature that Dostoevsky was receiving creative suggestions linked with the genesis of Prince Myshkin.

One of the few amusements of the Dostoevskys in Dresden, aside from listening to concerts in the gardens of restaurants and in the public parks, was to visit the Dresden Gallery and other local sights of cultural and artistic interest. Anna Grigoryevna soon became an assiduous sight-seer, and Dostoevsky comments on this proclivity with some amusement and relief to Apollon Maikov. "For her, for example, it's a thoroughly satisfying undertaking to go examine some silly town hall, make notes about it, describe it (which she does in her own stenographic marks, and has filled up seven tablets), but more than anything else she has been taken and struck by the Gallery, and I am very glad for that, because too many impressions were revived in her soul for her to get bored."[33] After rising late and working the first part of the day, Dostoevsky would meet her at the gallery in the afternoon; and many impressions of his own soul were thus constantly being revived as well. What these impressions were may be gathered indirectly from Anna's account of one of their first visits. "At one end of the Gallery is the Holbein Madonna, at the other end the Raphael. At last Feodor took me to the Sistine Madonna. . . . What beauty, what innocence, what sorrow are in that divine countenance, what humility and suffering in those eyes. Feodor thinks there is pain in her very smile."[34]

They returned a day later, and Anna records: "On our way our attention was attracted by the Murillo Madonna hanging in the first room of all. What a wonderful face it is, how tender is the coloring! The Christ Child, too, is so sweet with the loveliest possible look on its little face. We

... stopped for a time before Titian's *Tribute Money*—a magnificent picture, and worthy to be compared, as Feodor said, with Raphael's Madonna. All the suffering in Christ's face is shown so wonderfully, the sublimity, the sorrow.... In another room is to be found the Redeemer of Annibale Carracci that Feodor loves particularly and sets so much store by.... Feodor took me to see Claude Lorrain's pictures that are mostly mythological." Anna remarks elsewhere that Dostoevsky, when he arrived to pick her up, "hurried from one room to another ... and never will stand except in front of his favorite pictures."[35] These pictures were all—with the exception of Claude Lorrain's *Acis and Galatea*, which Dostoevsky would interpret as embodying the Age of Gold, mankind's innocent, presinful, Edenic past—representations of Christ or of Christ and the Madonna.

Just a few months before he began to struggle with creating a new novel, Dostoevsky was thus immersing himself in the emotions derived from contemplating the images of Christ and the Mother of God painted by some of the greatest artists of the Western Renaissance tradition. These were no longer the highly formalized iconic images he would have seen in Russian churches, but depictions of Christ as a flesh-and-blood human being, existing in and interacting with a real world in which money existed and tribute had to be paid. He was evidently stirred and moved by these pictures, to which he responded not primarily as aesthetic objects but in terms of the feelings aroused by some of the most hallowed moments of the divine narrative of the Christian faith. Never before had he been exposed so abundantly to such imagery; and one can hardly gauge the impact it may have had on his sensibility at this particular moment. Can it really be simply coincidence that his next novel came into being only when he discovered a character called "Prince Christ" in his notes and when, in effect, he set out to provide a Russian literary counterpart to the pictures he had so much admired in the Dresden Gallery?

CHAPTER 11

Turgenev and Baden-Baden

Dostoevsky and Anna Grigoryevna spent five agitated weeks in Baden-Baden, with their fortunes and their future riding on the turn of the roulette wheel. The sojourn of the Dostoevskys in this famous watering place reproduces the predictably monotonous, sadly familiar, and demeaning pattern of his gambling misadventures. During this time, however, an unavoidable call on Turgenev, now residing in Baden-Baden as a more or less permanent resident, led to an epochal quarrel that left its mark in the annals of Russian literature. Often thought to be merely a rancorous personal altercation, the dispute between the two men had explicit social-cultural implications of much greater scope that would re-echo in both *The Idiot* and *The Devils*. Dostoevsky's visit to the Basel Museum, where he saw Holbein the Younger's upsettingly realistic picture of the dead Christ, was also a notable event marking the termination of this turbulent period.

2

The Dostoevskys arrived in Baden-Baden with very little money and, able to afford only the most modest accommodations, rented two rooms over a smithy in which work began at four in the morning. Anna Grigoryevna, suffering some of the symptoms of her pregnancy, often felt weak and queasy, and was, not surprisingly, subject to accesses of depression and apathy. For the most part, however, she gallantly concealed her fears and misgivings from her husband, and exhibited an extraordinary staunchness in coping with the nerve-racking demands placed on her by Dostoevsky's shortcomings.

He began to gamble immediately, with the more or less usual results, but occasionally winning sums large enough to give them a certain security for the moment while allowing him to continue gambling for smaller stakes. This was, in fact, what he intended to do, and he turned over the amounts he gained to Anna for safekeeping; but after losing the allotted amount, he always returned and begged for more. Anna found his pleadings impossible to withstand because he was so tormented by the conflict between his remorseful sense of baseness and his irresistible obsession. A typical scene occurred on their third day, when half their money had vanished; after losing five more gold pieces, Dostoevsky made his usual pleas. "He was terribly excited, begging me not to think him a rogue who robbed me of my last crust of bread only to lose it, while I implored him only to keep calm, and that of course I did not think all those things of him, and that he should have as much money as he liked. Then he went away and I cried bitterly, being so cast down with sufferings and self-tormentings."[1]

In the midst of her own well-founded worries about the future (she worked to improve her shorthand skills, and began to practice translating from the French as a possible source of family income), Anna found herself continually called upon to calm Dostoevsky's own despondency and self-castigations. Once he went out to gamble, promising to return home quickly, and came back only seven hours later without a penny and "utterly distracted." Anna tried to quiet him, "but he would spare me none of his self-reproaches, calling himself stupidly weak, and begging me, Heaven knows why, for forgiveness, saying that he was not worthy of me, he was a swine and I an angel, and a lot of other foolish things of the same kind . . . and to try and distract him I sent him on an errand to buy candles, sugar and coffee for me. . . . I was terribly disturbed by the state he was in, being afraid it may lead to another fit."[2] This last sentence explains a good deal about Anna's remarkable self-control; nothing was more important than to guard Dostoevsky against the over-excitement that might bring on his epilepsy.

One such attack is described in detail, and helps us to understand why Anna felt that almost anything—even yielding without protest to Dostoevsky's mania—was better than risking the possibility of provoking an epileptic seizure. "I wiped the sweat from his forehead and the foam from his lips, and the fit only lasted a short while and was, I thought, not a severe one. His eyes were not starting out of his head, though the convulsions were bad. . . . As, bit by bit, he regained consciousness, he kissed my hands and then embraced me. . . . He pressed me passionately to his heart, saying he loved me like mad, and simply adored me. After the fits he is always seized with a fear of death. He says he is afraid they will end in his death, and that I must look after him. In order to quiet him I said I would lie down on the sofa that is close to his bed." Dostoevsky also asked Anna to make sure, when she awoke the next morning, to check whether he was still alive.[3]

Dostoevsky himself was quite astonished at Anna's extraordinary tolerance of his failings, even when this meant, at times, pawning not only their wedding rings but the earrings and brooch he had given her as a present and, as a last resort, Dostoevsky's overcoat and Anna's lace shawl and spare frock. He even commented to her that, "if I had been older . . . I should have behaved quite differently and told him I had been foolish before, and that if my husband was trying to do some stupid things, I, as his wife, must not allow anything of the kind." On another occasion, when she had given way once more to his entreaties, he said, perhaps half-seriously, that "it would have been better for him to have a grumbling wife who would be scolding instead of pardoning him, and nagging instead of comforting him, and that it was positively painful to him the way I was so sweet."[4] Anna's refusal to blame or berate Dostoevsky, we may adduce from such words, could well have increased his sense of guilt by blocking the possibility of turning angrily and self-defensively against an accusatory judge. Prince Myshkin's all-comprehending mansuetude will have much the same effect; but no more than in the case of Dostoevsky will such a surge of guilt lead, in the novel, to more than a momentary access of moral self-scrutiny.

Anna's forbearance, whatever prodigies of self-command it may have cost her, was amply compensated for (at least in her eyes) by Dostoevsky's immense gratitude and growing sense of attachment. When Anna remarked once that she may have affected his luck adversely, Dostoevsky replied: "'Anna, my little blessing, whenever I die remember only how I blessed you for the luck you brought me,' adding that no greater good fortune had ever come his way, that God had been lavish indeed in bestowing me upon him, and that every day he prayed for me and only feared one day all this might alter, that to-day I both loved and pitied him, but once my love were to cease, then nothing would be the same. That, however," Anna hastens to write, "will never happen, and I am quite certain we shall always love one another as passionately as we do now."[5]

Dostoevsky was not only lavish with such sentiments, which surely expressed everything he had begun to feel about Anna, but also clearly tried to atone in other ways for all the material and emotional hardships she was forced to endure. The moment he won a little money, and this occurred with fair frequency, he would return home laden with fruit, flowers, and wine. "He is a sweet person, this husband of mine," Anna wrote of one such occasion, "with a nature all loving and gentle, and I am happy beyond words."[6] Such moments did not last very long, and the couple went from relative plenty to total destitution from one day to the next; but these instants of fleeting festivity, which showed that Dostoevsky was not a completely self-preoccupied monster, should not be left out of the picture. Anna seems to have succeeded, like Dostoevsky himself, in divorcing his gambling mania from his moral personality, and in regarding it as something extraneous to his true character.

"One had to come to terms with it," she wrote in her memoirs many years later, "to look at his gambling passion as a disease for which there was no cure."[7] Such a conclusion merely extended to gambling the same attitude she took toward Dostoevsky's personal irritability and irascibility. Although this trait often led to an abusive treatment of herself as well as others, she blamed Dostoevsky's epilepsy and refused to accept it as his genuine nature. On the morning after the seizure already mentioned, she notes that "Feodor is always very difficult to please after one of his fits," and then adds: "Poor Feodor, he does suffer so much after his attacks and is always so irritable, and liable to fly out about trifles, so that I have to bear a good deal in these days of illness. It's of no consequence, because the other days are very good, when he is so sweet and gentle. Besides, I can see that when he screams at me it is from illness, not from bad temper."[8]

3

Struggle though she might, however, Anna could not prevent herself at times from giving way to furious resentment. And as the nerve-racking days passed without noticeable change, so that no end seemed in sight, even her seemingly infinite indulgence began to wear thin. "I had suffered beyond words waiting for Feodor," she writes on their fourth day in Baden. "I cried, and cursed myself, roulette, Baden-Baden, and everything on earth; I am ashamed now to confess it, and never remember to have been in such a state before." Ten days later, just after Dostoevsky had gone to pawn her brooch and earrings, "I could no longer control myself and began to cry bitterly. It was no ordinary weeping, but a dreadful convulsive sort of sobbing, that brought on a terrible pain in my breast, and relieved me not in the slightest. . . . I began to envy all the other people in the world, who all seemed to me to be happy, and only ourselves—or so it seemed to me—completely miserable."[9]

What drove her into a frenzy was the thought that "yesterday we had one hundred and sixty gold pieces and now not one of them left, and that we had been fools not to leave the place when we could." At such moments, her loneliness and isolation became crushing, and we remember that she was still only twenty-one years old. "I am so utterly alone here," she writes piteously, "with no Mama to come and bring me crumbs of comfort." Anna confesses to herself that she wished Dostoevsky to stay away as long as possible; but when he returned that day to tell her he had lost the money obtained for her jewelry, and wept as he said "Now I have stolen your last things from you and played them away!" she sank on her knees before his chair to try and calm his wretchedness. "Do what I might to comfort him, I couldn't stop him from crying."[10]

Many such complaints about her lot can be found in Anna's *Diary*, but there are only a few instances in which she openly criticizes her husband; and these outbursts are always motivated by his incessant concern for the family of his dead brother. By contrast, Dostoevsky never expressed much sympathy for the financial difficulties of poor Mme Snitkina, assailed by Dostoevsky's creditors, struggling to pay interest on their belongings, and yet also sending them money in response to Anna's calls for help. None of the torments of her present situation would bother her at all, Anna insists, "if I knew that all this misery was unavoidable, but that we should have to suffer so that an Emilya Feodorovna and her lot can live in clover, and that I should have to pawn my coat so that she can have one, arouses a feeling within me the reverse of nice, and it hurts me to find such thoughtlessness and so little understanding and human kindness in anyone I love and prize so much." This is the most extreme upsurge of revolt in the Baden pages of the *Diary*, and, just a few sentences later, Anna shrinks back timidly from her own audacity: "I am furious with myself for harboring such horrid thoughts against my dear, sweet, kind husband. I am a horrid creature, surely."[11]

Dostoevsky had written Katkov again for another advance, though he had long hesitated doing so from Baden-Baden, whose reputation as a famed gambling spa would make the reason for this new appeal all too evident; but he swallowed his pride in the face of dire necessity. Meanwhile, scenes of the kind already described were repeated daily with inessential variations, and when their last resource—her mother—seemed to be exhausted, Anna began to display her disaffection more openly. "I told him I simply couldn't help crying at the way we had been all this time in Baden-Baden . . . and that we should probably go on like this for four months on end, and lose Katkov's money into the bargain. . . . For a whole month I had borne it and said not a word, even when there was nothing else left to us, for still I could hope for some help from Mama, but that now everything was finished, it is impossible to ask Mama for any more, and I would be, moreover, ashamed to do it." Nonetheless, she ended by giving him some money as usual, and he returned home unexpectedly only an hour later with what, in their position, was a considerable win. It may well have been her censure that galvanized him into breaking off play while he was still ahead; she notes that "my recent remarks seem to have rankled dreadfully with him."[12]

More and more entries in the *Diary* indicate a hardening of Anna's attitude, or at least a much more undisguised expression of her unhappiness. During one such incident, Anna turned on Dostoevsky just after receiving a letter from her mother and learning that their furniture might be lost. "When Feodor began to speak of 'the damned furniture,' it hurt me so that I began to weep bitterly, and he was quite unable to calm me down. . . . I simply could not control myself, and said the very idea of winning a fortune through roulette was utterly ridiculous, and in my anger I jibed at him, calling him a 'benefactor of humanity.' . . . I am quite convinced that, even if we did win, it would only be to the benefit of all those horrid people, and we should not profit one jot or tittle." Very much hurt by Anna's phrase, Dostoevsky accused her the next day of being "harsh"; and this charge led to an explosion in the *Diary*, where she lists all her many grievances and regretfully compares her own forbearance with the abusiveness of Dostoevsky's first wife. "It isn't worthwhile controlling oneself," she writes. "Marya Dimitrievna never hesitated to call him a rogue and a rascal and a criminal, and to her he was like an obedient dog."[13]

Dostoevsky's luck improved toward the latter half of July, perhaps because Anna's reproaches were having some effect and he left the tables earlier, perhaps because his gambling fever was waning and produced the same result. His thoughts, in any case, began to turn elsewhere. In mid-July he spent a day on his Belinsky article and told Anna he wished to work on it again. On July 21/August 2, Anna received another money order from her mother, and with this amount, combined with Dostoevsky's recent winnings, they at last had enough to pay their debts, redeem everything in pawn, cover their fare to Geneva, and live there until Katkov's next advance arrived. "We could quite well get away from this place now—but we are mad beyond all manner of doubt," Anna declares bitterly. The *Diary* indicates that she had now made up her mind to leave, though whether she had announced this decision is not clear; but she mentions beginning to pack and making "various preparations for the journey."[14] Dostoevsky promptly began to gamble furiously on the very day these entries were made, encouraged by his recent success; and Anna, who was feeling quite unwell, flared up with indignation as he returned home with the usual litany and demands. Luckily he managed to win that evening and replenish their treasury.

Nonetheless, they decided to leave the next day, after Dostoevsky, having gone off to reclaim Anna's jewelry and ring in the morning, returned at eight in the evening and "at once turned on me in an outburst of wrath and tears, informing me that he had lost every single penny of the money I had given him to redeem our things with. . . . Feodor called himself an unutterable scoundrel, saying that he was unworthy of me, that I had no business to forgive him, and all the time he never stopped crying. At last I succeeded in calming him down, and we resolved to go away from here tomorrow." She then accompanied him to the pawnbroker, fearing to entrust him with another sum, after which they both went to the station to inquire about schedules and the price of tickets. They also decided to make a stopover at Basel, "as it would have been too unpardonably stupid to have gone traveling through Switzerland without seeing anything, absolutely nothing, of the beautiful places."[15*] It would also break the journey for Anna, who constantly notes, with stoic fortitude, the various pains and malaises attendant on her advancing pregnancy.

Dostoevsky continued to gamble on their very last day and lost fifty francs that Anna had given him, as well as twenty more obtained from pawning a ring. Now short of funds for the trip, they pawned Anna's earrings again, redeemed the ring, and bought their tickets. Just an hour and a half before departure, Dostoevsky returned to the casino with twenty francs for a last fling—of course to no avail. Anna jots down laconically: "I told him not to be hysterical, but to help me fasten the trunks and pay the landlady."[16] After settling accounts, which turned out to be an unpleasant affair, they finally left for the station. Nobody—not even the servant girls, whom Anna thought she had treated with consideration, and whose ingratitude she censures—bothered to bid them farewell.

4

In the opening pages of his novel *Smoke* (*Dym*, 1867), Turgenev vividly sketches the fashionable crowd thronging about the Konversationshaus in Baden-Baden. This was the name of the large, columned main building of the spa, looking rather like a barracks, set in spacious, parklike surroundings; it contained the notorious gambling rooms in its central portion, a reading room in the right wing, and a famous restaurant and café on the left. A motley-colored multitude always could be found swarming around its approaches and strolling among its tree-lined paths. The ladies in their glittering frocks recalled for Turgenev "the intensified brilliance and light fluttering of birds in the spring, with their rainbow-tinted wings."[17] Poor Anna Grigoryevna disliked going there because of the shabbiness and dullness of her one black dress, though

---

* Anna's diary makes it seem as if the stopover in Basel was planned simply from a general desire not to miss a chance to see the tourist sights. In her *Reminiscences*, however, she indicates that the pause in Basel may have been for the specific purpose of seeing Holbein's picture of the dead Christ, "which someone had told Feodor Mikhailovich about."

Whoever that "someone" may have been, Dostoevsky had long ago come across a reference to this picture in a book he had known since childhood, N. M. Karamzin's *Letters of a Russian Traveller*. "As for me," wrote Karamzin, "I studied with the closest attention and pleasure [on a visit to Basel] the paintings of the famous Holbein, a native of Basel and friend of Erasmus. How beautiful is the face of the Saviour at the Last Supper! . . . Although there is nothing divine in the Christ taken from the cross. He is portrayed with remarkable naturalness as a dying man. According to legend, Holbein took a drowned Jew as his model." Anna Dostoevsky, *Reminiscences*, 133; N. M. Karamzin, *Letters of a Russian Traveller*, trans. and ed. Florence Jonas (New York, 1957), 113.

she was driven by sheer tedium to visit the reading room stacked with French, German, and Russian newspapers and journals.

Not far from the café was a spot known as the "Russian tree," where the numerous Russian visitors were accustomed to assemble, exchange the latest gossip, and, if Turgenev is to be believed, bore themselves to the point of stupefaction. Most such Russians came to drink the waters of the spa and/or to gamble; those with pretensions to culture might also hope to catch a glimpse of the most distinguished Russian inhabitant of the city, Ivan Turgenev, who had constructed a house in Baden-Baden adjoining that of his largely platonic (or so it would seem) inamorata, the renowned diva Pauline Garcia-Viardot. Dostoevsky never frequented the "Russian tree," and he was perhaps the only Russian who had no interest whatever in seeing or being seen by Turgenev—indeed, who hoped fervently that neither he nor Turgenev would catch sight of the other at all.

The reasons for such reticence are many and complicated, and go back a long way. In the 1840s, when both had been fledgling writers, they had met in the circle gathered around the great critic Belinsky, who had presciently recognized their burgeoning talents. They had struck up an enthusiastic, youthful friendship, certainly more fervent in the case of the inflammatory Dostoevsky than on the part of the polished man-of-the-world Turgenev; but that congeniality rapidly cooled when Dostoevsky's excessive vanity at the literary success of *Poor Folk* made him a laughingstock among his literary competitors. Turgenev joined in composing some satirical verses that branded Dostoevsky as "a pimple on the nose of Russian literature," and the friendship ended abruptly. It was revived after Dostoevsky's return from exile in 1860, when they met again in Petersburg on a new footing of cordiality, and was considerably strengthened during the furious quarrel that broke out in 1862 over *Fathers and Children.* Even before they joined forces over Turgenev's novel, which Dostoevsky admired enormously, the illustrious Turgenev, whose name as a contributor was enough to increase the circulation of any journal, had agreed to give one of his shorter pieces to Dostoevsky's new magazine—not a story, but a prose-poetic "fantasy" entitled *Phantoms.*

When *Time* was suddenly banned by the government, Turgenev acceded to Dostoevsky's urgent request that he continue to reserve the piece, and it was published in *Epoch* in 1864. Dostoevsky wrote Turgenev a very flattering letter about this lyrical vignette, and his words of praise should not be considered as *merely* serving editorial diplomacy. Although he spoke of *Phantoms* to his brother Mikhail as containing "a lot of rubbish; there is something sordid, morbid and senile about it; it evidences *lack of faith* due to impotence—in a word, the whole of Turgenev and his convictions," he adds, all the same, that "the poetical element"

211

will go a long way "in making up for its weaknesses" and that it is one of the best items in their journal.[18]*

Dostoevsky's letter reveals both his genuine admiration for Turgenev as an artist as well as a deep-rooted antipathy to his pessimistic world-view; but such antipathy, for the moment, had no effect on their personal relations. Turgenev was one of the few people to whom Dostoevsky had felt it possible to turn while trapped in Wiesbaden; and whether he ever suffered an occasional twinge of conscience over the failure to repay his debt to the wealthy Turgenev cannot be determined. But there is an ironic acerbity in the remark he made in 1866 to Anna Korvin-Krukovskaya, which compares the conditions under which he was forced to write with the situations of other Russian authors. Explaining his plan to work on *Crime and Punishment* at night and *The Gambler* in the morning, he added: "The very thought of it would kill Turgenev."[19] This envious image of Turgenev polishing his works at leisure and in repose, rather than being forced to write at top speed, could well have stifled any incipient qualms about reneging on a debt of honor. But the debt hung over him nonetheless, and the last person in the world he wished to meet was Turgenev. As luck would have it, just a few days after arriving in Baden-Baden, Dostoevsky was strolling with Anna when he ran into Ivan Goncharov, the author of *Oblomov*, whom he once described as a person with "the soul of a petty official, not an idea in his head, and the eyes of a steamed fish, whom God, as if for a joke, has endowed with a brilliant talent."[20] Goncharov told the Dostoevskys "how Turgenev had caught sight of Feodor yesterday, but had said nothing to him knowing how gamblers do not like to be spoken to."[21]

On learning the unwelcome news, Dostoevsky may well have recalled Turgenev's highly unflattering picture of the gambling salons in *Smoke*, around whose green tables, he had written, "crowded the same familiar figures, with the same dull, greedy, half-stupefied, half-exasperated expression, which the gambling fever lends to all, even the most aristocratic features."[22] Turgenev's hesitation in approaching Dostoevsky implicitly included him among those overcome by the gambling fever; and Goncharov's words probably account for Anna's notation that "when we got home we decided to move to Geneva to-morrow" (they actually departed over a month later). It was now incumbent on Dostoevsky, however, to pay a call on Turgenev. "As Feodor owes Turgenev fifty rubles, he

---

* Dostoevsky's criticism of one detail in the first version of this text prompted Turgenev to make a change. A mysterious figure was called a "vampire," and, when Dostoevsky suggested that its supernatural power would be better expressed if left unspecified, the word was dropped. Other changes have also been linked to Dostoevsky's remark that Turgenev should have allowed *Phantoms* to be even *more* fantastic than it was. See the variants and commentary in I. S. Turgenev, *Polnoe Sobranie Sochinenii i Pisem*, 28 vols. (Moscow-Leningrad, 1960–1968), 9: 348, 475.

must make a point of going to see him, or otherwise Turgenev will think Feodor stays away from him for fear of being asked for money."[23] Dostoevsky told Anna he planned to call on Turgenev the next day, and did so with no success; it was only three days later that their meeting took place.

If we are to understand what occurred during their stormy interview, it is necessary to say a few words about Turgenev himself at this point in his career. Badly bruised by the altercation over *Fathers and Children*, he had retired to Baden-Baden to lick his wounds. Not only had he been savagely manhandled by the partisans of Chernyshevsky, but his defender Dimitry Pisarev had turned him into a propagator (an unintentional one, to be sure) of an all-destroying Nihilism. To make matters worse, even an old friend and natural ally such as Alexander Herzen, now more and more disillusioned with a European civilization unable to transcend its inherent limitations, had turned against Turgenev's moderate pro-Western liberalism, which shrank back before the specter of revolution. A brilliant series of articles, "Ends and Beginnings," published by Herzen in *The Bell* during 1862–1863, constituted a direct onslaught on Turgenev's most cherished convictions.

Herzen expresses here once again, with all his incomparable *brio*, his faith in the nascent potentialities of the Russian people, whose position in the face of a declining European civilization resembles that of the German barbarians confronted by the decaying magnificence of the late Roman Empire. Eventually, like those barbarians, the Russians were destined to create a new world out of the crumbling fragments of the ruins of the old. Europe, for Herzen, had lost sight of any ideal except that of *meshchantsvo*, the ideal of the shopkeeper and the petty bourgeoisie; but the natively socialist institutions of the Russian peasantry would regenerate Europe and create a brave new world of equality and justice far surpassing what the much-vaunted civilization of the West had been capable of achieving.[24]

This forthright attack on Turgenev's pro-Western faith brought forth a famous reply, in a personal letter, accusing the superlatively civilized Herzen of "kneeling before the Russian sheepskin, and you see in it the supreme good, the novelty and originality of future social forms." One cannot live without a God, Turgenev bitingly added, and Herzen "has raised [his] altar at the feet of the sheepskin [that is, the Russian peasant], the mysterious God of whom one knows practically nothing."[25] This sharp divergence of political ideals was further envenomed by a nasty reference in *The Bell* that described Turgenev (without mentioning his name) as "a gray-haired Magdalena" who was "losing sleep, appetite, his white hair and teeth" because of fear that the Tsar did not know of his repentance.[26] This was an allusion to a letter from Turgenev to the

Tsar, written when his name became involved in an investigation, futilely requesting that he not be recalled to Russia to testify, and quite untruthfully disclaiming any connection with the revolutionary propaganda emanating from London through Herzen's Free Russian Press.

Echoes of this fierce quarrel resound all through *Smoke* and are responsible for some of its harshest passages, aimed at the Slavophilism of both the right and the left. Turgenev satirizes both the scabrous immorality of the highest court circles and the empty maunderings of the radical intelligentsia; but his sharpest barbs are reserved for those of whatever political stripe who harbor any hope of a special destiny reserved for Russia and its people. Turgenev's spokesman is a minor character, oddly named Sozont Ivanich Potugin, whose role in the intrigue is accessory but who is given several lengthy speeches. In one he declares that "Russia for ten whole centuries has created nothing of its own, either in government, in law, in science, in art or even in handicraft."[27] Even more scathingly, he tells of a visit to the Crystal Palace exhibition near London (constantly evoked in the literary-cultural polemics of the 1860s), where all the creations of "the ingenuity of man" were put on display, "an encyclopedia of humanity one might call it." If Russia, he says, were suddenly to disappear from the face of the earth, with everything it had created, the event could occur "without disarranging a single nail in the place ... for even the *samovar*, the woven bast shoes, the yoke-bridle and the knout—these are our most famous products—were not invented by us."[28] His interlocutor, a liberal young landowner named Grigory Litvinov, makes some feeble objections, but these are far outweighed by the crushing assault of Potugin's diatribes.

The publication of Turgenev's novel in April 1867 blew up a storm even more furious than the one attending *Fathers and Children*, and this time the novelist was assailed from all sides and by everybody. P. V. Annenkov wrote him, just after its appearance in the pages of *The Russian Messenger*, that "Petersburg at this very minute is reading *Smoke*, and not without agitation. . . . The majority are frightened by a novel inviting them to believe that all of the Russian aristocracy, yes, and all of Russian life, is an abomination."[29] So outraged was good society, to which Turgenev belonged by birth and breeding, that the members of the exclusive English Club were on the point of writing him a collective letter excluding him from their midst (the letter was never sent, but a zealous "friend" informed Turgenev of the incident). N. N. Strakhov, who had sprung to the defense of *Fathers and Children*, wrote that the novelist he admired so much had now gone badly astray, and he concluded that "only someone who looked at Russian life with detachment" and from a great distance (an obvious allusion to Turgenev's residence abroad) could have composed such a book.[30] Writing to Dostoevsky in late May 1867, Apollon Maikov brought him up to date on the Russian reaction: "The admirers of *Smoke*," he says, "are found only among the Polonophils." And he adds: "How much does this disclosure in *Smoke* of the poverty of his love and understanding deprive of their foundation even the best of his earlier works: yes! for if you do not understand and love this [Russia], on what pedestal do you stand when you utter this or that."[31] Dostoevsky's reaction to the novel, which he had read before leaving Russia, was much the same; and the quarrel between the two men thus contained a social-cultural dimension as well as a purely personal and temperamental one.

5

Two accounts exist of Dostoevsky's meeting with Turgenev: one, contained in Anna Grigoryevna's *Diary*, was set down on the evening of the day it occurred; the other, in a letter from Dostoevsky to Apollon Maikov, was written a month later in Geneva; and both coincide in their recital of the main facts. Not a word was said about Dostoevsky's debt; rather, the conversation turned on other matters, particularly on *Smoke*. The letter to Maikov is much more detailed than Anna's version, and also harsher and more embittered; it is possible that Dostoevsky did not wish to reveal to Anna the depths of his feeling, or that he himself had not as yet fully allowed the impact of the encounter to sink in. Another reason for softening his words to Anna may well have been the desperateness of their economic plight in Baden-Baden. On the very same day as the meeting, when Dostoevsky came home with some winnings, Anna was delighted because it meant "that we shouldn't have to go to Turgenev and borrow from him till we get the money from Katkov."[32] These words suggest some earlier conversation about another appeal to Turgenev as a last resort; and perhaps Dostoevsky was reluctant to close off for Anna this source of hope. Her report, in any event, concludes with the thoroughly misleading assertion: "But on the whole they parted friends, and Turgenev promised to give him the book," presumably *Smoke*.[33]

There are no such mollifying afterthoughts in Dostoevsky's letter. He begins with the flat assertion: "I'll tell you candidly: even before that [the obligatory visit] I disliked the man personally." Dostoevsky's discomfiture, he admits, was made worse because of his unpaid debt; but "I also dislike the aristocratically farcical embrace of his with which he starts to kiss you but offers his cheek. The horrible airs of a general." Turgenev's upper-class manners always had rasped on Dostoevsky's nerves, and he will use this very detail in his withering portrait of the famous author

215

Karmazinov (a deadly caricature of Turgenev) in *The Devils*. It was not so much Turgenev's manners, though, that now accounted for Dostoevsky's hostility; "most important, his book *Smoke* put me out."[34]

The talk immediately turned to the book, apparently, if we follow Anna's text, at Turgenev's instigation. Dostoevsky told her that Turgenev "talk[ed] the whole time about his new novel, Feodor never even so much as mentioned it."[35] During the conversation, Turgenev affirmed that "the main point of the book" was contained in the speech of Potugin already noted: "If Russia disappeared, *there would not be* any loss or any agitation among mankind." Turgenev also expostulated on the virulence of the negative reaction he had encountered, perhaps expecting, as in the days of *Fathers and Children*, that Dostoevsky would take a more sympathetic view. If so, he could not have been more mistaken. "I didn't know," Dostoevsky tells Maikov, "that he had been given a lashing everywhere, and that at Moscow, at a club, I think, people were collecting names in order to protest his *Smoke*. I confess to you that I should never have imagined that one could expose the wounds to one's vanity as naively and awkwardly as Turgenev does."[36]

The conversation presumably then shifted to the perennial Westerner-Slavophil debate in Russian culture, and Turgenev forcefully reiterated the extreme Westerner position of his novel. "He criticized Russia and the Russians monstrously, horribly ... " Dostoevsky writes. "Turgenev said that we ought to crawl before the Germans, and that all attempts at Russianness and independence are swinishness and stupidity." When Turgenev remarked that "he was writing a long article against Russophils and Slavophils," Dostoevsky replied with the most often-quoted retort in their exchange of unpleasantries: "I advised him, for the sake of convenience, to order a telescope from Paris. 'What for?' he asked. 'It's far from here,' I replied. 'Train your telescope on Russia and examine us, because otherwise it is really hard to make us out.' "[37] Dostoevsky thus echoes the widespread opinion that Turgenev's self-imposed exile had alienated him from the Russian reality on which his outstanding talent had previously been nourished. Immersion in his native milieu was a primordial need for Dostoevsky, and elsewhere in the same letter he complains bitterly to Maikov about being forced to live in Europe "where not only is there not a Russian face, Russian books, or Russian thoughts and concerns to be found, but not even a friendly face.... And how can one spend one's life abroad? To be without one's native land—it's suffering, honest to God!"[38]

Taken aback by Dostoevsky's sarcasm, Turgenev "got horribly angry"; and Dostoevsky then, with an air of "extraordinarily successful naiveté" (evidently savoring his own aplomb in retrospect!), momentarily abandoned his antagonistic stance and slipped into the role of reassuring fellow author: "But I really didn't expect that all this criticism of you and the failure of *Smoke* would irritate you so much; honest to God, *it isn't worth it*, forget about it all" (italics in text). This sound advice only increased Turgenev's exacerbation, and, "turning red," he replied: "'But I'm not at all irritated? What do you mean?'" Dostoevsky then directed the conversation to personal and domestic matters, and finally took up his hat; but before going, "somehow, absolutely without intention," he assures Maikov (though one suspects his candor), "said what had accumulated in my soul about the Germans in three months." As we know from Anna's *Diary*, this accumulation was one of undiluted bile; and Dostoevsky launched forth on a denunciation of the German common people as "rogues and swindlers ... much worse and more dishonest than ours."

Even more, Dostoevsky then linked his intense dislike of the Germans with the social-cultural issues that the two men had spoken of the moment before: "Well here you go on talking about civilization, well what has civilization done for them [the Germans] and what can they boast of so very much as superior to us?" These words drove Turgenev into a paroxysm of rage: "He turned pale (literally: I'm not exaggerating a bit, not a bit!) and said to me: 'In talking like that you offend me *personally*. You should know that I have settled here permanently, that I consider myself a German, not a Russian, and I'm proud of it!' I replied: 'Although I have read *Smoke* and have been speaking with you for a whole hour, I couldn't at all have expected you would say that, and therefore please forgive me for having offended you.' Then we parted quite politely, and I vowed to myself never again to set foot at Turgenev's."[39] Turgenev presumably also resolved never again to set eyes on Dostoevsky, calling on him the next day at ten in the morning and leaving a card, although (or rather because) Dostoevsky had made a point of informing him that he was never available before noon.

Dostoevsky's letter to Maikov, so far as the essentials are concerned, jibes with what Anna jotted down in her notebook entry, which recorded her husband's words while his memory was still fresh. His thrust about the telescope is mentioned, with the additional comment that "Turgenev declared he was a realist, and Feodor said he only thought he was." The quarrel over the Germans is also confirmed: "When Feodor declared he found the Germans extremely stupid and very apt to be dishonest, Turgenev promptly took offense, assuring Feodor that he had irreparably insulted him for he himself was not a Russian any more, but had now become a German. Feodor said he didn't know that, and greatly deplored the fact." So, for that matter, did the staunchly patriotic Anna, who writes indignantly: "What an awful thing for a Russian to talk like that"—and especially for a Russian writer![40]

Indeed, the statement attributed to Turgenev is so startling that one cannot help wondering whether Dostoevsky's testimony should be accepted at face value. There is, however, other evidence that the normally mild-mannered, well-bred, and circumspect Turgenev, exasperated by the fiasco of *Smoke*, was now inclined to give way to intemperate verbal excess. To the poet A. A. Fet, for example, much more of an intimate than Dostoevsky and who had ventured to express an adverse judgment on *Smoke*, Turgenev wrote insultingly: "That *Smoke* did not please you surprises me not at all. . . . And just imagine, *it leaves me completely indifferent*, and I would not spend as much as a penny for your approval . . . your words are just *nothing* in my eyes, once and for all."[41] If this was Turgenev's tone with a longstanding and genuine friend, one can well believe that, driven beyond endurance and in a burst of rage, he could have defended Germany and the Germans by declaring himself one of them in response to Dostoevsky's unrestrained and vituperative denigrations.

One other passage in the letter to Maikov describing the interview is rather mysterious but of great importance, because it leads Dostoevsky into remarks foreshadowing *The Idiot*. "And these people," Dostoevsky declares, "boast of the fact, by the way, that they are *atheists*! He [Turgenev] declared to me that he is an atheist through and through." Since nothing in *Smoke* touches on religion, it is difficult to see what might have prompted such a confidence; perhaps there was also some unreported talk about *Phantoms*, which has a metaphysical theme and expresses a cosmic pessimism strongly influenced by Schopenhauer. If the conversation had turned to this work, it might well have elicited a remark about atheism; and there is reason to believe that the literary topics touched on were by no means limited to *Smoke*. Four days later the Dostoevskys bought a copy of *Madame Bovary* (alluded to in *The Idiot*), because in Anna's words "Turgenev declares it to be the best thing that has happened in the literary world within the last ten years."[42]

Whatever its origin, Turgenev's declaration caused Dostoevsky to explode to Maikov: "But my God, Deism gave us Christ, that is, such a lofty notion of man that it cannot be comprehended without reverence, and one cannot help believing that this ideal of humanity is everlasting! And what have they, the Turgenevs, Herzens, Utins, and Chernyshevskys presented us with? Instead of the loftiest, divine beauty, which they spit on, they are so disgustingly selfish, so shamelessly irritable, flippantly proud, that it's simply incomprehensible what they're hoping for and who will follow them." One can see here quite clearly the burgeoning impulse in Dostoevsky to present an image of the "loftiest, divine beauty" in face of the jeering, mocking unbelievers, whose names somewhat indiscriminately represent all shades of opinion and two generations of the godless Westernized intelligentsia.

Dostoevsky then goes on, in a manner anticipating *The Devils*, to draw a contrast between the generation of the 1860s and that of the 1840s,

> all those trashy little liberals and progressives, primarily still of Belinsky's school, [who] find their greatest pleasure and satisfaction in criticizing Russia. The difference is that Chernyshevsky's followers simply criticize Russia and openly wish for its collapse (particularly for its collapse!). These people, Belinsky's offspring, add that they *love Russia*. But meanwhile not only is everything of the slightest originality in Russia hateful to them, so that they deny it and immediately take enjoyment in turning it into a caricature, but that if one really were to present them finally with a fact that they could not overturn or ruin in a caricature, but to which they definitely would have to be reconciled, I think they would be unhappy to the point of *torture*, to the point of pain, to the point of despair.[43]

Here we can already see emerging the rough outlines of Stepan Trofimovich Verkhovensky, whose ideological profile is unmistakably that of a member of "Belinsky's school," and who, in his claim to love Russia and its people, forms a stark contrast with his cynically destructive son Peter. The inclusion of the novelist Karmazinov (Turgenev) in the same book seems to acknowledge this Baden-Baden meeting as one of the sources of its inspiration.

This encounter between Turgenev and Dostoevsky soon became public knowledge, at least in literary circles, because the portions of Dostoevsky's letter concerning Turgenev were sent to the editor of a journal called *Russian Archives* (*Russkii Arkhiv*), who was requested to preserve the information it contained "for posterity" but not allow its publication before 1890. Learning of this document through his informal literary factotum P. V. Annenkov, Turgenev promptly sent a disclaimer to the same editor through Annenkov, denying the views attributed to him and authorizing his intermediary to make no secret of the denial. Turgenev assumed that Dostoevsky himself had sent the document, but Dostoevsky was quite innocent; it was Maikov who showed his letter to P. N. Barsukov, the nephew of the editor of *Russian Archives*, and Barsukov promptly transcribed the incriminating passages and dispatched them to his uncle. Dostoevsky had no knowledge of the matter at all, so far as we know, though Turgenev's own letter states that the document bore "the signature of F. M. Dostoevsky."

Referring to "the shocking and absurd opinions about Russia and the Russians that he [Dostoevsky] attributes to me ... [and] which are supposed to constitute my intimate convictions," Turgenev denies that he ever would have expressed his "intimate convictions" before Dostoevsky. "I consider him," he writes, "a person who, as a consequence of morbid seizures and other causes, is not in full control of his own rational capacities; and this opinion of mine is shared by many others." During Dostoevsky's visit, Turgenev urbanely explains, "he relieved his heart by brutal abuse against the Germans, against me and my last book, and then departed; I hardly had the time or desire to contradict him; I repeat that I treated him as somebody who was ill. Probably his disordered imagination produced those arguments that he attributed to me, and on whose basis he composed against me his . . . message to posterity."[44] The editor responded reassuringly to Turgenev, noting as well that the document did not bear Dostoevsky's name; and the matter ended there. Whether Dostoevsky's "disordered imagination" did or did not invent the utterances ascribed to Turgenev can only remain an open question. In my view, Dostoevsky's letter is entirely credible, and Turgenev was attempting to obfuscate some embarrassing and compromising words that he strongly regretted ever having allowed to pass his lips.

6

The Dostoevskys arrived in Geneva on August 13/25, spending a day en route in Basel. Anna's *Diary* gives a full account of the most minute details of their journey, sprinkled with such remarks as: "Of course there are people among them [the Germans] no worse than the Russians, but, taken as a whole, they are a race of swindlers."[45] With only one day to see Basel, they hurried out to take in the sights and first went to the cathedral. Anna found it rather imposing, but Dostoevsky thought it very inferior to that of Milan—which greatly annoyed Anna, who had not the faintest idea of what the cathedral in Milan was like! A copy of Holbein's *Dance of Death* was also dismissed by Dostoevsky as "a lot of fuss about nothing," and Anna took this to mean that the copy was an inferior one. But if Dostoevsky remained unimpressed by the cathedral, his reaction to the museum—or to one painting in the museum, which they went to visit next—was of quite a different temperature.

The first room of the museum contained nothing special, "only various copies of pictures hardly worth looking at"; but then their guide "invited us to pass on and showed us the pictures of Holbein the Younger." Anna's words at this point must be quoted at length:

There are only two really priceless pictures in the whole Museum, one of them being the Dead Savior, a marvelous work that positively horrified me, and so deeply impressed Feodor that he pronounced

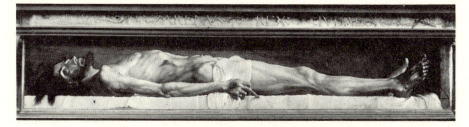

6. Hans Holbein the Younger, *Dead Christ* (1521–1522)

Holbein the Younger a painter and creator of the first rank. As a rule, one sees Jesus Christ painted after His death with His face all tortured and suffering, but His body with no marks on it at all of pain and suffering ... though of course they must have been there. But here the whole form is emaciated, the ribs and bones plain to see, hands and feet riddled with wounds, all blue and swollen, like a corpse on the point of decomposition. The face too is fearfully agonized, the eyes half open still, but with no expression in them, and giving no idea of *seeing*. Nose, mouth and chin are all blue; the whole thing bears such a strong resemblance to a real dead body that I should not like to be left with it in a room alone.... Feodor, nonetheless, was completely carried away by it, and in his desire to look at it closer got on to a chair, so that I was in a terrible state lest he should have to pay a fine, like one is always liable to here.[46]*

This chance visit to the Basel Museum was to have the most momentous consequences for the creation of *The Idiot*, in which the picture of Holbein the Younger plays an important symbolic role. No greater challenge could be offered to Dostoevsky's own faith in Christ the God-Man than such a vision of a tortured and decaying human being, whose face bore not a trace of the "extraordinary beauty" with which, as Dostoevsky was to write in the novel, Christ is usually painted. Instead, to continue

---

* A somewhat different account is given in the *Reminiscences*, with details not included in the *Diary*. "The painting had a crushing impact on Feodor Mikhailovich. He stood before it as if stunned. And I did not have the strength to look at it—it was too painful for me, particularly in my sickly [pregnant] condition—and I went into the other rooms. When I came back after fifteen or twenty minutes, I found him still riveted to the same spot in front of the painting. His agitated face had a kind of dread in it, something I had noticed more than once during the first moments of an epileptic seizure.

"Quietly I took my husband by the arm, led him into another room and sat him down on a bench, expecting the attack from one minute to the next. Luckily this did not happen. He calmed down little by little and left the museum, but insisted on returning once again to view this painting which had struck him so powerfully" (Anna Dostoevsky, *Reminiscences*, 134). There is surely something suspicious here. No reference is made to a possible epileptic fit in the *Diary*, and the description of Dostoevsky's indecorous behavior is suppressed.

quoting the book, this picture expresses the subjection of the supernatural Christ to the physical order of nature, conceived of "in the shape of an immense, merciless, dumb beast, or more correctly . . . in the form of a huge machine of the most modern construction which, dull and insensible, has clutched, crushed, and swallowed up a great priceless Being, a Being worth all nature and its laws, worth the whole earth, which was perhaps created solely for the appearance of that Being" (8: 339).

Holbein the Younger thus had created a work that relentlessly probed the basis of Christian belief with unflinching honesty, while presumably, at the same time, remaining loyal to its supernatural tenets. Dostoevsky's excitement at encountering such a painting may well be attributed to having discovered a fellow artist whose underlying inspiration was so close to his own. For Holbein the Younger—the friend of Erasmus and Sir Thomas More, who left portraits of both these illustrious humanists— had been affected like them by the new currents of ideas flowing from the world of classical learning; and he had struggled to reconcile such secular influences, so contrary to the irrational dogmas of the Christian faith, with the renewal of such faith inspired by the iconoclastic fervors of the Reformation.* In Holbein the Younger, Dostoevsky sensed an impulse, so similar to his own, to confront Christian faith with everything that negated it, and yet to surmount this confrontation with a rekindled (even if much less triumphant, indeed humanly tragic) affirmation. Such a picture had to be scrutinized at close range, even if it meant behaving indecorously and risking a fuss and a fine.

---

* Julia Kristeva, in a book whose subject is depression and melancholy, devotes some well-informed pages to Holbein the Younger. Of his *Dead Christ*, after citing Dostoevsky, she remarks: "Italian iconography embellished, or at least ennobled, the face of Christ in his Passion, but especially it surrounded him with personages plunged in sorrow as well as in the certitude of the Resurrection, so as to suggest the attitude we should adopt in face of the Passion. Holbein, on the contrary, leaves the cadaver strangely alone. It is perhaps this isolation—*a matter of composition*—which imparts a major weight of melancholy to the picture, much more than does its drawing or color-scheme."

Very little is known about Holbein the Younger except for the external facts of his life. Just after painting the *Dead Christ* in Basel (1521–1522), he fled to England to escape the iconoclasm of the Reformation, carrying a letter from Erasmus to Sir Thomas More. He returned to Basel in 1528, and in 1530 was converted to Protestantism—but not before demanding, and presumably receiving, "a better explanation of Holy Communion before committing himself" (a citation from the church registers). If nothing else, such a detail indicates a serious interest in religious matters, on the level of dogma as well as faith. Julia Kristeva, *Soleil noir* (Paris, 1987), 124 and chaps. 5, 7.

CHAPTER 12

Geneva: Life among
the Exiles

Dostoevsky arrived in Geneva in mid-August 1867 and remained until the end of May 1868, at which time he and Anna Grigoryevna moved to Vevey for the summer months. During this period, relatively stable and tranquil compared to what had gone before in Baden-Baden, Dostoevsky seriously settled down to work. His first order of literary business was to write an article on Belinsky, which he completed with great difficulty. The deadline for his next novel was also looming just ahead; and he began to make the first notes for *The Idiot*.

Life in Geneva brought Dostoevsky into sporadic contact with the colony of radical exiles who lived there, and the prickly Dostoevsky rather unexpectedly struck up an amicable acquaintance with N. P. Ogarev, who had recently been mockingly caricatured by Turgenev in *Smoke*. Alexander Herzen had written that Ogarev was "endowed with a peculiar magnetism, a feminine quality of attraction. For no apparent reason others are drawn to such people and cling to them."[1] Despite Dostoevsky's increasing detestation of the radicals, Ogarev's magnetism must have exercised its influence on him as well. It was because of Ogarev that the Dostoevskys were present at one of the sessions of the congress organized by the League of Peace and Freedom, a gathering of the European left wing in Geneva, whose clamorous proceedings were to provide some of the inspiration for *The Devils*.

2

A few days after settling in Geneva, where the Dostoevskys took a furnished room in a house owned by two kindly old ladies, Dostoevsky sat down to write a long letter to his old and staunchest friend, the poet Apollon Maikov. Maikov's letter to Dostoevsky in late May had remained unanswered because, as Dostoevsky explained, "I felt myself to be too unstable and was waiting for the slightest settled way of life in order to begin a correspondence with you."[2] Such a time had finally arrived, and his epistle marks the decision to take himself in hand. It is quite clear, however, that the letter is prompted as much by necessity as by courtesy or friendship. Dostoevsky makes no bones about asking Maikov for a loan, and goes into considerable detail about the bleakness of his economic prospects.

He had already received three advances from Katkov, whose generosity he found astonishing ("What a wonderful person he is! What a heart the man has!"), and he now owed the editor four thousand rubles in all. This debt he planned to repay with his novel, of which he speaks with perhaps more security than was warranted by the situation, since what he may have had in mind scarcely resembled what he finally wrote. But he tells Maikov, all the same: "I have a novel, and with God's help it will turn out to be a long thing and, perhaps, not a bad one. I like it an awful lot, and will be working on it with pleasure and anxiety." Meanwhile, it was necessary to survive before he could begin to supply Katkov with copy in January (the promised deadline), after which he would be in a position to ask for a new advance.[3]

Disclosing Anna's pregnancy, which he asks Maikov to keep secret for the time from Dostoevsky's relatives, he praises her in terms already familiar from her diary: "What an angel! How she tried to comfort me, how she languished in thrice-cursed Baden, in our two rooms over a blacksmith's shop, where we had moved." But now all their money had been spent on the most immediate necessities, and they could count on nothing except fifty rubles to be sent by Anna's mother, to whom Katkov had been instructed to remit the last advance. Dostoevsky thus asks Maikov for a loan of one hundred and fifty rubles for two months, which would be repaid directly by *The Russian Messenger*. Fully aware that Maikov's means were limited, Dostoevsky writes piteously: "But really, I'm drowning, have utterly drowned. In two or three weeks I'll be absolutely without a kopek, and a drowning man extends a hand without consulting reason . . . except for you—I don't have *anyone*, and if you don't help me I'll perish, utterly perish."[4]

The letter also contains a frank admission of his recent gambling escapades, which Dostoevsky explains, in his usual fashion, in terms of the lure of freeing himself from debt in one miraculous stroke, "in one fell swoop to get out of all these proceedings [with his creditors], provide for myself for a time and for all my family: Emilya Feodorovna, Pasha, and the others." But Dostoevsky is honest enough to add that gambling contains its own vertiginous attraction ("You know how that draws you in"), and, exactly like Aleksey Ivanovich, appears to take some satisfaction that his motives are not exclusively those of sordid gain. "No, I swear to you, it's not just self-interest, although above all I needed the money as money." All the same, to yield to his mania was a serious breach of his new moral responsibility: "none of that justifies me in the least, because I wasn't alone, I was with a young, kind, and wonderful creature who believes in me entirely, of whom I am defender and protector, and consequently, whom I could not bring to ruination and thus risk everything, even if by risking only a little."[5]

In the course of these self-revelations, Dostoevsky strikes off a sentence that has attracted a good deal of attention from commentators. Describing his passion for gambling as a moral-psychological flaw of character, he remarks: "And worst of all is that my nature is vile and very passionate; everywhere and in everything I go to the last limit; I've been going over the line my whole life."[6] This last statement has sometimes been given the most extravagant interpretation and taken to infer that Dostoevsky, seemingly by his own admission, confesses to being quite capable of committing all the worst moral excesses depicted in his novels. Before leaping to any such conclusion, however, it is well to remember the context of this remark. Dostoevsky is really talking about extreme imprudence rather than vice or perversity, and he does so against the background of the "vileness" of which he had constantly accused himself in the midst of his gambling frenzy. Moreover, because he was writing to Maikov, he may well have been alluding obliquely to his commitment to an underground revolutionary conspiracy nineteen years before. Maikov, whom Dostoevsky had unsuccessfully tried to recruit for the clandestine group, was one of the few people who knew how far Dostoevsky had gone "over the line" at that time. It thus seems illegitimate, so far as other episodes of Dostoevsky's life are concerned, to use these words as a buttress for accusatory inferences in the absence of firm supporting evidence independent of such unspecific self-condemnation.

Dostoevsky's letter, by no means confined to his practical affairs, is one of those in which, not having been in touch with someone for a protracted period, he stands back to survey recent events and bring his correspondent up to date. It is here that he describes the quarrel with Turgenev; and the letter contains much else that helps us to understand why Turgenev's apostasy with regard to his homeland should have filled Dostoevsky with such implacable fury. Maikov's letter, as well as providing information about the reception of *Smoke*, had also contained news about a Pan-Slav congress that had taken place in Moscow after Dostoevsky's departure under the auspices of the Russian Slavophils. Many of the Western Slav delegates had inquired about Dostoevsky, and his friend urges him to make a trip to Prague, if possible, where he has many admirers. Maikov also expresses his horror, which we have seen Dostoevsky fully sharing, at the assassination attempt made on the life of Alexander II. Above all, Dostoevsky gratefully refers to "the conviction about the similarity and agreement in our views and feelings" that made the letter so welcome and precious to him. Urging Maikov to continue to write regularly, Dostoevsky says that without such letters he would feel totally abandoned: they "will take the place of Russia for me and will give me strength."[7]

Dostoevsky's intense nostalgia for his homeland, and his despair over the impossibility of returning, reflects both a personal homesickness aggravated by his xenophobia and a gnawing fear that a prolonged residence in Europe would cripple his creative capacities. "And I need Russia, need it for my *writing* and work (not to mention the rest of my life) and how badly I need it! It's just like a fish being out of water; you lose your strength and means." On arriving in Dresden, Dostoevsky remarks, "I had wanted to set immediately to work and sensed that I absolutely couldn't work, that the impression was absolutely the wrong one." As a result, "I read, wrote a bit, suffered from ennui, and then from the heat." To relieve the tedium and, more important, to renew contact with the Russian sources of his inspiration, "I read Russian newspapers and relieved my heart. I sensed myself at last that enough material had accumulated for a whole piece about Russia's relations to Europe and about the whole Russian upper stratum. But what's the point of talking about all that! The Germans upset my nerves, and the life of our Russian upper stratum and its faith in Europe and *civilization* did too!"[8]

It is no accident that these irritable words are followed by a reference to Berezowski, whose murderous exploit had now become associated in Dostoevsky's sensibility with the pro-Western proclivities of the Russian upper stratum. Berezowski's trial had just taken place in Paris, where, in a stridently pro-Polish and anti-Russian atmosphere, the unsuccessful regicide had been sentenced to life imprisonment instead of execution. Referring to a demonstration in Berezowski's support by French lawyers, Dostoevsky writes rancorously: "The Paris lawyers who shouted 'Vive la Pologne' are fine ones too. Ugh, what vileness and most importantly— stupidity and conventionalism."[9] The reference to "conventionalism," which implies that the French are mired in old prejudices, probably alludes to a passage in Maikov's letter about the actions of Russian authorities in Poland. After the uprising had been crushed, and for the purpose of weakening the Polish nobility, the Russians broke up large estates and distributed the land to the peasants. But, of course, the French paid no attention to what, from the point of view of Maikov and Dostoevsky, had been such a beneficially democratic initiative. It is worth noting that, while offended by the demonstration, Dostoevsky presumably did not object to the decision to spare Berezowski's life.

Dostoevsky had always been intensely patriotic and nationalistic, even in the days of his short-lived revolutionary fervor, but never had his love for his native land reached such a pitch of fanaticism as during these years of involuntary expatriation. And never, as a result, did Russia appear to him, with the beguiling eyes of distance, more radiant and more full of hope and promise for the future. As he poured over the Russian newspapers containing news from home, Dostoevsky became convinced that he was obtaining a better and clearer view of Russian moral-social realities than if he had remained on his native soil. "From here Russia also seems more distinct to people like me. The extraordinary fact of the stability and unexpected maturity of the Russian people in encountering all our reforms (if only the legal one alone), and at the same time the news about the merchant of the first guild of Orenburg Province flogged by the chief of police."[10] The police chief in this case had asked for a bribe from a wealthy merchant and then illegally ordered him flogged when he refused to pay up (merchants of the first and second guild were supposedly immune from such corporal punishment). It is not clear if Dostoevsky sees in this press report a regrettable hangover from the old days, or takes the fact that a complaint was filed as evidence of the growth of the new legal order coming into being.

Whatever the answer, there is no doubt that he believed great and salutary events were now taking place in Russia. "One thing can be felt: that the Russian people, thanks to its benefactor and his reforms, has finally been put little by little into such a position that it is being forced to become accustomed to efficiency and self-observation, and that's the whole point. Honest to God, the present time, with its changes and reforms, is almost more important than that of Peter the Great's." Referring to the project of building more railroad lines in Russia, Dostoevsky says: "Let's have some to the south as soon as possible. . . . By that time there will be *true justice* everywhere, and then what a great renewal! (All that is being thought about, dreamed of, and wished for with all one's heart here.)"[11] These words are intermingled with the passages from the same letter in which Dostoevsky excoriates Turgenev and the Russian "atheists," whose ideal of man, presumably modeled on themselves, cannot stand comparison with the "lofty notion of man" given by Christ. Here we can observe how Dostoevsky's belief in the impending moral-social regeneration of the Russian people—a belief greatly nourished by his exile—blends with his religious convictions and his abhorrence of those who worship before the alien god of Western civilization. Just a few months later, such feelings will certainly contribute to his creation of a specifically Russian image of the highest type of moral beauty possible to humankind.

3
———

At the time he wrote to Maikov, Dostoevsky was working at the essay on Belinsky for which he had made some notes in Dresden. Anna remarks happily that dictation of the piece resumed at the beginning of September, and "perhaps we shall be able to send this essay to Babikov [the editor] very soon," she writes hopefully.[12] It was in fact finished three days later and dispatched to Maikov, along with a second letter, with the request to transmit it to the editor. But although Maikov followed Dostoevsky's instructions and deposited the text with a bookstore owner in Moscow for delivery to Babikov, the almanac never appeared and Dostoevsky's pages were lost. Just what the essay contained can only be inferred, and we shall speculate about its contents in a moment; what we do know is that the writing caused Dostoevsky an inordinate amount of trouble. "The fact is," he reports to Maikov, "that I have finished that damned piece, 'My Acquaintance with Belinsky,' . . . but it so wore me out and it was so hard to write that I dragged it out until now and finally, grinding my teeth, I have finished it. . . . Just as soon as I began writing it I saw at once that there was no way of writing it *so that it would pass the censorship* (because I wanted to write everything)." After rewriting it five times, Dostoevsky still remained unsatisfied: "How many valuable facts I was forced to throw out! . . . all that was left was the trashy and golden mean. Loathsome!"[13]

Belinsky had been one of the most important figures in Dostoevsky's life as a young writer, and he was also a major symbolic personality in Russian nineteenth-century culture. It was Belinsky whose praise of *Poor Folk* had catapulted Dostoevsky into instant fame in the 1840s, and the critic had then taken him under his wing not only as a literary but also as a moral-spiritual mentor. Even after Belinsky had renounced his former protégé by harshly criticizing *The Double*, and after the two had quarreled personally and ideologically, Dostoevsky still passionately admired his famous *Letter to Gogol*, with its fierce diatribe against serfdom and Russian Orthodoxy (though the *Letter* also spoke of Christ, in Utopian Socialist fashion, as the harbinger of liberty and freedom). One of the charges on which Dostoevsky was sent to prison camp was that he had read the *Letter* aloud to other members of the Petrashevsky circle.

Whatever their disagreements in the 1840s, Dostoevsky alluded quite positively to Belinsky in a critical article of 1861, where he remarks that "two pages" of Belinsky's work contained more historical insight into Russian literature than all the articles in *Notes of the Fatherland* (the journal with which he was polemicizing) from 1848 to the present (18: 71). Two years later Belinsky's widow, with whom Dostoevsky had been out of contact for fifteen years, unexpectedly sent him a friendly letter. He was touched, and replied: "I so much loved and admired your never-to-be-forgotten husband, and at the same time it was so pleasant for me to recall all of that best time of my life, that in my thoughts I thanked you from the bottom of my heart for your taking it into your head to write to me."[14] In the same year, nonetheless, Dostoevsky remarked in *Winter*

Notes that Belinsky, though "a passionate Russian personality," was still a Westerner and "presumably despised everything Russian"; and this hostility against Belinsky's Westernism rapidly gained the upper hand in Dostoevsky's view of his erstwhile friend and patron (5: 50). Turgenev had published a celebratory article about Belinsky in 1860 (one of the first to appear, after mention of his name had been banned by the censorship for a number of years), calling him a "central figure" whose ideas had gone to the core of the issues agitating Russian social-cultural life. And the result of Belinsky's influence, so far as Dostoevsky could now judge, was the contempt for Russia displayed in *Smoke* and in Turgenev's unabashed relinquishment of any claim to Russian nationality.

Some notion of the mood in which Dostoevsky wrote his article can be obtained from his comment, quoted in Chapter 11, about "all those trashy little liberals and progressives, primarily still of Belinsky's school," who "find their greatest pleasure and satisfaction in criticizing Russia" while still proclaiming their *love* for it. Whether he gave voice to any such sentiments in the text is highly unlikely; but he surely would have tried to include some of the reminiscences later incorporated in one of the first entries in his *Diary of a Writer* (1873). Here he evokes the image of Belinsky at a time when the critic had just been converted to Left Hegelian atheism under the influence of Feuerbach and was, with his usual uninhibited enthusiasm, indoctrinating his disciples with such freshly acquired convictions. Dostoevsky and Belinsky, as we know, had quarreled (or at least disputed) over the question of the immortality of the soul. The critic had ruthlessly discarded such a dogma, but Dostoevsky immovably clung to this hope and would not surrender it even to Belinsky's well-known vehemence in argument. The incident recounted in the *Diary* is a continuance of the same sort of disagreement, which centered on this occasion around the crucial question of whether Christ and the moral-social values he embodied still had any role to play in the modern world. Dostoevsky depicts himself, Belinsky, and two nameless others discussing this highly charged issue; and while Belinsky argues that old-fashioned Christian morality had been totally superseded by the decrees of "modern science," Dostoevsky inferentially maintains an opposing point of view.

"I'm really touched to look at him [Dostoevsky] ... ," Belinsky is quoted as declaring. "Every time I mention Christ his face changes expression as if he were ready to start weeping." Such a reaction could only have been provoked by words about Christ that were deeply offensive; and then, turning to Dostoevsky, who does not convey any of his own responses in the conversation, Belinsky goes on: "Yes, believe me, you naive person ... believe me that your Christ, if He were born in our day, would be the most ordinary and insignificant person; he would simply vanish in the face of contemporary science and of the contemporary movers of mankind." But when someone else volunteers the opinion that "if Christ appeared now, He would join the movement and would head it," Belinsky hastens to agree. "He would, as you say, join the Socialists and follow them" (21: 11).

Such memories, we may assume, would have flooded back to Dostoevsky as he was writing his article; and if so, then the image of a returning Christ, that is, a Christ re-entering the modern world and required to adjust Himself to its new moral-social challenges, would have been insistently hovering before him in the period immediately preceding the commencement of work on his new novel. The effect of such recollections, stirring in Dostoevsky's sensibility at this moment of creative ebullition, cannot be defined with any pretense at precision. It is not at all implausible, however, to imagine that Prince Myshkin's attempt to live by the highest Christian values in the modern world, and to cope with Young Nihilists who considered him as ludicrously outmoded as Belinsky had considered Christ Himself, is linked in some subconscious fashion with Dostoevsky's struggles to tell the truth about "My Acquaintance with Belinsky."

4
―――――

Life abroad for the Dostoevskys involved endless difficulties and hardships, most of them deriving from their acute lack of funds; and Dostoevsky's sporadic gambling only worsened their misery. But they also suffered because they had no society of any kind to relieve their loneliness; and their contacts with the local population were more a source of irritation than of welcome succor from isolation. Dostoevsky's intense dislike of the Germans had provoked the wrath of Turgenev; and though Anna was more good-natured, easygoing, and tolerant, her diary reveals that the Germans frequently got on her nerves as well. Life in Geneva put less of a strain on their easily aroused susceptibilities, and perhaps the shield of French manners served to ward off any overt unpleasantnesses that might have occurred. However, Dostoevsky's epileptic attacks became more frequent in Geneva, and he believed that the sudden changes of climate were to blame for this misfortune. He very soon thought of moving elsewhere; but with barely enough resources to cover their room and meals (they were constantly in arrears and forced to pawn belongings from time to time in order to get through a bad stretch), they could not think of leaving. Moreover, Anna would be giving birth in a few months, and Dostoevsky wanted to stay in a large, French-speaking city where medical care would be easily available and he could count on his command of the language.

What annoyed the Dostoevskys most about the French Swiss was their complacent self-satisfaction and rabid local patriotism. In the first entry in her Geneva diary, setting down a conversation with the two accommodating elderly ladies who had rented them a room, Anna notes: "They began to speak to me about the imminent arrival of Garibaldi, and that every other government absolutely envied their free country and certainly wished to conquer Switzerland because everything here is so fine that everyone is full of envy." The entry concludes with the sarcastic remark: "Although the city of Geneva boasts of its freedom, it turns out that freedom consists only in everyone being drunk and bawling out songs."[15] In October, Dostoevsky takes up the same refrain with Maikov. After complaining about the terrible effects of the rapid changes of weather on his health, he irascibly goes on: "Everything here is vile, rotten, everything is expensive. Everyone here is drunk! There aren't as many brawlers and loud drunks even in London. And everything they have, every stone, is elegant and majestic." Even "the puniest, trashiest rococo, in bad taste . . . can't fail to be praised even if you only ask for directions."[16]

One assumes that the Dostoevskys had often rehashed these particular impressions in their conversation; and since they had nobody but each other to talk to, it is not surprising that such similarities should emerge in their reactions. In Dresden, Dostoevsky and his wife had avoided all contact with whatever Russian colony existed in the city; and though they had stopped to chat with Goncharov in Baden-Baden, where Dostoevsky was also forced to pay his reluctant call on Turgenev, no other instances are recorded of any conviviality with fellow Russians. Geneva, however, was filled with a large number of Russians living abroad as political exiles, and they frequented the same cafés where Dostoevsky would have gone to read the Russian newspapers with devoted regularity. Some sort of occasional intercourse with them was thus inevitable, though it was very probably limited to a curt exchange of salutations. The only fellow exile of this kind with whom Dostoevsky struck up any sustained relation (it could hardly be called friendship) was Nikolay P. Ogarev, a distant cousin and boon companion of Alexander Herzen, who was himself quite prominent in radical circles. Just a few years earlier, in a famous chapter of *My Past and Thoughts* (*Byloe i Dumi*), Herzen had portrayed the two young men, still in their teens, climbing to the heights of the Sparrow Hills outside Moscow and "suddenly embracing . . . vow[ing] in the sight of all Moscow to sacrifice our lives to the struggle we had chosen."[17] This struggle, initially inspired by the reading of Schiller, involved a declaration of war against tyranny and despotism, and Herzen and Ogarev had remained faithful to their youthful oath by becoming leaders of the Russian revolutionary movement. Unquestion-

7. N. P. Ogarev

ably, too, the vibrant pages of Herzen's brilliant chapter had sparked more than one later revolutionary vocation.

The son of a wealthy landowning family, Ogarev was a rather gentle, softhearted, and quite sympathetic soul, whose life had been passed in the shadow of Herzen's more vital and vigorous personality. His private existence had been a very unhappy one, and a good part of his considerable fortune had been dissipated by his frivolous and pleasure-loving first wife, whose infidelities, however, had never caused him to renounce her completely. His second wife, when the pair left Russia and moved to London, became the mistress of his best friend, the recently widowed Herzen, to whom she bore three children. But this matrimonial reshuffling did not disturb the intimacy and close collaboration between the two men—which tells us a good deal about the mildness and all-suffering gentleness of Ogarev's character. Many years before, Herzen had written him, in jesting fondness, that "you have a broad comprehension of everything that is human, and a dull incomprehension of everything that is particular to Ogarev."[18] This observation proved to be quite accurate when Herzen put it to the test; but Ogarev's "comprehension of everything human" was not restricted only to his personal relationships. When his father died and he became master of the considerable estate, what part of his fortune had not been squandered by his first wife was further diminished because he freed his serfs on terms so advantageous to them and so economically disastrous for himself. By the time he met Dostoevsky in Geneva, Ogarev was almost as poor as the indigent novelist and lived, with an English ex-prostitute who had become his devoted companion and her son, on a small stipend provided by the affluent Herzen, whose money had always received the most careful supervision.

For all his misadventures as a man and husband, Ogarev worked zealously for the cause he had pledged to advance on the Sparrow Hills. He had become co-editor with Herzen of *The Bell*, the most important Russian radical periodical of the late 1850s and early 1860s, which the two men issued from London; and he also edited a special journal, *Obschee Veche* (these words, in an obsolete Russian, mean something like "The Common Assembly"), whose purpose was to stir up discontent among the Old Believers (*raskolniki*), the lower orders of the clergy, and peasants and soldiers unlikely to pay attention to propaganda cast in a more modern linguistic and ideological idiom. The co-editor of this journal was V. I. Kelsiev, whose name will soon turn up in Dostoevsky's correspondence with Maikov. Ogarev had also acquired a quite honorable reputation as a poet, which endures to the present day, and Dostoevsky had rather daringly praised one of his works, "The Tale of a Way Station Officer," in an article of 1861.

Ogarev was thus very publicly linked with the revolutionary agitation of the intelligentsia that Dostoevsky had come to abhor; but he was not a member of the brashly arrogant Nihilist generation of the 1860s, nourished on Chernyshevsky's crass atheism and materialistic Utilitarianism. Like Herzen, he was a highly cultivated, Romantic Idealist man of letters of the 1840s, with a refinement of taste and sensibility that Dostoevsky could appreciate and respect independently of the partisan enmities of politics. Dostoevsky would also have responded positively to Ogarev's evident desire to reach out to the less educated portions of the Russian people, his attempt to understand what they were thinking and feeling, and his manifest consideration for their values and beliefs. Politically, he advocated the convening of a *zemski sobor* (an assembly of representatives of *all* the people, including the peasantry) to cope with the problems created by the liberation of the serfs. The call for such an assembly, responsible for having appointed the Romanovs to the throne several centuries back, would later become a mainstay of Dostoevsky's own political articles in his *Diary of a Writer*. Ogarev too, it should be added, was subject to epileptic seizures, and this might also have created a personal bond between them as fellow sufferers.

5

The two men had probably met during Dostoevsky's visit to London in 1863, when he called on Alexander Herzen several times and was introduced to his entourage. How they made contact in Geneva is not known;

but they may have run into each other accidentally in the Café de la Couronne on the Grand Quai that Anna mentions as their usual place of rendezvous. The amiable Ogarev soon also visited the Dostoevskys at home: "I have just been at the house of the dead," he informs Herzen on September 3, "who sends you his greetings. He's in poor health."[19] Ogarev returned frequently thereafter, to Anna's great satisfaction, bringing books and newspapers and behaving toward her with great courtliness, as if she were a young girl—which of course she was! It was because of Ogarev that the Dostoevskys attended one session of the congress that took place in Geneva a week later under the auspices of a group of progressives and radicals calling themselves the League of Peace and Freedom, who had appointed Mikhail Bakunin, Ogarev, and another more obscure Russian émigré to represent their native land.

The mention of Garibaldi in Anna's diary refers to the excitement among the Genevans caused by the expectation of his arrival to take part in the congress, and additional entries record the imminence of this great event: "Today and yesterday evening, in every corner, hung proclamations announcing the arrival of Garibaldi and inviting everyone to give him an enthusiastic welcome." The next day she notes that his appearance had been delayed, but speaks of other posters outlining the planned events. On the final day of the congress, "there will be an outing on the lake and a dinner paid for personally by Victor Hugo [but Hugo, in fact, never showed up—J.F.]. I would like to see all that," jots down poor Anna, craving for some excitement or diversion in the unrelieved monotony of her days.[20]

Garibaldi finally came to Geneva on Sunday, September 8, to be greeted by a cannonade, the roll of drums, and a parade of local firefighters marching in stately procession and pulling their equipment by hand. Anna, quite scornful of their elaborate uniforms fitted out with epaulettes, remarks that if they proceeded to a fire at the same speed as they marched, everything would be burned down before they reached the scene! While Dostoevsky went off to read the newspapers, Anna remained in one of the main streets, very annoyed to be left alone but determined to stay; and she finally caught a glimpse of Garibaldi as he passed in an open carriage, waving his hat and bowing to the crowd. His prominent forehead, from a distance, reminded her of Dostoevsky's; and the impression he made on closer inspection was equally favorable: "What a good, kind, simple face; he must really be a remarkably good and intelligent man."[21]

Anna's reaction may well have been influenced by Dostoevsky's own very positive opinion of Garibaldi, who always unwaveringly refused to separate his radicalism from a religious foundation, and whose integrity and honesty Dostoevsky had defended in *Winter Notes*. In his speech at

8. Giuseppe Garibaldi

the congress, which aroused hostile reactions on both the left and the right, Garibaldi bitterly attacked Catholicism and the Papacy, but advocated that the League of Peace and Freedom march forward under the banner of "the religion of God." Posters instantly appeared, as we learn from Anna, accusing Garibaldi of having insulted half the population of the canton of Geneva, equally divided between Protestants and Catholics.

The Dostoevskys had had no intention of attending any sessions of the congress for a very simple reason: they did not wish to spend the sum required for admission. But "today Fedya met Ogarev," Anna writes, "who asked him whether he had been at the congress. Fedya replied that he was not a member, and [Ogarev] answered that admission cost only twenty-five centimes [actually, it turned out to be fifty]. So Fedya said: 'Then of course I will go.'"[22] Bakunin was scheduled to speak the next day, and it was long thought that the Dostoevskys had been present when the celebrated revolutionary warrior—whose leonine personality made him an electrifying platform presence, further heightened by his exotic garb of a Cossack freebooter—made a stirring impromptu speech in French calling for the breakup of the Russian Empire and expressing the hope that its armies would be defeated in the future. He also assailed the principle of nationality as a tool of reaction, and called for the destruction of all "centralized states" to make way for the formation of a United States of Europe organized freely on the basis of new groupings once the old state frameworks had been demolished.

In her *Reminiscences*, Anna mistakenly writes that she and Dostoevsky attended the second session of the congress—which would have meant that they had been in the audience when Bakunin delivered his ringing peroration. In fact, as her diary proves, the Dostoevskys attended the *third* session, and so could not have heard Bakunin's impassioned denunciation of everything that Dostoevsky held dear. This considerably undermines the view, questionable on other grounds as well, that the impact of hearing Bakunin made such an impression on Dostoevsky that he later used the career and personality of the great anarchist as a model for the character of Stavrogin in *The Devils*. What the Dostoevskys heard were two or three orators whose names Anna does not record, one of whom, an Italian, refused to stop speaking even when admonished by the president of the session, and gesticulated so violently that he upset a glass of water over an unfortunate gentleman in the front row. The crowd made so much noise that it was difficult to hear the speakers, and what they had to say, when it was audible, is labeled by Anna as nothing more than "bombastic phrases."[23]

But although Dostoevsky did not experience in person the full onslaught of Bakunin's legendary eloquence, his visit to the congress left some vivid recollections all the same. The sessions were covered thoroughly in the local and international press, which Dostoevsky read with great diligence, and he was thus quite well informed about what Bakunin had so thunderously advocated at the second meeting. Not all of the delegates by any means had been in agreement, as Dostoevsky well knew, with Bakunin's vision of total destruction as a necessary prelude to the advent of a new anarchist utopia; but it was this vision that dominated the impression left by the congress on his imagination.

Several of his letters at this time contain references to the congress, and they all ridicule its confusion and absurdity, as well as the self-contradiction of its presumably Bakuninian goals. "Not only had I never imagined such nonsense in all my life," he wrote to Maikov, "but I had not even imagined that people were capable of such stupidity."[24] To his favorite niece, Sofya Ivanova, he sets down the most detailed evocation:

What these gentlemen—whom I was seeing for the first time in my life instead of in a book—socialists and revolutionaries blathered on about from a podium before 5,000 listeners was indescribable! No description can convey it. The comicality, the weakness, the nonsense, the disagreement, the self-contradictions—unimaginable! And that trash stirs up the unfortunate working people! That's sad. They began with the fact that in order to achieve peace on earth the Christian faith has to be exterminated; large states destroyed and turned into small ones; all capital be done away with, so that every-

thing be in common, by order, and so on. All this without the slightest proof, all of this was memorized twenty years ago and that's just
how it has remained. And most importantly, fire and sword—and
after everything has been annihilated, then, in their opinion, there
will in fact be peace.[25]

Three years later, such reactions will be poured into *The Devils*, where
Dostoevsky also stresses the self-contradictions in which the radicals become involved as they try to think through the consequences of their
cherished ideas. The theoretician of the revolutionary group in that
novel will be reduced to despair because his "conclusion is in direct contradiction to the original idea with which I start. Starting from unlimited
freedom, I arrived at unlimited despotism" (10: 311).

Dostoevsky wonders why such congresses are forbidden in France,
where, if they were allowed, they would display all the futility of such
revolutionary agitation and make the poor aware of "what these propa-
gandists are capable of, whether they can say or do anything serious or
useful."[26] Obviously not, in Dostoevsky's opinion; and he notes approv-
ingly that Garibaldi had quit the congress very rapidly (this sudden departure aroused much comment and was interpreted as a sign of disapproval). Such vitriolic observations, however, were reserved for Dostoevsky's correspondence, or for the ears of Anna alone. Good relations
with Ogarev were maintained, though perhaps Dostoevsky took a more
circuitous route, disguised as a small, friendly gesture, to convey what he
could not say more overtly. On learning that his café companion had not
read *Crime and Punishment*, he obligingly loaned him a copy of the journal containing the first installments. Ogarev reciprocated by presenting
Dostoevsky with a volume of his poems published in London in 1858.

PART III

A Russian Ideal

CHAPTER 13

In Search of a Novel

Once having sent off his ill-fated Belinsky article, Dostoevsky settled into his larger task, and in mid-September Anna jots down, "today Fedya began to sketch the program of the new novel."[1] This preliminary preparation of a "program," the outline of what he intended to write, was always a very important step in the creative process for Dostoevsky. In this instance it continued, with increasing uncertainty and anxiety, up to the moment when submission of the first segment of the promised manuscript was required. The notebooks for *The Idiot* amply document this first stage and illustrate how persistently Dostoevsky struggled to find his artistic path through the maze of incidents and situations that he piles up in such profusion. An analysis of these notebooks, however, is reserved for the next chapter. Here we shall follow the course of Dostoevsky's life, both the external events and the inner accumulation of impressions, up to and slightly beyond the time at which the composition of the novel was begun.

Such a separation, though, is quite artificial, and we can constantly observe the interweaving of his specifically creative labors with the routine events of his day-to-day existence. It may be only a coincidence, but another entry in Anna's Geneva diary on this very date records a conversation between the pair about death (Dostoevsky was everlastingly haunted by the fear of dying in an epileptic attack), and also about the Christian faith. "This evening we spoke of the Gospels, of Christ, and spoke quite a long time. I am always happy," she writes appealingly, "when he speaks to me not only about ordinary matters, like coffee or sugar, but when he finds me capable of listening to him and speaking to him on other, more important and abstract matters."[2] Dostoevsky's new novel, which so far has little or nothing to do with *The Idiot* as we know it, already seems to be linked with its later religious thematic at some still latent level of his creative sensibility.

2

Dostoevsky's most immediate problem was, as usual, the financial one, and he wrote to everyone who might be willing to lend a helping hand. Maikov sent one hundred and twenty-five rubles; and Dostoevsky also appealed to Dr. Stepan Yanovsky, an old friend from the 1840s, reminding him that some years back the affable and prosperous doctor had told Dostoevsky to call on him if he were ever in dire need. Explaining all the difficulties of his present situation, including Anna's pregnancy, Dostoevsky requests the loan of seventy-five rubles, or at least fifty. The reply arrived on a day when Anna was particularly gloomy because the pair had no money left at all. "I got up terribly sad and terribly mournful because today I would certainly have to go to that dressmaker and pawn my lace mantilla. God! How much I wish I didn't have to go," she writes, adding that she would rather remain hungry for three more days than bow humbly before the condescending dressmaker.[3] Putting off the humiliating visit as long as possible, she went first to the post office—where the daily visits of the Russian couple had made them an all-too-familiar sight—and rushed home to tell Dostoevsky that a registered letter had arrived for which he would have to sign. On returning, he announced the joyful news that Yanovsky had sent one hundred rubles; and Anna breaks out into heartfelt exclamations of relief and gratitude at being spared her impending ordeal.

Matters were not always arranged so happily, and more than once both Anna and Dostoevsky were forced to pawn their clothing like the merest paupers under the supercilious gaze of the impassive Swiss. Letters from both Pasha Isaev and Emilya Feodorovna complained that *they* were short of funds, thus driving Anna into her usual rage at their exigencies. In fact, Mikhail's family was hardly living in circumstances as straitened as the Dostoevskys themselves. They had just returned to Petersburg from the summer dacha at Lublino and had moved into Dostoevsky's old apartment, for whose rent he had made himself responsible. Anna was particularly incensed at finding listed among her sister-in-law's grievances a lack of money to redeem her pawned best overcoat: "That is really killing, my overcoat has also been pawned, for more than six months, and before hers mine must be redeemed."[4] Dostoevsky replied by explaining how impoverished he was himself, but holding out some hope of relief in the next two months. He had asked for a new advance of five hundred rubles, to be sent in monthly installments of one hundred; and if the advance was forthcoming, Apollon Maikov would distribute sixty rubles to Emilya Feodorovna and Pasha. Even in his worst moments, much to Anna's suppressed bitterness, Dostoevsky never neglected to share what little he had with those he felt obligated to support. Katkov again exhibited his usual generosity, and the Dostoevskys finally had a regular but pitifully small income to tide them over until the novel could be gotten under way. Dostoevsky estimated, with his usual overoptimism, that once writing began he would complete it in five months.

Despite the pressure of his impending deadline, Dostoevsky nonetheless found time to make two short trips to Saxon-les-Bains for another fling at roulette. The lure of winning a large amount revived once more, and Anna can only mark its reappearance with incredulity and stoic resignation. On September 17, she notes: "He definitely has the intention of going there; what a strange man. It would seem that fate has punished him so strongly, and showed him so many times that he cannot get rich by roulette. No, this man is incurable, he still is convinced all the same—and I am sure he will always be convinced—that he will certainly become rich, will certainly win, and then will be able to help his wretches" (meaning his brother's family and Pasha).[5]

The usual results occurred; and after the second catastrophe, in a letter filled with the familiar frantic apologies and self-flagellations, he sketches a plan to ask Ogarev for a loan of three hundred francs (obviously unaware of the veteran radical's own circumstances). "In the first place," he writes revealingly, "he's not Herzen, and in the second, although it's distressing for me to the point of agonizing pain, I nonetheless won't obligate myself with anything morally. I'll *state* that when I borrow from him. . . . After all, he's a poet, a writer, he has a heart, and in addition he himself comes to me and seeks me, which means he respects me."[6] When Dostoevsky put the question to Ogarev, the mention of such a large sum "almost frightened him,"[7] according to Anna, but he thought he might scrape together sixty francs. Two days later, the unfailingly generous Ogarev visited the Dostoevskys and brought the smaller amount, which they promised to return in two weeks (but whether they managed to keep their word remains unknown).*

If perpetual tension had marked their life together in Dresden and Baden-Baden, Anna in Geneva records a growing tenderness and sense of dependency on Dostoevsky's part that filled her with intense satisfaction, and compensated in good measure for the insecurity and gloomy monotony of their lives. Once, walking past the theater in Geneva and looking at the program, Dostoevsky remarked that they should see a play sometime for amusement; but Anna knew that this tempting prospect was just an empty phrase. "I am fully convinced that during our entire stay in Geneva we will not be there even once," she writes sadly, in a prediction that proved correct.[8] To amuse themselves they composed a long comic poem called "Abracadabra," and Anna lovingly set down in

---

* Anna later gave a different version of this incident in her memoirs. She speaks of Ogarev as having lent them only ten francs, and adds "which we promptly returned at the first receipt of some money." Soon afterward, Ogarev was overcome by an epileptic fit while walking alone, fell into a ditch, and lay there all night with a broken leg. His friends took him to Italy to recover, and, after three months, the Dostoevskys were deprived of their sole acquaintance in Geneva. Anna Dostoevsky, *Reminiscences*, trans. and ed. Beatrice Stillman (New York, 1975), 136.

her diary, not only what was occurring from day to day, but also memories of her first meeting with Dostoevsky and the events leading to his proposal. Dostoevsky remained touchy and irritable, and there were temporary tiffs about one matter or another that led to periods of coolness; but these were quickly patched up and, in Dostoevsky's case, replaced by overflowing effusions of gratitude and love. One such can stand for many entries. Waking Anna to kiss her good-night, he declared: "I cannot live without you, Anya, we have grown so much together that a knife couldn't cut us apart." It was "for those like you," he tells her, "that Christ came. I say this not because I love you but because I know you. Soon there will be Sonya [their expected child], there will be two angels," and this vision fills him with happiness.[9]

Dostoevsky's entire future, of course, depended on the success of his next novel, which only increased the pressure and tension under which he was working at his notes. What he counted on, as he wrote to Maikov, was the sudden flash of inspiration that would enable him to discover, among the swarming multiplicity of his scenarios, the one that he could most profitably develop. Usually, he explains, "my seeds of artistic thought always occur and give notice of themselves," and they "are felt both in my head and in my heart. But, you see, this only occurs in a flash, and what is needed is a complete embodiment, which always rises unexpectedly and suddenly, but you can't calculate when precisely it will come about; and then finally, having received the complete image in your heart, you can undertake its artistic realization."[10] All through the fall and winter months Dostoevsky sought this moment and tried to provoke its appearance—with so little success, however, that he feared his capacities might be fading because of the frequency of his epileptic attacks. Writing to Dr. Yanovsky in a moment of depression, he gives voice to such misgivings and complains that "this epilepsy will end up by carrying me off. My star is fading—I realize that. My memory has grown completely dim (completely!). I don't recognize people anymore. I forget what I read the day before. I'm afraid of going mad or falling into idiocy."[11]

Nonetheless, work stubbornly went on, though hardly in a manner that could provide Dostoevsky with any satisfaction. And as time passed without the necessary spark of insight flashing forth from his notebook pages, he became more and more discouraged. At the end of October, Anna remarks that he "is terribly saddened because the novel is not going well and he worries that he will not be able to send it by the month of January."[12] One night she awoke to find him lying on the floor in prayer; and while there were many blessings for which he might have been imploring God, inspiration for his next novel may well have been one of them. Above all, though, he had determined that he would not compromise his artistic integrity, whatever the cost. "Worst of all," he tells his niece, "I fear mediocrity, I think it's better for a thing to be either very good or quite bad. Thirty signatures [a page measurement] of mediocrity is an unforgivable thing."[13] Two months later, explaining to Maikov why he had abandoned a considerable first draft, he declares: "I said to hell with it all. I assure you that the novel could have been satisfactory, but I got incredibly fed up with it precisely because of the fact that it was satisfactory and not *absolutely good*."[14] Dostoevsky thus remained faithful to his commitment against producing a satisfactory mediocrity, and instead chose to launch himself, almost unprepared, into the writing of one of the most extraordinary and thematically unprecedented novels in the history of the genre.

3

One should not imagine, however, that Dostoevsky's intense absorption in work on his novel cut him off from the outside world, or that the horizon of his concerns narrowed appreciably as a result of his persistently unyielding labors. Quite the contrary, he continued to read the newspapers every day, particularly the Russian ones, and perhaps even more carefully and attentively than in the past. For this was his only way of maintaining contact with the moral-social and cultural atmosphere of Russia that he felt was so indispensable a nourishment for his work, and of which he had now been deprived by his exile.

Indeed, the importance he always attributed to the daily press is well illustrated in the advice he gives to his niece just at this moment. "Read them [the newspapers], please," he admonishes her, "nowadays one cannot do otherwise, not because of fashion, but because the visible connection among all matters, general and private, is becoming stronger and stronger and more and more obvious."[15] The particular context of this injunction is the growing threat of an impending European war provoked by France (which broke out, as Dostoevsky foresaw, two years later in the Franco-Prussian conflict); but the words also express Dostoevsky's deep-rooted conviction, on which he continuously drew for artistic purposes, that the "general and the private" were inextricably interconnected. In the same letter, he remarks that "I definitely want to publish something like a newspaper when I get back (I think I even recall mentioning it to you casually, but here the form and goal have now become absolutely clear)."[16] This project, which gave birth some years later to the *Diary of a Writer*, would approach public events in a manner different from an ordinary newspaper and integrate them with a personal vision in an unprecedented fashion. The same idea is mentioned in *The Devils*, when the ill-fated Liza Tushina, wishing to do something "useful" with her life, hits upon the idea of publishing a volume of "facts" culled from the press that would "give, as it were, a picture of the spiritual, moral, and inner life of Russia for a whole year" (10: 104).

It is not surprising, then, to find that for *The Idiot*, at least in its initial stages, Dostoevsky also drew on material from the newspapers. His early notes were considerably affected by what he read of a court case involving the Umetsky family, whose fourteen-year-old daughter Olga had tried to burn down the family house four times—although she had warned everyone after setting the blazes—and was then brought to trial. Investigation uncovered an unspeakable picture of family tyranny, cruelty, and revolting neglect on the part of the parents. Their inhumanity had led the poor child to attempt to take her own life several times before turning to arson as a last resort.

Dostoevsky kept Anna apprised of the news from home by reporting on what he had read during their daily walks together, and she singles out for special mention the calvary of Olga Umetskaya. "If I could do so," she confides to her diary in fury, "I believe I would hang them [the parents], they are so repulsive to me."[17] In fact, although Olga Umetskaya herself was acquitted of any wrongdoing, the court imposed only minimal punishment on the parents; and this is probably what Dostoevsky is referring to when he mentions the case in a letter. "I'm just dying to get back to Russia," he tells Maikov in mid-October. "I wouldn't let the Umetsky case go by without having my word; I'd publish it. As soon as I arrive, I'll go around in person, to the courts, and so on. Our jurors are as good as can be. But as for our judges, one could wish for somewhat more education and practice. And you know for what else: moral principles. Without that basis, nothing can be established."[18] These last words probably refer to the failure to punish the monstrous Umetsky parents more severely for the mistreatment of their children.

The figure of Olga Umetskaya appears in Dostoevsky's notes linked to that of a female character called Mignon, whose name is taken from Goethe's *Wilhelm Meister*. In the margin of the notes he had already made about Mignon, Dostoevsky writes: "The history of Mignon—in all respects the same as the history of Olga Umetskaya" (9: 142). This should not be taken as a statement of fact (which makes no sense), but rather as an indication that the Goethean literary prototype will be fleshed out with some of the horrors of Olga Umetskaya's life. Mignon, a beautiful and wayward young girl haunted by some mysterious tragedy, wanders from place to place in the company of an old man called the Harper, who accompanies her on his instrument when she sings one or another piercingly sad and melancholy song. Olga Umetskaya's tormented life and desperate actions reveal a desire to take revenge, but this urge is countered by a need for love and family feeling; and Dostoevsky may have wished to combine her tortured history with the haunting dolefulness of Goethe's character. He will also use some of the details that came to light about the Umetsky family, though considerably softened, in his depiction of the disorder reigning in the household of the mythomaniacal General Ivolgin. Eventually, the fusion of Olga Umetskaya and Mignon would result in the creation of Nastasya Filippovna, the most genuinely tragic and enchanting of all Dostoevsky's heroines.

The harrowing fate of Olga Umetskaya was not the only case that attracted Dostoevsky's attention and, as he pored over the Russian press, left its traces on *The Idiot*. It is very likely that the character of Rogozhin, not mentioned at all in the early notes, is linked to the trial of a Moscow merchant named V. F. Mazurin, who killed a jeweler. This crime had made headlines in March 1867, before Dostoevsky left for abroad; but the trial and sentence took place at the end of November, just as he was drafting his novel. Mazurin, the son of a rich merchant like Rogozhin, had inherited a fortune of two million rubles, and lived in a house very similar to the one that Dostoevsky describes. The murder was committed in this gloomy dwelling, and the corpse, concealed in the house, was covered with an American oilskin; it was also surrounded, exactly as would be the corpse of Nastasya Filippovna, by two containers of something called Zhdanov fluid, used in Russia as a disinfectant and deodorant. Nastasya Filippovna herself mentions having read about this crime just before Prince Myshkin enters her life, and its recollection, foreshadowing her own end, haunts her throughout the succeeding sequence of events.

Two other crimes culled from the newspapers are also referred to frequently in *The Idiot*. One is the murder of six people by an eighteen-year-old student named Gorsky, who came from a noble family, had received an excellent education, and had exhibited a penchant for reading and study. Hired as a tutor by the Zhemarin family, he carefully prepared for his crime before carrying it out, killing a doorman and a cook as well as four family members, including his pupil. Lebedyev speaks, with the self-parodying exaggeration that is his wont, of his Young Nihilist nephew as being capable of committing a similar deed; and Dostoevsky thus brings this mass murder, even if only as a piece of grotesque black humor, into the orbit of his conviction that Nihilist ideas were weakening the power of moral conscience in the younger generation.

The second crime, which takes on a crucial symbolic significance, involved the murder of a servant by an acquaintance for the sake of a silver watch. Investigation established that, just before slitting the throat of the watch's owner, with whom he been chatting peacefully, the criminal uttered a prayer: "Bless me, O Lord, and forgive for the sake of Christ." The murderer's motive in real life appears to have been poverty: he wished to pawn the watch and return to his starving family in a village. But Dostoevsky uses the incident rather to indicate the deep, instinctive religiosity of the Russian people even in the midst of their worst excesses. Myshkin remarks, in what for Dostoevsky is a self-referential allusion, that if such a detail had been invented by a novelist, critics would have severely taxed it for being "improbable; but reading it in the newspapers as a fact, you feel that in such facts you are studying the reality of Russian life" (8: 412–413).

Another case to which Dostoevsky paid special attention was linked to the publication of the early chapters of *Crime and Punishment* just the year before. Shortly after these had appeared, with their terrifying images of Raskolnikov's slaughter of the two helpless women, a similar murder, as we know, had been committed by a student from a family of noble rank. A. M. Danilov impressed everyone at his trial by his culture, refinement, and self-possession, and many commentators at the time drew a comparison between Raskolnikov and Danilov. Some new information about this old case was reported in late November 1867, at the very moment Dostoevsky was recasting his projected novel; and he picked up one particular detail that appears in his text, again on the lips of Lebedyev, almost verbatim. Danilov had committed the murders after informing his father that he wished to marry; and the elder Danilov had given his son the following advice: "Do not despise any means; for one's happiness it is necessary to acquire money, even if this is done by way of crime."[19] Such a paternal injunction was just another flagrant example, in Dostoevsky's eyes, of the weakening of moral standards throughout Russian society caused by the inordinate emphasis on the importance of money.

4

Time and again, in his letters of this period, Dostoevsky reiterates his frustration at composing a new novel in the absence of any firsthand contact with Russian life. To his niece he explains: "As a writer (unless he is a specialist or a scholar), it is particularly difficult . . . to remain abroad for a long time. In our work, reality is primary; and here, well, reality is Swiss."[20] To supplement his devoted scrutiny of the newspapers, he was dependent on letters from friends like Maikov and from his immediate family, and his responses to these letters also display some of the other effects of his exile. They reveal, on the one hand, a growing antipathy toward European life in all its aspects; and on the other a compensating idealization of Russia that increased in proportion to his hostility.

Sometimes his disgruntlement descends to the most prosaic details of his surroundings in Geneva—for example, the freezing cold and the problem of heating their room. The Swiss, he complains (though he thinks, *pace* Turgenev, that they are infinitely superior to the immeasurable stupidity of the Germans), "do not have enough intelligence to better adapt their homes" to the rigors of the climate, which is much like northern Russia for three months of the year. "All they need do is install double windows to be able to live—and even only with chimneys [fireplaces]. I don't even say—to install a stove."[21] Instead, without double windows, they burn wood in the fireplaces all day long without taking off the chill, and thus needlessly destroy the few forests still remaining in Europe (Dostoevsky appears here in the unexpected role of pioneer ecologist, for which he has never been given any credit). He can hardly contain his rage at such negligence, though in *The Idiot*, when Mme Epanchina exclaims that the Europeans "in winter are frozen like mice in a cellar," another character sagely remarks that "she was bitter and unfair in her criticism of everything European" (8: 510). These mollifying words, however, were written when Dostoevsky was living in the much more temperate climate of Italy.

For the moment, his objurgations against Europe knew no bounds, and he seizes on every pretext he can find to undermine the congenital Russian assumption of European superiority. Just because Russians are used to importing foreign merchandise, he complains to Dr. Yanovsky, many "among us set off for abroad persuaded, as a result of a certain prejudice, that everything abroad is beautiful and cheap. I am now persuaded by experience that with the exceptions of items of the first necessity, only in Paris and London are products good and inexpensive. In all the other cities of Europe everything is more expensive and less good than at home." He also rails against the Russians who live in Europe and "raise their children there and do their utmost to have them forget Russian."[22] It is not accidental, of course, that he continues by informing Yanovsky of Turgenev's declaration that "he considered himself a German." Three months later, Dostoevsky objects vigorously to the news that his sister Vera intends to employ a French governess for her children. In the first place, he insists, it is not at all necessary: "Believe me . . . when your children are grown, French will no longer be spoken in our drawing rooms." Moreover, French is now spoken with a Parisian pronunciation that Dostoevsky finds "guttural, nasty, exuding baseness in every syllable." Worst of all, "what will that Frenchwoman teach the children?" She will merely "inculcate in them her foul, distorted, ridiculous and preposterous rules of behavior and deformed ideas about society and religion."[23]

Dostoevsky's aversion to everything European was easily transferred to the Russian Westerners—now incarnated mainly by Bakunin and Turgenev, but also including the tempestuous progenitor of them all, Belinsky—who continued to support the negative opinions about Russia that Dostoevsky could no longer regard as anything but self-hatred and betrayal. Referring to some information from Maikov about editorial changes in the leading radical journals, he remarks scornfully that these journals in any case all exhibit "the same scabby hatred of Russia and the same interest in workers' associations in France—and that's all. That Saltykov [-Shchedrin] belabors the zemstvos just had to happen. Our liberal cannot help but be at the same time an ingrained and quite conscious enemy of Russia. Just let something succeed in Russia or something happen to its advantage—and their venom starts to flow. I've noticed it a thousand times. Our extreme liberal party comes together seamlessly with *The News* [*Vest*] and it couldn't be otherwise."[24] *The News* was an extreme right-wing journal unalterably opposed to liberal government reforms (such as the establishment of elected and self-governing zemstvos to take charge of local administration), and it had gone so far as to declare Katkov himself, the terror of the radicals, as infected by Socialist tendencies. It is thus clear that Dostoevsky considered himself, far from being a partisan of reaction, to stand somewhere in the middle as an enthusiastic supporter of all the liberal innovations, beginning with the abolition of serfdom, instituted by Alexander II.

When Maikov wrote that he had undertaken to translate *The Tale of Igor's Campaign*, the famous twelfth-century epic, into modern Russian, Dostoevsky became quite excited at the news. This task was, as Maikov explained, his "small *monumentum*, an offering on the 'altar of the fatherland'";[25] and Dostoevsky's headlong decision to write *The Idiot* may well have been at least partly inspired by the same impulse to celebrate, or at least pay tribute to, the highest values of Russian culture as he conceived them. Otherwise, the field would be left to those whom Dostoevsky rails against in a choleric outburst. "The Slavs and their aspirations," he writes (meaning the struggle of the Serbians and Bulgarians against Turkey), "must have stirred up a whole swarm of enemies among the Russian liberals. When will we finally scrape away these cursed dregs, ingrown and retrograde. They are our previously so-called 'educated society,' a heap of everyone that has renounced Russia, not understanding her and becoming Frenchified—there's your Russian liberal—just recall our best liberals, recall Belinsky: wasn't he really a quite conscious enemy of the fatherland, wasn't he really retrograde?"[26] This view of Russian liberalism will soon find its way into *The Idiot*, where it is expounded by the highly intelligent Evgeny Pavlovich Radomsky; and he is seconded by Prince Myshkin—though with the slight reservation that there are probably among the liberals some exceptions who do not hate Russia per se.

5

Dostoevsky grasped at every indication he could find, or that happened to come within his ken, to justify his belief that Russian life—however much appearances might seem to indicate the contrary—was, at its moral core, superior to the much-vaunted European civilization. A striking example of such superiority, for him as well as for Maikov, was furnished by the vicissitudes of V. I. Kelsiev, the former associate of Ogarev, about whom Dostoevsky was informed in a letter from his friend. After references to the anti-Russian jeremiad of Turgenev's character Potugin in *Smoke*, and noting that Bakunin and Potugin were not very far apart, Maikov continues with a dash of irony: "Here from us, from our barbarous shores, I can give you more consoling, more touching news." He then recounts how Kelsiev, after years of unbelievable hardship and personal self-sacrifice—years spent trying to enlist various denominations of the Old Believers for the revolutionary cause—had appeared at the Russian border one day, declared himself a political criminal, and surrendered to the authorities.

Taken to Petersburg, he was brought before a special commission and his case then sent to the Tsar, who, after reading Kelsiev's confession and the other documents, ordered him to be pardoned unconditionally and set free. His decision about Kelsiev, Maikov continues, "is one of those spontaneous traits of his character. You know, all this moves me to tears. How Russian this is! How much far and away higher and better this is than all that humanistic bedlam in Geneva." What carried the day, according to Maikov, was Kelsiev's autobiographical confession, in which he explained that "only in the Slavic question and in the role of Russia in Slavdom" was he able to discover a resolution for "all his own ideal, deracinated strivings for liberty and activity, that only this question illuminates the significance of Russia, and once having seen it in this light . . . you receive a goal for your activity, one that is palpable, living, historic, with roots in the past and fruitful consequences for the future."[27]

Dostoevsky, as may well be imagined, was ecstatic at such news and replied: "I read about Kelsiev with great sympathy. That's the way, that's the truth, that's the way to do things. You should know, though, that all our trashy little liberals of a seminarian-social hue . . . will fall on him like wild beasts . . . well, what can they say now, whom can they throw mud at? . . . But now they'll be saying of Kelsiev that he denounced everyone.

Honest to God, mark my words. And is there anything now to denounce them for? (1) They have compromised themselves and (2) who worries about them? Are they even worth denouncing at all?"[28] Dostoevsky scoffs at the idea that the radicals are now important enough to be taken seriously, and he will depict his Young Nihilists in *The Idiot* as more ridiculous and pitiable than menacing. Moreover, the abused Prince Myshkin treats them with the same magnanimity that the Tsar displayed toward the hapless and remorseful Kelsiev (who, as a matter of fact, honorably refrained from denouncing anybody, and even defended his collaboration with Herzen and Ogarev). If Dostoevsky's reaction to the history of Kelsiev may well have influenced his handling of the Young Nihilists, there is no question that the figure of Kelsiev himself served as one of the sources of Shatov, the passionately honest and repentant revolutionary-turned-nationalist in *The Devils*.

Dostoevsky's fanatical belief in the moral elevation of the Russian spirit, and the Messianic destiny marked out for it in the future, is unabashedly proclaimed in an important letter to Maikov written just after sending off the first chapters of *The Idiot*. Comparing Russia and Germany, he mentions the admiration of their mutual friend, the critic and philosopher N. N. Strakhov, for the achievements of German culture, and he objects to such deference because "that's the way their life has worked out! And we at that time were putting together a great nation, had stopped Asia forever, endured endless suffering, *were able* to endure it all, did not lose the Russian idea, which will renew the world, but strengthened it. . . . Our people are infinitely higher, more noble, more honest, more naive, more capable, and full of a different, very lofty Christian idea, which Europe, with her sickly Catholicism and stupidly contradictory Lutheranism, does not even understand."[29] Dostoevsky had just taken the decision to attempt to embody this "lofty [Russian] Christian idea" in the character of Prince Myshkin; and some of the thoughts in this letter, especially the contrast between "the Russian idea" and Roman Catholicism, will appear in the Prince's harangue during his so-called engagement party in the very last chapters of the book.

The same fervent conviction is repeated to Maikov a month later, this time in response to an account from his friend of having served on one of the new juries for two weeks. "In those two weeks," Maikov had written, "one can live through the equivalent of five lives—I don't recall my heart ever having beaten so strongly." All the members of the jury (which included a *starosta*, or headman, of a local district, and a doctor specializing in caring for the insane) "went to their stiff benches as if to confession and communion, and even more reverently."[30] Maikov's account of his jury service had the same uplifting effect on Dostoevsky and "caused his heart to beat with excitement." The reason is that "the moral essence

9. Apollon Maikov, ca. 1861

of our judges and, more important, our juries, is infinitely higher than the European: they [Russian juries] look on crime as Christians." Dostoevsky is concerned, however, that the notorious leniency displayed by Russian juries was perhaps a result of the growing instability of moral principles that he feared so strongly. "It seems to me," he remarks, "that in this *humanity* toward the criminal there is still something bookish, liberal, not really independent," though he admits he might be mistaken in judging from abroad. Nonetheless, Dostoevsky repeats once again that "our [Russian] essence, in this respect, is infinitely higher than the European. And in general, all the Russian moral concepts and aims are higher than those of the European world. There is a more direct and noble belief in goodness, as in Christianity, and not as a solution to the bourgeois problem of comfort."[31]

Dostoevsky reiterates his faith that "Russian thought is preparing a grandiose renovation for the entire world (you are right, it is closely linked with Russian Orthodoxy), and this will occur in about a century— that's my passionate belief." But, for such a renovation to take place, the *rights* of the Great Russians over the other Slav nationalities must be definitively and unquestionably affirmed. Dostoevsky's Messianism, then, in one context stresses what Reinhold Niebuhr would call its "ethical-universalistic" component—the notion that Russia was destined to install a Christian reign of goodness and justice on earth—and in another becomes "egoistic-imperialistic" and emphasizes the importance of extending Russian political power.[32] For Dostoevsky, the two were more or less identical: he viewed the second as the precondition of the first and, unlike many later critics, refused to see any insoluble conflict between them. When it came to individual human life, however, Dostoevsky's nationalistic hubris was tempered by an acute sense of human fallibility and of the impossibility, which he would dramatize in Prince Myshkin, for any terrestrial being fully to realize the Christian ideal. Only the God-Man Christ had been capable of doing so, and the Incarnation had set before mankind a goal toward which it must eternally aspire. This helps to account for some of the discrepancy, which has often been commented on, between the disquieting political ambitions of Dostoevsky's Messianism and the quite different compassion and sympathy with human suffering displayed in his fiction.

For Dostoevsky, it was only in the afterlife of immortality that a perfect accomplishment of the Christian ideal of love could be realized; and his letters at this time contain several strong affirmations of his belief in such an afterlife. These letters were written to the family of his brother-in-law, Dr. A. P. Ivanov, who had died quite unexpectedly from a blood infection contracted while performing an operation. Dostoevsky had been close to the Ivanov family, with whom he had spent the summer of 1865 in Lublino, and he wrote to console his sister Vera immediately on learning of the misfortune. He asks his sister and his favorite niece Sofya Ivanova, perhaps intending to use the information for his work, "to give me all the details about the deceased and his last days, and then about all of you—what were your first thoughts, your first intentions, your first actions. Verotchka, my dear, lament and shed tears, but don't give way, in the name of Christ, to despair. . . . Look, you believe in a future life, just as all of you do; none of you has been infected by the rotten and stupid atheism. Remember that he really knows now about you; never lose the hope of reunion and believe that this future life is a necessity, not only a consolation."[33]

These last words express Dostoevsky's conviction, inscribed in a revelatory notebook entry written at the bier of his first wife five years earlier, that a future, immortal life after death could be reasonably inferred from the necessarily imperfect and deficient nature of human existence on earth.* Two months later, when *The Idiot* had already begun to appear,

---

* For more information, see *Dostoevsky: The Stir of Liberation* (Princeton, N.J., 1986), chap. 20.

he addresses himself again to his niece Sofya and, in consoling her, uses some of the language he had employed in his notebook. "Dear Sonya,* do you really not believe in the continuation of life and, above all, in the progressive and the infinite, in the consciousness and universal fusion of all [that is, the complete realization of the law of love—J.F.]? But, you know, 'le mieux n'est trouvé que par le meilleur.' That's a great thought! So let us become worthy of the best worlds, of resurrection rather than death in the lower worlds! Have faith!"[34]

This theme of immortality hovers in the background of *The Idiot* as an accompaniment to the theme of atheism—with which, as we see here, it is intimately related in Dostoevsky's sensibility. The plight of the dying young atheist Ippolit as he contemplates Holbein's *Dead Christ*, with its suggestion of the triumph of blind nature over Christ, is deepened into irremediable torment precisely because of this lack of religious faith and thus of the hope of immortality. Prince Myshkin, on the other hand, experiences a sense of "the universal fusion of all"—a foretaste of immortality, as it were, though not designated as such—in the moment of aura just preceding the onset of an epileptic seizure. But Dostoevsky had then only begun to create his novel, and it is doubtful whether the thematic use he would make of Prince Myshkin's epilepsy, or the scenes involving Ippolit, were as yet very clear in his mind. The moment has come, in any case, to retrace our steps and return to examine the abundant and bewilderingly protean notes with which Dostoevsky had been struggling between mid-September and mid-November of 1867.

* In Russian, Sonya is the diminutive of Sofya.

CHAPTER 14

"A Perfectly Beautiful Man"

Three notebooks exist in which Dostoevsky set down his ideas for what was to become *The Idiot*. Two of these contain scenarios written before publication of the first installment of the novel; the third sketches out continuations and possible lines of action for characters who already exist on the page. From the prepublication notebooks, it is clear that Dostoevsky had great difficulty in defining a satisfactory central character. The future Prince Myshkin appears only embryonically in notes written between November 10 and the beginning of December 1867; but by this time Dostoevsky had already set to work on an early draft. It was only after this initial version (unfortunately lost) began to displease him by its "mediocrity" that the suggestions contained in these later notes suddenly crystallized into a new artistic inspiration.

Dostoevsky himself, as can well be understood, tended to exaggerate somewhat the gap between his discarded manuscript and the definitive one; no doubt his decision to start from scratch seemed an entirely new undertaking. Some of the early Russian scholarship took him literally at his word, and one editor of these notes wrote that "nothing remains of the former Idiot" when the character became transformed into Prince Myshkin.[1] In fact, however, this change is not nearly as thorough as Dostoevsky affrmed: sketches of a Myshkin-like figure appear throughout these early stages. Many of the other situations, incidents, and events of the notes are also taken over and given a new artistic function in the altered context. Indeed, one of the fascinations of these notes, quite apart from their value as information, is that they allow us to observe, like a piece of sculpture arising out of an amorphous mass of clay or stone, the gradual emergence of the finished work of art under the restless probing of Dostoevsky's creative imagination.

2

Dostoevsky's notes for *The Idiot* are extremely complicated and detailed, and there is a learned dispute, into which we need not enter, over the exact number of his separate plans. Nor is it necessary to spend time on all the twists and turns of the plot situations that he envisaged. Some general sense of their nature is well conveyed in the remarks of Edward

Wasiolek, who has done so much to clarify these notes and, indeed, to make all of the notebooks for Dostoevsky's novels accessible to English readers:

> The relationships between characters fluctuate from plan to plan: sisters are and are not sisters, nephews become sons, fathers become uncles. The Idiot is sometimes the son of the Uncle, sometimes the nephew, sometimes the foster son, sometimes illegitimate, and sometimes legitimate; acts are committed and die abortively in the next plan, or even a few lines later; people hang themselves but then perhaps don't hang themselves; the same people die by hanging, poisoning, broken hearts or drowning. It is not always clear who is who, where they come from, and where they are going. Characters appear and disappear, crowd on the periphery, nudge their way into the author's consciousness for a time and then melt away; some appear without names and personalities, take on flesh, then waste away. Some persist to the very threshold of publication and immortality, only to find no place in the final conception.[2]

There would hardly be much point in attempting to unravel each of these variations; and the following account will be limited to those elements in the notes that anticipate, or help to throw some light on, either the final text or one or another work by Dostoevsky.

In the notes Dostoevsky jotted down between September 14 and mid-October, we immediately find the social framework that he will retain throughout. His characters belong to three families. One of them is described as "ruined gentry" struggling to maintain their social position; the father had deserted this family, gone to live abroad, been pursued there for debt, then returned to Russia and gone to pieces completely. This family may be considered the precursor of the Ivolgins in *The Idiot*, who are also of gentry stock and ruined by an errant father with the rank of general—a drunkard and a prodigious liar. It has been suggested that Dostoevsky may have been thinking, at this early stage, of a figure similar to the prodigal and featherbrained General in *The Gambler*, whom he has now brought home from abroad. The mother of the family is "a woman worthy of respect, of a noble but capricious nature"; and such words can well apply to the impetuous and surely noble-hearted Mme Epanchina, although as yet there is very little trace of her husband and daughters as later conceived (9: 140).

The so-called Idiot is a member of this ruined household, and the very opposite in temperament from what he will later become. Even though he is already afflicted ("he is an epileptic and has nervous seizures"), "his idiocy was in reality merely his mamma's invention"; and although "he has never finished his university studies," he "supports the whole family" and is very far from being (or having been) any sort of invalid. Another member of the family is a stepdaughter, "the wrathful Mignon, a Cleopatra (Olga Umetskaya)." The Idiot is in love with the member of a second family, "an extraordinarily beautiful, arrogant girl," who is a foreshadowing of Aglaya Epanchina; but "she detests him and treats him worse than an idiot or a footman." She also teases and taunts him, and "*after one of these occasions* he rapes Mignon. *He sets fire to the house.* On her [presumably the "beauty's"] command he burns his finger." (This motif of the burnt finger or hand as a testimony of violent amorous passion continues to reappear, and will be used finally for humorous effect rather than employed seriously.) A first characterization of the Idiot reads as follows: "*The Idiot's* passions are violent, he has a burning need of love, a boundless pride, and out of pride he means to dominate himself, conquer himself. He takes delight in humiliation. Those who do not know him make fun of him; those who do know him begin to fear him" (9: 141).

A later depiction of the Idiot among the same notes adds another trait to his character. "Domination of himself out of pride (not morality) and rabid self-license in everything. Consequently he could turn into a monster, but love saves him. He becomes imbued with the most profound compassion and forgives faults in others. . . . In compassion he progressively develops a high moral sense and performs a heroic action" (9: 146). This schema both anticipates Stavrogin in *The Devils* and points backward to Raskolnikov at the conclusion of *Crime and Punishment.* Dostoevsky had spoken of Raskolnikov's conversion to a new, Christian outlook on life as the subject for another novel, and he was still largely inspired by the ambition to depict such a conversion in action. Indeed, the desire to create such a character goes even further back in Dostoevsky's creative itinerary and is first given expression in *Winter Notes,* where he delineated a moral ideal of self-sacrifice presumably identical with that of the Russian (common) people. Denying that such an ideal implied any weakening or surrender of individual personality, he wrote: "Understand me: a voluntary, totally conscious sacrifice of oneself in the interests of all, made under no sort of compulsion, is in my opinion a sign of the highest development of the personality. Voluntarily to sacrifice one's life for all, to die on the cross or at the stake, is possible only with the very strongest development of the personality" (5: 79).

The ambition to create such a character—the transformation of a "strong" individual, whose prideful egoism is naked and undisguised, into a compassionate and loving soul—continues to haunt Dostoevsky through most of these preliminary notes for *The Idiot.* It was one thing, however, to project such a character; it was quite another to imagine him acting concretely in reasonably convincing and verisimilar dramatic situations. What is curious, moreover, is that, while no other personage in these notes receives as much analytic attention as "the idiot," in fact Dostoevsky did not yet conceive him as his central figure. On the contrary, we read that "the uncle is the chief character in the whole novel. A hypochondriac, with a deep-seated vanity, pride. . . . Fundamentally, he is even magnanimous, but everything in him has been warped and corrupted." He is "a usurer living a solitary life, but a usurer with a certain poetry in his nature" (9: 142), and he has amassed a fortune after living on the Petersburg streets in abject poverty. No such character as the Uncle appears in the final text, though the usurer motif is retained and distributed among Ganya Ivolgin, Lebedyev, and Lebedyev's son-in-law Ptitsyn. A character like the Uncle will later appear in Dostoevsky's superb short story *A Gentle Creature* (*Krotkaya*).

Many hints of later thematic developments already appear in this early stage of creation, but attached to a different plot situation; and perhaps the mass of spectacular intrigue obscured for Dostoevsky the thematic idea he was instinctively groping for. The Idiot, for example, is in love with the heroine, the proud beauty also coveted by the Uncle. She herself is in love with the Uncle's son (there is a sexual rivalry between father and son that anticipates both *A Raw Youth* and *The Brothers Karamazov*). Nonetheless, "the Idiot's love is of a strange kind: it is simply a spontaneous sensation devoid of all reason. . . . To love is the whole of his necessity. If she married another man, very likely his reaction would be quite different from what one would expect. 'Let her marry him, I will love her just the same.' If she were a whore, it would come to much the same thing: 'But I will love her just the same.' Eventually he begins to lose all sense of reality. He even goes to the son and talks about her without concealing his own love, yet as if supporting the son, so that the latter marvels and begins to believe him out of his mind" (9: 150). This notation encompasses both Myshkin's pitying devotion to the defiled Nastasya Filippovna and, more important, his crucial loss of all sense of reality in the final pages of the novel, when he continues to attempt to visit Aglaya while the preparations for his nuptials with Nastasya are being organized.

There are also strong suggestions of Aglaya in some notes where Dostoevsky begins by talking to himself: "*The lines of her character are emerging*. She is extraordinarily proud, she rides roughshod over all the conventions and *therefore* the worst extravagances of the Idiot neither shock nor outrage her (once he almost killed her, another time he broke her hands). . . . In general, she is unquestionably of an original, frivolous, capricious *provocative* and poetic nature, superior to her environment." This passage refers to "the heroine," who also rejects a rich and highly eligible suitor, to the consternation of her family, and turns to the Idiot instead after further complications. "Then she appeals to the Idiot to take her away. The Idiot is not at all her slave, on the contrary. (Their relationship is a far more romantic one)" (9: 151). Here Dostoevsky already seems to catch a glimpse of the Aglaya who, to everyone's amazement, prefers Myshkin to the elegant and extremely personable Radomsky.

Even though the Idiot of the early notebooks bears only an external and superficial resemblance to the later Myshkin (both are called idiots and are epileptic), Dostoevsky wished, all the same, to include a character *somewhere* in his plans to represent his positive moral ideal. This character initially is the Uncle's son, whom his father describes, significantly, as a "socialist." But, Dostoevsky writes, "he is not a socialist; on the contrary; he finds in socialism little besides an unrealizable ideal. Economic redistribution, the problem of bread." This last phrase prefigures the tipsy maunderings of Lebedyev about "the wagons that bring bread to humanity without any moral basis for conduct." The son pities the Uncle (his father), and the Idiot explains "that this is precisely why the Uncle detests him"; when the son refuses his father's money, he only increases the degree of such detestation.

This ideal figure is also given the ecstatic sense of life so important for Myshkin: "The son preaches about how there is a great deal of happiness in life, that each moment is a happiness," and is also "carried away by his compassion for Mignon." The word "Christ" then suddenly appears, followed by the sentence: "To an extent, the son has already impressed the Idiot some time earlier." It is as if the son and the Idiot were about to fuse here, and Dostoevsky came within an inch of finding the figure he was ultimately to create; but the initial conception of the Idiot continues to dominate, and "he is carried away on the full tide of passion" (9: 151–152). Still, Dostoevsky seems to have attained a certain clarity at this point, which is expressed in a sentence written in the margin and taken over almost verbatim in the novel: "The one thing in the world is spontaneous compassion. As for justice—that is a secondary matter" (9: 152n.2).

Along with important anticipations of this kind, as well as fascinating hints of missed and as yet uncomprehended opportunities, Dostoevsky's notes also contain certain action nuclei (as they may be called) that will be retained and ultimately shifted from one kind of employment to another. An example already given is the burning of the hand; another is the theft of a wallet, which Lebedyev will use to torment General Ivolgin, though it is first mentioned as a mistreatment of the Idiot. "The lost wallet. They accused the Idiot of having stolen the money. The Uncle drove him out of the house." In fact, the Idiot had found the wallet in the attic of the house, but "it was the father of the family who had put it there. The housemaid and Mignon had seen him in the act." The Idiot, as Myshkin will do in the case of General Ivolgin, "says they should pity him [the father, another ruined general—J.F.], and he restrains *the handsome youth,* who was about to tell everyone that the father was the thief" (9: 144–145). Still another such act is the rape of Olga Umetskaya by the Idiot, a violation that turns up in all the scenarios as a supreme example of the Idiot's savage and uncontrollable passions. Vanishing as such in the novel, it was perhaps softened into the background defilement of the young Nastasya by her guardian Totsky. All these recurring motifs illustrate how Dostoevsky could rely, as it were, on a repertory of such actions—thrown up in the course of mulling over his plethora of plot intrigues—and refocus them in the new conjuncture of a scenario revolving around Prince Myshkin.

3
———

Several versions of the projected novel were sketched by Dostoevsky between mid-October and the beginning of November; but they reveal no basic change in conception. Most attention is given to reshuffling the particularities of the family relationships among the characters and the external motivations of the plot intrigues. The Uncle is still designated as the main character, and the basic image of the Idiot remains unaltered: a "wild downtrodden creature" who "seeks the solution and his salvation in pride," and "ends up with a sublime deed" (9: 156). But Dostoevsky now includes an admonitory reflection: "If he is merely an oppressed character, nothing will come of it but oppression. An old, worn-out theme, whereas the new and major idea of the novel vanishes" (9: 156). Regrettably, Dostoevsky does not explain this "new and major idea"; but he will very soon distinguish Prince Myshkin from such a figure as Hugo's Jean Valjean precisely on the ground that Myshkin is not a victim of social injustice. Even though there are references to the Idiot's suffering and humiliations as a child and young man, Dostoevsky may have felt that too great an emphasis on these would obscure his new theme of inner transformation.

The relation between the Idiot and the heroine takes on an increased intensity in these notes because the Idiot's "savage pride captivates the heroine. (Nonetheless, she perceives that on occasion and under extreme provocation he is capable of a crime. The heroine is carried away with him and at the same time is terrified of him)" (9: 157). These observations are very close to what Nastasya will come to feel about Rogozhin; and in a jotting labeled "the main point," Dostoevsky writes: "The reader and *all the characters* in the novel must remember that *he can kill the heroine* and that everyone is expecting him to kill her" (9: 156). Such a sense of foreboding will be preserved in the Nastasya-Rogozhin entanglement; and though Dostoevsky did not definitively decide on his actual ending until much later, the possibility of such a dénouement, as we see, already existed long before. But here "the spontaneous force of development impels him [the Idiot] eventually *to reflection and to a new path in life*" (9: 157). The vagueness of this presumed happy ending sufficiently indicates how difficult it was for Dostoevsky to envisage such a resolution.

In the second half of October, some important changes are made in the basic plan: the Idiot becomes the son of the Uncle and is no longer a member of the General's family. More important, he is given a more active and aggressive role—perhaps to counteract the effect of portraying him only as "oppressed." Now he becomes an insidious plotter who turns all the characters against each other by his underhanded slanders. Dostoevsky compares him to Shakespeare's creation: "The Idiot's character—an Iago. But he ends up divinely. . . . He has slandered everyone, carried on intrigues in full sight of everyone, he has got what he wanted, money and his fiancée, yet he renounces it all" (9: 161). This idea is developed more fully in another entry, preceded by a depiction of the Idiot's emotions in the strongest terms yet used about him. "The Idiot, always cold-blooded, suddenly frightens the heroine with the violence of his passion, a passion as steely and chill as a razor. . . . But this passion is not love but the passion of gratified vanity." A sentence then follows, underlined to indicate its importance: "*But when he really feels and perceives what love is, he renounces her and immediately sends the heroine back to his brother*" (that is, the other son of the Uncle, with whom the heroine is in love) (9: 161).

These notes also contain a previsionary sketch of how others regard the relations between the Idiot and the heroine: "In the General's household they ridicule both her and him, in *a highly innocent manner*, saying that he is in love with her and that she is his betrothed. He himself pretends to take all this as a joke. . . . But actually he is in love and conceals the fact" (9: 161). Here we surely have the origin of all the background rumors of Aglaya's attraction to Myshkin, the reading of Pushkin's poem "The Poor Knight," Myshkin's refusal to take the matter seriously, and his inability to accept his own feelings. One should also note the appearance of a character called "the Jumper" (*prygunchik*; 9: 164), the husband of a new family and a member of a heretical religious sect given to ecstatic dancing (hence the odd designation). Dostoevsky clearly wished to include some form of religious sectarianism in his canvas, and ultimately would do so by linking Rogozhin with the Old Believers and alluding to his father's great respect for the Skoptsy, who practiced castration as the supreme form of spirituality.

Other elements of the later novel also now begin to turn up, such as the meeting between the two sons of the Uncle in a railway carriage, one "the natural son," the other legitimate. Sometimes the Idiot is one and sometimes the other; but the "natural son" is looked on by others as Myshkin will be by both Rogozhin and the Epanchins. "They all say: 'How odd he is!' The son: 'Yes, but he doesn't seem to me to be stupid. He is odd, that's true.' 'He's a regular *yurodivi.*' Again, they meet in the railway carriage" (9: 163). In another note, the relation between the brothers comes to resemble the reaction of Rogozhin to Myshkin. "Though the Idiot has slandered the son, still, oddly the son is *ingenuous* (Fedia) and the Idiot is more and more taken with this ingenuousness. And finally by the gentleness with which the son forgives him the Idiot *grows enamored* with the son, though he laughs at himself" (9: 163). This "ingenuousness" of the "son" is identical with one of the most important qualities of Myshkin's character and the source of the sympathy he arouses in everyone after initial mistrust.

In the next sheaf of notes, written in the last week of October, this Myshkin-like character—the brother of the Idiot, now called Ganechka—is further elaborated. "*Ganechka.* Pure, beautiful, virtuous, strict, very nervous, with a profoundly Christian, compassionate lovingness. He is anguished because of this, for despite his *ardent compassion* he is sensible, devoted to duty, and unshakable in his convictions" (9: 170). The intimation that Ganechka's "ardent compassion" can lead to an inner conflict with "duty" connects this passage with Myshkin's struggle between Nastasya (a love of compassion) and Aglaya (not simply "duty," of course, but earthly and fleshly love). We are further told of Ganechka that "*feeling* dominates his nature. He lives by feelings. He lives ardently and passionately. In a word, he is a Christian nature" (9: 170). The relation between Ganechka and the Idiot then becomes similar once again to that between the future Myshkin and Rogozhin: "He [Ganechka] loves the Idiot and forgives him, but does not agree with him. *At moments* the Idiot loves him passionately, but *in general* he [the Idiot] is spiteful, sneering, obdurate and rejects him" (9: 170). The fluctuations of Rogozhin's feelings about Myshkin follow exactly the same pattern.

Even though the psychology of the Idiot thus remains essentially unchanged, he now moves to the dead center of Dostoevsky's artistic preoccupations. "Dominating all the characters is the Idiot, an anguished, contemptuous, endlessly proud personality who delights in his own superiority and others' worthlessness. . . . *in the end he is agonized by his own role*, and suddenly he perceives a solution in love" (9: 171). Elsewhere, Dostoevsky goes into more detail about the Idiot's inner evolution: "The three stages of love: revenge and self-love, passion, a loftier love. Man becomes purified" (9: 168). On a later page, this note is expanded: "(1) Revenge and self-love (a *causeless* revenge, he himself [the Idiot] sees this, and that it is *characteristic* of him). Then: (2) Frenzied and merciless passion. (3) Lofty love and regeneration" (9: 171). Various characters in the finished novel will be adapted to this schema—Ganya Ivolgin to the first, Rogozhin to the second, Myshkin to the third (though the very "loftiness" of Myshkin's love leads to tragedy and not regeneration).

The notes of this period show Dostoevsky desperately trying to clarify the general significance of the various plots that he has been mulling over and continually revising. "N.B. *Boundless pride and boundless hate. The chief idea of the novel*: how much strength, how much passion, in contemporary youth, yet they are unbelievers. Boundless idealism together with boundless sensuality" (9: 166). The next sentence reveals how little such reflections yielded in the way of tangible inspiration. "Notes. *Well, now there opens up a new path*? What is to come now?" (9: 166). No answer is given to this query; and the last lines of these notes acknowledge defeat: "No good. The main idea as to the Idiot does not emerge. Essential: that the Idiot should be the Uncle's son" (9: 174). As we see, Dostoevsky still believed that his inspiration might emerge if he found the Idiot's proper place in the family structure.

4

The sentences just quoted, which confess to a sense of failure, are dated November 1. In the days following, further notebook entries introduce entirely new elements into the scenario, probably prompted by Dostoevsky's awareness that a new tack was necessary if he were to make progress. The Idiot is now sent to Switzerland, as a boy or young man, without the knowledge of his real family (he is brought up by others), and then he returns. This complication already comes close to an important aspect of the final text. Another note refers to what presumably occurs on the Idiot's return from abroad: "The most important scene: the Idiot at the General's. The Idiot captivates everyone with his childish naiveté" (9: 174). Exactly the same occurs when Myshkin unexpectedly shows up at the home of distant relatives, the family of General Epanchin; the Idiot in the notes is also a relative of the General, his unknown nephew. Not only was the Idiot sent to Switzerland, but he has also been secretly married, supposedly while drunk, "to a young girl who had had a baby." Although believed to be ignorant of her past, "he did know that there was a baby kept hidden" (9: 179). This plot twist allows Dostoevsky to motivate an inner conflict between the Idiot's compassionate love (the wife) and his passion for the heroine who loves but torments him, and on whom he wishes to take revenge—another hint of Myshkin's future struggle between his differing loves for Nastasya and Aglaya.

The motif of a secret marriage will later be used in *The Devils*, and, not surprisingly, we find the Idiot now defined in terms that come very close to the future Stavrogin: "The chief and paramount idea of the novel, on which everything hinges, is: namely, that he is filled with ... morbid pride to such a degree that he cannot help considering himself a god, and *at the same time* he has so little esteem for himself (he analyzes himself with great clarity) that he cannot help despising himself intensely, infinitely and unjustifiably. (At the same time he feels that for him to take blind revenge on everyone would be despicable, still, he acts like a scoundrel and he does take revenge)" (9: 180). The Idiot's pride previously had never reached such a pitch of self-deification; and the resemblance to Stavrogin becomes even closer when Dostoevsky turns to the motif of the secret marriage. "*Characteristic trait.* At first he has a morbid, cowardly fear (considering all the escapades and ruptures) of announcing that he is married. But now, since they have found it out, he suddenly holds up his head and prides himself on such a marriage and that he recognizes a different and higher destiny" (9: 191). But such a situation, or one resembling it, will be reserved for the later novel.

Even though Dostoevsky thus appears to be moving away from his final text at this point, other passages indicate an increasing attention to the Christian implications of his thematics. Some of these had appeared earlier, particularly in relation to the "positive" characters; but in the notes from mid-October we find: "He [the Idiot] and Olga Umetskaya (*the decapitated heads*)," which refers to an earlier entry: "[Conversations about decapitated heads—there is no God]" (9: 161–162). Two weeks later, this overtly religious motif is developed: "Umetskaya reads *The New Testament*. In her demented state, she sermonizes.... About heads being cut off, about fingernails being torn out, in the beginning she had set a fire" (9: 183). A snatch of dialogue that seems attributable to the Idiot significantly shows him taking over this religious preoccupation. "In Switzerland—we used to read *The New Testament* often, and after Renan's book I questioned the doctor *about the cross* (we were strangely at one on the subject of fingernails torn out and needles)" (9: 183).

In this context, a dialogue then occurs, presumably between the Idiot and his wife, introduced by a remark about Umetskaya's fascination with decapitation and death. "Umetskaya's speculations about what thoughts flash into the head of a man about to be decapitated" (9: 183). Myshkin will of course indulge in the same kind of conjecture; and there is also an exchange that highlights the future role assigned to Holbein's *Dead Christ*. " 'But the passion on the cross shatters one's mind.' 'But He has triumphed over mind.' 'Was it a miracle then?' 'Certainly it was a miracle, nonetheless ... ' 'What?' 'Nonetheless, He gave a terrible cry' '[What cry?]' '[Eloi! Eloi!]' '[There was an eclipse?]' 'I don't know—but it was a terrible cry.' The account of Holbein's 'Christ' in Basel" (9: 185). The Idiot is also defined in terms that will fit Myshkin's atheistic alter ego Ippolit: "He is a Christian yet at the same time he does not believe. *The dualism of a deep nature.* N.B. *The tongue in the mirror*" (9: 185). No doubt this last phrase refers to what will become Ippolit's self-mocking proclivities, his defiance of death as being an ultimate jest of fate on humankind.

What continues to plague Dostoevsky, however, is how to make the Idiot a convincing figure, and particularly how to motivate the totally opposed mixture of elements in his character. Over and over again, in the midst of piling one increasingly melodramatic complication on top of another, Dostoevsky worries over whether to make the Idiot a legitimate or illegitimate son of the Uncle. One notation reads: "To domineer over them all, to triumph over them all, to take revenge on them all (but for what reason—unknown). (He is the natural son)" (9: 178). The sentence in parentheses provides the hidden "reason" for the Idiot's behavior. But then, a few pages farther on, Dostoevsky suddenly asks himself in italics: "*Perhaps it would be better to make him a legitimate son*" (9: 184). Soon we read: "*Major problem.* Regarding the personality of the Idiot, is it more interesting, more romantic, and more graphic to express the idea that he is legitimate or that he is illegitimate?" (9: 187). This question is then followed by snippets of dialogue and action deriving from one or the other alternative. Dostoevsky's preoccupation here with the legitimacy of birth and its effect on character foreshadows a major thematic motif of *A Raw Youth*, where he becomes concerned with the problem of "accidental families."

Dostoevsky continues to debate this issue all through the remainder of these notes. If legitimate, the Idiot can exhibit "greater pride" by showing "that he alone, without the aid of wealth or any other person, can triumph over them all." But this choice would exclude an abrupt awakening to success if he were a social outcast, when he "dreams of the heroine and of high society" and then "everything becomes a vivid possibility" (9: 187). If illegitimate, his hatred becomes explicable, and he would be "a terribly proud and tragic person." If legitimate, he could be repudiated and "repudiates himself," exhibiting both "unaffected magnanimity of heart" and "vengefulness and envy" (9: 189). Dostoevsky's vacillation continues without any resolution, as he futilely toils to unite "magnanimity of heart" with "vengefulness and envy."

5
———

By November 4, Dostoevsky was becoming quite desperate, and among the notes written on that day, within a detailed outline of what he had decided upon up to that point, he suddenly jots down in italics: "*(Give me an idea!)*" (9: 196). Indeed, nothing very much seems to have changed, and the scenario rehearses once again most of the sensational events that have already been envisaged. These become even more theatrical and hyperbolic, and sometimes descend to the sheerest melodramatic clichés: "He [the Idiot] found her [his wife] with the baby and Umetskaya on the deserted bank of the Neva—near a rift in the ice. She had handed the baby to Umetskaya. He brought her back home. He falls at her feet: 'I love *only you!*' She forgives everything. But she did not forgive the rape of the heroine, and poisoned herself" (9: 198). In another version the wife hangs herself, or drowns herself, and Dostoevsky cannot decide if the Idiot finds the corpse in the company of the Uncle, who is in love with the wife, or accompanied by the heroine, who is in love with the Idiot himself. His total uncertainty about his theme, not to mention the sequence of events that he endeavors to set down meticulously in a "Plan for the 1st Part," is indicated by a question to himself. "*Enigmas.* Who is he? A terrible scoundrel or a mysterious ideal?" (9: 194). This query seems to leave Dostoevsky exactly where he began. But the notion that the Idiot might represent some sort of "mysterious ideal" has never been suggested before, and may have well led Dostoevsky's imagination along a new path.

At this time, as his notebooks also reveal, he was simultaneously jotting down ideas for other works; and one of these plans—entitled "*A Thought* (Poem), Theme called 'The Emperor'"—appears in the midst of the pages we have been examining. The dates assigned to these notes are October–November 1867, exactly the moment when Dostoevsky had reached a dead end in grappling with his novel. The theme mentioned, taken from Russian history, goes back to the middle of the eighteenth century (1740–1764), when a one-year-old child named Ivan Antonovich was declared emperor on the death of Empress Anna Ivanovna. A year later, he was imprisoned by the new empress, Elizabeth Petrovna, and kept in isolation for the remainder of his life. He died at the age of twenty-four, killed by a guard in an unsuccessful attempt, made by a young officer named Mirovich, to liberate him from the Schlusselberg fortress and reestablish him on the throne. Dostoevsky's knowledge of this obscure incident has been traced to an article published in 1866, which was based on some archival material that had recently become available.[3]

His main figure, Ivan Antonovich, is blocked in very quickly as someone "not able to speak" even though he is "almost twenty years old. Description of the *nature* of this person. He developed by himself, fantastic pictures and figures, dreams, a young girl (in a dream)—invented, saw through a window" (9: 113). Mirovich gains access to the prisoner and plans an uprising to free him: "the meeting of two human personalities. His amazement. And joy and fear, friendship" (9: 113). The daughter of

the commandant, engaged to Mirovich, joins the plot and dreams of becoming empress. Her fiancé, jealous, casts hostile glances at the prisoner; and, without understanding why, Ivan Antonovich "senses what
the matter is about" (9: 114).

Mirovich is described as "an enthusiast. Tells him [the emperor] about
God, about Christ." "Shows him God's world. 'Everything is yours, if only
you want it. Let us go!'" Of great importance are the reactions of the
prisoner as he becomes acquainted with the world; for example, when
told that Mirovich is not his equal, he replies: "If you are not my equal,
I do not wish to be emperor." When he learns about death, and that
others might be required to die for him, he says: "I do not wish to live."
But when told how much good he might do with his power, "he becomes
inflamed." The revolt takes place, the commandant runs him through,
and "he dies majestically and sorrowfully" (9: 114).

There is an evident similarity between the history of Ivan Antonovich
and that of the main character of Pedro Calderón's *La Vida es Sueño* (*Life
is a Dream*); and Dostoevsky, though he never mentions the Spanish
dramatist, was probably familiar with this play. The plan also indicates
Dostoevsky's evident desire to dramatize his moral-spiritual themes
against the background of Russian history—the first indication of a creative impulse that will have a significant effect on *The Devils*, with its
strongly accentuated social-historical coloring. More immediately, the
resemblance between Ivan Antonovich and Prince Myshkin is quite
clear. Both awaken to the world from the isolation of idiocy, respond to
life with the same instinctive and spontaneous goodness, are exposed to
the ravages of jealousy, and become acquainted with evil and death. It
may well be that the princely Ivan Antonovich served as a transition between the tyrannical and egoistic idiot-character of Dostoevsky's first
conception and the sudden appearance of the former "Idiot" as Prince
Myshkin.

Whatever the reason, a decisive breakthrough occurs almost at the
conclusion of the notes made in early November. Suddenly a new idea
flashes forth, though it is still part of the established framework: "*He is a
Prince*. Idiot. Everything is based on vengeance. A humiliated creature.
... Refuses the Uncle's money. In the office he sulks." The Idiot, even
though now a Prince, still remains the downtrodden and vengeful creature of the past; but the next entry evokes an entirely opposite image:
"Prince *Yurodivi*. (He is with the children)?!" (9: 200). In the manuscript,
Dostoevsky traces out "PRINCE" in capital letters, as if musing over its
implications; and the question mark and exclamation point suggest a
feeling of excitement. Nonetheless, no substantial change occurs as yet
in the main outline of the action, and the last sentences of this segment
read: "Main point: envy and pride, exasperated pride, he recounts to the

Uncle (at his house with a group including Ilya and the Madonna) how he longed for gold when he was living with the Uncle" (9: 201). Ilya is the Uncle's other son, and the Madonna is the Idiot's wife, whose long-suffering sweetness is compared to the expression on the face of Holbein's Madonna.

Dostoevsky, in a letter already cited, had explained to Maikov that while "embryonic artistic ideas" constantly streamed through his head and heart, they required a "complete incarnation" to be truly useful. This incarnation always occurred so suddenly and unexpectedly, however, "that it is impossible to count on it in advance." But once having received in his heart a "full image," he could then proceed to its artistic realization. Dostoevsky unquestionably received, if not the "full image" he was searching for, then at least the glimmer of one in the totally new conception of the Idiot as "Prince *Yurodivi*"; and in the notes written between mid-November and the beginning of December, we find the Idiot being elaborated in ways that begin to resemble the future Myshkin. "N.B. The Idiot with the children, 1st conversation ('And we thought you were so boring') . . . about Mont-Blanc, about Switzerland, about the story of a teacher and a little boy, about Olga Umetskaya, about the existence of God, and finally about the ward and her engagement. . . . he brings about a reconciliation between her and the children" (9: 208). The ward, living with the General's family, had appeared before, and there is a plan of the General to marry her (his wife had died recently), to the horror of the children. The reconciliation of the children with the ward, brought about by the Idiot, is roughly analogous to the change of attitude toward the defiled and despised outcast Marie that Myshkin effectuates among the children of his Swiss village.

His new vision of the Idiot clearly intrigues Dostoevsky, and he tells himself: "Essential: to set forth the personality of the Idiot in a masterly fashion" (9: 208). A bit later, the outlines of this personality begin to emerge: "The Idiot of the 1st marriage is 26 (is well-to-do), has been abroad. Directly on returning from abroad he goes to the country to the Umetskys. He is educated, an odd creature" (9: 205). Dostoevsky realizes quite clearly that the previous image of the Idiot must be discarded and now shifts his negative attributes to the son Ganechka, who had been the embodiment of love and forgiveness in the earlier plans. Of Ganechka, Dostoevsky now writes: "(This is the character that was formerly the Idiot's: magnanimous, bitterness, pride and envy)" (9: 204).

With the Idiot no longer caught in a struggle between revenge and love, Dostoevsky turns to the task of developing him in a totally different light. "The Idiot's *personality*. A bizarre creature. His oddities. Gentle, at times he says not a word. For example. Somewhere in Petersburg he has a little boy. He visits him. (He is always with the children.) At times he suddenly begins to hold forth to them, all about the bliss in store" (9: 201–202). The Idiot's unhappy childhood no longer leads to hatred and a desire to dominate, but rather a will to relieve the suffering of others: "A son rejected ever since childhood, the Idiot is wrapped up in his passion for children. Everywhere he has children about him" (9: 202). When a character named Nastia is seduced, abandoned, and gives birth to an illegitimate child, the Idiot takes her in, "and he took over the child, etc. In her anguish and rage at having been deserted, she inveighed against *him* and jeered at him ... in the end she fell in love with him, he offered his hand, and she *ran away* ('I am furious, I won't ask pardon, I am defiled')" (9: 202). Dostoevsky senses the importance of this raging defiance combined with a sense of defilement (exactly the feelings of the future Nastasya Filippovna), and remarks: "*Absolutely has to be worked out.*" When the Idiot accepts and even assents when Nastia abuses him, "she is stunned by his *simplicity and humility*" (9: 202).

The last notes made in the prepublication notebooks do not develop this image of the Idiot any further. Only the facts of his early life and upbringing are mentioned, and Dostoevsky seems to take his new personality more or less for granted. Otherwise, these notes are concerned with details of the plot action, which centers on a sexual rivalry between the General and his son over a character called Ustinaya, who will blend into Nastasya Filippovna. Ustinaya, incidentally, has been seduced by a rich landowner named Trotsky (the future Totsky), and she plays off the lecherous old General and his son against each other in a manner resembling Nastasya Filippovna's toying with Ganya and General Epanchin. At the conclusion of these entries, which are even more random and disconnected than usual, Dostoevsky tells himself: "Set up a detailed plan and tonight *begin*" (9: 215). Just when this command was set down is not clear; but if we accept Dostoevsky's own account in his letters, it would probably be sometime in early November.

6

"I spent the entire summer and autumn working on various ideas (some were very entangled)" Dostoevsky writes to Maikov at the end of December. "But a certain experience always allowed me to intuit in advance either their falsity, or difficulty, or lack of promise. Finally, I fixed on one of these ideas, began working on it, and wrote a great deal. But then, on December 4 (New Style) I threw it all out." As we know, the prospect of writing a "mediocre" novel repelled him, and he then began from scratch (at least in the major scenario, if not, as we have tried to show, in many of the details of his action). "Then (since my entire future depended on it), I set about the painful task of inventing a *new novel*. Nothing in the world could have made me continue with the first one. I simply could not. I turned things over in my mind from December 4 through December 18. I would say that on the average I came up with six plans a day (at least that). My head was in a whirl. It's a wonder I didn't go out of my mind. At last, on December 18, I sat down and started writing a new novel."[4] The first five chapters of the final text were mailed on January 5, and two more followed on the eleventh. Dostoevsky considered these seven chapters to form the first part of his novel according to the new plan; later he altered its organization to make them part of a larger unit.

Just having emerged from this intense spurt of creativity, Dostoevsky confesses that "I have no idea myself of what the thing I have sent them is like." But he explains that it finally emerged from a long-cherished ambition: "For a long time already, there was an idea that had been bothering me, but I was afraid to make a novel out of it because it was a very difficult idea and I was not ready to tackle it, although it is a fascinating idea and one that I am in love with. The idea is—*to portray a perfectly beautiful man. . . .* The idea used to flash through my mind in a somewhat artistic form, but only *somewhat,* not in the full-blown form that was needed. It was only the desperate situation in which I found myself that made me embark upon an idea that had not yet reached full maturity. I took a chance, as at roulette: 'Maybe it will develop as I write it!' This is unforgivable."[5]

Dostoevsky was quite accurate in referring to this idea as one that had long tempted him; in fact, though he implies the opposite, he had already made several attempts to give it artistic life. Colonel Rostanev in *The Village of Stepanchikovo,* some of whose utterances overlap literally with those of Myshkin, was a tentative effort in this direction. This robust, handsome, and Herculean retired Army officer rather incongruously shares Myshkin's ecstatic apprehension of life and declaims rapturously about the marvel of the sunrise, the glory of trees, and the sheer beauty of the world itself. But Colonel Rostanev is a comic character who is shamefully hoodwinked by that hypocritical literary Pecksniff, Foma Fomich; and though the Colonel is the embodiment of goodness, the young and sophisticated narrator treats him with amusedly affectionate condescension rather than unqualified admiration.*

Another and quite different attempt by Dostoevsky to represent positive goodness (or at least a certain innocent naiveté, which resembles goodness in the spontaneity of its affectionate attachment to others) can be seen in the character of Aleksey Valkovsky in *The Insulted and Injured.* If we are to look anywhere in Dostoevsky for a precursor of Myshkin, it would be to the burbling and irresponsible Aleksey, who lives like

---

* See the analysis of this story in *Dostoevsky: The Years of Ordeal* (Princeton, N.J., 1983), 276–289.

a child totally in each moment, loves everyone with the same uncritical devotion, and has no awareness of the often extremely regrettable consequences of his warmhearted behavior. Aleksey is a proto-Myshkin still viewed from the perspective of worldly common sense, a point of view that will be expressed in *The Idiot* but transcended by a more profound vision of tragic self-sacrifice. Another reminiscence of this early and rather weak novel may be found also in the disastrous confrontation between Nastasya Filippovna and Aglaya. This encounter resembles the competition for Aleksey's affections in the earlier novel, where, however, the rival women agree amicably that he will move from one to the other in his own best interests.*

The same letter to Maikov contains some further observations that reveal just how perplexed and uncertain Dostoevsky still was about the future course of his undertaking. "On the whole," he says, "a plan has taken shape. As I go along, various details crop up that I find fascinating and stimulating. But the whole? But the hero? Somehow the whole thing seems to turn on the figure of *the hero*. . . . I must establish the character of the hero. Will it develop under my pen? And imagine what uncontrollable horrors have emerged: it turns out that, besides the hero, there was a heroine, which means that there were TWO HEROS!! And apart from the two heros there are two other characters of absolutely major importance, that is, *semi-heros*. . . . Of the four heros, two are already clearly outlined in my *mind*, one is not yet outlined at all, and the fourth, the main hero, is still extremely pale. Perhaps he is not so vague in my heart, but he is terribly difficult."[6]

It is generally assumed that the "two heros" are Prince Myshkin and Nastasya Filippovna, while the "semi-heros" are Rogozhin and Aglaya Epanchina. The two that are clearly outlined would seem to be Rogozhin and Nastasya. Dostoevsky conceded that his "main hero" was still only a nebulous outline in his mind, not a truly realized figure. As for Aglaya, it is she who "is not yet outlined at all," and Dostoevsky even works an admission of her elusiveness into the novel itself. During the first scene in the Epanchins' sitting room, when Myshkin is submitted to the examination and scrutiny of the sisters, he remarks that "he knows their faces" and then is challenged to tell what he knows. He acquits himself satisfactorily with the eldest, Alexandra ("a happy face, the most sympathetic of the three"), and the second, Adelaida (her face combines kindness and a hint of sorrow, like Holbein's Madonna); but before Aglaya he can only comment that "you are so beautiful that one is afraid to look at you." And then, when pressed, he adds: "It's difficult to judge beauty; I am not ready yet. Beauty is a riddle" (8: 65–66). If uncertain at first, however,

---

* See the analysis of this novel in *Dostoevsky: The Stir of Liberation* (Princeton, N.J., 1986), chap. 9.

Dostoevsky will allow Aglaya's pride, vanity, and jealousy ultimately to triumph over the high-minded idealism that first draws her to Myshkin.

Some further comments on the novel, which show how deeply Dostoevsky had been thinking about Prince Myshkin's relation to previous literary types, were made to his niece Sofya Ivanova. Sofya, who had made a strong and very favorable impression on Dostoevsky, had written to her uncle to complain bitterly about the pressure being exerted on her to enter into a loveless marriage. Dostoevsky answers primarily to console her and, even if only implicitly, to encourage her resistance against such a self-betrayal. "My wish for you is that you be vigorous and firm of character," he says, "although I am sure you are anyway. So, my dear girl, attend to your education and bear in mind the importance of acquiring a specialty, but, above all, do not be in too much of a hurry; you are still very young, everything will take its course, but I want you to know that the question of women's rights, and especially where it concerns the Russian woman, is certain to take a few great and beautiful steps during your lifetime. Of course, I am not speaking here of our precocious lady-wonders—you know yourself what I think of them. But a few days ago I read in a newspaper that a former friend of mine, Nadezhda Suslova [Apollinaria Suslova's sister], had passed the exams for the degree of doctor of medicine at the University of Zurich and had defended her doctoral dissertation brilliantly. She is still only a very young girl . . . a

10. Sofya Ivanova

273

rare person, generous, honorable, and noble!"[7] Clearly, Dostoevsky was holding up Nadezhda Suslova as a sterling example for his niece to follow.

At the very beginning of his work on *The Idiot*, sometime in mid-October, Dostoevsky had written Sofya that he would dedicate his next novel to her; and the chapters he had just sent off contain her name following the title. Perhaps for this reason his letter is not confined to avuncular advice, or personal and family matters, but also provides extremely enlightening information about Dostoevsky's musings over his main hero. Repeating what he had written to Maikov, he explains again that "the main idea of the novel is to portray a positively beautiful man. There is nothing more difficult in the world, and this is especially true today. All writers—not only ours but Europeans as well—who have ever attempted to portray the *positively* beautiful have always given up. Because the task is an infinite one. The beautiful is an ideal, and this ideal, whether it is ours or that of civilized Europe, is still far from having been worked out. There is only one positively beautiful figure in the world—Christ—so that the phenomenon of that boundlessly, infinitely good figure is already in itself an infinite miracle. (The whole of the Gospel of St. John is a statement to that effect; he finds the whole miracle in the Incarnation alone, in the manifestation of the beautiful alone.)" It is precisely this "manifestation of the beautiful alone" that Dostoevsky will find himself attempting to re-create within a human rather than a divine-human perspective; and the letter shows him to be fully aware of some of the problems he would necessarily be called upon to confront in doing so.

"I will mention only," he continues, "that, of the beautiful figures in Christian literature, the most complete is that of Don Quixote.* But he is good only because at the same time he is ridiculous. The figure of Dickens's Pickwick (a conception infinitely weaker than that of Don Quixote, but still a tremendous one) is also ridiculous, and that's the only reason it succeeds. Compassion for the beautiful man who is ridiculed and who is unaware of his own worth generates sympathy in the reader. And this ability to arouse compassion is the very secret of humor. Jean Valjean is another powerful attempt, but he engenders sympathy because of his terrible misfortune and society's injustice toward him. But there is noth-

---

* We tend to take Dostoevsky's comparison of Don Quixote with Christ more or less for granted, but it was still a novelty at the time he made it. In his highly informative study, Eric Ziolkowski singles out Kierkegaard as "the first and, aside from Turgenev, the only person before Dostoevsky to compare Christ with Don Quixote" (94).

Dostoevsky was of course well acquainted with Turgenev's essay, *Hamlet and Don Quixote*, in which the inevitable defeat of the Don Quixotes of this world is called "the derisive blow of the Pharisees," thus paralleling Don Quixote with Christ (112). As Ziolkowski rightly comments, such a comparison was made possible by the Romantic (especially German) interpretation of Don Quixote as a "tragic idealist struggling in an imperfect society" (110). See Eric Ziolkowski, *The Sanctification of Don Quixote* (University Park, Pa., 1991).

ing of this sort in my novel, absolutely nothing, and that is why I am terribly afraid it will be a positive failure."[8] The response of Dostoevsky's contemporaries, as we shall see, confirmed his worst fears. But though *The Idiot* is the most uneven of Dostoevsky's four best novels, it is the one in which his personal vision of life, in all its tragic complexity, is expressed with the greatest intimacy, with the most poignancy, and with a lyrical pathos that touches on sublimity.

CHAPTER 15

An Inconsolable Father

The publication of the first seven chapters of *The Idiot* in *The Russian Messenger* (January 1868) successfully crowned the months of torturing gestation that Dostoevsky had just lived through. But his uncertainties about the novel's continuation were far from over. Writing itself was never a problem for Dostoevsky once he had a scenario firmly in mind; he could count on his ability to create the details of scene, character, and action as he went along. In fact, however, despite his assurances to Katkov that the remainder of the novel would follow in substantial regular installments ("and there can be no mistake about it on my part," he boldly asserted),[1] he knew very well that there was little hope of providing what he had promised and the editors expected. "I lied [to the journal]," he confesses to Maikov, "by claiming that much was already on the page and that I was only rewriting and polishing."[2] Far from being able to meet his commitments, Dostoevsky sent the remainder of *The Idiot* in small segments, sometimes so late that they were printed as the last item in the journal; the final chapters did not meet the deadline at all and were published as a special supplement. A primary reason for Dostoevsky's dilatoriness was, quite simply, that he was forced to create *both* a scenario and a final text for each new installment, and he remained in continual uncertainty until the very last stage of composition.

Another reason, however, was that no other of Dostoevsky's works was written under such distracting conditions as *The Idiot*. Although he constantly referred to the importance of being settled in one place in order to write, he moved five times while the novel was under way. Twice the Dostoevskys were forced to change quarters in Geneva, and then they shifted from Geneva to Vevey, on the other side of the lake, which supposedly had a milder climate. Three months later the Dostoevskys went to Italy, living for two months in Milan and then for the remainder of the year in Florence, where the final chapters were completed.

Work was also interrupted by the birth of his first child, a very joyful event then followed by the tragedy of her death—a terrible blow to the couple, whose anguish is movingly expressed in Dostoevsky's letters. Moreover, even though no longer harassed by creditors, as he might have been in Russia, Dostoevsky was continually plagued by worry over the wayward conduct of his stepson Pasha, as well as by the indigence of his late brother's family. All these and other matters constantly distracted him, and it is not difficult for an observer to share the admiring astonishment expressed by Maikov, the only person of his literary world with whom Dostoevsky remained in contact, and who was also familiar with all the details of his onerous situation. After an inquiry about his friend's epilepsy, Maikov goes on: "Anna Grigoryevna in her condition, poverty, exile, no close friends or family nearby, how do you bear all this, yes, and while bearing it, to write a novel into the bargain!"[3] These were the circumstances under which Dostoevsky toiled away at *The Idiot*; and he had ample justification for claiming that no major Russian novelist of his time had worked under such disheartening impediments.

2

Dostoevsky's most immediate and pressing concern during the remainder of January was to furnish the copy promised to Katkov, and he sat at his desk day and night struggling to embody his artistic intuitions into living figures on the page. To Sofya Ivanova, he provides an image of his working routine: "As for my life here: I get up late, light the fire in the fireplace (it's awfully cold here), and we drink our coffee; then I get down to work. At four o'clock I go out for dinner in a restaurant, where I eat for 2 francs, wine included. Anna Grigoryevna prefers to eat at home [that is, because of the advanced state of her pregnancy]. After that I go to a café, where I drink coffee and read the *Moscow Gazette* and *The Voice* down to the last syllable. When I am through I take a walk for half an hour or so to get some exercise and then return home and go back to work. Later I stoke the fire again, we drink tea, then I get back to work again. Anna Grigoryevna says that she is frightfully happy."[4]

Whether Dostoevsky gave complete credence to Anna's reassurances may be left undecided. There is other evidence, though, that he was much concerned over the state of her health and spirits. Six weeks later, he informs Maikov: "Anna Grigoryevna is waiting in awe, loves our future guest with all her heart, and bears up bravely and staunchly, although of late her nerves have given way a bit. She is occasionally assailed by somber thoughts, worries that she may die, etc. This makes things rather depressing and wearisome."[5]

The importance of Maikov's letters to Dostoevsky at this time cannot be overestimated, not only because of the practical services he was willing to undertake for his old friend, but also because through them Dostoevsky could obtain restorative draughts of the oxygen of Russian culture without whose stimulus he felt spiritually asphyxiated. "I wish you knew, my dear friend," he thanks Maikov, "with what joy I read and reread, again and again, every letter I get from you! If you could only imagine what my life here is like and what it means to me to receive letters from you! I see no one here, I have no news of anything, even the Russian newspapers (*Moscow Gazette* and *Voice*) have not been arriving since the beginning of the year." It was only with Maikov that he could exchange literary ideas and impressions, and he comments very favorably on a poem of Maikov's (sent to him in manuscript) whose protagonist is Sofya Alekseevna, the sister of Peter the Great. "Wouldn't it be great if 'Sofya Alekseevna' became an episode in a *whole poem* about that period," Dostoevsky remarks enthusiastically, "that is, a *Raskolnik poem*, or part of a novel in verse about that period? . . . I feel that such a poem would make a tremendous impression."[6]* Such advice indicates Dostoevsky's desire to further a contemporary literature steeped in the Russian moral-cultural values he was himself engaged in portraying. If we are to judge from Maikov's response, he evidently felt, on the basis of *The Idiot*, that Dostoevsky was accomplishing just such a task. "Your poem—is a novel, and not a novel in verse," he commented. "Those poems—you are writing them!"[7]

Dostoevsky had been sent the January issue of *The Russian Messenger*, which contained the first installment of his novel; and he conveys his reactions to the other contents of the journal for the benefit of his friend. A poem by their mutual friend Ya. P. Polonsky was quite "lovely," but Turgenev had contributed "a very weak story." The story in question, *Lieutenant Yergunov*—an insignificant anecdote about a young officer bewitched and robbed by an enchanting Gypsy girl—in truth scarcely redounds to Turgenev's artistic credit. Dostoevsky mentions this trifling work again at the end of the letter, where he complains about the pressures under which he is forced to work. "And to think that everything, my whole future, depends on whether this novel succeeds or fails. How different is the life, say, of Turgenev, and how dare he, under the circumstances, come up with a Yergunov! And when I tell you that he himself told me literally that he is a German and not a Russian, and that he feels it is to his honor to consider himself a German rather than Russian—that is the *literal* truth!"[8] Dostoevsky simply cannot put Turgenev's extraordinary declaration out of his mind.

He also comments in passing on Tolstoy's *War and Peace*, prompted by an article about the book and also by Maikov's own remarks. Maikov's nationalism was equal to, if not even more fervent than, Dostoevsky's own, and he had observed—with some justice, it must be acknowledged—that European culture had produced nothing in recent years to compare with *Crime and Punishment* and now *War and Peace*. Critics

* The full title of this poem is "A Streltsy Tale of the Tsarevna Sofya Alekseevna." The *streltsy* were regular soldiers in the Russian Army at the time of Peter the Great, and these regiments contained many Old Believers; hence Dostoevsky's allusion to the *raskolniki*.

like Strakhov, he reports, were "in ecstasy" over the book: "A majestic historical novel! The characters are depicted in all their historical and everyday shortcomings, but the sweep, the great sweep of the epoch captures the heart of the reader: it reeks of the Russian soul."[9] Dostoevsky had read about half the novel, which ran simultaneously with *Crime and Punishment* in alternate months in Katkov's journal, and replied: "I read the review of *War and Peace* [written by a historian, and little more than a précis—J.F.]. I should so much like to read the whole thing. . . . It seems to me to be quite a major work, although unfortunately, it has too many psychological details. I wish there were fewer of them. On the other hand, though, perhaps just because of these details it has so many good things."[10]

The ardent nationalism of Maikov's letters provoked a similar statement of Dostoevsky's own patriotic sentiments, which, as we have already seen, had become intensified by his exile. Maikov had written to him enthusiastically about the popularity of the Tsar and the Crown Prince, and rather unctuously declared: "What are the Russian people capable of enduring in the name of love! Why, everything! The people's love—that is our constitution! That's what a non-Russian will never understand!"[11] Dostoevsky hastened to agree, and wrote that Maikov had expressed what he had tried to proclaim in *Time* and *Epoch* several years earlier without being understood. "Yes, love, not conquest, is the foundation of our state (something, I believe, the Slavophils were the first to discover) and it is a sublime idea on which many things will be built. This is the idea we shall proclaim to Europe, which understands nothing whatsoever about it."[12] By "we" Dostoevsky presumably means Russia itself; but he wasted no time in proclaiming exactly this idea through the exhortations of Prince Myshkin to the disconcerted representatives of "aristocratic" Russian society assembled at the Epanchins. They were Russians, to be sure, not Europeans; but for Dostoevsky the Russian upper class had become so "Europeanized" that they were equally incapable of understanding the religious essence of Russia's world-historical mission.

This "religious essence" had now become fully identified with Tsarism, which for Dostoevsky embodied the quite illusory and utopian notion of a state founded on love rather than conquest. "Here abroad," Dostoevsky tells Maikov in a revealing admission, "I have definitely become an uncompromising monarchist when it comes to Russia." One can only infer that Dostoevsky had *not* been such a dedicated monarchist previously, whatever his ineradicable conviction that all attempts at revolution in Russia were futile and misguided. Dostoevsky had supported Tsarism in the past, but largely because, as he writes, "if anyone has accomplished anything in Russia, it has certainly been he [Alexander II] alone." Now, however, he sees something more deeply rooted at work: the Tsar "is beloved by the Russian people both for himself and because he is the Tsar. In our country, people have given and continue to give their love to every one of our Tsars, and it is only in him that they finally believe. For the people this is a mystery, a sacrament, an anointment. The Westerners understand nothing of this and they, who pride themselves on basing their theories on facts, have overlooked the primary, the greatest fact of our history."[13]*

This sacralization of Tsarism and the Russian state did not involve any contradiction with Christianity because Dostoevsky had persuaded himself that the Russian state incarnated the Christian principle of "love." It was only other forms of Christianity (particularly Roman Catholicism, which sought power through force and conquest) that violated the spirit of the Christian faith. All the same, neither Dostoevsky nor Maikov was deluded enough to believe that the *existing* Russian state really coincided with the ideal image they had formed of it; both knew they were projecting a prospective vision that could easily be deflated by a glance at the newspapers. "Let people blame me," Maikov conceded, "because I see everything in a rosy light—but we [Dostoevsky and himself] are *Vates* [prophets], we see farther than our noses and the abuses of a district overseer, or the stupidity of some governors, or the senselessness of a censor, or the stupid despotism of a Moscow merchant and the chicken-like blindness of a Petersburg columnist!"[14] Dostoevsky replied that he shared Maikov's sentiments exactly; but he had too much artistic and literary tact, as well as too much experience of life, ever to present this newfound religious-political faith except as an idealistic aspiration completely at odds with terrestrial realities. Moreover, Dostoevsky well knew that, like Christ Himself, such an aspiration was always exposed to the skepticism and scorn of a mocking and merciless world.

Despite the intensity of pressure under which he was working, Dostoevsky still found time to pay a visit to the ailing Ogarev (Herzen lists Dostoevsky's name among others, including Bakunin, who dropped in at the sickbed).[15] Herzen and Dostoevsky also met quite accidentally in the

* It is interesting to compare this passage with what one of the shrewdest and most clear-headed Western analysts of Russian culture, Anatole Leroy-Beaulieu, wrote about the attitude of the Russian people toward the Tsar just two years after Dostoevsky's death (1883). He was talking about the relations between church and state in the Russian Empire: "If the Tsar remains a secular layman, and if, in religious as well as in civic matters the Emperor acts in his capacity as head of state, it is not as head of a secular state in the modern or occidental sense. If he has no ecclesiastical status, the Tsar, for the mass of the people, has a religious one. He is the anointed of the Lord, established by the divine hand to safeguard and lead the Christian people. His anointment under the narrow cupola of the Uspensky Cathedral has endowed him with the virtue of the sacred. His dignity has no equal under Heaven. His subjects of all classes have, collectively and individually, taken an oath of fidelity to him on the Gospel." Anatole Leroy-Beaulieu, *L'Empire des Tsars and les Russes* (Paris, 1990), 1033.

street; and though Dostoevsky's sentiments toward Herzen had been quite friendly in the past, he had now reached such a pitch of exasperation with *all* opponents of the Tsarist regime that even a modicum of genuine affability was excluded. "It makes me sick when I run into our *know-it-alls*," he explodes to Maikov. "Oh, the poor wretches, oh, the nonentities, oh, the garbage swollen with vanity, oh, the turds. Disgusting! I met Herzen by chance in the street, and for ten minutes we spoke to each other in politely hostile tones, made a few digs at each other, and parted. No, I can't take them any more. They have fallen so far behind the times! The extent to which they understand nothing! And you should see how puffed up they have become, so very puffed up!"[16]

By the time this letter was written in mid-March, Dostoevsky had already sent off the remaining nine chapters of Part I (he completed them between January 13 and the beginning of February). These had initially been thought of as the second part of his novel, which had been planned as a work in eight parts; but this outline was gradually reduced to four as time went on, though Dostoevsky confusingly continues to use the old numbering in his notes and letters. A month earlier he explained to Maikov, with the usual exaggeration of his capacity to produce, that he intended to write two more parts in February and March; this would be sufficient to allow him to ask for a new advance. "And then, when I have also sent off [the March installment], I hope we shall be able to leave Geneva. That should be somewhere around May."[17] The second batch of chapters, printed in the February issue of the journal, was accompanied, however, by a note from the editors explaining that no further installment would appear until the April issue. This was in accordance with Dostoevsky's request that, in view of his wife's impending childbirth, he be granted a temporary respite from the obligation of uninterrupted publication.

3

The most important event in the lives of the Dostoevskys during their Geneva sojourn was the birth of their daughter Sofya (named after their favorite niece) on March 5, 1868. Anna had been aware of a possible pregnancy ever since their Dresden residency and, as time passed, began to feel the various discomforts connected with her condition. But it was only in mid-October, five months after their departure from Russia, that she decided to consult a midwife whose advertisement was posted in one of the hotels where the couple took their meals. It is clear from her diary entry that Dostoevsky had long urged her to visit a doctor; but she had refused for reasons that will become evident in a moment. At last, however, she chose to call on the midwife, who made no physical examination but concluded from descriptions that her pains were caused by a growing embryo. "I returned home," Anna writes, "terribly happy, all the more because now I was completely certain that I had not been mistaken and that I was really pregnant. I had been upset by the smallness of my belly, and continued to think that I had deceived myself, that I was not pregnant at all, and that my monthlies did not arrive because of some other illness; because, perhaps, I even had tuberculosis."[18]

There are many references to this expected and very welcome baby in Anna's Geneva diary, and the couple often spoke touchingly and affectionately with each other about the little Sonya or Misha who was on the way. Dostoevsky insisted that Anna consult a leading gynecologist, recommended by Ogarev, and the doctor gave them the name of a reliable midwife, to whose care Anna was entrusted. If we are to believe Anna's *Reminiscences*, Dostoevsky then began to walk every day through the street where the midwife lived so that, in case of a nighttime emergency, he would be able to fetch her without mistaking the house among others that resembled it closely. Ever since arriving in Geneva the couple had lived in one room, and the expectation of a child obviously made this no longer feasible if Dostoevsky were to work. They thus began to search for a two-room apartment, which was no easy task given their limited means. Luckily, they found suitable and comfortable quarters; and though Dostoevsky had engaged a nurse to look after Anna until her complete recovery, he also invited Anna's mother to join them (she did manage to come, but only several months later) to help her daughter in the early period after birth.

After several false alarms the great event finally arrived, unfortunately on the very night during which Dostoevsky had suffered a severe epileptic attack and was completely incapacitated. Anna remained silent all through the succeeding hours of labor pain, praying to God for strength and succor and awakening Dostoevsky only at seven in the morning. Refreshed by his sleep, he rushed to summon the midwife, who displayed an indifferent stolidity that both the frantic father and the apprehensive mother found absolutely infuriating. Anna's delivery was extremely prolonged, partly, according to the midwife, because Dostoevsky's own agitation and transparent fears so much upset his wife. Anna recalls that "at times I saw him sobbing, and I myself began to fear that I might be on the threshold of death."[19] He was finally denied access to her room, and in the midst of her contractions Anna would ask either the nurse or the midwife to peek outside and report on the state of her husband. At last Dostoevsky heard the whimpering cry of a child among Anna's moans, broke into the room even though the door had been hooked against him, and knelt at her bedside to kiss her hands with overflowing joy.

Dostoevsky later enshrined the emotions he had experienced during the birth of Sofya in *The Devils*, which indeed contains one of the most touching and tender scenes he ever wrote. Stavrogin's discarded mistress Marie, who is carrying his child, comes home to her deserted husband Shatov to give birth. He is not aware of her condition and mistakes her birth pangs for some illness; but she finally tells him the truth, and he responds with all the inchoate and unspoken love for her that he still feels. Just as with Dostoevsky, he is driven out of the room by the midwife, and "he was shaking like a leaf, was afraid to think, but his mind was already clinging to every image as it does in dreams. . . . At last the groans that were coming from the room turned into dreadful animal cries, unbearable, incredible. . . . Then at last, there came the sound of a cry, a new cry, which made Shatov shudder and jump up from his knees—the cry of an infant child, weak and discordant." All the figures in the scene, even the hard-boiled radical midwife, cannot resist the happiness of the moment; all are transfigured by a joyful exaltation. "There were two," Shatov declares, "and now there is a third human being, a new spirit, whole and complete, which no human hands can fashion—a new thought and a new love—it makes one feel frightened. And there's nothing greater in the world!" (10: 451–452). Such words convey Dostoevsky's own recollections of this transcendent moment in his life, whose radiance, alas, was destined to be blotted out very quickly.

Dostoevsky announced the birth of Sofya in letters to his family and friends, contenting himself with reassuring and conventional phrases in all except the one to Maikov, from which a more worrisome picture emerges. To his sister Vera, Dostoevsky reports: "Anna has presented me with a splendid, healthy, bright little girl resembling me to a ridiculous degree. Both, mother and daughter, are in a satisfactory condition, and I hope, with God's help, that everything will continue to go well."[20] A week later, he writes to Maikov: "On February 22 (our style) my wife (after terrible sufferings that lasted thirty hours) gave birth to a daughter and is still quite ill; you know how nerves become disordered in this situation. . . . Sonya, my daughter, is a healthy, robust, lovable, marvelous child, and I spend practically half the day kissing her and can't tear myself away."[21] The exuberant parade of adjectives about Sonya confirms Anna's testimony that Dostoevsky was "the tenderest possible father," who helped with the baby's bath and "would sit by her crib for hours on end, now singing songs to her, now talking to her, and was convinced that she recognized him in her third month."[22]

For the moment, though, Dostoevsky was terrified that Anna might suffer a relapse and that he would be unable to pay for a doctor and medicines. Even though the Dostoevskys were not in dire want, thanks to the regular payments received from Katkov, they lived from month to month without a penny to spare and were often forced to pawn belongings to meet an unexpected expense. Meanwhile, he was feverishly working on the plans for the next several sections of *The Idiot*, and the unremitting strain increased the frequency of his epileptic crises.

Dostoevsky was also greatly upset by a report—unfounded, and spread by Anna's mother—that Pasha Isaev had gone to Moscow to importune Katkov for some of the allowance sent his stepfather. The news of this presumed intervention threw Dostoevsky into a panic, not only because of the humiliating position in which it placed him, but also because he had requested a new advance of five hundred rubles over and above his stipend and was afraid that Katkov might take offense and refuse any further payments. Worst of all, surprised not to hear anything about the supposed trip from Maikov, Dostoevsky could not establish whether his information was true or false; but he wrote a humbly apologetic letter to Katkov nonetheless, on the deceptive assurance of his mother-in-law that the incident had occurred. The machinations of Anna's mother, determined to stop at nothing to end Dostoevsky's support of his stepson, thus only added to his vexations at this trying juncture.

Despite all these tribulations, Dostoevsky's next letter to Maikov was somewhat less harried (no doubt because the new advance had arrived in the interim), though there were still enough causes for disquietude. Anna's recovery had been disappointingly slow, and the Dostoevskys were packing up to move again because the baby's crying was disturbing their neighbors. Still, there is no mistaking the new note of unalloyed pleasure—so rare in Dostoevsky—resulting from the sensations attendant on fatherhood. Maikov had written him that becoming a parent would bring with it a whole range of new feelings, and Dostoevsky happily confirms this prediction. "For almost a month, ever since I saw Sonya for the first time up to the moment when we bathed her together in the laundry basin, I have felt much that is terribly new and totally unknown to me up to now. Yes, an angelic soul had really flown down to us."[23]

Dostoevsky frequently, and with a touching wonder, mentions as "amusing" and almost "ridiculous" the extent to which Sonya resembles her father. "The child is only a month old, and she already absolutely has my expression, my physiognomy even to the wrinkles on my forehead— when she is lying down—it's exactly as if she were writing a novel!" Despite the immense pleasure derived from contemplating his likeness in his daughter, it leads to some fatherly concern about her future. "From all this, you might conclude that she really cannot be all that beautiful (because I am *a beauty* only in the eyes of Anna Grigoryevna—and I say that in all seriousness!). But you, as an artist, know very well that one can be pretty and yet resemble someone who is not at all good-looking!" The humorous candor of these words allows us to catch Dostoevsky in a rare moment of relaxed and amused self-mockery.

Maikov's letter had not only accurately forecast the arousal of such paternal emotions in Dostoevsky's bosom but had also taken him gently to task for not reserving all his badly needed income for the benefit of his family. It was Maikov whom Dostoevsky had asked to look after the distribution of part of his new advance to Emilya Feodorovna and Pasha; and while accepting the chore, Maikov also advised Dostoevsky to be more of an "egoist" for the sake of Sofya and his wife. "If you were healthy, single, rich (or even moderately provided for)—oh, that would be a different matter!" he wrote. But, given Dostoevsky's present situation, his friend's opinion was that "you, Feodor Mikhailovich, busy yourself about yours here with *unpardonable* zeal. So that I dislike going and handing out your money. You, I believe, look through spectacles that are too kindly and make things seem worse."[24] In addition, Maikov advised Dostoevsky to make a will so that, in case of his death, there would be no ambiguity about who would inherit the right to the income from his works. Apparently he had heard rumors that Mikhail's family and Pasha had been pleased that Anna had given birth to a girl; with a son they would have had no legal claim to any of Dostoevsky's property.

Dostoevsky followed this excellent advice and in the same month wrote a "declaration" unambiguously assigning the rights of all his works to his wife. So far as his other dependents were concerned, however, he explained to Maikov why his obligations to them during his lifetime would continue to remain sacred. "In Pasha's case, he was entrusted to my care by poor Marya Dimitrievna on her deathbed. And so how can I abandon him altogether? He is like a son to me.... If I leave an impression of goodness and kindness on his heart now, it will stand him in good stead, as he matures." As for Emilya Feodorovna and her children, "there again, my late brother Misha is involved. Surely I don't have to tell you what that man was to me from my first moments of consciousness."[25] Dostoevsky's overwhelming sense of gratitude to his deceased older brother, who had sprung to his aid unstintingly just after his release from prison camp, would never allow him to consider refusing to help his family.

4

The respite of a month accorded Dostoevsky by *The Russian Messenger* relaxed the extreme tension under which he had been working, though he was hardly able to take full advantage of the extra time it afforded. "I was overjoyed ... ," he tells Maikov on April 2, at the announcement "that the novel would be continued in the April issue instead of the March one." But he still found himself with only twenty days left before a continuation had to be sent, "and I still have not written a single line! ... But what can I do—the whole month has been exceptionally hectic, fraught with anxiety and concern. There were nights on end when I couldn't get to sleep, not only because of mental strain, but because I actually had no other choice. That is a horrible thing for a man suffering from epilepsy. My nerves are now unstrung in the extreme."[26] Nonetheless, Dostoevsky's notebooks reveal that, with whatever time he had available during March and April (aside from a brief excursion to gamble), he continued to sketch out various possibilities contained in the action already initiated by his first sixteen chapters. These notes not only deal with the immediate problem of the next chapters, but also lay the groundwork for much of the later development of the novel as a whole.

Nothing could be clearer, on the evidence of these notes, than Dostoevsky's complete uncertainty about the future direction of his story. Edward Wasiolek once again well describes Dostoevsky's artistic perplexity:

> He [Dostoevsky] is not even sure of how much time elapses between the end of the action of the first part and the beginning of the second part. In the notes, he gives variously three weeks, five weeks, five days, one and one-half months, three months and six months. ... Dostoevsky is not sure whether Nastasya Filippovna will marry Rogozhin or the Prince; whether the marriage to the Prince, if it happens, is to be secret or open; whether Nastasya Filippovna will kill herself, be killed, or die naturally; whether Aglaya will marry Ganya or not; whether Nastasya Filippovna and Aglaya will hate each other or be reconciled to each other; whether Rogozhin will be a murderer or whether he will be redeemed by the Prince's teachings. Dostoevsky's mind teems with possibilities, but the tyranny of art and the tyranny of publishing require a choice.[27]

Rather unexpectedly, in view of the closeness of his next deadline, the earliest of Dostoevsky's March notes center around the conflict between Aglaya and Nastasya Filippovna. This conflict will openly appear only at a much later stage of the novel, but Dostoevsky already senses that the dynamics of his plot will depend on the rivalry between the two women. "The Prince is engaged to Aglaya. *Finally* seeks out N.F. Account of Aglaya's incessant ridicule and hatred. ... On the eve of the wedding Aglaya breaks everything off or else runs away with the count. The Prince and N.F., he marries N.F." (9: 216). This is altered, a day later, to bring it closer to what occurs in the novel: it is now Nastasya Filippovna who runs away on the eve of marriage to the Prince. "Rogozhin looks for her (N.B. Falls in love with Aglaya)" (9: 216). There has already been a previous reference to this highly improbable infatuation of Rogozhin for Aglaya, and Dostoevsky happily drops the notion very quickly.

Dostoevsky also sketches the encounter between Aglaya and Nastasya Filippovna that will precipitate his climax, even indicating some of the heated insults that will be exchanged. "Aglaya visits N.F., says that it is vile to play the role of Mary Magdalene, that she would do better to perish on a Japanese dagger in a brothel, out of sight and hearing. Laughs at the vileness of her soul. Offers her arsenic, calls her 'thou' [a demeaning usage]. N.F. declares that she is already a princess (mutual derision)" (9: 217). This scene will eventually lead to the Prince's agonizing and unwilling decision to marry Nastasya Filippovna, but very little is said here as yet about his attitude, only that "the Prince forgives everything" (9: 217). Nastasya's feelings for the Prince are then explored in notes on the following day. "She senses at heart that she loves the Prince. But considers herself unworthy of him. She wants to become a laundress—runs away to a brothel. N.B. At this point Aglaya visits her, tells her 'she should take refuge in a brothel.'" Aglaya calls the Prince "a rich idiot" in her conversation with Nastasya, but "from certain intonations in her voice and from a certain odd behavior, N.F. guesses that she loves the Prince. N.F. is jealous of Aglaya. Jealousy impels her to marry the Prince." But, once "having married him, she plunges into debauchery. The General again" (presumably General Epanchin, who lusts after Nastasya in the novel). Nastasya's death is envisaged, but apparently not by murder: "Her death in a brothel (description)" (9: 217–218).

Dostoevsky, as we know, had been greatly worried by the "vagueness" of his grasp of the Prince's character, and he now tries to fill it in a little more concretely. "The chief trait of the Prince's character: Downtroddenness. Timorousness. Self-abasement. Humility. He is fully aware that he is an *Idiot*. N.B. At every moment (inwardly) he asks himself the question: 'Am I right or are they right?' Ultimately he is always ready to accuse himself." On the other hand, the Prince is capable of standing against the world when he believes this to be right. "N.B. But when his heart and conscience tell him: 'No, it's like that,' then he acts against everyone's opinion." Dostoevsky also endows his character with the gift of psychological clairvoyance: "He sees clearly into the thoughts of those around him. He perceives perfectly that they think him an Idiot and [he] is convinced of this." As a result, "he thinks himself inferior and worse than others." Also, "he finds grown men in children, and makes them his companions" (9: 218).

Dostoevsky had linked Prince Myshkin very strongly with children in the already published Swiss episode concerning the dying shepherdess Marie, ostracized in the village after being seduced by a passing traveler, and he planned to continue such an association in later episodes. "N.B. *As for the relations with the children*, arrange matters in *this way*. At the beginning, when the subject matter is especially concerned with Aglaya, Ganya, N.F., the intrigues and so on, why not mention casually and *almost enigmatically* the Prince's relation with the children, with Kolya, etc. Do not mention the club, but rather introduce it abruptly, intimating that there are vague rumors as to its existence, and present the Prince like a tsar in its midst, in the 5th and 6th part of the novel?" (9: 220). This idea, though abandoned here, was to be revived in *The Brothers Kara-mazov*. Another idea was to end the novel with a "confession" (it is not clear whose), which reappears in Stavrogin's confession terminating *The Devils*.

In my view, one of the most important clarifying notes was made on March 12, when Dostoevsky jots down: "*Three* kinds of love in the novel: (1) Passionate and spontaneous love—Rogozhin. (2) Love out of vanity—Ganya. (3) Christian love—the Prince" (9: 220). Dostoevsky had defined these various types of love earlier as mutations in a single character, but he now assigns them to different individuals. In general, the importance of this love theme in the book, especially the tragic antinomy implicit in the Prince's "Christian love," has been neglected by interpreters; but Dostoevsky already has given a hint of it in the confusion of the Swiss children over the exact nature of Myshkin's "love" for the suffering Marie. Several times in the margin of his notes Dostoevsky puts down the phrase, standing by itself: "Prince Christ" (9: 246). This title is usually taken as confirming Dostoevsky's ambition to create a Christ-like figure in the Prince; but the phrase also suggests the tension between the human and the divine that Myshkin will be forced to confront—the tension between living in the world as a "Prince" and wishing to marry Aglaya, while being, at the same time, a seraphic visionary inspired by a self-sacrificing Christian love for Nastasya.

Another extremely important note indicates Dostoevsky's further reflections on the problem broached two months earlier in his letter to his niece. On March 21 he writes: "*The synthesis of the novel. The solution of the difficulty. How make the hero's personality sympathetic to the reader?*" Earlier he had, as we have seen, rejected the solution of Dickens and Cervantes, and he now sets down his own alternative. "If Don Quixote and Pickwick as philanthropists are sympathetic to the reader, it is because they are comical. The hero of this novel, the Prince, is not comical but does have another sympathetic quality: he is innocent" (this last word is enclosed by a box in Dostoevsky's manuscript). Such "innocence" was evidently to be highlighted by the Prince's already mentioned relation with children: "All the problems *concerning the personality of the Prince* (in which the children play an active role) as well as general problems are solved and in all this there is a great deal that is touching and naive" (9: 239–240).

Even though this involvement of the Prince with children was to remain only lightly sketched, Dostoevsky succeeded in conveying the Prince's "innocence" without exposing him to comic derision. Both Don Quixote and Pickwick are also innocent, but become laughable because of the mocking attitude taken toward them by others. In the case of the Prince, Dostoevsky is careful, after indicating an initial response of surprise and mistrust, to counter it by means already evident in the published chapters. The "innocence" of the Prince is displayed by his total candor, by his lack of any normal social vanity, and by his impassioned sympathy with human suffering (as in his discourses about capital punishment). He overcomes the initial suspicions by the evident sincerity of his ingenuousness; and there is as well an implicit recognition that his innocence, which discloses what others strive to keep hidden, possibly embodies a higher wisdom in the manner of the Russian "holy fools" (*yurodivi*). Myshkin is immediately singled out as such a "holy fool" by Rogozhin, whose merchant origins mark him as closest of all the characters to the roots of Russian religious life; and so Myshkin's bizarreries are very early endowed with a suggested religious aura.

Well into the month of April, Dostoevsky sets down one of his major difficulties, which in fact he never solved satisfactorily. "The main problem: the Idiot's character. Develop it. Here lies the idea of the novel. How Russia is reflected. Everything that would have come to maturity in the Prince lies extinguished in the tomb. And therefore little by little showing *the Prince in a field of action* will be sufficient. But! For that *the plot of the novel* is essential." The "plot" that Dostoevsky envisaged, however, was not one that he was able to incarnate artistically, no matter how much he might have wished to do so. "He [Myshkin] rehabilitates N.F. and exerts an ascendancy over Rogozhin. He induces humility in Aglaya, he drives the General's wife to distraction with her attachment to the Prince, her adoration of him" (9: 252). Except for this last reference to Mme Epanchina's affection for the Prince (and even this is more tempered than the note would have it), none of these happy results of Myshkin's influence are found in the text; and the lack of such a plot in the middle sections of the novel constitutes a major structural deficiency.

Much is broached in these notes and then discarded (such as the idea, clung to quite stubbornly, that the Prince will marry Nastasya very early in the sequence of events), but much will also be retained. The entry of March 12 contains a reference to Lebedyev as a "philosopher" (which is hardly how he had been seen previously) and then mentions his hobby of interpreting the Book of Revelation and his serio-comic story of the repentant monk. "The star *Wormwood*. He ate sixty monks, people were stronger in those times than ours, he ate and ate and confessed and for this he was burned" (9: 221). The scene of Ippolit's confession (the notion

of such a confession is shifted to him) is suggested by a group of disconnected sentences. "Why is it necessary in the construction of the world
that there should be people condemned to die? But is it possible to love
for *two weeks*?" (9: 223). Probably a remark of the Prince is given in the
following sentence: "Then die well; one can die well even when spitting
out one's last, vanity, the baby, your suffering, mountains—" Unattrib-
uted, but very likely a reference to Ippolit's "Necessary Explanation," are
the words: "Sick thoughts—still, there is nothing more intelligent in the
world" (9: 222). Here we can catch all the ambiguity and complexity of
Dostoevsky's own relation to the question of theodicy.

The death of Nastasya Filippovna appears in many variants in the
notes, but the one eventually used—the murder by Rogozhin, with
Myshkin and Rogozhin holding a vigil over the corpse—appears very
early as a possibility. On March 12, there are a number of detached jottings: "When Rogozhin shows him N.F.'s corpse. She was screaming. He
kisses the corpse. There's an undeniable smell from the corpse. He kisses
her foot." Two days later, Dostoevsky returns to this motif in the context
of a discarded plot arrangement. "Marries Rogozhin. She suffers terror,
blows, jealousy, reproaches, and desperate love. Rogozhin cuts her
throat. Zhdanov fluid" (9: 229). On April 8, the murder takes place in circumstances approximating the final version: "Rogozhin implores her
to marry him. She refuses repeatedly. After each refusal Rogozhin's despair and carousing. Finally she tells him: 'I'll marry you when the Prince
marries Aglaya.' Rogozhin is her slave (and at the end he cuts her
throat)" (9: 242). The actual scene in the book will synthesize these various *aperçus*.

As well as wrestling with the problems of theme and temporal sequence (time and again Dostoevsky outlines one or another proposed
order for the development of his action), he was also concerned with the
technique he should use as narrator. Here we can follow the excellent
analysis of Robin Feuer Miller, who points to the following passage as a
key statement: "N.B. Why not present the character of the Prince enigmatically *throughout the entire novel*, from time to time defining by
means of details (more fantastically and more questioningly, arousing
curiosity) and suddenly to elucidate his character at the end.... N.B.
With all the other characters *from the very beginning* more defined and
elucidated to the reader? (as, for example, Ganya?)" (9: 220).

On the basis of this passage, Miller characterizes Dostoevsky's narrative stance in *The Idiot* as a combination of "enigma with explanation,"
and cites other notes in which Dostoevsky indicates his wish to balance
one with the other.[28] There was to be an aura of mystery created around
the Prince, which the explanations of the garrulous narrator only en-
hance rather than dispel. "Write more concisely: only the facts," Dosto-

evsky admonishes himself at one point, "without reasoning and without a description of feelings. . . . Write using only the facts" (9: 235). But then he adds: "Write in the sense of *people say* . . . " (9: 236). In other words, the narrator would report the facts as he knew them but would not be omniscient, and many "facts" would be simply gossip and rumor—the legend, as it were—that accumulates around the Prince's actions and behavior. As Miller acutely remarks, "this grouping of narrative methods has the effect of placing facts on the side of rumor and mystery rather than on the side of description and explanation."[29]

Not specifically concerned with narration, but nonetheless important for its relation to the narrative stance already indicated ("write in the sense of *people say*"), is a passage sketching the final chapters in which the Prince prepares for his wedding with Nastasya. "(The Prince is insane—according to general rumor that is), and except for a few people they all desert him" (9: 258). A bit later: "In the 5th part the scandal about the Prince must be too great. . . . In the 7th and 8th parts the picture of the wandering Prince. . . . They take the Idiot abroad" (9: 260). This desertion of the Prince in face of the scandal he has provoked prefigures the attitude of the narrator in these concluding pages, who relays all the various distorted and malicious explanations of the Prince's decision, and even expresses his "sympathy" with some highly critical remarks about it made by Radomsky. Dostoevsky thus quite consciously envisages in advance the abandonment of the Prince by the narrator, who continues to remain on the level of "people say" when the scandal becomes "too great," and for whom the Prince becomes an inexplicable enigma. This limitation of the narrator, however, is not at all meant to indicate a definitive evaluation of Myshkin by the author (as distinct from the narrator). What Dostoevsky sought to convey was the sense of a character transcending *all* the categories of worldly moral-social experience.

5

Sometime in the latter part of April, Dostoevsky interrupted his work on the plans for the novel as a whole and managed to write the opening two chapters of Part II by the end of the month. These appeared in the May issue of *The Russian Messenger*, and he continued to work without interruption on the next three chapters. The five together form a kind of self-contained sequence marking Myshkin's return to Petersburg after a six-month absence.

Meanwhile, Dostoevsky's financial situation had worsened because of a few day's gambling at Saxon-les-Bains, from which he returned almost immediately. Hovering before his imagination was always the tempting will-o'-the-wisp of at last acquiring enough money to return home to Russia in safety. The birth of Sofya, aside from all the extra expenses entailed, had only made this desire to end his exile more pressing and acute; he abhorred Russians who brought up their children in Europe and possibly began to envisage such a dire fate for his beloved Sofya. Closer to home, Anna's mother was scheduled to arrive at the end of the month to help her daughter in the early period of nursing care, and her presence would mean additional outlays.

Dostoevsky's luck was even worse than usual on this occasion, and he gambled away all his money in the first half-hour of play. His letters to Anna (two on the same day) are filled with the usual semi-hysterical apologies, this time with additional self-castigations. Referring to his wife's "troubles" in caring for Sofya, he adds: "Of whom I am not worthy. What kind of a father am I?"[30] His losses, as had more than once happened in the past, drove him again to survey his situation and decide on a drastic resolution. He had intended to write Katkov and apologize for the scantiness of the chapters he had barely managed to send after a month's respite, but for obvious reasons of literary pride had put off this demeaning task. Now, however, he sketches for Anna's benefit a planned letter to Katkov—it was written and sent, but lost—in which he asks for a new advance to allow him to work more productively by moving his family to Vevey, just a short distance from Geneva and reputedly with a more clement climate. The health of himself and his family, he will explain to Katkov, had been suffering in the city, and this interfered with his work; but in the village of Vevey, where he will live as if in a *dacha* in the countryside, "I will remain in complete solitude until I finish the novel, and for that I absolutely need solitude and quiet. . . . Meanwhile, my wife's health will improve and we can bring up our child without fearing that she will catch cold in being exposed to the sudden local *bise* [the north wind from the mountains]."[31]

Alas for the poor Dostoevskys, the very thing they feared the most and had wished to guard against was exactly what happened. Anna's mother arrived in the early days of May, and Sofya was christened on May 4; her godparents were Mme Snitkina and Apollon Maikov. With Anna's mother now on the scene, Dostoevsky's household worries might have been expected to lessen, giving him more time for *The Idiot*; but misfortune struck just at the moment when the worst seemed over. Anna had been advised by the doctor to walk in the park with Sofya so that she could benefit from the fresh air, and when the weather turned mild and radiant in early May his counsel was zealously followed. But the hated *bise* blew in unexpectedly one day and Sofya caught a chill; it developed into an inflammation of the lungs in the course of a week, and though the worried parents were assured of recovery by the doctor (one of the best in the city, Dostoevsky remarks bitterly) just three hours before the end, she was carried off on May 12. Dostoevsky "sobbed and wept like a woman," his wife writes, "standing in front of the body of his darling as it grew cold, and covering her tiny white face and hands with burning kisses. I never again saw such paroxysms of grief."[32]

A week later, the depth of Dostoevsky's grief is fully revealed in a heartrending letter to Maikov. "Oh, Apollon Nikolaevich, what does it matter that my love for my first child may have been ridiculous, that I expressed myself ridiculously about her in letters to those congratulating me. For them alone I was ridiculous, but to you, *you*, I am not afraid to write. This tiny, three months old being, so pitiful, so minuscule—for me was already a person, a character. She began to recognize me, to love me, to smile when I approached, when I, with my ridiculous voice, sang to her, she liked to listen. She did not cry or wrinkle her face when I kissed her; she ceased to cry when I approached. And now they tell me, in consolation, that I will have other children. But where is Sofya? Where is that little individual for whom, I dare to say, I would have accepted crucifixion so that she might live?"[33]

All the more pathetic, and indicating the abyss of loneliness and desolation into which Dostoevsky had been plunged, is his request that Maikov say nothing as yet of Sofya's death to Dostoevsky's family. "It seems to me that not only will none of them feel sorry for my child but even, perhaps, feel the opposite, and the very thought of this fills me with bitterness. Of what is this poor little thing guilty in their eyes? Let them hate me, let them laugh at me and my love—it makes no difference."[34] After they buried Sofya on May 24, the atmosphere of Geneva became intolerable to the Dostoevskys, whose animosity toward the city had only been exacerbated by what they felt was the heartlessness of the Swiss to their loss. They would have dearly wished to quit the country and travel to Italy, but this was impossible financially. Besides, it would take too much time from *The Idiot*, and their livelihood depended on the continuation of the novel for which Katkov was waiting. With a liberality that astonished even Dostoevsky himself, Katkov again acceded to the plea of his tardy contributor and sent the requested new advance. The heartbroken pair, accompanied by Anna's mother, moved only as far as Vevey, where Dostoevsky, choking back his inconsolable sorrow, continued to toil unremittingly at his novel.

CHAPTER 16

Across the Alps

The next eight months of Dostoevsky's life were an exceedingly restless period marked by an increasing concern for his literary future and for the state of mind of his despairing wife. Vevey, far from being a restorative retreat where the harried couple could recover some of their depleted strength, turned out to be *too* provincial and isolated to be endured—especially for Anna, who needed cultural distraction of some sort to overcome her despondency. Dostoevsky soon realized that a change was necessary and determined, at whatever cost, to take her to Italy as soon as possible.

Life in Milan and Florence had the desired effect, and Anna's spirits gradually began to improve. Despite their displacements, Dostoevsky was able to keep *The Russian Messenger* supplied with copy, though he became more and more discouraged as time passed and felt that the pressures of publication were too great to allow him to do artistic justice to his great theme. He had pinned his hopes of returning to Russia on being able to sell the rights to republish the novel for a decent sum. But the tepidity of the critical reaction lowered the monetary value of such rights for future publishers, and the prospect of a substantial gain became more and more remote. Toward the end of this period, however, Dostoevsky was heartened by a renewal of his contact with Russian cultural life, from which he had begun to feel entirely cut off. He received an invitation to contribute to a newly founded journal whose literary editor would be his old friend N. N. Strakhov; and the ideological inspiration of the publication, he was assured, would revitalize the direction established by Dostoevsky's own journals *Time* and *Epoch*. This news provided an encouraging confirmation that his past editorial labors had not vanished into oblivion.

2

The very first letter that Dostoevsky wrote from Vevey was an answer to one received from his stepson Pasha, who congratulates his stepfather very affectionately on the arrival of Sofya (the absence of such congratulations earlier had wounded Dostoevsky to the quick). But by this time he could only respond with a despairing lamentation. "I am very unhappy, Pasha. God has dealt me a blow. My Sonya is dead and we have just buried her. Thanks, my dear boy, for your warm wishes and congratulations, but you see what my happiness is. Oh, Pasha, I feel so low, so bitter that I would rather be dead. If you love me, pity me."[1]

Most of the letter, however, is given over to more practical matters, which could not have been worse. With the aid of Dostoevsky's friends, especially Apollon Maikov, Pasha had obtained two jobs as a clerk in various offices; but he had left both after a short time because he had felt insulted by the treatment received from his superiors. When Dostoevsky heard this news from Maikov, he could not control his anger: "What a mentality, what opinions and ideas, what braggadocio!" he exploded to Maikov. "It's typical. But then, on the other hand—how can I abandon him?" And Dostoevsky goes on, in a sentence very reminiscent of the buffoon Lebedyev, "Well, just a little bit further and out of such ideas will come a Gorsky or Raskolnikov."[2] Gorsky, it will be recalled, was the highly educated young man who had murdered the Zhemarin family; and it is as a future Gorsky that Lebedyev wryly introduces his Young Nihilist nephew to Prince Myshkin. Dostoevsky, it would seem, simply transferred his own reaction to Pasha directly into the novel.

But just as Lebedyev was in fact supporting "the future murderer" living in his home, so Dostoevsky, after a mild rebuke—"whatever happens, my dear boy, *I urge you* very much to be more patient, modest and docile with your superiors in the future"[3]—accedes to Pasha's request that his stepfather guarantee a loan from someone called Gavrilov, with whom Dostoevsky had had business dealings in the past. Indeed, Dostoevsky asks that Pasha, after obtaining *his* loan, explore tentatively the possibility of a larger one for Dostoevsky himself, to be secured by the money that Dostoevsky will receive from a contract providing for the re-publication of *Crime and Punishment* in 1870. Nothing came of this idea, but it indicates how desperately Dostoevsky clutched at every possibility of raising funds. Dostoevsky also asked Pasha, if he obtained a loan from Gavrilov, to keep only one hundred rubles for himself and to give twenty-five to Anna's sister (probably to pay interest on the Dostoevskys' mortgaged belongings), with the other thirty-five to go to the ailing Emilya Feodorovna.

At the end of June, Dostoevsky apologizes to Maikov for the delay in answering his good friend. Work on *The Idiot* had not left him a moment to spare, because: "alas, I note with despair that somehow I am no longer able to work as speedily as just a little while ago and previously. . . . It's terrible, and I don't know what will become of me." It was "shameful" that he was supplying the magazine only with "bits and fragments" rather than substantial segments, and this could only damage his reputation. "I injure myself, not to mention the opinion of the editors of *The*

Russian Messenger, an opinion that is more important to me than that of the public." Dostoevsky had just sent off four more chapters of Part II, and had promised to finish the remainder of this section for the July issue—which left him about three weeks to get them on the page. With a sad irony, he remarks: "I am resting today, that is, I will write three letters."[4]

Dostoevsky was certainly unfair to himself in blaming his delays with *The Idiot* on a faltering of his creative capacities; it is a powerful testimony to their strength that he was able to write at all. The death of little Sofya haunted him continually, and it is in his letters to Maikov that he expresses the full extent of his mourning. "Apollon Nikolaevich, my friend," he writes pitiably, "I know, I believe, that you are sincerely sorry for me. Never have I been as unhappy as in the time just past. I will not describe anything for you, but, as time passes, the memory and the image of the departed Sonya stands before me more and more sharply etched. There are moments that are almost impossible to bear. She already knew me; when, on the day of her death, not imagining at all that she would die in two hours, I went out to read the newspapers, she followed me with her little eyes, she looked at me in such a way that up to this time I continue to see her more and more clearly. Never will I forget, and never will I stop torturing myself!"[5]

Besides his own torment, Anna "is terribly melancholy, cries through entire nights, and this has a very bad effect on her health." Coming to Vevey, he now realizes, was a frightful mistake; but given their limited resources, no other alternative had been possible. Vevey was not only as bad as Geneva; it was even worse. Although the panorama of the lake seen from there was very beautiful, "the rest is mediocrity itself, and we are afraid of having to pay too high a price for the panorama alone."[6] Dostoevsky repeats this withering characterization of his new abode a day later to Sofya Ivanova, to whom he remarks that "there are no Russian journals here [in Vevey], and they are very important for me. Just one bookstore; not a trace of galleries or museums: Bronnitsi and Zaraisk—that's Vevey!" These are the names of small towns on the road to the country property of Dostoevsky's parents, where he had spent summers in his childhood; the closest was Zaraisk, and in a final thrust he adds: "But Zaraisk is better and richer."[7]

Informing his niece about the death of her namesake, Dostoevsky again reiterates his inconsolable sadness: "It is now a month since she is gone, and not only have I not forgotten her, but the more time passes the greater is my sorrow and the more vividly she appears in my memory." He also sets down a more plausible explanation than the one given to Maikov of his inability to write more abundantly. "In spite of my sorrow, all this month I sat writing my novel day and night (and how I cursed my

J. J. 6843 Vevey — Rue du Centre et Fontaine St. Martin

11. Vevey, Switzerland

work, how difficult and disgusting it was to write!), and I wrote very little." It was only necessity, not any creative urge that kept Dostoevsky at
his work table; every sentence was forged in the teeth of an inner resistance caused by the artistic uncertainties revealed in his notes and by the
unrelieved wretchedness of both Anna and himself. "I do not know," he
tells his niece, "what will become of her, but she is certainly ill. She is
getting thinner, her nerves are on edge, and I do not know what may
happen."[8] But Dostoevsky repeats a previous invitation that Sofya come
to live with them when they return to Russia (which he was still hoping
to do sometime around the new year), study stenography to make herself independent, and thus escape the pressure to marry an unwanted
suitor. He even offers to attempt to find her a position through the editor
Katkov once she acquires the necessary skills and if he is still on good
terms with the journal. In fact, Sofya Ivanova soon succeeded in finding
employment with *The Russian Messenger*, without her uncle's aid, as an
English translator.

3
———

Dostoevsky's hatred of Europe (as represented by the Germans and the
Swiss) reached a new pitch of rancorous venom just at this time, no
doubt increased by his disappointment with Vevey. "Oh, if you had any
idea of how filthy it is to live abroad in one spot," he angrily tells Maikov,
"if you had any idea of the dishonesty, the meanness, the incredible stupidity and backwardness of the Swiss. Of course, the Germans are worse
[so much for Turgenev again!—J.F.], but these are not far behind! . . . But

to hell with them! There is no limit at all to how much I hate them!"⁹ As
if to confirm these apoplectic sentiments, Dostoevsky's name now became involved in a curious episode that served only to reinforce his repulsion against European civilization. Anna mentions this incident in
her memoirs, and it is equally attested to by the unfinished draft of an
unsent letter included in Dostoevsky's correspondence.

The affair began with the publication sometime in 1868 in Würzburg,
Germany, of a book in French entitled *Les Mystères du Palais des Czars
sous l'Empereur Nicolas I.* The author was a certain Paul Grimm, a pseudonym that suspiciously resembled the name of an honorable gentleman (August Theodore Grimm) who had served as tutor to the children
of the Russian royal family. The events take place in 1855, and a Theodore
Dostoiewsky, whom it is impossible to mistake for anyone but the novelist, is the chief character. He has presumably just returned from Siberia
(actually, he returned in 1859), where he had been sent because of the
Petrashevsky affair; and once again he cannot resist joining a revolutionary conspiracy. The group to which he belongs holds its meetings melo-
dramatically in an underground cellar, but the members are tracked
down and arrested. Dostoiewsky is depicted as heroically unwilling to
betray his comrades (this, at least, accurately portrays his behavior in
1849), and, after being flogged for his stubborn refusal to talk, is sent for
the second time to the Peter and Paul Fortress. In despair, his wife goes
to Nicholas I to plead for a pardon, and the magnanimous Tsar accedes
to her impassioned entreaties; but when she arrives at the prison with
the pardon, she finds Dostoiewsky has already been shipped off to Siberia. When he dies shortly afterwards en route, his woebegone spouse
enters a convent, and Nicholas I, realizing that his throne is tottering,
poisons himself. The book, incidentally, is also spiced with scandalous
details about Nicholas's well-known amatory adventures.

Dostoevsky could hardly believe his eyes when he came across this
production, and his wife reports that "he was outraged and even wanted
to write a refutation."¹⁰ After thinking it over, and burdened as he was
with so much else, he decided to let the matter rest rather than increase
the importance of a sleazy publishing venture by a public protest. But he
drafted a letter, in the first upsurge of wrath, intended to be sent to some
unspecified European journal or newspaper and objecting to the slanderous use of his name. On the one hand, he remarks, the number of
European publications concerned with Russia reveals a great interest in
the country; but on the other, "I am struck very strongly by the extraordinary ignorance of Europeans about anything concerning Russia." Europeans are ready to accept the most ridiculous nonsense published about
Russia, apparently written by someone who had lived there and become
privy to all sorts of titillating information, without realizing that they

were being sold, "by the kilo and the liter," a "speculation on the feelings of the reader ... for a noble indignation clearly fabricated to the detriment of Russia and the profit of the author."[11] What Dostoevsky objected to most of all was that the work was not frankly called a "novel" or "story" (this would at least have been honest), but that the ridiculous farrago was passed off as history—and the history of his own life! At this point, the pen dropped from his grasp.

Even while protesting dignifiedly against the supposedly distorted image of Russia so widespread in Europe, Dostoevsky became aware, ironically enough, that he was exposed to the surveillance of the Russian secret police. In mid-July he wrote to Maikov, from whom he had not heard in some time, complaining that he was sure his correspondence was being intercepted and delayed. Some well-wisher of Dostoevsky's had informed him anonymously that an order had been issued by the secret police to search him very carefully if and when he crossed the Russian border. These instructions, circulated at the end of November 1867, no doubt are the result of the following notation in the files of the Third Section: "Among the overexcitable [eksaltirovannikh] Russians now present in Geneva, [our] agent names Dostoevsky, who is very friendly with Ogarev."[12] Dostoevsky's frequentation of the notorious revolutionary had thus brought him under suspicion.

"The Petersburg police," he told Maikov, "open all my letters, and since the Orthodox priest in Geneva, according to everything known (note that these are not suspicions, but facts), works for the secret police, the post office in Geneva (with whom he has secret connections) delays letters addressed to me, and this I know full well. This is why," Dostoevsky continues, "I am firmly convinced that my letter never reached you, and that your letter has gone astray." And then the outrageousness of the situation suddenly sweeps over him, and he cannot contain his anger: "N.B. But how can someone like myself, an honest man, a patriot, who has delivered himself into their hands to the point of betraying my previous convictions, idolizing the Tsar—how can I bear to be suspected of some sort of connections with some sort of Polacks or The Bell! Fools, fools! Involuntarily, one pulls back from serving them. How many guilty among us they do not even notice, but a Dostoevsky is suspect!"[13]

At the end of this letter, which indicates just how much Dostoevsky was compelled to overlook and forgive in his support of Tsarism, and how few illusions he could have about the perspicacity of its servitors, he again returns to his own distressing situation. "Ought I not appeal to some personage and ask him to free me of the suspicion of betraying the Fatherland and in having relation with the Polacks, and also to not have my correspondence intercepted? It's disgusting! Really, they should know that the Nihilists, the liberals of The Contemporary, for three years running now have thrown mud at me because I broke with them, hate the Polacks and love my Fatherland. Oh, the scoundrels!" Maikov had already told Dostoevsky three months earlier that "among us, it is said, even in the higher circles, many do not know the difference between Katkov and Chernyshevsky, between writers devoted to Russia and the Sovereign to the marrow of their bones and the revolutionaries."[14] Now he attempted to console his friend with a story making the rounds that the letters of Katkov and Ivan Aksakov (the Slavophil editor) were also being read, and in the list of their suspicious correspondents was found the inheritor to the Russian throne. "Why should we take offense," Maikov asked jocularly, "if even he is listed in the category of suspects by the temporarily dominating party?"[15] Whether learning of these rumors provided any relief for Dostoevsky's indignation cannot be ascertained.

4

All through this period Dostoevsky was turning out chapter after chapter of his novel and making notes for its continuation. One entry, dated May 24, indicates just how uncertain he still was about the future course of his plot. "N.B. The complete account of the rehabilitation of N.F., who is engaged to the Prince. (The Prince declares when he marries N.F. that it is far better to resurrect one woman than to perform the deeds of Alexander of Macedon)" (9: 268). This contrast between an individual act of moral redemption and the warlike triumph of a conqueror may be reflected in Aglaya's opposite desire to turn the pacific and all-forgiving Myshkin into a warrior capable of fighting a duel.

The notes for May–June 1868 give a good deal of attention to the character of Radomsky, whose name initially was Velmonchek (*velmozha* means a dignitary or high official) and who was conceived as the very finest incarnation of a certain upper-class type. "Velmonchek—a brilliant character, flippant, skeptical, *a genuine aristocrat*, devoid of any *ideal* (not the kind of man we like, and this is what distinguishes him from the Prince)" (9: 273). The role sketched for him is much more ambitious than what finally emerged, and Dostoevsky here is already beginning to imagine a Stavrogin-like figure. "*Don Juan*. (Marries Lebedyev's daughter out of perversity after Aglaya refused him, out of braggadocio)" (9: 270). His relation to the Prince is caustic and ironic (it is critical in the novel, but not actually hostile), and "Velmonchek laughs incessantly at the Prince and makes fun of him. To him everything in the Prince is *truly* absurd up to the last moment" (9: 274). Dostoevsky regards him as similar to the French poet-murderer Lacenaire: "(In part, the vanity of a *Lacenaire*). 'The only thing left me' [Velmonchek is speaking], 'is the life of a profligate, but I am too cultivated for that, and I cannot make myself over into a Gogolian landowner'" (9: 274). In the notes, Velmonchek shoots himself like Svidrigailov; in the book he becomes an expatriate, like that other elegant aristocrat Pavel Petrovich in *Fathers and Children*, but one who visits the deranged Myshkin and thus proves that "he has a heart" (8: 508). Dostoevsky surely does not intend that the judgments of such a character about Myshkin, contrary to what some critics have maintained, should be taken as an authorial rejection of the Prince's values.[16]

Among the most interesting entries are some remarks to be made by the narrator—in this instance unquestionably speaking for the author—at the conclusion of the book ("after the scene of the two rivals"), that is, after the encounter between Nastasya Filippovna and Aglaya (9: 276). These observations are important as the first announcement of Dostoevsky's aesthetic of "fantastic realism," and they were probably evoked by some comments made by Maikov about the first two installments of the book (the entire Part I). Maikov had been enthusiastic after reading the first seven chapters, but for the next nine his unqualified praise became mixed with reservations. Of these he writes: "Here's the impression: an awful lot of strength, genial lightning-flashes (for example, when the Idiot is slapped and what he said, and several other instances), but in the whole action more *possibility and verisimilitude than truth*" (italics in text).[17]

Maikov found Myshkin to be the most convincing character of all (he knew this opinion would surprise Dostoevsky), while the others "as it were live in a fantastic world, on all of them there is, though powerful, still some sort of fantastic, exceptional lighting. One can't stop reading, and at the same time—you don't believe it." Trying to cushion these rather discouraging words, Maikov continues by a renewed reference to the novel's merits: "But how much power! How many marvelous stretches! How great the Idiot is!" Yet he cannot resist referring once more to the "electrical spark" by which all the characters seem illuminated, and "through which the most ordinary and well-known person, and the most ordinary flower, receives a supernatural brilliance and it is as if one wishes to examine them again." Whether this last phrase is praise or criticism remains unclear; but Maikov very perceptively adds, probably referring to the atmosphere of doom hanging over Nastasya Filippovna, that the "lighting of the novel is similar to that of *The Last Days of Pompeii*."

These reactions from a fellow writer and intimate friend, whose opinions could not be suspected of bias or antagonism, made a deep impression on Dostoevsky, and he responded to them in two ways. One was to stress that he had used real-life prototypes and actual events in his narrative (we shall return to this point). Another was to define his own independent conception of "realism" in contrast to the prevailing one by which he was being judged; and the first draft of his ideas are to be found in these Vevey notes. "We admit that we are about to describe strange happenings [the final chapters—J.F.]. Since it is difficult to explain them, let us confine ourselves to facts. . . . Let us bring to an end the story of a person who has perhaps not been worthy of so much of the reader's attention—we agree to that. Reality above everything. It is true perhaps that we have a different conception of reality, a thousand thoughts, prophecy—a fantastic reality. It may be that in the Idiot man is visible in a truer light" (9: 276). Dostoevsky here anticipates the detached stance taken by his narrator in these closing chapters; and though he did not include such thoughts about "realism" in the novel, they define Dostoevsky's explanation of why his characters should seem illuminated by an "electrical spark." A few months later, he would defend his novel in these very terms in replying to Maikov.

5

At the beginning of August, Dostoevsky makes clear that "the moment I have the means I intend to leave Vevey," adding that "if I travel elsewhere, the main reason is to save my wife."[18] Anna was clearly languishing and failing, and early in September, come what might, Dostoevsky decided to strike out for Italy. The pair crossed the Alps at the Simplon Pass, walking, as Anna describes it, "alongside an enormous mail coach which was climbing the mountain. We went in front of it, climbing the footpaths and gathering Alpine flowers along the road. We made the descent to the Italian side in a cabriolet."[19] A month later, Dostoevsky wrote to his niece that "the liveliest imagination cannot represent the picturesqueness of that mountain route,"[20] but Wordsworth made an effort to do so all the same. "The immeasurable height / Of woods decaying, never to be decayed / The stationary blasts of waterfalls / . . . The torrents shooting from the clear blue sky"—these are some of the impressions that the poet gathered when making the same crossing on foot.[21] Like Herzen, Dostoevsky found that the peasants of northern Italy reminded him of Russian ones, and this lightened his usual gloom. In a little Italian mountain town, where Dostoevsky went into a store to buy Anna a trinket, he was shown a chain for which so enormous a price was asked that "Feodor Mikhailovich had to laugh at the gap between the price and the amount of money he had on hand, and this was almost his first cheerful reaction since our loss."[22]

Their funds took them only as far as Milan, where they settled for the next two months. Dostoevsky found the climate much better for his health than Vevey; but it rained a good deal, and the general atmosphere of this bustling industrial metropolis was dismal and depressing. "The city is large and important," Dostoevsky writes his niece, "but lacking in picturesqueness, and almost not like the real Italy. The only notable thing in the city is the famous Milan Cathedral, enormous, marmoreal, Gothic, everything carved *à jour* and as fantastic as a dream."[23] The Dostoevskys took rooms on a street near the main Corso, so narrow that conversations could be (and certainly were) carried on between opposite windows, and they spent whatever time Dostoevsky could spare from his work exploring the cathedral. One day they even climbed to the roof so as to obtain a panorama of the city from this height, and to examine the statues at closer range.

All this provided some much-needed distraction for Anna, but Milan was from the first only a way station for them. Dostoevsky cherished some very pleasant recollections of his stay in Florence in 1862, and this time he had additional reasons for wishing to make this cultural landmark the goal of his Italian journey. "I intend to move to Florence at the end of November," he tells Sofya at the beginning of that month, "because there are Russian journals there and life is perhaps cheaper."[24] On the same day, he describes his situation to Maikov in more detail: "My life here is becoming really too painful for me. There is nothing Russian around—I haven't read a single Russian book or newspaper for six months now. And then there is the complete isolation. . . . Anna Grigoryevna is patient, but she is homesick for Russia and we both cry when we think of Sonya. Our life is gloomy and monastic. Anna Grigoryevna, who is a very active and enterprising person, has nothing to do here. I can see that she is bored, and, although we love each other if anything even more than 1½ years ago, it is still oppressive that she must share my sad, monastic life. It is very bad for her."[25] To his niece he complains once more of how difficult it is to write "without continuous and firsthand Russian impressions."[26]

It was not literally true, however, that Dostoevsky had not read a single Russian journal in these past six months, for he regularly received issues of *The Russian Messenger* in which his novel was appearing. The September issue contained a report on a recent meeting of the British Society for the Advancement of Science, and he urged his niece to be *certain* to read it carefully. Several English scientists, among them the famous physicist and popularizer of science John Tyndall and the well-known botanist Sir Joseph Hooker—a friend of Darwin's—had vigorously rejected the idea that religion and science were inimical and antithetic to each other. Science was legitimate in its own material sphere; but it had nothing to say—and *should* have nothing to say—about the spiritual life of mankind and the ultimate meaning of the universe. The world had been created by a power inaccessible to the mechanistic-materialistic methods used by science, and religion and science could thus go hand in hand. Dostoevsky had just completed Part II of *The Idiot*, with its vision, contained in Ippolit's "Necessary Explanation," of Nature as "an immense, merciless dumb beast" or "a huge machine of the most modern construction" that had succeeded in crushing and annihilating Christ (8: 339). Here was reassurance, however, that Ippolit's vision was only a terrified reflex of the crippling despair of his fatal illness. Belief and faith in Christ, and in the moral values that Christ had brought to the world, had not been vanquished by Nature.

Whether this article had anything to do with a sudden mutation in Dostoevsky's notes cannot be asserted, but on September 15 Dostoevsky suddenly jots down: "Ippolit—the main axis of the whole novel." He then sketches Ippolit's relations to the main characters, all of whom, except the Prince, he dominates and manipulates in one way or another. "*The main point.* N.B. The Prince has not once given way to Ippolit and because of his insight (which Ippolit himself has experienced and which drives him wild) and because of his gentleness to him, he reduces him to despair. The Prince overwhelms him by his trustfulness" (9: 277–278). Dostoevsky may have thought of expanding Ippolit's role as intriguer in order to provide more of a plot structure than he had so far managed to invent; this would seem to be the sense of a note like the following: "Write tersely and powerfully about Ippolit. Center the whole plot on him" (9: 280). But perhaps, thematically, Dostoevsky also felt the need to counter the power of Ippolit's negation by blackening his character. For example: "Little details about Ippolit. *An enemy to Kolya* (he slanders the Prince), a despot to his little brother and sister" (9: 278). There is even the notation that "Ippolit kills" (it is not clear whom, perhaps Nastasya Filippovna) (9: 280). None of these intentions, however, were ever developed in the final version.

The notes Dostoevsky made in Milan are much scantier than his previous ones, no doubt because the already published chapters narrowed the range of possible variation. Some notes are concerned merely with specifying the particular dominant for each character that he wished to maintain: "In the Prince—*idiotism*. In Aglaya—*modesty*. Ippolit—*the vanity of a weak character*. N.F.—derangement and beauty. (A victim of fate). Rogozhin—*jealousy*. Ganya: weakness, propensity for good, intelligence, *shame*, he becomes an emigrant. Evgeny Pavlovich: the last representative of the Russian gentleman landowner. Lizaveta Prokofeyevna—untamed honesty. Kolya—the new generation" (9: 280). Another note refers to what probably became Myshkin's fateful outburst at the party given to introduce him to society, and links him again with Don Quixote: "'Each blade of grass, each step, Christ—' The inspired discourse of the Prince (Don Quixote and the acorn). 'To the health of the sun'" (9: 277).

The Prince's "inspired discourse" is thus compared with Don Quixote's evocation of the Golden Age, when all men lived in innocence and concord. Dostoevsky also, at this time, settled on the presentation of the final scene, whose murder he had anticipated since the beginning. "2nd half of the 4th Part. N.F. is engaged to the Prince—. Eccentricity. One scene in church. Goes to Rogozhin in despair. (He murders). Summons the Prince. Rogozhin and the Prince beside the corpse. Finale. *Not bad*" (9: 283).

It was in the midst of working on these notes that Dostoevsky wrote sadly to Maikov: "Now that I see, as through a magnifying glass, I am bitterly convinced that never in my literary life have I had a better and richer poetic idea than the one now becoming clear to me in the detailed plan of the fourth part. And so what? I must rush full speed ahead, work without re-reading, whip up the posthorses and, in the end, all the same fail to keep my schedule." Maikov had praised the "idea" of the novel somewhat feebly, and Dostoevsky replied that "so far the execution of it has not been all that brilliant. What distresses me deeply is that, if I had started writing this novel a year earlier and then could have spent two or three months correcting and re-writing, it would have come out differently, I answer for it."[27]

Dostoevsky's disquietude about *The Idiot* certainly added to his woes; but he was somewhat heartened otherwise by Maikov's news that "in Petersburg for a long time the need has been felt for a new Russian journal," and that one to be called *Zarya* (*Dawn*) was now being planned.[28] Maikov had been entrusted with the task of asking Dostoevsky to join his name with the others (A. F. Pisemsky, A. A. Fet, and Tolstoy were mentioned) who had already agreed to collaborate. The publisher was a certain Kashpirev, an unknown quantity, but the editor in charge would be Dostoevsky's old friend N. N. Strakhov, formerly chief critic on his own journals. Dostoevsky, as a matter of fact, had received a letter from Strakhov in March 1868, congratulating him on the birth of Sofya and also on the publication of the first chapters of *The Idiot*. "Your Idiot interests me personally almost more than anything you have written," declares Strakhov, who had published one of the best early articles on *Crime and Punishment*. "What a beautiful idea! The wisdom of an open-hearted childish soul, and inaccessible to the wise and the intelligent—that is how I understand your aim."[29] Strakhov also complains, however, about being forced out of *Notes of the Fatherland*, where he had been publishing, and thus finding himself at loose ends.

Dostoevsky greets Maikov's news with enthusiasm and then, after echoing the usual doleful complaints of recent months, metamorphoses into the erstwhile successful editor of two important magazines. He rejoices that Strakhov has at last "found an occupation worthy of him," and thinks "it would be desirable that the review be unmistakably *Russian in soul*, as you and I understand it, although, naturally, not purely Slavophil." Dostoevsky had always maintained a certain distance from the Slavophils, although he shared many of their basic ideas; but he had never accepted their tendency to glorify and idealize the Russian past, with its shameful heritage of serfdom, or their refusal to acknowledge the achievements of contemporary Russian literature. Now he also exhibits a certain reticence about their more recent turn to Pan-Slavism and remarks that "it is not necessary to run after them [the Western Slavs] *too much*, and I mean too much."[30]

To make an impact, *Dawn* would have to assert its literary independence from the very first moment, and also exhibit its ability to attract established writers—though Dostoevsky advised firmly against paying large sums simply for the sake of a name. A comedy of A. N. Ostrovsky's set in a merchant milieu would be worth a considerable amount, but Dostoevsky hoped that Strakhov would not waste good money on "a rotten rice-pudding [the word refers to a dish eaten after funerals—J.F.] like *Minin* or other [more recent] historical dramas of Ostrovsky." The list of proposed contributors included the name of N. Kokhanovskaya, a now forgotten but once popular female author, and Dostoevsky shuddered at the possibility of finding himself in her suffocatingly pious company. He recalled "all the loathing and shame I had to endure two years ago [actually four and a half] on reading *Roya*—that hallelujah swimming in icon oil, which made Aksakov [the Slavophil editor] knit his brows." As for "that pompous Yergunov [Turgenev], who has written himself out," one should not pay except for a decent manuscript.

Dostoevsky also laments, in response to Maikov's recommendation that he read a new book by the Slavophil Yury Samarin, that it is impossible to find any Russian books in Milan. "Even in Geneva, where one can find Russian books, the only thing on the shelf is *What Is To Be Done?* and the rubbish of our émigrés. If there are [other] Russian books—some volume or other of Gogol or Pushkin—it's just an accident." Dostoevsky had already forgotten how grateful he had been in Geneva to find copies of *The Polar Star*, *The Bell*, and Herzen's memoirs; whatever sympathy he may have had for such émigré literature in the past had now vanished completely. Samarin's book, *On the Russian Borders* (*Okraini Rossii*), dealt with the Baltic provinces and the situation of the local (Estonian and Lettish) populations there, whom the Slavophil Samarin thought could be weaned away from fidelity to their Baltic German overlords if offered economic advantages by the Russian government. The book, Maikov reported, was causing quite a stir (many Baltic German noblemen, of whom Governor-General von Lembke in *The Devils* may be considered a specimen, held very high rank in government and bureaucratic posts), and Dostoevsky regrets being unable to read the work because "I have thought about all this incessantly myself."

The letter ends with a renewed expression of concern about Pasha and Emilya Feodorovna, though Dostoevsky stresses that he bears Pasha no ill will and refuses to judge him harshly. Mostly, though, he apologizes to Maikov for not yet having paid a debt owing to his loyal friend while asking him to distribute money to others. "It torments me terribly just because you have behaved toward me like a blood brother, and, really, not many brothers would have acted like that. You have a family too. But I still receive money, and I'll repay. Dawn will break for me too, but how much I would like to return to Russia." And then Dostoevsky reveals a hidden wound referred to nowhere else, but about which he and Anna no doubt had had many mournful conversations: "And to think, besides, that Sonya would certainly be alive if we had been in Russia!"[31]

Sometime in the early days of November the Dostoevskys moved to Florence, where they stayed for about a week at a hotel before renting two rooms on the Via Guicciardini just opposite the Pitti Palace. Dostoevsky immediately inscribed his name in the register of the famed Gabinetto Scientifico-Letterario Vieusseux, which subscribed to Russian periodicals and newspapers, and where his signature joined those of Henri Beyle, Hector Berlioz, Heinrich Heine, Lamartine, and Franz Liszt (among many others well known to posterity), who had used the library at various times.[32] Anna, who had begun to study Italian at Vevey and quickly picked up a smattering of the language, was delighted with the liveliness and animation of the streets and the wealth of treasures in the museums. Dostoevsky was tied hand and foot by *The Idiot*, but he spent some time with Anna just after arrival in visiting the sights. "Florence is beautiful but too humid," he writes to Maikov in his first letter from there. "The roses are still flowering in the open air in the gardens of the Boboli. And what treasures in the galleries! My God, in 1863 I had not paid any attention to the 'Madonna of the Chair' [by Raphael], I passed by it an entire week without seeing it, it's only now that I have discovered it. How many wonderful things there are, even aside from this painting. But I postpone everything till the end of the novel. I have closed myself off."[33]

Dostoevsky was now faced with completing the fourth and final section of *The Idiot*, which he very much wished to do by the end of the year. He had promised Katkov to finish by that date, and felt he should renounce all payment for chapters appearing later. Also, he had been counting on the fourth part, with its crescendo of climactic scenes and haunting finale, to induce publishers to offer substantial sums for the reprint rights; and the impact of this concluding section would be badly weakened if printed in small installments. At first, he did not think it possible to meet the deadline; but then he wrote to Katkov that, if publication of the December issue were slightly delayed (the journal rarely came out exactly on schedule), he would be able to furnish the remainder of his manuscript.

"I suddenly realized," he tells Maikov, "that I was in a condition to do it without really spoiling the novel. If there are readers of *The Idiot*, they perhaps will be somewhat stunned by the unexpectedness of the ending; but, on reflection, they will finally agree that it had to end in this way. In general, the ending is quite successful, that is, just as an ending; I am not speaking of the value of the novel in itself; but when I finish, I'll write something to you as a friend about what I think of it myself."[34] The uncertainty betrayed here about the quality of his own achievement, and particularly the self-deprecatory doubt about whether the novel still had any readers, express all of Dostoevsky's dubiety about his latest creation. Nor would Maikov's reports about his own reaction, as well as that of the public, have quieted his fears, although his old friend tried to be as encouraging as possible. But just as he had not withheld his comment about the "electrical spark" surrounding Dostoevsky's characters, so he repeated, in conveying reader reaction six months later, that "the chief criticism is in the fantasticality of the characters."[35]

It was in response to this reiterated charge that Dostoevsky now sets down the famous declaration of his aesthetic credo of "fantastic realism." "Oh, my friend," he writes, "I have a totally different conception of reality and realism than our novelists and critics. My idealism—is more real than their realism. God! Just to narrate sensibly what we Russians have lived through in the last ten years of our spiritual development—yes, would not the realists shout that this is fantasy! And yet this is genuine, existing realism. This is realism, only deeper; while they swim in the shallow waters. Really, is not Lioubim Tortsov in essence a nobody—and yet that's all that their realism allows itself of the ideal.... Their realism—cannot illuminate a hundredth part of the facts that are real and actually occurring. And with our idealism, we have predicted facts. It's happened."[36]

Here we have Dostoevsky's own conception of what he was striving to achieve: an illumination of all the heights and depths of the moral chaos of Russian life as he saw it at present. Lioubim Tortsov is a lower-class, all-forgiving character from one of Ostrovsky's plays, who had been singled out by Apollon Grigoryev as a sterling, if somewhat disreputable, incarnation of Russian values; and the claim that "we have predicted facts" alludes to the Danilov murder case. Dostoevsky thus sees his own "realism" as becoming "fantastic" because it delves beneath the quotidian surface into the moral-spiritual depths of the human personality, while at the same time striving to incarnate a more-than-pedestrian or commonplace moral ideal.

This same important letter also contains a passage that, although not referring to *The Idiot* specifically, nonetheless helps us understand how Dostoevsky wished this "ideal" to be understood—and how, consequently, we should regard the ending that he thought would so surprise his readers. Maikov had sent Dostoevsky the manuscript of one of his poems, and Dostoevsky responded with lavish praise. "Your 'In Front of the Chapel' is incomparable," he enthused. "Where have you found such words! This is one of your best poems." It is, indeed, a beautiful descriptive lyric in Maikov's restrained, neoclassical style, which conveys the poet's reflections as he stands contemplating the candles dimly illuminating the icons in a chapel. They were placed there by unknown hands, and, as the choir sings solemnly, "someone's woe is comforted / Someone's tears gently flow." The candles are the images of souls that are trembling and palpitating:

> This is a widow's copper penny
> This is the mite of a poor peasant wife
> This is—perhaps—of a murderer
> The yearning to repent. . . .
> This is a radiant moment
> Amidst savage darkness and silence
> A memory of tears and the tender feelings
> Of a soul peering into eternity.[37]

It is not hard to understand why Dostoevsky should have been enchanted by this poem, whose rhythmic delicacy can hardly be conveyed in my literal translation. Less expected, however, is the objection that he makes to it. "Everything is lovely," he explains, "but there is one thing only that I am not satisfied with: the *tone*. You seem to *excuse* the icon, to *justify* it; well, you say, this is barbarism, but after all there are the tears of a murderer, and so forth. You know, even the famous words of Khomiakov about the Miraculous Icon, which once almost filled me with rapture—now no longer please me, they seem weak. In a word: 'Do you believe in the icon or not!' (My dear friend, believe more bravely and courageously)."[38] Dostoevsky's memory has played him false here: the words about the miraculous icon are those of Ivan Kireevsky, another prominent Slavophil, and come from a conversation with him reported by Herzen in the fourth part of *My Past and Thoughts*.

There is, indeed, a close relationship between Maikov's poem and Kireevsky's words, which describe a very similar experience of imaginative penetration into the mystery of religious faith. Kireevsky had stood before a chapel containing a miraculous icon of the mother of God, and "I thought of the childish faith of the people [peasants] praying to it; some women, the ill and elderly, were on their knees and, crossing themselves, bowed down to the earth." As Kireevsky continued to gaze at the icon, he was suddenly overcome by the feeling that it was not merely a wooden board painted with images. For centuries that board had soaked up all the passion and all the prayers addressed to it and had become "a living organism, a meeting place between the creator and people." As he looked again at the praying mass of sufferers and back to the icon, "then I myself saw the features of the mother of God come alive; she looked on all these simple people with pity and love. . . . And I fell on my knees and humbly prayed to her."[39]

In the past, as Dostoevsky said, these words had filled him with rapture, and for perfectly comprehensible reasons: they depicted the process of his own conversion, not from atheism, but from a semi-secularized Christian socialism to a reverence for the people and their "childish faith." But now he found even such reverence unsatisfactory, because it accepted faith solely for its consoling and compensatory effects on human life. Such faith was not spontaneous and instinctive, not treasured for its own sake and divorced from any practical consequences it might bring about. For Dostoevsky, faith had thus now become completely internal, irrational, and non-utilitarian; its truth could not be impugned by a failure to effect worldly changes, nor should it be defended *rationally*, as it were, because of the moral-psychological assuagements it might offer for human misery. Myshkin's life ends tragically; but for Dostoevsky, poised to write his final pages, this in no way undermines the transcendent ideal of Christian love that he tries to bring to the world, and whose full realization is beyond the power of any earthly human to achieve.

Despite his assurances to Maikov that the entire fourth part already existed in draft "and that I know every word by heart,"[40] Dostoevsky was unsuccessful in his strenuous endeavor to allow *The Idiot* to end with the maximum possible aesthetic power. Only three chapters of the final section made the December issue, and the remainder was printed as a supplement to the second issue of 1869; but Dostoevsky was not really to blame. On the very day that he expected his final section to have arrived in Russia, he explained to his niece: "Now it's finished at last! I wrote the final chapters day and night in anguish and terrible uncertainty. . . . I had two epileptic attacks, and I was ten days behind the fixed limit."[41] Once again fate had played him a nasty trick, and his epilepsy had been responsible for the delay. Still, his long and arduous labors on *The Idiot* were now finally over; but this did not mean that he could enjoy even a temporary respite from the strain of uninterrupted composition. Indeed, he was already thinking of a huge new novel, one that he regarded as the culmination of his life's work. For the moment, though, let us complete this account of *The Idiot* by discussing one more aspect of its genesis.

6

All through the publication of *The Idiot*, Dostoevsky eagerly awaited word from his friends about their responses, as well as the reaction of the public, to his novel. "You know, my dear fellow," he complained to Maikov, shortly after the appearance of his first seven chapters in January 1868, "you promised me that the minute you finished [reading them] you would write and tell me what you thought of it. And I go and hang around the post office every day, but there is nothing from you. . . . I have drawn the quite obvious conclusion that my novel is weak and that out of consideration for my feelings, out of pity and conscience, you are putting your reply off rather than confront me with the truth."[42]

In answer to this plea, Maikov wrote: "I can report to you very pleasant news: success, the arousal of curiosity, the interest of much personally experienced terrible moments, the originality of the hero's mission (whose identity, it would seem, I can make out, would you believe through whom? . . . through yourself!). . . . Madame the General [Epanchina], the promise of something powerful in Nastasya Filippovna and much, very much that caught the attention of all to whom I spoke."[43] When such praise became tempered with later reservations, Dostoevsky countered by enunciating his aesthetic of "fantastic realism"; but his initial defense was also to claim "realism" for his characters in the more ordinary and narrower meaning of the term.

He was disappointed that Maikov did not seem to appreciate the finale of Part I (the riotous birthday party at Nastasya Filippovna's, during which Myshkin proposes marriage to her and she throws Rogozhin's hundred thousand rubles, wrapped in copies of the *Stock Exchange News*, into the fireplace). "I had really counted on that!" he wrote regretfully. And while conceding that Maikov's judgment "perhaps may be true," he affirms the veracity of his characters within Maikov's own assumptions: "I still believe, however, that the character of Nastasya Filippovna is absolutely true. By the way, there are many little things at the end of Part I that are taken directly from life, and some of the characters are straight portraits, e.g., General Ivolgin and Kolya."[44] Dostoevsky says nothing about some of the other episodes of the book that are also drawn from life, though Maikov alludes to them obliquely ("personally experienced terrible moments"); and these moments contribute an important stratum to this most intimately autobiographical of his novels. Moreover, although Dostoevsky's claim to have taken other characters besides Prince Myshkin "directly from life" aroused skepticism in the past, new research has given some plausibility to what had seemed an unconvincing insistence on literality.

At the time of his initial reaction, Maikov had read only Part I of the novel, and his reference to the "terrible moments" can thus refer only to Prince Myshkin's narrative about the man condemned "to be shot for a political offense. Twenty minutes later a reprieve was read to [him], and [he] was condemned to another punishment" (8: 51). This is, of course, exactly what happened to Dostoevsky in 1849, when he was sentenced to death in the Petrashevsky affair and then reprieved by Nicholas I; many of the details of this scene are reminiscences of the actual event. Dostoevsky was the same age as the man mentioned (twenty-seven), and, just as described, the gilt spire of a church adjoining Semenovsky Square suddenly was lit up by the rays of the sun while the prisoners were waiting for the sentences to be carried out by a firing squad. Dostoevsky thus re-creates the indelible sensations of this decisive instant in his own life, when "the uncertainty and feeling of aversion for that new thing which would be and was just coming was awful." But "nothing was so dreadful" for the man of whom Prince Myshkin speaks as the thought of what he might do with his life if he were not to die: "What if I could go back to life—what eternity. . . . I would turn every minute into an age. . . . I would count every minute as it passed. I would not waste one" (8: 52).

These were exactly the thoughts of Dostoevsky himself, as recorded in a letter written to his brother immediately upon returning from his mock execution. "When I turn back to look at the past," he exclaimed, "I think how much time has been wasted, how much of it has been lost in misdirected efforts, mistakes and idleness, in living in the wrong way, and, however I treasured life, how much I sinned against my heart and spirit. . . . *Life is a gift, life is happiness, and each minute could be an eternity of bliss*" (italics added). Moreover, this realization of the infinite value of the gift of life also brought with it a moral transformation: "If anyone remembers me unkindly," Dostoevsky continued, "and if I quarreled with anybody or left him with an unpleasant impression of me, ask him to forget about it, if you happen to come across him. There is no bile or malice in my soul, and I should like so much at this instant to love and to press to my heart any of these former acquaintances. It is a joy; I experienced it today as I was taking leave of those who were dear to me before I was to die."[45]

This eschatological apprehension of life, of life as lived under the impending shadow of eternity, has sometimes been attributed to the early Christians and considered the source of the Christian ethic of love. Albert Schweitzer has argued that this ethic, with its exorbitant demands on the human personality for self-conquest and self-sacrifice, is in fact an "interim" ethics, appropriate only to the short period of time between the Incarnation of Christ and the imminence of the Second Coming.* Whatever one thinks of this view, there is no doubt that Prince Myshkin inherited such an eschatological apprehension from Dostoevsky, who assimilated the full force of its revelation into his own sensibility. And he was thus able to portray this ethic—not only in *The Idiot*, but in his other works as well—with an uncompromising purity and tragic pathos unrivaled up to his time and unsurpassed ever since. Myshkin's character incorporates those values arising from the moral transfiguration that Dostoevsky reports as having occurred within himself. Is there not even a sad biographical poignancy in the admission of the "condemned man" (that is, Dostoevsky) that "he didn't live like that at all; he wasted many, many minutes" (8: 53)?

Prince Myshkin and Dostoevsky are also linked by the disease of epilepsy, which appears as part of the Idiot's character from the very first conception of the book, but the importance of which, especially after Part I, is not mentioned in the notes at all. Dostoevsky's use of his own epilepsy for Myshkin, however, was for him the height of "realism," even though the experiences he records are extraordinary enough to seem "fantastic." For Dostoevsky himself had felt, as Myshkin does in the "aura" preceding the onset of a fit, the supernatural illumination of a realm embodying "the acme of harmony and beauty," which aroused in him "a feeling, unknown and undivined till then, of completeness, of proportion, of reconciliation, and of ecstatic devotional merging in the highest synthesis of life" (8: 188). Even though fearing that "stupefaction, spiritual darkness, idiocy stood before him conspicuously as the conse-

---

* It was Albert Schweitzer's famous book, *The Quest for the Historical Jesus* (1906), that first focused attention on the importance of such eschatological expectations as the source of the Christian ethic of love. Ever since, this theory has been subjected to a flood of analysis and criticism, without really being shaken as a *psychological* basis for understanding the more extreme aspects of the Christian doctrine of love (or *agape*).

A good summary of the issue is provided by Amos N. Wilder, who argues against considering *all* of Christ's teachings to be an "interim" ethics, created to govern life only in the brief interval between the First and Second Comings, but who acknowledges the importance of such a sense of imminent End in shaping the Christian ideal. "More than one element," he writes, "went to make up the original antecedents and circumstances of this [Jesus'] teaching, of which the most important were the standing ethical norms of the time, the Torah and the tradition and their practice. Strains of ethical teaching cognate with one or another element in Jesus' own can be found in the ethics of the prophets, of the wisdom teachers, of the apocalytists and of the rabbis. When all such matters are noted, it still remains that a most significant factor in the presentation, if not in the content, of the ethical teaching was the eschatological expectation. It is difficult to deny that Jesus' whole call to repentance and his urgent summons to the righteousness he preached were set against the background of vivid eschatological rewards and punishments which he saw as imminent. And it is difficult to deny that some of his demands, certainly as laid on certain individuals, were extraordinary demands conditioned by an extraordinary situation." Amos N. Wilder, *Eschatology and Ethics in the Teaching of Jesus* (New York, 1950), 11.

quence of these 'higher moments,'" Dostoevsky had also "actually said to himself at that second that, for the infinite happiness he had felt in it, that second really might be worth the whole of life." It was not only the fictional creation Myshkin who could affirm, in words taken from the Book of Revelation, that "at that moment I seem somehow to understand the extraordinary saying that *there shall be no more time*" (8: 188–189).

Such aspects of *The Idiot*, which come directly from Dostoevsky's own life, would certainly have made the charge of "fantasticality" less telling in his eyes; and much else as well also derived from his personal history. Many of the episodes involving the Epanchin family are based on Dostoevsky's courtship of Anna Korvin-Krukovskaya, who probably also furnished some of the features for Aglaya Epanchina. Aglaya's rebelliousness and restlessness, her desire to break out of the confines of her family and devote herself to the "useful" work she had learned about in reading "forbidden books," are neatly paralleled by Anna's life. Anna's adolescent infatuation with tales of knightly adventure, which Dostoevsky could easily have heard about in conversation, may well have inspired Aglaya's choice of Pushkin's poem "Poor Knight" as a deceptive analogue for Myshkin, who is very far from being a heroic warrior. Like Myshkin in the drawing room of the Epanchins, Dostoevsky also rather frightened the Korvin-Krukovsky women by describing for them the scene of his mock execution and, no doubt, many of the sensations evoked in *The Idiot*.

Recent speculations about the possible prototypes for various other characters also help to explain why Dostoevsky might have insisted so forcibly that even his most extravagant figures had a certain anchoring in the reality of his time. A very wealthy Count Kushelev-Bezborodko, who was afflicted with Saint Vitus' dance and married to a well-known St. Petersburg hetaera, was among Dostoevsky's literary acquaintances. He had also met in society a garrulous general with a pert and lively grandson called Kolya. This worthy gentleman, an inexhaustible raconteur, had translated several books about Napoleon and aroused widespread amusement by his penchant for inserting himself among the important historical and military matters on which he discoursed. One of Dostoevsky's uncles had raised a female ward in a manner suspected of being similar to that of Totsky, and then married her off to a nephew with a large dowry. A. P. Milyukov had written ethnographic sketches of merchant life on which Dostoevsky drew for details about Rogozhin and his father.[46]

Other episodes in the book are also taken from well-known incidents of the period. During the scene at the concert in Pavlovsk, Nastasya Filippovna is publicly rebuked by an officer offended at her appearance in respectable society, and Myshkin restrains the enraged officer, who had raised his whip to strike her. Dostoevsky's notes for this scene contain the enigmatic sentences: "The public insult (Ch—s wife). The Prince's explanation" (9: 260). The parenthesis indicates that Dostoevsky modeled this episode on an actual one at the same spot a few years earlier, which had involved the wife and sister of Chernyshevsky. Mistaking them for prostitutes strolling among the very proper residents of the elegant watering place, an officer had threatened to horsewhip them and was only stopped by a number of students who sprang to their defense.

Another specific reference to actual events, this time involving Dostoevsky himself, is in the chapters dealing with the protests made to Myshkin by the "son of Pavlischev" and his Nihilist friends, outraged because the Prince has unjustly (in their view) inherited the fortune of his benefactor. After sending off these chapters, Dostoevsky wrote to Maikov that in them "I have tried my hand at an episode with contemporary youthful positivists of the most extreme kind. I know that I have written truthfully (for I write from experience; no one has had more experiences or observed them more than I have), and I know that everyone will curse me, and say that this is ridiculous, *naive and stupid*, and untrue."[47] The slanderous article about Myshkin read aloud here is a skillful parody, down to stylistic minutiae, of the denunciatory diatribes regularly appearing in the radical journal *Spark* (*Iskra*); and the insulting poem in the article is a takeoff on some mocking verses about Dostoevsky that Saltykov-Shchedrin had printed five years earlier.

Dostoevsky thus never felt, in the course of writing, that he was transgressing "reality" because so much of his material was taken from his own life experiences, or could be found in the lives and behavior of others with whom he was familiar. In this sense, he remained faithful to the demands of "realism" that he, along with all the Russian novelists of his time, accepted as prescriptive. But realism for Dostoevsky never meant the acceptance of the factual and literal *in itself*; it meant, rather, its transformation in the light of what he called the "beginnings and ends" of factuality, its significance in a larger framework of moral-religious meaning; and as for these "beginnings and ends"—"all this is still," as he wrote, "as yet fantastic for humankind." Dostoevsky's realism, however justified his claims may be to a strict veracity, inevitably became "fantastic" because he was always reaching out to grasp the ultimate meaning of such beginnings and ends. And nowhere is this effort more apparent than in *The Idiot*, where Prince Myshkin himself "kept fancying that if I walked straight on, far, far away, and reached that line where sky and earth meet, there I should find the key to the mystery" (8: 51).[48]

CHAPTER 17

The Idiot

> The final majesty, the ultimate freedom, and the perfect disinter-
> estedness of divine love can have a counterpart in history only in
> a life which ends tragically.... It is impossible to symbolize the
> divine goodness in history in any other way than by complete
> powerlessness.
>
> Reinhold Niebuhr, *The Nature and Destiny of Man*

Writing to a correspondent more than ten years after finishing *The Idiot*, Dostoevsky remarks that he is always particularly gratified to receive letters from people who consider this novel his finest creation. "All those who have spoken of it as my best work have something special in their mental formation" he writes, "that has always struck and pleased me."[1] Such a remark may easily be taken as little more than an epistolary flourish; but there is good reason to believe that Dostoevsky meant it seriously. For *The Idiot* is the most personal of all his major works, the book in which he embodies his most intimate, cherished, and sacred convictions. Readers who took this work to their hearts were, he must have felt, a select group of kindred souls with whom he could truly communicate.

In all his larger novels, Dostoevsky's positive convictions appear mainly as a foil and background for the noxious doctrines he wishes to undermine and destroy—or to depict as doomed to self-destruction. In *The Brothers Karamazov*, for example, though his religious ideal is extensively portrayed in Father Zosima, this ideal does not spring so directly from the living roots of his own personal experiences. It is only in *The Idiot* that Dostoevsky includes an account of his ordeal before the firing squad, his own encounter with the imminence of death. This experience had given Dostoevsky a new apprehension of the meaning of life, and Prince Myshkin struggles to bring this revelation to a world mired in the sloth of the material and quotidian. Also afflicted with the epilepsy from which Dostoevsky suffered, the Prince is overcome, at the onset of this disease, with the same ecstatic intuition of supernatural plenitude that his creator both cherished as a divine visitation and feared as the harbinger of madness.

The particular form assumed by the tragic fate of Prince Myshkin, quite aside from its general parallel with the Passion of Christ, is also linked with some other of Dostoevsky's most hallowed and sacrosanct beliefs. "To love man *like oneself*, according to the commandment of Christ, is impossible," Dostoevsky had written at the bier of his first wife. "The law of personality on Earth binds. The *Ego* stands in the way" (20: 172). In a passage of the deepest relevance for Prince Myshkin's unhappy fate, Dostoevsky continues: "Marriage and the giving in marriage of a woman is, as it were, the greatest deviation from humanism, the complete isolation of the pair from everyone else. . . . The family, that is the law of nature, but [it is] all the same abnormal, egotistical." Even that "most sacred possession of man on earth," the family, is thus a manifestation of the Ego, which prevents the fusion of individuals into an All of universal love (20: 173). Only at the end of time—only when the nature of man has been radically transformed into that of an asexual, seraphic being—will the total realization of the Christian ideal of love become possible. Prince Myshkin approximates the extremest incarnation of this ideal that humanity can reach in its present unregenerate form; but he is torn apart by the conflict between the contradictory imperatives of his apocalyptic aspirations and his earthly limitations.

Although Prince Myshkin, the child of Dostoevsky's own theological musings, is certainly one of his author's most original creations, it is possible to construct a summary genealogy for him all the same. Myshkin can be related to all those romantic seekers for the absolute in Balzac—Louis Lambert, for example—whose absorption with the infinite wrecks their subliminal existence. From Balzac as well comes a perhaps closer analogue for Myshkin than any other character in the modern novel: the irresistibly attractive, androgynous hero-heroine of the fantastic *Seraphitus-Seraphita*, who ascends into a Swedenborgian heaven at the end of the book. Within Dostoevsky's own creative universe, as already pointed out, Myshkin may be seen as prefigured by Colonel Rostanev in the *Village of Stepanchikovo* and Aleksey Valkovsky of *The Insulted and Injured*. The naively good-hearted Colonel also feels, if only sporadically, the same ecstatic apprehension of life that Myshkin struggles to impart to others; and the childlike ne'er-do-well Aleksey anticipates Myshkin's incapacity to live in time and his inability to choose between two women. Dostoevsky works out the character schema for Prince Myshkin by spiritualizing the spontaneous and whole-souled goodness of the Colonel and blending it with Aleksey's discontinuity and irresolution. The result is a discontinuity that springs from a total surrender of self in each human encounter, and an irresolution that becomes sublime in its aspiration toward a universality of love.

2
___

The first part of *The Idiot* was written at white heat, under the inspiration of Dostoevsky's decision to center a major work around the character of a "perfectly beautiful man"; and the singular spiritual fascination of Prince Myshkin derives very largely from the image of him projected in these early pages. Later in the book, Myshkin tends to be somewhat submerged by the flood of talk among the characters; and though he remains the implicit center of the action, his presence is much less strongly felt. In Part I, however, we see him in the clearest focus and receive the strongest impression of the Fra Angelico radiance that illuminates his personality.

The moral halo that surrounds the Prince is conveyed in the very first scene, set in a railway carriage on the way to Petersburg, where he confronts the turbulent merchant's son Rogozhin and the amusingly cynical scrounger Lebedyev. What strikes Rogozhin is the perfect un-selfconsciousness with which the Prince replies to his insolent questions, the complete lack of resentment toward his condescension. The Prince's behavior is marked by a total absence of vanity or egoism; he simply does not seem to possess the self-regarding feelings on which such attitudes are nourished. Even more, he displays a unique capacity to take the point of view of his interlocutor—to such an extent, indeed, that he fully understands the other's view of himself. This does not mean that the Prince necessarily agrees with these views (as when he rebukes Ganya Ivolgin for continuing to refer to him insultingly as "an idiot"); but he attributes their source to the strangeness of his appearance and behavior, and thus forgives them in advance. This explains the Prince's failure to take umbrage at his reception by others; and his capacity to transcend himself in this way invariably disarms the first response of amused and superior contempt among those he encounters.

Max Scheler, in his admirable book, *The Nature and Forms of Sympathy*, distinguishes what he calls "vicarious fellow feeling," which involves experiencing an understanding and sympathy for the feelings of others without being overcome by them emotively, from a total coalescence leading to the loss of identity and personality.[2] The underlying movement of *The Idiot* may be provisionally defined as the Prince's passage from the first kind of fellow feeling to the second; but in Part I there are no indications of such a loss of identity. Rather, all the emphasis is placed on the Prince's instinctive and undifferentiated capacity for completely lucid vicarious fellow feeling even under great stress. As an example, we may take the scene where the Prince intervenes in the bitter altercation between Ganya Ivolgin and his sister, and himself receives the blow intended for the young woman. His response is to hide his face in his hands, turn to the wall, and say to Ganya in a breaking voice: "Oh, how ashamed you will be of what you've done" (8: 99).

This quality of the Prince's character is not motivated psychologically in any way; but, in a suggestively symbolic fashion, it is linked with certain leitmotifs. On the one hand, the Prince is much possessed by death: twice in these early pages he speaks of an execution he has recently witnessed; and he also recounts vividly the feelings and thoughts of a man first condemned to death by a firing squad and then unexpectedly reprieved. The first two descriptions dwell on the unutterable agony of the certainty of impending death—an agony mitigated only by the priest holding a cross to the lips of the condemned man as he mounts the scaffold. The third stresses the immense value assumed by each moment of existence as the end approaches, the infinite importance that suddenly seems to fill every precious instant of life.

Despite the obsessiveness of the death motif in these early pages, the Prince also admits to having been "happy" in the years just preceding his arrival in St. Petersburg; and the relation between these two motifs provides the deepest substratum of his values. The Prince's "happiness," we learn, began with his recovery from a state of epileptic stupor. A sudden shock of awareness woke him to the existence of the world in the form of something as humble and workaday as a donkey. The donkey, of course, has obvious Gospel overtones, which blend with the Prince's innocence and naiveté; and this patiently laborious animal also emphasizes, quite in accord with Christian kenoticism,* the absence of hierarchy in the Prince's ecstatic apprehension of the wonder of life. The same point is

---

* *Kenosis* is a theological term defined in Webster's International Dictionary as "Christ's action of 'emptying himself' on becoming man, humbling himself even to suffering death; also, any of the various Christological theories based upon this, as that in becoming incarnate the Son surrendered all or something of the divine attributes." One of the distinguishing aspects of the Russian religious tradition, as defined by its greatest modern historian, G. P. Fedotov, is the stress placed on this aspect of the Christian faith. It is the suffering and humiliated Christ, according to Fedotov's generally accepted thesis, who lies at the heart of Russian spirituality.

Writing of the first Russian martyred saints, the Princes Boris and Gleb, who were killed for political rather than religious reasons, Fedotov compares their meek acceptance of their fate with the teachings of the monk Theodosius, the founder of the Russian kenotic tradition. "Boris and Gleb followed Christ in their sacrificial deaths—the climax of His kenosis—as Theodosius did in His poverty and humiliations. . . . From the outside, it must give the impression of weakness as Theodosius' poverty must appear foolish to the outsider. Weak and foolish—such is Christ in his kenosis in the eyes of a Nietzsche just as he was in the eyes of the ancient pagan world." See G. P. Fedotov, *The Russian Religious Mind*, vol. 1 (New York, 1946), 130, and chap. 4 ("Russian Kenoticism").

Fedotov's reference to Nietzsche is by no means fortuitous. There is good reason to believe that Nietzsche was familiar with *The Idiot*, and that Dostoevsky's novel helped to shape his whole interpretation of Christianity. A convincing argument for this view, based on all the relevant material, has been advanced by the excellent German historian of religious philosophy Ernst Benz. See his *Nietzsche's Ideen zur Geschichte des Christentums und der Kirche* (Leiden, 1956), 92–103.

made in the Prince's remark that, in the early stages of his recovery, he had been consumed by restlessness and had thought to find "the key to the mystery of life" in his transcendent yearning to reach "that line where sky and earth meet," or in "some great town like Naples, full of palaces, noise, roar, life." But then, he adds, "I fancied that one might find a wealth of life even in prison" (8: 51).

Nothing arouses the suspicion and antagonism of the Epanchin sisters more than this expression of what seem to them pious platitudes. The haughty and arrogant Aglaya tells Myshkin quite bluntly that he resembles the widow of a government clerk who comes to beg from her family and whose sole aim in life is "to live as cheaply as possible . . . that's your wealth of life in prison; perhaps, too, your four years of happiness in the country for which you bartered your Naples." The girls see in the Prince's words only the utterances of a conventional "quietism" that complacently accepts evil and injustice as God's will and selfishly looks after its own creature comforts with a hypocritical sigh of commiseration. "If one shows you an execution or if one holds out one's finger to you," Aglaya bluntly tells Myshkin, "you will draw equally edifying reflections from both and be quite satisfied" (8: 51). This remark, however, leads to Myshkin's description of the agony of the condemned criminal kissing the cross; and the girls realize that no imputation of indifference or "quietism" can fairly be assigned as the source of his "happiness."

Far from being complacently indifferent to suffering—and particularly to the universal and ineluctable tragedy of death—Myshkin imaginatively re-experiences its tortures with the full range of his conscious sensibilities; but this does not prevent him, at the same time, from marveling in ecstasy before the joy and wonder of existence. Indeed, the dialectic of this unity is the point of the story about the man reprieved from execution—the story that embodies the most decisive and crucial event in Dostoevsky's own life. Most dreadful of all in those last moments, Myshkin says, was the regret of the poor victim over a wasted life and his frantic desire to be given another chance. "What if I were not to die? . . . I would turn every minute into an age; I would lose nothing, I would count every minute as it passed, I would not waste one!" But on being asked what happened to this man after his reprieve, Myshkin ruefully admits that his frenzied resolution was by no means carried out in practice.

> "Well, there you have it tried [says Alexandra Epanchina]. So it seems it's impossible really to live 'counting each moment.' For some reason it's impossible."
>
> "Yes, for some reason it's impossible," repeated Myshkin. "So it seemed to me also . . . and yet somehow I can't believe it." (8: 52–53)

Here is the point at which Myshkin's love of life fuses with his death-haunted imagination into the singular unity of his character. For Myshkin feels the miracle and wonder of life so strongly, he savors the inexpressible beauty and value of its every manifestation so deeply, precisely because he lives "counting each moment" as if it were the last. Both his joyous discovery of life and his profound intuition of death combine to make him feel each moment as one of absolute and immeasurable ethical choice and responsibility. The Prince, in other words, lives in the eschatological tension that was (and is) the soul of the primitive Christian ethic, whose doctrine of totally selfless *agape* was conceived in the same perspective of the imminent end of time.

Very little is said about God or religion directly in Part I; but there is a constant play of allusion around the Prince that places him in such a Christian context. Rogozhin, the merchant's son still close to the religious roots of Russian life, labels him a *yurodivi*, a holy fool; and though the gentlemanly and well-educated Prince bears no external resemblance to these often extravagantly eccentric figures, he does possess their traditional gift of spiritual insight. The Prince himself, speaking to General Epanchin's doorman of the inner suffering of a condemned man awaiting death, says passionately: "It was of this torture and of this agony that Christ spoke, too. No, you can't treat a man like that" (8: 21). Again, there is the mention of the cross, which the criminal going to the gallows kisses convulsively and which somehow helps him to sustain the torment. "But he was hardly aware of anything religious at this minute," the Prince adds, meaning that the consolation of the cross operated instinctively, below any level of conscious awareness or doctrinal commitment.[3] The idyllic New Testament note is struck very strongly in the Prince's story of the poor, abused, consumptive Swiss peasant girl Marie, who had been reviled and mistreated as a fallen woman, and whose last days the Prince and his band of children manage to brighten with the light of an all-forgiving love. In this way the figure of the Prince is surrounded with a pervasive Christian penumbra that continually illuminates his character and serves to locate the exalted nature of his moral and spiritual aspirations.

The story concerning Marie also brings sharply to the foreground another leitmotif, one that may be called the "two loves"—the one Christian, compassionate, nonpossessive, and universal, the other secular, ego-gratifying, possessive, and particular. Alexandra Epanchina's remark that the Prince must have been in "love" prompts him to tell the story of Marie. But while the young woman was referring to the second kind of normal, worldly love, the Prince's "love," as he takes care to explain, was only of the first type. Even the children clustered around the Prince were confused by this difference and happily believed that the Prince was in "love" with Marie when they saw him kissing her. But "I kissed her," he explains, "not because I was in love with her but because I was sorry for her, and because I had never, from the beginning, thought of her as guilty but only as unhappy" (8: 60). On first reading, one is tempted to take this inset story as a foreshadowing of what will redemptively occur in Myshkin's relations with Nastasya Filippovna; and it is possible—indeed, quite likely—that Dostoevsky may have initially meant it to be viewed as such. But the confusion of the children (and Myshkin is also a good bit of a child) will turn out rather to anticipate his own entrapment in the "two loves," whose mutually incompatible feelings and obligations will later result in the Prince's disastrous inability to choose between Nastasya and Aglaya.

3

The world into which the Prince is plunged upon his unexpected arrival in St. Petersburg is one that lives by standards directly opposite to those he embodies. It is a world locked in the grip of conflicting egoisms, a world in which the desire for wealth and social advantage, for sensual satisfaction, for power over others in one form or another, dominates and sweeps away all other humane and less self-centered feelings. All these motives are given full play in the intrigue, which parallels that of *La Dame aux camélias* by Dumas the younger, a work to which Dostoevsky alludes in the text and whose background presence serves to contrast the moral fiber of two different worlds: one French (and French-influenced Russian), the other purely Russian at its moral core. Part I of *The Idiot* turns on the plan to marry off Nastasya Filippovna with a handsome dowry, so as to allow Totsky—first her guardian, then her seducer—to wed the eldest Epanchin daughter. Much the same situation confronts the ex-courtesan Marguerite Gautier, *la dame aux camélias*, who, after being redeemed by love, is asked to abandon her devoted paramour so that his virginal sister can enter into a proper union. Marguerite "nobly" sacrifices herself on the altar of family pride and hypocritical virtue; but Nastasya refuses to be treated merely as a pawn in this sordid game of social chess. One can be sure that Dostoevsky, in thus reversing the situation, intends to contrast the moral superiority of Nastasya's inconsolable outrage at her violated human dignity with the docile acceptance of the tawdriest social prejudices by her French predecessor.*

* Totsky, of course, is a great admirer of Dumas the younger's book and declares that "it's a work which, in my opinion, is not destined to die or tarnish with age" (8: 128). Quite appropriately, the story he tells about "the worst of all the evil actions in his life" (8: 120) completely ignores his seduction of Nastasya and concerns the betrayal of a friend by obtaining a bouquet of camellias. It is no surprise that he is last seen becoming "fascinated by a Frenchwoman of the highest society, a marquise and a legitimist [royalist]" (8: 154).

No work of Dostoevsky's up to this time contains a comparable gallery of figures, among whom so many modulations and nuances of egoism are depicted with such vivid power. Every major character in the book (including the Prince, though this point has invariably been missed) is susceptible to the imperative promptings of the ego inherent in the human condition; but, of course, definite degrees of moral value are assigned to its various manifestations in each character. Lowest of all on the moral scale is the pursuit of some personal utilitarian advantage or the satisfaction of some physical appetite. To this level belongs the greedy Ganya Ivolgin, ready to sell his soul to marry the abused Nastasya and thereby gain the dowry that will enable him to attain the wealth he craves. Here too belong the epicurean sensualist Totsky (who does not feel the slightest twinge of conscience at having ruined Nastasya forever, though he behaves well according to his lights in trying to arrange her future) and the harmless, hen-pecked General Epanchin, who also has abortive designs on Nastasya. The pompous General, though, is elevated a notch by his genuine devotion to his family and by the remorse he feels for having unknowingly berated an old woman on the point of death.

A significantly higher position on the moral scale is attained by those characters whose egoism, even though taking a self-destructive form, testifies to a genuine capacity for some sort of moral-spiritual experience. In this category we find the passion-mad Rogozhin, ready to squander a fortune and endure any suffering if only he can win Nastasya's love. And here is also Nastasya herself, whose plunge into degradation is the supreme example in Dostoevsky's work of what he called "the egoism of suffering," that is, the egoism of the insulted and injured, who revenge themselves on the world by masochistically refusing all attempts to assuage their sense of injury.* A place here can also be assigned to the dying young consumptive Ippolit Terentyev, whose rage against God parallels Nastasya's against society, and who refuses to reconcile himself with a Creator responsible for the supreme injustice of bringing human consciousness to birth and then condemning it to death.

On the next level may be placed such characters as Aglaya Epanchina and her mother Lizaveta Prokofeyevna, Aglaya's wealthy and brilliant suitor Radomsky, and the Prince himself. The egoism of all these characters does not assume any overtly aggressive form and is combined with

---

* Dostoevsky first refers to this idea in *The Insulted and Injured* while depicting the character of little Nellie. The narrator speaks of her as having been "ill-treated," and "purposely trying to aggravate her wound by this mysterious behavior, this mistrustfulness of us all; as though she enjoyed her own pain, by this *egoism of suffering* [italics in text], if I may so express it. This aggravation of suffering and this revelling in it I could understand; it is the enjoyment of many of the insulted and injured, oppressed by destiny and smarting under the sense of injustice" (3: 385–86).

admirable qualities of mind and heart; but each displays an egoistic trait in one form or another. Aglaya's besetting sin is the prideful arrogance and hauteur of her youthful beauty. Her mother—whose impulsive and childlike directness of vicarious fellow feeling brings her closest of all to the Prince—still cannot resist giving way to the vanity of her birth and social position. Radomsky is the perfect model of a sympathetic and well-bred Russian gentleman, whose delicacy and courtesy is beyond reproach; but his worldly, skeptical intellect does not allow his emotions to go beyond the rules of decorum that protect his inner complacency. As for the Prince, his "egoism" will consist in the purest and most chaste of earthly attachments to Aglaya and the desire to marry.

A. Skaftymov, in what is still the best Russian analysis of *The Idiot*, has pointed out that each of the major characters is caught in an inner struggle between his or her own particular manifestation of egoism and a desire to overcome it in some appropriate form.[4] The role of the Prince in Part I, who brings with him the atmosphere of a sublimely selfless moral ideal, is to serve as a catalyst for each in this secret struggle. Rogozhin spontaneously offers to clothe the Prince properly on first meeting him. Even the busy financial operator General Epanchin cannot resist giving him twenty-five rubles, and he becomes concerned about the Prince's future. Nastasya, witnessing the incident of Ganya slapping the Prince, "was evidently stirred by a new feeling." A few moments later the Prince addresses her: "Surely you are not what you are pretending to be now. It isn't possible!" he cries reproachfully (8:99). Under the influence of these words Nastasya, who had come to pay back with contemptuous mockery the resentment of Ganya and the disapproval of his family, kisses the hand of Ganya's mother with remorse. Ganya himself later comes to apologize to the Prince and confesses that, while he plans to go through with the disgraceful marriage, it makes him feel like a scoundrel. "Scoundrels love honest men," he tells the Prince. "Don't you know that?" (8: 104).

The climax of the first part of the book is the tumultuous birthday party at Nastasya Filippovna's; all the characters gather here to await her decision on whether to accept Totsky's arrangement. Nastasya, of course, has carefully prepared the evening to culminate in the scandalous irruption of Rogozhin, whose brutal frankness in bidding for her favors (his hundred thousand rubles are wrapped in a copy of the *Stock Exchange News*) rips off the mask of hypocrisy from the whole sordid scheme. It is in the midst of this wild confusion that the moral appeal of the Prince's presence also receives its strongest affirmation. Nastasya turns to him to decide the question of her marriage to Ganya because, as she says, the Prince "is the first man I have met in my whole life that I believed in as a sincere friend. He believed in me at first sight and I in him" (8: 131). But while the Prince's word stops her from marrying Ganya, his own offer of marriage, as she rises to a paroxysm of bitter self-hatred, is powerless to prevent her from running off with Rogozhin. The masochistic satisfaction of debasing herself, and thus of symbolically debasing Totsky and all her respectable "admirers" at the same time, proves stronger than the Prince's appeal to her need for disinterested compassion and his recognition of her essential purity.

Nastasya is so majestic and overwhelming a figure in this early part of the book, and so much emphasis is placed on her victimization, that there has been an understandable tendency to see her only as a latter-day Iphigenia innocently doomed to destruction. It is quite clear, however, that Dostoevsky also wished to convey the festering and embittered pride that poisons all her relations with others, a pride that ultimately makes it impossible for her either to forgive herself or to accept the aid of the Prince. This aspect of her character is indicated very explicitly in Myshkin's reaction to Nastasya's picture, which is repeated twice in the early chapters. His first response is to the traces of suffering that he sees in her features; but he immediately adds: "It's a proud face, awfully proud, but I don't know whether she's kindhearted. Ah, if she were! That would rescue everything!" (8: 32). A second look at the photograph strengthens and sharpens this first impression: "There was a look of unbounded pride and contempt, almost hatred, in that face," Myshkin thinks, "and at the same time something confiding, something wonderfully simple-hearted. The contrast of these two features aroused a feeling of some sort of compassion" (8: 68). Both these aspects of Nastasya must always be kept in mind if we are to do justice to the complexity of Dostoevsky's artistic aims.

4

The first part of *The Idiot* was conceived and written as a self-contained unity and perhaps may best be read as an independent novella. It is clear from Dostoevsky's notebooks and letters that he had no satisfactory idea of how to continue. This uncertainty persists all through the middle sections of the book (Parts II and III), which are written from scene to scene with only the loosest thread of any central plot line. As a result, *The Idiot* possesses a kind of wayward charm and narrative spontaneity that is not artistically inharmonious with its thematic emphasis on the moral importance of impulsive sympathy and emotive frankness. However, the haphazardness of the action also makes this novel the most disorganized of Dostoevsky's longer works and the one most difficult to see in any unified perspective.

Essentially, the book now breaks down into three plot strands that alternate with one another more or less randomly. One continues the Nastasya-Myshkin-Rogozhin relationship, though this rivalry sinks almost totally out of sight for long stretches. A second is the Aglaya-Myshkin love affair (with a new character, Radomsky, as the putative third in the triangle). Dostoevsky makes a feeble attempt to link these two plot lines by the device of Nastasya's unsolicited attempt to abet the Aglaya-Myshkin romance from the wings. This effort allows for Nastasya's return into the action from time to time and prepares for the crucial confrontation scene between the two women; but Dostoevsky's refusal to present more of Nastasya, except through indirect accounts, weakens the effect of her reappearances and makes them shrilly melodramatic. Moreover, neither of these narrative components is more than superficially related to a third, which roughly comprises the lengthy scenes involving a group of "Young Nihilists," the "Necessary Explanation" of Ippolit Terentyev, the antic lucubrations of Lebedyev, and the marvelous mendacities of that inspired liar, General Ivolgin.

One's problems with *The Idiot* are further increased by the curious intermezzo of the five chapters that begin Part II, which present Myshkin—as well as other characters like Rogozhin and Lebedyev—in an unexpectedly new light. Nine months have elapsed between the end of Part I and the beginning of Part II, and important changes are supposed to have occurred in the Prince during this period; but Dostoevsky evades the challenge of describing this inner evolution. It is clear, in any case, that Myshkin is now being seen from a perspective for which there was no earlier foreshadowing. This becomes obvious in Chapter 5 of Part II, where Dostoevsky depicts the Prince in the state of mind engendered by an imminent epileptic fit. The contours of reality have here begun to cloud and blur for the poor Prince, and he finds it difficult to distinguish between what he ardently longs for and what the true situation (as regards Rogozhin and Nastasya) really is. Under the influence of this confusion, he convinces himself that Rogozhin would be capable of compassion for Nastasya, despite the mountains of humiliation that she has heaped on him as revenge for accepting his attentions. "Compassion would teach even Rogozhin and awaken his mind. Compassion was the chief and perhaps the only law of all human existence" (8: 192). The Myshkin of Part I would certainly have subscribed to this sentiment; but there has been no previous indication that his outlook was a sublime illusion distorting a true vision of reality. The Myshkin of Part I, on the contrary, possessed an ideal that gave him uncanny insight into the hearts of all those whose lives he touched.

This change in Myshkin is a function of the new role that is now assigned to the Prince's epilepsy. Epilepsy had no particular significance in Part I; Myshkin had awakened to the inestimable beauty of life—the foil for his universal compassion—only on *emerging* from his epileptic stupor. Now, however, it is in the "aura" of the moment before the epileptic onset that the Prince experiences "gleams and flashes of the highest sensation of life and self-consciousness" and is filled with a feeling, "unknown and undivined till then, of completeness, of proportion, of reconciliation, and of ecstatic devotional merging in the highest synthesis of life." This quasi-supernatural revelation becomes the source of the Prince's impassioned faith in a universal harmony; but this faith stands in absolute contradiction to the normal conditions of earthly existence. For the Prince was well aware that, if his epileptic attacks resumed, "stupefaction, spiritual darkness, idiocy stood before him conspicuously as the consequence of these 'higher moments'" (8: 188). Myshkin is thus inevitably doomed to catastrophe because the unearthly light of love and universal reconciliation cannot illuminate the fallen world of man for more than a dazzling and self-destructive instant.

From all the evidence, it is likely that Dostoevsky had no clear idea while writing Part I that the book was heading in this direction. The manner in which the Prince overcomes incomprehension and hostility in the earlier pages, along with the foreshadowing provided by the story of Marie, would seem to indicate an original inclination to stress the regenerating effects of Christian love. But from the beginning of Part II, the Prince is cast in a tragic (or, at least, self-sacrificial) role; the inner logic of his character now requires that the absolute of Christian love should conflict irreconcilably with the inescapable demands of normal human life. This new grasp of the Prince very probably accounts for the change in the tonality of these chapters, with their menacing Gothic atmosphere of mystery and impending doom—a tonality that contrasts sharply with the even, unclouded, novel-of-manners lighting of Part I, despite the heightening of tension in certain scenes.

This altered projection of the Prince also leads to the introduction of a new thematic motif, which first appears in the strange dialogue between Myshkin and Rogozhin about religious faith. Somewhat improbably, a copy of Holbein's *Dead Christ* turns up in Rogozhin's living room; and, with no transition whatever, the erstwhile drunken rowdy of Part I is shown as tormented, not only by Nastasya, but also by a crisis of religious doubt.* Holbein's picture, as we know, is an image of Christ after the Crucifixion as a bruised, bloody, and broken man, without a trace of supernatural or spiritual transcendence, though it is described as such only much later in the book. All we learn here is that "a painting of our Saviour who had just been taken from the Cross" has begun to undermine Rogozhin's religious faith; and Myshkin attempts to allay Rogozhin's disquietude by a lengthy and crucial speech.

---

* Dostoevsky betrays his uneasiness at this unexpected metamorphosis by the awkward comment that "in Moscow they [the Prince and Rogozhin] had met frequently and spent a great deal of time together, and there were moments during their meetings which had left an indelible impression on their hearts" (8: 171).

This speech consists of four anecdotes grouped in pairs, which illustrate that the human need for faith and for the moral values of conscience based on faith transcends both the plane of rational reflection and that of empirical evidence. On the one hand, there is the learned atheist whose arguments Myshkin cannot refute; on the other, there is the murderer who utters a prayer for forgiveness before slitting his victim's throat. There is the drunken peasant soldier selling his cross; but there is also the peasant woman, perhaps the soldier's wife, comparing a mother's joy in her child with God's gladness at the heartfelt prayer of a sinner. The point of these stories is to show religious faith and moral conscience existing as an ineradicable attribute in the Russian people independent of reason, or even of any sort of conventional social morality. "The essence of religious feeling," Myshkin explains, "does not come under any sort of reasoning or atheism, and has nothing to do with any crimes or misdemeanors. . . . But the chief thing is that you will notice it more clearly and quickly in the Russian heart than anywhere else" (8: 184).

This thematic motif is of key importance for understanding the remainder of the book. For in depicting religious faith and the stirrings of conscience as the totally irrational and instinctive needs of "the Russian heart," whose existence shines forth in the midst of everything that seems to deny or negate its presence, Dostoevsky is surely indicating the proper interpretation of Myshkin's ultimate failure and tragic collapse. The values of Christian love and religious faith that Myshkin embodies are, in other words, too deep a necessity of the Russian spirit to be negated by his practical failure, any more than they are negated by reason, murder, or sacrilege. If Holbein's picture and Myshkin's tirade are introduced so awkwardly and abruptly at this point, it is probably because Dostoevsky wished immediately to establish the framework within which the catastrophic destiny awaiting the Prince would be rightly understood.

The action of these chapters, which serves as a coda to the central triangle of Part I, clearly dramatizes the Prince's altered role. Myshkin's efforts to save the crazed Nastasya from destroying herself has placed him athwart the raging passion of Rogozhin, though the latter is fully aware that the Prince's "love" for Nastasya is not carnal but Christian. The drama of Rogozhin's inner struggle is played out by the Prince's obsession with Rogozhin's new knife, by the exchange of crosses between the two men, and by the blessing given the Prince by Rogozhin's mother. Rogozhin thus tries to place the Prince within a sacrosanct circle of religious awe that will shield him from the menacing knife; but it is the Prince himself who provokes Rogozhin by breaking his promise not to seek out Nastasya. The euphoric influence of the pre-epileptic "aura" betrays Myshkin into a heinous breach of faith that uncovers the dangerous discrepancy between the real and the ideal; and Myshkin's neglect of this gap leads to the flash of Rogozhin's upraised blade. It is symbolically appropriate that the onset of the sacred illness, whose first symptoms are responsible for Myshkin's delusion, should save him from its fatal consequence when he collapses before Rogozhin can strike his blow.

5

The Idiot is filled with all sorts of minor characters who are related to the main plot lines only by the most tenuous of threads and who take over the book on the slightest of pretexts. The plethora of such digressions no doubt accounts for Dostoevsky's feeling that he had lost control of the novel; but it is not too difficult to see the thematic rationale of most of these episodes, even if, structurally, they come and go with very little motivation. Many of them have the function of the comic interludes in medieval mystery plays, which parody the holy events with reverent humor and illustrate the universality of their influence. Others serve to bring out facets of the Prince that Dostoevsky was unable to develop from the central romantic intrigue.

Lebedyev, General Ivolgin, and the "boxer" Keller make up a group with common characteristics—a group that affirms, sometimes in a grotesquely comic form, that the inner moral struggle precipitated by the Prince in the major figures also can be found among the smaller fry. To be sure, Dostoevsky abandons all attempts to maintain any psychological verisimilitude in the case of Lebedyev and Keller; their mechanical shuttling between devotion to the Prince and petty swindling and skullduggery sometimes reaches the point of self-parody. This is particularly true of Lebedyev, transformed from the randy scrounger of Part I into the compassionate figure who shares Myshkin's horror of capital punishment and prays for the soul of the guillotined Mme Du Barry.

Without ceasing to be an unscrupulous scoundrel, ready to sell his soul for a ruble, Lebedyev also piously interprets the Apocalypse and rails against the "materialism" of the modern world in drunken tirades. His long, mock-serious historical "anecdote" on the famines of the Middle Ages is manifestly a burlesque exemplum of the significance of his character and that of others like him. Similar to the starving medieval "cannibal"—who devoured sixty fat, juicy monks in the course of his life and then, despite the prospect of the most horrible tortures, voluntarily confessed his crimes—the behavior of Lebedyev and his ilk testifies to the miraculous existence of conscience in the most unlikely places. Another example is the broken-down, Falstaffian General Ivolgin, whom Dostoevsky uses very effectively in Part I to parody the "decorum" surrounding Nastasya's life, and whose colossal mythomania is a protection against the sordid reality of his moral and social decline. The General dies of a stroke brought on by his torments over having stolen Lebedyev's wallet, torments caused not so much by the theft itself—he returned the wallet untouched—but by the fear that he would henceforth be regarded as a thief in his own family.

The most extensive of these digressions is Prince Myshkin's encounter with the group of so-called Young Nihilists, an episode that, in the special key required by *The Idiot*, continues Dostoevsky's polemic with the ideology of the radicals of the mid-1860s. As already mentioned, this subplot provides a parodistic answer to attacks made on Dostoevsky in the past, and particularly a tit-for-tat riposte to Saltykov-Shchedrin.* The Young Nihilists themselves are nothing but insolent little schoolboys, whose pathetic innocence and insecurity are strongly stressed as an implicit apologia for their aggressiveness. The point of this episode is to contrast the true selflessness of the Prince, based on Christian love, with a doctrine of social justice blind to its own egoistic roots.

Dostoevsky's merciless caricature of the Young Nihilists was, of course, a calculated affront to the susceptibilities of the radicals; but it has not been sufficiently noticed that he depicts their motives as entirely honorable. The claim they advance to a share of the Prince's fortune—on the ground that one of their number is the illegitimate son of the Prince's deceased benefactor—has no basis in truth. But, as the Prince points out, they had good reasons to believe they were rectifying a crying social injustice, and so no moral onus can be attached to their intent. What Dostoevsky attacks is not their aim to right a presumed social wrong but, rather, the unscrupulous means they adopt to attain their goal and the resulting inner contradiction in their position. For they scornfully reject all old-fashioned ideas of "morality," yet insist that the Prince behave like "a man of conscience and honor"; and they always assume that their own motives, though deriving from a philosophy of egoistic self-interest, are perfectly pure and untainted, and do not require the moral self-scrutiny demanded from their opponents.

What distinguishes the Prince, on the contrary, is precisely his capacity to respond in terms of the "other" and to avoid the pharisaism of the Young Nihilists' self-righteousness. He understands that the claimant to a share of his wealth, Burdovsky, has been downtrodden and humiliated all his life; and he forgives the young man's impossible behavior as a consequence of all the battering that his self-respect has been forced to endure. Instead of responding, like the other "respectable" characters, with contempt, outrage, or indignation, the Prince apologizes for having

* For more information, see *Dostoevsky: The Stir of Liberation* (Princeton, N.J., 1986), 208–210.

offended Burdovsky by offering in public to help him. Indeed, the figure of Burdovsky momentarily becomes a "double" for the Prince, who remembers how pathetic and ridiculous a figure he has often cut himself. Confronted for the first time in his life with truly active and selfless sympathy (the Prince matches words with deed), Burdovsky finally acknowledges a feeling of gratitude inconsistent with his ideology ("I regard it as a weakness," he writes) (8: 266). By this admission, he overcomes the egoism of his resentments and enters the world of mutual moral obligations.

The acridly satirical scenes involving the Young Nihilists are perhaps too didactic to serve Dostoevsky's purpose successfully; and he is always least convincing when he offers his moral-religious point of view as an answer to concrete social dilemmas. Far more effective is the spotlight focused on the dying young consumptive Ippolit Terentyev, who detaches himself from the group of Young Nihilists to rise to major heights and become the first in Dostoevsky's remarkable gallery of metaphysical rebels. For Ippolit is revolting not against the iniquities of a social order but, anticipating Kirillov and Ivan Karamazov, against a world in which death, and hence immitigable human suffering, is an inescapable reality. With Ippolit, Dostoevsky picks up a major thematic motif of Part I and presents Myshkin with the strongest challenge to the "happiness" that the Prince had declared himself to have discovered. Like Burdovsky, Ippolit is another quasi double for Myshkin—one who shares his obsession with death and his ecstatic sense of life, yet lacks the Prince's sustaining religious faith in an ultimate world-harmony. For this reason, Ippolit cannot achieve the self-transcendence that is the secret of the Prince's moral effulgence and the response he evokes in others.

Ippolit's semi-hysterical "Necessary Explanation" is carefully composed to contain all the main features of Myshkin's Weltanschauung, but combined with an *opposite* human attitude. His preoccupation with death does not lessen but strengthens his self-concern, and turns it into a pathetic megalomania, as can be seen from the touchingly incongruous epigraph, "après moi le deluge!" that he appends to his "Necessary Explanation" (8: 321). He reveres the infinite beauty and value of life ("it is life, life that matters, life alone," he exclaims); but so precious does the gift of life *in itself* seem to the dying boy that he simply denies the existence of other evils and misfortunes less absolute than death (8: 327). "I knew one poor fellow, who, I was told afterwards, died of hunger, and I remember that it made me furious: if it had been possible to bring the poor devil back to life, I believe I'd have him executed" (8: 326). Instinctively, Ippolit's feelings are on the side of the victims of social injustice (for example, the story of the starving doctor); and when he is carried on the current of such benevolent feelings, he admits "that I forgot my death sentence, or rather did not come to think of it and even did work" (8: 328). Only such concern with others can ease the tragedy of Ippolit's last days; but he finally abandons all such endeavors to brood over his own condition. Death, the universal portion, he comes to regard as a personal insult and "humiliation" aimed at him by "nature," or rather by the Creator of a world that requires the individual's consent to the indignity and injustice of being destroyed.

The thematic contrast between Ippolit and the Prince is brought out most forcefully by their differing reactions to the key religious symbol of the book: Holbein's *Dead Christ*, whose unvarnished realism Ippolit finally expatiates on at length. Holbein's picture had led Myshkin to affirm the irrational "essence of religious feeling" as an ineradicable component of the human spirit; but for the Young Nihilist, it is only a confirmation of his own sense of the cruel meaninglessness of life. To Ippolit, the picture conveys a sense of nature "in the form of a huge machine of the most modern construction," which "has aimlessly clutched, crushed, and swallowed up a great priceless Being [Christ], a Being worth all of nature and its laws, worth the whole earth, which was created perhaps solely for the advent of that Being" (8: 339). Ippolit simply cannot grasp how the first disciples of Christ, who witnessed in reality what he sees only at the remove of art, could still have continued to believe in the triumph over death that Christ proclaimed; but this is precisely the mystery of faith to which Ippolit is closed, and whose absence poisons his last days with bitterness and despair.

Ippolit, like the other characters, instinctively regards the Prince as the standard for his own conscience. The Prince's "humility," however, is the ideological antithesis of Ippolit's "revolt," and it is Myshkin who must bear the brunt of the Young Nihilist's vituperative shifts of feeling. "Can't I simply be devoured without being expected to praise what devours me?" Ippolit asks caustically, in rejecting the Prince's "Christian meekness" (8: 343). This question comes from such a depth of suffering in Ippolit that no offense on his part can lessen his right to an absolute claim on the indulgence of the other characters. For as Myshkin tells the ironically tolerant and distant Radomsky, it is not enough simply to be willing to overlook Ippolit's offensiveness out of condescending pity: "The point is that you, too, should be willing to accept forgiveness from him"—an unprecedented rebuke from the Prince. "How do I come in?" asks the bewildered Radomsky. "What wrong have I done him?" (8: 280). None whatsoever, to be sure; but the Prince understands that, for Ippolit, the untroubled possession of life by others is a supreme injustice, which should burden them with guilt and a sense of moral obligation.

The doomed and suffering Ippolit is thus entitled to boundless tolerance and compassion; but he too has an obligation to overcome his envy and resentment of those who, though now untouched, will eventually share his fate. Ippolit knows, as he tells the Prince, that he is "unworthy" of what could be the purifying experience of his death; he uses its imminence only to harass and discomfit the living, and he is unable to conquer his malice up to the very last. Hence the Prince's moving and beautiful reply to Ippolit's question on how best to die: "Pass by us and forgive us our happiness," says Myshkin in a low voice (8: 433). Hence, too, the macabre quality of gallows humor in several of the scenes with Ippolit, the grating callousness that some of the characters display toward his plight. No pages of Dostoevsky are more original than those in which he tries to combine the utmost sympathy for Ippolit with a pitiless portrayal of what may be called "the egoism of dying." Dostoevsky wishes to show how the egocentricity that inspired Ippolit's "revolt" also impels him to a behavior that cuts off the very sympathy and love he so desperately craves. By turns pathetic and febrilely malignant, the unfortunate boy dies offstage, unconsoled and inconsolable, "in a state of terrible agitation" (8: 508).

6

The major action of *The Idiot* after Part I centers on the Prince's budding romance with Aglaya Epanchina. The Prince does not cease to preoccupy himself with Nastasya; but though he continues to pity her with all his heart, there is, nonetheless, a significant change in his attitude. Nastasya's behavior is now portrayed as alternating between extravagant displays of reverence for moral purity—revealed in the hysterical bathos of her letters to Aglaya, which deludedly idealize her rival as capable of the totally selfless love to which Myshkin aspires—and continual relapses into the masochistic cultivation of her own sense of depravity. "Do you know," the Prince tells Aglaya, "that she seems to derive some dreadful unnatural pleasure from the continual consciousness of shame, a sort of revenge on someone" (8: 361). The Prince at last becomes persuaded that Nastasya literally has gone mad, especially when he hears of her letters; and he speaks of them, almost on the point of tears, as "proof of her insanity" (8: 362). It is likely that Dostoevsky's continual later emphasis on Nastasya's "madness," which has the effect of absolving her of responsibility, is intended to hold the balance with this stronger stress on her self-destructive "egoism."

Prince Myshkin's note to Aglaya at the beginning of Part II clearly expresses his attraction for the haughty and high-spirited beauty; but it is only in Chapter 7 that their eccentric courtship is solidly established in the foreground. By reading Pushkin's poem "The Poor Knight" in the Prince's presence, with obvious reference to his intervention on behalf of

Nastasya, Aglaya reveals to what extent her lofty imagination has become inflamed by the Prince's self-sacrificing magnanimity toward a victimized "fallen woman." This open display of admiration, which scandalizes the assembled company and terribly embarrasses the Prince, strikes the note on which their relation will henceforth be depicted. Because the Prince's humility and total lack of self-assertiveness make it impossible for him to act in his own interest, it is Aglaya who must take the initiative; and the manner in which she forces his hand, with a combination of girlish high spirits, temperamental petulance, and true feminine instinct, results in some of Dostoevsky's most engaging scenes.

Aglaya's whole relation to the Prince, however, is tainted with misunderstanding from the very start. To Aglaya, Myshkin is the Poor Knight of Pushkin's poem—a poem in which she sees united "in one striking figure the grand conception of the platonic love of medieval chivalry, as it was felt by a pure and lofty knight," a knight who was a "serious and not comic" Don Quixote. (8: 207). These words have usually been taken as objectively relevant to the Prince; but although they apply to him in part, their more important function is to bring out the illusory nature of Aglaya's image of his character. Certainly one can say of Myshkin:

> He had had a wondrous vision:
> Ne'er could feeble human art
> Gauge its deep, mysterious meaning,
> It was graven on his heart.

But nothing could be less characteristic of the Prince than the deeds of military valor performed during the Crusades by the Poor Knight in the service of the Christian faith:

> *Lumen coeli*, Sancta Rosa!
> Shouted he with flaming glance
> And the thunder of his menace
> Checked the Mussulman's advance.
>
> (8: 209)

The Poor Knight, in other words, represents the Christian ideal of the Catholic West in its days of glory and in all its corrupting confusion of spiritual faith and temporal power. The Russian Christian ideal, as Dostoevsky understood it, sharply splits off one from the other and accepts all the paradoxical and even demeaning social consequences of the Prince's humility, meekness, and all-forgiving love.

Aglaya's love for the Prince is thus vitiated from the beginning by this misconception of the true nature of his values—a misconception that mirrors her own character, with its combination of ardent idealism and personal arrogance and pride. Aglaya is capable of loving the purity of spirit that she finds in the Prince, but at the same time she wishes her ideal to be socially imposing and admired by the world. This fusion had attracted her to militant Catholicism, and she misguidedly seeks for it in the Prince. By introducing the Young Nihilist scenes right after the "Poor Knight" reading, Dostoevsky forcefully dramatizes the opposition between Aglaya's image and the actual values that inspire the Prince's conduct. The combative Aglaya welcomes the intrusion of the group because, as she says, "they are trying to throw mud at you, Prince, you must defend yourself triumphantly, and I am awfully glad for you" (8: 213). Far from emerging "triumphant," though, Myshkin reacts to insult and provocation with a docility and passivity that drive Aglaya into a towering rage. "If you don't throw out these nasty people at once, I shall hate you all my life, all my life!" she whispers to the Prince "in a sort of frenzy" (8: 250).

Aglaya will continue to exhibit the same sort of dualism: irresistibly attracted by the Prince's spiritual elevation and selflessness, she cannot reconcile herself to the ludicrous figure that he presents because of his lack of pride and normal social self-regard. When the Prince, in defending Nastasya, insults an Army officer who asks for his name, Aglaya automatically assumes that he will fight a duel and instructs him on how to load a pistol; but the Prince never has any intention of engaging in such a conventionally heroic enterprise. Similarly, before the party scene at which he will be introduced officially as Aglaya's betrothed, she tries to have a "serious" talk with him to make sure that he will not commit any *faux pas*. Nonetheless, once more under the influence of the pre-epileptic "aura," the Prince launches into a Slavophil attack on Roman Catholicism as "unchristian" because "Roman Catholicism believes that the Church cannot exist on earth without universal political power" (8: 450). He is thus denouncing in Roman Catholicism the very confusion of the temporal and the spiritual that, on the personal level, Aglaya wishes him to incarnate. It is no hazard that this speech appears precisely at the point where his personality is shown as most hopelessly incompatible with her requirements.

Myshkin's disastrous harangue also incorporates other motifs of great importance to Dostoevsky. The Russian need for religious faith is reasserted yet again as Myshkin describes the Russian proclivity to be converted to false faiths—such as Roman Catholicism or atheism. "Russian atheists and Russian Jesuits are the outcome not only of vanity," he declares, "not only of a bad, vain feeling but also of spiritual agony, spiritual thirst, a craving for something higher ... for a faith in which they have ceased to believe because they have never known it! ... And Russians do not merely become atheists, but they invariably *believe* in atheism, as though it were a new religion without noticing that they are putting their faith in a negation" (8: 452). Myshkin here utters some of Dostoevsky's profoundest convictions, which the author well knew would be looked on by the majority of his compatriots with the same rather frightened and pitying incredulity as that displayed by the Epanchins' guests.

Despite the catastrophe of the Prince's outburst and epileptic attack at the engagement party, Aglaya is still capable of conquering her dismay; for her the ultimate test of Myshkin will be his relation with Nastasya. No more than Rogozhin can Aglaya view the Prince's "Christian love" for Nastasya—his boundless pity and sense of obligation—as anything but a threat to her own undisputed possession of the man she loves (though it was the Prince's attitude toward Nastasya that had first stirred Aglaya's admiration). In the powerful confrontation scene between the two women, each tells the other some harsh truths; but Aglaya's cruel vindictiveness, from the height of her virtue and social position, is less forgivable than the delirious rage of Nastasya's self-defense in invoking her claim on the Prince. The climax of the scene finds Myshkin called upon to choose between the two women and utterly unable to do so. Nastasya's "frenzied, despairing face" causes him to reproach Aglaya for her cruelty to the "unhappy creature"; Aglaya looks at him with "such suffering and at the same time such boundless hatred that, with a gesture of despair, he cried out and ran to her, but it was already too late." He is stopped by Nastasya's grasp, and remains to comfort the fainting and half-demented creature whose tortured face had once "stabbed his heart forever" (8: 475).

The Prince thus finds himself helplessly caught in the rivalry of clashing egoisms, and he responds, on the spur of the moment, to the need that is most immediate and most acute. Each woman has a differing but equally powerful claim on his devotion; and his incapacity to make a choice dramatizes the profoundest level of Dostoevsky's thematic idea. For the Prince is the herald of a Christian love that is nothing if not universal; yet he is also a man, not a supernatural being—a man who has fallen in love with a woman as a creature of flesh and blood. The necessary dichotomy of these two divergent loves inevitably involves him in a tragic imbroglio from which there is no escape, an impasse in which the universal obligation of compassion fatally crosses the human love that is the Prince's morally blameless form of "egoism."

Three years earlier, sitting at the bier of his first wife, Dostoevsky had meditated on the situation to which he gives artistic life in Myshkin's tormented irresolution. "The family—this is the most sacred possession of man on earth" he had noted, "for by this law of nature man attains development (i.e., the succession of generations), the goal. But at the same time, by this very law of nature, in the name of the final ideal goal, man must unceasingly negate it (Duality)." In the same document, Dostoevsky states that Christ had given mankind only one clue to the future nature of this "final ideal goal" of humanity—a clue contained in the Gospel of Saint Matthew: "They neither marry, nor are given in marriage, but are as angels in Heaven" (20: 173). The "final ideal goal" of humanity is thus the total fusion of the individual Ego with All in a mystic community literally (and not metaphorically) freed from the constraints and limits of the flesh; it is the transcendent "synthesis" that Myshkin had glimpsed in the ravishment of the pre-epileptic "aura."* Hence even the most chaste and innocent of earthly loves constitutes an abrogation of the universal law of love, whose realization, prefigured by Christ, is man's ultimate, supernatural goal. The closing pages of *The Idiot* strikingly present this insoluble conflict between the human and the divine that Dostoevsky felt so acutely, and which could achieve its highest pitch of expressiveness and poignancy only as embodied in such a "perfectly beautiful man" as Prince Myshkin.

7

The three concluding chapters that follow the confrontation scene contain a significant shift in the narrative point of view; and this shift is closely correlated with the unprecedented conflict focused through Myshkin's remarkable character. Up until these chapters, the omniscient narrator has usually been able to describe and explain what the Prince is thinking and feeling. Now, however, the narrator confesses that he is unable to understand Myshkin's behavior and must confine himself to a "bare statement of facts"; "we find it difficult in many instances," he says, "to explain what occurred" (8: 475). The facts referred to are these: on the one hand, Myshkin has become the fiancé of Nastasya, and the plans for their wedding are going forward; but, on the other, the Prince still tries to visit Aglaya as if nothing had changed, and he cannot comprehend why the impending marriage should affect his relation to her. "It makes no difference that I'm going to marry her [Nastasya]," he tells Radomsky. "That's nothing, nothing" (8: 483). The strain of the Prince's impossible position has finally caused him to lose all touch with reality. No longer able to distinguish between his vision of universal love and the necessary exclusions and limiting choices of life, he is presented as having passed altogether beyond the bounds of accepted social codes. To express this transgression, Dostoevsky adopts the guise of the baffled and puzzled narrator, whose bewilderment accentuates the impossibility of measuring the Prince's comportment by any conventional standard.

---

* For a more extensive discussion of this diary entry, the only explicit and detailed statement we have of Dostoevsky's religious convictions, see *Dostoevsky: The Stir of Liberation* (Princeton, N.J., 1986), 296–309.

This ever-widening distance between the Prince and the world, the paradox of his behavior, is then placed at the center of a lengthy dialogue with Radomsky. The elegant man of the world gently but firmly criticizes Myshkin for having failed to side with Aglaya; and he analyzes the Prince's behavior toward Nastasya both as the result of inexperience and as a consequence of "the huge mass of intellectual convictions which you, with your extraordinary honesty, have hitherto taken for real, innate, intuitive convictions." Radomsky detects an "element of *conventional democratic* feeling" in the Prince's attitude toward Nastasya, "the fascination, so to say, of 'the woman question'" (8: 481). The narrator, unexpectedly, prefaces such words by associating himself firmly with Radomsky's observations: "We are in complete sympathy with some forcible and psychologically deep words of Evgeny Pavlovich, spoken plainly and unceremoniously . . . in conversation with Myshkin" (8: 479).*

How is one to interpret this disconcerting volte-face of the narrator? Certainly not as Dostoevsky's repudiation of his hero, but rather as a calculated shift in narrative stance from relative omniscience to ignorance and incomprehension; and this shift is meant to correspond with the inevitable trivialization of the Prince's plight. For the ideas that Radomsky expresses are precisely the same as the wild rumors and ridiculous conjectures floating around Pavlovsk about the events in which the Prince has been involved. Like Radomsky, who is even hinted to have aided the spread of such rumors, the gossips attribute the Prince's conduct to "the gratification of marrying a 'lost' woman in sight of all the world and thereby proving his conviction that there were neither 'lost' nor 'virtuous' women . . . [since] he did not believe in the old conventional division, but had faith only in 'the woman question'; that in fact a 'lost' woman was, in his eyes, somewhat superior to one not lost" (8: 477).

The moral profundities of the Prince's conflict are thus distorted and reduced to the level of spiteful tittle-tattle and current clichés over female emancipation; and the narrator's declared agreement with Radomsky only adds to the melancholy irony of the Prince's total isolation. Like Abraham in Kierkegaard's *Fear and Trembling*, who alone hears the secret commandment of God to sacrifice his son, the Prince has now become a knight of faith whose obedience to the divine makes his conduct appear to others, more often than not, a sign of madness. Quite appropriately, Lebedyev comes to this conclusion and tries to have the Prince

* Robin Feuer Miller has argued that, in various ways, Dostoevsky begins to undermine the reader's trust in the narrator starting with Part III. This may well be so, and her perceptive analysis is of the greatest interest; but the narrator's earlier uncertainties and inconsistencies are qualitatively different from the adoption of Radomsky's belittling point of view. See Robin Feuer Miller, *Dostoevsky and "The Idiot"* (Cambridge, Mass., 1981), chap. 4.

committed to a mental institution before the wedding ceremony. Radomsky too shares the same conviction that the Prince "was not in his right mind"; but his thoughts come closer to Dostoevsky's thematic mark: "And how can one love two at once? With two different kinds of love? That's interesting . . . poor idiot" (8: 485).

The closing pages show us the Prince helplessly trapped between the conflicting claims of his human nature and his divine task, deprived of all comprehension and almost all sympathy, and overwhelmed by events over which he has no control. His grasp of the real world becomes weaker and weaker as all hope of human happiness for him vanishes irrevocably; he now lives at the mercy of the shifting moods of the unbalanced Nastasya, the spiteful whims of Ippolit, and the antic machinations of Lebedyev. At the end his personality simply dissolves, abandoning all claims for itself and becoming a function of the needs of others. The Prince's final destruction is brought about by the murder of Nastasya, who, in a last access of remorse over having ruined his life, flees to the destruction she knows awaits her with Rogozhin. In the eerie and unforgettable death-watch scene over Nastasya's corpse, the Prince loses himself completely in the anguish of the half-mad Rogozhin and sinks definitively into the mental darkness that he had long feared would be the price of his visionary illuminations. So ends the odyssey of Dostoevsky's "perfectly beautiful man," who had tried to live in the world by the divine light of the apocalyptic transfiguration of mankind into a universal harmony of love.

Two or three details in these final pages deserve a brief additional mention. One is the underscored reference to *Madame Bovary*, which Myshkin finds in Nastasya's room and insists on carrying away in his pocket. Are we not invited here to compare the agonies of Nastasya's tortured conscience with the despairing cynicism of Flaubert's French adulteress, who is driven to suicide by the ignominy of her life but not by any moral revulsion or change of heart? If so, this moment would reinforce the implied comparison already made with *La Dame aux camélias* to the detriment of the European moral consciousness. The anti-European note is struck again in relation to Aglaya, who continued to seek her ideal in the worldly and glamorous form she had been unable to find in the Prince. It should be no surprise, if we have read *The Idiot* aright, to learn that Aglaya marries a shady Polish Catholic émigré-adventurer and quondam nobleman who "had fascinated [her] by the extraordinary nobility of his soul, which was torn with patriotic anguish" over the unhappy fate of his native land, but who then, appropriately, turns out to be a complete fake (8: 509).

The last words, though, are given to Aglaya's mother, Lizaveta Prokofeyevna, the character who has always been closest in spirit to the Prince but has managed to keep her feet successfully on the ground. Her typically explosive and matronly denunciation of Europe—"they can't make decent bread; in winter they are frozen like mice in a cellar"—concludes the book with a down-to-earth affirmation of the same faith in Russia that Myshkin had expressed in the Messianic eloquence of his ecstatic rhapsodies (8: 510).

8

The Idiot is perhaps the most original of Dostoevsky's great novels, and certainly the most artistically uneven of them all. It is not hard to point out its flaws if we take the nineteenth-century conception of the well-made novel as a standard; more difficult is to explain why it triumphs so effortlessly over all the inconsistencies and awkwardnesses of its structure and motivation. One reason, perhaps, is that the very gaucheries and grotesqueness of its treatment of plot and character, after several readings, generate an intriguing quality of their own. Its appeal might be compared with the effects created by such artists as Rouault and Chagall, who also play fast and loose with realistic conventions and return to earlier naive forms of folk art to revive feelings of religious awe and wonder. Moreover, as we have seen, Dostoevsky poured himself more personally and unconstrainedly into this book than into any other; readers sense they come very close in its pages to touching the quick of his own values, and so perhaps are inclined to overlook technical defects, or even to take them as a testimony of authenticity. Whatever its faults, *The Idiot* also contains some of the greatest scenes that Dostoevsky ever wrote: Nastasya Filippovna's birthday party; the black comedy, anticipating Beckett, of the reading of Ippolit's "Necessary Explanation"; the tenderly touching tryst in the park between Myshkin and Aglaya; the haunting, dreamlike vigil of Rogozhin and the Prince over Nastasya's corpse. Nor can any other Christ figure in modern literature rival Prince Myshkin in the purity of his appeal.

Taken in the perspective of Dostoevsky's work as a whole, *The Idiot* may also well be considered his most courageous creation. As we know, the inspiration for his most important works in this period was provided primarily by his antagonism to the doctrines of Russian Nihilism. The underground man and Raskolnikov had assimilated its ideas into their hearts and minds, and Dostoevsky dramatized the disastrous aftermaths of such acceptance when taken to their ultimate limit in action. His next major novel will renew the same attack even more ferociously, and *The Idiot* is often contrasted with these works because Prince Myshkin, far from being a member of the intelligentsia spiritually infected by Nihilism, is rather an iconic image of Dostoevsky's own highest Christian ideal. In fact, however, there is much less structural difference between *The Idiot* and these other works than may appear at first sight.

For with an integrity that cannot be too highly praised, Dostoevsky fearlessly submits his *own* most hallowed convictions to the same test that he had used for those of the Nihilists—the test of what they would mean for human life if taken seriously and literally, and lived out to their full extent as guides to conduct. With exemplary honesty, he portrays the moral extremism of his own eschatological ideal, incarnated by the Prince, as being equally incompatible with the normal demands of ordinary social life, and constituting just as much of a disruptive scandal as the appearance of Christ himself among the complacently respectable Pharisees. But whatever the tragedy that Prince Myshkin and those affected by him may suffer in *this* world, he brings with him the unearthly illumination of a higher one that all feel and respond to; and it is this response to "the light shining in the darkness" that for Dostoevsky provided the only ray of hope for the future.

CHAPTER 18

Historical Visions

The termination of *The Idiot* allowed Dostoevsky, who had been writing steadily for a year and a half, to catch his breath for a moment; but it also brought new anxieties in its wake. Dostoevsky's only source of income was publication, and the end of *The Idiot* meant the end of the monthly stipend he had been receiving from Katkov. To make matters worse, Dostoevsky calculated that the amount of copy he had furnished still left him with a debt to Katkov's journal of one thousand rubles. Money had always been forthcoming in answer to his requests, but now he had no idea what his relation to the journal would be in the future. "I am free beginning in January," he wrote Maikov, "but in my position I cannot sit with hands folded: I have to live and to pay my debts."[1] Dostoevsky thus now begins to mention all sorts of new plans and projects, and the relation of these crisscrossing ideas to the works he then wrote is sometimes difficult to unravel.

Both Dostoevsky and his wife yearned to return to Russia, but residence in Florence was much less oppressive than in Dresden or Geneva and offered numerous cultural compensations. "Often the two of us would go to the Pitti Palace," Anna wrote in her *Reminiscences*, "where he [Dostoevsky] was entranced by Raphael's painting, *Madonna della Sedia*. The same artist's other painting, *St. John in the Desert*, which hangs in the Uffizi Gallery, also enchanted him, and he always stood before it a long time. After visiting the art gallery he would invariably go to see the statue of the Medici Venus, located in the same building. . . . My husband considered this statue a work of genius."[2] The Dostoevskys also explored the numerous architectural masterpieces dotting the city, and he was particularly captivated by Ghiberti's famous bas-reliefs on the bronze doors of the Baptistery. "He assured me [Anna] that if he should happen to get rich he would certainly buy photographs of these doors, in their actual size if possible, and hang them in his study where he could admire them."[3]

The Vieusseux library was also a place of refuge for Dostoevsky, who assiduously read the Russian newspapers there every day and followed from afar the events and clash of opinions in his homeland. For recreation, he borrowed some works of Voltaire and Diderot from the collection (unfortunately, Anna does not give their titles) and perused them through the winter. Most important of all, Anna became aware in January that "God had blessed our marriage and that we might hope to have another child."[4] This welcome news helped lift Dostoevsky's gloomy spirits, still weighed down by the loss of Sonya, and the couple could now look forward to a happier family future instead of brooding sadly over the past. Anna recalls how they even began to joke about their unrelieved poverty and to refer to each other as Mr. and Mrs. Micawber (a name that Dostoevsky applies to himself in a letter a year later). But their destitution was no laughing matter, and, along with plans for future works, Dostoevsky also pondered various ways of escaping his unenviable fate of being a literary proletarian forced to write for wages.

2
———

Even before finishing the fourth part of *The Idiot*, and in the same letter in which he defines his "fantastic realism," Dostoevsky outlines to Maikov the idea for a major new novel. (Indeed, this outline immediately precedes the statement of his aesthetic, which may have emerged not only as a response to criticisms of *The Idiot* but also as a generalization of the approach to Russian life and reality expressed in his new creative project.) Dostoevsky had in mind

a huge novel whose title will be *Atheism* (for God's sake, let this remain between us); but before getting to work on it, I shall have to read practically a whole library of atheists, Catholics, and Orthodox Christians. It will not be ready, even with complete financial security while working, before at least two years. The main figure is: a Russian of our society, *of a certain age*, not very well educated but not uneducated either, not without rank—*suddenly*, already advanced in years, he loses faith in God. All his life he was concerned only with his service, did not go off the beaten path, and for forty-five years was in no way other than ordinary. (The psychological clue: deep feeling, a man and a Russian man.) His loss of faith in God has a colossal effect on him. (The proper action of the novel, the surroundings—are very variegated.) He darts about among the young generation, the atheists, the Slavs and Europeans, the Russian fanatics, anchorites, the priests; he is strongly affected, among others, by a group of Jesuits, propagandizers, Poles; he slips away from them to the depths of the flagellants—and in the end finds Christ and the Russian God. (For God's sake, don't tell anyone; this is how I feel: let me write this final novel, and even if I die—I will have spoken out about everything.)[5]

Dostoevsky never wrote such a novel; but this outline soon developed into a much longer work that also remained unwritten, *The Life of a Great Sinner* (*Zhitie Velikogo Greshnika*), and both then fed into *The Devils*. Dostoevsky's ambition, it is clear, was to present a large fresco of Russian opinions and religious experiences, and to dramatize his main character in terms of such competing views and ideologies (including those of "the young generation").

Other passages in the same letter show how eagerly Dostoevsky was then scanning the cultural horizon for signs that the evolution he wished to depict in his main character (and which roughly corresponds to the pattern of his own inner history) was also a more general phenomenon portending a renewed and more affirmative phase of Russian culture. N. N. Strakhov had written to Dostoevsky a month earlier about the new journal *Dawn*, urging him once again to become a contributor and enticing him to consent by various items of information. On closer acquaintance with the publisher Kashpirev, Strakhov had discovered that he was "a pupil of *Time* and *Epoch*, that he was educated by them, as other Russians had been by *The Contemporary*, *The Russian Word*, etc." Moreover, the first issue would contain, besides a new novel of Pisemsky's, a lengthy work by Nikolay Danilevsky, which Strakhov called "a complete doctrine, Slavophilism with a better defined and clearer shape."[6]

Danilevsky, an ex-Fourierist involved in the Petrashevsky case, had been given only a light sentence of administrative exile. Afterward, making a name for himself as a naturalist and government expert on Russian fisheries, he had vanished from public view. Maikov had mentioned his name and new work in a much earlier letter, and Dostoevsky now replies to him: "I was very pleased, among other things, to hear the news [from Strakhov] about the articles of Danilevsky—I confess that I haven't heard anything about Danilevsky since 1849, but I sometimes thought about him. I recall what a fanatical Fourierist he was. And now from Fourierism he returns to Russia, becomes Russian again and loves his country again and its essence! That's how you recognize an honest man! Turgenev, from being a Russian writer, became a German—that's how you recognize a worthless man!"[7]

The name of Turgenev evidently evokes that of Belinsky, whom Dostoevsky now places in the same negative category, and he speaks of his old mentor with an insulting harshness that he would later considerably soften. "Equally, I will never believe the words of the late Apollon Grigoryev that Belinsky would have ended as a Slavophil. Belinsky would not have ended this way. He was only a louse—nothing more. A great poet in his time; but he was not capable of developing any further." And in a few sentences that already anticipate some of the caustic treatment of radical types in *The Devils*, Dostoevsky blocks in a humiliating future for a Belinsky who had survived to go into exile and dragged out his days as one of the Russian radicals scurrying about in Geneva. "He would have ended by becoming an errand boy for some local Mme Gegg [a well-known Swiss feminist—J.F.], her adjutant on the woman question at meetings and would lose his command of Russian without being able for all that to learn German."[8] Belinsky, though deeply influenced by German philosophy, had notoriously remained ignorant of the language.

Those incapable of what Dostoevsky called "development"—that is, the return to their Russian roots—were thus doomed to become the servile instruments of their Western inspirers. But not all of Russian culture was condemned to such a fate; and just as Dostoevsky was consoled by the news about Danilevsky, whose book he would read with the intensest interest, so too was he encouraged in his hopes for the future by learning about another such figure—unknown to him till then—through the pages of *The Russian Messenger*. The July and August issues, which contained articles on the publications of Old Believers abroad, had given special attention to the writings of one K. E. Golubov, the editor and chief contributor of a journal issued in Prussia and called *Truth* (*Istina*). Golubov, a self-educated theologian and peasant philosopher, was the disciple of an Old Believer patriarch known as Pavel Prussky. Ample extracts from Golubov's writings were included in the article, among them a correspondence with N. P. Ogarev, who, as we know, had edited with Kelsiev a publication intended to win over Old Believers to the cause of social revolution. In 1868 Golubov and his master Pavel had returned to Russia and rejoined the ranks of Orthodoxy.

Just after belaboring Belinsky, Dostoevsky singles out Golubov as the harbinger of a rebirth amidst the sterilities of the Russian cultural landscape. "And do you know who the new Russian people are? There is that peasant [*muzhik*], a former *raskolnik* with Pavel Prussky, about whom *The Russian Messenger* printed an article with citations. . . . He is not the type of the coming Russian man, but certainly one of the coming Russian people."[9] Dostoevsky would surely have been struck by the resemblance of some of Golubov's ideas to his own, particularly Golubov's emphasis on the importance of self-discipline and self-mastery as the sole basis of true freedom. Even more, he insisted that such true freedom could be won only through adhering to the teachings of the Orthodox faith. "True good," wrote Golubov, "is contained in our conscience; the kingdom of God is within us. . . . Without awareness of the presence . . . [within us] of true good, we will never seek it, but only false goods, in our surroundings." In opposition to Ogarev, whom he nonetheless addressed with great respect, Golubov argued that social inequality was the result of "immorality" and the "uncontrolled disunion" of people from each other, and that "prosperity is dependent on morality."[10] The teachings and figure of Golubov would enter importantly into the early stages of *The Devils*, and Dostoevsky's imagination was unquestionably stimulated by the juxtaposition of Ogarev's radical atheistic thought with the moral-religious teachings of an Orthodoxy revitalized by some of the fanatical faith of the ex–Old Believers.

It would require considerable time, however, before Dostoevsky's next novel would emerge from such sources. For the moment, even the very idea of immediately undertaking the major work he was dreaming of was very far from his thoughts. "I will not put up my *Atheism* for sale (and about Catholicism and the Jesuits I have a good deal to say compared with Orthodoxy). I have an idea for a rather longish story, about twelve signatures in length, that tempts me. There is still another idea."[11] Just what "longish story" Dostoevsky has in mind remains unclear; and he finds himself in a quandary, not only about which of the many ideas strewn through his notebooks he should undertake to develop, but also about where to place it. He was greatly tempted to contribute to *Dawn*, whose ideological position strongly appealed to him, but he knew nothing about its financial resources; and he inquires anxiously of Maikov whether the editor would be in a position to furnish the advances on which he depended for his subsistence. Moreover, a contribution to *Dawn* would place him in an awkward position vis-à-vis Katkov, to whose journal he still owed a considerable debt. But he did not wish to mortgage himself to one magazine, and he rather resented the taciturnity exhibited by the editors, who never deigned to say a word about his contributions in their businesslike letters.

Money worries never ceased to preoccupy Dostoevsky; and he ends with a request that Maikov once again distribute one hundred rubles, soon to arrive from Katkov, between Emilya Feodorovna and Pasha. The latter, meanwhile, had found another job thanks to Dostoevsky's friends; as for his brother's widow, "although she has always been my enemy (I do not know why), although she hates me, I cannot *this time* give her less than fifty rubles."[12] In fact, Dostoevsky knew very well why this hatred existed, and he goes on for several more pages to unroll for Maikov the whole calamitous history of his brother's death, his single-handed efforts to keep *Epoch* alive, the final collapse, and his disastrous assumption of all the debts incurred. All sorts of slanderous rumors had been spread about by the impoverished family—such as the one, strictly false, that he had persuaded Mikhail to sell his cigarette factory and establish a magazine solely to publish his own works. What exasperated him above all was that the family considered it his *duty* to support them (and thus, presumably, need feel no gratitude to him for doing so), while he was only sharing his all-too-meager resources with them out of pity and reverence for the memory of his dead brother.

On the very next day, Dostoevsky replied to the earlier letter of Strakhov's announcing the appearance of *Dawn*, though without saying anything specifically about a future contribution. Writing from Florence, Dostoevsky evokes memories of their common sojourn there for a week in the summer of 1862, when they had spent pleasant evenings in talk over a café table laden with several bottles of the good local wine. This idyllic recollection conveniently neglects the occasional sharp exchanges between them, which have only recently become known, over the attitude to be adopted toward the radicals.* Dostoevsky had been much more conciliatory toward them in those days than Strakhov, and perhaps he has such ancient quarrels in mind when he regrets not being able to speak with Strakhov face-to-face, because "after two years, I think, even views and convictions must in part be changed." Expressing intense pleasure at the news about *Dawn*, he is cheered by the knowledge that "our tendency and our work in common has not died. *Time* and *Epoch* . . . have produced their fruits, and the new undertaking is obliged to begin from where we left off. This is very, very reassuring."[13]

Although then engaged in turning out an important series of articles on Tolstoy, Strakhov had complained about a certain weariness and lack of desire to write. Dostoevsky, refusing to take him at his word, praises his criticism in highly flattering terms. He expresses sympathy, though, with Strakhov's distaste for meeting deadlines and acknowledges that "we are all in the same boat. The deadlines and commands finally overcome all one's disposition and every spark, especially as the years advance." As for Tolstoy, Dostoevsky offers some reflections of his own. "I see," he writes, "that you hold Lev Tolstoy in very high regard; I agree that here is much of *our own*; but not that much. And yet, of *all of us*, in my opinion, he has succeeded best in expressing more of what is us, and is thus worth talking about."[14] The italicized phrases evidently refer to the strongly national and patriotic character of Tolstoy's new work; but the mixture of admiration and reservation reveals all the ambiguities of Dostoevsky's relation to Tolstoy, whose immense talent he could not fail

---

* This quarrel was first disclosed in 1973, when an unpublished fragment, written by Strakhov in the form of an open letter to Dostoevsky, became available in the Russian scholarly annual *Literaturnoe Nasledtsvo*. See *Dostoevsky: The Stir of Liberation* (Princeton, N.J., 1986), 193–196.

Despite the seeming amity of the two men on the surface, there was always an underlying tension in their relationship, which would be displayed in a particularly vicious form after Dostoevsky's death.

to admire although he could never regard him with the same unqualified reverence as Strakhov. There was more than a touch of envy in Dostoevsky's attitude; and this led to a sense of rivalry soon to become evident in the plans for *The Life of a Great Sinner.*

3

The Dostoevskys, much against their will, spent six and a half more months in Florence. Of all the places in Europe in which they lived, Florence was the city that Dostoevsky wrote about with the most appreciation—or, better, the least depreciation. Nor, *mirabile dictu,* does he say anything derogatory about the Italians. Whether the climate was better or worse for his epilepsy remains unclear (he offers different opinions in different letters), but he was fully responsive to the natural beauty of the location. "It rains too much in Florence," he writes his niece, "but then, when the sun appears—it is almost like paradise. It is impossible to imagine anything more beautiful than this sky, this air and this light."[15] Despite the attractions of Florence, however, there were very solid reasons why the Dostoevskys wished to settle elsewhere.

Ideally, they were aching to return to Russia, and Dostoevsky speaks of the agony of being separated from his homeland in accents that become more and more despondent. To his niece he confides that "I must absolutely return to Russia: here I will end by losing any possibility of writing for lack of my indispensable and habitual material—Russian reality (which feeds my thoughts) and the Russians. And then at any moment I need information nowhere to be had." The plan for *Atheism,* Dostoevsky says, will "require a great deal of preliminary study"; he also explains that "it is not a matter of denouncing contemporary convictions, it's something else—a genuine poem."[16] Beyond this overwhelming need to make contact once again with the vital source of his creations, Dostoevsky was convinced that his material interests were suffering because of his absence. Even though *The Idiot* had not aroused much critical enthusiasm, Dostoevsky believed that he might still have obtained a few thousand rubles for reprint rights if he had been on the spot. As it was, the terms negotiated through his sister-in-law and then Strakhov were so disadvantageous that he simply refused.

Another practical reason to return was to explore the feasibility of some plans that might enable Dostoevsky to break loose from his wage-slavery to editors. One idea, as he told Sofya Ivanova, was for a publication that would provide a very good income but "would require all my working time, that is, would not give me time to undertake novels." Dostoevsky probably has in mind what became his *Diary of a Writer.* The other idea was for a publication that would be "almost only . . . a compilation" and could be put together mechanically; he conceived it as "a large *annual*, useful, and a necessary bedside book for everyone," a volume that would appear each year in January and was certain to have a widespread sale. Of course the material would be organized around "an idea, and with a considerable knowledge of the matter";[17] but this type of publication would not interfere with Dostoevsky's own writing. No publication of this kind ever appeared, but Liza Tushina in *The Devils* takes up the same notion and tries to enlist Shatov as a collaborator.

Meanwhile, it was necessary for Dostoevsky to think of his immediate financial situation, and he wrote to *The Russian Messenger* again asking for an advance on a new novel that he promised to provide in about a year. But this was the holiday season, when all the journals were busy paying bills and attempting to attract new subscribers, and Dostoevsky did not expect to receive any funds for some time. Faced with temporary indigence once more, he decided to respond to another invitation from Strakhov at the end of January, in the name of the editor and all the important collaborators of *Dawn*, to honor them with a contribution. An advance from *Dawn* would allow him to meet his most pressing needs until the money from Katkov was forthcoming.

While expressing all his gratitude for the invitation, and to those who took such an interest in him, Dostoevsky rather embarrassedly explains to Strakhov (who must surely have known it) that he lived only from his writings and was thus forced always to ask for advances. At present he had a desperate need for money, though he continued to remain on good terms with *The Russian Messenger*. "I have, at present," he said, "three ideas that I value. One of them will make a long novel. I believe that they [Katkov] will choose the novel, and I will begin with it next year. I thus have several free months." Dostoevsky proposes that he be sent an advance of a thousand rubles with no delay, and in return he would engage to write "a story, that is, a novel," which would be about the size of *Poor Folk*. He assures Strakhov that "the idea for the novel strongly attracts me. This is not something for money, but quite the opposite. I feel that in comparison with *Crime and Punishment* the effect of *The Idiot* on the public was weaker." Dostoevsky's vanity has thus been aroused, and "I want to produce an effect again."[18] Employing a little flattery, he assures Strakhov that it will be more advantageous to do so in *Dawn* than in *The Russian Messenger*.

Dostoevsky's references to future works are so unspecific that it is difficult to know just what he had offered *The Russian Messenger*; nor do we know what he intended to write for *Dawn*. But if uninformative on this score, his letter is of considerable interest because, in communicating his reactions to the first two numbers of *Dawn*, he offers an important restatement of his aesthetic. As might be expected, Dostoevsky is enthusiastic about the journal, though he knew very well that the patriotic and more or less Slavophil orientation of *Dawn* would run into stiff opposition. Nonetheless, he assures Strakhov, he is certain the review will succeed. Whether he believed this himself is difficult to say; certainly he wished it to be true, because "there is an *idea* in the journal and just the very idea that is now necessary and unavoidable, and which *alone* will grow in the future while all the others die off."

Dostoevsky knew that in expounding and defending this idea "you will be called retrograde, savages and perhaps accused even of having sold out, when for us and in our time this is the only leading and *liberal* idea." He warns that "the routine mind always sees liberalism and new ideas in what is old and outdated," that is, the radical ideas and doctrines of the early 1860s. Dostoevsky was afraid that Strakhov, who temperamentally was not a fighter, would lose heart along with the others at the vastness of the task. They were battling upstream against a flood tide; and he knew, having been in the same position himself just a few years back, just how arduous it was to make any headway. All the more so because, as he admits, "neither *Time* nor *Epoch*, as you know, expressed their ideas with such openness and frankness, but remained mostly in the middle, especially at the start."[19]

Dostoevsky compliments Strakhov on his development as a critic (the first two issues of *Dawn* contained his lengthy and quite penetrating articles on *War and Peace*) and remarks that every important Russian critic had made his reputation by devoting himself to one author and developing his own thoughts in this context. Belinsky was inspired by Gogol (though he also wrote an important series of articles on Pushkin), Apollon Grigoryev by Ostrovsky, and now Strakhov by Tolstoy. Agreeing in general with Strakhov's interpretation, which draws heavily on Grigoryev (whom Dostoevsky had always admired), he objects to the "stupidity" of a critic who had accused Strakhov of sharing Tolstoy's "historical fatalism." What Strakhov had defined was really the "national, Russian idea," which he saw embodied in Tolstoy's depiction of the battle of Borodino; and because Dostoevsky clearly accepts this idea as his own, it is worth quoting what Strakhov wrote:

> Facing each other stood two peoples—one attacking, the other defending. Thus with great clarity the strength of two *ideas* here becomes clear, which on this occasion moved these peoples and placed them in such a mutual situation. The French were revealed as the representatives of a cosmopolitan idea—capable, in the name of a general principle, of resorting to force and to the murder of a people. The Russians were revealed as the representatives of a national idea—standing guard with love over their soul and their organically formed life and particular organization. The question of

nationalities was posed on the battlefield of Borodino, and the Russians resolved it for the first time in the interest of nationality.[20]

Dostoevsky then moves on to offer some technical criticisms of the journal's format and to regret that it is not more combative in tone. "You avoid polemics? Wrongfully so. Polemics is a very useful method of clarifying thought, and our public likes it very much. All the essays of Belinsky, for example, were polemical." While praising the clarity and calm of Strakhov's own manner, Dostoevsky adds insidiously that his lack of aggressive ardor "gives your essays an air of *abstraction*. One must sometimes get excited, use the whip, sink to the most particular, commonplace, and contemporary circumstances."[21] Such barbs, wrapped in compliments, in all likelihood were prompted by Dostoevsky's irritation at a remark slipped into Strakhov's essay, which he could only take as a concealed criticism. One of the great merits of *War and Peace*, Strakhov had written, was that Count Tolstoy "did not attempt to entice the reader with any complicated and mysterious adventures, or the description of any scabrous and horrifying scenes, or the depiction of terrible spiritual agony, or, finally, any sort of daring, new tendencies" that unhealthily stimulate the imagination of the reader.[22]

A week or so later, in a letter to his niece, Dostoevsky notes laconically that Strakhov "hardly counts among my admirers" as a novelist.[23] And this concealed polemic no doubt explains why, when he mentions to Strakhov having just completed *The Idiot* (though the final chapters had not yet appeared), Dostoevsky, seemingly out of the blue, breaks into a defense of his own approach to reality. Urging Strakhov to give him his impressions of later sections of the book, Dostoevsky continues:

I have my own particular view of reality (in art), and what the majority calls almost fantastic and exceptional, for me sometimes constitutes the very essence of the real. The ordinariness of events and a routine view of them is not realism in my view, and even the opposite. In every issue of a newspaper you run across an account of actual, most surprising facts. For our writers, they are fantastic; they pay no attention to them, and yet they are reality because they are *facts*. Who notices them, explains them, and sets them down? They occur all the time and every minute, and are by no means *exceptional*.... We just let reality pass by our nose. Who will note the facts and delve into them? ... Is not my fantastic *Idiot* reality, yes, and the most ordinary! Just right now such characters must exist in the strata of our society detached from their soil—strata which have in truth become fantastic![24]

Whether Dostoevsky is referring to Prince Myshkin or to the novel as a whole is not clear; but he insists that only through the extremes of con-

duct he depicts—and, presumably, only through the melodramatic devices that he employs—can the full depth of the moral-social crisis now
plaguing Russian society be truly grasped.

After this outburst, though, Dostoevsky reveals all the uncertainty
about *The Idiot* that continued to plague him. "But it's no good talking!"
he exclaims. "Much in the novel was written hastily, much is dragged out
and does not come off, but something still does come off. I do not stand
by my novel but by my idea." Whatever its defects, he staunchly maintains—and with much justification—that, compared to other works then
being published (such as Goncharov's *Precipice* [*Obriv*]), he was at least
striving for something new. Of Goncharov's chief character, he asks
scornfully, "Who is Raisky? He is a cliché depiction of pseudo-Russian
traits, a person who busies himself about a lot of things, strives for much,
and cannot even accomplish a little! What old stuff! What a decrepit,
empty idea, and yes, totally untrue into the bargain. Such a slander on
the Russian character was already common in Belinsky's time. What a
trivial and base point of view and comprehension of reality. Always, always the same thing!" Raisky, in Dostoevsky's eyes, was a latter-day version of that famous Russian type, "the superfluous man," whom Dostoevsky would soon delineate in his own unsurpassable portraits of two
varieties: the liberal Idealist of the 1840s, Stepan Trofimovich Verkhovensky, and a new incarnation, towering over all previous ones, of the Byronic type, Nikolay Stavrogin. As for the latest story of Turgenev's (*The
Unhappy Woman* [*Nechastnaya*]), the less said the better; it was so vapid
that "the devil only knows what it is!"[25]

4

Ten days later Dostoevsky finally received an advance from Katkov,
meanwhile having been forced to borrow one hundred francs from some
unknown benefactor and to pawn whatever he and Anna could spare for
another hundred francs. Dostoevsky was relieved to receive the money,
not only for obvious reasons, but also because he had been worried
about his status at the journal on which his livelihood depended.
"Katkov told me himself in 1867 . . . " he wrote his niece, "that the number of their subscribers had increased by five hundred and attributed this
to *Crime and Punishment*. I don't believe that *The Idiot* will bring them
new subscribers; I am very sorry about that, and that's why I am very
happy that they hold on to me despite the obvious lack of success of my
novel." Also, the advance had been accompanied by a letter apologizing
for a delay in printing Dostoevsky's final chapters; and even though, as
Dostoevsky said, "this is what is worst of all for me," he was pleased at
being treated with such consideration.[26] Careful about maintaining good
relations with *The Russian Messenger*, he advised his niece very strongly

to read *Dawn*, but asked her not to breathe a word to anyone on Katkov's staff that he planned to write for the new journal.

Dawn agreed to send Dostoevsky one thousand rubles, but not immediately and only in several installments—which did not suit his requirements at all. He thus reduced his demands and asked for only three hundred rubles to be sent immediately; in return he offered "a story, rather short, about two signatures, perhaps a little more. . . . I had considered writing this story four years ago, the year my brother died, in response to something Apollon Grigoryev said at the time in praise of *Notes from Underground*. He said: 'Keep on writing in that vein.' But this is nothing like *Notes from Underground*, it is completely different from it in form, although in essence it is the same, the essence of all my work, that is, Nikolay Nikolaevich, if you will grant me that, as a writer, I have a special individual essence."[27] Dostoevsky was clearly dubious that Strakhov would be willing to recognize any striking originality in his work at all.

It was assumed until recently that the story mentioned here was *The Eternal Husband*. This work, published by *Dawn* at the beginning of 1870, was written between the completion of *The Idiot* and the conception of *The Devils*; and it also corresponds very neatly to what Dostoevsky says about his idea. One can see a thematic relation in the story to *Notes from Underground*, and Dostoevsky could well have considered such a theme to be his "essence" as a writer. Even more, the work contains an explicit allusion to Apollon Grigoryev's theory about cultural types in Russian literature, and the reference would appear to be Dostoevsky's graceful acknowledgment of the inspiration and encouragement of his friend. But what had seemed so textually self-evident has turned out to be erroneous: the work that Dostoevsky was offering, as revealed by his notebooks, was not at all the one he came to write.

The story idea in question was sketched in an entry clearly entitled "Plan for A Story (in Dawn)," which has been dated between the end of February 1869 and the beginning of March. It begins with a remark on the technique Dostoevsky wished to employ: "A story in the manner of Pushkin (concise and without explanation, psychologically candid and artless)." In fact, Dostoevsky maintained such a manner to a great extent even when his story idea changed character, probably clinging to Pushkin's classic sobriety as a model to counter Strakhov's charge of "sensationalism." The plan, which involves a young girl called the Pupil living on the bounty of a rich gentlewoman, anticipates the relation of Mme Stavrogina and Darya Shatova in *The Devils*. The central male figure is a Nephew, who arrives to inherit the estate and whose character shows Dostoevsky returning to the early drafts of *The Idiot*.

Of the Nephew, Dostoevsky writes: "In general, he is a *type*. Principal trait: misanthropy, but with the underground [which here indicates a need for love—J.F.]. This is the essence, but the principal trait: a need to confide in others that appears through a terrible misanthropy and a hostile and offensive mistrust" (9: 116). There is also a "crippled girl" among the characters, who again points forward to *The Devils*, and the Nephew fights a duel like Stavrogin. The notes trail off without resolution, though the possibility is raised that "perhaps he [the Nephew] blows out his brains." Closest of all to the final *Eternal Husband* is one notation: "Either a nice type à la O-ff [identified as Ogarev] or a serious murderer comes from the underground" (9: 117–118). The eternal husband combines both these psychological traits, and one wonders if this sentence may not have turned Dostoevsky's attention toward such a character. In any case, it would be several months before he began to work on what became his novella.

Meanwhile, let us return to Dostoevsky's running commentary on *Dawn* for the benefit of Strakhov. Strakhov's letters were full of complaints about the difficulties of his editorial tasks and the lack of public response to the journal and to his own articles. Dostoevsky continues to buoy up his obviously flagging spirits, even though, as he told his niece, "in my view, Strakhov . . . is not really made for the uninterrupted work that a periodical requires."[28] Yet Dostoevsky was eager for *Dawn* to be a success, and a very heartening event for him was the publication of Danilevsky's book, to which he responded with ever-increasing enthusiasm. "The articles of Danilevsky," he exclaimed, "in my eyes are becoming more and more important and central. Yes, they are the future bedside book of all Russians for a long time to come; . . . they agree with my conclusions and convictions to such an extent, that I am even amazed in certain pages at the resemblance of the conclusions." What impressed Dostoevsky was that his own ideas should now be put forward by Danilevsky in so organized, harmonious, and logical a form, "and with that degree of scientific method which I, of course, despite all my effort, would never be able to realize."[29] Dostoevsky was so eager to read each installment that he scolded *Dawn* for not printing the book in larger segments.

Despite his fervent approval of Danilevsky's historiosophical thesis, which predicted the advent of a new and world-dominating Slavic civilization in the near future, Dostoevsky was troubled by a deplorable omission in his arguments. "I am not at all certain," he worriedly confides to Strakhov, "that Danilevsky will show *in its full strength* the definitive substance of the Russian mission, which consists in the revelation to the world of the Russian Christ, unknown to the world and whose principle lies in our native Orthodoxy. As I see it, in this lies the essence of our future civilizing role, and the resurrection, perhaps, of all of Europe, and the whole essence of our mighty future."[30] Strakhov replied reassuringly that "there will be Orthodoxy in Danilevsky, though I suspect that you, as an artist, must see it from another perspective. Danilevsky does not directly touch on the content [of Orthodoxy], but only indicates the historical significance of our confession."[31] This was, Strakhov rightly surmised, very far from satisfying Dostoevsky. After having read the entire work, Dostoevsky wrote disappointedly to Maikov that "even among people of a level as high as that of the author of *Russia and Europe*," he had not found the idea that Russia's mission was to bring the true Christ to the peoples of the West, who had been deluded and pushed into atheism by the quest of the Catholic Church for temporal power.[32] By this time Dostoevsky was hard at work on *The Devils*, and we shall soon see that his opinions about Danilevsky can help to clarify one of the much-debated questions concerning that novel.

5

The editors of *Dawn* accepted the proposal for a shorter work, and at the beginning of April Dostoevsky asked Strakhov, who had told him the advance would be sent in the middle of the month, if the money could not be dispatched earlier. The weather in Florence was turning torrid, and the Dostoevskys had been advised to leave because Anna was expecting a child in four months. They planned to move to Dresden, a city they already knew and where (since Dostoevsky had not learned a word of Italian) they could find a doctor and nurses "who express themselves in a comprehensible language and are competent." In addition, they were awaiting the arrival of Anna's mother in a few days and planned to depart as soon as means were available. Dostoevsky also complained to Strakhov that he received *Dawn* very tardily and asked him to request a bookstore to send copies of the book by Samarin (that Maikov had mentioned), along with the entire *War and Peace*. He had read only portions of the novel, of which the fifth volume had just appeared, "and I have quite forgotten what I read." Evidently beginning to lose patience with Strakhov's lamentations, his tone is now rather sharp: "Once and for all—stop talking of your '*feebleness*' and your '*dashed-off-drafts*.' It makes me sick to hear this. One would think you are shamming. Never have you had so much clarity, logic, and *convincing opinions and conclusions.*"[33]

Continuing his usual survey of the contents of *Dawn*, Dostoevsky waxes enthusiastic about a now-forgotten play, *Frol Skobeev*, from the pen of D. Averkiev, himself hardly remembered at present. A romantic comedy set in the seventeenth century, the play details the amorous adventures of an engaging rogue—a nobleman, but from impoverished stock—who runs off with a boyar's daughter and finally wins acceptance from her wealthy and high-toned family. Dostoevsky is carried away to such an extent (though he cooled off somewhat after a second reading) that he claims to have read "nothing like it" since *The Captain's Daughter*," Pushkin's classic historical novel. What pleased him particularly was the uncondescending acceptance of Russian life that Averkiev managed to achieve. Comparing him in this respect to Ostrovsky, he remarks that the much more famous playwright "is something of a dandy, and presents himself as incomparably higher than his merchants. If he represents a merchant as a human being, it's almost as if he is telling the reader or spectator: 'Look, after all he is also a human being.' "[34]

Averkiev avoids such an implicit self-display of his own superiority; and praising the play for this quality, Dostoevsky even expresses agreement with Dobrolyubov's two famous articles on Ostrovsky. Such accord with one of the most virulent radical spokesmen of the 1860s indicates Dostoevsky's relative freedom from political prejudice when it came to literary-cultural matters; he was quite capable of conceding the truth of an insight even though uttered by someone whose politics he abhorred. "You know," he tells Strakhov, well aware that his correspondent would be profoundly irritated by his words, "I am sure that the opinion of Dobrolyubov on Ostrovsky is more accurate than that of Grigoryev. Perhaps Ostrovsky himself really never became aware he was showing a Realm of Darkness [the title of one of Dobrolyubov's articles—J.F.], but Dobrolyubov *prompted him well*, and it fell on fertile soil." Grigoryev had denied that Ostrovsky's plays were meant to "expose" the backwardness and obscurantism of merchant life; but Dobrolyubov had stingingly raised into prominence all the elements in this milieu that reinforced such an impression, and Dostoevsky intimates that the power of his criticism had affected Ostrovsky's own attitude toward his material. Averkiev's characters, on the other hand, even such easy targets as the grand boyars, are portrayed without a trace of superiority. "Not only is it impossible to caricature them with a smile à la Ostrovsky, but on the contrary their gentlemanliness must be admired. . . . They are the *grand monde* of that time in the highest and truest degree, so that if you laugh at anything it is only at the cut of their clothes."[35] Such an overestimation of Averkiev probably stems from Dostoevsky's increasing desire, soon to become evident in *Life of a Great Sinner*, to discover and depict the *positive* elements of Russian life in his own creations.

The arrangement with *Dawn* had seemed to solve Dostoevsky's immediate monetary problem; but matters turned out otherwise, and he again found himself in desperate financial straits. The promised advance was sent, not through the post as he had specified, but to a special agent in Florence to be delivered personally. Unfortunately, this precaution added almost two weeks to its arrival, and by this time his extra expenses had eaten up what he finally received. Expecting the money promptly, and intending to quit Florence immediately, the Dostoevskys had moved out of their apartment to save on rent; but the single room was more expensive for a prolonged period, and Strakhov's unfortunate choice of transmission meant that they were forced to prolong their stay in Florence under the worst possible conditions. Anna's mother had by now arrived to look after her, and Dostoevsky gives an exasperated image of their highly uncomfortable circumstances. "The heat in Florence is unbearable," he wrote to Maikov in mid-May, "the city is white-hot and stifling, our nerves are overwrought—which is particularly bad for my wife; right now we are packed together (still *attendant*) in a small narrow room giving on the marketplace. I have had enough of this Florence, and now with no space and the heat, I cannot even write. In general, a terrible anguish—and worse, because of Europe; I look at everything here like a wild beast."[36]

The marketplace was surrounded by arcades adorned with graceful granite columns, and in the center played a municipal fountain dominated by an enormous bronze boar ("a classic work of great beauty," Dostoevsky admitted), from whose mouth the water flowed picturesquely. But the sun made the bronze boar, along with all the arcades and columns, as torrid as a furnace, and Dostoevsky compared the result to living perpetually in a Russian steam bath. What baffled him was why the numerous and elegant foreigners who thronged the city remained there when they obviously could afford to flee. The temperature cooled off and became tolerable at night; but the Italians sang in the streets at all hours, at five o'clock in the morning the market life began, the donkeys brayed, and sleep was impossible. "Most of all, I felt sorry for my poor Anya," he wrote after escaping to Dresden. "She, poor thing, was in her seventh or eighth month, and suffered terribly from the heat."[37]

Even though Dostoevsky was not able to work under such conditions, he was very far from being idle; on the contrary, it is thanks to this slackening of literary pressure that he produced a document of extraordinary interest. Written to his literary and ideological intimate Apollon Maikov, this letter contains the most extensive statement he ever made about his conception of artistic creation; and it also sketches a vast fresco of Russian and world history that fills in the background of his worldview. Maikov had informed his friend that he planned to write a series of poems about Russian history for use in public schools, an idea that Dostoevsky greeted with rapturous approval. "You see, my idea is that these ballads could become a great national book, and do a good deal for the rebirth of the self-consciousness of Russian man. Believe me, Apollon Nikolaevich, in every school the boys will know them and learn them by heart."[38] Dostoevsky was particularly pleased to hear about this intention because he had suggested the plan for such a historical sequence just a year earlier.

What Dostoevsky then had in mind was the writing of a series of *biliny* (he uses the term for Russian epic verse)—they might be ballads, songs, short poems, romances—whose form would emerge spontaneously from the soul of the poet almost as if independent of his will. And this leads Dostoevsky into a long digression (for which he apologizes), in which he develops his view of the artistic process. Creation takes place in two stages, the first of which is inspiration. The poem appears at this moment "like a natural precious stone, a diamond in the poet's soul, complete in all its essence. . . . We can even say that the actual creator is not he but rather life itself, the mighty essence of life, God, living and real, manifesting his power in the diversity of creation here and there and most often in great hearts and in powerful poets, so that, if the poet himself is not the creator . . . the poet's soul is the mine in which the diamonds are formed and outside of which they cannot be found."

The second stage is that of putting this inspiration into the best possible artistic form. "Once [the artist] has received the diamond he must polish and mount it," and "at this point the poet is not much more than a jeweler."[39] Problems of form and technique, even though Dostoevsky gave them careful attention, were nonetheless secondary for him; primary was the afflatus of inspiration obtained from life itself, and ultimately, he believed, from God. Such words reveal the persistence of the Romantic Schellingian influence of Dostoevsky's youth, when he had absorbed the notion of the artist as the vehicle for some sort of supernatural truth. Dostoevsky's literary criticism, as a result, always places the works he discusses, particularly those he admires, in the broad perspective of some eternal moral-spiritual dilemma or some epochal historical clash or crisis; they are never merely the personal and idiosyncratic expressions of particular individuals. Similarly, the events used in his works are always magnified and transformed by what he called his "fantastic realism," which means that he invariably grasps them in terms of some larger—ultimately moral-philosophical or social-religious—issue or situation.

Dostoevsky then sketches some of the possible subjects for such a series of "epic legends in verse." And his notations are so scenic and pictorial, so bent on obtaining striking *montage* effects of contrast, that they resemble nothing so much as film scripts that could have provided inspiration for Sergey Eisenstein. He begins with the Muslim capture of Constantinople by the armies of Muhammad II, and Dostoevsky himself remarks on the oddity of including such an event as part of *Russian* history. But this starting point only reveals his implicit acceptance of the famous "Third Rome" ideology of Russian nationalism, the idea that Russia had inherited the mantle of Rome from the conquered and dese-crated Byzantium (the second Rome), and was thus destined to found a new Christian world empire to which there would be no successor. The momentous catastrophe is evoked by Dostoevsky in vivid strokes: "the Emperor walking through the palace . . . as he goes to pray before the icon of Our Lady of Vlakhern; the prayer; the assault; the battle; the Sultan entering Constantinople on horseback, the blood dripping from his sword."[40]

The Sultan finds the Emperor's body among a pile of corpses, and the scene shifts: "Hagia Sophia; a trembling Patriarch, the last Mass, the Sul-tan, still on horseback, galloping up the steps and entering the Cathedral (*historique*); reaching the middle of the Cathedral, he pulls up his horse in perplexity; looking around musingly and confusedly, he utters the words: 'This is the house of prayer for Allah!'" Cut to "a Russian wed-ding, Prince Ivan III [who married the last of the Byzantine royal fam-ily—J.F.] in his wooden hut instead of a palace, and there enters into that wooden hut the great idea of the Pan-Orthodox significance of Russia and the cornerstone laid for her supremacy in the East; . . . she is not to be simply a mighty country, but a whole new world whose destiny it is to know Christianity through the Pan-Slav Orthodox idea and offer man-kind a *new* message when the West has decayed, and it will decay when the Pope has completely distorted the image of Christ and thus engen-dered atheism among the defiled peoples of the West."[41]

There would then be a sudden transition, in another ballad, "to the end of the fifteenth and the beginning of the sixteenth centuries in Eu-rope, to Italy, to the Papacy, to church art, to Raphael, to the cult of Apollo Belvedere, to the first rumors about the Reformation, about Lu-ther, America, gold, Spain and England." This unrolling of European splendor would be starkly juxtaposed against "the tableau of the wise Prince, inspired by a grand and profound idea, sitting next to the humbly dressed Metropolitan and the Russified 'Fominishna' [the Byzantine Princess—J.F.] in the wooden shack." And this "vast, vivid tableau" of European glory would be filled with "intimations of what that tableau portends for the future, of science, atheism, *human rights* in the Western sense, not in ours—everything that has contributed to bringing about what is and what will be."[42]

Dostoevsky had originally thought that the series should end with Peter the Great; but now he would like to see it go forward in time—"to the emancipation of the serfs, and to our boyars scattered all over Eu-rope with the last paper rubles, and to the Russian ladies whoring around with the Borgheses, to our seminarists preaching atheism, to the Russian counts, the super-humanitarian citizens of the world who write criticism, stories, etc., etc." As for the future, "I would have ended with fantastic pictures—Russia in two hundred years alongside torn and darkened Europe with all its civilization reduced to a brutish state. I wouldn't have stopped short of *any flight of the imagination.*" Well aware of how extravagant all this sounded, he ends with the remark: "I'm sure you must think I'm mad right now, specifically and chiefly because I have let my pen run on and on."[43] But this sweeping overview indicates how inflamed Dostoevsky's imagination could become by such historical visions, and how he could use them to express his deepest hopes and values. The future creator of "The Legend of the Grand Inquisitor," who will eventually set it against the background of "the first rumors of the Reformation" mentioned here, is already present in these soaringly panoramic, if manifestly jaundiced, pages.

6

By the time the advance from *Dawn* finally arrived, it was no longer sufficient to cover the cost of travel, and Dostoevsky was forced to appeal to Katkov for succor once again. The suffocating Dostoevskys left Florence only at the end of July, departing not for Dresden but for Prague, though there had been no mention of such a destination earlier. The abrupt change of itinerary was the result of Anna's desire to find a possible remedy for Dostoevsky's dispiriting isolation from any literary or intellectual milieu. Never had they been so much alone as in Florence, where "we did not know a single soul ... with whom we could talk, argue, exchange reactions. Around us, all were strangers and sometimes hostile ones; and this total isolation was sometimes difficult to bear."[44] Maikov had written that Dostoevsky had many admirers in Prague, and there, too, they would be immersed in a Slavic world once again. Prague could also be reached by way of Venice, which Dostoevsky had long desired to show to the zealous tourist Anna as a small reward for all the deprivations of their life together.

Proceeding by way of Bologna, where a stopover was made to view Raphael's *St. Cecilia*—Dostoevsky had seen it only in reproduction—they stayed for several days in Venice, hardly leaving the Piazza San Marco and the cathedral, but also visiting the nearby Palazzo Ducale and the Palace of the Doges. "How lovely Venice is!" Dostoevsky wrote Strakhov several weeks later.[45] To his niece he described how "Anna could only utter exclamations and cries of admiration in looking at the palaces and the piazza. In San Marco Cathedral (astonishing, incomparable!) she lost her sculptured Swiss fan that she adored (she had so little jewelry!). My God, how she cried!"[46] Despite this minor misadventure, Venice evidently made its incomparable impact. On departing, the Dostoevskys took a boat to Trieste, running into a rough sea that caused Dostoevsky a good deal of anxiety over the pregnant Anna, and then, changing to a train on shore, arrived in Prague at the beginning of August.

Their plan to settle in Prague for the winter, however, was thwarted by a lack of available accommodations. No furnished apartments could be found for rent in the city, and they could not afford to equip an unfurnished dwelling or live in hotels or rooming houses. Dostoevsky regretted this very much and wrote to Maikov that "I had hoped and dreamed of the usefulness for me of a stay in Prague. I even imagined that in the soon to be celebrated festival [in honor of the five-hundredth anniversary of the birth of Jan Huss—J.F.], among the Russians I might even meet you."[47] In fact, Maikov was not invited to the celebration, whose organizers had first intended to give it a Pan-Slav character but then decided to aim at a more cosmopolitan appeal. Dostoevsky's hopes of living in a congenial circle even outside Russia thus came to naught, and he and Anna fell back on their original Dresden goal. He had written to Maikov from Florence that "in Dresden I will work without raising my head."[48] And so he did, as we shall see in the next chapter.

PART IV

The Pamphlet and
the Poem

CHAPTER 19

The Life of a Great Sinner

The return of the Dostoevskys to Dresden marked the last period of their sojourn abroad, which was becoming more and more difficult for them to endure. Their nostalgia for Russia only increased as the hope of return proved an ever-elusive phantom, and it was impossible to imagine accumulating sufficient funds to guarantee against the threat of debtor's prison once Dostoevsky crossed the Russian border. His absence also injured his business affairs, which could not be conducted satisfactorily from a distance and through unreliable intermediaries. Time and again Dostoevsky was forced to appeal to the goodwill of friends, particularly the truly devoted and loyal Apollon Maikov, and his apologies for imposing on him become increasingly troubled and embarrassed. The situation was clearly impossible; and Dostoevsky made up his mind to return home in the near future, come what may, certainly now with the strong approval of Anna.

During the last twenty months of their stay, Dostoevsky wrote *The Eternal Husband* and the first part of *The Devils*. Even while composing his novella, however, he did not cease to think of his novel (which was not initially *The Devils* at all, but a mutation of his original *Atheism* project). The history of his literary career in this period is extremely intricate and complex, and we must follow it very closely to untangle its interweaving strands.

2

The Dostoevskys arrived in Dresden in mid-August and quickly managed to find satisfactory quarters. Ten days after getting settled, Dostoevsky shot off four letters to various correspondents. One of them went to a lawyer he did not know personally but who was co-trustee, along with Dostoevsky's younger brother Andrey, of the business affairs of their wealthy aunt, A. F. Kuminina. Shortly before, Maikov had conveyed the supposedly reliable information that this aunt had passed away and that her will contained a bequest of forty thousand rubles to a monastery. The lawyer in question, V. I. Veselovsky, was a great admirer of Dostoevsky, and through mutual acquaintances knew of his straitened circumstances. In his opinion, as Maikov had learned, Mme Kuminina had become addled in her last years when she made this donation. The will could thus easily be broken, and the money, reverting to the family, would help to relieve Dostoevsky's penury.

This report of his aunt's death eventually turned out to be false, but for the moment Maikov's news presented Dostoevsky with something of a quandary. In *Crime and Punishment,* one of the arguments used to justify the murder of the old pawnbroker was that she had willed her money to a monastery—money that could have been much better employed in relieving the suffering of the needy. Would Dostoevsky now align himself with the type of reasoning that he had combated in his novel?* In writing to Veselovsky, Dostoevsky makes it perfectly clear that he would not contest the will if there was any reason to believe that such a bequest had been a longstanding intention of his aunt, made when she was still in full possession of her faculties. But if, in fact, dotage had overtaken her at the time, then the possibility of a lawsuit should not be excluded.

Two weeks later, Dostoevsky worriedly wrote his favorite niece for additional information about the (presumed) death. If the bequest had been made when she was mentally competent, "what sort of a man would I be," he asks, "and what would I consider myself, in my conscience, if I went against her will and the disposition of my aunt of her own money, whatever the substance of the will and the disposition might be?"[1] But Dostoevsky also remarked that a practical and experienced lawyer like Veselovsky would not have come forward without knowing all the circumstances under which the bequest had been made; and thus there might really be something suspicious about the will. Dostoevsky's uncertainties about this prickly problem, caused by lack of reliable information, later led to unjust accusations that he wished to break the will unconditionally in his own selfish interests.

On the same day that he wrote to the lawyer, Dostoevsky also replied to Strakhov, who had recently appended an apologetic postscript to a letter of Maikov's excusing his own recent silence. Dostoevsky replies in a manner indicating the continuing strain in their relationship, which had not been improved by recent events—it was Strakhov's precautions, after all, that had been chiefly responsible for the scorching delay of their departure from Florence. "Do not excuse yourself, my esteemed Nikolay Nikolaevich, for your silence; it is well known that life is like that, and besides, does an editor have time to write even to friends, not to mention contributors? But from your postscript to the letter of my dear and es-

---

* During the tavern scene in which Raskolnikov hears his own ideas expressed, the reader also learns that the all-suffering Lizaveta, the half-sister of the pawnbroker, "did not stand to get a penny from [her] will; all the money was to go to a monastery in N—y province, for the eternal remembrance of her soul" (6: 53).

teemed Apollon Nikolaevich, I see and conclude that you continue to be my well-wisher." The sententious irony of this seemingly friendly pardon is quite obvious, and Dostoevsky was clearly smarting from the casualness with which he was being treated. After a brief account of the Florentine inferno (though of course without a word of direct accusation), he goes on: "You can well imagine, my dear and very kindly Nikolay Nikolaevich, that at thirty degrees Reaumur in the shade, to write—that is, to invent—is literally impossible. Nonetheless, I have already begun here on the novella for *Dawn*; I am only afraid it may be a little long (though I hope not long-winded)." Dostoevsky also informed Strakhov that "in three weeks I [and Anna—J.F.] will have a child. I wait with nervousness, fear, hope, and tremulousness."[2]

In his third letter of the day, Dostoevsky is more relaxed and expansive. He writes Maikov about the Veselovsky matter, complains once more (as he had already done to Strakhov) of the ingratitude of Emilya Feodorovna—"if they were to know that I had pawned my wife's things in order to come to their aid! If it's not very much, how can I be blamed!"—and notes offendedly that in her last letter she does not mention Anna even though knowing of her pregnancy. To Maikov, Dostoevsky elaborates on the state of agitation that he had merely mentioned to Strakhov. "I have terrible fears about [Anna's] health," he confesses. "She bore her first pregnancy very bravely. This time it's entirely different. She is constantly unwell, and besides this, worried, nervous, impressionable, and in the bargain seriously fears that she will die in childbirth (remembering the suffering of the first birth). Such fears and worries in someone whose nature is not at all frail or flabby is really dangerous, and that's why I am very worried too."[3]

In the midst of these gloomy forebodings, Dostoevsky complains that "I must begin to write, first for *Dawn*, and then begin the major work for *The Russian Messenger*. I have not written anything for eight months. I will of course begin to write with ardor, but what will happen as I continue? I have all kinds of ideas, but I need Russia." This need is expressed even more vehemently a bit later: "Yes, now things have so turned out for me that it would be more useful to sit in debtor's prison than remain abroad. If I remain here another year, I do not know whether I will be in a condition to write, not even well but at all, so much have I become cut off from Russia." Besides, Anna also missed Russia dearly, and both believed, with a growing sense of guilt, that Sonya had died "solely because we could not adapt ourselves to the foreign manner of nurturing and rearing a child."[4] Europe was thus to blame for this lacerating blow to their happiness; and if they were to lose the second child, both he and Anna would give way to total despair.

Happily, their second daughter, Lyubov, was born on September 26 without untoward incident; but Dostoevsky was so concerned about Anna's state of mind that he hid from her the volume of *War and Peace* depicting the death of Prince Andrey's wife in childbirth. Strakhov had sent them the book in the last weeks just before Anna's lying-in, and Dostoevsky pretended that the volume had been misplaced so as not to increase Anna's misgivings. The presence of Anna's mother was also a source of aid and reassurance because she could look after the child in the Russian fashion considered so all-important. Lyubov's birth, however, brought a flood of new expenses that far surpassed the family's very limited means; and once again Dostoevsky found himself with his back to the wall. Three days after the birth, he writes Maikov that he will now be forced to sell (or pawn) his linen, his topcoat, and perhaps even his jacket, unless he receives the advance he had requested from *Dawn*.

3

To his niece, Dostoevsky describes his two literary obligations and admits: "I have not yet begun anything for either the one or the other." Lamenting that he is forced to write out of necessity rather than inspiration, he continues: "I have an idea to which I am completely devoted; but I cannot, I must not, undertake it because I am not yet ready; I have not thought it out completely, and I need material. I shall thus have to compel myself to invent new stories; this is disgusting. I cannot imagine what is going to happen to me now, and how I will manage to take care of my affairs!"[5] What stirred Dostoevsky's creative ambition was clearly his *Atheism* idea, and he undertook the story for *Dawn* only with reluctance and even distaste.

By the end of September, as Dostoevsky informed Maikov, he had completed half of the still-untitled work, which would be longer than anticipated; he also expected to be finished by the end of October, an estimate that as usual proved much too sanguine. Meanwhile, in view of its increased length, he felt justified in asking for a further advance of two hundred rubles. Dostoevsky did not know Kashpirev personally, and he found it difficult to expose all the indignity of his circumstances to a stranger; but need left him no alternative. His letter has been lost, but he outlines it to Maikov and asks his friend to visit the editor and reinforce his own plea that he receive an *immediate* reply. Dostoevsky had told Kashpirev that "*the time and the rapidity of the aid is almost more important than the money itself,*" and that if a delay occurred, "I would be forced on the spot to sell my remaining and most necessary things, and for things worth one hundred thalers would receive twenty . . . in order to save the lives of three beings."[6] Dostoevsky added, for Maikov's eyes alone, that he was here telling an untruth: everything worth a hundred thalers had long since been pawned.

Kashpirev replied favorably within a week and dispatched a letter of credit from a Petersburg bank to one in Dresden; but Dostoevsky's financial relations with *Dawn* were dogged by misfortune. The letter of credit, by mistake, had been written in such a way as to require another document in order to be cashed; and Dostoevsky waited in vain for this all-important paper to arrive, hopefully going to the bank every day and being told, after a while, that such letters of credit were sometimes issued *as a joke*. Desperate with fear for the well-being of Anna and the new-born Lyubov, and literally reduced to his last penny, Dostoevsky wrote a week later to Kashpirev asking him to rectify the error and send seventy-five rubles immediately. It took twelve days for him to receive a reply, even though letters from Petersburg usually arrived in three days, and no seventy-five rubles were forthcoming. Noting that Kashpirev's letter, dated October 3, was postmarked as having been sent on the sixth, he dashed off a furious and frantic letter to Maikov asking him to intercede.

Dostoevsky's missive to Maikov on this occasion is one of the most angry and indignant that he ever wrote—a letter in which he releases all his pent-up resentment at the constant humiliations arising from his impecunious and precarious literary situation. Dostoevsky had written to Kashpirev deferentially, almost pleadingly; and the apparent negligence with which he was being treated, when he had confessed that both he and his family were being forced to pawn and sell their belongings, filled him with a quite pardonable fury: "Doesn't he understand how much this is *insulting* for me? After all, I wrote him about the needs of *my wife* and my child—and after that such carelessness! Is this not insulting!" Dostoevsky felt that Kashpirev was behaving toward him "as only a *barin* behaves with his lackey"; and he returns to this comparison again and again as the tempestuous sentences pour forth in a wave of bitterness and wounded pride.[7]

"Kashpirev writes me (in his letter, on the twelfth day) about my story, demands that I give him the title for advance publication, etc. But can I really write at this moment? I walk up and down and tear my hair, and at night I can't sleep! I think all the time and become furious." After enlarging on the enormity of the insult dealt both him and Anna, he exclaims defiantly: "Let him know that Feodor Dostoevsky can always earn perhaps more than he can by my own work! And after that they demand artistry from me, pure poetry without strain, without tension, and refer to Turgenev, Goncharov! Just let them look under what conditions I work!" Dostoevsky also compares the offhandedness with which he had been treated with the attitude of the magazine toward its own subscribers, since the issues that he received were never sent on time. "How can they edit a journal after this, with such carelessness and lack of skill. I can well imagine what the subscribers in the provinces have to endure! I now understand why they have been met everywhere with general hatred" (as Dostoevsky had been told by Strakhov).[8]

Coming to the rescue, Maikov sent one hundred rubles and another letter of credit, along with the apologies of Kashpirev and the editor's offer to reimburse Dostoevsky for all his extra expenses. Gratified by such contrition, Dostoevsky insists that he is content simply by the offer being made, and "that I don't want any compensation. I'm not a usurer!" Despite his agitations, he had been able to continue working on the novella, whose title he thought would be *The Eternal Husband*, and it would be even lengthier than previously reported. Dostoevsky was also worried because Kashpirev intended to advertise the work in advance, and he asks Maikov to persuade him not to do so if possible. He requested that the manuscript, which he expected to send in two weeks' time (the letter was dated October 27/November 8), be printed in the November or December issue of *Dawn* and not held over. "It would be very, very burdensome for me," he writes, "if it were set aside for the following year."[9] Presumably, it would be in *Dawn*'s best interests to publish the novella soon, because important contributions appearing just before the end of the year brought in new subscribers. The real reason, of course, was that he had promised *The Russian Messenger* the first chapters of a new novel by January 1870, a promise he knew very well he could not keep; and Katkov would become aware that he had been writing for *Dawn* instead.

Dostoevsky continues to complain about the tardiness with which he was receiving issues of *Dawn* and insists that, "even if they had Pushkin and Gogol among their contributors, their journal would fail because of their negligence. They are killing themselves." Other business affairs involved the possibility of publishing *The Idiot* as a volume with Stellovsky, the publisher with whom he had signed the ruthless contract requiring him to write *The Gambler*. This contract also committed Stellovsky to reprint *Crime and Punishment* in 1870; and Dostoevsky would be paid a royalty depending on the size of the printing. With *Crime and Punishment* in hand, the publisher might, Dostoevsky thought, be amenable to expending an extra thousand rubles for the rights to *The Idiot* as well. The prospect of acquiring a thousand rubles was too tempting to resist in face of his desperate situation, despite his well-founded mistrust of the wily cultural entrepreneur; and he entrusted Pasha with the negotiations, asking Maikov, in addition, to keep a watchful eye on the proceedings. In conclusion, Dostoevsky asks Maikov to give twenty-five rubles to Emilya Feodorovna, remarking ruefully: "My heart is saddened by them; it's been so long since I helped them!"[10]

Dostoevsky worked uninterruptedly at his novella from September through December; and to his niece Sofya Ivanova, whose bustling family household is affectionately depicted in the work, he described the routine of his daily life in Dresden. First and foremost was the delight he took in his daughter Lyubotchka, as he lovingly called her, who was exactly three months old on the day he wrote. "I cannot tell you how much I love her. . . . The little girl is healthy, precocious, she listens when I sing to her and laughs all the time; she is a quiet child, not capricious." Anna was breast-feeding Lyubov and apparently finding it a great strain; Dostoevsky was worried that her health was being undermined. "Dresden, besides, is a very dull city," he writes. "I find these Germans unbearable."[11] Happily, his epilepsy had let up for the last three months despite the nervous intensity of his concentration; but he was discomfited by what he called an excess rush of blood to his head and his heart.

"I rise at one o'clock in the afternoon," he specifies, "because I work at night. I work from three to four [in the afternoon]. I take a walk for a half-hour to the post office, and I return through the Royal Garden. We eat dinner. At seven, I take another walk and return always by the same route. I then have some tea, and at half-past ten I start to work until five o'clock in the morning. I go to bed and fall asleep as six o'clock sounds. That's my life, complete. During my evening walk, I stop at the reading room where there are Russian newspapers and read the *St. Petersburg Gazette*, the *Voice*, and the *Moscow Gazette*."[12] Poor Anna, he adds, could not take walks at all because of Lyubov, and her life was even more tedious than his own. This description of Dostoevsky's timetable, besides providing information about his working habits (Balzac too wrote regularly only in the hours just before dawn), is also important for its confirmation of Dostoevsky's zealously regular scrutiny of the Russian press.

Such scrutiny is highly relevant to the problem of the origin of *The Devils*; but for the moment there is no trace of any such project to be found in Dostoevsky's letters or notebooks. Having finished *The Eternal Husband* in the first week of December, he wrote Maikov that "it is terribly long: exactly ten signatures in the type of *The Russian Messenger* [this is how Dostoevsky evaluated what he was to be paid—J.F.]. (Not because it stretched out as I wrote but because the subject changed as I wrote and new episodes came in.) One way or the other, good or bad (I think it is not entirely unoriginal)—I should get at least a thousand rubles for it (maybe a little more)." Dostoevsky, however, was once again so badly short of funds that he could not even afford the postage required for such a bulky manuscript, and he asks Maikov to urge Kashpirev to send fifty rubles immediately. By this time, he was so convinced of *Dawn's* business incompetence that he preferred to approach the editors with his friend acting as intermediary. He also remarks that he had so far received no further advance from *The Russian Messenger* and that *Dawn* could print his manuscript whenever it pleased.[13]

Two weeks later, having sent off his text, Dostoevsky once more pleaded with Maikov to put pressure on Kashpirev for advance payment on everything he had earned. Or if not, "since it is impossible for me to remain absolutely without any money during the Christmas season," then at least to forward one hundred rubles immediately. It was necessary to buy woolens for both Lyubov and Anna, and also to christen the baby—which had not yet been done for lack of funds. "In three days," Dostoevsky also informs him, "I will go to work on my novel for *The Russian Messenger*. Don't think that I just write anything [the literal Russian is: that I bake *blinis*, that is, Russian pancakes]: no matter how terrible and awful what I write may be, the idea of a novel and work on it— is yet to me, poor author, more important than anything in the world! This is not nothing [*blinis*], but the dearest and most longstanding of my ideas."[14] Dostoevsky can only be referring here to his *Atheism* plan, which by this time had metamorphosed into *The Life of a Great Sinner*. It was this novel, or one of its parts, that he was now setting out to compose.

4

Dostoevsky's artistic reputation had been badly tarnished by *The Idiot*, but *The Eternal Husband*, whose analysis is reserved for the next chapter, succeeded in restoring some of its gloss. Strakhov was delighted by the novella's taut limpidity, which avoided all those melodramatic trappings he had underhandedly criticized, and immediately offered his congratulations. "Your story produces a lively impression and will unquestionably be a success. In my opinion, it is one of your most polished works—one of the most interesting and deepest, as only you can write."[15] A month later, he told Dostoevsky that his prediction had been confirmed; the notices in the newspapers were uniformly favorable and quite flattering for Dostoevsky's literary self-esteem. Despite this reassuring reception, Dostoevsky wrote his niece later that she "wouldn't believe how much I abhor writing such stories, when my head is filled with many ideas already formed—in a word, not to write what I should really like."[16] Sheer necessity had driven him in this instance, and he had querulously told her after sending off the manuscript in December that "I have hated this story from the very start."[17] Not even the recognition that he had turned out a small masterpiece could decrease his resentment at having been deflected from a work that, he was convinced, would definitely establish his claim to a place in the pantheon of major Russian writers.

Dostoevsky had initially, as we know, refused to contemplate embarking on his cherished plan while still living abroad. "It is impossible to write [*Atheism*] here [in Europe]," he explains to his niece at the beginning of 1869, because the materials he would need simply were not at hand.[18] Moreover, the theme itself inspired him with reverence, and he approached it with a certain solemnity that precluded the pressure of hastening to meet deadlines. By the time *The Eternal Husband* had been completed, however, Dostoevsky's *Atheism* had evolved into *The Life of a Great Sinner*, which he sketched in his notebooks mainly between December 1869 and January 1870. And as this was to be a work in several volumes, the new plan opened up new possibilities.

In mid-December 1869 Dostoevsky speaks of his obligation to *The Russian Messenger* with a good deal of anxiety and indicates how he hopes to comply with his promise. He has become engaged on a vast novel, he tells his niece, "only the first part of which will be published in *The Russian Messenger*. It [the entire work] will not be finished sooner than in five years, and will be divided into three separate novellas. This novel is the whole hope and whole dream of my life—not only as regards money. . . . But I mustn't be in any hurry to write it. . . . This idea is everything for which I have lived."[19] Dostoevsky has thus decided to embark immediately on the first of these three works, though he continues to voice all his qualms about taking such a decision. In fact, even "in order to write this novel—I would need to be in Russia," he insists. "For instance, the second half of my first novel takes place in a monastery. I need not just see it (I have seen a lot) but to live in a monastery for a while too."[20] The first half, though, could still presumably be written abroad; and a glance at Dostoevsky's notes will help to explain why, even if with great reluctance, he now believed this to be feasible.

The bulk of Dostoevsky's notes deal with the childhood and boyhood of the "great sinner," who is a member of an "accidental family"—as Dostoevsky liked to call households with no settled traditions of order or decorum. The central figure here is thus an illegitimate child, sent to live with an elderly couple in the countryside and raised in isolation from his father (a situation that will later be used for *A Raw Youth*). Dostoevsky's rivalry with Tolstoy is apparent in the definition he sets down of what he wishes his character to represent. "A type entirely contrary to the scion of that noble family of Counts, degenerate to the point of swinishness, which Tolstoy had depicted in *Childhood and Boyhood*. This is simply a primitive type, subconsciously agitated by a primitive strength, a strength which is completely spontaneous and ignorant of any basis of support" (9: 128). From such "primitive strength" came Stenka Razin, the legendary leader of a peasant rebellion in the eighteenth century, and Danilo Filippovich, the equally legendary founder, revered as a reincarnation of the deity, of the sect of the Khlisty, whose secret rites often included self-flagellation.*

The great sinner was to possess such an elemental force, symbolic of that contained in the Russian people, "an extraordinary innate power hard to bear for those who possess it, a power which demands a foundation to stand on and a cause to lead, which demands peace out of the storms of life to the point of suffering, yet cannot help stirring up storms before it finds peace. He finally comes to rest in Christ, but his whole life is storm and disorder." Such a type "joyfully throws itself—in its period of searches and wanderings—into monstrous deviations and experiments until it comes to rest on an idea powerful enough to be fully proportionate to its own immediate primitive strength—an idea so powerful that it can at last organize this strength and calm it down to a tranquilizing stillness" (9: 128).

As a boy, the great sinner is surrounded by a moral laxity that fills him with loathing and contempt. "Disrespect toward people around him, but not yet consciously, solely because of disgust with them" (9: 127). He is beaten and whipped, but this only increases his hatred and nourishes his ferocious pride. "Disgust with men from his first childish awareness (because of his pride and passionately domineering nature)" (9: 131). His companion is a "little cripple" named Katya, over whom he tyrannizes unmercifully; but he confides to her his most secret thoughts (such as a desire to be "king"). This intimate linkage between a crippled girl and the great sinner anticipates that between the future Stavrogin and his crippled, demented wife in *The Devils*. Dostoevsky rapidly indicates the great sinner's initiation into social injustice (a serf girl is sold), sex (he reads *Thérèse-philosophe*, but also Karamzin, Walter Scott, Pushkin, and Gogol), and the accursed questions of religion. "The first confession, what is there in the little boxes and in the chalice. Does God exist?" (9: 133). Dostoevsky sums him up, at this stage, in a sentence: "1st period. A savage boy, but who has an immense opinion of himself" (9: 139).

The next period begins with a return home, at the age of eleven, to live with his father and stepmother. Now made to feel his illegitimate status very acutely, he responds with the prideful arrogance of his nature: "And an immense design of domination—(the spontaneous feeling) is so strong in him that he feels incapable of adapting himself to these people" (9: 129). Instead, he turns for friendship to the family lackey (Kuli-

---

* The name of this sect was actually Khristy (Christians), or, as they called themselves, "the people of God." Their self-flagellation, however, led their adversaries to label them Khlisty (*khlist* means whip). See Anatole Leroy-Beaulieu, *L'Empire des Tsars at les Russes* (1881–1883; rpt. Paris, 1990), 1209–1225. See also "Pisma o raskole," in P. I. Melnikov-Pechersky, *Sobranie Sochinenii*, 6 vols. (Moscow, 1963), 6: 193–376.

kov or Osip), who affects him profoundly: "In the extravagance of his fantasy infinite dreams, to the point of overthrowing God in order to be in his place (Kulikov influences him strongly)" (9: 130). The lackey may be a member of the Khlisty sect, who believed that their ecstatic rites led to literal self-deification, and the two unmistakably converse about the sect. The motif of self-deification, developed so impressively later through Kirillov in *The Devils*, is expressed in a snatch of dialogue: "'I am myself God' and he [the great sinner—J.F.] forces Katya to worship him" (9: 130). These dreams of replacing God, however, do not destroy a subliminal reverence for religion also evident in Kirillov: "The little cripple refuses to be an atheist. He does not beat her because of this" (9: 131).

The great sinner is sent to school, but runs away with Osip and Katya and accidentally becomes involved in the murder of an escaped convict turned bandit. This incident "has a shattering impact and, to a certain extent, bewilders him, so that he feels a natural urge to retire into his shell . . . so as to settle his thoughts. (He then settles on money after all. So far *he has not given any thought* to God)" (9: 129). Money, or the idea of acquiring it, becomes a means of psychic self-protection and security as well as a source of power (a familiar Dostoevskian motif derived from Pushkin's *The Covetous Knight*, which will be developed in *A Raw Youth*). "Sometimes it seemed to him again that in case he did not become extraordinary and were completely ordinary, money would give him everything—that is, power and the right to have contempt—" (9: 136).

Six months later, he confesses to his part in the crime and is sent off to a monastery as a means of disciplining his rebellious behavior, also portrayed through other incidents. He and a fellow student named Albert (of French origin) desecrate an icon; but though it was the great sinner's idea, "when Albert starts to blaspheme, he beats him. After which he declares himself an atheist to the court" (9: 130). The motif of a subliminal struggle with faith thus appears again; and Dostoevsky also suggests an inner evolution toward higher forms of ego satisfaction: "NB the sciences and poetry, etc., expel him from that height [his immeasurable pride—J.F.] in this sense that it is higher and better and that in consequence he must in that also be higher and better" (9: 129). Nor can he be satisfied with debauchery like a schoolfellow now called Lambert (another French name), who will reappear in *A Raw Youth*. Lambert "finds nothing higher" than sensuality because of "the frivolity of national character," but "the emptiness, dirtiness, and absurdity of debauchery unhinges him [the great sinner—J.F.]" (9: 135). The conflict between these higher and lower forms of egoism, if we are to judge from the following note, was to make up the theme of the first novel: "Although money supplies him with a *solid* support and resolves all questions, yet sometimes the *support* wavers (and he) poetry and many other things and he cannot find a solution. This state of *wavering* is precisely what constitutes the novel" (9: 130).

If we assume that the great sinner's childhood and boyhood were to make up Dostoevsky's first novel in the series, we can see why he came round to altering his decision not to undertake his great theme before returning to Russia. A major obstacle had been the lack of available documentary material; but the background of this first segment would require no such sources. All the people mentioned in the notes by name are easily identifiable as members of his own family, their servants, or their friends and acquaintances. The day school and boarding school that the great sinner attends—Souchard and Chermak—are the very ones in which Dostoevsky had been educated. Clearly, he was planning to draw on the background of his own life to provide the experiential context for his great sinner's early moral-psychological struggles; and this background, he must have felt, could be created from his own recollections.

5

The confession of the youthful great sinner brings him to the monastery, where he encounters a saintly monk named Tikhon. Dostoevsky had spoken of this setting initially as belonging to the second half of his first novel, but this second half soon acquired the status of an independent work. The monk Tikhon is based on the figure of Saint Tikhon Zadonsky, a Russian clergyman of the mid-eighteenth century who was elevated to sainthood in 1860 and who left an abundant literary legacy (fifteen volumes) strongly revealing the influence of German Pietism. Just when Dostoevsky became acquainted with these writings is difficult to say, but in the spring of 1870 he told Apollon Maikov that "I took [him] into my heart with rapture a long time ago,"[21] perhaps when an edition of Tikhon's works was published at the time of his canonization. Whatever the date, the theology of this Russian saint, as well as his exemplary life, left a deep and lasting impression on the novelist.

Father George Florovsky, the greatest modern historian of Russian theology, is by no means a partisan of Saint Tikhon from a doctrinal point of view; but he describes him as "possessing a great gift of the word, both artistic and straightforward at the same time. He writes always with a somewhat surprising limpidity" and is "a great writer ... [whose] books fascinate by their light yet plastic images." Saint Tikhon's literary gifts would certainly have attracted Dostoevsky; and the novelist would also have been greatly taken by another aspect of this quite remarkable figure. Florovsky notes, as an especially unusual trait for a revered Russian clergyman, Saint Tikhon's open and unconcealed expression of moods of depression, despair, and susceptibility to temptation. He speaks of Saint Tikhon as undergoing what Saint John of the Cross called *la noche oscura*, the "dark night of the soul."[22] Such features of Saint Tikhon's psychological makeup would surely have appealed to Dostoevsky, who also found in his writings many of the moral-religious precepts that the novelist accepted as the basis of his own conception of Russian Orthodoxy.

Evil, according to Saint Tikhon, was necessary in the world to bring about the birth of the good, and the chief Christian task of mankind was to conquer its own evil proclivities, to conquer "pride by humility, anger by gentleness and patience, hatred by love." Tikhon taught that mankind should be grateful for the existence of temptation, misfortune, and suffering because it was through them that men came to knowledge of all the evil in their souls. It is only through the experience of wrestling with the evil in itself that humankind discovers the value and meaning of human existence. Surely such ideas are the source of the famous notebook entry in which Dostoevsky defined what was for him "the Orthodox point of view" dominant in his work. Here he declares that "man is not born for happiness . . . because the knowledge of life and consciousness . . . is acquired by experience *pro and contra*, which one must take upon oneself. (By suffering, such is the law of our planet, but this immediate awareness, felt with the life process, is such a great joy that one gladly pays with years of suffering for it)" (7:155).

For Tikhon, indeed, even crime was a way of clearing the path to such a discovery of Christian truth; in principle, the possibility of enlightenment and purification was never closed, no matter how burdensome the crime weighing down a human conscience. A chapter of one of his major works, *Treasury of the Spirit*, is entitled "Criminals and Joyous News for Them." According to Tikhon, "the Son of God came to save sinners, not only such and such, but all, whoever they may be." Elsewhere he declared that "there is no kind of sin, and there cannot be any such on earth, that God would not pardon to someone who sincerely repents." There are many references in Tikhon's works to "a great sinner," and he insists that, whatever the multitude and magnitude of sins, God would always pardon a contrite and remorseful heart. Also, one of the best known incidents of Saint Tikhon's life involved a quarrel with a landowner reputed to be a "Voltairian." Disputing about questions of faith with Tikhon, the irascible landowner flared up and struck the clergyman in the face. Although known for his fiery temper, Tikhon immediately kneeled and begged forgiveness for having provoked the blow. Such an incident would certainly have been taken by Dostoevsky as an early symbolic instance of that clash between the disintegrating effects of Western reason and the kenotic Russian faith which had now become the great theme of his life.[23]

The tenor of the monk Tikhon's relations with the adolescent great sinner, once he arrives in the monastery, is indicated in the following notes: "The limpid stories of Tikhon about life and earthly joy. Of the family, father, brothers. Extremely naive, and because of this touching, stories of Tikhon, of his sins toward those close to him, vanity, mockery (how I should like to change all that now, Tikhon says)" (9: 138). During his stay in the monastery, and under the tutelage of Tikhon, the egoism of the great sinner turns inward on itself. He is still obsessed by a need for power and domination; but he begins to believe that this need can be satisfied only by first conquering himself. An earlier stage of this motif is indicated by a reference to self-mutilation, which recalls Rakhmetov's sleeping on a bed of nails: "The strengthening of the will, the wounds and burnings—pride nourishes this. He wishes to be ready for anything" (9: 130).

This tendency is developed into a doctrine of ascetic self-domination with the aid of Tikhon's guidance. Under the title, "The Principal Idea," we read: "After the monastery and Tikhon the great sinner again goes into the world to be the *greatest of men* ... he is the proudest of the proud and treats people with the greatest arrogance.... But (and this is the essential) thanks to Tikhon he had been seized by the idea (conviction): that to conquer the entire world it suffices to conquer oneself. Conquer thyself and thou wilt conquer the world" (9: 138–139). This is the teaching of Tikhon as defined succinctly: "Tikhon. Of Humility (how powerful humility is). All on humility and free will" (9:138).

Self-conquest is thus the highest expression of the freedom of the will, the most exalted goal of the most powerful personality; and the great sinner, as Dostoevsky imagined him, would show that the greatest strength is self-domination and hence, ultimately, the capacity for self-sacrifice. The subsequent career of the great sinner is rapidly sketched: "Suddenly adolescence and debauchery. Exploit and atrocious misdeeds. Abnegation. Insensate pride. Out of pride he becomes ascetic and pilgrim. He travels through Russia.... *Traits*: out of pride and immeasurable arrogance toward people he shows himself as gentle and humble toward all—precisely because he is infinitely higher than all" (9: 138). The great sinner thus reaches the stage of humility and self-abasement out of pride and arrogance; but the temptation of sanctity is only the last and supreme test, the subtlest form taken by the sin of pride. The great sinner was presumably to succeed in overcoming this final temptation as well, though Dostoevsky was unable to imagine anything better than a sentimental Dickensian climax: "NB He wished to blow his brains out (a small child is left before his door). He ends up by installing a school for orphan children in his home. . . . Everything becomes transfigured. He dies confessing his crime" (9: 139).

As with all the notes he made for future works, Dostoevsky is much concerned with questions of narrative technique and form. Here he sets down remarks on the "tone" of his narrative, which was to be that of a *vita*, the hagiographic life of a saint. "N.B. *Tone* (the narrative is a *vita*, i.e., even though it comes from the author's pen, it is concise, not sparing with explications, yet presented in scenic forms." He wants the tonal texture to maintain the "matter-of-factness" of Alain-René Lesage's *Gil Blas* (the French picaresque novel that he much admired), but at the same time to insinuate constantly that the events are more significant than they seem at first glance. "Yet it is also important that the dominant idea of the *vita* be apparent, i.e., even though the whole dominant idea may never be explained in so many words. . . . The reader still ought to know at all times that the whole idea is a pious one." The selection of the narrative elements, he told himself, "should continually convey a certain *something*," and "the man of the future is to be exhibited for everyone to see, and to be placed on a pedestal" (9: 132–133). Dostoevsky would later return to these notes for both *A Raw Youth* (where the peasant "wanderer" Makar Ivanovich also regales an adolescent with naive and touchingly edifying parables and apothegms) and *The Brothers Karamazov*, where Father Zosima's life is narrated as a *vita* and the semi-hagiographic treatment of the "man of the future" would be realized in Alyosha.

6

Dostoevsky did not, so far as we know, settle down to the redaction of the novel sketched in these notes. Instead, as he told Maikov just a month later, he was swept away by a new inspiration, one that changed all his literary plans. "I have tackled a rich idea," he informs his friend enthusiastically. "I am not speaking of the execution, but the idea. One of the ideas that has an undoubted resonance among the public. Like *Crime and Punishment*, but even closer to reality, more vital, and having direct relevance for the most important contemporary issue. I will finish by fall; I'm not hurrying and not rushing." These words are the first reference to *The Devils*, which was indeed conceived with "direct relevance to the most important contemporary issue," that is, to the recent discovery of a murder committed by a group of revolutionary conspirators. Dostoevsky thus set aside his "eternal" theme, that of atheism, for one that was burningly topical because he was persuaded that such a book would solve all his problems. He would pillory the radicals once and for all, satisfy *The Russian Messenger* with a novel, reap a rich financial reward, and do all this in record time. "I hope to make at least as much money as for *Crime and Punishment*, and therefore, by the end of the year there is hope of putting all my affairs in order and of returning to Russia. . . . Never have I worked with such enjoyment and such ease."[24]

Work on the new novel began immediately and relegated *The Life of a Great Sinner*, which Dostoevsky must have given up with some relief, to a less uncertain, less economically harassed, and happily repatriated future. But his imagination could not relinquish the stately vistas it had created, and continued to toil at their elaboration. In late March, Dostoevsky speaks of five novels to Maikov, instead of three (the size of *War and Peace*, he remarks, again disclosing the competition with Tolstoy), and defines his "main question" as being "the same one that I have been tormented by consciously and unconsciously all my life—the existence of God." He also confesses how painfully he suffers from a sense of inferiority to his two great rivals, Turgenev and Tolstoy, and his hope of enhancing his status by the exalted thematic heights he would be attempting to scale. "Perhaps people will at last say," he complains sadly, "that I did not spend all my time writing trifles."[25]

Just how sublime these heights were meant to be is suggested by some additions to his original scenario. The monastery would harbor not only Tikhon and the future great sinner, but also representatives of various currents of Russian thought. Peter Chaadev would be there,* also Belinsky, T. N. Granovsky, and perhaps even Pushkin, as well as Pavel Prussky and the monk Parfeny (the author of a famous account, much admired by Dostoevsky, of travels to holy sites). Dostoevsky was thus envisaging a vast panorama of Russian ideological attitudes, not just those of the intelligentsia, as well as a clash between secular and religious views; and some of this ambition to create a symbolic fresco of Russian culture will be carried over into the purely up-to-the-minute events of the novel on

---

* Chaadev was a famous Russian thinker of whom Herzen has left a scintillating portrait in *My Past and Thoughts*. A dandy and friend of Pushkin's, he wrote a series of *Philosophical Letters*, only the first of which was published in his lifetime; but it was enough to have him declared legally insane and condemned to house arrest by Nicholas I. Chaadev argued, with impressive erudition, that Russia was the stepchild of European civilization, doomed to backwardness because it lacked the spiritual and cultural heritage of Greco-Roman civilization preserved for Europe by the Roman Catholic Church. Later, in a work ironically called *The Apology of a Madman*, he reversed himself by maintaining that Russia's "backwardness" was a great advantage because it would enable Russian culture to make a fresh start. This second thesis exercised an enormous influence.

See Alexander Herzen, *My Past and Thoughts*, trans. Constance Garnett, rev. Humphrey Higgens, 4 vols. (New York, 1968), 2: 516–526. An excellent introduction to Chaadev's thought can be found in Andrzej Walicki, *A History of Russian Thought from the Enlightenment to Marxism* (Stanford, 1979), chap. 5. See also P. Chaadev, *Philosophical Letters and Apology of a Madman*, trans. Mary-Barbara Zeldin (Knoxville, Tenn., 1969).

which he was then busily engaged. More than anything else, however, and with Saint Tikhon as model, Dostoevsky wished to produce "a majestic, *positive*, holy figure."

Dostoevsky's great ambition was now to provide Russian culture with an august image expressing its highest religious values. The disappointing reception of his first attempt, *The Idiot*, had not quenched his aspiration; and the historical stature of Saint Tikhon would shield his literary eulogist from the all-too-familiar accusation of giving rein to his weakness for "the fantastic." "This is not," he assures Maikov, "Kostanzhoglo [in the second part of *Dead Souls*], and not the German (I have forgotten his name) in *Oblomov*, and not Lavretsky [*A Nest of Gentlefolk*], nor Chichikov [also in *Dead Souls*], and not the Lopukhovs and Rakhmetovs [in *What Is To Be Done?*]. True, I will not be creating anything; I will just portray the real Tikhon."[26] Side by side with Saint Tikhon would stand the type of character Dostoevsky had been struggling to delineate ever since the epilogue to *Crime and Punishment*—a great sinner, who would convincingly undergo a religious conversion and display the regenerative effects of Saint Tikhon's teaching and example.

Dostoevsky clearly intended to keep his "contemporary" theme separate from his more "exalted" one of atheism, postponing the second for more propitious working conditions while quickly (and profitably) dispatching the first. In so doing, however, he was allowing his contest with Tolstoy, whose elevation of subject matter he envied and wished to emulate, to tempt him into running counter to the distinctive idiosyncracy of his talent. Dostoevsky always found his inspiration in the most immediate and sensational events of the day—events that were often commonplace and even sordid—and then raised such material in his best work to the level of the genuinely tragic. This union of the contemporary and the tragic was the true secret of his genius, and he finally found it impossible to maintain the forced and artificial disjunction of one from the other that he thought he could impose. What he called his "poem" could not be kept distinct from the social-political "pamphlet" into which he had thrown himself, and the two eventually blended together into his unprecedented novel-tragedy, *The Devils*. But before examining the process by which this remarkable fusion took place, let us first pause for a closer look at *The Eternal Husband*.

CHAPTER 20

The Eternal Husband

No information exists concerning the origins of *The Eternal Husband*, but it has been plausibly linked to some events that occurred between 1854 and 1856, during the period of Dostoevsky's Siberian exile. In those years, his young friend Baron Wrangel was carrying on an impassioned love affair with Mme E. I. Gerngross, the libidinous wife of the general commanding this distant outpost of the Russian Empire. Dostoevsky, it would seem, had planned to make Wrangel's romantic liaison, as well as his own tortured courtship of his first wife (who, after relocating several hundred versts away, took a lover in Dostoevsky's absence before their marriage), the basis for a novel. As late as 1865, after reading *House of the Dead*, Wrangel inquired of Dostoevsky whether he still planned to use "our Semipalatinsk life" for his work.[1] It has been conjectured that, in search of a subject for a story to be written quickly, Dostoevsky fell back on this old creative intention.

Aside from this biographical source, two intertextual connections also help to throw some light on the novella. One, mentioned by name, is Turgenev's play *A Provincial Lady*, first published in 1851 and reissued in 1869. The two main characters of *The Eternal Husband*, Velchaninov (whose name implies grandeur) and Trusotsky (whose name suggests cowardice), discuss this one-act comedy and compare its situation with their own. The play revolves around a good-hearted and good-natured husband betrayed by a scheming and unfaithful wife, who is bored by her provincial existence and quite willing to use her charms to escape from its tedium. Dostoevsky's novella takes its point of departure from a similar situation, and may be considered an implicit commentary on Turgenev's amusedly man-of-the-world treatment of his theme. For Dostoevsky reveals the tragic outcome that may result for the hood-winked husband as a result of his wife's amorous dalliances.

The most important subtext for this seemingly uncomplicated novella, however, is provided by Apollon Grigoryev's theory of Russian culture. Velchaninov and Trusotsky also speak—rather obscurely, for a reader unfamiliar with Russian literary polemics—of "peaceable" (*smirny*) and "predatory" (*khischny*) types of personalities. These terms were used by Grigoryev to characterize Russian literature and culture, which he views as a struggle between such types; and the same terms had just been revived and employed by Strakhov in his essay on Tolstoy. Types of this kind were understood not only as moral-psychological categories but, in addition, possessed a strong social-cultural significance. The "predatory" figures—masterful, heroic, brilliant, often glamorously Byronic— were identified with Western European culture; the "simple" or "peaceable" ones with Russia and the Russian national character. *War and Peace*, according to Strakhov, had borne out Grigoryev's views to perfection, and offered the greatest depiction so far achieved of this memorable internecine warfare taking place within the Russian national psyche.[2]

Dostoevsky, a great admirer of Grigoryev, had been deeply influenced by his typology of Russian culture; but he had never accepted all of its details. Indeed, as Grigoryev revealed in a series of articles, "The Paradoxes of Organic Criticism"—subtitled "Letters to F. M. Dostoevsky"— the novelist had once taxed him personally with being too "theoretical." Just what Dostoevsky meant by his remark to Grigoryev may perhaps be inferred from *The Eternal Husband*, in which both the lordly Velchaninov and the docile cuckold Trusotsky momentarily exchange personalities and exhibit characteristics of each other under the stress of events. The novella may thus be taken not only as a comment on Grigoryev but also as a reply to what Dostoevsky considered Strakhov's excessive praise of Tolstoy, against whose pure personality types he was presenting his own more tangled view of the mutabilities and indeterminacies of human character.[3]

2

In *The Eternal Husband*, Dostoevsky employs a plot situation, that of the cuckolded husband, on which endless changes had been rung in the lighter literature of the nineteenth century. Indeed, in his travel articles, *Winter Notes*, Dostoevsky had ridiculed the exclusive preoccupation of the French stage with this time-honored and titillating *topos*; and the popular novelist who specialized in cuckoldry with immense success— Paul de Kock—is invariably the favorite author of characters whom Dostoevsky wishes to satirize (Foma Fomich in *The Village of Stepanchikovo* and the soon-to-be created Stepan Trofimovich Verkhovensky in *The Devils*). His own choice of such a subject for *The Eternal Husband* may thus seem surprising; but in Dostoevsky's hands the threadbare intrigue of countless farces—the intrigue, as he entitled one of his chapters, of "The Wife, the Husband, and the Lover"—becomes the exploration of a double moral crisis. And just as, in his first novel *Poor Folk*, Dostoevsky had transformed the comic bureaucratic scribbler of Gogol's *The Overcoat* into the moving image of the sensitive and suffering Makar Devushkin, so here too the stock comic butt, the husband abundantly adorned with horns, becomes a profoundly self-conscious and lacerated human being despite all the grotesque and even distasteful features that he continues to retain.

To achieve his own perspective, Dostoevsky shifts the time of the action from the illicit events themselves to their long-delayed consequences. *The Eternal Husband* takes place nine years after Pavel Pavlovich Trusotsky had been deceived by his wife and the man he considered his friend. Velchaninov, the lover, had carried on an all-engulfing year-long affair with the provincial philanderess—neither the first nor last for that "passionate, cruel, and sensual" woman, whom he has since come to compare with "the Madonna of the Flagellants who believes implicitly herself that she is the mother of God" (9: 27). Dostoevsky here is drawing on his intense interest in, and fascination with, Russian sectarian religion to express all the power of Mme Trusotskaya's personality and the serene self-righteousness she always exhibited. Dismissed by his imperious mistress unceremoniously when a replacement appears, Velchaninov has long since forgotten the affair and betaken himself to the delectable pursuit of amorous pleasures elsewhere. Mme Trusotskaya dies just a few months before the story begins, leaving all her correspondence intact for her innocent husband's perusal; here he learns about her betrayals, and, in an unsent letter, that his eight-year-old daughter Liza is really Velchaninov's illegitimate child. He arrives in Petersburg with Liza shortly thereafter, and the story concerns the relation between the two men, as well as, in the first part, the tragic fate of little Liza.

The opening chapters give an extended portrait of Velchaninov, partly through objective narration and partly through the filter of his own mocking self-consciousness. He is a handsome and prepossessing gentleman approaching forty, whose life has been devoted more or less exclusively to sexual philandering and the protection of his considerable vanity. He is, we are told, "full of the most unshakable, the most aristocratically insolent self-confidence," even though this self-assurance of late has been seriously undermined by a "nervous depression" that he sardonically acknowledges to be a moral crisis. "Yes, he had even come to that, he was worrying about some sort of *higher* ideas of which he would never have thought twice in his earlier days. In his own mind and in his conscience he called 'higher' all 'ideas' at which (he found to his surprise) he could not laugh in his heart—there had never been such hitherto—in his secret heart only, of course; oh, in company it was a different matter!" (9: 6). This passage adroitly captures the conflict between Velchaninov's sudden access of moral questioning and his sophisticated skepticism, which makes it absolutely impossible for him to imagine courting ridicule by any public manifestation of his embarrassing respect for "higher ideas." Still, he is haunted by memories of his past peccadillos, not only sexual but including even casual acts of social sadism—gratuitous remarks, supposedly jokes, that had deeply wounded and injured perfectly inoffensive people. But he is convinced—and this only depresses him all the more—that he does not have sufficient strength to undergo any fundamental moral change.

Velchaninov is analyzed with an amplitude of expository detail rare in Dostoevsky, who usually prefers to bring out character traits in the course of a developing action. But here the action primarily involves Velchaninov's attempt to comprehend the behavior of Trusotsky, "the eternal husband" (as Velchaninov might be called "the eternal lover"), and thus it is necessary to establish and motivate him very solidly so as to bring out the nature and limitations of his point of view. Velchaninov's attitude toward Trusotsky is the result of his own inner conflict, which combines a feeling of guilt and a need for expiation with an unconquerable aversion to admitting to himself—or, even worse, to others—the presence of any such inadmissible sentiments. As a result, he stubbornly refuses to feel any sympathy whatever for Trusotsky, because to do so would break down the wall protecting him from his own guilt. His view of Trusotsky is thus consistently colored by this need to safeguard the facade behind which he conceals the undermining ravages of his "higher ideas." It is only at the climax of the story that he is able to face Trusotsky—and himself—with any degree of honesty.

No similar analysis is given for Trusotsky, who is always seen from the outside through Velchaninov precisely because Velchaninov's relation to him provides the crux of the story. To stress this relation, Dostoevsky employs one of his frequently used technical devices: Trusotsky appears on the scene as another guilt-laden fragment of Velchaninov's past, who floats up from the depth of his subconscious to plunge him into a particularly acute state of nervousness and ill humor. The two brush by each other several times on the street, apparently by chance, but really because Trusotsky desires an encounter; and Trusotsky's evanescent face in the crowd, which Velchaninov is unable to identify, begins to obsess him unpleasantly and to intensify his already existing morosity and spleen. At last Trusotsky materializes in the middle of the night, just after Velchaninov had dreamed that he was being accused by a crowd of a "crime which he had committed and concealed" and that his fate lay in the hands of one man, "once an intimate friend of his who was dead, but now suddenly come to see him." The crowd expected "from this man a final word that would decide Velchaninov's guilt or innocence," but "he was mute and would not speak." Velchaninov struck the man, and continued to beat him with "a strange enjoyment" (just as Raskolnikov had tried to rekill the murdered pawnbroker, the image of *his* guilt)—and is awakened by a ring of the doorbell (9: 15). The dream manifestly expresses the exasperated struggle of Velchaninov's subconscious (and conscience) both to recognize Trusotsky and to suppress the silent accusation stirred by his reappearance.

The manner in which Trusotsky seems to emerge as the emanation of Velchaninov's guilty psyche has often led critics to call him a "double," but Dostoevsky's use of this feature of his technique is here given a very subtle variation. Velchaninov and Trusotsky are not linked to each other, as are similar quasi doubles who exist independently, by any similarity in their personalities or moral attitudes. There is, instead, a remarkable parallel in the *pattern* of their relation to the situation in which they find themselves. Both become split personalities, torn between love (or at least tolerance and sympathy) for each other and hatred; each feels a need to punish the other as well as himself; both are victims of the same domineering female deity who had manipulated their lives. Dostoevsky weaves a delicate web of such parallels into the background without underlining them explicitly; but they serve to counterpoint ironically the refusal of Velchaninov to identify with the plight of the seemingly repulsive and abjectly obstreperous Trusotsky. They also serve to reinforce structurally the fusion between the two that finally emerges.

3

The lengthy analysis of Velchaninov's inner conflict serves as a preparation for the appearance of Trusotsky; but although no such dissection of Trusotsky's character occurs until the final pages, the symptoms of his crisis are evident from the very first encounter with his erstwhile friend. On the one hand, he provocatively expresses his resentment against Velchaninov by sardonic insinuations that leave no doubt about his knowledge of the past. On the other, he continues to insist on his continued "friendship" for the man he manifestly knows has betrayed him so shamefully. The perversity of Trusotsky's attitude, with its mixture of barely concealed resentment and supposedly unbroken amiability, clearly recalls the underground man; and this idea of the "underground"—that is, behavior expressing an unresolved struggle between love and hate (or, in this instance, between feelings of sympathy and cordiality and the need for revenge)—is used as a key thematic motif. For the moment, though, Velchaninov is revolted by Trusotsky's self-demeaning and humiliating conduct, and totally unable to explain it except as the result of a general moral collapse since the death of his wife. "'What if he's simply a "buffoon"' flashed through his mind, 'but n-no, n-no! I don't think he's drunk—he may be drunk, though: his face is red. Even if he were drunk—it comes to the same thing. What's he driving at? What does the low fellow want?'" (9: 22).

Velchaninov's bewilderment becomes fully explicable only in the light of his previous opinion of Trusotsky, which is evoked in a retrospective chapter following their first meeting. In the past, Trusotsky had been nothing but the docile and well-disciplined appendage to the fascinating adulteress. For the lover, Trusotsky had been nothing but an "eternal husband," whose essence consisted "in being, all his life, a husband and nothing more.... The chief sign of such a husband is a certain decoration. He can no more escape wearing horns than the sun can keep shining, he is not only unaware of the fact, but he is bound by the very laws of nature to be unaware of it" (9: 27). This is Velchaninov's patronizing and completely external view of the man he had deceived and dishonored, and who is thus denied the very possibility of being considered a responsive and vulnerable human being.

Just as Velchaninov had seen Trusotsky in the past solely in terms that dignified his own treacherous conduct, so now he continues to regard him from the same self-defensive point of view. And the discovery of the existence of little Liza only increases Velchaninov's conviction that the sole explanation for Trusotsky's actions is a sadistic need to seek revenge. The drunken and irascible Trusotsky has been shamefully mistreating the child, and has even taunted her with being illegitimate. Velchaninov immediately (though silently) recognizes her as his daughter, and removes her from the sordid conditions in which she is living to stay at the home of some friends. Explaining the situation to his confidante Klavdia Petrovna, Velchaninov says: "He came to me yesterday from an irresistible malicious desire to let me know that he knew of the wrong done him.... He simply came to work off his resentment! ... I tell you, he's even been tormenting Liza, tormenting the child, and probably that, too, was to work off his resentment—to vent his malice, if only on a child!" (9: 40).

There is ample evidence in the text to justify Velchaninov's judgment, and we should be misreading if we attempted to make Trusotsky any more appealing or sympathetic a figure than Dostoevsky meant him to be. His conduct toward Liza *is* odious, and he *is* working off his resentment against both his dead wife and Velchaninov on the unfortunate child. But what Dostoevsky wishes us to understand—and what Velchaninov stubbornly refuses to acknowledge—is that Trusotsky is not merely a degraded monster. To make the point, Dostoevsky introduces details about Trusotsky's past life that show him to have been an inoffensive, kindly, and generous man—indeed, far too obliging and trusting for his own good. And he is also shown to have been lovingly attached to his little daughter, who "became everything to me as soon as she came to me, so that I used to think that even if my tranquil happiness should, by God's will, be at an end, Liza would always be left me; that I reckoned upon for certain!" (9: 34). These words, because they are addressed to Velchaninov, have a double edge that might make their sincerity suspect; but they are confirmed by Liza herself, who confides to Velchaninov "that she loved her father more than her mother, because he had always been fonder of her, and her mother had not cared so much for her" (9: 38).

This image of the earlier Trusotsky constantly intrudes in the course of the action to suggest a complexity of response, a torment of conflicting feelings, from which Velchaninov carefully keeps his eyes averted. The parting between Trusotsky and Liza offers additional dramatic confirmation of his love for the child, and Liza is terrified, as she drives off, that Trusotsky will hang himself as he had threatened to do, though Velchaninov hesitates to take this seriously. And when Velchaninov reproaches Trusotsky for failing to visit Liza (who meanwhile has fallen ill out of chagrin at being abandoned to the care of strangers), the latter blazes back: "'Liza? Do you know what Liza has meant and means to me? Has meant and still means!' he cried all at once, almost frantically" (9: 48).

All these signs point to the terrible turmoil taking place in Trusotsky's own breast—a turmoil that drives him to abandon what he loves the most, out of a hatred as much directed against himself as against its helpless object. Liza is a living reminder of his humiliations, and his love for her has turned to hatred precisely because, unable to detach himself from her emotionally, he cannot escape the past that he wishes to blot out. This is the infernal circle of Dostoevsky's dialectic of pride and humiliation, which can be broken only by a transcendence of the ego, an act of selflessness overcoming the festering poisons of wounded pride. But Trusotsky is no more capable of accomplishing such a moral-psychological feat than was the underground man.

The action of the first part of the novella centers around the pitiable fate of little Liza, and the relations between the two men are determined by her situation. But Dostoevsky takes care, all the same, to indicate the similarity between Trusotsky's tortured ambiguity of feeling about Liza and his attitude toward Velchaninov. Just as his overflowing love for Liza has now become mixed with hate, so his previous friendship for Velchaninov has turned into masked insolence and aggressiveness. When he insists almost insultingly that Velchaninov drink with him and even kiss him, despite his "friend's" evident resistance, Velchaninov suddenly realizes that his previous notion of Trusotsky had been far too limited. "Damnation!" he suddenly exclaims. "Why, you are really a 'predatory type.' I thought you were 'the eternal husband' and nothing more!" (9: 47).

Velchaninov disgustedly accedes to this request for the sake of Liza, whom he wishes Trusotsky to go and visit, and by doing so he behaves in the same morally convoluted manner as his despicable visitor. But while the haughty Velchaninov feels only repulsion for his interlocutor, there are moments when Trusotsky, dropping his "predatory" tone of sarcasm and provocation, reveals quite other feelings. After the drink, for example, he first kisses Velchaninov's hand, and then, when the two men kiss on the lips, he breaks into tears at the thought that Velchaninov too, like all the rest, had betrayed him so unconscionably. Velchaninov, though, remains unwilling to recognize the agonies that lie behind Trusotsky's revolting behavior:

> "Ah! a drunken fool and nothing more!" He [Velchaninov] waved his hand dismissing the subject.
> "Absolutely nothing more," he repeated energetically as he undressed and got into bed. (9: 49)

Liza's death provides a poignant minor climax to the first sequence of *The Eternal Husband*, and her pathetic demise plunges Velchaninov into a torpor of despair all the more anguishing because the discovery of her existence had seemed to show him the path of redemption. By his love for Liza, he had thought, "all my old putrid and useless life would be purified and expiated" (9: 62); but with her disappearance he returns once again to the nagging misery of his "higher ideas." Meanwhile, Trusotsky is stumbling drunkenly from one brothel to another and, despite Velchaninov's urgings, fails to visit Liza in her illness or even to attend her burial. He learns of her death in a drunken stupor, but retains enough awareness to taunt Velchaninov by naming another of his wife's lovers as Liza's father. And when Velchaninov accuses him of lying, Trusotsky turns to curse him, "his face . . . contorted by a frenzy of hatred" (9: 61). In the two weeks following Liza's funeral Velchaninov neglects everything in his grief, incessantly haunted by the events that have just occurred and particularly by one question: "How could that monster be so cruel to a child whom he had loved so much, and is it credible? But every time he made haste to dismiss that question and, as it were, brush it aside; there was something awful in that question, something he could not bear and could not solve" (9: 63). To face that question squarely would mean to face himself and his own responsibility.

4

The events of the next sequence have the effect of a play within a play— one thinks of the trap "to catch the conscience of the King" in *Hamlet*— which, by re-creating the past under changed circumstances, forces Velchaninov to confront that past in a manner he has so far avoided. This confrontation takes place under the guiding inspiration of the memory of Liza, whose grave he visits just before the action resumes, and who, he believes, has sent him the consolation of faith. At her graveside, "a rush of pure, calm faith flooded his soul, there was something like hope in his heart after many days" (9: 63). This memory of Liza remains with Velchaninov all through the next chapters as a symbol of purity and goodness by which he constantly measures himself, even though she is no longer alive to motivate a transformation of his life.

Trusotsky himself has been affected in a totally different way by Liza's death. On meeting him again outside the cemetery where Liza has been interred, Velchaninov notes that "the attire, the hat with the crepe band, and the whole appearance of Mr. Trusotsky were incomparably more presentable than they had been a fortnight ago" (9: 64). Even his manner toward Velchaninov entirely lacks the strain and tension so manifest previously. The death of Liza, ghoulish though the idea may seem, has freed Trusotsky from the pressure of his love-hate relationship with the child, and with both her and Velchaninov as the living testimony to his shame. Indeed, he now proposes to Velchaninov that they pay a visit together to the family of a fifteen-year-old girl whom he intends to marry in a year with the permission of her parents. The perversity of this unhealthy desire indicates again how little Dostoevsky wishes to arouse any facile sympathy for Trusotsky. His marriage plan is clearly still a twisted expression of his ego, which has transferred its new need for self-assertion in an effort to assume Velchaninov's role as triumphant seducer.

Velchaninov's reaction to this strange request is at first a refusal, and a revival of all his feelings of loathing for the impossible creature appealing to him so deferentially and pleadingly. But he suddenly agrees, prompted by an "oppressive and malignant impulse. This evil impulse had been faintly stirring within him from the very beginning, ever since [Trusotsky] had talked of his future bride" (9: 68). This impulse turns out to be the assumption of his old role as the practiced and irresistible Don Juan, "the eternal lover," and he slips into it with all his accustomed grace and success in the midst of the festive atmosphere of the Zahlebinin household. These pages, written in a Turgenevian tonality unusual for Dostoevsky, draw on those summer evenings in the Ivanov household at Lublino, also filled with high-spirited young people, when games were played, theatricals were staged, and Dostoevsky had been the master of the revels. The charm of these scenes provides some welcome relief from the strained perversities of the earlier section; and one should also note the tone of amusement, touched ever so lightly with caricature, that Dostoevsky employs to depict the innocent "radicalism" of his adolescent characters.

Velchaninov succeeds in winning the confidence of Trusotsky's "betrothed," who cannot bear the sight of her intended fiancé, and her girlish candor is troubled by his well-tested gallantry. Meanwhile, Trusotsky is publicly and repeatedly humiliated by all the young people in league against him; and he finally drags Velchaninov away in a fury of renewed resentment. These scenes revive the initial relation between the seducer and the cuckold—though this time under circumstances that are happily more comic than tragic. Nonetheless, the ease with which Velchaninov has slipped into his old posture as seducer fills him with horror and remorse. "I consider," he tells Trusotsky, "that I have never lowered myself as I have today—to begin with, by consenting to go with you, and then, by what happened there. . . . It was so paltry, so pitiful. . . . I've defiled and debased myself for mixing myself up in it . . . and forgetting" (9: 85). Velchaninov is here talking about the present, but the emotional pressure behind his words comes from the memory of Liza and the past; it is the past that he judges when he acknowledges its comparatively inoffensive repetition to be a debasement and defilement.

Matters are made even worse for Velchaninov because Trusotsky chooses just this moment to reveal that it has always been impossible for him simply to hate Velchaninov straightforwardly. What could only be inferred in the first part of the novella now is openly expressed when Trusotsky confesses: "I loved you, Aleksey Ivanovich . . . and all that year at T—I loved you. . . . I always thought of you as a man with a passion for every noble feeling, a man of education . . . and therefore believed in you—in spite of anything" (9: 87). The incongruity and mawkishness of this confession does not make it any less genuine or pathetic; and it confronts Velchaninov openly with his fatal involvement in Trusotsky's life and all the shabbiness of his past. Nothing could be more intolerable for Velchaninov at this moment than such an appeal from Trusotsky for "reconciliation." To respond would be to break down the barrier he has so carefully built up against any feeling of sympathy; and his only reaction is a hysterical outburst of rage expressing all the suppressed tension of his sense of guilt.

Dostoevsky nonetheless indicates a subterranean change as having taken place in Velchaninov by a telling repetition of the word "underground." Early in the story, in a similar outburst, Velchaninov had said to Trusotsky: "Go to hell with *your* underground vileness" (9: 56; italics added). Now he repulses the flattering image of himself offered by Trusotsky as "nothing but delusion, mirage, and falsity, and shameful, and unnatural, and—exaggerated—and that is what's worst. . . . And it's all nonsense; we are *both* vicious, underground, loathsome people" (italics added). This significant admission does not prevent Velchaninov, however, from continuing to insist that he and Trusotsky "are men of different worlds" and that between them "lies a grave." But this reference to Liza rekindles all of Trusotsky's old fury: "'I know that little grave here, and we both stand at the side of the little grave, but on my side there is more than yours, more . . .' he whispered as though in delirium, still thumping at his heart with his fist, 'more, more, more'" (9: 87–88).

The climax occurs when Velchaninov, having brought Trusotsky to his flat, is suddenly seized by a severe and intensely painful liver attack that could be fatal. The old, kindly Trusotsky suddenly comes to life again in this emergency, and he springs to the aid of the suffering man with compassionate zeal. With the last vestiges of his arrogance swept away by his helplessness and his gratitude, Velchaninov murmurs: "You, you . . . you are better than I am. I understand it all, all. . . . Thank you" (9: 97). He then falls into a feverish dream, in which exasperated and irate figures threaten him with some obscure, approaching menace. On opening his eyes, he finds Trusotsky standing over him with an open razor in his hand. Velchaninov's breakthrough to repentance has been too late and too long delayed; the memory of Trusotsky's humiliations are no longer possible for him to endure, and the resurrection of his former self while nursing Velchaninov has only fueled his murderous rage.

During a struggle in the dark. Velchaninov's hand is badly cut but he finally masters his assailant and ties him up. In the morning, he releases Trusotsky without a word—and feels an "immense, extraordinary relief . . . a weight of depression had vanished and was dissipated forever" (9: 100). All through the story, Velchaninov had been struggling between his vanity and the sense of guilt induced by his "higher ideas"; but it had been impossible for him to humiliate himself by acknowledging any culpability, especially in front of the despicable "eternal husband." The physical assault has freed him from this debasing obligation by allowing him, as it were, literally to expiate his past sins in blood and to acknowledge his atonement by the silent liberation of Trusotsky. The relief he feels is the joy of at last being able to obey his "higher ideas," without, miraculously, any overt derogation of his self-esteem.

This resolution of the inner conflict between his conscience and his vanity at last enables Velchaninov to grasp the truth about Trusotsky and himself. "He had been thinking of me with respect, cherishing my memory and brooding over my utterances for nine years. Good Lord! and I had no notion of it!" (9: 102). Even more, this moment of empathy brings with it a glimpse of the possibility of another relation between them that had not been realized. "H'm! He comes here 'to embrace and to weep,' as he expressed it in the most abject way—that is, he came here to murder me and thought he came 'to embrace and to weep.' . . . He brought Liza too. But, who knows? If I had wept with him, perhaps, really, he would have forgiven me, for he had a terrible longing to forgive me!"

(9: 103). Velchaninov was right in calling both Trusotsky and himself "underground men": neither had been capable of rising to the challenge of accomplishing a selfless act of love—Trusotsky toward Liza, Velchaninov toward Trusotsky by accepting him as more than a contemptible and ridiculous "eternal husband."

What has just transpired, however, elevates Velchaninov above himself for a fleeting moment; and he goes to seek, of his own free will, the man who tried to take his life. Their roles have now become reversed, and Velchaninov is behaving exactly as Trusotsky had done at the beginning of the story. " 'Can it be, can it be?', he cried, turning crimson with shame. 'Can it be that I'm crawling there "to embrace and shed tears"?' That senseless abjectness was all that was needed to complete his ignominy!" (9: 104). The delicious irony of these lines shows that Velchaninov can hardly believe his own reactions, and is still fundamentally the same insolently incorrigible man-of-the-world. What he feels is only a passing moment of truth, not the beginning of any deep-seated moral conversion; and Dostoevsky rings down the curtain with admirable tact at the point necessary to preserve him from being put to the test. Trusotsky's conflict has been resolved by his attack on Velchaninov, and he has departed from Petersburg for good, leaving behind for Velchaninov's perusal the unsent letter from Mme Trusotskaya revealing all the secrets of their affair and the parentage of Liza. Velchaninov imagines Trusotsky reading the letter while reading it himself; and the story thus comes full circle, returning to its beginning as the two figures blend into one at this climactic moment.

Dostoevsky might well have terminated his story here, but he adds a brief epilogue. Several years later, Velchaninov and Trusotsky meet at a railroad station during a change of trains. Both have become very much themselves after the derangement of their past encounter: Velchaninov is once again a debonair and self-confident social butterfly; Trusotsky, remarried to a very pretty and overdressed lady accompanied by a handsome young officer, clearly has reassumed his predestined status of "eternal husband." Dostoevsky rapidly brushes in a tentative flirtation between the new Mme Trusotskaya and Velchaninov, who saves her from an embarrassing situation. The story seems about to begin again, but the appearance of Trusotsky cuts short the rising hopes of the fluttered lady. Velchaninov affably reassures his old "friend" with a patronizing laugh and holds out his hand at parting; but Trusotsky recoils, and for an instant the past flames back to life. Velchaninov, furious at this rebuff, thrusts before Trusotsky the palm of his hand, scarred in their struggle. Trusotsky "too, turned pale, and his lips trembled too; a convulsive quiver ran over his face. 'And Liza?' he murmured in a rapid whisper, and suddenly his lips, his cheeks and his chin began to twitch and tears gushed from his eyes" (9: 112). Of the two, it is the "eternal husband" for whom the memory of Liza has truly stayed alive.

5

The Eternal Husband, the most perfect and polished of all Dostoevsky's shorter works, can truly be called "classical" in its construction. The almost ballet-like organization of the encounters between the two main characters, with the gradual shift in position of one toward the other and finally the complete reversal, is brilliantly worked out. Its effect is that of a controlled symmetry rarely encountered elsewhere in Dostoevsky, and in sharp contrast with the rather slapdash plotting of *The Idiot*. In this novella, too, Dostoevsky's mastery of his special type of dialogue—a dialogue whose words are charged with *unspoken* significance—perhaps reaches its peak of perfection. The scenes between Velchaninov and Trusotsky, in which each responds not to what is being said but to what he knows or senses the other has left unuttered, are filled with a mesmerizing tension fully the equal of those between Ivan Karamazov and Smerdyakov, and perhaps more psychologically subtle as the lover and cuckold exchange roles.

Dostoevsky had initially written, concerning the story he intended to create for *Dawn*, that it would contain his "individual essence" as a writer; and his remark applies equally well to *The Eternal Husband*. Both of the main characters are engaged in Dostoevsky's typical struggle between egoism and conscience, and both are entrapped in the dialectic of pride and humiliation, whose infernal circle can be broken only by the self-transcendence of the ego. The finely shaded figure of Velchaninov is one of Dostoevsky's most persuasive depictions of such an inner moral transformation—temporary, it is true, but all the more convincing for this reason. Trusotsky's self-lacerating behavior is more familiar, but captured with equal skill. A major flaw, however, is the unpardonably masochistic mistreatment of Liza by Trusotsky, which leads to her death. Dostoevsky clearly wishes the reader to accept Trusotsky's abuse of Liza as a bitterly pathological distortion of his previous overflowing adoration; but it is difficult to summon up much sympathy for Trusotsky in the face of such inexcusable victimization of an innocent child. The balance between the two main characters thus becomes tilted with a weight that goes heavily counter to Dostoevsky's aim of undermining Velchaninov's patrician contempt for the ignominious and risible cuckold.

Of great interest in the story too, as has already been remarked, is the ideological play with Grigoryevian categories. Both characters turn out to contain possibilities of *either* type, the predatory and the peaceable, when a crisis occurs in their lives; human nature, at least in its contemporary Russian incarnation, is more fluid and amorphous than depicted in Tolstoy and glorified by his great admirer Strakhov. *The Eternal Husband* thus may be seen as Dostoevsky's first artistic answer to Tolstoy's increasing fame. The second would have been the great work he was planning, on as vast a scale as *War and Peace,* under the title of *The Life of a Great Sinner.* And even though this work was never written as such, the three novels that emerged from Dostoevsky's notes—essential features of *The Devils,* and then *A Raw Youth* and *The Brothers Karamazov*—unquestionably established his right to rank as a worthy rival of Tolstoy among Russian authors.

CHAPTER 21

Fathers, Sons, and
Stavrogin

Between December 1869 and February 1870, Dostoevsky suddenly shifted his literary course, set aside the *Life of a Great Sinner,* and threw himself into a book with "direct relevance to the most important contemporary issue." What issue had so riveted Dostoevsky's attention? It was the "Nechaev affair"—the murder, by a secret revolutionary group led by Sergey Nechaev, of a student named Ivan Ivanov at the Petrovsky Agricultural Academy in Moscow. Why the group killed Ivanov, one of their own members, still remains in dispute.

As it happened, Dostoevsky's young brother-in-law Ivan Snitkin, visiting in Dresden at the time, was on leave from that very institution. Always intensely interested in the state of mind, the attitudes, and the values of the young generation, the novelist had avidly welcomed the opportunity provided by Snitkin's presence to obtain some firsthand impressions of his distant homeland. Indeed, the very appearance of Snitkin in Dresden, if we are to believe Anna's version, was a result of the sharp eye that Dostoevsky kept on radical activity both in Russia and abroad. He had advised the family to send Ivan to join his sister because he had foreseen trouble in the Petrovsky Academy during the fall of 1869; and Ivan confirmed on arrival that revolutionary agitation had been spreading through the student body. He had spoken with special warmth about a student named Ivanov, who, at first attracted by Nihilist radicalism, had then "in a thoroughgoing fashion altered his convictions"; everyone admired him for "the staunchness of his character." It was such conversations, according to Anna Grigoryevna, that first prompted Dostoevsky to begin a novel with Ivanov as hero, and "how profoundly was my husband shaken when he learned in the newspapers of Ivanov's murder!"[1]

Although long accepted as reliable, not much credence should be given to this account, which of course adds a bit of luster to the family escutcheon; but it contains a modicum of truth all the same. For reasons that will become clear, Dostoevsky could well have foreseen disruptive unrest in Russian schools of higher education in the fall of 1869. He was of course horrified by the news of Ivanov's murder; but that he learned anything specific about Ivanov's supposed "change of convictions" *be-*

fore the murder is highly questionable, though the student's name may well have been mentioned. Nor is there any evidence in Dostoevsky's notes that he ever thought of a novel dealing with revolutionary conspiracy before the Nechaev affair made headlines.

The Devils thus did not spring full-grown from familial conversations about Ivanov and the sudden surge of indignation caused by learning of his fate. Rather, it emerged from the gradual infiltration of this horrendous event, which seized Dostoevsky's imagination, into various plans for other kinds of novels that he had been mulling over between completing *The Eternal Husband* and taking the plunge into a new literary commitment. For the decision to begin writing the first part of his *Life of a Great Sinner* had at best been tentative, and he could not overcome the nagging fear of creative self-betrayal if he launched into it before returning to Russia.

2
———

Dostoevsky's notebooks always contained a plethora of plans that he jotted down on the spur of the moment, and he would often return to them later while seeking new inspiration. During these pivotal December–February months, he accordingly took up some notes written in September 1869 and tinkered with them to see what they might yield. Entitled *Death of a Poet*, these notes are an offshoot of *Atheism*, and include a debate among a young priest who is a zealous defender of Orthodoxy (his fervor is curiously compared to that of Archpriest Avvakum, a martyr of the Old Believers), an atheist, a Nihilist doctor, and a bona fide Old Believer. The argument concerns freedom and what it means to be a free man "according to Saint Paul." Here Dostoevsky is referring to the passage in 1 Corinthians (7:22): "For he that is called in the Lord, being a servant, is the Lord's freeman: likewise also he that is called, being free, is Christ's servant." When the Orthodox priest falters, the Old Believer springs to his defense and turns out to be the most successful advocate of this Christian idea of freedom, which is independent of external enslavement and social distinctions.

Dostoevsky links this religious thematic with a romantic intrigue involving the Poet's wife and a gentleman returning from abroad. The Poet himself, only twenty-six years old, either dies a natural death or shoots himself. He is described as "a pagan" who "deifies nature," and does so even in his final hours: "Delirium, last moments, *Götter Griechenlands* [the poem of Schiller—J.F.]."* He bids farewell to the world with an assembled company present "at the request of his wife—charming, pretty, excitable—it finished with champagne" (9: 120). Dostoevsky instructs

---

* This poem of Schiller's, it might be mentioned, was translated into Russian by Mikhail Dostoevsky, whose version was published in 1861. See *PSS*, 9: 497.

himself to render this final confession of the worn-out Poet, who has badly gone to seed, with "touching humor and elevated art" (9: 121). The faint outlines of Stepan Trofimovich Verkhovensky are already discernible in such entries; and *The Devils* distinctly looms into view with another notation. "Nechaev, Kulishov has denounced Nechaev.... The police enter and capture [presumably Nechaev—J.F.]" (9: 121). The romantic entanglement, whose further details are superfluous, is thus combined with a debate about faith, the portrait of a dilapidated devotee of the Romantic Schillerism of the 1830s, and a representative of the Nihilist politics of the late 1860s. The name of Kulishov also indicates how fluid the boundaries were between *The Life of a Great Sinner* and Dostoevsky's other creative ideas.

Another group of notes, recalling some of the early drafts for *The Idiot*, is also linked with what became *The Devils*. The main figure here is Dostoevsky's omnipresent Usurer, an atheist, who brings home a terrified young bride and attempts to isolate her from the world. The lame girl from the Great Sinner scenario, who here has been violated and beaten by Kulishov, is in love with the Usurer. "Well educated, she is the daughter of a drunken lieutenant who goes begging." Marya Lebyadkina and her disreputable brother thus make their first appearance, and the future Captain Lebyadkin, still only a drunken lieutenant, "goes begging in a noble manner" and is a "phrasemonger" who distributes petitions for financial aid (9: 122–123). He will use more drastic methods in the novel; but his incongruously lofty eloquence and resentment at his lowly position are already suggested. He derives from another series of notes of uncertain date dealing with a Captain Kartuzov, a comically importunate figure who writes mock-heroic and titillatingly erotic poems to an Amazon (a horsewoman) with whom he becomes madly infatuated, and his passion only increases when she breaks her leg. These details will all be taken over into the preposterous courtship of Liza Tushina by the sodden and obstreperous Captain Lebyadkin.

The Poet also turns up in these notes, and Dostoevsky continues to relish the prospect of his farewell scene: "The Poet's adieu to life, and 'I do not believe' (a brilliant chapter)" (9: 124). In a variation of the plot, the Usurer is only engaged instead of married; his rival for the Fiancée is a Prince, "a pathetic figure" who is "envious, aspiring to high human dignity without cost, proud without having the right to be." He "has made a girl pregnant and turned her over to the Schoolteacher," who is clearly a moral exemplar ("leaving babes on people's doorsteps: a simple, live, and grandiose feat") (9: 124). This moral contrast between the Prince and the Schoolteacher then becomes the center of other notes entitled *Envy*, which date from the end of January to February 1870; and here we see the first outlines of the plot of *The Devils*.

The intrigue revolves around a young girl, the Pupil or Ward, who was later to become Darya Shatova. She lives with a wealthy female land-owner (Mme Stavrogina) and is seduced by the son of her patroness, Prince A. B.; other figures include a Teacher, "a weak and timid character, terribly absentminded and strange" (11: 59). Marriage between the Prince and the Pupil is out of the question, and the Prince's mother suggests that she marry the Teacher with a large dowry. The Teacher neither accepts nor refuses; but he goes to see the Ward, indicates that he wishes to marry her without the dowry, and a friendship springs up between them. But the Ward loves the Prince, who himself covets the Beauty (the future Liza Tushin), and the latter is attracted by the moral nobility and courage that the Teacher suddenly displays. He sustains a blow unflinchingly, challenges his opponent to a duel, but then refuses to fire. The Prince "envies the superiority of the Teacher" (which explains Dostoevsky's title), and out of envy—an envy that inspires a moral transformation—he decides to emulate the Teacher's example by marrying the Ward "to the horror of his mother" (11: 61, 60).

Many of the plot ingredients of *The Devils* are evident in this schema, whose background setting is also that of a populous provincial society ("a large group gathered in the rural countryside"). The tranquillity of this peaceful backwater, however, is being undermined by the infiltration of Nihilist ideas. Even the Teacher is characterized as "a Nihilist up to a certain point, does not believe ... NB) Another neighbor a Nihilist, very wealthy, with students. The Teacher notices that all the Nihilists are terribly anxious to get rich. (Proclamations. Fugitive appearance of Nechaev, to kill the Teacher(?)" (11: 59). The romantic and political plots begin to intertwine, and the fleeting reference to Nechaev earlier is now directly connected with a politically inspired murder. This is the novel that Dostoevsky initially set out to write as a "pamphlet," which would compete with Turgenev's *Fathers and Children* as a more up-to-date portrayal of the conflict of generations in Russia and its fearful results.

3
———

Because the revolutionary machinations of Sergey Nechaev make a sporadic appearance in several plans for works that Dostoevsky was mulling over at this time, the question inevitably arises of how much he actually knew about the Nechaev group. From where would he have obtained his information? The brother-in-law hypothesis is superficially plausible but cannot withstand scrutiny. Ivan Snitkin left Russia probably in mid- or late October, and the conflict within the Nechaev circle, leading to Ivanov's murder on November 26, occurred in the weeks just preceding that date. Nor is there any convincing evidence that Ivanov had abandoned his former Nihilist convictions; what he objected to, so far as can be established, was Nechaev's assertion of his right to absolute dictatorial control over the members of his group of five.[2] It is possible that Snitkin had become aware of Nechaev's organizing activities among the students, but he would scarcely have been able to inform Dostoevsky of anything else. Dostoevsky himself admitted to Katkov, as he sent off his first chapters a year later, that "I know nothing at all about Nechaev, nor Ivanov, nor the circumstances of the murder, except from the newspapers."[3] These words should be taken quite literally.

The fascinating, extraordinary, and sinister figure of Sergey Nechaev, who seemed to exercise an almost hypnotic effect on all those who came into contact with him (with a few exceptions, such as Alexander Herzen), probably first came to Dostoevsky's notice in the Russian press that he read every day with such nostalgic assiduity. At the end of May 1869, M. N. Katkov published an article in the *Moscow Gazette* (*Moskovskii Vedomosti*) dealing with the recent student disorders that had broken out in St. Petersburg and Moscow (including incidents at the Petrovsky Academy), and he designated among their leaders "a certain Nechaev." He was described as a "very hardened Nihilist," an "inflamer of youth," who had been arrested but managed the unprecedented feat of escaping from the Peter and Paul Fortress (in which Dostoevsky had once been imprisoned himself) and fleeing abroad. In Europe he had produced a series of incendiary proclamations calling on students to revolt, "printed them very handsomely," and sent bales of them back to Russia through the public mails.[4] In fact, Nechaev had never been arrested, much less escaped from the impregnable fortress; but this was the legend that he spread about himself, in accordance with his calculated tactic that deception was perfectly permissible in the service of the revolution. M. A. Bakunin and N. P. Ogarev, who eagerly aided Nechaev in his proclamation campaign, at first greeted him admiringly in Geneva as the resurrected incarnation of the revolutionary aspirations of their youth. It was only later, when his total unscrupulousness had been turned against them, that their initial enthusiasm changed to regretful repudiation.

The Nechaev-Bakunin-Ogarev proclamations posted to Russia were also available in those Russian bookstores in Europe that Dostoevsky occasionally sought out and in which, as he complained, all he could find were the works of exiles and radicals. It may have been after coming across these ringing appeals addressed to students, as well as Katkov's article, that he spoke to Anna about inviting her brother to spend some time in Dresden during the fall. He could well have foreseen trouble ahead, not only in the Petrovsky Academy, but in all the Russian universities of the empire.

Six months later, the *Moscow Gazette* carried news of the murder of a student on the grounds of the Petrovsky Academy; but no connection between the crime and any revolutionary group was at first indicated. Nechaev's name, however, appeared in another story a month later, along with excerpts from two of the leaflets he had sent from abroad. It was only on December 29 that the agitator's name finally was linked to the murder; and thereafter stories about Nechaev appeared regularly, with references to "some kind of wild conspiracy with proclamations" and to Ivanov as having "died because he wished to denounce the criminal scheme."[5] On January 4, 1870, a leading article by Katkov, which summarized and commented on foreign newspaper reports covering the Nechaev affair, devoted a good deal of space to Bakunin, who, along with the weak-willed and compliant Ogarev, had participated with Nechaev in launching his propaganda campaign. Katkov had known Bakunin all too well as a young man (he had once almost faced him in a duel), and he quoted Bakunin's anarchist call for the total destruction not only of the Russian state but of every and any existing state.* He also cited Bakunin's advice to the younger generation to foster in themselves that "fiercely destroying and coldly passionate fervor that freezes the mind and stops the blood in the veins of our opponents."[6] All through the month of January, Katkov's newspaper continued to print reports about the gradually unfolding story of the Nechaev case, often using corroborating information from foreign (particularly German) newspapers, which of course Dostoevsky could read independently.

It is thus hardly surprising that references to Nechaev, the proclamations, and the murder begin to creep into Dostoevsky's notes from this time. He was then daily poring over the flood of rumor and speculation, and the few snippets of hard fact that emerged in the various press accounts; and he must have immersed himself in such pages with a mixture of fury and gnawing despair. After all, had he not practically predicted this outcome of radical ideas when he created Raskolnikov? Nechaev and his group had merely drawn the conclusions, and taken the actions, that in *Crime and Punishment* Dostoevsky had only imagined as extreme and "fantastic" possibilities.

And who was ultimately responsible for this perversion of Russian youth, now capable of the most atrocious crimes for the sake of revolution, if not the generation of the 1840s, the generation of Dostoevsky

---

* In 1840 Bakunin spread the word that Katkov was carrying on an affair with Ogarev's first wife (the Russian intelligentsia constituted a very small world). After a furious quarrel in Belinsky's quarters, during which Katkov called Bakunin "a eunuch" (the revolutionary firebrand appears to have been in truth sexually impotent), Bakunin challenged him to a duel. But no date was set, and Bakunin soon left for Europe in June 1840. See Aileen Kelly, *Mikhail Bakunin* (New Haven and London, 1947), 64–65.

himself and such luminaries as Belinsky, Herzen, Bakunin, and Turgenev (whose *Rudin* was well known to be an image of Bakunin in his youthful heyday)? Indeed, had not Turgenev himself, in a recent preface to a new edition of his *Fathers and Children* (1869), practically claimed such responsibility in his attempt to overcome the hostility of the radicals to his work? A "witty lady" of his acquaintance, he informed his readers, had said after perusing the novel: "You are a Nihilist yourself." And Turgenev adds musingly: "I will not undertake to contradict: perhaps the lady spoke the truth." In another passage he declares that, with the exception of Bazarov's views on art, "he almost shares all his [Bazarov's] convictions."[7] A shocked Strakhov, in the December issue of *Dawn*, had exclaimed in amazement: "Turgenev—a Nihilist! Turgenev shares the convictions of Bazarov!"[8]*

All through the past several years, as we have noted, Dostoevsky's bile against his own generation had been steadily accumulating. His reminiscences of Belinsky had brought back the abusive insults to Christ made in his presence, and the bitter quarrel with the self-declared renegade Turgenev had only aggravated his animosity. The Nechaev affair reopened all these old wounds, and, in the midst of turning the pages, what he learned from the newspapers became amalgamated not only with Strakhov's ironic article on Turgenev but also with an earlier one by the same critic, whom he read so carefully and so admiringly. A biography of one of the most eminent members of the generation of the 1840s, T. N. Granovsky, was published in 1869 and greeted by Strakhov with a detailed review. "He was," Strakhov wrote, "a *pure* Westerner, that is, a Westerner still totally undefined, who embraced with an equally sympathetic glance the entire history of Europe, all its vital manifestations. . . . The sole formula that can grasp the tendency of Granovsky is: a sympathy for the sublime and the beautiful wherever and however it may appear."[9]

Strakhov then defines this Russian type further with the help of some lines from N. A. Nekrasov—lines that Dostoevsky would pick up and cite in the first chapter of *The Devils*: "A living monument of reproach . . . / Thou stoodst before thy country / O liberal-idealist." Without denying the virtues of this type, Strakhov nonetheless pillories its representatives

---

* The hostile reaction of Dostoevsky and Strakhov to Turgenev's preface was by no means isolated or unusual. Even so close an intimate of Turgenev's as P. V. Annenkov wrote him an angrily indignant letter about it. And his attempt to curry favor on the left was met with at best a tolerant condescension. "Let us be generous . . . " wrote D. D. Minaev. "Despite the clumsiness of Mr. Turgenev's excuses, his explanations regarding *Fathers and Children* still have the character of a certain repentance; from all this we must understand that our venerable novelist is asking for pardon from the young generation." I. S. Turgenev, *PSSiP*, 14: 470–471.

as "superficial people, leading purposeless lives . . . incapable of genuine effort, impotent, and dejected." And yet they believed themselves worthy of being placed on a pedestal. To be sure, "they were honorable in thought and pure in heart," and one should not treat them too harshly; but "we will not take a symptom of disease for something worthwhile." Strakhov sees contemporary Russian Nihilism as a direct consequence of the influence of such "pure" Westerners, even though the surviving members of that generation refuse to recognize their offspring in the "impure" progeny they have engendered.[10] Indeed, these survivors "have begun to defend their starting point—the worship and imitation of the West—and yet, at the same time, to deny all the consequences that such worship has given birth to in our cultural world."

On the other side, the young generation has little respect for such "pure" Westerners as Granovsky, "and they naturally prefer Belinsky, Dobrolyubov, and Pisarev, who advanced the same position much further." The Nihilist children themselves have now taken to renouncing their fathers, "and it is in vain that one can try and persuade us that one can stand at present in the same position of pure Westernism as Granovsky."[11] The battle of the generations was thus joined once again in Russian culture, as it had been in *Fathers and Children*. Sometime in January or early February 1870 Dostoevsky put down in his notebook, under the heading *T. N. Granovsky*, a few sentences depicting "a pure and idealistic Westerner in his full splendor," whose "*characteristic traits*" are sketched in as "aimlessness and lack of firmness in his views . . . which . . . used to cause him suffering before, but *have now become his second nature* (his son makes fun of this tendency)" (11: 65).

It was Strakhov's article, in all likelihood, that clarified for Dostoevsky how he might turn to creative profit his smoldering anger against his own generation and his blazing hatred of the Nechaevian avatar they had produced. Shortly after setting down his note, he dashed off a request to Strakhov for "the book of Stankevich on Granovsky. You will do me a great service, which I will always remember. I need that little book as I do the air I breathe, and as quickly as possible, as the most necessary material for my book—material that I cannot do without."[12] A month later, he wrote to Maikov: "What I am writing now is something tendentious, I want to speak out as passionately as I can. All the Nihilists and Westerners will cry out that I am *retrograde*. To hell with them, I will speak my mind to the very last word."[13] He has high hopes for his new novel, he tells Strakhov, "but not on the artistic, rather on the tendentious side; I wish to speak out about several matters even though my artistry goes smash. What attracts me is what has piled up in my mind and heart; let it give only a pamphlet, but I shall speak out."

4
———

Once he had fixed on T. N. Granovsky as the prototype of the generation of the 1840s (though many others will be amalgamated into the type, particularly Alexander Herzen), Dostoevsky's imagination began to work very rapidly. His notes show him developing both the private intrigue, which mainly follows the pattern of *Envy*, as well as the ideological clash of generations. Granovsky, the future Stepan Trofimovich Verkhovensky, is pinned down almost immediately and will remain unchanged throughout. "Places himself unconsciously on a pedestal, in the style of relics to be worshiped by pilgrims, and loves it. . . . Shuns Nihilism and does not understand it. . . . 'Leave me God and art, and I will let you have Christ. . . . Christ did not understand women.' Fifty years old. Literary recollections. Belinsky, Granovsky, Herzen . . . Turgenev and others" (11: 65). Dostoevsky here was manifestly summoning up all *his* memories and using them to fill out his ideological canvas.

The action involves, instead of the Schoolteacher, an ex-student named Shaposhnikov, "who has been involved in student disorders." His sister has been dishonored by the Prince, and he has come to the locality where the events take place to keep an eye on her seducer. Dostoevsky notes: "Sh—type of a person with roots. His convictions—the Slavophils an aristocratic fancy, the Nihilists, children of landowners. We have passed Russia by. Now are unable to recognize our particularity and do not know how to keep our independence vis-à-vis the West." Suddenly, "the Student [Nechaev] *appears* with the aim of counterfeit money, proclamations and groups of three. . . . Troubles his father (Granovsky) by his Nihilism, his sarcasms, contradictions. Simple, straightforward. Rebuild the world. . . . The *Student* is in town and moves around in society (*Bazarov*)" (11: 66–67). There is also another characterization, written in capital letters, of Nechaev as a literary type: "THE STUDENT IN THE FORM OF A HERO OF OUR TIME" (presumably a reference to Pechorin, the hero of Lermontov's novel) (11: 115). For all his Bazarovian coarseness and insolence, Nechaev was also to be given a dashing, Romantic coloring sufficient to attract the Beauty and become a rival in seduction to the Prince.

Just as Dostoevsky almost immediately fixed on the main outlines of his ideological collision, so too he very quickly found the narrative posture he wished to adopt. The mock-heroic tone is suggested from a very early stage: "The novel has the form of an epic poem about how Granovsky wanted to get married, but did not." Dostoevsky also defines his point of view as mimicking what one might expect "*from a provincial chronicle*," and he then gives a sample of the tonal stance: "Start from how everybody is discussing this whole business, and how so-and-so many were carried away by it all, and how people were wondering about many things, such as broken marriages and suicides, and how could we possibly have such an *échevelée* [disorderly] literature. Just as they are saying God knows what about the last days of Timofey N. Granovsky (it's known for a positive fact that the Princess had been paying him a pension). Whereas actually, everything happened quite simply" (11: 92). Here we already have the gossipy, intimate, slightly ironic narrator of *The Devils*, worried about the social breakdown he observes all around, but concerned to preserve the proprieties and to reduce the shocking events to the proportions of a juicy local scandal.

The romantic complications of *Envy* remain at the center of the plot line, but in an altered form: the Ward now becomes engaged (or married) to Granovsky, a friend of the Prince, so as not to cause a scandal. But she drowns herself out of despair, and Shaposhnikov is thus given an unimpeachable motive for hating the Prince. Meanwhile, Shaposhnikov has been attracted by the Student and "is stupid enough to go to meetings" (11: 66); but he makes no secret of his disagreement with the views he hears expressed. Fearing that he will denounce the group's underground activities, the three members kill Shaposhnikov and, because of his well-known animosity against the Prince, try to throw the blame on this enemy of the victim. Eventually this schema will lead to the plan for Kirillov's voluntary assumption of the murder of Shatov through suicide and a false confession. This group of notes also contains a clear delineation of the ideological role assigned Granovsky: "What is Granovsky doing in the story? He is there to mark the meeting between *the two generations*, and Sh. who is a new man (taciturn, simple, strong, and latterly impetuous)" (11: 68). Nothing is said about any moral transformation of the Prince, and Shaposhnikov is the "new man"—but his murder precludes the emergence of any positive ideological perspective.

Dostoevsky tries to remedy this deficiency by developing the idea of pinning the murder on the Prince. The plot line now comes closer to the final text: the Ward is no longer in trouble because of the Prince, but there is an undeclared romance between the two. The Prince's mother, to prevent unwelcome developments, decides to marry her off to Granovsky, and the rumor spreads that the engagement is being used to cover up the Prince's sins. Nechaev (the Student) also hints to the Prince of an affair between the Ward and Shaposhnikov (now called Shatov, and obviously no longer her brother). This leads to open enmity between the two rivals, and the purpose of such rumors is to throw suspicion on the Prince for Shatov's murder. But "when the accusation rings out that the Prince has killed Shatov, the Prince immediately unravels everything, goes to Uspensky [the actual name of one of Nechaev's accomplices— J.F.], obliges him to confess and firmly denounces to the Governor" (11: 101). In this version, as in *Envy*, the Prince then marries the Ward, and

Dostoevsky comments: "The principal idea (that is, the pathos of the novel) is the Prince and the Ward—*new people* who have surmounted temptation and have resolved to begin a *new* regenerated life" (11: 98).

This is not, to be sure, the only dénouement that Dostoevsky envisages; but it is the one that points forward to the final text. For the Prince is thus placed at the intersection of both the romantic intrigue and the Nihilist conspiracy. Yet Dostoevsky also realizes that, if the Prince is to emerge as "a new person," he will require considerably more elaboration. Accordingly, a good many entries are devoted to exploring the Prince's personality as a way of motivating his decisive action. At first Dostoevsky conceived him as a somewhat unimpressive figure who suddenly reveals an unexpected strength: "In general, at the end of the novel nobody suspects such a strong and ardent character in the Prince" (11: 99). But to portray the Prince as a mediocrity for most of the book was not very promising; and Dostoevsky alternates that image with one of a haughty lordling—"The Prince is an aristocrat: I, he says, hate and despise them all" (11: 100)—perhaps so as to make his climactic regeneration more dramatic and socially symbolic. Then we find another image of the Prince, closer to how Stavrogin will finally be portrayed, arriving on the scene in the midst of a moral metamorphosis: "He [the Prince] returns home *a well-tempered bar of steel*, having secretly sworn to break with all the reality, even though his mother should disinherit him for it" (11: 114).

To motivate this altered Prince, Dostoevsky now assigns him religious ideas and aspirations: "The Prince, for example, never disputes with the atheists, although he passionately believes in God." Again: "Despises the atheists to the point of fury, *believes* furiously. Wishes to be a *muzhik*, Old Believer" (11: 100). This reference to the *raskolniki* is certainly linked with another note: "*Nechaev*. Has arrived also to arrange the affair with Golubov about the secret printing press of the Old Believers" (11: 113). Golubov, the converted Old Believer whom Dostoevsky considered one of the types of the "future Russian man"—a type whose advent he so eagerly and impatiently awaited—thus now becomes the inspiration of both Shatov and the Prince. His ideas, as summarized by Dostoevsky, are "those of humility and self-possession, also that God and the Kingdom of Heaven are within us . . . and that's where freedom is too. He [the Prince] is thunderstruck, awed, and wholeheartedly submits to his influence" (11: 131).*

* This stage in the Prince's evolution is expressed through lengthy speeches, dialogues, and reflections in the notes that reveal some of Dostoevsky's own ideological dilemmas in a striking and quite fascinating fashion. Dostoevsky writes, for example, that "the main idea from which the Prince suffers and which keeps him preoccupied is this: We have *Orthodoxy*, our nation is great and wonderful because it believes and because it has Orthodoxy. We Russians are strong, and stronger than anybody else, because . . . we have immense masses

Until the end of February, Dostoevsky clung to his portrayal of the Prince and the Ward as "new people" who end the novel on a note of regeneration. But in March a decisive change takes place in his basic conception, though the plot outlines, including the behavior of the Prince, remain unaltered. He arrives at the beginning of the novel "a *new* man," having resolved all his doubts, and "he reconciles himself with those he has offended, supports a slap in the face. Intervenes in the affair of the sacrilege, discovers the assassin, and finally declares solemnly to the Ward that he loves her, establishes his conditions. These consist in that he is henceforth a Russian and that it is necessary to believe even what he said at Golubov's (that Russia and Russian thought will save humanity). He prays before icons. . . . And then, suddenly he blows his brains out—(Enigmatic personage, said to be mad)" (11: 133). This note from March 11 marks the crucial transition between Dostoevsky's initial "pamphlet" and *The Devils*, in which the central figure, Stavrogin, is tragic rather than satiric, for his inability to believe in his own rebirth leads to self-destruction.

Dostoevsky, as we see, gives no explanation for the Prince's mysterious act except in the final, cryptic parenthesis; but he now devotes himself to filling in this evident lacuna. A few days later (March 15), he returns to the problem: "The Prince—a man who has become bored.

---

of people who are believers in Orthodoxy. But if the faith in Orthodoxy were shaken among our people it would immediately begin to decay, as the nations of the West have already begun to decay (naturally, our own upper class is an import, actually borrowed from them, therefore it is just so much grass on fire, and of no consequence), as their religion (Catholicism, Lutheranism, and various heresies, a distortion of Christianity) has become lost and must remain lost. Now this question: who then can believe?"

A bit further on, the Prince's reflections continue, as he thinks that "it all boils down to one urgent question: can one believe while being civilized, i.e., a European? i.e., believe without a reservation in the divine nature of Jesus Christ, the Son of God? (For this is what faith amounts to.) N.B. To this question, civilization gives a factual answer in the negative (Renan), also stating that society has failed to preserve a pure interpretation of Christ's teaching (Catholicism being the Antichrist, the Whore, and Lutheranism no better than the teaching of the *molokane* [a Russian sect close to Protestantism]."

"If this is so," the Prince reasons, "can society exist without faith (on the basis of science alone, for instance)? (Herzen). The moral foundations of a society are given through revelation. Eliminate one thing from religion, and the moral foundation of Christianity will collapse entirely, for everything is mutually linked together. So, then, is a different, scientific morality possible? If it is not, this means that morality rests with the Russian people alone, since it possesses Orthodoxy. But if it is impossible for an enlightened person to be Orthodox (and in a hundred years half of Russia will be enlightened), this is all nothing but hocus-pocus, and this whole Russian strength is a temporary phenomenon only. For in order to be eternal, a complete faith in everything is a must. But is it possible to believe?" (11: 178–179).

Whatever one may think of such ideas, which have lost none of their relevance more than a hundred years later, they surely indicate how lucidly and honestly Dostoevsky faced the difficulties of his own most cherished convictions and beliefs.

Product of Russian century [italics added]. He is haughty and knows how to be himself, that is, to keep apart from the aristocrats, the Westerners, the Nihilists, and Golubovs (but the question remains for him—what is he himself?). He replies—nothing. . . . But this is an elevated nature and to be nothing does not satisfy him and torments him. He does not find any foundation in himself and is bored." This version of the Prince now motivates the suicide: "Leaves for his property, asks pardon by letter for having carried her [the Ward] away (had been carried away himself, lied to himself for the last time) but he is bored and will not make her happy—and shoots himself." A few lines later, Dostoevsky writes: "But the idea of the author: to show a man who becomes aware that he has no roots" (11: 134–135).

The Prince thus now receives a social-cultural dimension as a "product of the Russian century," a blasé victim of the ubiquitous *mal de siècle* like Eugene Onegin and Pechorin, consumed like them by ennui and despairing of ever finding an aim for which to live. Dostoevsky had depicted such a type before in Prince Valkovsky (*The Insulted and Injured*) and in Svidrigailov; but their malaise had taken the form of a cynical libertinism that hardly gave their characters any dignity (though Svidrigailov had the decency to kill himself in the end). This new reincarnation of the type, however, was one into which Dostoevsky could pour all his complex feelings about the spiritual malady of the literary idols of his youth—a malady that had come to represent for him the beginning of the European invasion of the Russian soul. What was "the Russian century" if not the history of a culture whose most brilliant and gifted representatives had become alienated from their people and, as a result and most fatefully, from their people's faith? This enlargement of the Prince's character into a symbol of "the Russian century" soon led to a definitive change in orientation. By the end of March, it is no longer the Prince who goes to others, such as Shatov and Golubov, for ideological inspiration, but he now becomes a source of such inspiration for Shatov, and eventually for Kirillov and even Nechaev (Peter Verkhovensky).

The most immediate result of this fresh grasp of the Prince was recorded at the very end of March: "Golubov is not necessary." And the reason is: "WITHOUT GOLUBOV it appears that the main hero of the novel is the Prince. He associates with Shatov, inflames him to enthusiasm, but does not believe himself. Observes and remains indifferent even with respect to the murder of Shatov, about which he knows" (11: 135). The character of Stavrogin, whose name appears in these March entries, is thus beginning to emerge, and Dostoevsky says strikingly that "all the rest moves at his [the Prince's] side like a kaleidoscope. He also replaces Golubov. Of an immeasurable height." The next page contains a reference to the Prince having "violated a child of thirteen years of age, which created some stir (for no reason, brusquely, in passing, a fantasy)." He is described as "gentle, modest, quiet, infinitely proud and bestially cruel. ... Thus all the pathos of the novel in the Prince; he is the hero" (11: 136–137).

By April 1870, Dostoevsky had thus developed the Prince-Stavrogin, hitherto an accessory to the main conflict-of-generations theme, to the point where he had become the hero and taken the book away from both Granovsky and Nechaev. Presumably, the first had been the central figure at the start; he was then replaced by Nechaev in the impressive guise of a mixture of both Bazarov and Pechorin. But now Stavrogin had preempted their place, and Dostoevsky could no longer contain him within the confines of his initial idea of the novel as a tendentious "pamphlet." Indeed, at this time a process of fusion took place between the two creative projects that Dostoevsky had intended to keep separate, and it becomes difficult to distinguish one from the other.

In some May notes, the Great Sinner is said to be "gentle and humble" toward everyone "out of pride and immeasurable arrogance," and also to have committed "atrocious crimes." The heros of his two novels are thus almost identical, and the barriers between the "pamphlet" and the "poem" broke down completely at this time: the Lame Girl, the future haunting Marya Lebyadkina, moves from one to the other, and Tikhon appears as well as the confessor and interlocutor of Stavrogin. It turned out to be impossible for Dostoevsky to write a novel that would be *only* a politically satiric denunciation of the Nihilist generation and its Liberal-Idealist forebears; his book had now taken on an entirely different and much richer character, one that engaged Dostoevsky's deepest convictions and values. For Stavrogin has absorbed the religious thematic originally reserved for the Great Sinner's struggle with faith—a struggle that for Dostoevsky inevitably involved the theme of Russia itself and the Messianic role that he believed it had been selected to fulfill in the destiny of humankind.

6

Dostoevsky had promised Katkov—in return for the resumption of his monthly stipend, interrupted after the publication of *The Eternal Husband*—that he would be able to furnish the beginning of a new novel not later than June 1870. This commitment, however, was based on the rash assumption that he could dash off his relatively undemanding pamphlet in just a few months. But the increasing complexity of his plans made this promise impossible to keep; and at the beginning of July Dostoevsky tells his niece that he hopes to meet a new deadline at the end of August or early September. Five months later, he described to Strakhov some of the difficulties he had experienced even in the very early stages of composition: "All year I only tore up and made alterations. I blackened so many mounds of paper that I even lost my system of references for what I had written. I have modified the plan not less than ten times, and completely rewrote the first part each time."[14] To his niece, he explains in mid-August that "the novel I was writing was long, very original, but of an order of ideas quite new to me; it required a good deal of self-confidence to cope with it. But I did not cope with it and failed. The work went slowly, I felt that there was an important error in the whole thing, but what it was—I could not figure out."[15]

During the month of July, suffering from weekly epileptic attacks, Dostoevsky found it impossible to write at all;* but this imposed respite gave him the opportunity, when he returned to his desk in August, to look afresh at what he had already succeeded in putting on the page. "Two weeks ago," he writes Sofya Ivanova, "getting back to work, I suddenly saw all at once what the trouble was, and where I had made a mistake, and with this, as if by itself and through inspiration, a new plan appeared in all its proportions. Everything had to be radically changed; not hesitating for a moment, I struck out everything I had written (roughly fifteen signatures [approximately 240 pages]), and I began again on page 1. The work of a whole year was wiped out."[16] In fact, as often happened, Dostoevsky here is exaggerating somewhat; for he told Katkov a month later that "of the fifteen signatures already written [in the first version—J.F.], probably twelve will go into the new version of the novel."[17] Dostoevsky did not exaggerate, however, in describing as "inspiration" what occurred in early August, when he at last saw where his problem had lain. He could now confidently promise his text to Katkov, and enough copy was supplied to the journal in the next few months to ensure the beginning of publication in January 1871.

Dostoevsky does not explain to Sofya Ivanova what he had seen his "trouble" to be or what new plan had finally given him the structure he had been seeking; but he furnishes some further details to Katkov. One of the most important events in the novel, he tells his editor, will be "the

---

* Dostoevsky's notebooks for 1869–1870 contain a number of descriptions of his epileptic crises. On January 7/19, 1870, he records: "Crisis at six o'clock in the morning . . . I was not aware of it, woke at eight o'clock with the feeling of an attack. My head ached, my body felt shattered. NB in general, the results of an attack, that is, nervousness, weakening of the memory, a state of cloudiness, and some sort of pensiveness—now lasts longer than in previous years. Earlier, this passed in three days, now not before six. In the evening especially, by candlelight, a sick sadness without cause and as if a red coloration, bloody (not a tint) on everything. Almost impossible to work these days."

On July 1/13, 1870, the period we are speaking of, he writes: "An attack while sleeping this morning. I had just fallen asleep. Anya told me about it at 1:30. Not strong, she thought." On July 17, "my body is not *too* shattered, but my head even now is still not clear, especially toward evening. Anguish. I remark in general that the attacks even of a moderate kind at present (that is, as I get older) have a greater effect on my head, my brain, than strong attacks in the past. . . . I struggle with the 1st part of my novel and am in despair." E. M. Konshina, *Zapisnie Tetradi F. M. Dostoevskogo* (Moscow-Leningrad, 1935), 83–84.

well-known murder of Ivanov in Moscow by Nechaev," though he hastens to add: "my Peter Verkhovensky may not at all resemble Nechaev; but it seems to me that my aroused mind has created by imagination the person, the type, that really corresponds to the crime. To be sure, there is some value in depicting such a man, but he alone would not have enticed me. In my opinion, these pitiful freaks are not worthy of literature. *To my own surprise, this figure half turns out with me to be a comic figure*" (italics added).[18] Nechaev, as we know, had not at all been conceived in this light earlier, and the "surprise" Dostoevsky expresses obviously arises from the unexpected alteration of his original character image.

As a result, Dostoevsky continues, "even though the whole incident [the murder] forms one of the main events of the novel, it is nonetheless only accessory and a setting for the actions of another character, who could really be called the main character. . . . This other character (Nikolay Stavrogin)—is also a sinister character, also a villain. But he seems to me a tragic character, although many will probably ask after reading: 'What on earth is this?' I embarked on the poem about this character because for much too long I have wished to portray him. In my opinion he is Russian, and a typical character." Although worried that his presentation of this type may be considered "stilted," Dostoevsky nonetheless assures Katkov: "He comes straight from my heart. Of course, this character seldom appears in all its typicality, but it is a Russian character (from a certain stratum of society)." At the same time, to balance these "somber figures," there will also be "radiant ones," and "for the first time I intend to touch upon a category of people still rarely treated in literature. As the ideal of such a character I take Tikhon Zadonsky. He is that bishop, living in retirement in a monastery. I confront the hero of my novel with him, and make them acquainted for a time."[19]

What happened in August, then, was the recognition by Dostoevsky of what we have seen taking place in his notebooks during April and May: the transformation of the Prince into Stavrogin, whom he found more and more difficult, as he continued writing, to fit into the framework originally established. As Stavrogin increased in stature, complexity, and tragic significance, he began to duplicate some of the lineaments of Nechaev as a "hero of our time" and an irresistibly attractive and powerful Satanic figure. It was thus necessary to re-create Peter Verkhovensky as partly comic; and in some notes from mid-August, under the title "Something New," we find among other items: "And Nechaev's appearance on the scene as Khlestakov" (11: 202). No longer Bazarov or Pechorin, Nechaev (Peter Verkhovensky) is here reimagined as the ingratiating, fast-talking, and totally deceptive impostor in Gogol's *Inspector-General*, who now, like everyone else, revolves around Stavrogin and becomes an insidiously dangerous and semicomic rogue. Once this change had been made, the structural problem that had been plaguing Dostoevsky solved itself.

Dostoevsky's erstwhile political novel had now become *The Devils*, a "tragic poem" about the moral-spiritual ills that had been afflicting Russian culture and had climaxed in the appearance of Nechaev and his accomplices. Writing to Apollon Maikov the day after he sent off his first chapters, Dostoevsky explains how he saw the book he was just setting out to write (or rewrite): "It is true that the facts have also proved to us that the disease that afflicted cultured Russians was much more virulent than we ourselves had imagined, and that it did not end with the Belinskys and the Kraevskys and their ilk. But at that moment what happened is attested to by Saint Luke: the devils had entered into a man and their name was legion, and they asked Him: 'suffer us to enter into the swine,' and He suffered them. The devils entered into the swine, and the whole herd ran violently down a steep place to the sea and was drowned. When the people came out to see what was done, they found the man who had been possessed now sitting at the feet of Jesus clothed and in his right mind, and those who saw it told them by what means he that was possessed of the devils was healed."[20]

Dostoevsky dearly wished to believe that Russia too would be healed in the same way; but he knew that such hopes remained as yet only a remote possibility, visible, if at all, solely to the farseeing eyes of *Vates* (prophets) like Maikov and himself. What he saw all around, and what he would depict in his novel, was the process of infection and self-destruction rather than the end result of purification. "Exactly the same thing," his letter continues, "happened in our country: the devils went out of the Russian man and entered into a herd of swine, that is, into the Nechaevs and Serno-Solovieviches, et al. These are drowned or will be drowned, and the healed man, from whom the devils have departed, sits at the feet of Jesus. . . . And bear this in mind, my dear friend, that a man who loses his people and his national roots also loses the faith of his fathers and his God. Well, if you really want to know—this is in essence the theme of my novel. It is called *The Devils*, and it describes how the devils entered into the herd of swine."[21]

This self-interpretation is usually taken only as a loosely allegorical explanation of why Dostoevsky chose the passage from Luke that he uses as one of his epigraphs; it is rarely brought into any direct relation with the actual text. But in my opinion the explanation is meant much more literally than has usually been assumed, and furnishes a valuable clue to the manner in which Stavrogin is related to the other characters and to the ideological construction of the book. Just in what way, however, will be left for clarification to a later chapter.

CHAPTER 22

Exile's Return

Despite the enthusiasm with which Dostoevsky had plunged into work on *The Devils*, his mood changed as he ran into complications and the initial idea for a "pamphlet" began to mutate and expand. "I started this novel; it enticed me," he wrote his niece in July 1870; "but now I regret it. It occupies me very much now, but I would like to write about something else."[1] Once the book had become a "poem," however, his attitude again became positive. As he confided to Strakhov, "then I was visited by genuine inspiration and I suddenly came to like the work, went at it with both hands—crossing out what I had written."[2]

But although the composition itself was no longer a painful chore, Dostoevsky was gripped by another anxiety. "I have suddenly taken fright," he confesses to Strakhov. "I am afraid that I have taken on a topic that is beyond me. I am seriously afraid; it is painful."[3] On the same day, just after sending off his first chapters, he wrote his niece: "The idea [of his novel] is bold and big. The whole problem is just that I keep taking topics that are beyond me. The poet in me always outweighs the artist, and that is bad."[4] Two months later, he complains despairingly to Strakhov that "if there were more time now to finish writing it without hurrying (without meeting deadlines), then perhaps something good would result." If only, he exclaims, he was not forced "to work . . . for a deadline" but could create "the way the Tolstoys, Turgenevs, and Goncharovs write!"[5]

Besides such editorial pressure, work on *The Devils* was hampered by Dostoevsky's usual tormenting conditions of financial incertitude, a nostalgia for the homeland verging on melancholia, and the outbreak of the Franco-Prussian War. The book was only half completed when the Dostoevskys finally returned to Russia in early June 1871; and the magazine publication dragged on, for reasons beyond Dostoevsky's control, almost to the end of 1872.

2

When Dostoevsky decided to throw himself into his novel-pamphlet, he genuinely believed it could be dashed off at top speed. "What I am writing for *The Russian Messenger*," he confidently tells Maikov in April 1870, "will be finished in three months or so for certain."[6] Very short of funds as usual, and unable to obtain any further advances from Katkov before providing some manuscript, Dostoevsky turned to *Dawn* for aid. He had already concluded that it would be possible to write the first volume of his Great Sinner cycle even while living abroad; and he offered this idea to *Dawn*, in exchange for an advance, with publication to begin by December 1870. After receiving nine hundred rubles, he was forced to write to Kashpirev in August that he could not keep his commitment because work on his present novel would continue through the remainder of the year. Dostoevsky pledged to furnish a new text sometime toward the end of 1871; but nothing had appeared under his signature when *Dawn* ceased publication in 1873. The journal for which he felt the most ideological sympathy was, in fact, the one he treated rather shabbily.

Dostoevsky was quite apologetic about this unfortunate situation, and insisted on his good faith. His letters do not suggest any duplicity, but rather an overestimation—which we have noted time and again—of the speed at which he could turn out a text satisfying his own standards despite the unpredictable fluctuations of his creative imagination. In any event, the dispiriting conditions of his life at this time could well have excused a certain self-beguiling subterfuge. To his niece, with whom he was franker about the details of his home life than with other correspondents, he sent this joyless picture of his existence: "About us in general, I will say that we are still living in Dresden, and for the meanwhile, all right. Lyuba is a sweet and quite healthy child; we look after her with fear since we have already lost a baby. Anya is nursing her, and with every day that seems to be too much for her. She has gotten very weak, very thin, and moreover misses Russia. I also miss it, and that is precisely the basis of all my worries and concerns."[7]

Half a year later, he continues in the same vein: "Anna Grigoryevna has even fallen ill from missing Russia, and that torments me. She is sad and pining away. True, she is very exhausted physically from nursing the baby a whole year. Since then her health has been severely shaken, and add to that her homesickness. The doctors said that she has symptoms of severe exhaustion of the blood, and specifically from nursing. . . . She's been walking little, mostly sitting or lying down. I am terribly afraid." Anna had become so depressed that she even refused to take the iron prescribed for her by the doctors, and Dostoevsky attributed much of her despondency to the melancholy of exile: "there's no way her inner longing, her homesickness can be chased away."[8]

More and more Dostoevsky felt it imperative to return, and the couple decided to do so whenever they could scrape together enough to meet the expenses of the trip; the fear of prison now took second place to their irrepressible need to regain their native soil. Meanwhile, on sending off the first chapters of *The Devils* in October 1870, Dostoevsky accompanied them with a plea to Katkov for an advance of five hundred rubles, and the sagacious editor came to his rescue again when the beginning of a new novel finally crossed his desk. Dostoevsky was also still in correspondence with Maikov about the possibility of selling the rights to *The Idiot*; and he worried that his stepson Pasha, to whom he had given a broad power of attorney, might use it to obtain money for himself. Much to Dostoevsky's relief, Maikov assured him that, although Pasha might be light-headed and flighty, he was not dishonest. "How I suffered, how I prayed for him," Dostoevsky replied, "and finally, your letter dispelled my doubts . . . you have healed a wound in my soul."[9]

Pasha had been negotiating about *The Idiot* with the cunning publisher Stellovsky, with whom Dostoevsky soon became involved in another altercation at the end of 1870. An advertisement had apprised him that a new edition of *Crime and Punishment* was to be published by Stellovsky; and Dostoevsky immediately asked Maikov to collect the three thousand rubles the publisher was required by contract to pay the author. All of Dostoevsky's financial tribulations momentarily seemed at an end: this windfall would be enough to ensure a safe and secure return to Russian soil. But Stellovsky, engaging in his usual delaying tactics, pleaded a poverty that Dostoevsky knew was totally fictitious, and even the threat of being forced to pay damages for breach of contract over and above the amount of his obligation could not bring the wily businessman to heel. Dostoevsky was unable to obtain a single ruble when he needed it most, and it would take five years to manage to extract from Stellovsky what was clearly Dostoevsky's fee.

Dresden harbored a large Russian colony that included some admirers of their resident author, a celebrity of sorts even if his convict past made him rather suspect. The Dostoevskys thus no longer suffocated in the almost complete isolation of their earlier years; but this renewal of social life hardly brought Dostoevsky satisfaction or pleasure. Indeed, he tolerated as much of it as he did solely in the hope of alleviating Anna's crippling ennui. The home of the Russian priest was the gathering place of their compatriots, and the Dostoevskys showed up there from time to time; but the novelist disliked this local clergyman, whom he found too animated, somewhat erratic in judgment, and lacking in the gravity appropriate to his office. Nor, since Dostoevsky himself abhorred living in exile, could he suppress a subliminal hostility against all those Russians who did so voluntarily. As Anna later remarked, "our Russian friends in Dresden were in his opinion not Russians but voluntary emigrés, who did not love Russia and had left it forever."[10] He looked on them as members of a class who, resenting the abolition of serfdom and the loss of their privileges, had fled from the new and more democratic Russia in the course of creation.

Dostoevsky's reluctance to mingle with his fellow countrymen is clearly voiced in a comment made to Sofya Ivanova at the beginning of 1871. "Hard as we tried to avoid acquaintances here with Russians, of which there are many, we have been unable to avoid them. Some of them started up all on their own. Just imagine: I had to celebrate the New Year at a ball given by our local consul. Anya also has several acquaintances among the ladies here."[11] All the same, Dostoevsky was quite happy to lend these Russians his literary services when they appealed to him in a patriotic cause. In October 1870 the Russian government announced that it was unilaterally abrogating one of the clauses of the Treaty of Paris, which had been signed after its humiliating defeat in the Crimean War. No longer would the Russian government accept the prohibition against stationing its fleet in the Black Sea. On this occasion the Russians in Dresden decided to send a message of support to the Russian chancellor; and when Dostoevsky was asked to write it, he gladly complied. This assertion of Russian national pride certainly corresponded to his own deepest sentiments.

3
———

The defiant action of the Russian government was one of the consequences of the quick defeat of France by Prussia, allied with the south German states, in the Franco-Prussian War. Dostoevsky had foreseen such a clash two years previously, and five days before the declaration of war (July 19, 1870) he concluded from the newspapers that it would not be long in coming. "God forbid," he writes his niece, "that Russia should enter into anything European, since we have enough to do on our own."[12] But Dostoevsky's hope that Russia would not become a party to the conflict did not stem from any aversion to the prospect of war as such. Indeed, he disagrees with Sofya's protest against the horrors of war, about which she had written him sadly: "they will wound and kill, and then they bandage them up and treat them." To which Dostoevsky replies, quoting Saint Matthew: "Remember the greatest words in the world: 'I will have mercy, and not sacrifice.'"[13] Perhaps he meant that, since war is an inevitable part of human life, mercy and compassion should be preserved in its midst.

For Dostoevsky, however, war was not an unmitigated evil, and he tells her outright: "I do not agree with you at all about war. Without war a person grows numb in comfort and wealth and completely loses the capacity for generous thoughts and feelings and imperceptibly becomes hardened and lapses into barbarity. I am speaking of nations as a whole. Without suffering you will not even understand happiness. An ideal passes through suffering the way gold does through fire."[14] Such a moral justification of war sounds rightly repellent to modern ears; but this no longer bearable view of the beneficial effects of war on a population was once held very widely by highly respected thinkers. Even the unbellicose Kant believed that "a long peace generally brings about a predominant commercial spirit and, along with it, low selfishness, cowardice and effeminacy, and debases the disposition of the people."[15]

Dostoevsky's sympathies were unmistakably with the French, and he followed the campaign very closely as it unfolded. Even though he concluded, quite wrongly, that the Germans had committed a strategic error, he believed they would win eventually; but defeat would help to bring about a rejuvenation even of France itself. "France has grown too callous and petty. Temporary pain is of no importance: it will endure it and rise again to a new life and a new idea." Europe itself will embark on a new era, and "the change . . . will be great everywhere. What a stimulus! How much new life will be produced everywhere! Even science and learning, after all, were declining in narrow materialism, for the lack of a noble idea," and the war will presumably lead to a replacement of such materialistic tendencies by more exalted values.[16]

Although Dostoevsky refused to condemn war as such, neither did he glorify it in any way. "Well, is he not really a babe . . . who believes that the Prussian conquered by virtue of his schooling," he exclaims indignantly to Maikov. "That is even obscene. Is it not a fine schooling that plunders and tortures like Attila's horde! (And perhaps even worse)." Despite his "deep revulsion" against everything in Europe, which he acknowledges has reached "the point of hatred," Dostoevsky still cannot close his eyes to the human reality of the conflict as seen through the far from triumphant reactions of ordinary German soldiers. "I have read several letters myself from German soldiers in France, near Paris, to their mothers and fathers here (shopkeepers, tradesmen). Lord, what they write! How sick they are, and hungry!" He notes that the crowds in the street are no longer singing the patriotic "Wacht am Rhein," and only the educated class seems filled with warlike ardor. One "hoary and influential scholar," whom Dostoevsky had come to know by sight in the reading room of the library, had shouted: "Paris muss bombardiert sein" (Paris has to be bombed). "These are the results of their learning," he comments caustically. "If not of their learning, then of their stupidity."[17]

The rising power of Germany filled both Dostoevsky and Maikov with trepidation for the future of Russia, and Maikov wondered if Nikolay the Miracle Worker—a saint much revered by the Russian people as helper, comforter, and protector—would come to Russia's aid in this critical moment as he had done in the past. Dostoevsky's reply in October 1870, in a letter already cited in connection with *The Devils*, reassures Maikov by giving his own version of the saint's efficacy. "You write me about Nikolay the Miracle Worker. He will not abandon us, because Nikolay the Miracle Worker is the Russian spirit and Russian unity." And Dostoevsky is convinced that such unity, in the hour of need, will come to the fore even "in the most un-Russian part of Russia, that is, a liberal—a Petersburg official or student, even they become Russians . . . even though they are ashamed to admit it."

As proof, Dostoevsky recalls his own reaction during the Crimean War, when "even though I still had a strong ferment of the mangy Russian liberalism preached by shitheads like the dung beetle Belinsky and the like, I did not consider myself inconsistent in feeling myself to be a Russian." On the contrary, "I was in prison back then and was *not* happy at the Allies' success, but together with my other comrades, unfortunates and soldiers, I felt myself to be a Russian, wished the Russian arms success."[18] Linking this reminiscence with the theme of *The Devils*, Dostoevsky continues with his explanation of the epigraph from Luke, which predicts the expulsion of the liberal "herd of swine" from the body of "Russian man," who will sit at the feet of Jesus after being healed.

The Franco-Prussian War appears in *The Devils* as the title of a piano composition by the servile, obsequious Jew Lyamshin, whose piece is a musical battle, as it were, between *La Marseillaise* and *Mein lieber Augustin*. At first the two works sound separately, with the *Marseillaise* ringing out "a flamboyant challenge" and filled with "the flush of future victories." But *Augustin* doggedly continues, refusing to be shaken off, and "suddenly the strain of *Augustin* begins to blend with the strains of the *Marseillaise*." *Augustin* becomes more and more "full of joy and arrogance," and starts to drown out the *Marseillaise* entirely: "only from time to time could a snatch of the original tune be heard: *'qu'un sang impur.'*" At last the *Marseillaise* disappears entirely: "hoarse sounds are heard, one has the feeling of countless barrels of beer, the frenzy of self-glorification, demands for milliards, expensive cigars, champagne and hostages; *Augustin* passed into a wild uproar" (10: 251–252).

This sarcastic musical rendition of the conflict is the only overt reference to the war in the novel; but an aftermath of the French defeat, the establishment of the Paris Commune by the extreme radical left, may be brought into connection with a key thematic motif. Like many others in France and Europe, Dostoevsky had been horrified at the uprising of the Commune and the destruction of the city that ensued (partly as a result of the desperate defense of the Communards, in whose ranks could be

12. Barricades of the Paris Commune

found Dostoevsky's erstwhile beloved Anna Korvin-Krukovskaya*). Writing to Strakhov, who had objected to his scatological insults against Belinsky, Dostoevsky replied by linking the critic—and thus the theme of his novel—directly to the cataclysmic events taking place in the French capital.

"But take a look at Paris, at the Commune," he admonishes. "Can you really also be one of those who say that it again failed for lack of people, circumstances, and so on? For the whole nineteenth century that movement has ... been dreaming of paradise on earth (beginning with the phalanstery). . . . In essence it is all the same old Rousseau and the dream of re-creating the world anew through reason and knowledge ... (positivism). . . . They desire the happiness of mankind, and still cling to Rousseau for their definition of 'happiness,' that is, with a fantasy not con-

* By this time, Anna Korvin-Krukovskaya had linked her fate with Charles Victor Jaclard, a French ex-medical student who became an important radical politician and commanded a regiment of the National Guard that fought for the Commune. She is described in the memoirs of the Communard Louise Michel as a "heroine," and she was active in a commission appointed to reorganize the education of the people and particularly that of women. She was also one of the founders and editors of an evening newspaper, *La Sociale*, published from the end of March 1871 to the middle of May, which "was the most consistently Socialist organ of the Commune" and noted for the seriousness of its articles. I. S. Knizhnik-Vetrov, *Russkie Deyatelnitsi Pervogo Internatsionala i Parizhkoi Kommuni* (Leningrad, 1964), 185–190.

firmed by any experience. The burning of Paris is a monstrosity: 'It did not succeed, so let the world perish because the Commune is higher than the happiness of the world and of France.' But after all, to them (and to lots of people) that madness does not seem a monstrosity, but, on the contrary, *beauty*. And so, the aesthetic idea in modern humanity has become muddled."[19] Much of the symbolism of *The Devils* is based on this very idea of such a false and perverted "beauty" having replaced the true "beauty" of Christ.

Dostoevsky remains impenitent toward Belinsky, but retreats somewhat from the insulting intemperance of his language. "I criticized Belinsky," he explains, "more as a phenomenon of Russian life than as a person: that was the most foul-smelling, obtuse, and ignominious phenomenon of Russian life." But though he tries momentarily to separate the man from his ideas, Dostoevsky returns to the charge when he places Belinsky and his generation in exactly the same perspective as the one used for Stepan Trofimovich in his novel. "If Belinsky, Granovsky, and that whole bunch of scum were to take a look now, they would say: 'No, that is not what we were dreaming of, that is a deviation; let us wait a bit, and light will appear, progress will ascend to the throne, and humanity will be remade on sound principles and will be happy!' There is no way they could agree that once you have set down that road, there is no place you can arrive at other than the Commune." Indeed, Dostoevsky even imagines Belinsky arguing that the "Commune was a failure because it was French," and that Russia could do better because it had *no* nationality at all to impede the building of a brave new world.[20] Such bitter words indicate the unappeasable fury of Dostoevsky's indignation; and his anger leads him to deprecate Belinsky's literary judgments, once valued so highly, in ways that manifestly exaggerate their presumed wrongheadedness and dogmatism.

What Dostoevsky could never forgive was Belinsky's animadversions against Christ during their conversations in 1845, just after the two had met and Belinsky was preaching his Left Hegelian atheism, under the influence of Feuerbach, with his usual unbridled tempestuousness. "But here is something more: you never knew him," he writes Strakhov vehemently; "but I knew him and saw him and now fully comprehend him. That man reviled Christ to me in the foulest language, but meanwhile he himself was never capable of setting all the movers and shakers of the whole world side-by-side with Christ by way of comparison. He was not able to notice how much petty vanity, spite, intolerance, irritability, vileness, and most important vanity there was in him and in them. In reviling Christ he never asked himself what we would set up in place of him— surely not ourselves, when we are so vile. No, he never pondered the fact that he himself was so vile. He was extremely satisfied with himself, and that was personal, foul-smelling, ignominious obtuseness."[21] Belinsky, to do him justice, could often be harshly self-critical and self-condemnatory; but Dostoevsky's recollection of the insults to Christ, combined with their now-evident (to him) Nechaevist consequences, now drove the novelist beyond all bounds. Just a few years later, even while depicting Belinsky holding forth condescendingly about Christ, Dostoevsky would be much more equable in tone.

4
———

All through these Dresden months, as can be seen from his comments on Russian literary and cultural matters, Dostoevsky was following very closely the course of events in his homeland. To Maikov, Dostoevsky asserts that his own "knowledge of what was happening in Russia" was probably better than that of his correspondent. "I go through *three* Russian newspapers to the last line daily (!), and receive two journals."[22] A constant preoccupation was the fate of *Dawn*, which had failed to attract subscribers, and whose lack of success Dostoevsky repeatedly attributes to a deficiency of editorial skills and a sloppiness in meeting publication and distribution schedules. "The first issues of *Dawn* for this year [1871] make a very dull impression: the complete absence of anything contemporary, vital, burning (that is always true of them), paltry prose fiction. ... Even the translated novel [*Old-Town Folks*, by Harriet Beecher Stowe—J.F.] is junk." How could it compete with the liberal Westerner *European Messenger*, "which has united in itself all the most brilliant names (Turgenev, Goncharov, Kostomarov), which publishes every issue in the most interesting and rich manner, and which has gotten into the habit of coming out on the first day of each month!"[23]

Though Dostoevsky strongly supported the nationalist and quasi-Slavophil stance of *Dawn*, his sympathies with the journal's problems had been considerably strained by an article written under a pseudonym by the brilliant and ultrareactionary Konstantin Leontiev (who would later attack *The Brothers Karamazov*). Leontiev had referred to Dostoevsky's journal *Time* as a "failure"; and the ex-editor, in a pained letter to Strakhov, protests against such a defamation of the truth. It was not, Dostoevsky said, a matter of literary vanity—he had not objected, for example, when in a novel of Pisemsky's serialized by *Dawn* one of the characters had called *Poor Folk* "talented, but tedious." The reason he now raised his voice was that accusations had been circulated by his brother Mikhail's family "that I had allegedly *ruined* my brother by distracting him from his earlier commercial pursuits and persuading him instead to publish a journal. That accusation is made with bitterness," and "a line in a journal will greatly strengthen that accusation against me in their hearts."[24] Strakhov apologized for the "oversight," but one may suspect an ulterior motive. It was an article of Strakhov's that had led to the suppression of *Time*, and to consider the journal as having been a failure in any case removed some of the onus from his shoulders.*

Dostoevsky worried not only about the fate of *Dawn* but also about the future of its chief literary critic, his putative friend Strakhov. He told Maikov, who evidently did not share his admiration, that Strakhov "is the only critic in our time";[25] and he was liberal with advice on ways to increase Strakhov's feeble popularity, which suffered from his erudite but rather tepid manner. Sometimes, Dostoevsky admonishes him, it is necessary "to write with whip in hand." Strakhov was just "too, too gentle. . . . Nihilists and Westerners require an absolute whip" and should be attacked "more passionately and *coarsely*." In one article, Strakhov had criticized a writer for citing the fashionable German materialists Moleschott and Büchner rather than Plato and Hegel. Dostoevsky comments: "But you know . . . they [the Nihilists] will consider you a backward old man who is still fighting with bow and arrow, while they have long since been using rifles."[26] Dostoevsky's preferred tactic was to fight the Nihilists on their own terrain, and by turning their own weapons back on themselves; but such combative skill and ardor was entirely foreign to Strakhov's furtive, involuted temperament and scholarly disposition.

Strakhov's article on Granovsky, as we know, had been very important for the genesis of *The Devils*; and another of his contributions to *Dawn*, a major series on Herzen, can also be linked to Dostoevsky's presentation of the character of Stepan Trofimovich. After reading the first installment, Dostoevsky wrote appreciatively that "you have done an extremely good job of establishing Herzen's main point—pessimism." Dostoevsky wonders whether Herzen's "doubts" were *really* insoluble, and he anticipates a strong reaction "when you prove that Herzen said before lots of others that the West is rotting." Of greatest interest is Dostoevsky's own view of Herzen, whom he sees in terms not mentioned by Strakhov at all: "the main essence of all of Herzen's activity—namely, that he has been, always and everywhere, *primarily a poet*" (italics in text).[27]

"The poet wins out in him everywhere and in everything, in all his activity. The propagandist is a poet; the political activist is a poet; the socialist is a poet; the philosopher is a poet in the highest degree! That quality of his nature, I think can explain a great deal in his actions, even his flippancy and inclination to pun about the loftiest moral and philosophical questions (which, by the way, is very revolting in him)." The "poetic" quality of Herzen's temperament, his inability to commit him-

---

* For more information on the suppression of *Time*, see *Dostoevsky: The Stir of Liberation* (Princeton, N.J. 1983), chap. 14, sec. 7.

self wholeheartedly to whatever intellectual or practical activity he was involved in, will constitute one of the most engaging traits of Stepan Trofimovich's whimsically volatile character. This Herzen component of Stepan Trofimovich also provides the historical background for his stormy relations with Peter Verkhovensky and the Nihilist ideas of his offspring (we shall return to this matter in Chapter 24).

Strakhov wrote a number of articles about Turgenev at this time, and Dostoevsky, who partly took issue with their lack of severity, refers to them frequently in his letters. More fuel for Dostoevsky's already red-hot animosity was added by the publication of Turgenev's article, "The Execution of Troppmann," in the *European Messenger*. Turgenev, like Dostoevsky, opposed capital punishment, and he had written an eyewitness account of the execution of a famous criminal to protest against this extreme penalty. But, as Dostoevsky saw it, Turgenev had concentrated more on his own discomfiture and distaste than on the sufferings of the condemned. For Dostoevsky, who had once undergone such torments himself, and had compared them in *The Idiot* with the agonies of Christ at Gethsemane (8: 21), Turgenev's finickiness at such a moment filled him with a scarcely controllable rage.

"You may have a different opinion, Nikolay Nikolaevich," he fumed to Strakhov, "but that pompous and refined piece made me indignant. Why does he keep on being embarrassed and repeating that he does not have the right to be there? Yes, of course, if he only came to see a show; but no person on earth has the right to turn away and ignore what happens on earth, and there are supreme *moral* reasons for that. *Homo sum and nihil humanum*, and so on. . . . The main impression of the piece . . . is a terrible concern, to the point of extreme touchiness, for himself, for his safety and his peace of mind, and that in sight of a chopped-off head!"* Dostoevsky would parody this article in *The Devils*, and also make use of the further observation that "I consider Turgenev the most written out of all written-out Russian writers—no matter what you write 'in favor of Turgenev' Nikolay Nikolaevich."[28] The phrase cited is the title of an article in which Strakhov gently chides Turgenev's newly announced allegiance to Nihilism, but insists that the nature of his artistic talent made such an alliance impossible.

---

* For a less partisan view of Turgenev's article, see the deeply felt reflections of Robert L. Jackson in *Dialogues with Dostoevsky* (Stanford, 1993), 29–54; also, William C. Brumfield, "Invitation to a Beheading: Turgenev and Troppmann," *Canadian-American Slavic Studies*, 1 (Spring 1983), 79–88.

One of Dostoevsky's jottings about his epilepsy (January 7/19, 1870) mysteriously remarks that an attack occurred on "the day and almost the very hour of Troppmann's agony." Dostoevsky presumably felt some sort of subterranean linkage between Troppmann's torments and his own psychic upheavals. See E. M. Konshina, *Zapisnie Tetradi F. M. Dostoevskogo* (Moscow-Leningrad, 1935), 83–84.

When Strakhov wrote that Turgenev's *King Lear of the Steppes* had produced a "rather strong impression" on its readers, Dostoevsky fired back: "I did not like Turgenev's 'King Lear' *at all.* A pompous and empty thing. The tone is low, oh, landowners who have written themselves out! Honest to God, I am not speaking out of envy."[29] Strakhov nonetheless continued to praise Turgenev's artistry and to maintain that his literary gifts more than compensated for his ideological vacillations. Dostoevsky could hardly believe it, and thought that perhaps he had misread Strakhov's words. "If you recognize that Turgenev has lost the point and is hedging," he objects, "and *does not know what to say* about certain phenomena of Russian life (treating them mockingly *just in case*), then you ought to have recognized that his greatest artistic ability had weakened (and this was inevitable) in his latest works. That is exactly what has occurred: he has weakened as an artist." But Strakhov had not arrived at any such conclusion, much to Dostoevsky's surprise: "You recognize his former artistry even in his latest works. Is that really so? But perhaps I am mistaken (not in my opinion of Turgenev, but in your article). Perhaps you just did not state your opinion quite correctly."[30]

Dostoevsky had not been mistaken, however, and this defense of Turgenev leads him into more general considerations that go beyond the question of individual talent. They lead him, in fact, to an insight that has since become classic about the evolution of Russian literature and his own position in its ranks. Dostoevsky had once accepted the opinion that Turgenev's work had been enfeebled by his prolonged residence in Europe; but now he feels that "the reason is more profound" and goes far beyond Turgenev personally because "it really is all gentry-landowner literature. It has said everything that it had to say (superbly by Lev Tolstoy). But this in the highest degree gentry-landowner word was its last. There has not yet been a *new word* to replace that of the gentry-landowners, and besides, there has been no time for it. (The Reshetnikovs have not said anything. But the Reshetnikovs nevertheless express the idea of the necessity of something new in the artistic word, something no longer *gentry-landowner*, though they express it in a hideous form.)"[31]

F. M. Reshetnikov was a minor social realist whose novel, *The People of Podlipov* (*Podlipovtsy*), created a considerable stir by its unsparing depiction of the primitive and almost bestial conditions of the life of the peasants (mostly of Finnish stock) in the neighborhood of Perm. Nothing could be further from the country-house and upper-class world of Tolstoy and Turgenev, or even from the lyrical and poetic depiction of peasant life in Turgenev's *A Sportsman's Sketches.* Dostoevsky certainly thought of himself as capable of supplying such a *new word*—not in copying the manner of Reshetnikov and those like him (though he had been their precursor in *House of the Dead*), but in dramatizing and combating the moral-spiritual confusion and chaos that had led to the rise of Nihilism.

Dostoevsky's reactions to Strakhov's articles about Herzen and Turgenev fed directly into the creation of his new novel; and he was also keeping a watchful eye on literary competitors dealing with the same subject. In *The Russian Messenger* he had been reading installments of a recent anti-Nihilist novel, *At Daggers Drawn* (*Na Nozakh*), which N. S. Leskov was publishing under a pseudonym. Although Dostoevsky had published Leskov in *Epoch* and admired his talent, he comments dismissively to Maikov that the book "contains a lot of nonsense ... it is as though it takes place on the moon." Dostoevsky of course is thinking of his own novel by contrast, in which he takes great pains to delineate a verisimilar social framework. He singles out for praise, however, Leskov's portraits of Russian clergymen ("what a master at depicting our priests! How is Father Evangel for you?") and his grasp of a character called Vanskok.

This nickname designates the feminine head of a radical circle notable for her unswervingly fanatical, honest, and unselfish devotion to the cause, which she accepts with an almost childlike faith. "Gogol never had anything more typical and accurate ... you know, I have seen that *Vanskok*, heard her myself. ... A most amazing character. If the Nihilists of the beginning of the Sixties die out, that figure will remain to be remembered forever."[32] Dostoevsky also is careful to present his Nihilists in *The Devils* not as evil villains acting out of dishonest or purely selfish motives, but as vain, pretentious, frivolous, or simply naive—easy prey for someone like Peter Verkhovensky who knows how to play on their human weaknesses. One should never forget that Dostoevsky himself had been an underground revolutionary conspirator as a young man, and knew very well that those who had joined with him were far from being scoundrels or reprobates.

5

It was in the spring of 1871, just before embarking on the return trip to Russia, that Dostoevsky took his final stab at gambling. This was the last time he ever approached a roulette table—surely an event worthy of notice—but so much attention has been lavished on the pathology of his gambling mania that no scrutiny at all has been given to its disappearance. Indeed, it has been argued that he never gambled again only because, on his four later trips to Germany for his health, the casinos had been closed. But one must agree with his wife that, if he had not truly conquered his addiction, it would have been easy enough to travel to where the wheels were still alluringly spinning; distance had never stopped him in the past from gratifying his then irresistible obsession. It must be assumed, therefore, that Dostoevsky overcame his desire to gamble—a desire that Freud considered a symptom of his masochistic need for self-punishment, stemming ultimately from a parricidal death-wish. Oddly enough, Freud never says a word about this quite remarkable self-cure.*

If we are to believe Anna's memoirs, it was her idea and not her husband's at all that he once again try his hand at Wiesbaden. He was laboring industriously at the first chapters of *The Devils*, but in a mood of depression and anxiety, harassed both by the loss of his "feel" for Russian life and by the bleakness of his financial prospects. Anna had become pregnant with another child, and the expectation of an addition to the family only increased Dostoevsky's paternal torments about their lack of means. They both desired desperately to return to Russia before the new child was born, which meant a departure by the beginning of July. It so happened that Anna had managed to accumulate a small surplus of three hundred thalers and was willing to sacrifice one hundred of them to provide some needed distraction for her husband. She also knew that after every gambling misadventure he returned to writing with renewed devotion and vigor. One day she brought the conversation round to Wiesbaden, and Dostoevsky jumped at the chance. Some subterfuge was necessary because of the presence of Dostoevsky's mother-in-law, who disapproved of gambling, and the couple concocted a little code that Dostoevsky could use in telegraphing for money. Anna writes with hindsight that she was convinced her husband would lose as usual; but perhaps even she harbored a shred of hope that he might, as had occasionally happened, bring home some winnings.

But Dostoevsky lost all his money almost immediately, and, to make matters worse, also gambled away the thirty thalers sent him for the return home. Once more he writes the familiar pitifully pleading, imploring, self-castigating letters, not even asking for pardon but rather the opposite: "if you feel sorry for me at this moment, do not do so, I am not worth it." He is frantic about how the news will affect Anna, now in her final months of pregnancy, and also feels guilty when he thinks of his little daughter: "And Lyuba, Lyuba, how vile I have been!" In asking Anna to dispatch thirty more thalers, which he swears not to use for gambling, he envisions the terrible prospect of what might happen if he betrays her trust yet again. "But, my angel, try to understand, after all, *I know that you will die if I were to lose again!* [italics added]. I am not at all a madman! After all, I know that then I am done for. . . . Believe me *for the last time*, and you will not regret it."[33]

* For a critical view of Freud's article, see my "Freud's Case-History of Dostoevsky," printed as an appendix in *Dostoevsky: The Seeds of Revolt* (Princeton, N.J., 1976), 379–391.

The last phrase in italics refers to Dostoevsky's promise, a few sentences later, that he would never gamble again—a promise he had made often enough in the past and often enough broken. But with the benefit of hindsight, one may perhaps detect a new note of resoluteness in his vehement declarations, a desire at last to come to terms with himself once and for all. "Anya, my guardian angel! A great thing has been accomplished within me, a vile fantasy that has *tormented* me almost ten years has vanished. For ten years (or, rather since my brother's death, when I was suddenly crushed by debt) I kept dreaming of winning, I dreamed seriously, passionately. Now all that is finished. This was ABSOLUTELY the last time! Will you believe, Anya, that my hands are untied now; I had been bound by gambling." As usual, too, the letter is filled with affirmations of a desire to return to work, and he proclaims that "I will think about serious things now, and will not dream whole nights on end about gambling, as I used to. And therefore *the serious business* will move better and more quickly, and God bless it."[34] Anna, who had heard all this before, was understandably skeptical; but time would show that something decisive *had* occurred, and it is worth dwelling on what might have been its cause or causes.

One should not underestimate, it seems to me, the increasing depth and intensity of Dostoevsky's love for, and dependence on, his wife as a result of their living together and being thrown back on each other under extremely difficult practical conditions in almost total isolation from a normal social milieu. The bonds between them had become very strong and close-knit, and Dostoevsky's references to Anna in his letters, as well as the words recorded in her diary, become increasingly warm, appreciative, and heartfelt. There can be no doubt that his guilt at making Anna suffer because of his gambling became more and more tormenting as the years passed. "Will you believe, my angel," he writes from Wiesbaden, "that I dreamed all year of buying you the earrings that I have not given back to you? You have pawned everything of yours for me in these four years and roamed after me homesick for your native land!"[35] Dostoevsky had always been haunted by the fear that Anna's infinite tolerance might one day vanish, and he was now concerned that her health—at this moment quite precarious—could be affected by his losses and his untrustworthiness. The specter of her dying from the grief brought on by his follies should be taken as more than a rhetorical flourish.

Indeed, this fear had already manifested itself to him palpably in two terrifying dream images. "I dreamed of my *father* last night," Dostoevsky tells her, "but in such a horrible way as he has appeared to me only twice in my life, foretelling a terrible disaster, and twice the dream came true. (And now when I also recall my dream three days ago, that you had turned gray, my heart stops! Lord, what will happen to you when you get this letter!).”[36] Anna later commented on this missive: “Feodor Mikhailo-vich believed in the importance of dreams. He was always particularly upset when he saw his brother Misha, or particularly his father, in a dream. Dream images foretold misfortune or calamity, and I was the wit-ness several times that shortly (two or three days) after such a dream image, there would be a sickness or death in the family, healthy up until then, or a severe epileptic attack of Feodor's, or some kind of material calamity. Happily, nothing of the sort occurred this time.”[37] Dostoevsky may well have felt that he was being warned of a looming disaster to Anna if he continued to gamble; and the frightening dream images, whose impact on him may be compared to that of Raskolnikov's final dream, perhaps was taken as a warning of catastrophe if his gambling fever continued.

Another incident recounted in the letter—and to which little attention has been paid—is curious enough to deserve some comment. Dostoev-sky not only took dream images very seriously, but he also believed in signs and premonitions; in general he was quite superstitious and sus-ceptible to being influenced by any intimations of the dictates of a higher will.* In Wiesbaden, after playing until 9:30 P.M. and losing everything, he ran off to seek the Russian priest. “I thought on the way,” Dostoevsky explains to Anna, “running to see him, in the dark, down unfamiliar streets, that after all he is the Lord's shepherd, that I would talk to him not as with a private person, but as at a confession.” Lost in the obscu-rity, he saw looming before him a building whose vaguely Oriental out-lines seemed to mark out his destination. “When I reached the church that I had taken for a Russian one, I was told at a shop that it was not a Russian one, but a Jewish one. It was as though I had had cold water poured over me. I came running home; it is now midnight, I am sitting and writing to you.”

Why should this simple mistake of one building for another have had such a powerful effect on Dostoevsky? Clearly, he intended to convey that he had received a shock to his entire nervous system; and this sensa-tion may perhaps be interpreted to mean that he had felt something like an ominous sign. The Jews in the background of *The Gambler* knew how to control their play and had warned Aleksey Ivanovich not to return to the casino; there was also, to be sure, the inevitable, age-old association of Jews with money and money-grubbing. It could be that Dostoevsky took this error to indicate, by a signal from on high, that his gambling mania was bringing him into a degrading proximity with those people

---

* Writing about Dostoevsky in Siberia in 1854, when he was worried about the sentiments of his future wife, Baron Wrangel remarks: “Suddenly he became superstitious, began to tell me about clairvoyance, visited fortune-tellers, and as I was twenty years old and had my own romance, he dragged me to an old woman telling fortunes with beans.” Baron A. E. Wrangel, *Vospominaniya o F. M. Dostoevskom* (St. Petersburg, 1912), 53.

traditionally linked with the amassing of filthy lucre. Perhaps, whenever he was tempted to gamble in the future, this (for him) demeaning and chilling recollection continued to recur and acted as a barrier. A post-script to the letter confirms that he felt a decisive turning point in his life had been reached: "I *will not go to see* a priest, not for anything, not in any case. He is one of the witnesses of the old, the past, the former, the vanished! It will be painful even for me to meet him!"[38]

Dostoevsky came back from Wiesbaden determined, despite the loss of one hundred and eighty thalers, to make plans for returning to Russia in July. He had calculated that he needed three or four thousand rubles to arrive in safety, but he now resolved to make the journey even though only a thousand might be available. "Staying in Dresden for another year," he wrote Maikov, "is the most impossible thing of all. That would mean killing Anna Grigoryevna with despair that she is unable to con-trol. . . . It is also impossible for me not to move for a year."[39] Katkov had promised him the thousand by the end of June; but Dostoevsky wrote immediately, as he had done so often after a gambling disaster, to retail his woes and ask that the money be sent as soon as possible. Although the trip would be difficult—the Dostoevskys would be traveling without help and with Lyuba on their hands—there was no time to lose: Anna was expected to give birth at the beginning of August.

The ever-compliant Katkov agreed to send the money requested, and the Dostoevskys prepared for departure, which meant redeeming the be-longings they had pawned, paying their bills, and packing up. This raised the question of what to do with Dostoevsky's papers, because he had been warned that an order had been issued to search his luggage very carefully at the border. Much to Anna's sorrow, Dostoevsky insisted on throwing early drafts of *The Idiot, The Devils,* and *The Eternal Husband* into the fire. What clinched his argument was that, if they carried the papers, they might be detained at the border for a number of days while the documents were examined, and this would be quite risky in view of Anna's condition. Luckily, Anna managed to rescue Dostoevsky's note-books, which she confided to her mother to bring back in the autumn.

The Dostoevsky family departed on July 5, and it was Dostoevsky's task to keep Lyuba content and amused through the sixty-eight hours of the journey. Apparently he acquitted himself in exemplary fashion, tak-ing her for walks on the platform at stopping places, playing games with her, and buying milk and food; the then-enfeebled Anna is warm in her retrospective praise of his talents as a nanny. As expected, they were de-tained at the border, and Dostoevsky's papers were put aside for closer scrutiny. All the other passengers left the customs hall to catch the con-necting train for Petersburg, and the Dostoevskys were afraid they would miss it and be stranded. But Lyuba saved the day: she cried so loudly and insistently for food that the officials hurriedly returned the confiscated documents and hustled the family out of earshot. So much for the border search, and the orders of the secret police! At last back in their homeland, the Dostoevskys still had a twenty-four-hour train trip ahead; but they felt as if they were living through the wondrous realization of a long-cherished dream. "Our consciousness of the fact that we were riding on Russian soil," Anna recalls, "that all around us were our own people, Russian people, was so comforting that it made us forget all about the troubles of our journey."[40]

6

Work on *The Devils*, of course, went on unabated as the Dostoevskys settled down to life in Petersburg, where a son, Feodor, was born on July 16, 1871. In the spring of 1872, they moved to a country town called Staraya Russa to escape both the stifling Petersburg summer heat and the distracting pressures of social life. Composition went smoothly enough, though the laboriously toiling author complains about the difficulty of obtaining the exact effects he wants; but there are no uncertainties about the conception or direction of the book, or even about some of the major scenes that lay ahead.

Dostoevsky's unusually firm grasp of his future text may be attributed to several causes. One, as he tells Katkov, was that Stavrogin's character had come to him "sketched in scenes, actions, and not in statements"; this meant that he did not have to invent dramatic situations as he went along to display Stavrogin's personality. Another was that Dostoevsky worked on *The Devils* in a wholly unprecedented manner, which gave him some of the overall command of his manuscript that he so envied in his more affluent literary rivals. They could survey their novels as wholes or in large portions *before* publication, while Dostoevsky, under the pressure of need, had been forced to write from month to month with only a few notes and sketches indicating what his next installment would contain. With *The Devils*, however, he informs Katkov, "something happen[ed] ... that has never happened before; I stopped the work at the beginning for weeks and wrote from the end."[41] Dostoevsky thus had a much clearer view of the book as a whole, at a much earlier stage of composition, than had been the case with his two previous major novels.

Just how clear this image was may be seen in a remark to Maikov after the first chapters had been published and his confidant had dispatched an enthusiastic letter of praise. One sentence from it, quoted by Dostoevsky in his reply, gave him the greatest satisfaction. "In your comments you had a brilliant statement: 'Those are *Turgenev's heroes in their old age.*' That is brilliant! While writing, I myself was dreaming of something like that, but in these words you have designated everything, as in a formula." Maikov thus confirms Dostoevsky's own sense of the book's relation to *Fathers and Children*; but the novelist warns his friend against taking Stepan Trofimovich, to whom the comment refers, as the main character. "Stepan Trofimovich is a secondary character; the novel will not be about him at all; but his story is closely linked to other events (main ones) in the novel, and therefore I have taken him as though the cornerstone of everything. But still and all Stepan Trofimovich's star turn will be in the fourth part [actually the third]: at that point there will be a highly original conclusion to his fate. I cannot vouch for anything else, but for that passage I can vouch ahead of time."[42] Dostoevsky here pinpoints one of the structural problems of the work (the relation of Stepan Trofimovich and Stavrogin), and also illustrates how distinctly he had already envisaged the marvelous pages devoted to "Stepan Trofimovich's Last Pilgrimage."

A similar instance of Dostoevsky's foreknowledge can be seen in what he told his niece, to whom *The Idiot* had been dedicated in its journal text. This honor had aroused some envy in her older sister, Marya Alexandrovna, who also aspired to have her name attached to one of her uncle's novels. When this desire was conveyed by Sofya to Dostoevsky, he wrote that, although he would have dearly liked to comply with her request, he felt it would be unseemly. The reason was that "there will be passages in the novel (in the second and third parts) which, even though they could be read by a girl, all the same it would be unfitting to dedicate to her. One of the main characters in the novel secretly confesses to another character a crime he has committed. The psychological influence of that crime on the character plays a large role in the novel; the crime, however, I repeat, even though it can be read about, is not suitable for a dedication. When you dedicate something, it is as though you are saying publicly to the person to whom you make that dedication: 'I thought of you as I wrote this.'"[43]

Dostoevsky is here referring to a chapter of the novel that was never published during his lifetime: the chapter sometimes called "Stavrogin's Confession" or, more literally, "At Tikhon's." It was initially meant to be Chapter 9 of Part II and to provide a conclusion to this section, though there are indications that Dostoevsky also toyed with placing it at the beginning of Part III; but the internal logic of the thematic structure would make the first choice more suitable. This chapter narrates the visit of Stavrogin to a nearby monastery in which the monk Tikhon is living and his confession, in the form of a written document, of the violation of a twelve-year-old girl. Dostoevsky wrote this chapter in the fall of 1871 and finished it not later than November. Chapters 7 and 8 were printed in the November issue of *The Russian Messenger*, but then the serialization came to a halt. Katkov refused to accept the decidedly shocking episode, and Dostoevsky could not persuade him to change his mind; the pages thus never appeared during Dostoevsky's lifetime, though some inoffensive portions of the text would be used in *A Raw Youth*. The chapter was found among Dostoevsky's papers in 1921, published in 1922, and since then has been the subject of considerable critical controversy.

The text exists in two versions: one consists of the galleys Dostoevsky received from the journal before the decision was made not to publish; the second is a copy, transcribed by Anna, containing the alterations and corrections Dostoevsky undertook in an effort to meet the editors' objections. Dostoevsky was very upset by the rejection of this cornerstone of his creation, which contains not only the crucial revelation of the full range and depth of Stavrogin's depravity but also his moral-philosophical motivation, his inner torments, and his longing for redemption. To test his own judgment, Dostoevsky read the galleys aloud to friends like Maikov, Strakhov, and a new acquaintance, K. P. Pobedonostsev, then tutor to Crown Prince Alexander. When they unanimously agreed that one section (part 2 of Chapter 9, containing Stavrogin's confession) was "too realistic," he began to invent variations, one of which described Stavrogin's encounter with an adolescent girl who had been brought by her governess to a bathhouse to meet him. Someone had told Dostoevsky about such an incident; but his "advisers" warned against using it because it might be taken as an insult to governesses and thus run afoul of the "woman question."[44] Incidentally, this variation of the confession grew into the legend that Dostoevsky himself, unexpectedly showing up in Turgenev's room one day when his fellow novelist was visiting Petersburg, confessed to having committed this very crime.*

Dostoevsky traveled to Moscow in January 1872 to consult with the editors about the chapter, and he informs Sofya Ivanova the next month that, after much head-breaking indecision, he has decided not to invent a new version of the crime. Instead, "remaining with the substance of the matter, I changed the text only enough to satisfy the chaste editors. And in this sense I have sent an *ultimatum*. If they do not agree, then I really

---

* This persistent rumor, which continues to dog Dostoevsky's reputation, has been thoroughly investigated by V. N. Zakharov. Beginning with its first appearance in press reports dating from 1908, he tracked down all the utterances that put it into circulation and demonstrated that the various versions are inconsistent and contradictory. Also, on the basis of everything we know about the lives of Dostoevsky and Turgenev, he proves that such a visit could not physically have occurred in the time period in which it was placed.

Zakharov believes that Turgenev invented the story in the last years of his life, as a satirical anecdote to characterize Dostoevsky and as revenge for the caricature of himself in *The Devils*. It was then converted into fact on retelling. Other varieties of the legend, which was retailed by Strakhov in a letter to Tolstoy in 1883, are convincingly traced to Dostoevsky's efforts to rally support for his rejected chapter by reading it to friends. See V. N. Zakharov, "Fakti protiv legendi," in *Problemi Izucheniya Dostoevskogo* (Petrozavodsk, 1978), 95–109.

do not know what to do."[45] Dostoevsky's revision left in doubt whether any seduction had actually occurred: Stavrogin refuses to give part of his manuscript to Tikhon, but affirms categorically that nothing untoward happened except for an innocent embrace. "Calm yourself," he tells Tikhon, "it is not my fault if the girl was stupid and did not understand me. There was nothing, nothing at all." To which Tikhon replies, "Thank God!" and crosses himself (12: 111). There is also an intervention by the narrator, speculating that the document was "a morbid work, the work of the devil who took possession of that man," and suggesting that what it recounted may be just an invention. It is compared to the scene in which Stavrogin bites the Governor's ear, causing a scandal but doing no real harm. But then the narrator backtracks: "I certainly do not maintain that the document is false, that is to say, that it has been completely made up and invented. More likely, the truth is to be sought somewhere in between" (12: 108).

In March 1872, Dostoevsky wrote N. A. Lyubimov, Katkov's assistant editor, with reference to the revision: "I believe that what I have sent you . . . can now be printed. Everything too scabrous has been removed, the substance shortened, and all this half-mad escapade sufficiently revealed, although it will be revealed more strongly later. I swear to you, I cannot do without the core of the matter. This is a full-fledged social type (in my opinion), *our* type, Russian, an idle person, not out of a desire to be idle, but having lost his ties with everything national, and, most important, his faith, depraved out of *melancholy longing*—but conscience-stricken, and making an effort through convulsive suffering, to renew himself and again begin to believe. Along with the Nihilists, this is a serious phenomenon. I swear to you that it exists in reality. This is a person not believing in the belief of our believers and demanding a totally different faith. . . . But all this will be cleared up even more in the third part."[46]

Despite such insistences and justifications, the journal still hesitated to accept the chapter. No final decision was made, however, and Dostoevsky was told that Katkov, no longer wishing to print in small installments, would wait for the remainder of the novel before resuming publication. Dostoevsky thus forged ahead, sending in several more chapters, on the assumption that his disputed section would be included. It was only in early November that he learned there was no further hope of publishing even the revised variant of Stavrogin's confession. By this time, publication had been scheduled to begin with the November issue; and so Dostoevsky, his back to the wall, reworked as much of the manuscript as he could to cope with the new situation.

It is not necessary here to detail all the differences that exist between the manuscript of Part III and its published form; but one is of particular importance. In Chapter 7, which narrates the touchingly pathetic "pilgrimage" of Stepan Trofimovich, he listens to a reading of passages from the Gospel and then takes on himself the primary responsibility for having infected the body of Russia with the devils. No such scene is found in the manuscript, which means that it was added *after* Dostoevsky had learned that his confession chapter would not be printed. The omission of this scene in the manuscript may indicate that Dostoevsky had originally intended to portray Stavrogin as having assumed this burden of guilt (which would make more thematic sense); but he was unable to do so because, without the glimpse he had hoped to give into the torments of Stavrogin's conscience, a sudden display of such conscience in the final pages would have been insufficiently motivated.

The remainder of *The Devils* was finally published, after a year's delay, in the November and December 1872 issues of *The Russian Messenger*. When the novel appeared in book format the next year, it had once more been extensively revised. Several passages in Part II foreshadowing and motivating the encounter with Tikhon were eliminated, and these, along with the suppressed chapter itself, now must be taken into account in any consideration of the book. Since Dostoevsky himself did not include this chapter in later editions, some question has been raised about its importance; but both internal and external reasons provide a plausible answer for his failure to reinstate it. For one thing, he had altered the still-unpublished text as much as possible *before* magazine publication to meet the crisis he had not foreseen; the work thus no longer represented his original conception, and extensive rewriting would have been required to transform it once again. Also, he would then have had to face the formidable hurdle of the *official* censorship, and perhaps fail.

Hence Dostoevsky decided to leave well enough alone, and Stavrogin thus remains a far more enigmatic and mysterious figure than he was initially meant to be, though Dostoevsky could scarcely have conceived him as entirely pellucid in any case. But he lacks the clarifying moral-philosophical motivation that Dostoevsky had intended to provide, and it is remarkable that so much is still conveyed of the stature of his personality even without the dignifying effect such motivation was meant to furnish. If Dostoevsky could not give us the book as he had originally conceived it, however, we should not allow ourselves to be limited by his constrictions. To understand and appreciate the full grandeur of Dostoevsky's extraordinary endeavor, which is nothing less than to write a symbolic history of the moral-spiritual travails of the Russian spirit in the first half of the nineteenth century, we must analyze the printed text with all of the means that scholarship has since placed at our disposal to illuminate its complexities.

CHAPTER 23

History and Myth in
The Devils: I

The Devils takes its place, along with *Notes from Underground* and *Crime and Punishment*, as part of Dostoevsky's continuing struggle against the Russian Nihilism of the 1860s. Unlike these earlier works, however, it is not solely an imaginative projection of the personal and moral-emotive consequences of radical ideology as Dostoevsky envisaged them. The book is based to a great extent on material that Dostoevsky collected about the Nechaev affair—word-of-mouth accounts, newspaper reports, the propaganda he may have come across in Europe, and then all the numerous documents published in connection with the trial of Nechaev's followers in Petersburg.

Although Nechaev himself, like Peter Verkhovensky, left Moscow after Ivanov's murder and escaped across the border, the members of his Moscow group in the Petrovsky Academy of Agriculture, along with many others (sixty-four in all), were arraigned on July 1, 1871, and tried throughout the summer. Political trials in Russia were ordinarily held in secret; but the evidence uncovered by the investigation was considered so damaging to the revolutionaries that the Tsarist authorities decided to air all their misdeeds in public. By this time, Dostoevsky had published only the first and second chapters of Part II, and he could make full use of this additional data in the remainder of the book.

The Devils, to be sure, is a work of art and not either literal history or quasi reportage (like *House of the Dead*). Nor did Dostoevsky ever pretend that it had any claim to truth other than as a creation of his imagination. "Several of our critics have observed," he wrote in 1873, "that in my novel I used the plot of the well-known Nechaev affair. But they hastened to add that my book did not contain any actual portraits or a literal reproduction of the Nechaev history—having taken an event, I tried only to clarify its possibility in our society, and precisely as a social event, not as an anecdote, not as a description of a particular occurrence in Moscow. All this, I may observe, is quite correct. In my novel, I have not handled the well-known Nechaev and his victim Ivanov in any personal way" (21: 125).

It is true that, in a letter to Crown Prince Alexander Alexandrovich accompanying a presentation copy of the book, Dostoevsky referred to it as

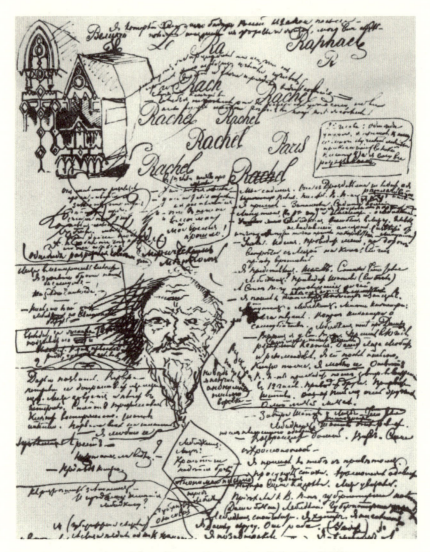

13. A page from Dostoevsky's notebooks for *The Devils*

"almost a historical study";[1] but the qualification is indicative of his cau-
tion. His notion of "history," moreover, had always involved grasping it,
like so many other Russian writers beginning with Pushkin's *Evgeny Onegin*, in terms of historically representative but artistically created literary
types. As he wrote of the underground man, such a figure "not only may,
but *positively must*, exist in our society, given the circumstances under
which our society was in general formed" (5: 99; italics added). The un-

derground man was not only a private individual, existing as a particular kind of personality, but also someone who manifested a symbolic truth about the nature of Russian society as a whole.

Dostoevsky had thus in the past created fictional characters who, as the embodiment of certain social-cultural ideas and attitudes, could be considered "historical" in a broad sense; but not until *The Devils* had he ever based himself on actual events that were a matter of public knowledge. Even though his characters might still be freely invented, they (or their prototypes) were also known from other sources and through their real-life histories. This aspect of the novel poses the question, which had never yet arisen so centrally for Dostoevsky's fiction, of what use he made of such documentation. To what extent does he offer an acceptable image of what he is portraying, within the range of liberty allowed a novelist to reshape his factual point of departure? Such a question arises for *The Devils* particularly in relation to the social-political stratum of the book.

Quite obviously, Dostoevsky did not limit himself to the actual, rather insignificant dimensions of the Nechaev affair, which were repugnant and reprehensible but hardly of notable importance. If he had done so, "the facts" would have given him only a rather pitiful tale of a distressing event that had occurred among a handful of students and hangers-on in the student milieu, who had been duped and misled by a revolutionary zealot into the useless murder of an innocent victim. Rather, this incident furnished only the nucleus of Dostoevsky's political plot; and he enlarged and magnified it, according to the technique of his "fantastic realism," into a full-blown dramatization of the far more ambitious tactics and aims set down in the writings of Nechaev and his supporters. What happens in *The Devils* is thus myth and not history (using the word *myth* to mean the imaginary amplification of the real), art and not literal truth—just as Raskolnikov may be considered a "myth" engendered by the "immoderate Nihilism" of Pisarev and Zaitsev. But while in *Crime and Punishment* this myth is entirely of Dostoevsky's own devising (Pisarev had not actually advocated the murder that Raskolnikov committed), in *The Devils* Dostoevsky merely gives artistic life to what he found already inscribed in the documents at his disposal. Much of what he learned, in any case, hardly taught him anything new, for he could draw on recollections from his own days as a revolutionary conspirator when his secret group had worked in the shadows to manipulate the larger Petrashevsky circle.

To what extent, however, does Dostoevsky remain faithful to the spirit, if not the letter, of what his documentation revealed about the Nechaev affair? Time and again, from 1872–1873 to the present, *The Devils* has been attacked as a vicious slander on the Russian revolutionary movement of his day. More recently, as Russians have begun to speak freely about life in the former Soviet Union, the book has come to be seen as far more prophetic than defamatory;* but some consideration of these persistent accusations is still definitely called for all the same. Does Dostoevsky, in fact, portray characters and depict behavior and events that by no stretch of the imagination could have occurred among people committed to the Russian revolutionary cause? If so, he is guilty of slander; if not, the charges must fall. That he was an opponent of the radicals does not make him slanderous; neither does his use of material that hardly places them in a favorable light. For the indictment to be upheld, it must be shown that he drastically distorted or perverted the conduct and aims of the actual personages and circumstances on which he based his narrative.

2
—————

Upon first reading, nothing could seem to support such a charge against Dostoevsky more glaringly than his depiction of Peter Verkhovensky. This monster of deviousness and duplicity, who resembles Shakespeare's Iago as a destructive inciter of evil in others, would seem to be light-years removed from any conceivable image of a nineteenth-century Russian revolutionary. Has he not been created from whole cloth by Dostoevsky's malevolent imagination? Certainly the real Nechaev bears little actual resemblance, either physically or socially, to Dostoevsky's character. Yet the actions taken by Peter Verkhovensky with such masterful relish are exactly the same ones that Nechaev accomplished, or would have accomplished had it been within his power to turn desires into deeds.

An indelibly vivid portrait of Nechaev at work is sketched in a letter we are fortunate to possess from no less a pen than that of Mikhail Bakunin. He had been—along with Dostoevsky's Geneva acquaintance, the sym-

---

* As an example of a recent reaction, let me cite Yury Karyakin, a well-known literary critic and cultural historian who has a particular interest in Dostoevsky and who had been at one time a Stalinist true believer. He recalls the period of the Twentieth Party Congress, when Krushchev first lifted the curtain on the true nature of Stalinism, and remarks: "For me, and most of my friends, this was a veritable earthquake. But someone close to me (now dead), a classic Russian *intelligent*, a typical Stepan Trofimovich Verkhovensky, with a doctorate in chemistry, a professor, seeking relief from personal and political troubles in Dostoevsky, Leskov, and Chekhov, or departing every Thursday to the House of Teachers (where he played flute in the orchestra)—said to me with a sorrowful smile: 'But you know, all this is in *The Devils*. I was almost arrested in '36 because I read that novel. Someone denounced me.' . . .

"These were frightening and enlightening nights: we read *The Devils* and the notebooks for the novel (we managed to get them). . . . We read, and did not believe our eyes: all this we knew, had believed it all, all this we recalled only too well. We read and interrupted each other almost on every page: *'It can't be. How could he have known all this?'* " Yury Karyakin, *Dostoevsky i Kanun XXI Veka* (Moscow, 1989), 204–205.

pathetic but weak-willed N. P. Ogarev—one of Nechaev's most enthusiastic supporters. Many scholars have speculated on the curious personal
relations between the fiercely determined young revolutionary and the
passionately eloquent veteran of a hundred subversive plots, who was
crowned with the aureole of his fabulous insurrectionary past. For
Bakunin soon found himself in thrall to the young man, whom he admiringly called an *abrek* (a pitiless Muslim warrior of the Caucasian peoples)
and "a young eagle." But this was before Nechaev, after escaping to Europe in the wake of the Ivanov murder, began to use the methods they
had both agreed upon against Bakunin himself and the circle of their
common friends. Once Nechaev did so, Bakunin felt it necessary to write
in July 1870 to a family with whom Nechaev had entered into contact.
The letter is so revelatory, and so precise in its depiction of Nechaev's
limitless unscrupulosity, that it must be cited at length:

> My dear friend, I have just learned that N[echaev]. has called on you
> and that you hastened to give him the address of your friends (M.
> and his wife). I conclude that the two letters by which I warned you,
> and begged you to turn him away, arrived too late; and, without any
> exaggeration, I consider the result of this delay a veritable misfor-
> tune. It may seem strange to you that we advise you to turn away a
> man to whom we have given letters of recommendation addressed
> to you and written in the warmest terms. But those letters date from
> the month of May; and since then we have been obliged to admit
> the existence of matters so grave that they have forced us to break
> all our relations with N. . . . . Now I shall try to explain briefly the rea-
> sons for this change.
>
> It remains perfectly true that N. is the man most persecuted by
> the Russian government, which has covered the continent of Eu-
> rope with a cloud of spies seeking him in all countries; it has asked
> for his extradition both from Germany and Switzerland. It is equally
> true that N. is one of the most active and energetic men I have ever
> met. When it is a question of serving what he calls the cause, he does
> not hesitate; nothing stops him, and he is as merciless with himself
> as with all the others. This is the principal quality which attracted
> me, and which impelled me to seek an alliance with him for a good
> while. Some people assert that he is simply a crook—but this is a lie!
> He is a devoted fanatic, but at the same time a very dangerous fa-
> natic whose alliance cannot but be harmful for everybody. And here
> is why: at first he was part of a secret committee which really existed
> in Russia. The Committee no longer exists; all its members have
> been arrested. N. remains alone, and alone he constitutes what he
> calls the Committee. His organization in Russia having been deci-
> mated, he is trying to create a new one abroad. All this would be

14. Sergey Nechaev

perfectly natural, legitimate, very useful—but the methods he uses are detestable. Very much struck by the catastrophe that has destroyed the secret organization in Russia, he has gradually succeeded in convincing himself that, to found a serious and indestructible organization, one must take as a foundation the tactics of Machiavelli and totally adopt the system of the Jesuits—violence as the body, falsehood as the soul.

Truth, mutual confidence, serious and strict solidarity only exist among a dozen individuals who form the *sanctus sanctorum* of the Society. All the rest must serve as a blind instrument, and as exploitable material in the hands of the dozen who are really united. It is allowed—even ordered—to deceive all the others, to compromise them, to rob them and even, if need be, to get rid of them—they are conspiratorial fodder. For example: you have received N. thanks to our letter of recommendation, you have taken him into your confidence, you have recommended him to your friends. . . . Here he is, transplanted to your world—and what will he do first? First he will tell you a pack of lies to increase your sympathy and your confi-

440

dence; but he will not stop there. The tepid sympathies of men who are devoted to the revolutionary cause only in part, and who, besides this cause, have other human interests such as love, friendship, family, social relations—these sympathies are not, in his eyes, a sufficient foundation, and in the name of the cause he will try to get a hold on you completely without your knowledge. To do this, he will spy on you and try to gain possession of all your secrets; and in your absence, being alone in your room, he will open all your drawers and read all your correspondence. If a letter seems interesting to him, that is, compromising from any point of view either for yourself or one of your friends, he will steal it and preserve it very carefully as a document either against you or your friend. . . . when, at a general meeting, we accused him of this, he had the nerve to say—"Well, yes, that's our system. We consider as our enemies all those who are not with us *completely*, and we have the duty to deceive and to compromise them." This means all those who are not convinced of their system, and have not agreed to apply it to themselves.

If you have presented him to a friend, his first concern will be to sow discord between both of you by gossip and intrigue—in a word, to cause a quarrel. Your friend has a wife, a daughter; he will try to seduce them, to make them pregnant, in order to tear them away from official morality and to throw them into a forced revolutionary protest against society.

All personal ties, all friendship, all [gap in text] . . . are considered by them as an evil, which they have the right to destroy—because all this constitutes a force which, being outside the secret organization, diminishes the sole force of this latter. Don't tell me that I exaggerate: all this has been amply unravelled and proven. Seeing himself exposed, poor N. is still so naive, so childish, despite his systematic perversity, that he thought it possible to convert me—he went so far as to implore me to develop this theory in a Russian journal that he proposed to establish. He has betrayed the confidence of us all, he has stolen our letters, compromised us terribly, in a word, behaved like a villain. His only excuse is his fanaticism! He is terribly ambitious without knowing it, because he has ended by identifying the cause of the revolution with that of himself—but he is not an egoist in the banal sense of the word because he risks his life terribly, and leads the existence of a martyr full of privations and incredible activity.

He is a fanatic, and fanaticism carries him away to the point of becoming an accomplished Jesuit—at moments, he simply becomes stupid. The majority of his lies are woven out of whole cloth.

He plays at Jesuitism as others play at revolution. In spite of his relative naiveté he is very dangerous because *each day* there are acts, abuses of confidence, treacheries, against which it is all the more difficult to guard oneself because one hardly suspects their possibility. With all this, N. is a force because of his immense energy.... His last project was nothing less than to set up a band of brigands and thieves in Switzerland, naturally with the aim of acquiring some revolutionary capital. I saved him by persuading him to leave Switzerland because he would certainly have been discovered, he and his gang, in a few weeks; he would have been lost, and all of us lost with him....

Persuade M. that the safety of his family demands that he break with them completely. He must keep N. away from his family. Their system, their joy, is to seduce and corrupt young girls; in this way they control the whole family. I am very sorry that they learned the address of M. because *they would be capable of denouncing him.* Didn't they dare to admit to me openly, in the presence of a witness, that the denunciation of a member—devoted or only partly devoted—is one of the means whose usage they considered quite legitimate and sometimes useful? ... I am so frightened at their knowledge of M.'s address that I beg him to change his lodgings secretly, so that they won't discover him.[2]

This letter, so far as Nechaev is concerned, hardly needs any commentary; but it contains a hidden irony that should not be overlooked. The "methods" that Bakunin now castigates so severely, and from which he so fastidiously dissociates himself, are merely the application of doctrines set down in the notorious *Catechism of a Revolutionary*, written either by Nechaev and Bakunin in collaboration or by one of them alone (scholars still dispute the issue). There is no doubt that Bakunin had full knowledge of this most sinister of handbooks of revolutionary strategy and had approved of its precepts. What horrified him was only that the recommended methods were now being used against *himself* and his friends. Dostoevsky of course had no knowledge of this letter; but Bakunin's bewilderment and outrage at becoming the victim of doctrines he had originally sponsored reminds one irresistibly of Stepan Trofimovich's reaction to the ideas and activities of his son Peter, whom he sees as distorting and vulgarizing the exalted ideals of *his* youth. Bakunin's letter is thus valuable not only as a source of information about Nechaev but also as proof of the uncanny accuracy, *mutatis mutandis*, with which Dostoevsky had captured the essence of the historically symbolic relation between the generations.

In view of Bakunin's letter, it is difficult to have much patience with the monotonously reiterated opinion that Dostoevsky willfully slandered and misrepresented what he had chosen to portray. Such a charge can be maintained only from ignorance (as in much non-Russian criticism), or from a diehard political partisanship that rejects the historical evidence. Bakunin's infatuation with Nechaev survived the parting of the ways recorded in his letter; and he wrote sorrowfully to Ogarev on learning of the arrest of his erstwhile protégé by the Swiss police, who would extradite him to Russia. "I don't know how you feel, but as for me, I feel very sorry for him. . . . He was a man of rare energy; and when you and I first met him, there burned in him a clear flame of love for our poor and downtrodden people, he had a genuine ache for the people's age-long suffering."[3]* Dostoevsky, much to his credit, did not deprive Peter Verkhovensky of this one redeeming feature, though it is not displayed very prominently. "Listen," Peter says to Stavrogin, "I've seen a child six years old leading home his drunken mother, while she swore at him with foul words. Do you suppose I am glad of that? When it's in our hands, maybe we'll mend things" (10: 324–325). Just as Dostoevsky remained true to Nechaev by including this one flicker of compassion, so there is not a single action of Peter Verkhovensky that Nechaev did not perform, or would not have performed if given the opportunity.

One can only agree with Georgy Chulkov, a survivor of the Silver Age of Russian literature who lived into the Soviet period to write one of the least tendentious works published on Dostoevsky in the 1930s, that "the political caricature of *The Devils* is not too far removed from the then-existing reality." "This, of course," he hastened to add protectively, "does not eliminate the counterrevolutionary character of the novel. But we

---

* That Nechaev was indeed a person of "rare energy" and extraordinary strength of will is proven by the amazing history of his later career. Extradited to Russia from Switzerland in 1872 as a common-law criminal accused of murder, he was tried in January of the following year and sentenced to twenty years of hard labor and exile to Siberia for life. His attitude in court was defiant, and he refused to recognize its authority. At the public ceremony of his "civil execution," he shouted that in three years the heads of those condemning him would be chopped off by the first Russian guillotine.

Alexander II personally ordered that, despite his sentence, Nechaev be secretly held for life in the Peter and Paul Fortress. There his rebellious attitude in solitary confinement led to further punishments, though he was provided with books he requested and apparently wrote a number of works that have disappeared. Most remarkable of all is that he gradually won over the soldiers assigned as his guard to the revolutionary cause, and they became his willing admirers, followers, and couriers.

In 1879, learning through new prisoners of the existence of the underground revolutionary *People's Will* (*Narodnaya Volya*), he sent a message to the Executive Committee that they could hardly believe. Nechaev was still alive, and not in Siberia but Petersburg! Plans were made to arrange an escape from prison, and, learning of the intention to kill Alexander II, Nechaev characteristically advised them to issue false manifestos at the moment of the attempt so as to confuse the population. The Tsar's assassination on March 1, 1880, put an end to a hope of escape with outside aid, though Nechaev attempted to organize one himself with the help of his allies in the prison garrison. But someone informed the authorities of his influence among the soldiers, his guard was replaced, and he died of scurvy on November 21, 1882. See Franco Venturi, *Roots of Revolution* (New York, 1966), chap. 15.

only wish to emphasize that Dostoevsky as an artist remained faithful to his predilection for factual accuracy. His sarcasm was directed against the ideology of the Nechaevists and his pamphlet was constructed for this purpose; but Dostoevsky did not distort the facts themselves. He ridicules with hatred the psychology of Peter Stepanovich, but there was no necessity for him to exaggerate the negative aspects of his activity."[4]

3

Dostoevsky's attention to factual accuracy is displayed not only in his portrait of Peter Verkhovensky but also in the entire social-political intrigue of the book. The power of Peter Verkhovensky in *The Devils* is based on his claim to be the representative of a worldwide revolutionary organization, vaguely located somewhere in Europe and with which he has made contact in Switzerland. Nechaev in fact carried credentials attesting him to be representative No. 2771 of the "Russian section of the World Revolutionary Alliance"; and these credentials, signed by Bakunin, were also stamped with the seal of the "Central Committee" of the "European Revolutionary Alliance." None of these bodies existed anywhere except in the vast reaches of Bakunin's conspiratorial imagination, and it is doubtful whether Nechaev placed too much faith in their power. After all, he had presented himself to Bakunin as the delegate of an equally fictitious organization of Russian students; but he was perfectly content to use the aura of Bakunin's prestige, and the looming shadow of these all-powerful organizations, to impress his dupes in Moscow. To reinforce his authority, he once arrived at a meeting of his group with a stranger (an inoffensive visiting student from Petersburg), whom he introduced as a member of the "Central Committee" in Geneva come to check on their activities.[5] Quite appropriately, Peter Verkhovensky instructs the glamorous Stavrogin to appear at a meeting as "one of the founding members from abroad, who knows the most important secrets—that's your role" (10: 299).

Almost from its start, Nechaev's career was marked by a systematic use of falsehood and deceit, not only against the enemies of his cause but also toward his allies and followers. Such a policy was explicitly affirmed as a principle in the *Catechism*: "the degree of friendship, of devotion, and of other obligations toward . . . a comrade is measured only by his degree of utility in the practical world of revolutionary pandestruction."[6] Peter Verkhovensky reveals the "secrets" of his activity—namely, that there really are no "secrets," that he is acting alone—only to Stavrogin, who is the key to his revolutionary plans. All the rest of his group he considers as "raw material," to be used and manipulated as he sees fit for the good of the cause. Such manipulation was foreseen in the paragraph of the *Catechism* devoted to "revolutionary chatterers" (a perfect description of the group at Virginsky's), who were to be "pushed and involved without ceasing into political and dangerous manifestations, whose result will be to make the majority disappear while some among them will become revolutionaries."[7]

It was in accordance with this ruthless application of the principle of utility that Nechaev disposed of Ivanov; and Dostoevsky's interpretation of the crime in no way violates the evidence. Whether Nechaev really believed that Ivanov would betray the underground group, or whether, as Dostoevsky was convinced, he wished to gain an indissoluble hold on his followers by involving them in a common crime against a troublesome dissident, has never been established. Yury Steklov, the Old Bolshevik and one-time editor of *Izvestia*, after reviewing all the evidence in his massive, four-volume biography of Bakunin, comes to the same conclusion as Dostoevsky. Nechaev was faced with the choice of abandoning the dictatorial methods against which Ivanov objected, or "carrying to its extreme logical conclusion his characteristic system of terror and deceit, kill Ivanov, and in this way intimidate the remaining members of his organization by linking them together in a bloody crime. Nechaev chose the second path, along which he was impelled by the logic of his chosen method of action on the one hand and, on the other, by his stubborn fanaticism and confidence in his great mission."[8]

Peter Verkhovensky arrives in the provincial town where the novel is set as the bosom companion of the gentry scion Stavrogin and also as an intimate of the equally wealthy Drozhdov family. Having learned the secret of Stavrogin's perverse marriage to Marya Lebyadkina, and aware of Liza Tushina's infatuation with Stavrogin, he manifestly hopes, whether by intimidation or by catering to Stavrogin's lusts, to gain a hold over Stavrogin and exploit him for his revolutionary purposes. Such maneuvers are completely in conformity with the doctrines of the *Catechism*: "with the aim of implacable destruction a revolutionary may, and often must, live in the midst of society, pretending to be quite different from what he really is."[9] The aim of this disguise, as with Peter, is to gain power over "the great number of highly placed animals who, by their position, are rich and have relations." Such dupes "must be exploited in every possible way, circumvented, confused, and, by acquiring their dirty secrets, be turned into our slaves. In this manner their power, their relations, their influence, and their riches will become an inexhaustible treasure and an invaluable aid in our various enterprises."[10]

The same tactics are used by Peter Verkhovensky to gain control over the von Lembkes—the governor of the province and his wife—whom he also exploits for his revolutionary aims. Through Stavrogin, Peter obtains a letter of introduction to Yulia Mikhailovna from "a very important old lady in Petersburg, whose husband was one of the most distinguished old dignitaries in the capital." Peter himself is rumored to have gained the approbation of certain mysterious and powerful government personages by repenting of his past sins and by having "mentioned certain names" (10: 169). Nothing in the *Catechism* would preclude sacrificing one or two comrades for the purpose of infiltrating the higher spheres; indeed, as Nechaev insolently told Bakunin, such an act was perfectly acceptable.

Once entrenched in Yulia Mikhailovna's good graces, Peter encourages the giddy lady, who liked to flirt with "liberal" ideas (and is a wonderfully clairvoyant anticipation of our contemporary "radical chic"), into believing that with his help she could scale the dizziest social heights and save Russia from disaster at the same time. "To discover the plot, to receive the gratitude of the government, to enter on a brilliant career, to influence the young 'by kindness,' and to restrain them from extremes—all these dreams existed side by side in her fantastic brain" (10: 268). Revolutionaries, the *Catechism* declares, should conspire with liberals "on the basis of their own program, pretending to follow them blindly" but actually compromising them so that they can be "used to provoke disturbances in the State."[11] Peter subverts Yulia Mikhailovna's innocent liberal fête for the benefit of the governesses of the province in exact accordance with these instructions, turning it into a riotous manifestation of protest against the authorities.

Peter's strategy toward the dim-witted, bewildered, and rather touching Russo-German von Lembke, who, for relief from the cares of office, turns to making mechanical toys and writing a novel, is to gain a hold over him by using the influence of Yulia Mikhailovna and by flattering his literary vanity. With him, Peter also plays the *agent provocateur*: he spurs von Lembke on to harsh suppression of signs of unrest among the Shpigulin workers and taxes him with being "too soft" and "liberal" in the performance of his gubernatorial duties. "But this has to be handled in the good old way," Peter jovially tells the hesitant von Lembke. "They ought to be flogged, every one of them; that would be the end of it" (10: 272). Peter's metamorphosis into an advocate of "the good old ways" is justified by a passage in the *Catechism* requiring the revolutionary to "aid the growth of calamity and every evil, which must, at last, exhaust the patience of the people and force them into a general uprising."[12] It can also be linked with two Bakunin-Nechaev pamphlets, supposedly issued by the "Descendants of Rurik and the Noble's Revolutionary Committee."[13] These pamphlets preached the most outrageously reactionary sentiments and were intended to stir up right-wing, oligarchical opposition among the old nobility to the reforming Tsar. They probably inspired Peter's friendship with the retired Colonel Gaganov, who resigned from the army partly because he "suddenly felt himself personally insulted by the proclamation" of the liberation of the serfs. Gaganov is described, quite specifically, as a person who "belonged to that strange section of the nobility, still surviving in Russia, who set an extreme value on their pure and ancient lineage and take it too seriously" (that is, "the descendants of Rurik") (10: 224).

4

Sources or parallels for almost every other politico-ideological feature of *The Devils* can be found either in the Bakunin-Nechaev propaganda or in other easily identifiable historical events and situations. Peter Verkhovensky's employment of Fedka the convict as the executive arm of the revolution brings to life (rather feebly, it must be said) advice given in the *Catechism*: revolutionaries must unite "with the fierce world of the bandits," who are "the sole and genuine revolutionaries in Russia."[14] This Romantic glorification of the fearsome bandit of Russian folklore is combined, in the Bakunin-Nechaev propaganda, with blood-curdling exhortations and apocalyptic images of total annihilation: "We must dedicate ourselves to wholehearted destruction, continuous, unflagging, unslackening, until none of the existing social forms remains to be destroyed." "Poison, the knife, the noose. . . . The revolution sanctifies everything in this battle."[15] Peter Verkhovensky only echoes such passages when he cries: "We shall proclaim destruction. . . . Why? Why? Well, because it is such a fascinating little idea! . . . Every scurvy 'group' will be of use. I'll find you fellows so eager in these groups that they'll be glad to shoot and will be grateful for the honor. . . . There's going to be such an upheaval as the world has never seen before" (10: 325).

Nothing about the Bakunin-Nechaev propaganda is more striking than its total negativism, the complete absence of any specific aim or goal that would justify the horrors it wishes to bring about. Such a positive purpose, in any determined sense, is outlawed on principle as a historical impossibility and must remain wrapped in the Messianic obscurity of the future. "Since the existing generation is itself exposed to the influence of those loathsome social conditions against which it is revolting, to this generation cannot belong the work of construction. This belongs to those pure forces that will be formed in the day of renovation."[16] This negativism helps to explain why Peter Verkhovensky sets himself off so sharply from "Socialists" like Shigalev, who *do* worry about the form of the future social order, and why, as a true Bakuninist revolutionary, Peter dedicates himself only to the work of uprooting the existing moral-social norms. "But one or two generations of vice are essential now," he tells Stavrogin; "monstrous, abject vice by which a man is transformed into a loathsome, cruel, egoistic reptile. . . . I am not contradicting my-self, I am only contradicting the philanthropists and Shigalevism, not myself! I am a scoundrel, not a Socialist!" (10: 325).

No passage in the book testifies more to Dostoevsky's integrity than this refusal to tar Socialism and the Socialists with the infamous brush provided by Peter Verkhovensky. Dostoevsky himself had once strongly sympathized with French Utopian Socialism in its initial, semi-Christian form, and he knew very well that, even in its Russian metamorphosis of the 1860s, it bore little resemblance to the unbridled amorality preached and practiced by Peter Verkhovensky. Marx and Engels took great care to make the same distinction, and thoroughly agreed with Dostoevsky's separation of Nechaev's tactics from Socialism as *they* understood it. In-deed, they used the Bakunin-Nechaev propaganda as one of their weap-ons in evicting Bakunin and his followers from the First International. "These all-destroying anarchists," they wrote sententiously, "who wish to reduce everything to amorphousness in order to replace morality by anarchy, carry bourgeois immorality to its final extreme."[17]

Peter Verkhovensky's contemptuous indifference to Socialism and So-cialist theory, so manifest in his behavior at the "birthday party" at Vir-ginsky's, echoes a constant keynote in the Bakunin-Nechaev writings: "The modest and far too cautious formation of secret societies, without any overtly practical consequences, is, in our eyes nothing more than a childish game, ludicrous and loathsome."[18] Peter is a little more tactful in his utterances, but he cannot contain his inexpressible boredom with such ideas. " 'You see, gentlemen'—he raised his eyes a trifle—'to my mind all these books, Fourier, Cabet, all this talk about the "right to work" and Shigalev's theories—all are like novels of which one can write a hundred thousand—an aesthetic entertainment'" (10: 313). The same tone of sarcasm can be found in remarks on this subject in the propa-ganda leaflets. "In the Cossack groups formed by Vassily Usom in Astra-khan at the time of Stenka Razin," one such document reads, "the ideal goal of social equality was achieved in an immeasurably superior fash-ion to the phalansteries of Fourier, the institutions of Cabet, Louis Blanc and other learned Socialists, better even than in the associations of Chernyshevsky."[19]

Even when commentators have not wished to defend Nechaev, very few have resisted the temptation to accuse Dostoevsky of misrepresent-ing the Russian radical movement as a whole. For while traces of Ne-chaev's systematic Machiavellianism can be found earlier in under-ground circles,* it was alien to other radical groupings then in existence. In fact, however, Dostoevsky never tries to give any other impression,

* See above, p. 52n, for remarks about Ishutin's organization "Hell."

and Peter Verkhovensky's relation to the members and sympathizers of his underground organization is one of continual struggle to overcome their opposition and mistrust. No one at the meeting really agrees with Verkhovensky, but he browbeats them into submission by playing on their vanity and curiosity: all agree to go "full speed ahead" in order to hear his mysterious "communication" from the all-powerful organization he claims to represent. Just before Shatov's murder, even the members of Verkhovensky's inner circle are panic-stricken at what has occurred—the fire, the various murders already committed, the riots and disorders—and decide that unless Verkhovensky gives them a "categorical explanation" they will "dissolve the quintet and ... found instead a new secret society 'for the propaganda of ideas of their own and on the basis of democracy and equality'" (10: 415–416). Shigalev, at the last moment, refuses to have anything to do with the murder as a matter of principle; Virginsky never stops protesting even while it is taking place. However unappealing or pathetically ridiculous Dostoevsky makes them out to be, the members of the quintet do not believe in systematic amorality and universal destruction as panaceas for the ills of the social order.

To be sure, Dostoevsky's satire is not much tenderer for Shigalev than it is for Verkhovensky; but at least he should be given credit for acknowledging the existing spectrum of radical opinion. Shigalev, in Dostoevsky's notes, is first called Zaitsev; and one of his physical features—his long ears—is probably derived from an adjective (*visloykhii*, lop-eared) applied to Zaitsev and Pisarev by Saltykov-Shchedrin during the "Schism among the Nihilists" controversy. Dostoevsky may have thought of Zaitsev in this connection—"an idiot, as I remember him," he jots down (11: 129)—because of his extreme theoretical élitism and his ill-starred defense of Negro slavery, presumably for humanitarian reasons. Without the protection of slavery, Zaitsev had argued, the black race would be doomed to extinction because of its inherent inferiority. Shigalev too is initially an honest democratic radical who ends up, much to his dismay, favoring the "slavery" of the masses to an omnipotent radical elite. "I am perplexed by my own data," he confesses, "and my conclusion is in direct contradiction of the original idea from which I start. Starting from unlimited freedom, I arrive at unlimited despotism" (10: 311).

Zaitsev's views derived from his Social Darwinism, and this doctrine is alluded to when Shigalev asserts that all previous social thinkers "have been dreamers, tellers of fairy tales, fools who contradicted themselves, *who understood nothing of natural science and the strange animal called man*" (10: 311; italics added). Shigalev's own theory for attaining "the earthly Paradise" is unmistakably biological, even though it is given only in an abbreviated version. (He solemnly asks for ten meetings to expound it properly, but, alas, the revolution cannot wait!) A "lame teacher" who has read his manuscript explains the chief idea: "Shigalev suggests ... the division of mankind into two equal parts. One-tenth enjoys absolute liberty and unbounded power over nine-tenths. The others have to give up all individuality and become, so to speak, a herd, and, through boundless submission, will by a series of regenerations attain primeval innocence, something like the original paradise. They will have to work, however. The measures the author proposes for depriving nine-tenths of humanity of their true will, and their transformation into a herd by means of the re-education of whole generations, are very remarkable. They are based on the facts of nature and very logical" (10: 312).

One might imagine that Dostoevsky here has simply let his satirical fantasy run wild à la Swift, and that there could be no textual source for Shigalev's plan to create "the earthly Paradise" by selective Socialist breeding. In fact, however, such a source exists in the radical journalism of the 1860s, and Dostoevsky's familiarity with all varieties of such journalism makes it more than likely that he drew on it for his purposes. It can be found in the writings of P. N. Tkachev, one of whose first articles was published by Dostoevsky in *Time*, and who had been associated with Nechaev in agitating among Petersburg students in 1869. Together they had written a *Programme of Revolutionary Activities*, which led to Tkachev's arrest in the roundup of Nechaev's followers after Ivanov's murder. Both Tkachev and Zaitsev developed the implications of Social Darwinism within the Russian radical context, but Tkachev drew conclusions even more extreme, and more shockingly inhumane, than the iconoclastic defender of Negro slavery.

Tkachev accepted the biological foundations of Darwinism but deplored the social-political conclusions that could be drawn from its tenets. If unchecked and uncontrolled, he argued, the struggle for existence could lead only to the eternal perpetuation of inequality and injustice. Justice could not be achieved except in a world of total equality, but this aim "must by no means be confused with political or legal or even economic equality"; rather, it meant "an organic, physiological equality conditioned by the same education and common living conditions." Such equality, Tkachev wrote, was "the final and only possible aim of human life ... the supreme criterion of historical and social progress"; it was thus the absolute goal and highest ideal of the coming Socialist revolution.[20] If Dostoevsky was not parodying Tkachev, it is surely a remarkable coincidence when Peter Verkhovensky exclaims that "Shigalev is a man of genius" because "he's discovered 'equality.'" "Great intellects cannot help being despots and they've always done more harm than good.... Cicero will have his tongue cut out, Copernicus will have his eyes put out, Shakespeare will be stoned—that's Shigalevism! Slaves must be equal: there has never been either freedom or equality without despotism, but in the herd there's bound to be equality, and that's Shigalevism!" (10: 322).

5
―――――

The ultimate aim of Peter Verkhovensky is to seize power by turning Stavrogin into Ivan the Tsarevich, the false pretender to the throne, and in this way to enlist the peasantry, unbeknownst to themselves, behind his revolutionary banner. This plan is part of a symbolic structure that will be discussed in the analysis of the novel; but even here Dostoevsky does not depart from a verisimilar transmutation of Russian historical reality into the "myth" of his creation. Deeply rooted in the Russian folk imagination was the idea of a "Tsar in hiding" who would someday appear to remedy the world's injustices. Time and again in Russian history a revolt has been justified by the claim that the reigning Tsar was "false."* The renegade monk Gregory Otrepeyev, who led the uprising against Boris Godunov in the early seventeenth century, claimed to be the "true" Tsar and the murdered son of Ivan the Terrible. Exactly the same legend arose at the end of the eighteenth century, when the rebellious Cossack leader Pugachev claimed to be Peter III, who had been killed in a court conspiracy. Peter Verkhovensky intends to exploit this folk tradition and use the quasi-religious status of the Tsar to achieve his overthrow in the interests of social revolution. Nor is such an idea as harebrained as it seems; several recent events had demonstrated the continued vitality of this tradition in the peasant mentality.

Anton Petrov, the leader of the peasant disorders at Bezdna in 1861 at the time of the liberation of the serfs (the event is mentioned in the opening pages of *The Devils*), told his followers that the manifesto of liberation was false and that the Tsar would ultimately send the "true" manifesto, granting the peasants much more land, by means of "a young boy of seventeen with a gold medal on his right shoulder and a silver medal on his left." (Petrov, a self-educated peasant *raskolnik*, probably believed this himself.[21]) Elsewhere in the empire, peasants became convinced that the manifesto was false because the "true" manifesto would have been written in letters of gold.

It was almost inevitable that small groups of isolated radicals should attempt to take advantage of the peasants' credulity and their faith in a

---

* In one of the most penetrating books written on the social-religious psychology of Russian culture, Michael Cherniavsky remarks: "What one may call the Tsar-centeredness of Russian popular uprisings has been noted many times in historical literature. Nearly all the peasant rebellions during the interregnum of the Time of Troubles advanced under the banner of the Tsar, utilizing for that purpose the most unlikely pretenders to the throne." Michael Cherniavsky, *Tsar and People* (New York, 1969), 70.

just and merciful Tsar. In 1863, at the time of the Polish rebellion against Russian rule, false manifestos purporting to be the long-awaited "golden charter" were circulated by the Poles and distributed by Russian radical sympathizers who hoped to instigate internal disruption. There is a jesting allusion to these peasant superstitions, attributed in Dostoevsky's notes to Stepan Trofimovich: "gr. At first, in a casual discussion with his son, he laughingly says of the Russian people: —the authors of these proclamations ought to spend some money, and print them on *papier d'argent* with golden letters, frame it in red and sign Golden Charter of the Tsar—then the people will destroy churches and families when they learn that this comes from the Tsar" (11: 80). Peter Verkhovensky's apparently insensate ideas may well have developed out of the "golden charter" forgeries and recollections of the aberrant claims of earlier rebel leaders. They were thus grounded, not only in the events of the decade covered by the novel, but also in the deepest historical recesses of the Russian folk imagination.

All this should be enough to illustrate on what a solid historical foundation Dostoevsky constructed what seems to be his most extravagant fictional edifice. One of the commonest charges made against *The Devils* in the mostly hostile early reviews was that the book was purely a product of Dostoevsky's "psychiatric talent"—his penchant, long ago noted and harshly criticized by Belinsky, for preoccupying himself with what could only be considered abnormal and psychopathological characters. But Dostoevsky was convinced, and time has proven him right, that his "fantastic realism" cut more deeply into the problems of Russian life than the more superficially verisimilar and equably average presentation of them favored by his literary contemporaries. While giving free rein to his "fantasy," however, he knew that the charges of his critics might be justified unless he took great pains to anchor its flights in the "realism" we have tried to document; and the next chapter will show that he took the same care with Russian culture as he had done with the "myth" of Nechaev and his group.

CHAPTER 24

History and Myth in
The Devils: II

The Nechaev affair and its ramifications is only one of the interweaving historical-ideological strands in *The Devils*. Another is the satirical confrontation between Stepan Trofimovich and his Nihilist son Peter—a confrontation that, before Stavrogin appeared to take over the book, had been intended to occupy the center of Dostoevsky's canvas. Even though this encounter became subordinate in the final text, Dostoevsky succeeded, all the same, in making *The Devils* one of the two classic portrayals in Russian literature of this momentous battle between the generations.

Turgenev had depicted its opening salvos in *Fathers and Children* (1862); but Stepan Trofimovich is much closer to the central figure of an earlier Turgenev novel, *Rudin* (1856), than he is to any of the characters who speak for the past face-to-face with Bazarov. Like Stepan Trofimovich, Rudin is also a Romantic-Idealist of the 1840s—a genuinely pure and noble spirit, but one too weak to live up to his lofty phrases and glowing ideals. *The Devils* may thus be seen as a disputation between two of Turgenev's characters at a later stage of their lives, when Rudin had sunk into a whimsically charming, self-pampering *poseur* and Bazarov had stiffened into a ruthless fanatic. Dostoevsky, we know, enthusiastically agreed with Maikov's remark that Dostoevsky's characters reminded him of "Turgenev's heros grown old."

The Devils thus has an extremely important literary-cultural dimension, which includes its relation both to Turgenev's novels and to Turgenev himself (malevolently but irresistibly caricatured in the figure of Karmazinov). In addition, it also encompasses a whole range of other literary, moral-philosophical, and cultural phenomena, whose richness can only be rivaled, in the nineteenth-century novel, by Balzac's *Les Illusions perdues* and Flaubert's *L'Éducation sentimentale*. The book is almost a compressed encyclopedia of the Russian culture of the period it covers, filtered through a witheringly derisive and often grotesquely funny perspective; and it creates a remarkable "myth" of the main conflicts of this culture, reconstructed on a firm basis of historical personages and events.

2
_____

The figure of Stepan Trofimovich, as we have seen, is primarily derived from that of T. N. Granovsky, a historian from the 1840s who was already half-forgotten by 1869; and one may well wonder why Dostoevsky should have chosen to fasten on him as a prototype. The accidental appearance of Strakhov's article provides one answer; but another possibility is that Dostoevsky had long been familiar with his image and had cherished it particularly because of the portrait given in Herzen's *My Past and Thoughts*. In a famous chapter of this brilliantly evocative work, Herzen describes the end of his friendship with Granovsky in the summer of 1846. This was the fateful moment when Belinsky and Herzen, under the influence of Feuerbach's *The Essence of Christianity*, had become militant atheists; but Granovsky refused to follow Herzen along this emotionally lacerating path. "I will never accept your desiccated, cold idea of the identity of the body and spirit," Herzen cites him as saying; "with that, the immortality of the soul disappears. Perhaps you don't need this, but I have had to bury far too much to give up this belief. For me personal immortality is a necessity."[1] Dostoevsky, who himself clung tenaciously to the hope of personal immortality, could thus have been attracted to Granovsky as a kindred soul: here was a liberal Westerner who refused to surrender the ultimate sanctuary of religious faith. And it was precisely such a figure, with all its inner contradictions, oscillations, and uncertainties, that Dostoevsky wished to highlight as the precursor, as well as the shocked opponent, of the amoral Nihilism exhibited by the new breed of Bazarovs.

Dostoevsky's attention may also have been drawn to Granovsky as a symbolic figure by some remarks in a letter of Maikov's, which he read just as *The Idiot* was being completed. Filling in Dostoevsky on new publications, Maikov mentions Nekrasov's *The Bear-Hunt* (later also referred to by Strakhov in his article on Granovsky) and Pisemsky's new novel, *People of the 1840s* (*Liudi 1840 godov*). Both he and Dostoevsky, Maikov remarks, were such people; and out of their generation had come the liberation of the serfs and all the other reforms initiated by Alexander II. So far, this generation had not been replaced; but Dostoevsky should not think, Maikov assures him, that they were the last of the Mohicans. Like the students now causing disorders in the universities, both he and Dostoevsky had also known their moments of rebellion; and he optimistically predicts that these students will also find their way back to patriotism and national loyalty. Russians would always remain Russians—and he instances the pure Westerner Granovsky as living proof during a moment of crisis for the country. "But already during the Crimean War, when the Westerners were rejoicing—look, they said, the English are coming and will set up a Parliament for us, and they would all rush there themselves to declaim speeches about humanity, Granovsky said indignantly: 'No, gentlemen, the moment they invade Russian territory—you will see, we all will move against them.'"[2*] Granovsky could not resist feeling himself in unity with his countrymen; and one may perhaps see here a first hint of Stepan Trofimovich's last wanderings, when he finally goes out to discover the Russian people about whom he had been pontificating for so long.

The sources for Stepan Trofimovich-Granovsky can be found not only in the personality and biography of the Moscow historian, who died in 1855, but also and more extensively in the controversies that began in the middle of 1858, when the tension between the generations exploded in public. Although these polemics have been discussed in an earlier volume,** it is necessary to return to them if we are to do justice to the cultural underpinning of Dostoevsky's creation. Dostoevsky had followed these fierce exchanges very closely throughout the 1860s; and he was all the better equipped to depict them impartially because he shared both the antipathy of the "sons" for the pampered, pretentious, self-indulgent Westerners of the 1840s and the aversion of the "fathers" for the provocatively insulting vulgarity and materialistic coarseness of their Nihilist offspring of the 1860s. In the last analysis, however, Dostoevsky could not help tilting the artistic scales in favor of his own generation's Romantic love of art and its refusal to relinquish human nature completely to the leveling grip of the materialism and determinism of the 1860s.

The campaign against the liberal-idealist "superfluous men" of the 1840s marked the emergence of a new, more radical group of *raznochintsy* intellectuals as a force on the Russian cultural scene. (The *raznochintsy* possessed no official rank or status [*chin*], many being sons of the lower clergy and graduates of seminaries.) The spokesmen for this newly vociferous group, N. G. Chernyshevsky and Nikolay Dobrolyubov, combined some of the fanatic intransigence of their religious education with a complete rejection of Orthodox precepts in favor of atheism and materialism. They soon unleashed a flood of derogatory articles against the generation of the 1840s, which reached its high point in the bitter and passionate mockery of Dobrolyubov. The generation of the 1840s, in his

---

* The editor of Maikov's correspondence cannot find any source for this anecdote, but cites a letter of Granovsky's from 1855: "If I were healthy," he writes K. D. Kavelin, "I would enlist in the militia without wishing for a Russian victory, but with the desire to die for her. My soul aches because of this time." The letter is cited from the very book of A. V. Stankevich about Granovsky that Dostoevsky read. "A. I. Maikov, Pisma k F. M. Dostoevskomu," ed. N. I. Ashimbaeva, *Pamyatniki Kulturi*, 1982 (Leningrad, 1984), 93.

** For more details, see *Dostoevsky: The Stir of Liberation* (Princeton, N.J., 1983), chap. 5.

influential pages, was dismissed as weak, indecisive, incapable of action and decision; its members were slaves to high-flown principles that only served to bolster their egoism and vanity:

> People of *that* generation were possessed by lofty but somewhat abstract strivings. They strove toward truth, longed for the good, they were captivated by everything beautiful; but highest of all for them was *principle*. . . . Withdrawing in this way from real life, and condemning themselves to the service of principle, they were not able truly to estimate their strength and took on much more than they were capable of performing. Hence their eternally false position, their eternal dissatisfaction with themselves, their eternal grandiose phrases of self-approval and self-encouragement, and their eternal failure in any practical activity. Little by little they sank into their passive role, and, of all that had gone before, they preserved only a youthful inflammability, yes, and the habit of conversing with well-bred people about good manners and dreaming of a little bridge over the stream [that is, local, insignificant reforms and improvements—J.F.].[3]

No better outline of Stepan Trofimovich's character profile could be sketched; all that remained was for Dostoevsky to fill in the traits.

Such attacks could hardly fail to elicit a reply; and one was soon forthcoming from Alexander Herzen, who, more than any other single individual, had been the original inspirer and propagator of whatever radical and Socialist currents of thought existed in Russia in the 1860s. Granovsky may have furnished an external schema for Stepan Trofimovich, but the pattern of his opposition to Peter, as the horrified "father" of a Nihilist "son," is historically based on Herzen's intransigent refusal to knuckle under to the generation of the 1860s. Herzen, indeed, was much on Dostoevsky's mind exactly at the moment when he was working on the early drafts of *The Devils*. His death in Paris in January 1870 immediately called forth an important series of articles by Strakhov summing up his career, and they were published almost simultaneously with Dostoevsky's decision to write a "pamphlet-novel."

Dostoevsky's reaction to these articles has already been cited; here we need only recall his remark that "the main essence of all Herzen's activity . . . [was] that he has been, always and everywhere, *primarily a poet*." It is this aspect of his nature, Dostoevsky believes, that explains "even his flippancy and inclination to pun about the loftiest moral and philosophical questions (which, by the way, is very revolting in him)." Such a comment indicates to what extent Stepan Trofimovich and Herzen blended together in Dostoevsky's imagination. For the quality that offended Dostoevsky in Herzen also offends the narrator in Stepan Trofimovich. "Why could not this week be without a Sunday—*si le miracle existe*?" exclaims the latter despairingly, anticipating a meeting with the formidable Varvara Petrovna Stavrogina on that fateful day. "What could it be to Providence to blot out one Sunday from the calendar? If only to prove His power to atheists *et que tout soit dit*!" "He wouldn't have been himself," the narrator comments acidly, "if he could have dispensed with the cheap gibing free-thought which was in vogue in his day" (10: 100).

Herzen's *The Superfluous and the Bilious* (1860) was the first reply of the generation of the 1840s to the onslaught of their detractors; and like Stepan Trofimovich, Herzen spoke for the fathers, or at least those among them who refused to abdicate their right to paternal respect. Voicing the attitude of the "bilious" sons, their unnamed spokesman (Chernyshevsky) sarcastically remarks that the "superfluous men" of the 1840s "were educated differently, the world surrounding them was too dirty, not sufficiently wax-polished, besmirched by hands and feet. It was far pleasanter for them to moan over their unhappy lot, and meanwhile eat and drink in peace." These are exactly the words, and this is unmistakably the condescendingly contemptuous tone, of Peter Verkhovensky about his father. But in Herzen, as in Dostoevsky, the son is not allowed to dominate the field. For all their good intentions, Herzen replies, the "bilious" would "drive an angel to fighting and a saint to cursing by their tone." And—wrongly, as it turned out—he predicts a short life for the type of "gloom-inspiring Daniels by the waters of Petersburg, who mournfully reproach people for dining without gnashing their teeth and for forgetting the miseries of the world while admiring a picture or listening to music."[4]

On the one hand, we have the reproach of impotence, inaction, posturing, and pretentious self-indulgence; on the other, that of intolerant, narrow-minded fanaticism, ready to condemn and destroy all the fruits and glories and civilization. What is at first so striking in the "bilious" generation, according to Herzen, is "the facility with which they despair of everything, the malicious pleasure of their negation, and their terrible mercilessness." They remind him "of those monks who, out of love for their neighbor, have come to hate everything human, and who curse the whole world out of a desire to bless something." But Herzen's "bilious" opponent remains unmoved by these accusations and only replies that the men of the 1840s "were idle, empty aristocrats, who lived quietly and well, and I see no reason why I should feel sorry for them." Herzen's reply to this thrust reveals an undogmatic sensitivity to human misery that would certainly have won Dostoevsky's approval. "Let each man decide for himself," Herzen answers, "whether they deserve his sympathy or not. Every human suffering, particularly if inescapable, arouses our sympathy; there is no suffering that would be impossible for us to share."[5]

Just as Stepan Trofimovich returns home in a shambles after his attempt to make a comeback in Petersburg in the early 1860s, having been discarded by the new breed of radicals as "*un vieux bonnet de coton,*" so Herzen is dismissed by Chernyshevsky as similar to "the fine skeleton of a mammal . . . that had been dug up and belonged to a different world with a different sun and different trees." But Herzen, refusing to be swept so easily into the dustbin of history, stubbornly rejects any obligation to say farewell, in the name of utility and revolution, to the significance of his own past and that of humankind as a whole. For if the blinkered view of the 1860s is accepted, then, as Herzen says in eloquent words that Stepan Trofimovich will echo, "farewell not only to Thermopylae and Golgotha, but also to Sophocles and Shakespeare, and incidentally to the whole long and endless epic poem which is continually ending in frenzied tragedies and continually going on again under the title of history."[6]

3

Hostilities between the two generations subsided somewhat during the mid-1860s but flared up again even more vehemently in the spring of 1867, after Karakozov's unsuccessful attempt to assassinate Alexander II. Herzen, we have seen, publicly reproved the attempt in *The Bell,* rightly predicting that it would lead to an intensified government reaction. But despite this disagreement over tactics, Herzen insisted that the goals of the indigenous Russian radical movement, which looked to Chernyshevsky as its leader, did not differ from the ones he had advocated in exile; and he urged that the two generations should go forward hand in hand. This plea for unity only provoked a furious reply from one of the leaders of the "young emigration," Alexander Serno-Solovievich, who dismissed Herzen even more unceremoniously than Chernyshevsky had done. In the eyes of the young generation—and in words that remarkably anticipate Dostoevsky's—he proclaimed that Herzen was just another *vieux bonnet de coton* exactly like Stepan Trofimovich:

> You are a poet, an artist . . . a storyteller, a novelist, anything you wish but not a politician. . . . Failing to perceive that you have been left behind, you flap your enfeebled wings with all your might; and then, when you see that people are only laughing at you, you go off in a rage and reproach the younger generation with ingratitude to their leader, to the founder of their school, the first high priest of

Russian Socialism.... Come down to earth; forget that you are a great man; remember that the medals with your effigy were struck not by a grateful posterity, but by yourself out of your blood-stained wealth.... you, Mr. Herzen, are a dead man.[7]

Herzen did not reply directly to this scurrilously abusive broadside. Instead, he sent the brochure, along with a letter, to Bakunin, whose indiscriminate sympathy with the younger generation would later lead to his association with Nechaev. Serno-Solovievich, in Herzen's view, "is insolent and a fool; but the worst is that the majority of the young Russians *are the same* and we're the ones who have contributed to make them *like this.*... This isn't Nihilism. Nihilism is a great phenomenon in the evolution of Russian thought. No. These are the dispossessed noblemen, the retired officer, the village scribe, the local priest and petty landowner disguised in costumes."[8]

Whether Dostoevsky had ever met Serno-Solovievich in Geneva is not known, but he had certainly read this harangue, and the young radical is mentioned, along with Nechaev (no others are identified), as belonging to "the herd of swine" infected by "the devils" who "came out of the body of Russian man." Dostoevsky, of course, could have had no knowledge of Herzen's letter, but he was able to intuit, with remarkable percipience, exactly its mixture of consternation and guilt. "I agree that the author's fundamental idea is a true one," Stepan Trofimovich says of *What Is To Be Done?*, the "catechism" of the Nihilists, "but that only makes it more awful. It's just our idea, exactly ours; we first sowed the seed, nurtured it, prepared the way, and, indeed, what could they say new, after us? But, heavens! How it's all expressed, distorted, mutilated.... Were these the conclusions we were striving for? Who can understand the original idea in this?" (10: 238).

For those who criticize Dostoevsky because he presumably chose an "atypical" event in the history of Russian radicalism on which to base his novel, it should be pointed out that Herzen's last important work, *Letters to an Old Comrade* (1869), was written expressly to counteract the turbulent torrent of vandalism running through the Bakunin-Nechaev propaganda. These open letters addressed to Bakunin were included in a collection of Herzen's posthumous writings that Dostoevsky certainly would have hastened to procure. "The savage clamors exhorting us to close our books, to abandon science, and to engage in an absurd combat of destruction," Herzen wrote, "belong to the most uncontrollable and baneful demagoguery. They always provoke the unleashing of the worst passions. We juggle with terrible words, without thinking at all of the harm they do to the cause and to those who listen to them."[9] Herzen certainly did not believe that the Bakunin-Nechaev movement, which led to the murder of Ivanov, was merely an isolated and aberrant episode, and he felt it his duty to raise his voice against the terrible consequences he could so clearly foresee.

One can well imagine Dostoevsky's satisfaction at reading Herzen's condemnatory words, which to him could well have sounded almost as a self-denunciation and recantation. And while Dostoevsky did not need Herzen to teach him the value of art and culture (he had defended them against Belinsky in 1849 and Dobrolyubov in 1861), he would surely have been gratified to find Herzen aligning himself so fervently against the Pisarevian iconoclasm (in the literal sense of the word) that had become endemic among the generation of the 1860s. "Woe to the revolution poor in spirit and weak in a sense of art," Herzen exclaims, "which will make of all that has been acquired by time a depressing workshop, and whose sole interest would be subsistence and nothing but subsistence!" (One recalls here the notorious slogan of Peter Verkhovensky: "Only the necessary is necessary, that's the motto of the whole world henceforward" [10: 323].) "The force of unleashed destruction," Herzen continues, "will wipe out, along with the limits of property, the *peaks* of human endeavor that men have attained in every direction since the beginning of civilization. . . . I have often felt this keenly when, overcome by a gloomy sadness and almost by shame, I have stood before some guide who showed me a bare wall, a broken sculpture, a coffin torn from its tomb, and who repeated: 'All this was destroyed during the Revolution.'"[10]

Only against this background can one fully appreciate Stepan Trofimovich's defiant "last word" in *The Devils*—a last word shouted at a hooting, jeering younger generation who hounded him as unmercifully as it had hounded Herzen in his last years, and to whom he replied with the voice of Herzen and that of Dostoevsky as well. "'But I maintain,' Stepan Trofimovich shrilled at the utmost pitch of excitement, 'I maintain that Shakespeare and Raphael are higher than the emancipation of the serfs, higher than Nationalism, higher than Socialism, higher than the young generation, higher than chemistry, higher than almost all humanity because they are the fruit, the real fruit of all humanity, and perhaps the highest possible fruit! A form of beauty already attained, without whose attainment I, perhaps, would not consent to live. . . . Oh, God' he cried—he clasped his hands—'ten years ago I cried exactly the same thing in Petersburg in exactly the same words, and they understood nothing in exactly the same way, they laughed and hissed as now; you pygmies, what do you need to make you understand?'" (10: 372–373). Ten years before, in *The Superfluous and the Bilious*, Herzen had indeed said the very same thing; and Dostoevsky's boisterously uproarious fête, which also includes other incidents and allusions taken from the stormy events of the early 1860s, is the artistic enshrinement of this momentous historical-cultural clash.

4
―――――

Stepan Trofimovich, to be sure, is not the only figure in the book who represents an eminent member of the generation of the 1840s. No account of *The Devils* would be complete without some discussion of the malicious but masterly caricature of Turgenev in the portrait of Karmazinov. (*Karmazin*, from the French *cramoisi*, means crimson in Russian and ridicules the presumed social-political sympathies of the Great Writer.) Dostoevsky's troubled and increasingly inimical relations with Turgenev have already been amply discussed, and it may seem unnecessary to look any further for an explanation of such a devastating depiction, which has few rivals in the nineteenth-century novel. Personal caricature was quite commonplace in Russian fiction, and Turgenev himself had not spared Bakunin in *Rudin* nor a whole host of well-known personalities (particularly Nikolay Ogarev) in *Smoke*. But to find an equally extended lampoon of a prominent literary personage one would probably have to look to Dickens's attack on Leigh Hunt in *Bleak House* through the character of Harold Skimpole.

It would be unfair to Dostoevsky, however, to attribute Karmazinov only to personal enmity, for there were ample literary-cultural reasons to include this caricature in a full-scale portrayal of the epoch. Dostoevsky had been outraged not only by *Smoke*, but also by Turgenev's later attempts to curry favor with the young generation through pretending to have agreed with Bazarov. We should not forget that Turgenev had once warmly praised Dostoevsky's comments on *Fathers and Children*, and told him he was one of the two people to have really understood the book; but Dostoevsky saw Bazarov as a tragic figure torn between his narrowly rationalistic-radical convictions and the sentiments of his "great heart." Could Turgenev, as he now intimated, really have agreed with the Nihilist ideas whose human limitations he had so brilliantly exposed?

Karmazinov, who is described as "a short, prim old man, though not over fifty-five, with a rather rubicund little face" (10: 70), bears no physical resemblance to the handsome figure of the stately Turgenev; but otherwise Dostoevsky's target is unmistakable, and he ridicules all those aspects of his fellow novelist that had long aroused his antipathy. Turgenev's aristocratic airs and manner, his preference for residence in Europe, his demolition of Russian culture in *Smoke*, the philosophical pessimism revealed most overtly in his prose poems, the squeamish, self-protective egoism that Dostoevsky saw most blatantly manifested in the article about the execution of Troppman—nothing is spared! The first encounter between the narrator and the Great Writer is accompanied by a derisory parody of the Troppman article, transposed into an account of the wreck of a steamer off the English coast. As a young man, Turgenev had been involved in such a wreck off Lübeck (he later wrote about it in 1883, after Dostoevsky's death), and widespread rumor in literary circles attributed to him a behavior that was very far from heroic.

The narrator recalls having read an article of Karmazinov's, "written with the most dreadful affectation of the crudest kind of poetry as well as psychology [describing] the wreck of a steamer ... which [Karmazinov] had witnessed himself, and how he had watched the drowning people being saved and the dead bodies brought ashore." Just as when Troppman was guillotined, Karmazinov-Turgenev is much more concerned with his own reactions than with the victims of the disaster. "All this rather long and verbose article was written solely with the object of self-display. One seemed to read between the lines: 'Concentrate yourselves on me, see how bravely I behaved at those moments. . . . Why look at that drowned woman with the dead child in her dead arms? Look rather at me, see how I was unable to bear the sight and turned away from it. Here I stood with my back to it, here I was horrified and could not bring myself to look; I blinked my eyes—isn't that interesting?'" "When I told Stepan Trofimovich my opinion of Karmazinov's article," the narrator adds, "he quite agreed with me" (10: 70).

Although Karmazinov's vanity and narcissism is thus displayed from the very start, his role is defined more broadly by the attempts of Turgenev to worm his way back into the good graces of the generation of the 1860s. In contrast to Herzen's forthright and staunch defense of his own values, which then became embodied in Stepan Trofimovich, Turgenev had ignominiously truckled to Nihilist browbeating, implicitly giving his stamp of approval to Bazarovism and, by extension, to its latest avatar, Sergey Nechaev. Wounded by Dostoevsky's assault, Turgenev later complained ruefully that Dostoevsky "had allowed himself something worse than parody, he depicted me under the name of K[armazinov] as secretly sympathizing with the party of Nechaev."[11] Of course, nothing of the kind was literally true, but in the symbolic myth of Dostoevsky's creation it is perfectly defensible. Karmazinov is responsible for Peter Verkhovensky's prestige in society, just as Turgenev had been responsible for the prestige of Bazarov and his later offshoots in real life, and he acts as the young man's mentor and advocate. "When I came, I assured everyone," he tells Peter, "that you were a very intelligent man, and now I believe everyone is wild over you" (10: 286). As A. S. Dolinin has shrewdly noted, even though Stepan Trofimovich is the physical father of Peter Verkho-vensky, the latter is much more the "spiritual son" of Karmazinov.[12]

Dostoevsky worked various details of his personal relations with Tur-genev into the scene between Karmazinov and Peter Verkhovensky (thus indicating how freely he used incidents from his own biography, often assigning them to characters like Peter with whose ideas and behavior he can in no way be identified). Dostoevsky had commented to Maikov that, although Turgenev made a pretense of greeting a visitor with an embrace and a kiss, in fact he merely touched the other person's cheek. Accord-ingly, "Peter knew from experience that while Karmazinov seemed eager to exchange kisses, he merely held up his cheek, and so he did the same this time; both their cheeks touched" (10: 285). The same scene contains another reference to an actual event: Dostoevsky's failure to read Turge-nev's prose poem *Phantoms* (*Prizraki*), which the author had lent him in Baden-Baden in the early fall of 1863.

Traveling at that time with the tantalizing but sexually aloof Apolli-naria Suslova and gambling furiously all the while, Dostoevsky never got around to casting an eye over the work, which Turgenev had obligingly offered him for publication in *Time*. Similarly, Karmazinov entrusts Peter with a manuscript copy of the composition he intended to read at the fête, and is surprised and disturbed when Peter says not a word about it, as if it had completely slipped his mind. Peter finally refers to it carelessly as *Bonjour* (instead of *Merci*), does not recall where he put it (much to Karmazinov's consternation), but finally fishes it out. " 'Wait, here it is!' Peter said, producing a bundle of notepaper from his back pocket. 'Got a little crumpled, I'm afraid. Would you believe it? It's been lying in my pocket with my handkerchief ever since I took it from you. Forgot all about it' " (10: 286). Dostoevsky had probably been far more apologetic than Peter, but he relished the opportunity to recall this (at the time surely inadvertent) slight to Turgenev's overweening literary vanity.

5

The climax of Dostoevsky's ridicule of Turgenev occurs during the fête scene, when Karmazinov condescendingly agrees to read his farewell work to the hungry and fractious assemblage, having decided—or so he pretends—to put down his pen forever after this last appearance in pub-lic. Turgenev, upon receiving a letter of sympathy from a friend after the publication of this chapter, replied in a hurt tone of restrained dignity: "It is surely curious that he [Dostoevsky] chose for his parody the sole work [*Phantoms*] that I placed in the journal he once edited, a work for which he showered me with grateful and flattering letters. I still have the letters. It would be amusing to publish them! But he knows that I will not do such a thing. I am only left with the regret that he employs his un-doubted talent to satisfy such unsavory feelings. Obviously he values it but little, if he debases it to pamphleteering."[13]

Turgenev could not have read Dostoevsky's pages very carefully, or perhaps, quite understandably, he could not resist the temptation to be-labor Dostoevsky for treacherous ingratitude. Whatever the reason, his accusation does not withstand a careful analysis of the text: *Phantoms* is by no means the main basis for Dostoevsky's parody, which in fact takes off from another prose poem, *Enough* (*Dovolno*). As for Karmazinov's introductory remarks, as well as his replies to the heckling audience, Dostoevsky makes use of the essay "Concerning *Fathers and Children.*" Such questions of sources are in any case irrelevant to the brilliantly hi-larious parody, certainly a small masterpiece in its own right. The Tur-genev of the prose poems is quite a different writer from the sober, often sharply satirical and coolly observant author of the novels. The conven-tions of realism in the novel restrained the melancholy lyricism of his temperament, which emerges only here and there to add an extra touch of emotive vibrancy to a scene or a dialogue. But this lyricism is given free rein in the prose poems, which employ a Romantic imagery heavily weighted with cultural and historical allusions; and their dominant mood, often expressed by dreamlike events unrestrained by the limits of time and space, is a sense of world-weariness and metaphysical despair. The preciosity of style and vocabulary in these works is much more rem-iniscent of the earlier part of the century, or of the Symbolist era, than of the materialistic 1860s.

Dostoevsky takes well-directed aim against these extremely vulnerable aspects of Turgenev's prose-poems, which are easy enough to ridicule simply by introducing a note of sober prosaicism into their lugubrious fantasy. Time and again, as he does so, Dostoevsky also mocks the self-importance impelling the great genius to reduce every event and inci-dent to a reflection of his own existential anguish. In one scene, the poet is presumably drowning after falling through the ice of the Volga in a thaw; but then "he caught sight of a tiny little ice floe, the size of a pea ... and ... its iridescent glitter recalled to his mind the very same tear, which you remember rolled down from your eyes when we sat beneath the emerald tree and you cried joyfully, 'There is no crime.' 'No,' I said, through my tears, 'but if that is so, there are no saints either.' We burst into sobs and parted forever" (10: 366–367). This is a hit at Turgenev's newly proclaimed adhesion to Nihilism, whose moral-metaphysical negation Dostoevsky here portrays in a ridiculously burlesque register rather than, as with Stavrogin, in a tragic one.

In a similar passage, the sublime poet has dug beneath the Sukharev Tower in Moscow for three years, finds a hermit in a cave with a lamp burning before an icon, and suddenly hears a sigh. "You think it was the hermit that sighed? What does he care about your hermit? No, this sigh simply reminds him of her first sigh, thirty-seven years ago, when do you remember how we sat beneath the agate tree in Germany, and you said to me, 'Why love? Look, ruddle is growing all around, and I am in love, but when the ruddle ceases to grow, I shall fall out of love'" (10: 367). Dostoevsky then travesties Turgenev's fondness for bestrewing his pages with learned references. "Here a mist rises again, Hoffmann appears, the water nymph whistles a tune from Chopin, and suddenly out of the mist Ancius Marcus appears over the roofs of Rome, wearing a laurel wreath. A shiver of rapture ran down our backs and we parted forever, and so on and so forth" (10: 367).

Dostoevsky's narrator finally admits that he finds it hard to make head or tail out of what Karmazinov had read, and he ends with a string of antitheses reproducing the moral-spiritual confusion engendered in such Russian geniuses after they have absorbed the sublime conquests of European thought: "There is crime, there is no crime; there is no truth, there are no truth-seekers; atheism, Darwinism, Moscow church bells. ... But, alas, he no longer believes in the Moscow church bells; Rome, laurels. . . . But he doesn't believe in laurels. . . . Here you get a conventional attack of Byronic spleen, a grimace from Heine, something of Pechorin—and off he goes full steam ahead, with his engine emitting a shrill whistle." Behind all this, the narrator finds only the author's egoism ("but do praise me, do praise me, for I like it awfully"), and he does not believe for a moment that, as Karmazinov-Turgenev promises, he will now lay down his pen forever in weariness and sorrow (10: 367). The takeoff on Turgenev's literary mannerisms and personal foibles could not have been deadlier, and it enriches *The Devils* with a dazzling display of Dostoevsky's satiric virtuosity.

6

The capstone of Dostoevsky's intricate thematic construction in *The Devils* is the figure of Stavrogin. No clues to any prototype for his character can be found in Dostoevsky's notes, and a debate has raged for many years over whether he may not have been inspired by Bakunin. But this hypothesis, first advanced by the noted Dostoevsky scholar L. P. Grossman, has now been generally rejected.* If we are to link Stavrogin with

---

* In a lively and witty summary of this question, Jacques Catteau authoritatively concludes: "Our decision has been made. *The Devils* is not at all a monograph about Bakunin, and Stavrogin is not a 'caricature of Bakunin' as Grossman has continued to affirm. . . . *All this is only legend.* Stavrogin comes from another world." See Jacques Catteau, "Bakounine, Combats et Débats," in *Collection Historique de l'Institut d'Études Slaves*, 26 (Paris, 1979), 103.

any actual person, the likeliest candidate would be the enigmatic figure of Nikolay Speshnev, whom Dostoevsky called his Mephistopheles during the days of his involvement in the Petrashevsky circle. The possibility that Speshnev served as the original of Stavrogin has already been broached in the first volume of the present work;* but some information about him may be resumed here briefly for convenience.

Speshnev was in real life just such a Byronic figure as Stavrogin, a wealthy and cultured aristocrat irresistibly attractive to women. He was also a political radical, a committed communist, and the center of a secret revolutionary group whose seven members included Dostoevsky (who kept this highly compromising affiliation a secret for the remainder of his life). This group operated *within* the larger Petrashevsky society and attempted to manipulate it for its own ends, just as Peter Verkhovensky manipulates his own little group, and society at large, for *his* ends—although, so far as is known, Speshnev did not preach the unrestrained Machiavellianism of Nechaev. Nonetheless, he was very well read in the philosophy then current in progressive left-wing circles, and his moral-philosophical views are very similar to those later attributed to Stavrogin. These views are expressed by Speshnev in private letters, none of them addressed to Dostoevsky; but it is highly possible that he uttered the very same thoughts in the course of philosophical conversations with an intimate such as Dostoevsky had become.

Speshnev closely followed the controversies that had arisen among the Left Hegelians following the publication of Feuerbach's *Essence of Christianity* (1841), and on these issues he sided with Max Stirner's totally subjective egoism. "Anthropotheism [the position of Feuerbach] is also a religion," he wrote quite perceptively, "only a different one. It divinizes a new and different object [Man, Humanity—J.F.], but there is nothing new about the fact of divinization. . . . Is the difference between a God-man and a Man-god really so great?" Speshnev refused to accept any authority over the individual Ego and concluded, as a result, that no objective criteria exist for anything. "Such categories as beauty and ugliness, good and bad, noble and base, always were and always will remain a matter of taste."[14]**

These words should be set against Stavrogin's confession in the suppressed chapter "At Tikhon's," where he explains that "I formulated for

---

* For Dostoevsky's relations with Speshnev and the Petrashevsky circle, see *Dostoevsky: The Seeds of Revolt* (Princeton, N.J., 1976), chaps. 17, 18, 19.

** Compare this with the famous dialogue between Arkady and Bazarov in *Fathers and Children*, during which Bazarov says: "There are no general principles—you've not made that out yet! There are feelings. Everything depends on them. . . . Take me, for example, I maintain a negative attitude, by virtue of my sensations; I like to deny—my brain's made on that plan and that's all. Why do I like chemistry? Why do you like apples?—also by virtue of sensations. . . . Men will never penetrate deeper than that." I. S. Turgenev, *PSSiP*, 8: 325.

the first time in my life what appeared to be the rule of my life, namely, that I neither know nor feel good and evil and that I have not only lost any sense of it, but that there is neither good nor evil (which pleased me), and that it is just a prejudice: that I can be free from any prejudice, but that once I attain that degree of freedom I am done for" (12: 113). That such a doctrine will lead to self-destruction is Dostoevsky's own conclusion; otherwise, Stavrogin's denial of any difference between good and evil remarkably coincides with Speshnev's. Indeed, the abominable violation of little Matryosha is really a terrible experiment designed to test such ideas in practice. There is thus every reason to believe that Dostoevsky recalled some of the features of Speshnev, his initiator into underground revolution and moral-metaphysical Nihilism, when the amorphous "Prince" of the early drafts began to evolve into Stavrogin.

But just as Peter Verkhovensky is not Nechaev, nor Stepan Trofimovich solely Granovsky, neither should Stavrogin be identified with Speshnev. For Dostoevsky "mythifies" this prototype into an image of the doomed and glamorous Russian Byronic dandy who haunted the literature of the 1820s and 1830s. Stavrogin, he had told Katkov, "seems to me a tragic figure. . . . In my opinion, this is a Russian and typical figure. . . . I took him from my heart. . . . Of course this figure rarely appears in all its typicality, but this is a Russian character (of a certain social class)." This declaration stems from Dostoevsky's long-held interpretation of the immense cultural and moral-religious importance of the Russian Byronic type as a clue to the subterranean changes taking place in the national psyche.

This interpretation is found most amply and explicitly in some of the articles that Dostoevsky wrote for *Time* in 1861. Arguing against the view that Pushkin's *Evgeny Onegin* had no connection with the life of the Russian people but was merely the portrait of an upper-class wastrel of the 1820s, Dostoevsky answers that, on the contrary, the work is the embodiment of a momentous crisis in the history of the Russian spirit: "Onegin precisely belongs to that epoch of our historical life marked by the very first beginnings of our agonizing consciousness and, as a result of this consciousness, our agonizing uncertainty as we look around us. . . . This was the first beginning of that epoch when our leading men sharply separated into two camps and then violently engaged in a civil war. The Slavophils and Westerners were also a historical manifestation and in the highest degree national. . . . But in Onegin all this as yet had only just become aware of itself, had only just begun to be glimpsed" (19: 10). Onegin thus contains within himself the source of what later became the opposition between the Slavophils and Westerners; and both these ideologies bear traces of the same inner crisis that determined his fate.

This crisis is that of the Russian spirit, which, having steeped itself in European culture, realizes that it has lost its native roots and accordingly turns back on itself with destructive skepticism. "The skepticism of Onegin contained something tragic in its very principle, and sometimes expressed itself with malicious irony" (19: 11).

Onegin, like the later Stavrogin, was a member of the Russian gentry, the group that "had most alienated itself from its native soil, and in which the externalities of civilization had reached their highest development" (19: 11). But while Onegin is one of the most brilliant products of this society, again like Stavrogin "he no longer respects it. He has begun to doubt, to oscillate; but at the same time, he hesitates in confusion before the manifestations of life, undecided whether to kneel before them or to cover them with mockery" (19: 11). Onegin's inner turmoil is thus caused by the lack of an ideal in which he can believe *absolutely*, because "in essence his soul hungers for a new truth." It is proof of his moral elevation that he cannot be satisfied with the cheap and easy satisfactions of worldly pleasures or social rank; he genuinely suffers from his idleness and emptiness and from the inner hollowness of his life. And he suffers because he does not know what to occupy himself with, "he does not even know what to respect, though he is firmly convinced that there is something that must be respected and loved. But he became exacerbated, and respects neither himself nor his thoughts and opinions; he does not respect even his own thirst for life and truth. . . . He becomes an egoist, and at the same time ridicules himself because he does not even know how to be that" (19: 11–12).

This type then enters into the consciousness of Russian society and develops new and more virulent variations with each new generation. "In the personage of Pechorin, it reached a state of insatiable, bilious malice, and of a strange contrast, in the highest degree original and Russian, of a contradiction between two heterogeneous elements: an egoism extending to the limits of self-adoration and a malicious self-contempt. And always this thirst for truth, and always the same eternal 'nothing to do!' Out of anger and as if in derision, Pechorin throws himself into outrageous, strange behavior that leads him to a stupid, ridiculous, and useless death" (19: 12). The most extreme and uncompromising development of this type, who coldly experiments with the farthest reaches of moral perversity and self-degradation, is of course Stavrogin himself.

Once Stavrogin is viewed from this perspective, it is not difficult to understand why he unexpectedly assumed such importance in Dostoevsky's early drafts. As the outlines of Stavrogin emerged from the character of the colorless Prince, Dostoevsky was seized by the temptation to extend his historical perspective backward in time and to link up the conflict of the 1840s and the 1860s with the Byronic type of the preceding years—the first manifestation of the disintegrating effects of Western influence on the Russian cultural psyche after such influence had been thoroughly absorbed. Here was the origin of the negation of Russia that had finally culminated in the abhorrent Nechaev; and since for Dostoevsky the idea of Russia was inseparable from that of the Russian Christ and the Orthodox faith, the tragedy of Stavrogin—like that of Onegin and Pechorin, as he saw it—takes the form of a moral-religious crisis. It is the search for an absolute faith that has been surrendered to the blandishments of the European Enlightenment and cannot yet be recaptured despite the torturing need for a "new truth."

This social-cultural significance of Stavrogin's Byronism suggests a more specific and concrete meaning for Dostoevsky's somewhat vague assertion that "the devils have come out of Russian man and entered into the Nechaevs and Serno-Solovieviches." It is Stavrogin—or the type of which he is the greatest incarnation—who is "Russian man" in the fullest meaning of that phrase for Dostoevsky; and it is this type that, historically, gave birth to all the ideological "devils" that have plagued Russian culture ever since. But Stavrogin's historical role as the original fount of "the devils" became obscured because Dostoevsky retains the plot structure that makes him the pupil of Stepan Trofimovich, in effect reversing the anteriority of the Onegin-type to the generation of the 1840s. It is possible that if Dostoevsky had been able to use his chapter "At Tikhon's," and thus to reveal the full ideological range of Stavrogin's supreme attempt to transcend the boundaries of good and evil, he might have allowed him to assume explicit responsibility for "the devils" despite the anachronism involved. (We shall see in the next chapter how he attempted to cope with this problem of anachronism.) Since the Gospel-reading scene, in which Stepan Trofimovich declares *himself* to be responsible for the "devils," was *not* contained in the original manuscript, such a possibility cannot be excluded.

In any event, Stavrogin's symbolic cultural status helps to throw light on the puzzling particularities of his relationships to Kirillov and Shatov, which have frequently been seen as arbitrary and enigmatic. Dostoevsky could not think of the Byronic type without also thinking of the two competing ideologies of the Westerners and Slavophils, who had offered divergent responses to its moral-spiritual dilemmas; and the structure of Stavrogin's linkage with these figures, as well as their own peculiar mixture of past friendship followed by antipathy, easily becomes comprehensible once seen in these historical-cultural terms. (Without wishing to allegorize the book too rigidly, we can nevertheless note that the Westerners and Slavophils originally maintained the most friendly personal contacts, but then broke off because of ideological incompatibilities.*) Dostoevsky dramatizes these ideologies strictly in relation to the problem of religious faith, which, as he saw it, lay at the root of the self-torments of the Byronic type. The beliefs of both Kirillov and Shatov, being derived from the tainted source of Stavrogin, are presented as secular substitutes for the genuine and spontaneous religious faith that both, like their mentor, yearn for but cannot attain.

In Kirillov, who is one of his greatest inspirations, Dostoevsky concentrates all the pathos and sublimity of the atheistic humanism inspired by Feuerbach, with its doctrine that the Man-God—that is, all of humanity—could take the place of the traditional God-Man. Shatov represents Dostoevsky's view that even the Slavophils, despite their declared adherence to the Russian Orthodox faith, were still too Westernized to accept the Russian Christ with a complete inward acquiescence. This opinion of Slavophilism had recently been reinforced by the publication of Danilevsky's *Russia and Europe*, in which the ex-Fourierist and ex-Feuerbachian writer had spoken of God as the "synthetic personality" of each people, just as, for Feuerbach, God had been the "synthetic personality" of humankind—a creation of humankind itself, in other words, and not a divine truth transcending reason. The ideas that Shatov took over from Stavrogin, and which he then repeats to his master, transcribe this Slavophil version of Feuerbachianism straight from the pages of Danilevsky's book. Dostoevsky, as we know, agreed politically with Danilevsky's glorification of Slavdom and Russia as the basis of a new world-culture; but he was troubled by the writer's failure to recognize the *universal* religious mission of Orthodoxy. Shatov thus embodies Dostoevsky's criticism of Danilevsky, and Shatov's elevation of the Russian people into a god fits very neatly into the tragic incapacity of Stavrogin, whose ideas Shatov is repeating, to attain the humility of self-surrender to a redeeming *religious* faith.

* See, for example, Herzen's account of saying farewell to Konstantin Aksakov:
"In 1844, when our differences had reached such a point that neither the Slavophils nor we wanted to go on meeting, I was walking along the street when Konstantin Aksakov drove up in a sledge. I bowed to him in a friendly way. He was on the point of driving by, but he suddenly stopped the coachman, got out of his sledge, and came towards me.

" 'It hurt me too much,' he said, 'to pass you and not say good-bye. You understand that after all that has happened between your friends and mine I shan't be coming to see you; it's a pity, a pity; but there is no help for it. I wanted to shake you by the hand and say good-bye.' He went quickly toward his sledge but suddenly turned round. I was standing in the same place, and I was sad; he rushed up to me, embraced me, and kissed me warmly. I had tears in my eyes. How I loved him at that moment of our quarrel!"

These quarrels were about Russia and its relation to Europe, but also, more fundamentally, about the relations between religion and science (or philosophy). Alexander Herzen, *My Past and Thoughts*, trans. Constance Garnett, rev. Humphrey Higgins, 4 vols. (New York, 1968), 2: 542.

One further context, provided by the Franco-Prussian War, also helps to enrich the symbolic significance of Stavrogin. Dostoevsky had been filled with horror and rage at the flames engulfing Paris during the last days of the Commune. Of the Communards, whom he held responsible, he said: "to them (and many others) this monstrosity doesn't seem madness but, on the contrary, *beauty*. The aesthetic idea of modern humanity has become obscured" (italics in text). These words surely bear on the scene in which Peter Verkhovensky, as he goes into raptures over Stavrogin's "beauty," finally reveals himself to be a passionately visionary fanatic and not simply a cold and ruthless tactician of terror. " 'Stavrogin, you are beautiful,' cried Peter Stepanovich, almost ecstatically. ' . . . I love beauty, I am a Nihilist, but I love beauty. Are Nihilists incapable of loving beauty? It's only idols they dislike, but I love an idol' " (10: 323).

The calm and impassive figure of Stavrogin is thus surrounded in Dostoevsky's imagination with the infernal halo of the flames that had recently been crackling in the heart-city of Western civilization. It is he who has brought to Russia all the "beauty" of this idolatrous negation, which, if allowed to go unchallenged by the "authentic beauty" of Christ, would light the same torch of destruction in Holy Russia that was already ravaging the West. For the "beauty" of Stavrogin is that of the demonic, the beauty of Lucifer in Byron's *Cain*, who, as Herzen wrote unforgettably, "is the gloomy angel of darkness, on whose brow shines with dim lustre the star of bitter thought, full of inner discords which can never be harmonized." He lures like "still, moonlit water, that promises nothing but death in its comfortless, cold, glimmering embraces."[15]

CHAPTER 25

The Book of the Impostors

The Devils, as we know, was initially begun as a "pamphlet-novel" in which Dostoevsky would unleash all his satirical fury against the Nihilists. It is thus not surprising that, of all his major works, this novel contains the greatest proportion of satirical caricature and ideological parody. Dostoevsky had always exhibited a taste and talent for satire and parody; even in his very first novel, the sentimental-humanitarian *Poor Folk*, there are parodies of the then-dominant literary genres (the high-society adventure novel, the Gogolian humorous local-color tale, the debunking physiological sketch). Indeed, this work as a whole can well be considered a "serious" parody, since Dostoevsky rewrites Gogol's *The Overcoat* to reverse its moral-social evaluations.* All of Dostoevsky's works thus contain characters who are satirical and parodistic; but for the most part, even in the sustained satire of *Notes from Underground*, they are subordinate to an overarching tragic perspective. It is only in such novellas as *Uncle's Dream* and *The Village of Stepanchikovo* that a comic-satirical tonality prevails. Critics have often noted resemblances between these two minor creations of the beginning 1860s and *The Devils*, because, among other reasons, the latter is written so extensively in such a mockingly derisive key.

The emergence of Stavrogin in the midst of Dostoevsky's plan gave *The Devils* another dimension, however, and the episodes involving Stavrogin's relations with the other characters, far from being comic, are hauntingly tragic. Dostoevsky has sometimes been criticized for this disparity of tone, but in a deeper sense it is quite suitable to his major thematic purpose. What had been, in the generation of the 1840s, an amiable, relatively harmless flirtation with European culture and intellectual fashions had turned vicious and deadly by the mid-1860s, and the darkening mood of the later chapters corresponds to this thematic mutation. Besides, the differences in coloring between the earlier and later chapters tend to blur and fuse as the action proceeds; the fête merges hysterical comedy with the threat of mob violence, while the touchingly absurd odyssey of Stepan Trofimovich is combined with the heartfelt seriousness of his edifying death.

* For an analysis of *Poor Folk*, see *Dostoevsky: The Seeds of Revolt* (Princeton, N.J., 1976), chap. 11.

A certain unity of tone is also provided by Dostoevsky's decision to write the book in the form of a "provincial chronicle" and to use as his narrator a young man attached to Stepan Trofimovich's "circle"—but not, like most of the others, a member of Peter Verkhovensky's secret group. Dostoevsky began, in other words, with a narrator who is a more or less detached observer, looking at events from the outside and, if not openly condemnatory, then certainly ironically critical. Such a narrator had been used for *Uncle's Dream*, and Dostoevsky returned to him here because he again wished to write a caustic exposure of provincial life. This chronicle-narrator, who was retained even after Stavrogin had become the center and the book changed character, thus gave rise to a certain technical inconsistency.

As a personal friend and particular confidant of Stepan Trofimovich, the narrator has privileged access to his consciousness. He is also vaguely attached to events through having nourished (like Captain Lebyadkin) a hopeless passion for Liza Tushina, who is herself enamored of Stavrogin. Otherwise, he is what Henry James called a *ficelle* (a piece of string), a character invented only as a device for the author to provide information about others, to help in their manipulation, and to tie the work together. When his source of information is Stepan Trofimovich, the narrator's means of acquiring his knowledge are not in question; but the same is not true of Stavrogin and his interlocutors, the meetings of Peter Verkhovensky's "quintet," the bedroom conversations of the von Lembke couple, the scene "At Tikhon's," and so on. Dostoevsky tries to cope with this anomaly by emphasizing the retrospective character of the narrator's account, which allowed him to gather information about what had taken place. "I will pass on," he writes at one point, "to the description of the succeeding incidents of my chronicle, writing, so to say, with full knowledge, and describing things as they became known to me afterwards, and are clearly seen today" (10: 173). It is evident, however, that the chronicler could not possibly have learned the exact words, the physical movements, and the thoughts and feelings of the characters as they appear in such scenes. Dostoevsky has simply substituted an omniscient narrator here for the chronicler's eyewitness account, or for what he may have gathered from the disclosures of Stepan Trofimovich.

There are, as a result, two narrators in *The Devils*, who alternate with each other and are hitched together with remarks like the one quoted above.* For those who, like Henry James, consider perspectival consis-

---

* To a contemporary reader, the claim of the narrator to be describing "things as they became known to me" seems quite perfunctory. But it may have carried more weight for the readers of Dostoevsky's day, who themselves had recently learned much that was unknown and kept secret because of the reprinting of the Nechaev trial testimony in the Russian newspapers. Mr. Anton G-v, Dostoevsky's narrator, had access to the same source of information.

tency a major artistic virtue, this feeble attempt to preserve it is no doubt a weakness; but Dostoevsky, in my view, was very well advised to follow the course he did. It enables him to narrow and widen his focus on the action easily and at will, and to step back from the intensity of his dramatic scenes to the sweeping and summarizing commentary of the chronicler whenever this was desirable; and while an objective, third-person narrator might have given him the same freedom, he would have been forced to sacrifice the effects he obtains with the chronicler. No third-person narrator could have had the same inflection as the narrator's personal "voice," which imparts a special quality and atmosphere to the events.

The "voice" of the chronicler, in the first place, is that of a "moderate liberal" who sympathizes with progress and improvement and is opposed to both extreme reactionaries and extreme radicals. It is the voice of the average, educated Russian, a good citizen and a faithful subject, for whom the designs of Peter Verkhovensky and the fears of Stepan Trofimovich are both nightmare and fantasy. They are the extravagances and excrescences that come and go on the surface of Russian life but do not really touch its inner depths. The chronicler's comments thus constantly *reduce* the turbulent events of the book to eccentric and isolated manifestations, and in this way work to soften and mute their importance. This effect is reinforced by turning the chronicler into a friend and neighbor of the main figures—a somewhat gossipy and by no means gullible, but fundamentally good-hearted soul, who wavers between exposure and apologia. He knows and retails all the petty (and hence excusable) human and personal weaknesses that lie at the root of so much of the chaos he depicts; thus the scale of events tends to be reduced to the level of personal fallibility and social carelessness or imprudence. The constant reappearance of the "voice" of the narrator, taking up the thread after the febrile tensions of the dramatic episodes, continually reminds the reader that these events are from a past now happily done with, and thus throws a certain veil of epic serenity even over the hecatomb of murders and deaths (thirteen in all) that occur in the final chapters. Without such a calming and soothing "voice," the clash between the tragic and comic-parodistic tonalities would be far more dissonant than it actually turns out to be.

2

Dostoevsky immediately establishes the social and historical dimensions of his theme by the leisurely and insidiously ironical portrait of Stepan Trofimovich Verkhovensky, the Liberal Idealist of the 1840s. (The name in Russian implies height and grandeur, but its root *verkh* is also used disparagingly.) Stepan Trofimovich is depicted against the background of a brilliantly parodistic re-creation of Russian culture from the 1830s up to the point at which the novel begins in 1869–1870.* Every cultural detail of this first chapter, which Dostoevsky slaved over and rewrote a number of times, refers to one or another actual source (as can easily be verified by consulting the notes in the great Academy of Sciences edition). But more important for our purpose than the plethora of references to matters well-known to Dostoevsky's literate contemporaries is the rhetoric of the narrator's account of Stepan Trofimovich's career, which both exalts and deflates him at the same time. Since the narrator feels a genuine sympathy for Stepan Trofimovich and wishes always to present him with his best foot forward, he begins by delineating the exalted and ennobling image that the eminent worthy has of *himself.* But he immediately undermines it by revealing the completely exaggerated, even illusory nature of many of the poses that his subject strikes (as a supposed "political exile," for instance, who was not an exile at all, or as a noted scholar). "Yet Stepan Trofimovich was a most intelligent and gifted man," the narrator affirms, "even, so to say, a man of science . . . well in fact he had not done such great things in science. I believe indeed he had done nothing at all. But that's very often the case, of course, with men of science among us in Russia" (10: 8).

In fact, Stepan Trofimovich had done *something* in "science," though the narrator's recollection of his accomplishments is quite vague. A famous article he wrote contained "the beginning of a very profound investigation into the causes, I believe, of the extraordinary moral nobility of certain knights at a certain epoch or something of that nature. Some lofty and exceptionally noble idea was maintained in it anyway" (10: 9). The choice of such a subject, of course, also defines the sublime elevation of Stepan Trofimovich's own ideal, which forms such a touchingly incongruous contrast to the circumstances of his life. These ideals are

---

* In a spirited and quite interestingly speculative book on *The Devils,* whose subtitle reveals the new Russian attitude toward this work—"A Novel of Warning" (*predupre-zhdenie*)—Ludmila Saraskina insists that all the action of the book takes place within thirty days, from September 12 to October 11, 1869—the day of Stavrogin's suicide. This conclusion is supported by a scrupulously minute collocation of *all* the dates supplied in the text about the characters, including what we learn about their past. In the course of this effort, Saraskina sharply takes issue—in my opinion quite justifiably—with Bakhtin's view that the past of Dostoevsky's characters has no influence on the present because his novelistic perspective does not unroll in time.

But Saraskina's quite convincing thesis gives rise to a new problem, for in the book Dostoevsky refers to events—such as the Paris Commune and the death of Herzen—that occurred in 1870. How can this anachronism be explained? Simply, in her view, by the fact that such events were part of Dostoevsky's present in the three years during which he wrote the book, and he allows his characters (and readers) to live through the current history of these years along with him in the course of his narrative. See Ludmila Saraskina, *Besi—Roman-Preduprezhdenie* (Moscow, 1990), 9–57.

also illustrated by the chronicler's account of Stepan Trofimovich's presumably inflammatory prose poem, written sometime in the 1830s, the manuscript of which "had been passed around in a circle consisting of two poetical amateurs and one student" (10: 9). Described as "some sort of allegory in lyrical-dramatic form, recalling the second part of *Faust*" (10: 9), the poem parodies Pecherin's *The Triumph of Death* and is much more textually important than has usually been recognized.

The extremely amusing lampoon of this composition is too long to quote entire; but its concluding passage must be given as the first announcement of the book's dominating symbolism:

> Then a youth of indescribable beauty rides in on a black steed, and an immense multitude of all nations follow him. The youth represents death for whom all the peoples are yearning. And finally, in the last scene we are suddenly shown the Tower of Babel, and certain athletes at last finish building it with a song of new hope, and when at length they complete the topmost pinnacle, the lord (of Olympus, let us say) takes flight in a comic fashion, and man, grasping the situation and seizing his place, at once begins a new life with a new insight into things. (10: 10)

For all its humor, this parody contains the major theme of the book and foreshadows the appearance of Stavrogin. He too is of an "indescribable beauty"; he too is death and not life; he too is followed, if not by a multitude of all nations, then by the multitude of all those who look to him for inspiration. He too believes that man can take the place not of the lord of Olympus, who has nothing to do with the Tower of Babel, but of the God of the Old Testament and His Son of the New. He is the pretender and the impostor aspiring to the throne of God, just as Death in the poem aspires to be the source of Life. Everything that stems from him is thus marked with the seal of supreme falsity and deception and leads to Death. He is a counterfeit and fraudulent facsimile of Truth; and this symbolism of the usurper, the pretender, the impostor runs through every aspect of the book, underlying and linking all its actions.

No one, to be sure, is more of an impostor—more of an endearing and charming old fake—than Stepan Trofimovich. Even hostile critics of *The Devils*, enraged at its lambasting of the radicals, greeted his appearance as a triumph. Dostoevsky paints him with such an overflowing abundance of traits that it is difficult to do justice to them all; but each reinforces the comic discrepancy between his rhetorical postures and his practical performances. To take only one example, the lazy, self-coddling Stepan Trofimovich, who is always on the point of beginning to write his great masterpiece (but somehow never quite gets started), is

476

very fond of indulging in a little homily on the virtues and importance of work for the Russian character. "For the last twenty years I've been sounding the tocsin and calling to work.... I shall hold on to the bell rope till they start tolling for my requiem," he declaims impressively to his deferential listeners (10: 23).

His alternately tender and stormy relationship with his domineering patroness, based on a pattern of successive moods of adoration and exasperation on both sides, is irresistibly funny broad comedy; and it shows, incidentally, that Dostoevsky could employ his famous love-hate situation in whatever key was required by the demands of his theme. Nor does Dostoevsky neglect, despite his personal detestation of Nihilism, to allow Peter Verkhovensky to puncture his father's self-protective poses with deadly accuracy. The pitiless realism of the Nihilist, always viewing everything in terms of the crudest self-interest, time and again reveals the skeleton in Stepan Trofimovich's beautifully bedecked closet. But this only serves to make the fickle old Idealist even more sympathetic and appealing. Whatever the material basis of his existence, he has never exploited it cynically or basely; in yielding to his weaknesses, he has always been aware that he is unworthy of the great ideals that he proclaims and reveres. Stepan Trofimovich, in other words, has never allowed his conscience to become dulled or blunted—and this, for Dostoevsky, always leaves the path open for salvation.

This first chapter not only establishes the historical framework in which the action will be placed but also serves a less-noticed and more implicit aesthetic function. These pages have a static quality that imparts an impression of calm tranquillity and lulling routine to the patterns of life soon to be upset by the incursion of "the devils," who will gradually filter into the provincial town (considered to be Tver, where Dostoevsky spent five months in 1859) and shake it to its very roots. The chronicler, appropriately, stresses the perfectly innocuous, commonplace, and almost ritual nature of the meetings of Stepan Trofimovich's group of visitors and "friends," some of whom will soon become the nucleus of Peter Verkhovensky's "quintet." "At one time it was repeated about the town that our little circle was a hotbed of Nihilism, profligacy, and godlessness.... And yet we did nothing but indulge in the most harmless, agreeable, typically Russian lighthearted chatter" (10: 30).

Life would have continued very much as before without the external stimulus provided by Peter Verkhovensky's determination to change words into deeds. The gradually tightening web of the plot, with its accelerating tempo and intricate network of concealed relations, conveys an almost physical sense of this gradual invasion of a long-established order by occult forces surreptitiously taking over its destiny. In this respect the undramatic and (for Dostoevsky) unusually slow opening chapter works to set off by contrast the tension of the rest of the book, and to provide an appropriate formal analogue to the theme of secret conspiracy and subversive encroachment.

3

We are next introduced to Stavrogin, and this is the point at which, if my reading of the book is correct, Dostoevsky runs into serious trouble. Up to the age of sixteen, Nikolay Stavrogin was the pupil of Stepan Trofimovich, who had been entrusted with his education; and this plot structure makes a Liberal Idealist of the 1840s the spiritual progenitor of a Byronic type associated with the 1820s and 1830s. Along with what has already been said on this point, we should remember that Dostoevsky was composing under intense pressure and that, as he told Katkov, "of the fifteen signatures that I've written [of the discarded first draft—J.F.], probably twelve will go into the new version of the novel."[1] By the time the Prince evolved into Stavrogin, Dostoevsky obviously wanted to preserve as much as he could of what he had already written and thus clung to his old pattern. Stavrogin's Byronism, however, loses much of its symbolic meaning when he is linked to Stepan Trofimovich as pupil to teacher; and this also weakens the nature of Stavrogin's relations to Shatov and Kirillov, which tend to seem more personal than historically representative.

Although the positions of Stavrogin and Stepan Trofimovich are chronologically skewed from this point of view, Dostoevsky nonetheless succeeds in making their relationship humanly convincing. He takes great care to underline the tradition of metaphysical-religious Idealism that constitutes a bond between teacher and pupil; but the heritage is conveyed in a form reflecting all the velleities of Stepan Trofimovich's highly volatile character, which exercises a morbid and unhealthy influence on his impressionable charge. "More than once he awakened his ten- or eleven-year-old friend at night, simply to pour out his wounded feelings and weep before him, or to tell him some family secret, without noticing that this was totally impermissible" (10: 35). The tutor communicated all his own moral uncertainty and instability to his unfortunate pupil without providing anything positive to counteract their unsettling effects, and the result was to leave an aching emptiness at the center of Stavrogin's being.

"Stepan Trofimovich succeeded in reaching the deepest chords in his pupil's heart, and had aroused in him a first vague sensation of that eternal, sacred longing which some elect souls, once having tasted and discovered it, will then never exchange for a cheap gratification. (There are some connoisseurs who prize this longing more than the most complete satisfaction of it, if such were possible)" (10: 35). This passage both defines Stavrogin as a personality emotionally engaged in the quest for an absolute of some kind and also suggests the perversity springing from his lack of any positive goal. His quest is a spiritual experimentation totally preoccupied with itself, totally enclosed within the ego, and hence incapable of self-surrender to the absolute presumably being sought.

All through this first presentation of Stavrogin, Dostoevsky accentuates the pure gratuity of his scandalous behavior, the impossibility of explaining it by any ordinary and commonplace motives. Stavrogin is not simply exhibiting the customary insolence of his class and personal position when he lives the riotous life of a Guards officer; his escapades are not merely the "cheap gratification" of an overbearing social vanity or of an uncontrollable drive for sensual pleasures. There is something mysterious about Stavrogin's violence, particularly about his taste for self-degradation, that transcends the norm. He is not, as Stepan Trofimovich consolingly suggests to Varvara Petrovna, a young Prince Harry out of Shakespeare's "immortal chronicle," sowing his wild oats and rubbing elbows with the people before settling down to assume his rightfully exalted position in society.

The sheer gratuitousness of this defiance of social convention, which so much fascinated André Gide in Dostoevsky, is stressed even more strongly in the episodes that scandalize his birthplace on his return. He suddenly pulls the nose of a harmless old gentleman who has been in the habit of asserting, "No, you can't lead me by the nose" (10: 38); on the spur of the moment he kisses Liputin's pretty wife with ardent passion; called in by his distant relative, the governor of the province, for some explanations, he surpasses himself by biting the governor's ear. All these incidents exemplify Stavrogin's refusal to bridle or check his impulses in any way, his rejection of any internal or external restraints on the absolute autonomy of his self-will. When he goes mad with an attack of "brain fever," the chronicler remarks that it was thought by some (and they were right) to be "neither here nor there" so far as an explanation of his actions was concerned (10: 44).

The first physical description of Stavrogin pinpoints his strange appearance of indefinable artificiality—an appearance that obviously derives from his symbolic function. "His hair was of a peculiarly intense black, his light-colored eyes were peculiarly light and calm, his complexion was peculiarly soft and white, the red in his cheeks was too bright and clear, his teeth were like pearls and his lips like coral—one would have thought the very acme of beauty, yet at the same time somehow repellent. It was said that his face suggested a mask" (10: 37). Stavrogin's masklike beauty reminds one of the vampires and ghouls of Gothic fictional mythology; like them, he is a living corpse whose unearthly beauty is the deceptive facade behind which festers the horror of evil and corruption. Several years later, however, when the chronicler observes him face-to-face again, a change has occurred. "Now—now, I don't know why he impressed me at once as absolutely, incontestably beautiful, so that no one could have said that his face was like a mask." Now he seemed "to have the light of some new idea in his eyes" (10: 145).

By this time, Stavrogin has decided to reject and transcend his past, to humiliate himself publicly and sincerely by acknowledging his marriage to Marya Lebyadkina and confessing his violation of Matryosha. By seeking forgiveness and absolution, he hopes to save himself from the madness that he feels to be his impending fate. On the purely moral-personal level, Stavrogin's character is defined by his despairing struggle to triumph over the egoism of his self-will and to attain a state of genuine humility. The first overt manifestation of this "new idea" is the self-control he exhibits under the provocation of Shatov's blow; but he lies about his relation to the crippled Marya, which he wishes to reveal only under conditions of his own choosing. And this is the first justification for Tikhon's later judgment that Stavrogin's egoism, far from having been conquered by his new resolution, has taken on its subtlest form of all as a carefully staged martyrdom of contempt.

At the end of this scene the chronicler attempts to define Stavrogin's character, explaining that in the past year, "and because of special circumstances" (10: 163), he has succeeded in gathering a great many facts about him. It is no surprise, at least according to my reading, that what comes to his mind is a comparison with the well-known figure of a legendary Decembrist, L—N (Lunin). By linking Stavrogin to a member of this group and to this period—that of Russian Byronism, *Evgeny Onegin*, and Lermontov's Pechorin—Dostoevsky is manifestly trying to compensate for the anachronism inherent in his plot structure. Consequently, Stavrogin turns out to be a *contemporary* development of the same type, its latest avatar in Russian culture, who, unlike his predecessors, is strangely afflicted by inner desiccation and emotional apathy.

In the past, such "predatory" Byronic types, as Apollon Grigoryev called them, had at least enjoyed the consciousness of their own superiority and strength. But while Stavrogin would have performed the same daring feats from which they derived pleasure, he would have done so "without the slightest thrill of enjoyment, languidly, listlessly, even with *ennui* and entirely from unpleasant necessity." Stavrogin had even more "malignancy" than such gentlemen of the past, "but his malignancy was cold, calm, and, if one may say so, *rational*—therefore, the most revolting and terrible possible" (10: 165). All the springs of human feeling have dried up in Stavrogin; his demonism is that of a total rationalism, which, once having emptied life of all significance and value, can no longer make any direct, instinctive response even to its most primitive solicitations. Byron's Manfred has different reasons for his despair with life (his crime of incest, which resembles Stavrogin's violation of innocence, is at least a crime of passion), but his self-characterization accurately applies to Stavrogin with equal force:

> Good, or evil, life,
> Powers, passions, all I see in other beings,
> Have been to me as rain unto the sands. . . .
> I have no dread,
> And feel the curse to have no natural fear,
> Nor fluttering throb, that beats with hopes or wishes,
> Or lurking love of something on the earth.[2]

4

The action in the first four chapters of Part II, which concentrates on Stavrogin as he makes a round of visits to Kirillov, Shatov, and the Lebyadkins, indirectly illuminates both his historical-symbolic significance and the tragedy of his yearning for an unattainable absolution through humility. The first two figures each represent an aspect of himself that he has discarded but that has now become transformed into one or another ideological "devil" permanently obsessing his spiritual disciples. In the case of Kirillov, this devil is the temptation to self-deification logically deriving from the atheistic humanism of Feuerbach. "The necessary turning point of history," Feuerbach had written in his *Essence of Christianity*, "will be the moment when man becomes aware of and admits that the consciousness of God is nothing else but the consciousness of man as species. . . . *Homo homini Deus est*—this is the great practical principle—this is the axis on which revolves the history of the world."[3] There is a transparent echo of these famous words in the scene between Kirillov and the chronicler in Part I, when Kirillov remarks that history will be divided into two parts, "from the gorilla to the annihilation of God, and from the annihilation of man ["To the gorilla?" ironically interjects the narrator—J.F.] . . . to the transformation of the earth and of man physically. Man will be God and be transformed physically" (10: 94).*

Kirillov is one of Dostoevsky's most remarkable creations, and, like Raskolnikov, displays Dostoevsky's intimate understanding of the moral

---

* The idea that once man overcomes God he will be physically transformed into a different kind of creature can also be found in Feuerbach. Andrzej Walicki cites a passage from the later *Lectures on the Essence of Religion* in which Feuerbach refers to "the future immortal man, differentiated from man as he exists at present in the body and flesh." See Andrzej Walicki, *A History of Russian Thought* (Stanford, 1979), 317.

passion inspiring many of the radical intelligentsia whose concrete politics he abhorred. Kirillov is a secular saint whose whole being is consumed by a need for self-sacrifice. Determined to take his own life for the greater glory of humankind, whom he wishes to free from the pain and fear of death, Kirillov has agreed to do so at the moment that would most aid "the cause"; and Peter Verkhovensky intends to exploit this demented but great-souled resolution to cover the murder of Shatov. God, Kirillov believes, is nothing but the projected image of this pain and fear, and he wishes to commit suicide solely to express the highest capacity of humankind's self-will—solely to free humanity from a God who is nothing but such fear. Kirillov is convinced that *such* a suicide will initiate the era of the Man-God predicted by Feuerbach; and his death will thus be a martyrdom for humankind, but a martyrdom that reverses the significance of that of Christ. Rather than testifying to the reality and existence of God and a superterrestrial world, it will mark their final elimination from human consciousness.

With a daring that has given rise to a great deal of confusion, Dostoevsky does not hesitate to endow Kirillov with many of the attributes of Prince Myshkin—his love for children, his ecstatic affirmation of life, his eschatological apprehension of the end of time. The symbolism of the book requires Stavrogin always to inspire a deformed and distorted image of the Truth—but one that resembles what it imitates as closely and uncannily as Stavrogin's "mask" resembles healthy human beauty. Hence Dostoevsky gives Kirillov the "mask" of Myshkin's apocalyptic intuitions and feelings while revealing the monstrosities that result when such religious emotions, divorced from a faith in Christ, are turned into secular and subjective ideas.

Kirillov's deification of Man leads to his own self-destruction as well as that of all humankind ("it will be the same to live or not to live"); his conviction that the Kingdom of God already exists, if people will only realize it, deludes him into denying the existence of evil ("everything is good"); and he sees no difference between worshiping "a spider crawling along a wall" and a sacred icon. Stavrogin's demonism is refracted in Kirillov through a religious sensibility haunted, like Ippolit Terentyev, by the loss of Christ; and Kirillov's apocalyptic yearning makes him oblivious of, and personally immune to, the horrible consequences of his own doctrines. Stavrogin, though, has lived through other experiences, and he indicates the most important of them in his question: "if anyone insults and outrages [a] little girl, is that good?" Throughout this scene he regards Kirillov "with a disdainful compassion," though, as Dostoevsky adds carefully, "there [was] no mockery in his eyes" (10: 187–189).

The dialogue with Kirillov is followed by a parallel scene with Shatov, and here again Dostoevsky uses some of his most cherished convictions to dramatize another of Stavrogin's "masks." Just as Stavrogin had inspired Kirillov with an atheistic humanism based on the supremacy of reason and the Man-God, so he has inspired Shatov, at the same time, with a Slavophilism founded on the very opposite principle. "Reason has never had the power to define good and evil," Shatov declares, repeating Stavrogin's teaching, "or even to distinguish between good and evil, even approximately; on the contrary, it has always mixed them up in a disgraceful and pitiful way; science has even given the solution by the fist." The distinction between right and wrong, as the Slavophils had argued, comes only from the irrational, only from religion and faith. "There has never been a nation without a religion, that is, without an idea of good and evil." And since, for a Russian, religion can only mean Orthodox Christianity, Stavrogin had affirmed that "a man who was not Orthodox could not be a Russian" (10: 197–199). Here, growing directly out of Stavrogin's preachments, is the metaphysical-religious essence of the two ideologies that succeeded the Russian Byronism of the 1830s.

The relation between Shatov and Stavrogin is much more complex, and much more difficult to describe accurately, than that between Stavrogin and Kirillov. Kirillov's attempt literally to incarnate the Man-God can lead only to self-destruction; he thus expresses the demonic and Luciferian side of Stavrogin's personality (but in a morally elevated form). Shatov, on the other hand, represents the need and the search for faith that is also deeply rooted in Stavrogin, the need that is impelling him to acknowledge and repent his crimes. Moreover, the effect of Stavrogin on Shatov has been the very opposite of what occurred with Kirillov: he helped Shatov to break with his radical past and imbued him with the Messianic idea of the Russians as a "god-bearing" people destined to regenerate the world. Stavrogin's influence has thus led Shatov along the path that Dostoevsky certainly considered that of salvation; but the symbolic pattern of the book requires that his path also be blocked by the fatality of Stavrogin's doom.

This does not mean, as has often been too hastily concluded, that Dostoevsky is here repudiating, or at least casting some doubt on, his own most hallowed convictions. It means, rather, that he wishes to emphasize the need for such convictions to be grounded in sincere religious faith. Shatov's ideas echo those of Danilevsky, who had, in Dostoevsky's view, reduced Orthodoxy simply to a national faith and thus betrayed the universal religious mission of the Russian Christ. Indeed, as we have seen in Dostoevsky's comment on Maikov's poem, he now felt that even the old Slavophilism of Khomiakov and Kireevsky, for all its overt religiosity, was still an artificial, Western-imported substitute for the spontaneity of the people's faith. "The Slavophil," Dostoevsky wrote in his notes, identifying such a doctrine with Danilevsky, "thinks that he can manage solely thanks to the natural attributes of the Russian people, but without Orthodoxy one will not manage at all, no attributes will do anything if the world has lost faith." On the same page, in a speech not included in the text, Shatov calls Slavophilism "an aristocratic whim" and then adds: "They [the Slavophils] will never be able to believe directly" (11: 186). This idea was finally assigned to Stepan Trofimovich, who says much the same thing—and here he certainly speaks for the author—when he declares that "Shatov believes *by forcing himself to*, like a Moscow Slavophil" (10: 33; italics in text). Hence Stavrogin and his pupil Shatov, for all their Slavophilism and Russian nationalism, cannot muster the simple and unquestioning faith that would infuse their ideas with the inner fire of true emotional commitment.

Stavrogin thus here again inspires a mutilated version of the Truth that falls short of its grounding in religious faith, even though he knows abstractly that such faith is the only means of rescue from the chaos of his unlimited freedom. Shatov diagnoses the malady afflicting Stavrogin (and himself) in a key speech that helps to explain how Dostoevsky saw them both:

> You're an atheist [Shatov says] because you're a nobleman's son, the last nobleman's son. You've lost the distinction between good and evil because you've ceased to know your people. A new generation is coming, straight from the heart of the people, and you will know nothing of it, neither you nor the Verkhovenskys, father or son, nor I, because I am also a nobleman's son, I, the son of your serf-lackey Pashka. (10: 202–203)

On the symbolic level of the book, this can only mean that *all* the ideologies deriving from Stavrogin—whether liberal or radical Westernism in its political or metaphysical-religious form, or Slavophilism of whatever tint or shading—are equally tainted with the original sin of their birth among a Western-educated "aristocracy" totally divorced from the people. All are doomed to be swept away by an authentically Russian culture springing from the people's faith.

Stavrogin's personal behavior in these scenes also makes it clear that he will never be able to achieve the total abandonment of self necessary for a religious conversion. Even with Shatov, whom he comes to warn about the impending danger and to whom he is closer than anyone in the book except Darya Shatova, he cannot confess the truth about Matryosha. He denies that he has "outraged children," just as he had lied earlier about his marriage to Marya Lebyadkina. And he refuses to answer when Shatov poses the question that was to be clarified in his visit to Tikhon: "Is it true that you saw no distinction between some brutal obscene action and any great exploit, even the sacrifice of life for the good of humanity? Is it true that you have found identical beauty, equal enjoyment, in both extremes?" (10: 201). Shatov displays the same insight into Stavrogin that Tikhon would later exhibit when he diagnoses the motives for his marriage to Marya: "You married through a passion for martyrdom, from a craving for remorse, *through moral sensuality*" (10: 202; italics added). The first two impulses in Stavrogin, genuinely moral, are always crippled and distorted by the third, which stems from his enjoyment of the outrageously perverse, shocking, and sheerly gratuitous manifestations of his absolute self-will.

Stavrogin's next visit, to the Lebyadkins (framed by his two encounters with Fedka the convict), completes the sequence unmasking Stavrogin as an "impostor." The Falstaffian Lebyadkin, whose drunkenly off-color poetry was actually picked up and imitated by some twentieth-century admirers,* anticipates some aspects of Dimitry Karamazov. He is also a sleazy, down-at-heels version of the extreme stretch of possibilities—a taste for poetry and beauty on one hand, for bestiality and cruelty on the other—at war with each other in Stavrogin on the level of tragedy. His sister Marya, Stavrogin's virginal wife, is one of Dostoevsky's most poetic and enigmatic creations, whose exact significance has excited a great deal of discussion. Childish and mentally feeble, unable to distinguish between objective reality and her dreams and desires, she yet pierces through the "mask" of Stavrogin with a clairvoyance that recalls Prince Myshkin and foreshadows Father Zosima. Her sense of the sacredness of the cosmos, her affirmation that "the Mother of God is the great mother, the damp earth," who brings joy to men when they "water the earth with [their] tears a foot deep" (10: 116), evokes the esoteric, heretical lore of certain sects of the *raskolniki*, who mingled their Christianity with remnants of pre-Christian paganism.

Various theological and allegorical interpretations have been offered of Marya, but it is not necessary here to decide among them. What seems undeniable is that she represents Dostoevsky's vision of the primitive religious sensibility of the Russian people, who continued to feel a mystical union between the Russian soil and "the Mother of God." The debasement and pathos of her condition, however, reveals Dostoevsky's ambiguity about the *raskolniki* and their sectarian offshoots: he tended to see them as a precious reservoir of Old Russian values, but kept his distance from their sometimes theologically suspect extremes. At one point, it should be recalled, Dostoevsky had thought of using Golubov, an Old Believer returned to Orthodoxy, as a positive source of moral inspiration.

---

* Oddly enough, Lebyadkin's poetry served as inspiration for a group of "absurdist" Russian poets just after the First World War. "The poetry meant as parody in *The Devils*," Ilya Serman has written, "turned out to be an indispensable ferment in the literary stirrings of the 1920s." See Ilya Serman, "Stikh Kapitan Lebyadkina i Poesiya XX Veka," *Revue des Études Slaves*, 53 (1981), 597–605.

In this context, Marya's poignant longing for a "Prince" who would not be ashamed to acknowledge her as his own takes on a good deal of historical-symbolic meaning. And her false and unconsummated marriage to Stavrogin surely indicates that no true union is possible between the Christian Russian people and the embodied essence of godless Russian Europeanism.

Symbolically again, it is entirely appropriate that Marya should finally unmask Stavrogin and label him unequivocally as an "impostor." Whatever confusions may exist in her mind, her demented second sight, like that traditionally possessed by a "holy fool" (*yurodivi*), has now pierced through to his ultimate incapacity for true selflessness. "As soon as I saw your mean face when I fell and you picked me up—it was as if a worm had crawled into my heart," she says; "it's not *he*, I thought to myself, not *he*! My falcon would never have been ashamed of me in front of a young society lady!" (10: 219). Stavrogin starts with rage and terror when she prophetically alludes to his "knife," that is, his lurking desire to have her murdered (on which Peter Verkhovensky hopes to capitalize). And while she reads his innermost soul, she also speaks for the Russian people in assigning him his true historical-symbolic dimension. He is not the "Prince," not the genuine Lord and Ruler of Russia, but only Grishka Otrepeyev, "cursed in seven cathedrals," the impious and sacrilegious "impostor" and "false pretender." On the plot level it is precisely as such a "false pretender"—as Ivan the Tsarevich—that Peter Verkhovensky wishes to use Stavrogin to betray and mislead the hapless Russian people.

How justly Marya has seen into Stavrogin becomes even clearer when he throws his wallet to Fedka the convict in the solitary darkness of the storm-tossed night. By this gesture, Stavrogin silently connives at the murder of the Lebyadkins, giving way once again to the temptation of evil. His inner defeat is dramatized again in his duel with Gaganov, when he strives to achieve self-mastery and to avoid useless bloodshed; but his arrogant and contemptuous manner only enflames the uncontrollable hatred of his opponent all the more. The truly good Kirillov, ready to give his life for humankind, tries to explain to Stavrogin that moral self-conquest means a total suppression of egoism and the patient acceptance of any humiliation, even the most unjust and insupportable. "Bear your burden," he says. "Or else there's no merit" (10: 228). But Stavrogin cannot bear the burden of good, whatever his desire to do so, because his irrepressible egoism continues to stand in the way.

This crucial sequence of scenes is climaxed by Stavrogin's unexpected meeting with Darya Shatova, an episode that, in the book text, is about a page and a half shorter than the earlier magazine version. The section that Dostoevsky cut contained Stavrogin's admission that he was haunted by hallucinations and "devils," which he knew were only parts of himself; but his self-absorption indicates that he is gradually beginning to believe in their reality. This menace of madness was meant to motivate the visit to Tikhon but became superfluous and incomprehensible without the confession chapter. One passage of the variant, however, is important in helping to reconstruct the original historical-symbolic meaning of Dostoevsky's conception. Stavrogin tells Darya that he has begun to be obsessed with a new "devil," very different from those in the past (as represented by Kirillov and Shatov): "Yesterday he was stupid and insolent. He's a thickheaded seminarian filled with the self-satisfaction of the 1860s, with the ideas of a lackey, the background, soul, and mentality of a lackey, fully persuaded of his irresistible beauty. . . . Nothing could be more repulsive! I was furious that my own devil could put on such a debasing mask" (12: 141). From these words, it is clear that Dostoevsky intended to make Stavrogin as much responsible for the devils of the 1860s as Stepan Trofimovich, if not indeed more so, because of his disdainful collaboration with Peter.

5

The scene with Darya Shatova, accordingly, serves as a transition between the first and second sections of Part II. Immediately following this dialogue, Dostoevsky shifts his focus from Stavrogin to the spread of the moral and social chaos he has brought in his wake in the form of Peter Verkhovensky. Here Dostoevsky gives full play to his immense satiric verve as he sketches all the people whose stupidity and lack of principle turn them into willing dupes of Peter's intrigues. The ambitious blue-stocking Yulia von Lembke, determined to impress the most exalted spheres by her magical influence on the young generation; her well-meaning but obtuse and incompetent Russo-German automaton of a husband, the governor of the province, literally driven out of his mind by the tumultuous course of events; even the normally hardheaded and domineering Mme Stavrogina—all fall under Peter Verkhovensky's spell, powerfully aided and abetted by the patronage of Karmazinov. Mme von Lembke picks up the jargon of the Nihilists from Peter and terribly impresses Mme Stavrogina with her mastery of the latest mode. "You carefully concealed all these new ideas from me," his protectress tells Stepan Trofimovich irately, "though everyone's familiar with them nowadays. And you did it simply out of jealousy, so as to have power over me. So that even now Yulia is a hundred miles ahead of me" (10: 265). Only poor Stepan Trofimovich, more and more lonely, isolated, and agitated, resists the general disintegration and still plans to vindicate his ideals.

Starting as the personal foible of a few foolish people, the corruption becomes a demoralization in the most literal sense. Dostoevsky introduces a whole series of incidents to illustrate it, ranging from a breakdown of standards of personal conduct and social propriety to disrespect for the dead and the desecration of a sacred icon. Politically, Peter Verkhovensky demoralizes von Lembke by encouraging him to take the harshest and most despotic measures; and Peter dupes, deceives, and manipulates his followers in exactly the same fashion. Just as with his general influence on society as a whole, the result of his pressure on the quintet is a collapse of their own moral-political standards and the approval of a wanton murder. There is a clear structural parallel between Stavrogin's round of visits in the first half of this section and Peter's calls in the second half on all the pawns he is engaged in maneuvering. Dostoevsky intended to bring these parallel sequences together by the two chapters of self-revelation that would conclude Part II: Verkhovensky's mad hymn to universal destruction, inspired by Stavrogin, and then a disclosure of the moral bankruptcy and despair of Verkhovensky's "idol" as he makes his confession to Tikhon.

From his first appearance in the novel, Peter Verkhovensky is depicted as the genius of duplicity; even the details of his physical appearance constantly alter, though the first description given of him is unmistakably meant to evoke something reptilian. Under the surface of simple frankness and disarming directness, Verkhovensky carries on his work of sowing demoralization and destruction. He is Stavrogin's demonism incarnated as a political will-to-power. "I invented you abroad," he cries furiously to Stavrogin. "I invented it all, looking at you. If I hadn't watched you from my corner, nothing of all this would have entered my head" (10: 326). What Peter has invented, under the spell of Stavrogin, is the plan to consecrate him as Ivan the Tsarevich—to use the very force he wishes to destroy, the faith of the Russian people in a just and righteous God-anointed ruler, as a means for their own destruction. This plan has obvious symbolic affinities with Stavrogin's effect on Kirillov and Shatov; in each of them he has inspired a "mask" of the Truth shorn of its true religious foundations. This mask is "beautiful," as Peter exclaims ecstatically while gazing at Stavrogin, but it is the beauty of the demonic. "You are my idol!" Peter passionately proclaims to Stavrogin (10: 323). Peter's plan, however, implicitly contains its own negation, for it reveals the impotence of his godless and amoral principles to establish any basis for human life. Falsehood and idolatry must speak deceptively in the name of Truth and God, thus confessing their own bankruptcy. Later, in *The Brothers Karamazov*, the same dialectic will be used when the Grand Inquisitor speaks in the name of Christ.

Following Verkhovensky's "confession" to the false god Stavrogin,

Dostoevsky had planned to portray Stavrogin's confession to the true God in the person of His servitor Tikhon. This would have dramatized all the horror and abomination of the "idol" that Peter Verkhovensky was worshiping. After a sleepless night spent in warding off his hallucinations, Stavrogin would visit Tikhon, and then the secret of his past, repeatedly hinted at up to this point, was to be finally disclosed. Like Onegin and Pechorin, Stavrogin is a victim of the famous *mal de siècle*, the all-engulfing ennui that haunts the literature of the first half of the nineteenth century and is invariably depicted as resulting from the loss of religious faith. Baudelaire, its greatest poet, called ennui the deadliest of the vices:

> Quoiqu'il ne pousse ni grands gestes ni grands cris,
> Il ferait volontiers de la terre un débris
> Et dans un baillement avalerait le monde.*

Ennui is a prominent symptom of that "romantic agony" whose dossier has been so industriously compiled by Mario Praz; and, as he has abundantly shown, its usual result is some form of moral perversion.[4] Dostoevsky had depicted it as such in Prince Valkovsky (*The Insulted and Injured*), in the sudden appearance of Cleopatra in *Notes from Underground* sticking gold pins into her slave girls for amusement, and in Svidrigailov (*Crime and Punishment*). With Stavrogin, it has led to the abominable violation of little Matryosha and his unspeakably vile passivity as she takes her life.

Such is the result of Stavrogin's attempt to pass beyond the limits of morality, to put into practice, with the maniacal determination of Dostoevsky's negative heroes, the conviction that there are no moral boundaries of any kind. "I formulated for the first time in my life what appeared to be the rule of my life," Stavrogin tells himself, "namely, that I neither know nor feel good and evil and that I have not only lost any sense of it, but that there is neither good nor evil (which pleased me), and that it is just a prejudice: that I can be free from any prejudice, but that once I attain that degree of freedom I am done for." (12: 113). For Stavrogin, these were "old familiar thoughts" that he was at last putting clearly to himself for the first time; they were thoughts that had been gnawing at his psyche and had shaped his behavior in the past. Like Raskolnikov's crime, Stavrogin's revolting and despicable escapades had been a great moral-philosophical experiment. This is why Dostoevsky had taken such pains from the very start to dissociate his conduct from any kind of banal and self-indulgent debauchery.

* "Without great gestures or loud cries / It would gladly turn earth into a wasteland / And swallow the world in a yawn." Charles Baudelaire, *Oeuvres*, ed. Y.-G. Le Dantec (Paris, 1954), 82.

Yet Stavrogin's ambition to transcend the human, to arrogate for himself supreme power over life and death, nonetheless runs aground on the hidden reef of conscience. No matter what he may think, Stavrogin cannot entirely eliminate his *feeling* for the difference between good and evil, This irrepressible sentiment breaks forth from his subconscious—usually, though not invariably, the guardian of morality for Dostoevsky—in Stavrogin's famous dream of "the Golden Age," inspired by Claude Lorrain's painting *Acis and Galatea*. Stavrogin saw in his mind's eye:

A corner of the Greek archipelago; blue, caressing waves, islands and rocks, a foreshore covered in lush vegetation, a magic vista in the distance, a spellbinding sunset—it is impossible to describe it in words. Here was the cradle of European civilization, here were the first scenes from mythology, man's paradise on earth. Here a beautiful race of men had lived. They rose and went to sleep happy and innocent; the woods were filled with their joyous songs, the great overflow of their untapped energies passed into love and unsophisticated gaiety. The sun shed its rays on these islands and that sea, rejoicing in its beautiful children. A wonderful dream, a sublime illusion! The most incredible dream that has ever been dreamed, but to which all mankind has devoted all its powers during the whole of its existence, for which it has died on the cross and for which its prophets have been killed, without which nations will not live and cannot even die. (11: 21)

This vision of a primeval earthly paradise of happiness and innocence fills Stavrogin's heart with overflowing joy. "I woke and opened my eyes, for the first time in my life literally wet with tears. . . . A feeling of happiness, hitherto unknown to me, pierced my heart till it ached." But then a tiny red spider, associated in Stavrogin's subconscious with Matryosha's death, replaces this blissful vision of Eden. He sees the little girl, in his mind's eye, standing on the threshold of his room and threatening him with her tiny fist. "Pity for her stabbed me," he writes, "a maddening pity, and I would have given my body to be torn to pieces if that would have erased what happened" (12: 127–128). Stavrogin finds this lacerating reminder of his own evil unbearable, but he willfully refuses to suppress the recollection; and this insupportable need to expiate his crime, which nothing he knows or believes in can help to absolve, is gradually driving him mad.

Stavrogin's confession thus reveals the source of his inner torment, but this torment has never been sufficient to overcome the supreme egoism and self-will that originally motivated his actions. Even his confession, as Tikhon senses, is only another and more extreme form of the "moral sensuality" that has marked all his previous attempts at self-

15. Claude Lorrain, *Acis and Galatea*

mastery. "This document," says Tikhon of his manuscript, "is born of a heart wounded unto death. . . . But it is as though you were already hating and despising in advance all those who read what you have written, and challenging them to an encounter" (11: 24). Tikhon discerns that Stavrogin by himself can never achieve the true humility of genuine repentance; his need for suffering and martyrdom can thus lead only to more and more disastrous provocations. Hence Tikhon urges that Stavrogin submit his will *completely* to the secret control of a saintly *staretz* and thus discipline himself, by a total surrender to another, as the first step along the path to the acceptance of Christ and the hope of forgiveness. But Stavrogin, irritably breaking an ivory crucifix he has been fingering during the interview, rejects this final admonition and goes to his self-destruction.

6

When it proved impossible to include the confession chapter in its proper place, Dostoevsky was forced to mutilate the original symmetry of his plan. Part II was to have exposed the origins of the chaos and confusion sown by Stavrogin and his "worshiper" Peter Verkhovensky; Part III would then have shown the practical results of their handiwork. Instead, Dostoevsky was forced to allow the present Chapter 9 of Part II ("Stepan Verkhovensky Is Raided") to replace the confession. From this point on, though, a continuous sequence unrolls the disastrous moral-social consequences of Peter Verkhovensky's intrigues. Their first result is the ridiculous raid on Stepan Trofimovich, prompted by the political leaflets and Peter's undermining of his father's prestige. The second is von Lembke's madness, brought on by jealousy and resentment of Peter and by the irresponsible frivolity of his purblind wife.

Von Lembke's hysteria, whipped up by Peter, causes the perfectly justified and peaceful demonstration of the Shpigulin workers to be broken up by brutal floggings. "I may mention, as characteristic of our society," remarks the narrator acidly, "that there were very few of the better-class people who saw reason to suppose that there was anything wrong with him [von Lembke]; his conduct seemed to them perfectly normal, and so much so that the action he had taken in the square the morning before was accepted and approved" (10: 360). Dostoevsky's depiction of the shortsightedness and stupidity of the von Lembkes castigates the reigning bureaucracy as mercilessly as he satirizes the revolutionaries.

Chaos reaches a climax in the weird and wonderful fête for the under-privileged governesses of the province, which is certainly one of the greatest comic mass scenes in the history of the novel. For sheer verve, it is approached only by the exuberance of similar depictions of mass mayhem in Smollett. But Dostoevsky's aim is far more serious than merely to ridicule some fashionable social stupidities. All the demoralization that had been brewing in the depths suddenly spouts forth like volcanic lava, beginning with the drunken Lebyadkin's bawdy poem, laden with sexual allusions, and ending with the glow of burning houses across the river in the night sky. Karmazinov, supposed to be the greatest attraction of all, provokes hostility in the audience by his highfalutin texts and pretentious mannerisms. Rudely heckled, he is thoroughly disconcerted by the time the obligatory laurel wreath arrives to honor his presence.

Stepan Trofimovich's turn is next, and finally screwing up the courage to denounce the Nihilists publicly, he restates the symbolic theme of the book in his own personal, aestheticized terms. "The enthusiasm of our modern youth," he declaims, "is as pure and shining as it was in our time. Only one thing has happened: a shift of aims, a substitution of one beauty for another. The whole misunderstanding lies only in this question: What is more beautiful, Shakespeare or boots, Raphael or petroleum?" (10: 372). Beginning with Stepan Trofimovich's prose poem glorifying the "beauty" of Death, and continuing with the various truncated and abortive ideologies inspired by the "beauty" of Stavrogin, the desecration of Divine Beauty has led to the grotesque vulgarization against which, his eyes opened at last, Stepan Trofimovich now protests: the replacement of the great creators of humankind's eternal ideals by the crudest and coarsest materialism.

Stepan Trofimovich's condemnation of Nihilism as "the most base, the most ingenuous, the most silly little stupidity" whips up the radicals scattered throughout the crowd into a rage (10: 371); breaking down and weeping under the hail of personal abuse, he finally flees. His place is then taken by some professor of literature, a newcomer to the town, whom the narrator had noticed walking backstage and rehearsing his speech. "Every time he turned round he raised his right hand, and then suddenly brought it down as though reducing an opponent to dust and ashes" (10: 365). Bounding onto the now-empty platform, he creates pandemonium by his unbridled attack, with his fist rising and falling, on Russia in the past and even more in the present. Later, at the evening ball, from which many respectable people had been frightened away by the turbulence of the afternoon, a ridiculous "literary quadrille" represents the triumph of "honest Russian thought" (radical thought, of course) over all attempts to suppress or crush it.* These events reach dizzy heights of farce, intermingled with the shocking news of Liza Tushina's flight to Stavrogin (arranged by Peter), the destruction caused by the fires, and the discovery of the murders of Captain Lebyadkin and his sister.

The most important episodes of these concluding chapters depict the end of Stavrogin's romance with Liza, the return of Shatov's wife bearing Stavrogin's illegitimate child, the climactic murder of Shatov, Peter's untroubled departure for parts elsewhere, and Stepan Trofimovich's last pilgrimage. Stavrogin's romance with Liza ends after a night in which she experiences his incapacity to love (not sexually, as some have claimed, but emotionally and humanly). The scenes between Shatov and his wife are in a mood of tenderness unusual for Dostoevsky, and the brief portrait of the disillusioned, betrayed, heartsick "new woman" is Dostoevsky's sole (but unforgettable) treatment of the burning "woman question" theme of the 1860s. Marie's self-contempt for her own femininity

---

* Both these incidents can be traced to actual events. The fiery professor is taken from an incident that occurred at a famous so-called literary-musical evening of 1862. Dostoevsky was one of the participants, and he heard a very similar speech, greeted by the crowd just as rapturously, made by Professor Platon Pavlov. For more details, see *Dostoevsky: The Stir of Liberation* (Princeton, N.J., 1983), 141–144.

The ridiculous "literary quadrille" performed at the end of the fête, and advertised as one of its chief attractions, was based on an actual "literary quadrille" much written about in the Russian newspapers in the spring of 1869. See S. Panov, "'Literaturnaya kadril' v romane 'Besi,'" *Zvenya*, 6 (1936), 573–582.

struggles with a natural joy at becoming a mother; her unwillingness to accept the humiliation of dependence wars with a genuine love for the pure-hearted Shatov. In this one scene, Dostoevsky captures all the moral-emotional complexities arising from the woman's liberation movement, which had been so blithely skipped over by Chernyshevsky's Utopian image of sexual velleities in *What Is To Be Done?* The pathos of Shatov's murder is also greatly intensified because it occurs just at the moment when the awkward, unhappy faith-seeker, who ecstatically welcomes the return of the unfaithful Marie and her child, has at last caught a glimpse of the possibility of family happiness.

Both the killing of Shatov and the suicide of Kirillov exhibit the same pattern of reversion and regression to the inhuman. The hapless conspirators are far from sharing Peter's insouciance about human life, and as the murder takes place, Lyamshin and Virginsky are overtaken by a panic return to animality. "Lyamshin gave vent to a scream more animal than human, [and] he went on shrieking without a pause, his mouth wide open and his eyes starting out of his head.... Virginsky was so scared that he too screamed out like a madman, and with a ferocity, a vindictiveness that one could not have expected of Virginsky" (10: 461). Nor is Kirillov's eerie death the triumphant assertion of a total self-will; it is, rather, the demented act of a crazed and terrified subhuman creature. The annihilation of God, far from leading to a mastery over the pain and fear of death, brings on the animal frenzy with which Kirillov sinks his teeth into Peter Verkhovensky's hand. Like Raskolnikov's crime, Kirillov's suicide is the self-negation and self-refutation of his own grandiose ideas.

Before shooting himself in a convulsive frenzy, Kirillov had written, under Peter's dictation, a false confession to the murder of Shatov and Fedka (defiantly signed in French with the revolutionary slogan: *liberté, égalité, fraternité ou la mort!*). Peter has thus carried his plan through to the letter, and he takes the next train, presumably for Petersburg, accompanied to the station by the subservient Lieutenant Erkel. He promises to return shortly; but as with everything about Peter, this too is a lie. Erkel, who suspects as much, devotedly assures him that even if he were to go abroad, that would be perfectly proper in the interests of the cause. Peter believes—or pretends to believe—that the members of his group will keep the secret of the murder, because "who will run the risk of utter ruin unless he's lost his reason?" The faithful Erkel, who had taken part in the murder himself, correctly predicts: "But they will lose their reason, sir" (10: 477).

The thumbnail sketch of the young Lieutenant Erkel, a very minor character, is worth dwelling on for a moment because it is not satirical at all and so well illustrates Dostoevsky's understanding of how the innately idealistic feelings of youth could become distorted and perverted. Erkel, a newcomer in town "who was very handsome and even gave the impression of being clever" (10: 415), had simply fallen under Peter's spell, and become his willing tool, out of purity and innocence of heart. "The sensitive, tenderhearted, and good-natured Erkel," writes the narrator, "was perhaps the most callous of the murderers who planned to kill Shatov and was quite ready to be present at his killing without a trace of any personal hatred and without batting an eyelid" (10: 439). Erkel himself was a model son devoted to his mother, to whom "he sent half of his scanty pay, and how she must have kissed that poor fair head of his! How she must have trembled and prayed over it! I speak so much about him because I am very sorry for him!" (10: 415). So, we may assume, was Dostoevsky.

If some characters may be said to sink below themselves by reverting to the level of animality, Stepan Trofimovich, on the other hand, surprises the narrator by rising above himself and finally overcoming his eternal hesitations and vacillations. His touchingly aimless peregrinations, which Dostoevsky had so much looked forward to composing, plunge him into entirely new and unexpected circumstances. Nothing is finer, in this book so filled with remarkable pages, than the bewildered contact between the sheltered, pampered "liberal," who has spent his life uttering fine phrases and depreciatory remarks about the Russian people, and the dumbfounded peasants whom he finally encounters.* The mutual incomprehension on both sides, as each observes the strange ways of the other with astonishment, is depicted with a sympathetic humor rare in Dostoevsky. Above all, the inspired meeting with the ex-nurse distributing copies of the New Testament allows Dostoevsky to introduce his religious thematic in the midst of Stepan Trofimovich's perplexity.

The startled lady immediately becomes the object of his affectionate attentions, and he dependently adapts himself to her as he had done for most of his life with Mme Stavrogina. "*Vous voyez, désormais nous le prêcherons* [the New Testament] *ensemble. . . .* The common people are

---

* These scenes are an astonishing anticipation of what actually occurred a year or so after *The Devils* was published, when, with the self-sacrificing zeal of the early Christians, the flower of Russian youth decided to abandon everything like Stepan Trofimovich and "go to the people." A good summary account of this event has been given by Richard Wortman: "In the summer of 1874 the radical youth, inspired by the signs of success that they had themselves projected on reality, abandoned their academic pursuits to plunge, inexperienced and untutored, into the countryside. Their hopes of an enthusiastic welcome evaporated on first contact with the peasantry. The image of the peasant as incipient revolutionary corresponded little with the sullen country folk they met, who, seemingly hostile in their trust of autocracy, met them with distrust and hostility. Hopelessly vulnerable to arrest once they strayed outside the capital, they were herded into prison by the hundreds." Richard Wortman, *The Crisis of Russian Populism* (Cambridge, 1967), 18.

religious, *c'est admis*, but they don't yet know the Gospel. . . . By expounding it to them verbally it is possible to correct the errors of that remarkable book, which, of course, I shall treat with the utmost respect" (10: 497). The scene in which, already running a high fever, he attempts to persuade her of his unacknowledged genius, only leaves her totally confused. "It was all 'much too clever,' she used to say afterwards dejectedly." When he reaches the secret of the great romance of his life, he embellishes it in a manner rivaling the finest flights of General Ivolgin in *The Idiot*. He had, it seems, been caught between a brunette (Mme Stavrogina) and a blonde (Darya Shatova), neither of whom would speak of her love for fear of wounding the other. "And so the three of them, pining away with magnanimity toward each other, kept silent for twenty years, locking their secrets in their breasts" (10: 494–495). Such pages carefully avoid anything harsh or condemnatory in their gently satirical depiction of Stepan Trofimovich's foibles.

Dostoevsky's handling of the dying Stepan Trofimovich is one of the most telling demonstrations of his artistic tact and scrupulosity. Deprived both of his positive Christian figure in Tikhon and of the opportunity to confront Stavrogin's despair with the divine mystery of Christ's all-forgiving love, Dostoevsky must certainly have been tempted to nudge Stepan Trofimovich's repentance in some conspicuously Christian direction. He scrupulously abstains, however, from violating the integrity of his masterful creation. From the very first pages, Stepan Trofimovich has been presented, not as an atheist to be sure, but as a species of Hegelian Deist. "I believe in God," he declares importantly, "*mais distinguons*, I believe in him as a Being who is conscious of himself in me only" (10: 33). Nothing that Stepan Trofimovich says in these last pages contradicts his aversion to the naive anthropomorphism of the popular faith, and the chronicler maintains a well-justified skepticism over "whether he was really converted, or whether the stately ceremony of the administration of the sacraments impressed him and stirred the artistic responsiveness of his temperament" (10: 505). Nor does he lose his taste for *risqué* jests about religion even on his deathbed. It is after an imperious outburst of Varvara Petrovna, who has finally arrived to take charge, that he smiles faintly and says: "God is necessary to me if only because He is the only being whom I can love eternally" (10: 505).

Stepan Trofimovich, then, does not die a Christian in any strict meaning of the word, but a reading of the Sermon on the Mount stirs him to acknowledge: "My friend, all my life I've been lying." And after listening to the passage from Luke about "the devils" who had entered the herd of swine, he declares: "They are we, we and those . . . and Petrusha and *les autres avec lui* . . . and I perhaps at the head of them" (10: 499). Such words, though consistent with the plot structure, scarcely accord sufficient importance to Stavrogin. More convincing, and entirely in character, is Stepan Trofimovich's final statement of his credo: "The whole law of human existence is merely this, that man should always bow down before the infinitely great. If people are deprived of the infinitely great, they will not continue to live and will die in despair. The infinite and immeasurable are as necessary to man as the little planet on which he dwells. My friends, all, all: Long live the Great Idea!" (10: 506). This is not Christian in any literal sense and could hardly have been meant to be taken as such; but it contains enough of a feeling for the transcendent to constitute an answer to the *hubris* of the purely human.

Stavrogin's suicide, which terminates the novel, had been foreseen by Dostoevsky from his very first grasp of this character; but it is difficult to say how it might have been presented if the confession chapter had been included. As we have seen in the excised conversation with Darya Shatova, it is Stavrogin who feels possessed by all the ideological "devils" and ultimately sees himself as their source. Whether, if the Tikhon chapter had been accepted, Dostoevsky would have picked up this foreshadowing can only remain a matter for speculation. As it stands, the book merely contains the somewhat feeble assertion, in Stavrogin's suicide note, that "from me nothing has come but negation, with no magnanimity and no force. Even negation has not come from me" (10: 514). This last sentence hardly jibes with Stavrogin's relations with the other characters, and may have been included to strengthen the final speech of Stepan Trofimovich. Without the confession chapter, there is no doubt that the book ends somewhat lamely: the reader does not know either that Stavrogin had made a sacrilegious, proto-Nietzchean attempt to transcend the boundaries of good and evil, or that his conscience has driven him to the point of madness. His suicide thus loses much of its symbolic-historical meaning as a self-condemnation of all the ideologies he has spawned.

The Devils, as a result, peters out rather inconsistently for reasons very largely outside Dostoevsky's power to remedy by the time he reached the final pages. But the scope of his canvas, the brilliant ferocity of his wit, the prophetic power and insight of his satire, his unrivaled capacity to bring to life and embody in living characters the most profound and complex moral-philosophical issues and social ideas—all combine to make this "pamphlet-poem" perhaps his most dazzling creation. It is an unprecedented historical-symbolic drama, intended to encompass all the forces of nineteenth-century Russian culture up to its time, and unlike any other work in the period in Russian or European literature except perhaps Flaubert's dispirited *L'Éducation sentimentale*. Its only rivals, a quarter of a century later, would be Conrad's *Nostromo* and *Under Western Eyes* (that remarkable reworking of *Crime and Punishment*) and

James's *The Princess Casamassima,* all equally disillusioned exposés of political and social revolution. And even with the flood of such novels in the twentieth century, *The Devils* remains unsurpassed as an astonishingly prescient portrayal of the moral quagmires, and the possibilities for self-betrayal of the highest principles, that have continued to dog the revolutionary ideal from Dostoevsky's day down (even more spectacularly) to our own.

CHAPTER 26

Conclusion

Dostoevsky's return to Russia in the summer of 1871 marked the beginning of a new phase in his life. But this new phase, though it can be physically assigned to that moment, actually commenced in a significant artistic-ideological sense only two years later. In the interval, Dostoevsky was continuously preoccupied with finishing *The Devils*, and it was only after completing this task that he could lift his eyes from his writing table and begin to take stock of his surroundings. His European years, during which his fury against Nihilism had been fanned to a white heat, continued to live within him imaginatively even though, as he was to discover, much had changed in the ideology of the radical intelligentsia during his absence. This is why the present volume, nominally terminating in 1871, plays a bit fast and loose with chronology by treating *The Devils* as a finished book.

Dostoevsky, in any case, still had nine more years left to live; and these years would be, if not as extraordinary in a literary sense as the six preceding, remarkable enough in their own way. For the lonely expatriate who had lived from hand to mouth in Europe, eagerly awaiting letters from home to keep in touch with Russian culture, would in a few years find himself the most important public voice in his country, whose every word was eagerly anticipated, commented on, and argued about. In November 1872, the same month as the publication of the last six chapters of *The Devils*, Dostoevsky agreed to become the editor of a weekly journal, *The Citizen* (*Grazhdanin*), whose proprietor was Prince V. P. Meshchersky. A minor author himself, Meshchersky was the center of a politically conservative literary circle that included Apollon Maikov and K. P. Pobedonostsev. Pobedonostsev was the tutor of Crown Prince Alexander, and Prince Meshchersky himself had very highly placed connections with the Russian court. Dostoevsky thus became a member of this influential social-literary grouping, though he tried to maintain a relative independence from its more obscurantist tendencies. Beside editing the weekly, he also contributed a column, under the title "Diary of a Writer," that later became an independent publication.

The ferocious satire of *The Devils* had naturally blackened Dostoevsky's reputation in the eyes of the radical intelligentsia, and his acceptance of the editorship of Meshchersky's magazine seemed to fix his social-political position once and for all. But Dostoevsky had always tried to maintain a balance between his opposition to revolutionary agitation and his recognition of the moral idealism that often inspired those who stirred up its flames. He saw his role in relation to the radical youth as that of a sympathetic critic rather than an immitigably hostile opponent. Moreover, radical ideology had changed once again, and those aspects of the 1860s that had repelled Dostoevsky the most—the contempt for religion, the attempt to base ethics on calculations of Utilitarianism, the denial of free will—had now been abandoned.

A new generation of radical Populist thinkers, led by N. K. Mikhailovsky and Peter Lavrov, based their appeals for social change on moral principles that any Christian could accept. Their influence, especially that of Mikhailovsky, had also given rise to a new appreciation, even idealization, of the moral-social values at the roots of peasant life— values directly linked to the religion of the peasantry, though the secular radicals preferred to disregard such an inconvenient relation to Russian Orthodoxy. Nonetheless, the new radical Populists (*narodniki*) saw peasant life, unlike their Nihilist predecessors, as the basis of a Russian moral-social order they wished to preserve and protect. Such views could hardly fail to arouse a responsive echo in the author of *House of the Dead* and the advocate of a doctrine of *pochvennichestvo*. Dostoevsky's columns in the "The Diary of a Writer" accordingly brought into prominence his old association with such revered radical figures as Belinsky and Herzen, and he defended even the Nechaevists—not Nechaev himself, to be sure—against the charge of being nothing more than ignorant and unscrupulous scoundrels. It is no accident, though it startled many at the time, that his next novel, *A Raw Youth*, was published by the most prominent radical Populist journal, *Notes of the Fatherland* (*Otechestvenniye Zapiski*). Dostoevsky himself initiated negotiations with this supposedly hostile publication, and his proposition was accepted with alacrity.

In the early 1860s, Dostoevsky had tried to serve as mediator among the competing extremes of Russian social-cultural opinion, but such a role no longer seemed possible for the author of *The Devils*. His choice of venue for his new novel, however, suggests that this ambition had revived, and the welcome he received also indicates the shift in the moral-philosophical foundations of radical ideology that had taken place since the 1860s, partly as a result of the influence of Dostoevsky's own novels. Over and above the immediate political question, this shift had once again made a dialogue possible between Dostoevsky and the new radical vision, and it was the hope of establishing a dialogue of this kind that shaped the ideological modality of his writings in the 1870s. To Dostoevsky's old friends and allies, including Maikov and Strakhov, his flirtation with the radicals seemed like betrayal, and there was a distinct cooling off in his relations with the two men.

It was in the *Diary of a Writer*, which he began to issue in 1876 as a monthly publication written entirely by himself, that Dostoevsky reached the height of his fame. His *Diary* became the most successful publication of its kind ever to have appeared in Russia, and it exerted an immense influence on public opinion. Letters from readers flowed in by the hundreds: Dostoevsky became, as it were, the voice of the national conscience as he took up one or another public issue in his own idiosyncratic, intimate manner, almost as if carrying on a private conversation. During this period, on the one hand, the ex-revolutionary and convict Dostoevsky was invited to meet with the grand dukes of the realm informally from time to time so as to give them the benefit of his wisdom. On the other, he was consulted by radical students asking him to clarify why the people, on whose behalf they were risking exile and imprisonment, had brutally broken up one of their demonstrations against the government. Nothing could better illustrate for Dostoevsky the "uniqueness" of the moral-social position he had managed to attain (and on which he commented himself) than the coexistence of these events.

Despite the enormous popularity of the *Diary*, Dostoevsky was a novelist first and foremost, and after two years he temporarily suspended the journal's publication to undertake *The Brothers Karamazov*. This majestic novel, intended only as the first of a series, is the culmination of Dostoevsky's artistic career. Its theme of parricide coincides with the repeated attempts of the radicals, who by this time had turned to terrorism, to assassinate the Tsar. Dostoevsky's last appeal for fraternal union and Christian compassion, which he saw as native endowments of the Russian national character, was made amidst the exploding bombs in his famous Pushkin speech of June 1880, which stirred the audience into hysterical raptures and led to his being hailed on the spot as "a prophet."

When he died seven months later, the huge funeral procession that accompanied his corpse to the grave demonstrated once again the extraordinary impact made by his life and work—an impact that, at least in the case of his work, has continued to the present day. But all this will be the subject of our next volume, and for the moment we will leave Dostoevsky poised to begin a new, much more tranquil and happier life, happier at least on the level of his personal existence if not—and very far from it—in relation to the travails racking his beloved country, to which he never ceased responding with anguish and apprehension.

DSiM   F. M. Dostoevsky, *Stati i Materiali*, ed. A. S. Dolinin, 2 vols. (Petersburg-Moscow-Leningrad, 1922–1924).

DVS   F. M. Dostoevsky v Vospominaniakh Sovremennikov, ed. K. Tyunkina, 2 vols. (Moscow, 1990).

LN   *Literaturnoe Nasledtsvo*

Pisma   F. M. Dostoevsky, *Pisma*, ed. and annotated by A. S. Dolinin, 4 vols. (Moscow, 1928–1959). This first edition of Dostoevsky's letters is still valuable for the richness of its commentary.

PSS   F. M. Dostoevsky, *Polnoe Sobranie Sochinenii*, ed. and annotated by G. M. Fridlender et al., 30 vols. (Leningrad, 1972–1990). This definitive edition of Dostoevsky's writings, which is now complete, contains his correspondence and provides an extensive and reliable scholarly apparatus.

PSSiP   I. S. Turgenev, *Polnoe Sobranie Sochinenii i Pisem*, 28 vols. (Moscow-Leningrad, 1960–1968). The volumes of this edition are not numbered consecutively, but are grouped according to creative works (15 volumes) and letters and other documents (13 volumes).

NOTES

CHAPTER 1

1. *PSS*, 28/Bk. 2: 120; March 31, 1865.
2. Ibid., 28/Bk. 1: 164; December 22, 1849.

CHAPTER 2

1. This letter is cited in V. S. Nechaeva, *Zhurnal M. M. i F. M. Dostoevskikh "Epokha," 1844–1865* (Moscow, 1975), 19.
2. *PSS*, 28/Bk. 2: 73; March 26, 1864.
3. The letters of Martha Panina were published by G. Prokhorov in "Nerazvernuvshiisya roman F. M. Dostoevskogo," *Zvenya*, 5 (1936), 582–598; the citation is on 588.
4. Ibid.
5. Ibid.
6. Ibid, 597.
7. Ibid.
8. Ibid., 600.
9. S. V. Kovalevskaya, *Vospominaniya* (Moscow, 1974), 70.
10. Ibid., 73.
11. Ibid., 65.
12. Ibid., 50.
13. *PSS*, 28/Bk. 2: 107–108; December 14, 1864.
14. Kovalevskaya, *Vospominaniya*, 73.
15. Ibid., 76.
16. Ibid., 77
17. S. V. Belov, "Z. A Trubetskaya, Dostoevsky i. A. P. Filosofova," *Russkaya Literatura*, 3 (1973), 117.
18. Kovalevskaya, *Vospominaniya*, 81.
19. Ibid.
20. Ibid., 88.

CHAPTER 3

1. *PSS*, 28/Bk. 2: 108; December 14, 1864.
2. Ibid., 120; March 31, 1865.
3. Ibid., 121–122; April 19, 1865.
4. I. S. Turgenev, *Polnoe Sobranie Sochinenii i Pisem*, 28 vols. (Moscow-Leningrad, 1960–1968), 28: 145.
5. N. S. Leskov, *Sobranie Sochinenii*, 11 vols. (Moscow, 1956–1958), 3: 279–380.
6. Benni's letters are published in Leonid Grossman, *Zhizni i Trudi Dostoevskogo* (Moscow-Leningrad, 1935), 148–149.
7. *PSS*, 28/Bk. 2: 127; June 8, 1865.
8. See the important essay by L. P. Grossman, "Gorod i Liudi 'Prestupleniya i Nakazaniya,'" which is the introduction to his edition of the novel (Moscow, 1935), 23.
9. *PSS*, 28/Bk. 2: 128; August 3/15, 1865.
10. Ibid., 129; August 20, 1865.
11. See Fyodor Dostoevsky, *The Gambler, with Polina Suslova's Diary*, trans. Victor Terras, ed. Edward Wasiolek (Chicago and London, 1972), 278. The Russian text is contained in *Godi blizhosti s Dostoevskim. Dnevnik. Povest. Pisma*, ed. with notes and introductory essay by A. S. Dolinin (Moscow, 1928).
12. Ibid., 296.
13. *PSS*, 28/Bk. 2: 129–130; August 10/22, 1865.
14. Ibid., 130–132; August 12/24, 1865.
15. Father Georgii Florovskii, *Puti Russkogo Bogosloviya* (Paris, 1983), 390.
16. N. N. Glubokovskii, *Russkaia Bogoslovskia Nauka v eia Istoricheskom Razvitii i Noveishem Sostoianii* (Warsaw, 1928), 17.
17. *PSS*, 28/Bk. 2: 259; February 18/ March 1, 1868.
18. Ibid., 135; September 10/22, 1865.
19. *F. M. Dostoevsky v Vospominaniyakh Sovremennikov*, 2 vols., ed. K. Tyunkina (Moscow, 1990), 1: 28. Extracts from Milyukov's memoirs are included in these volumes.
20. *PSS*, 28/Bk. 2: 136–138; September 15/27, 1865.

CHAPTER 4

1. *PSS*, 28/Bk. 2: 150; February 18, 1866.
2. Ibid.
3. Ibid., 151.
4. Dostoevsky, *The Gambler, with Polina Suslova's Diary*, trans. Victor Terras, ed. Edward Wasiolek (Chicago and London, 1972), 301–302.
5. Ibid., 302.
6. *PSS*, 28/Bk. 2: 151; February 18, 1866.
7. Cited in *PSS*, 7: 346.
8. Ibid., 349.
9. Orest Miller and N. N. Strakhov, *Biografia* (St. Petersburg, 1883), 289–290.
10. *PSS*, 28/Bk. 2: 329; December 11/23, 1868.
11. Ibid., 150; February 18, 1866.
12. Ibid., 151–152.
13. Ibid., 152.
14. The incident is recounted in the memoirs of Dostoevsky's niece Maria Ivanova. See *DVS*, 2: 48.
15. See the reminiscences of Z. K. Ralli, who knew the Ishutin group and Karakozov himself, and cites this passage of Weinberg in his own recollections. "Iz Vospominaniya Z. K. Ralli," in *Revolyutsionnoe Dvizhenie* 1860-godov, ed. B. I. Gorev and B. P. Kozmin (Moscow, 1932), 143.
16. Cited in A. A. Kornilov, *Obschestvennoe Dvizhenie pri Alexander II, 1835–1881* (Moscow, 1909), 175.
17. Cited in Henri Granjard, *Ivan Tourguénev et les courants politiques et sociaux de son temps* (Paris, 1954), 336.
18. Cited in Kornei Chukovsky, *The Poet and the Hangman*, trans. R. W. Rotsel (Ann Arbor, Mich., 1977), 40.
19. Ibid., 40–41.
20. Ibid., 18–19.
21. *PSS*, 28/Bk. 2: 153; April 25, 1866.
22. Ibid., 154
23. Ibid.
24. Ibid.
25. Franco Venturi, *The Roots of Revolution*, trans. Francis Haskell (New York, 1966), 332–334.
26. *PSS*, 28/Bk. 2: 154–155; April 25, 1866.
27. Ibid., 155.
28. Ibid., 156; April 29, 1866.
29. Ibid., 157; May 9, 1866.
30. Ibid., 158; April–May 1866.
31. Ibid., 160; June 17, 1866.
32. Ibid., 156; April 29, 1866.
33. M. A. Ivanova, "Vospominaniya," *DVS*, 2: 41.
34. Ibid., 47.
35. Ibid., 44.
36. *PSS*, 28/Bk. 2: 160; June 17, 1866.
37. Ibid., 165; July 10/15, 1866.
38. M. A. Ivanova, *DVS*, 2: 41.
39. N. Fon-Fokht, "K Biografia F. M. Dostoevskogo," *DVS*, 2: 56.
40. *PSS*, 28/Bk. 2: 166; July 10/15, 1866.
41. A. P. Milyukov, "Feodor Mikhailovich Dostoevsky," *DVS*, 1: 284, 289–290.

CHAPTER 5

1. *PSS*, 28/Bk. 1: 351; October 9, 1859.
2. See the remarks in *PSS*, 7: 308n.1.
3. Ibid., 315, 408.
4. *PSS*, 28/Bk. 1: 201; January 13/18, 1856.
5. A. F. Wrangel, *Vospominaniya o F. M. Dostoevskom v Siberii* (St. Petersburg, 1912), 35.
6. *PSS*, 28/Bk. 1: 187; June 4, 1856.
7. Ibid., 236; July 14, 1856.
8. I take this term from the excellent book of Dorrit Cohen, *Transparent Minds* (Princeton, N.J., 1978), 99–140.
9. D. I. Pisarev, *Sochineniya*, 4 vols. (Moscow, 1955), 1: 135.
10. N. N. Strakhov, *Iz Istorii Literaturnago Nigilizma, 1861–1865* (St. Petersburg, 1890), 34.
11. See Chernyshevsky's statement that "an open manifestation of Turgenev's hatred of Dobrolyubov was, as is well known, the novel *Fathers and Children*." He was, however, willing to admit later, in view of Turgenev's denial of any such intention, that the resemblance may have been involuntary. See the commentary in I. S. Turgenev, *PSSiP*, 8: 592–593.
12. Turgenev, *PSSiP*, 8: 243.
13. Pisarev, *Sochineniya*, 2: 8–11.
14. Ibid., 11, 10.
15. Ibid., 15.
16. Turgenev, *PSSIP*, 8: 325.

17. A. S. Pushkin, *Sobranie Sochinenii*, ed. D. D. Blagoi et al., 10 vols. (Moscow, 1959–1962), 5: 252.

18. See the extract from the article of F. I. Evnin in *Twentieth-Century Interpretations of Crime and Punishment*, ed. Robert Louis Jackson (Englewood Cliffs, N.J., 1974), 91–93.

19. Pushkin, *Sobranie Sochinenii*, 6: 343.

20. F. M. Dostoevsky, *The Gambler, with Polina Suslova's Diary*, trans. Victor Terras, ed. Edward Wasiolek (Chicago and London, 1972), 217.

21. See B. P. Kozmin, *Iz Istorii Revolyu-* *tsionnoe Mysli v Rossii* (Moscow, 1961), 46.

22. See the chapter on Zaitsev in V. Ya. Kirpotin, *Publitsisty i Kritiki* (Leningrad, 1932), 158.

23. Strakhov, *Iz Istorii Literaturnago Nigilizma*, 575.

24. These quotations are taken from the richly informative article of F. I. Evnin, who first called attention to the similarities of these writers with Dostoevsky. F. I Evnin, "Roman *Prestuplenie i Nakazanie*," in *Tvorchestvo Dostoevskogo*, ed. N. L. Stepanov et al. (Moscow, 1959), 127–172, esp. 134–138.

CHAPTER 6

1. See *The Notebooks for Crime and Punishment*, ed. and trans. Edward Wasiolek (Chicago and London, 1967), 101. My citations of the notebooks are taken from this indispensable work, with some slight alterations.

2. For a discussion of Bakhtin's views, see my "The Voices of Mikhail Bakhtin," in *Through the Russian Prism* (Princeton, N.J., 1990), 18–33, esp. 26–32.

3. See E. M. de Vogüé, *Le Roman Russe* (Paris, 1910), 253.

4. *PSS*, 28/Bk. 2: 166; July 10–15, 1866.

5. Cited in *PSS*, 7: 326.

6. *PSS*, 28/Bk. 2: 164; July 8, 1866.

7. Ibid., 167; July 19, 1866.

CHAPTER 7

1. Roland Barthes defines such an effect as being caused by details that have no place in a literary structure. As readers, "we will inevitably be confronted by *notations* which no function (not even the most indirect) will allow us to justify." See the extract from Barthes's essay on the "reality effect" in the useful anthology, *Realism*, ed. Lillian R. Furst (London and New York, 1992), 135.

2. Vyacheslav Ivanov, *Freedom and the Tragic Life*, trans. Norman Cameron, ed. S. Konovalov (New York, 1952).

3. D. I. Pisarev, *Sochineniya*, 4 vols. (Moscow, 1955–1956), 4: 351.

4. Mikhail Bakhtin, *Problems of Dostoevsky's Poetics*, trans. and ed. Caryl Emerson (Minneapolis, 1984), 258.

5. For this distinction, see Tzvetan Todorov, "Typologie du roman policier," in his *Poétique de la prose* (Paris, 1971), 55–56.

6. Ian Watt, *Conrad in the Nineteenth Century* (Berkeley and Los Angeles, 1979), 280.

7. K. Mochulsky, *Dostoevsky*, trans. Michael A. Minihan (Princeton, N.J., 1967), 303.

8. Lord Byron, *Complete Poetical Works* (Cambridge, Mass., 1905), 371.

9. Philip Rahv, "Dostoevsky in *Crime and Punishment*," in *The Myth and the Powerhouse* (New York, 1965), 115.

CHAPTER 8

1. Anna Dostoevsky, *Reminiscences*, trans. and ed. Beatrice Stillman (New York, 1975), 6, 7.

2. Ibid., 8.

3. Ibid., 7.

4. Ibid., 10

5. Ibid., 4.

6. Ibid.

7. Ibid., 12.
8. Ibid., 15, 16.
9. Ibid., 58.
10. Ibid., 16.
11. Ibid., 16–17.
12. Ibid., 18.
13. A. G. Dostoevskaya, "Dnevniki i Vospominaniya," *LN*, 86 (Moscow, 1973), 221.
14. *Reminiscences*, 20.
15. "Dnevniki," 222.
16. *Reminiscences*, 21.
17. Ibid., 19.
18. Ibid., 21.
19. Ibid., 22.
20. Ibid., 24.
21. Ibid., 26.
22. Ibid., 24.
23. Ibid., 26.
24. "Dnevniki," 225.
25. *Reminiscences*, 27.
26. Ibid., 27, 28.
27. Ibid., 27.

28. Ibid., 29.
29. "Dnevniki," 262.
30. *Reminiscences*, 30.
31. Ibid.
32. "Dnevniki," 243.
33. *Reminiscences*, 32.
34. Ibid.
35. "Dnevniki," 263.
36. *Reminiscences*, 36.
37. Ibid., 38.
38. Ibid., 39.
39. Ibid.
40. Ibid., 40.
41. Ibid., 41.
42. Ibid., 42.
43. Ibid., 44.
44. Ibid., 45; "Dnevniki," 273.
45. *Reminiscences*, 45.
46. Ibid., 46.
47. Ibid., 65.
48. Ibid., 69.
49. Ibid., 76.

CHAPTER 9

1. *PSS*, 28/Bk. 2: 50–51.
2. See D. S. Savage, "Dostoevsky: The Idea of *The Gambler*," reprinted in Robert L. Jackson, *Dostoevsky: New Perspectives* (Englewood Cliffs, N.J., 1983), 111–125. Savage's article, which first appeared in 1950, is generally accepted as a classic, and his interpretation has become standard. For a lengthier discussion of my objections to this view, see my article, "*The Gambler*: A Study in Ethnopsychology," *Hudson Review*, 46 (1993), 301–322.
3. Savage, "Dostoevsky," 116.
4. See the introduction to Fyodor Dostoevsky, *The Gambler, with Polina Suslova's Diary*, trans. Victor Terras, ed. Edward Wasiolek (Chicago and London, 1972), xxxv. I have used this translation for my quotations.

CHAPTER 10

1. Anna Dostoevsky, *Reminiscences*, trans. and ed. Beatrice Stillman (New York, 1975), 79.
2. Ibid., 80.
3. Ibid., 86.
4. Ibid., 91.
5. Ibid., 90
6. Ibid., 92.
7. Ibid., 97.
8. Ibid., 100.
9. Ibid., 109.
10. Ibid., 110, 112.
11. Ibid., 114.
12. *Dnevnik A. G. Dostoevskoi, 1867 g.* (Moscow, 1923), 120, 173. This work was translated into English, from a German rendering, as *The Diary of Dostoevsky's Wife*, ed. Rene Fülöp-Miller and Dr. Fr. Eckstein, trans. Madge Pemberton (New York, 1928). I have used this translation as a basis for my own quotations from the original text.
13. Ibid., 172, 33–35, 59.
14. Ibid., 35.
15. *PSS*, 28/Bk. 2: 182.
16. *Dnevnik A. G. Dostoevskoi*, 28.
17. Ibid., 48.
18. Anna Dostoevsky, *Reminiscences*, 32.
19. *Dnevnik A. G. Dostoevskoi*, 40.
20. *PSS*, 28/Bk. 2: 204; August 16/28, 1867.
21. Ibid., 184–185; May 5/17, 1867.
22. Ibid., 186; May 6/18, 1867.

23. Ibid.

24. Ibid., 196–198; May 12/24, 1867.

25. Ibid., 188–189; May 8/20, 1867.

26. Ibid., 195; May 11/23, 1867.

27. Ibid., 192; May 9/21, 1867.

28. *Dnevnik A. G. Dostoevskoi*, 105–106.

29. Anna Dostoevsky, *Reminiscences*, 127–128.

30. Alexander Herzen, *My Past and Thoughts*, trans. Constance Garnett, rev. Humphrey Higgins, 4 vols. (New York, 1968), 3: 1391–1393, 1394–1396.

31. *Dnevnik A. G. Dostoevskoi*, 91.

32. Ibid., 100.

33. *PSS*, 28/Bk. 2: 205; August 16/28, 1867.

34. *Dnevnik A. G. Dostoevskoi*, 15.

35. Ibid., 19, 116.

Chapter 11

1. *Dnevnik A. G. Dostoevskoi, 1867 g.* (Moscow, 1923), 185.

2. Ibid., 184.

3. Ibid., 311.

4. Ibid., 189, 186.

5. Ibid., 188.

6. Ibid., 195, 206.

7. Anna Dostoevsky, *Reminiscences*, trans. and ed. Beatrice Stillman (New York, 1975), 132.

8. *Dnevnik A. G. Dostoevskoi*, 312.

9. Ibid., 191.

10. Ibid., 223–224.

11. Ibid., 269–270.

12. Ibid., 280.

13. Ibid., 322–323, 326.

14. Ibid., 339, 342.

15. Ibid., 345–346.

16. Ibid., 352.

17. *PSSiP*, 9: 143.

18. *PSS*, 28/Bk. 2: 72–73; March 26, 1864.

19. *PSS*, 28/Bk. 2: 160; June 17, 1866.

20. Ibid., 28/Bk. 1: 244; November 9, 1856.

21. *Dnevnik A. G. Dostoevskoi*, 185.

22. *PSSiP*, 9: 143.

23. *Dnevnik A. G. Dostoevskoi*, 223.

24. Herzen's articles are collected in Alexander Herzen, *My Past and Thoughts*, trans. Constance Garnett, rev. Humphrey Higgins, 4 vols. (New York, 1968), 4: 1680–1749.

25. *PSSiP*, 5: 67.

26. Ibid., 628.

27. Ibid., 9: 170.

28. Ibid., 232–233.

29. *PSS*, 28/Bk. 2: 450n.31.

30. N. N. Strakhov, *Kriticheskye Stati ob I. S. Turgenev i L. N. Tolstom*, 2 vols. (Kiev, 1908), 1: 67.

31. "Pisma Maikova k Dostoevskomu," in *F. M. Dostoevsky, Stati i Materiali*, ed. A. S. Dolinin, 2 vols. (Moscow-Leningrad, 1924), 2: 338–339.

32. *Dnevnik A. G. Dostoevskoi*, 194.

33. Ibid., 199.

34. *PSS*, 28/Bk. 2: 210; August 16/28, 1867.

35. *Dnevnik A. G. Dostoevskoi*, 198.

36. *PSS*, 28/Bk. 2: 210n.36.

37. Ibid., 211.

38. Ibid., 203–204.

39. Ibid., 211.

40. *Dnevnik A. G. Dostoevskoi*, 199.

41. Cited in *Pisma*, 2: 384.

42. *Dnevnik A. G. Dostoevskoi*, 214.

43. *PSS*, 28/Bk. 2: 210.

44. *PSSiP*, 7: 17–18.

45. *Dnevnik A. G. Dostoevskoi*, 358.

46. Ibid., 361–366.

Chapter 12

1. Alexander Herzen, *My Past and Thoughts*, trans. Constance Garnett, rev. Humphrey Higgins, 4 vols. (New York, 1968), 2: 390.

2. *PSS*, 28/Bk. 2: 204; August 16/28, 1867.

3. Ibid., 207, 212.

4. Ibid., 208, 214.

5. Ibid., 208, 212.

6. Ibid., 207.

7. Ibid., 203, 204.

8. Ibid., 204, 206.

9. Ibid., 206

10. Ibid.

11. Ibid.

12. A. G. Dostoevskaya, "Dnevniki i Vospominaniya," *LN*, 86 (Moscow, 1973), 184.

13. *PSS*, 28/Bk. 2: 215–216; September 3/15, 1867.

14. Ibid., 28/Bk. 2: 30; January 5, 1863.

15. A. G. Dostoevskaya, "Dnevniki i Vospominaniya," 167–168.

16. *PSS*, 28/Bk. 2: 226; October 9/21, 1867.

17. Herzen, *My Past and Thoughts*, 1: 69.

18. Cited in the splendidly written, rather mocking classic of E. H. Carr, *The Romantic Exiles* (London, 1949), 194.

19. Cited in the notes to Anna Grigor-

yevna's "Geneva Diary," *LN*, 86 (Moscow, 1973), 284n.26.

20. A. G. Dostoevskaya, "Dnevniki i Vospominaniya," 170, 171.

21. Ibid., 173.

22. Ibid., 176.

23. Ibid.

24. *PSS*, 28/Bk. 2: 217; September 3/15, 1867.

25. Ibid., 224–225; September 29/October 11, 1867.

26. Ibid.

Chapter 13

1. A. G. Dostoevskaya, "Dnevniki i Vospominaniya," *LN*, 86 (Moscow), 197.

2. Ibid.

3. Ibid., 247.

4. Ibid., 227.

5. Ibid., 184.

6. *PSS*, 28/Bk. 2: 235; November 6/18, 1867.

7. A. G. Dostoevskaya, "Dnevniki i Vospominaniya," 276.

8. Ibid., 188.

9. Ibid., 200.

10. *PSS*, 28/Bk. 2: 239; December 31, 1867/January 12, 1868.

11. Ibid., 358; November 1/13, 1867.

12. A. G. Dostoevskaya, "Dnevniki i Vospominaniya," 250.

13. *PSS*, 28/Bk. 2: 223; September 29/October 11, 1867.

14. Ibid., 239n.10.

15. Ibid., 222n.13.

16. Ibid., 224.

17. A. G. Dostoevskaya, "Dnevniki i Vospominaniya," 215.

18. *PSS*, 28/Bk. 2: 228; October 9/21, 1867.

19. See the commentary in *PSS*, 9: 392.

20. *PSS*, 28/Bk. 2: 224n.13.

21. Ibid., 224; December 31, 1867/January 12, 1868.

22. Ibid., 353–354; September 28/October 10, 1867.

23. Ibid., 248; January 1/13, 1868.

24. Ibid., 258; February 18/March 1, 1868.

25. *DSiM*, 2: 343; November 3, 1867.

26. *PSS*, 28/Bk. 2: 259n.23.

27. *DSiM*, 2: 341; September 20, 1867.

28. *PSS*, 28/Bk. 2: 227n.18.

29. Ibid., 243n.14.

30. *DSiM*, 2: 344–345; January 7, 1868.

31. *PSS*, 28/Bk. 2: 260; February 18/March 1, 1868.

32. For this distinction, see Reinhold Niebuhr, *The Nature and Destiny of Man*, 2 vols. (New York, 1964), 2: 15–34. This profound discussion stresses how deeply rooted the messianic dream is in all cultures that believe God's purpose will be realized in and through history. Niebuhr also points out how inevitably these two types become entangled with each other.

33. *PSS*, 28/Bk. 2: 254; February 1/13, 1868.

34. Ibid., 294–295; March 29/April 10, 1868.

Chapter 14

1. *Iz Arkhiva F. M. Dostoevskogo. "Idiot". Neizhdannie Materiali*, ed. P. N. Sakulin and N. F. Belchikova (Moscow-Leningrad, 1931), 243.

2. Fyodor Dostoevsky, *The Notebooks for "The Idiot,"* trans. Katherine Strelsky, ed. with intro. by Edward Wasiolek (Chicago and London, 1967), 7–8. My quotations are taken from this translation.

3. See the commentary in *PSS*, 9: 486.

4. Ibid., 28/Bk. 2: 240; December 31, 1867/January 12, 1868.

5. Ibid., 240–241.

6. Ibid., 241.

7. Ibid., 252.

8. Ibid., 251.

Chapter 15

1. *PSS*, 28/Bk. 2: 238; December 24, 1867/January 5, 1868.
2. Ibid., 244; December 31, 1867/January 12, 1868.
3. "Pisma Maikova," *DSiM*, 2: 343.
4. *PSS*, 28/Bk. 2: 252; January 1/13, 1868.
5. Ibid., 258; February 18/March 1, 1868.
6. Ibid., 259.
7. A. N. Maikov, "Pisma k F. M. Dostoevskomu," ed. N. T. Ashimbaeva, *Pamyatniki Kulturi*, 1982 (Leningrad, 1984), 66.
8. *PSS*, 28/Bk. 2: 259n.5.
9. "Pisma Maikova," *DSiM*, 2: 344.
10. *PSS*, 28/Bk. 2: 258–259n.5.
11. "Pisma Maikova," *DSiM*, 2: 348.
12. *PSS*, 28/Bk. 2: 280; March 21–22/April 2–3, 1868.
13. Ibid., 281.
14. "Pisma Maikova," *DSiM*, 2: 349.
15. Leonid Grossman, *Zhizni i Trudi F. M. Dostoevskogo* (Moscow-Leningrad, 1935), 177.
16. *PSS*, 28/Bk. 2: 282n.12.
17. Ibid., 258n.5.
18. A. G. Dostoevskaya, "Dnevniki i Vospominaniya," *LN*, 86 (Moscow, 1973), 213.
19. Anna Dostoevsky, *Reminiscences*, trans. and ed. Beatrice Stillman (New York, 1975), 142.
20. *PSS*, 28/Bk. 2: 266–267; February 24/March 7, 1868.
21. Ibid., 272–273; March 2/14, 1868.
22. Anna Dostoevsky, *Reminiscences*, 146.
23. *PSS*, 28/Bk. 2: 277–278n.12; March 21–22/April 2–3, 1868.
24. "Pisma Maikova," *DSiM*, 2: 345.
25. *PSS*, 28/Bk. 2: 279–280n.12.
26. Ibid., 278.
27. *The Notebooks for "The Idiot,"* trans. Katherine Strelsky, ed. with intro. by Edward Wasiolek (Chicago and London, 1967), 160.
28. Robin Feuer Miller, *Dostoevsky and "The Idiot"* (Cambridge, Mass., 1981), 79. This is one of the best works written about this novel, an excellent analysis of its narrative technique that also explores the wider thematic context.
29. Ibid., 81
30. *PSS*, 28/Bk. 2: 285; March 23/April 4, 1868.
31. Ibid., 286.
32. Anna Dostoevsky, *Reminiscences*, 147.
33. *PSS*, 28/Bk. 2: 297; May 18/30, 1868.
34. Ibid., 298.

Chapter 16

1. *PSS*, 28/Bk. 2: 300; June 9/21, 1868.
2. Ibid., 298; May 18/30, 1868.
3. Ibid., 300n.1.
4. Ibid., 301–302; June 22/July 4, 1868.
5. Ibid., 302.
6. Ibid., 302–303.
7. Ibid., 308; June 23/July 5, 1868.
8. Ibid., 306.
9. Ibid., 303n.4; June 22/July 4, 1868.
10. Anna Dostoevsky, *Reminiscences*, trans. and ed. Beatrice Stillman (New York, 1975), 156.
11. *PSS*, 28/Bk. 2: 314; end August/beginning September 1868.
12. Ibid., 481n.3.
13. Ibid., 309–310; July 21/August 2, 1868.
14. "Pisma Maikova," *DSiM*, 2: 350.
15. *PSS*, 28/Bk. 2: 482n.13.
16. See Murray Krieger, "The Curse of Saintliness," in *The Tragic Vision* (New York, 1960), 209–227.
17. A. N. Maikov, "Pisma k F. M. Dostoevskomu," ed. N. T. Ashimbaeva, *Pamyatniki Kulturi*, 1982 (Leningrad, 1984), 67.
18. *PSS*, 28/Bk. 2: 310n.14.
19. Anna Dostoevsky, *Reminiscences*, 151.
20. *PSS*, 28/Bk. 2: 318; October 26/November 7, 1868.
21. William Wordsworth, *Poetical Works* (Boston, 1982), 167.
22. Anna Dostoevsky, *Reminiscences*, 156.
23. *PSS*, 28/Bk. 2: 318–319n.21.
24. Ibid., 319.
25. Ibid., 321; October 26/November 7, 1868.
26. Ibid., 319n.21.
27. Ibid., 320–321.
28. A. N. Maikov, "Pisma," 70.
29. "Pisma N. N. Strakhova F. M. Dos-

toevskomu," in *Shestidesyatie godi*, ed. N. K. Piksanova and O. V. Tsekhnovitsera (Moscow-Leningrad, 1940), 258–259.

30. *PSS*, 29/Bk. 2: 322n.21.

31. Ibid., 323–324; October 26/November 7, 1868.

32. Katherine Strelsky, "Dostoevsky in Florence," *Russian Review* 23 (1964), 149–163.

33. *PSS*, 28/Bk. 2: 333; December 11/23, 1868.

34. Ibid., 327.

35. A. N. Maikov, "Pisma," 73.

36. *PSS*, 28/Bk. 2: 329; December 11/23, 1868.

37. A. N. Maikov, *Izbrannye Proizvedeniya*, ed. L. S. Geiro (Leningrad, 1977), 171.

38. *PSS*, 28/Bk. 2: 333n.37.

39. Alexander Herzen, *My Past and Thoughts*, trans. Constance Garnett, rev.

Humphrey Higgins, 4 vols. (New York, 1968), 2: 539.

40. *PSS*, 28/Bk. 2: 327n.37.

41. Ibid., 29/Bk. 1: 9–10; January 25/February 6, 1869.

42. Ibid., 28/Bk. 2: 257; February 18/March 1, 1868.

43. A. N. Maikov, "Pisma," 65.

44. *PSS*, 28/Bk. 2: 283; March 21–22/April 2–3, 1868.

45. Ibid., 28/Bk. 1: 163–164; December 22, 1849.

46. For such speculations, see the commentary in *PSS*, 8: 385–393.

47. Ibid., 28/Bk. 2: 305; June 22/July 4, 1868.

48. For the quotation and an excellent discussion of this issue, see L. M. Rosenblyum, *Tvorcheskie Dnevniki Dostoevskogo* (Moscow, 1981), 153–154.

CHAPTER 17

1. *PSS*, 29/Bk. 2: 139; February 14, 1877.

2. Ibid., 28/Bk. 1: 163–4; December 22, 1849.

3. Max Scheler, *The Nature of Sympathy*, trans. Peter Heath (London, 1954), chap. 2.

4. A. Skaftymov, "Tematicheskaya kompositsiya 'Idiot,'" *Nravstvennie Iskaniya Russkikh Pisatelei* (Moscow, 1972), 23–87. I am greatly indebted to this article for my own analysis.

CHAPTER 18

1. *PSS*, 28/Bk. 2:330; December 11/23, 1868.

2. Anna Dostoevsky, *Reminiscences*, trans. and ed. Beatrice Stillman (New York, 1975), 153.

3. Ibid., 152–153.

4. Ibid.

5. *PSS*, 28/Bk. 2:329n.1

6. "Pisma N. N. Strakhov," in *Shestidesyatie godi*, ed. N. K. Piksanova and O. V. Tsekhnovitsera (Moscow-Leningrad, 1940), 260.

7. *PSS*, 28/Bk. 2:328n.1.

8. Ibid.

9. Ibid.

10. Quoted in *PSS*, 12: 179–180.

11. Ibid., 28/Bk. 2: 329n.1.

12. Ibid., 330.

13. Ibid., 335; December 12/24, 1868.

14. Ibid., 334

15. Ibid., 29/Bk. 1: 10; January 25/February 6, 1869.

16. Ibid., 11.

17. Ibid., 11–12.

18. Ibid., 20–21; February 26/March 10, 1869.

19. Ibid., 29/Bk. 1: 15–16n.17.

20. N. N. Strakhov, *Kriticheskiya Stati*, 2 vols. (Kiev, 1902–1908), 1: 213.

21. *PSS*, 29/Bk. 1: 18n.17.

22. Strakhov, *Kriticheskiya Stati*, 1: 187.

23. *PSS*, 29/Bk. 1: 24; March 8/20, 1869.

24. Ibid., 19; February 26/March 10, 1869.

25. Ibid.

26. Ibid., 24n.23.

27. Ibid., 32; March 18/30, 1869.

28. Ibid., 25n.23.

29. Ibid., 30n.28.

30. Ibid.

31. "Pisma N. N. Strakhov," *Shestidesyatie godi*, 263.

32. *PSS*, 29/Bk. 1: 147; October 9/21, 1870.

33. Ibid., 34–35; April 6/18, 1869.
34. Ibid.
35. Ibid., 36.
36. Ibid., 43; May 15/27, 1869.
37. Ibid., 56–57; August 29/September 10, 1869.
38. Ibid., 41n.37.
39. Ibid., 39.
40. Ibid., 40.
41. Ibid.

42. Ibid., 40–41.
43. Ibid., 41.
44. Anna Dostoevsky, *Reminiscences*, 154.
45. *PSS*, 29/Bk. 1: 53; August 14/20, 1869.
46. Ibid., 57n.37; August 29/September 10, 1869.
47. Ibid., 50n.46; August 14/26, 1869.
48. Ibid., 43n.37; May 15/27, 1869.

Chapter 19

1. *PSS*, 29/Bk. 1: 60; August 29/September 10, 1869.
2. Ibid., 52, 54; August 14/26, 1869.
3. Ibid., 49n.2, 51.
4. Ibid., 51.
5. Ibid., 58n.1.
6. Ibid., 63; September 17/29, 1869.
7. Ibid., 67, 69; October 16/28, 1869.
8. Ibid., 70.
9. Ibid., 71, 72–73; October 27/November 8, 1869.
10. Ibid., 75, 74.
11. Ibid., 88–89; December 14/26, 1869.
12. Ibid.
13. Ibid., 77–78; November 23/December 5, 1869.
14. Ibid., 81; December 7/19, 1869.
15. "Pisma N. N. Strakhov," in *Shestidesyatie godi*, ed. N. K. Piksanova and

O. V. Tsekhnovitsera (Moscow-Leningrad, 1940), 265.
16. *PSS*, 29/Bk. 1: 123; May 7/19, 1870.
17. Ibid., 88; December 14/26, 1869.
18. Ibid., 11; February 6/January 25, 1869.
19. Ibid., 93–94n.22.
20. Ibid., 94.
21. Ibid., 118; March 25/April 6, 1870.
22. Georgii Florovsky, *Puti Russkogo Bogosloviya* (Paris, 1983), 123–125.
23. For the citations from Saint Tikhon's works, see the commentary to *The Life of a Great Sinner* in *PSS*, 9: 511–514.
24. *PSS*, 29/Bk. 1: 107; February 12/24, 1870.
25. Ibid., 117; March 25/April 6, 1870.
26. Ibid., 118.

Chapter 20

1. Wrangel's inquiry, and other information on this possible source, may be found in *PSS*, 9: 472–474.
2. N. N. Strakhov, *Kriticheskiya Stati*, 2 vols. (Kiev, 1902–1908), 1: 247.
3. The relations of Grigoryev and Dostoevsky are informatively discussed by I. Z. Serman, "Dostoevsky i Grigoryev," in

Dostoevsky i Ego Vremya (Leningrad, 1971), 130–142. The polemic with Strakhov-Grigoryev in *The Eternal Husband* is mentioned but not developed. A lengthier analysis of this context is given by Richard Peace, "'The Eternal Husband' and Literary Polemics," *Essays in Poetics*, 3 (1978), 22–49.

Chapter 21

1. Anna Dostoevsky, *Reminiscences*, trans. and ed. Beatrice Stillman (New York, 1975), 158–159.
2. See Philip Pomper, *Sergei Nechaev* (New Brunswick, N.J., 1979), 112. There is a considerable literature on Nechaev, some of it quite sensationalist. Pomper's is a balanced, well-researched study.

3. *PSS*, 29/Bk. 1: 141; October 8/20, 1870.
4. See the commentary to *The Devils* in *PSS*, 12: 198. I am greatly indebted in general to the material contained in pages 192–218.
5. Ibid., 199.
6. Ibid., 200.

7. I. S. Turgenev, *PSSiP*, 14: 103, 100–102.

8. N. N. Strakhov, *Kriticheskiye Stati*, 2 vols. (Kiev, 1902–1908), 1: 82.

9. *Zarya*, 7 (1869), 159; cited in *PSS*, 12: 170.

10. See *PSS*, 12: 171.

11. Ibid., 172.

12. Ibid., 29/Bk. 1: 111; February 26/March 10, 1870.

13. Ibid., 116; March 25/April 6, 1870.

14. Ibid., 151; December 2/14, 1870.

15. Ibid., 136; August 17/29, 1870.

16. Ibid.

17. Ibid., 139–140; September 19/October 1, 1870.

18. Ibid., 141; October 8/20, 1870.

19. Ibid., 142.

20. Ibid., 145; October 9/21, 1870.

21. Ibid.

CHAPTER 22

1. *PSS*, 29/Bk. 1: 130; July 2/14, 1870.

2. Ibid., 148; October 9/21, 1870.

3. Ibid.

4. Ibid., 143n.2.

5. Ibid., 151; December 2/14, 1870.

6. Ibid., 117; March 25/April 6, 1870.

7. Ibid., 121; May 7/19, 1870.

8. Ibid., 163–164; January 6/18, 1871.

9. Ibid., 116n.6.

10. Anna Dostoevsky, *Reminiscences*, trans. and ed. Beatrice Stillman (New York, 1975), 164.

11. *PSS*, 29/Bk. 1: 165n.9.

12. Ibid., 131n.1.

13. Ibid., 138; August 17/29, 1870.

14. Ibid., 137–138.

15. Immanuel Kant, *Critique of Judgement*, trans. J. H. Bernard (New York, 1959), sec. 28; cited in Shlomo Avineri, *Hegel's Theory of the Modern State* (Cambridge, 1972), 197.

16. *PSS*, 29/Bk. 1: 138n.14.

17. Ibid., 161–162; December 30/January 11, 1871.

18. Ibid., 144–145n.4.

19. Ibid., 214; May 18/30, 1871.

20. Ibid., 215.

21. Ibid.

22. Ibid., 115; March 25/April 6, 1870.

23. Ibid., 106–107; February 12/24, 1870.

24. Ibid., 179; February 10/22, 1871.

25. Ibid., 112; March 24/April 5, 1870.

26. Ibid., 125; May 28/June 9, 1870.

27. Ibid., 113n.28.

28. Ibid., 127–129; June 11/23, 1870.

29. Ibid., 153; December 2/14, 1870.

30. Ibid., 216n.21.

31. Ibid.

32. Ibid., 172; January 18/30, 1871.

33. Ibid., 196–199; April 16/28, 1871.

34. Ibid., 199.

35. Ibid., 198.

36. Ibid., 197.

37. Cited in ibid., 467.

38. Ibid., 198.

39. Ibid., 205; April 21/May 3, 1871.

40. Anna Dostoevsky, *Reminiscences*, 168.

41. *PSS*, 29/Bk. 1: 142; October 8/20, 1870.

42. Ibid., 184–185; March 2/14, 1871.

43. Ibid., 164; January 6/18, 1871.

44. This is the version of events given in Anna Dostoevsky, *Reminiscences*, 378–379. It is accepted as accurate by the editors of the commentary to the novel, *PSS*, 12: 239.

45. Ibid., 29/Bk. 1: 227; February 4, 1872 (o.s.).

46. Ibid., 232; end March/beginning April 1872.

CHAPTER 23

1. *PSS*, 29/Bk. 1: 260; February 10, 1873.

2. This letter has been translated in *Daughter of a Revolutionary*, ed. Michael Confino (La Salle, Ill., 1973), 305–309; his translation differs somewhat in wording from my own.

3. Ibid., 323.

4. Georgy Chulkov, *Kak Rabotal Dostoevsky* (Moscow, 1939), 232–233.

5. Yury Steklov, *Mikhail Aleksandrovich Bakunin*, 4 vols. (Moscow-Leningrad, 1926–1927), 3: 489.

6. I cite the translation of *Catechism of a Revolutionary* given in Confino (see

note 2) as the most recent and readily available. See *Daughter of a Revolutionary*, 226.

7. Ibid., 228.

8. Steklov, *Bakunin*, 3: 491–492.

9. *Daughter of a Revolutionary*, 227.

10. Ibid., 228.

11. Ibid.

12. Ibid., 229.

13. Steklov, *Bakunin*, 3: 455–456.

14. *Daughter of a Revolutionary*, 230.

15. Steklov, *Bakunin*, 3: 465.

16. Ibid., 464–465.

17. Karl Marx and Friedrich Engels, *Werke*, 39 vols. (Berlin, 1959–), 18: 426.

18. Steklov, *Bakunin*, 3: 449.

19. Ibid., 453–454.

20. See the citation from Tkachev in Franco Venturi, *Roots of Revolution*, trans. Francis Haskell (New York, 1966), 399; also B. P. Kozmin, *P. N. Tkachev i revolutsionnie dvizhenie 1860-kh godov* (Moscow, 1922), 119–120.

21. See the citation from a speech of Petrov's in Franco Venturi, *Roots of Revolution*, 215.

CHAPTER 24

1. Alexander Herzen, *My Past and Thoughts*, trans. Constance Garnett, rev. Humphrey Higgins, 4 vols. (New York, 1968), 2: 586.

2. "A. I. Maikov, Pisma k F. M. Dostoevskomu," ed. N. I. Ashimbaeva, *Pamyatniki Kulturi*, 1982 (Leningrad, 1984), 92; September 17, 1868.

3. N. A. Dobrolyubov, *Izbrannoye* (Moscow, 1975), 156.

4. Herzen, *My Past and Thoughts*, 4: 1581, 1579.

5. Ibid., 1580, 1583.

6. Ibid., 1581, 1583.

7. Cited in the excellent book of Abbott Gleason, *Young Russia* (New York, 1980), 132–133.

8. B. P. Kozmin, *Iz Istorii revolutsionnoi mysli v Rossii* (Moscow, 1961), 547.

9. A. I. Herzen, *Sochineniya*, 10 vols. (Moscow, 1955–1958), 8: 417.

10. Ibid., 405, 417.

11. I. S. Turgenev, *PSSiP*, 10: 9.

12. A. S. Dolinin, "Turgenev v Besakh," in his *Dostoevsky i drugie* (Moscow, 1989), 173. Dolinin's article, written in 1924, is still the classic treatment of this subject.

13. Turgenev, *PSSiP*, 10: 9.

14. The letter is published in *Proizvedeniya Petrashevtsy*, ed. V. I. Evgrafova (Moscow, 1953), 496–497.

15. Herzen, *My Past and Thoughts*, 2: 744.

CHAPTER 25

1. *PSS*, 29/Bk. 1 :140; September 19/October 1, 1870.

2. Lord Byron, *Complete Poetical Works* (Cambridge, Mass., 1905).

3. Ludwig Feuerbach, *The Essence of Christianity*, trans. George Eliot (New York, 1957), 270–271.

4. Mario Praz, *The Romantic Agony* (Oxford and New York, 1970), 419–420.

INDEX

DATE DUE

			Printed in USA

ЫMITH #45230